D1568289

Unless Recalled Earlier

DATE DUE

DEMCO, INC. 38-2931

Diary, 1901–1969

Diary, 1901–1969

KORNEI CHUKOVSKY

Edited by Victor Erlich

Translated by Michael Henry Heim

Yale University Press   *New Haven & London*

Original text and annotations copyright © 1991, 1994 by Elena Chukovskaya. .... ,
annotations, and apparatus © 2005 by Yale University.

Photographs courtesy of the Chukovsky family.

This translation is of an abridged version edited by Elena Chukovskaya of the diary published
in Russian in 1991 (vol. 1) and 1994 (vol. 2).

Designed by James J. Johnson and set in Monotype Ehrhardt Roman type by Binghamton
Valley Composition.

Printed in the United States of America.

Library of Congress Cataloging-in-Publication Data

Chukovskii, Kornei, 1882–1969.
  [Diaries. English. Selections]
  Diary, 1901–1969 / Kornei Chukovsky ; edited by Victor Erlich ; translated by Michael
Henry Heim.
      p. cm.
  "This translation is of an abridged version edited by Elena Chukovskaya of the diary
published in Russian in 1991 (vol. 1) and 1994 (vol. 2)"
  Includes bibliographical references and index.
  ISBN 0-300-10611-4 (alk. paper)

1. Chukovskii, Kornei, 1882–1969—Diaries. 2. Chukovskii, Kornei, 1882–1969—
Friends and associates. 3. Authors, Russian—20th century—Diaries. I. Erlich, Victor,
1914– II. Heim, Michael Henry. III. Chukovskaia, E. TS. IV. Title.
  PG3476.C49Z46313   2005
  891.78'4203—dc22
2004025814

A catalogue record for this book is available from the British Library.

The paper in this book meets the guidelines for permanence and durability of the Committee
on Production Guidelines for Book Longevity of the Council on Library Resources.

10 9 8 7 6 5 4 3 2 1

Contents

Note from the Publisher   vii

Introduction, by Victor Erlich   ix

Diary 1901–1969   1

Appendix: Excerpts from "What I Remember; or, Fiddle-Faddle"   550

Periodicals, Publishing Houses, Abbreviations, and Acronyms   567

Biographical References   575

Index   611

Illustrations follow page 280

Note from the Publisher

The diary of Kornei Chukovsky is an immense document spanning seven decades and three generations, starting in prerevolutionary Russia and encompassing almost the entire Soviet era. Although little could be considered unimportant or uninteresting, about one-quarter of the original text had to be cut to make a book of readable length for the nonspecialist.

The diary, kept with some irregularity from 1901 to 1969, is contained in twenty-nine notebooks. Because of the scarcity of paper in the 1920s some entries were scribbled on reverse pages of letters to Chukovsky or on separate sheets that were later stapled into appropriate notebooks. In an entry dated 27 May 1957, Chukovsky says that dozens of his diaries were lost. In the diaries that survived a number of pages had been torn out. Some years are barely or not at all represented. There are no entries dated 1915 or 1938 and very few entries for the years 1916–1917 or for the late 1930s.

In this volume, the reader will find two kinds of ellipses: those originally made for the Russian edition, by Elena Chukovskaya, Kornei Chukovsky's granddaughter (marked with < . . . >), and those made specifically for this edition (marked with [. . .]).

Text in **boldface** indicates words that Chukovsky, an ingrained Anglophile, wrote in English. Footnotes followed by "(V.E.)" or "(M.H.H.)" were written with the non-Russian reader in mind by Victor Erlich and Michael Henry Heim. The others are translations of Elena Chukovskaya's notes for the Russian edition. The titles of journals and names of publishing houses appear in Russian; a list can be found at the back of the book. Titles of books, plays, poems, and magazine articles appear in English except when, in footnotes, they refer to secondary literature.

Introduction

VICTOR ERLICH

Kornei Chukovsky's *Diary*, which covers the years from 1901 to 1969, is a cultural document of major importance. At the dawn of the twentieth century, while yet a brooding adolescent, Chukovsky committed himself to jotting down his thoughts and impressions with some regularity; he was still at it as a venerable octogenarian. The voluminous record, whose abridged version follows, spans sixty-eight years of its author's adult life and ranges from the pre-1917 heyday of Russian modernism well beyond the cultural ferment of the post-Stalin era.

Chukovsky was born in 1882 in Saint Petersburg as Nikolai Korneichukov, the illegitimate son of a Ukrainian peasant woman and a Russian student. Soon abandoned by the latter, his mother moved with her two children to Odessa. The gymnasium (secondary school) Nikolai attended there gave him, as he put it, "nothing serious in the way of knowledge," a gap he filled by avid reading. In 1901 he published his first literary articles in a local newspaper, and in 1903 he went as its correspondent to London. "I proved a total failure as a correspondent," he was to write sixty-two years later in a brief autobiographical sketch. "Instead of attending the sessions of the Parliament and listening to speeches about high politics, I spent day after day at the library of the British Museum reading Carlyle, Macaulay, Hazlitt, de Quincey, and Matthew Arnold. I was excited about Robert Browning, Rossetti, and Swinburne."[1] This early exposure to the English classics proved invaluable for the future translator of Defoe and Chesterton. Not unpredictably, Chukovsky soon lost his job: his letters from London lacked the requisite topicality. But they drew the attention of Valery Bryusov, leader of the Moscow Symbolists and editor of *Vesy* (Scales), the most influential literary journal of the era. When Bryusov invited Chukovsky to contribute to *Vesy,* the budding writer's far-flung career was properly launched.

---

1. Kornei Chukovskii, "O sebe," *Sobranie sochinenii* (Moscow, 1965), vol. 1, 8.

A resourceful literary critic who combined alert monitoring of the current literary scene with pathbreaking studies of nineteenth-century masters, a splendid children's writer whose versified tales delighted and amused three generations of young Russian readers, an accomplished practitioner and theoretician of the art of translation, a prolific and perceptive memoirist, Chukovsky was a complete man of letters. Moreover, since his prodigious intellectual energy and versatility were matched by a zest for life and a gift for friendship, he remained for decades at the center of the Russian literary milieu. It is fair to say that he knew, at times intimately, everyone involved in shaping the course of twentieth-century Russian literature. The astute and often revealing records of encounters with such major literary figures as Anna Akhmatova, Isaac Babel, Alexander Blok, Maxim Gorky, Vladimir Mayakovsky, Boris Pasternak, and Alexander Solzhenitsyn are among the most valuable aspects of this chronicle. These close-ups are marked by an unfailing alertness to variety and complexity, to apparent or actual contradictions. A few examples will suffice.

During the early years of the Revolution, Chukovsky was an active and indispensable participant in the mammoth translation project designed to make many masterpieces of world literature available to the Russian reader, a project nurtured and masterminded by Maxim Gorky. Thus, at the dawn of Soviet culture he had ample opportunity to see this resourceful and influential writer in action. The image of Gorky that emerges from the 1918–21 entries is an altogether credible blend of shrewdness and naïveté, of heavy-handed didacticism and the practiced seductiveness of a consummate raconteur. Listening spellbound to Gorky's account of his visits with Lev Tolstoy, Chukovsky is struck by the contrast between Gorky's monochromatic, doctrinaire articles about Tolstoy the man, and his fascinating, complex, richly textured, and uncannily perceptive reminiscences. "It was an entirely different Gorky." Equally complex, and at times downright puzzling, is Gorky's attitude toward the Soviet regime as glimpsed in the course of candid, unguarded conversations. In point of fact, during the period reflected in the *Diary*, the relationship between Gorky and the Bolsheviks was more problematical than the official Soviet hagiographers could allow. Not until the end of the twenties did the celebrated revolutionary writer conclude that "since they [the Bolsheviks] had very big goals . . . everything was justified,"[2] thereby readying himself to don the mantle of the great old man of Soviet literature. To draw on his immense prestige on behalf of the large-scale publishing enterprise which, in addition to its cultural import, provided much-needed employment for uprooted writers and scholars, Gorky had to establish a modus vivendi with the Soviet authorities, but his initial ambivalence toward the new rulers was all too apparent.

2. Yevgeny Zamiatin, "M. Gorky," *Sochineniia* (Moscow, 1988), 355.

On 2 April 1919 Chukovsky notes: "He always refers to the Bolsheviks as 'they'! Never once have I heard him say 'we.' He always speaks of the Bolsheviks as the enemy." Elsewhere he cites Gorky's admission that in dealing with "our authorities" he often had to be devious: "Never before have I dissembled, and now I must dissemble, lie and pretend. I know that this is 'necessary.' I just sat there stunned." As the staggered narrative unfolds, it is difficult not to conclude that Gorky the man was more interesting or at any rate less predictable than the bulk of his oeuvre.

Another major contributor to the World Literature project was the great Symbolist poet Alexander Blok. Working side by side with him, Chukovsky was repeatedly struck by Blok's overwhelming sense of responsibility, his self-discipline, his obsessive and "pathological" neatness, a quality "not at all in keeping with the poetry of madness and destruction he does so well." So impatient was Blok's post-revolutionary recoil from the "merely literary," so intense his hankering after total engagement that it elicited from Chukovsky a radical prognosis: "The more I observe Blok," wrote Chukovsky on 7 December 1919, "the more clearly I see that by the time he's fifty [Blok was thirty-nine in 1919] he'll forget about poetry and start writing artistically prophetic journalism (in the spirit of *The Diary of a Writer*)."[3] This prediction was soon overtaken by events: the poet's untimely death in August 1921 provided an occasion for a totally different assessment. A deeply emotional entry, mourning an incalculable loss, proclaimed the centrality, indeed the indispensability to Blok's destiny of the lyrical impulse, of the urge "to sing": "His life had no events. 'I went to Bad Nauheim.'[4] He did nothing but sing. A never-ending song passed through him in a continuous stream. For twenty years, from 1898 to 1918. Then he ceased—and immediately started dying. His song was his life. Once the song was over, his life was over."

If Chukovsky's close association with Gorky and Blok was confined to a short though momentous period, his encounters with Anna Akhmatova extended for almost half a century—from her stunning prewar debut through the years of enforced silence and the ordeals of the Stalin era to a degree of recognition in the more liberal post-Stalin climate. Thus Chukovsky had occasion to observe Akhmatova in different roles and guises. His admiration for Akhmatova's poetic achievement and his fascination with the woman behind it did not prevent him from striking an occasional mildly critical note. Visiting the poet in 1920 at the peak of her richly deserved fame, he found her overly concerned with her reputation and a trifle too worldly for his taste. He came

3. A miscellany of essays, reviews, reportage, and short fiction that served as a vehicle for Dostoevsky's passionate ideological commitments.
4. A quotation from Blok's diary. Bad Nauheim is a German spa.

close to being put off by her mundane chatter only to construe it promptly as a protective device, a shield for the inner, real Akhmatova.

A keen sense of Akhmatova's precious, indestructible core dominates the last extended entry devoted to her. On 8 March 1954 Chukovsky writes: "[She is now] a self-possessed, gray-haired woman, very stout, very simple, nothing at all like the highly stylized, timid yet at the same time haughty woman with banged hair, the slender poetess Gumilyov brought to see me in 1912, forty-two years ago. Of the catastrophe she speaks calmly and with humor: 'I was very famous and became even more infamous, and I saw that the two conditions are essentially one.' [. . .] I experienced the same excitement from her presence as I had in my youth. One can't help feeling her grandeur, her nobility, the immensity of her gift and her fate."

Yet the *Diary* is more than a portrait gallery. An invaluable witness and a keen observer, Chukovsky was also an active participant in the era's travails. His distinguished if often impeded career, during which recognition alternated and at times coexisted with bureaucratic harassment, is a stark illustration of the predicament of a writer totally dedicated to the literary craft under an increasingly oppressive regime. To put it differently, it is a paradigm of the plight of the socially conscious but essentially apolitical literary intellectual destined to ply his trade in a blatantly and brutally politicized culture. Chukovsky's own priorities are clearly indicated in an entry written during the peak of the revolutionary turmoil on 19 June 1917: "This is the second night I've been reading Stendhal's *The Red and the Black*, a fascinating novel in two volumes. It robbed my entire morning too. I was so annoyed at being taken away from my work that I threw it out. Without a heroic gesture I'd never have torn myself from it. Five minutes later Masha told me about a Bolshevik demonstration that took place in Petrograd yesterday. It sounded less interesting to me than the fabricated sufferings of Julien Sorel dating from 1830."

Chukovsky's position in Soviet literature is not easily defined. He was neither a premature dissident nor, to use Trotsky's invidious phrase, an "internal émigré." For a number of years he shared the hopes and expectations aroused by the Revolution with many of his contemporaries. Yet although he had personal ties with the Soviet literary establishment, he was emphatically not an official or accredited writer. As will soon become apparent, one of the persistent themes in the diary is the immensely wearying and often exasperating wrangling with obtuse or hostile censors: Chukovsky's freewheeling sensibility, inherently resistant to systems and dogmas, made him suspect to literary watchdogs. An incredibly hardworking writer and scholar, he was compelled to spend many days away from his desk, running from one faceless bureaucrat to another, seeking to rescue his latest work, be it the full-length study of the major nineteenth-century poet Nikolai Nekrasov, an exuberant poem for children, or a translation of *The Playboy of the Western World*, by John Millington Synge.

As it happened, the latter experience proved especially galling. In 1923 Chukovsky submitted a carefully translated and edited version of *The Playboy* only to be met by a high-handed rebuff. Actually, the play itself proved more than acceptable: Synge was commended for having unmasked the "narrowness and dull-wittedness of Irish farmers and innkeepers." But Chukovsky's well-crafted introduction was brusquely rejected since in addition to offering some useful information he "gives his own views on the author's work." His perversely individualistic analyses, argued the publisher's reader, ought to be excised and replaced by a proper Marxist interpretation.

As the twenties wore on, Chukovsky's status as a critic was increasingly called into question. A man who by 1917 was developing into one of the most vital critics of his generation could write somberly on 25 December 1925: "When my Gorky book came out last year, there wasn't a review anywhere, though hacks pilfered its ideas right and left in their articles.[5] I'm forced into silence as a critic, because RAPP have taken over criticism and they judge by Party card rather than talent.[6] They've made me a children's writer. But the shameful way they've treated my children's books—the persecution, the mockery, the suppression, and finally the censors' determination to ban them—has forced me to abandon that arena as well."

Ironically, it is Chukovsky's most innocuous writings that became the source of major trouble. The grimly literal-minded official Soviet pedagogues had precious little use for the qualities that made such versified tales as "The Crocodile" or "The Giant Cockroach" classics of Russian children's literature—that is, for their irrepressible gaiety, wit, and inventiveness. A reference to "unclean chimneysweeps who should be ashamed of themselves" in "Wash 'Em Clean," a humorous plea for cleanliness, was enough to lay its author open to the charge of slandering men of honest toil. Lenin's widow, Nadezhda Krupskaya, a humorless Bolshevik schoolmarm, dubbed "The Crocodile"— in which a cigarette-smoking, German-speaking crocodile strolls down the streets of Saint Petersburg—a "bourgeois muddle." In 1928 a full-blown campaign against Chukovsky's verse tales was spearheaded by a strident article, "Chukovitis," and a scornful statement adopted by the Kremlin nursery equivalent of the PTA. The writer stood accused of "distorting the facts about the

5. A reference to *Dve dushi Maksima Gor'kogo* (Moscow, 1924).

6. RAPP (Russian Association of Proletarian Writers) was a doctrinaire literary faction that became increasingly influential in the mid-twenties. Between 1928 and 1932 it exercised a virtual dictatorship over literary policy.

world of animals and plants," of failing to provide a properly edifying (in other words, "class") perspective, and, worse still, of smuggling reactionary ideas into the seemingly innocent tales.

This preposterous attack was mounted at the very end of the relatively liberal twenties. The subsequent decades proved still more trying. Although Chukovsky kept soldiering on and recording his manifold activities and ordeals, the brutal pressures under which he and his confrères were laboring began to register through significant omissions, gaps, and silences: the dread year 1938, the high point of Stalin's prewar political purges, is altogether missing from the *Diary;* the year 1948, the high point of Stalin's postwar cultural purges, is represented by a mere three entries; and the first entry for 1949 is a cri de coeur: "1948 is not a year to look back upon. It was a year of mechanical, mind-deadening scribbling of one (dull) note after the other [. . .]. Not a single line of my own did I write, not a single original word, as if I weren't Chukovsky."

No less telling is the claustrophobic quality of some entries, the turn away from horrors occurring beyond the confines of the writer's immediate circle as well as some dismayingly conformist passages strongly suggesting that the diarist did not dare to face, let alone commit to paper, profoundly unsettling truths. In an admirably balanced preface to the second volume of the diary, which covers the years 1930–69, Yelena Chukovskaya, Chukovsky's grand-daughter and editor of the Russian edition of the diary, calls attention to "many blank spots, torn-out pages and crossed-out lines and the absence of or cryptic references to important events in the life of the diary's author": the arrest and subsequent execution of Matvei Bronshtein, the husband of his daughter Lidia, are reduced to two words: "Lidia's tragedy." Chukovskaya speaks further "of the mixture of sober and keen observations with fear-induced attempts to explain the inexplicable and to accept the unacceptable" that marked the perceptions of many writers in those years.[7]

A similar note is struck by a thoughtful and honorable contemporary who toward the end of his life bestirred himself to speak of the writer's plight under Stalin with remarkable candor and insight. In his excellent introduction to the first volume of the diary, which covers the years 1901–29, Venyamin Kaverin pauses before the entry recording Chukovsky's conversation with Mikhail Slonimsky, a personal friend and fellow writer, about the rigors of Soviet censorship: "Misha complained about being forced to lead a double literary life: 'I am now writing one piece for the soul,' he told me, 'a piece that will never be passed by the censors and will end up in my desk drawer, and another, perfectly horrendous, for publication.' " Chukovsky then chimes in to

---

7. "Ot sostavitelia," *Dnevnik, 1930–1969* (Moscow, 1994), 3.

recount his own troubles with the censor over "The Crocodile," which had been held up for half a year, and sums up the situation as follows: "We are in the grips of a censorship the likes of which Russia has never known." Quite unexpectedly, however, the joint jeremiad concludes on an incongruously upbeat note: "Yet even after talking over these topics, we decided we are still Soviet writers, because we can easily imagine a Soviet system in which these delays do not take place. What is more, we are certain it is the Soviet system that will enable us to overcome them."

"Only fear," comments Kaverin, "could dictate in the thirties so ultra-loyal a sentiment."[8] The fact that the above exchange actually occurred on 21 January 1928 does not invalidate Kaverin's diagnosis. By the late twenties the intimidation of Soviet intellectuals, which marked much of the following decade, was all too palpable. Yet what is operative here is not merely fear in the sense of intense concern over one's personal safety or livelihood but also fear of being discarded, declared marginal or obsolete, or, to put it less negatively, the overweening need to belong to the new society even at the cost of extending unlimited credit to its least plausible claims.

Another heart-to-heart talk recorded in the diary may be seen as proof, if proof indeed is needed, that political gullibility is not incompatible with literary sophistication. This time Chukovsky's interlocutor is Yury Tynyanov, one of modern Russia's most distinguished literary historians and theorists. The entry for 5 June 1930 contains the following: "Called on Tynyanov in the evening. When I told him my thoughts about the kolkhoz, he said, 'I agree. I'm a historian and it is the historian in me that admires Stalin. As the author of the kolkhoz, Stalin is, historically speaking, the greatest of geniuses to reshape the world. If he had accomplished nothing but the kolkhoz, he would deserve to be called the most brilliant man of the age. But please don't tell anyone I said so.'" Even allowing for the unfair advantages of hindsight, it is difficult to contemplate with equanimity the unabashed enthusiasm of two eminent literary intellectuals for an idea whose implementation was soon to prove an economic and human disaster.

Shortly after Stalin's death in 1953 the tenor of Chukovsky's diary changes radically. The evil spell is broken. With the lifting of the paralyzing fear and the gradual erosion of widely shared illusions, the strenuous attempts "to explain the inexplicable and to accept the unacceptable" increasingly give way to recurrent outbursts of outrage over the untold damage done by the Stalin regime to Russian culture. Reading *Prisons and Exiles*, an unsparing account by a brave heterodox writer, Ivanov-Razumnik, of his ordeal in the gulag, Chukovsky does not hesitate to call it "a chilling indictment of Stalin, Yezhov,

---

8. "Dnevnik K.I. Chukovskogo," *Dnevnik, 1901–1929* (Moscow, 1991), 7.

and the campaign against the intelligentsia. They and all their henchmen wanted to wipe it out. They hated everyone who thought for himself." When, after delivering a public lecture at an elite sanitarium, Chukovsky was asked by the wife of a Party dignitary, "Why did Mayakovsky shoot himself?" he had considerable difficulty restraining himself. "I wanted to ask her why she wasn't interested in why Yesenin hanged himself, why Tsvetaeva hanged herself, why Fadeev shot himself, why Dobychin threw himself into the Neva, why Mandelshtam died, why Gumilyov was executed, why Zoshchenko was persecuted."

But not until the last years of his long life did Chukovsky feel free to confide his profound disillusionment with the entire Soviet project: "Now that I'm so old I find it painful to see the dreams of so many—our Belinskys, Herzens, Chernyshevskys, Nekrasovs, and countless members of the National Will and Social Democrat Parties—to see their dreams crushed and the paradise on earth for which they were willing to give up their lives nothing but a debauch of lawlessness and police brutality." Not until then did he reveal how he really felt in the days of the Great Terror: "The year of Stalin's terror, 1937, was upon us. Our homegrown Red Guards were on the warpath, bent on the mass destruction of the intelligentsia. Many of those nearest and dearest to me—writers, translators, physicists, artists, actors—were arrested for no reason at all. Every night I awaited my turn."

In the more permissive climate of the post-Stalin era Chukovsky's literary situation improved significantly. The cultural "thaw" brought a virtual end to harassment and made possible an unimpeded republication of his major writings, including the "controversial" poems for children, which were at long last made freely available to millions of young Russian readers. The year 1962 saw a symbolic recognition of the aging writer's achievement both at home and abroad—a Lenin Prize for his lifetime work on Nekrasov and an honorary doctorate at Oxford. To an inveterate Anglophile the latter award was as deeply gratifying as it was richly deserved. The entries dealing with his visit to England—the festivities at Oxford and sightseeing in London in the congenial company of his daughter-in-law—are among the sunniest passages in this voluminous record. On 24 May 1962 "A group of students came for me. [. . .] In Carroll's honor we took a boat ride on the Isis, where precisely a hundred years ago he told the Liddell sisters the story of *Alice in Wonderland*. It's a lovely river with magnificent views and Magdalen Tower in the distance. A gray squirrel leaps through the grass like a kangaroo, swans glide along the water, and you have the feeling that both squirrel and swans have been here since 1320 or 1230."

The sense of having overcome overwhelming odds is a recurrent theme in the late entries, where delayed denunciations of the "Stalinist thugs" alternate with expressions of profound satisfaction over having outlasted and ultimately "vanquished" them: "In *From Two to Five*[9] I make it look as though my tales were attacked only by individual pedagogues; in fact, they were the target of the state as a whole, backed by millions of officials, turnkeys, and soldiers, backed by a terrorized press. They trampled me underfoot, banned my works, ran smear campaigns against me—and came a cropper." Chukovsky is no less emphatic in hailing the comeback of a long-silenced and much reviled great poet: "Stalin's police thugs have come a cropper, and it's all Akhmatova's doing. The man in the street may think it a miracle, [. . .] but *we* don't find it in the least surprising; *we* know that's how it always is. The poet's word is always stronger than the police's thugs."

Chukovsky's belated vindication of the modern masters was closely bound up with the literary ferment that began in the late fifties and spilled into the early sixties. Chukovsky listened closely, indeed avidly, to the new voices in Russian literature. The octogenarian extended a warm welcome to Yevgeny Yevtushenko, whose panache he thoroughly enjoyed and whose poetic gifts he vastly overestimated. He delighted in the indomitable spirit and robust talent of Alexander Solzhenitsyn even while shrewdly diagnosing his fierce singleness of purpose as both a source of his moral strength and a built-in limitation.

When the human rights movement, with its challenge to the sclerotic regime's lurch toward repression, got under way, Chukovsky was too old and infirm to have taken as active a part in the literary conclaves as he had done back in the 1920s, but there was no question as to where he stood: until his last days he sought to provide succor and counsel to heterodox young poets and writers and use his prestige to expedite the rehabilitation or release from the gulag of friends who had fallen victim to Stalinist terror. All his intimates, including his intrepid daughter Lidia, were on the firing line, whether monitoring the trials of leading dissidents, mounting the defense of Joseph Brodsky, or protesting the Soviet invasion of Czechoslovakia. At times the intransigence of his younger friends appeared to Chukovsky unduly reckless, if not self-destructive. "Now that the Longweibing [Chinese Red Guards] are ganging up against the intellectuals," he wrote on 13 October 1968, and "the word 'intellectual' has become a word of abuse, it is important to remain in the ranks of the intelligentsia and not abandon them—for jail. We need our intelligentsia to carry on our day-to-day intellectual existence."

A propensity for equating civic courage with folly was scarcely surprising in one who had spent a quarter of a century under a system where an overt challenge to authority was tantamount to suicide. Yet as the final sentence of

9. A perceptive and richly documented study of children's linguistic creativity, reprinted in the mid-fifties after a fifteen-year ban.

the passage just cited strongly suggests, what was at stake throughout was more than physical survival. What Chukovsky had salvaged and what he ultimately affirmed was a sturdy if unheroic commitment to the everyday work on behalf of cultural continuity, the ongoing project of keeping alive, in the face of the onslaught of totalitarian kitsch, a faith in genuine literature and genuine literacy. Small wonder that to Chukovsky's natural progeny—the searching young writers of the post-Stalin era—this aged man of letters appeared as an exemplar: a living link with world culture, a living testimony to the resilience of the literary sensibility.

Diary, 1901–1969

1901

+>->->->->->->->->-

24 February. Saturday evening.

Curious! I've been keeping a diary for several years and I'm used to its free form and informal content—light, motley, whimsical: I've filled several hundred pages by now. Yet coming back to it, I feel a certain reticence. In my earlier entries I made a pact with myself: it may be silly, it may be frivolous, it may be dry; it may fail to reflect my inner self—my moods and thoughts—granted, so be it. When my pen proved incapable of giving bold and concise expression to my hazy ideas, which the moment after they came to me I was unable to make out myself, when it ended up merely reflecting commonplaces, I bore it no particular ill will; I felt nothing more than mild frustration. But now, now I am ashamed *in advance* of every clumsy formulation, every sentimental outburst and superfluous exclamation mark; I am ashamed of the careless bumbling, the insincerity so characteristic of diaries, ashamed for her sake, for Masha.[1] I categorically refuse to show this diary to her. < . . . >

Heavens, the rhetoric! Can I show this to anyone at all? [. . .]

2 March.

An odd thing happened to me today. I gave Velchev his lesson and went on to Kosenko's. I worked with Kosenko for a while and then looked in on

---

1. Chukovsky's future wife, Marya Borisovna. (V.E.)

Nadezhda Kirianovna. She spoke to me about monasteries, Mount Athos,[2] and miracles. I was all unction and devotion, my expression changing every second—I'm good at that. I grabbed my head in horror to learn that there were people who go to church to gossip and show off rather than . . . , and so on. I made several modest points of my own, calling atheists fools and scoundrels.

And so on. Suddenly the news that Tolstoy had been excommunicated fell on that disingenuous soil. I disagree with everything Tolstoy says < . . . >, yet I surprised myself by bounding out of my chair and, arms waving, playing the Cicero with all the fire of a nineteen-year-old.

For forty years now, I said, a great man, a man bold in spirit, goes through public somersaults and contortions over his every thought, for forty years he's been shouting at us, "Don't just stand there with your hands in your pockets! You turn somersaults too, you twist and turn if you want to know the bliss of the correspondence of word and deed, thought and word," and all we've done is to stand there gawking and say, "He's not so bad, worth hearing out if you've nothing better to do," with our hands in our pockets. And now that we've finally deigned to take them out, what do we do but grab him by the throat and tell him, "How dare you bother us, old man? What right have you to go on thinking, shouting, clamoring, and provoking us all these years? How dare you suffer? People don't suffer at seventy-four!" And so on. In terms equally grandiloquent and equally foolish [. . .]

I fear banal conversations, the idyll of the tea table, a life of rules and constraints. I wish to flee that life. But for where? How does one start another life? An active, restless life of freedom. Tell me. Help me . . .

But even as I speak, I don't believe a word of it. Perhaps I don't need freedom. Perhaps all I need is to finish the Gymnasium. < . . . >

7 March.

< . . . > Beauty, nothing but beauty! How beautiful it is to say:

> Believe me, friend: the time will come,
> A dawn of blissful jubilation;
> When Russia rises with the sun
> And on the ruins of oppression

2. A mountain in Greece inhabited for centuries by monastic communities, the "Holy Mountain" of the Orthodox Church. (V.E.)

Inscribes your name and with it mine!
("To Chaadaev" 1818)[3]

Pushkin speaking. Yet he also makes this fine proclamation:

To be dependent on the people or the monarch
It's all one, is it not?
("Pindemonte" 1836, I believe)

Yes, those are Pushkin's words.

Yet the words do not matter so much as the mood. It is wonderful, intoxicating to be the prophet of one's native land. Think of "To Russia's Slanderers," where he calls Napoleon impudent, or "Pindemonte," where

It's all the same to me whether a press that's free
Befuddles nitwits' brains or whether subtle censors
Restrain prattlers from printing their misapprehensions.

It makes no difference! And then there's the 1824 epistle to the censor:

But tell me: are you not ashamed that Holy Rus
Because of you and yours has no books yet to speak of?

Shame on you. It's all the same to him, yet he says, "Shame on you." One might put it down to the difference in age: his convictions evolved. Under whose influence? Nonsense! People like him need no convictions. When he writes to Chaadaev, you think, "Now here's a stern moralist, a stalwart." Yet on that very day practically, he sends Krivtsov a note, the ending of which gives a clear picture of the content: "Love your unchaste brother, the victim of sensuous love." Perusing his letters is a treat. He is different in each. He writes letters to Vyazemsky as one person and to Chaadaev as another and maintains each personality over a span of thirty letters. He does so quite unintentionally, as a result of an inner sense of artistic truth. I might even say he does so against his better intentions. He didn't understand himself, this infinite man; he kept going on about something called personal freedom, something called rights, trying to explain himself to

3. A quotation from Pushkin's stirring political poem addressed to one of Russia's first dissidents, Pyotr Chaadaev. Pushkin strikes an entirely different stance in a later poem, presumably inspired by an obscure Italian poet, Pindemonte, where he eschews the dichotomy of autocracy versus the people to extol creative privacy and freedom from all societal pressures. The patriotic ode "To the Slanderers of Russia" represents a riposte to the outcry in the West over the brutal suppression of the Polish national uprising of 1830–1831. A. P. Kern was one of Pushkin's many love objects and the addressee of the famous love poem "I recall the wondrous moment." (V.E.)

himself. He wanted to make a type of himself, be a type, put himself in a frame. Read his letters to Kern. They make him out to be a regular wag, a rascal, a fine chap, a hail-fellow-well-met—and that's it: one can't add a thing to the characterization. Here is a sample of the tone of one such letter: "You write that I don't know your character. Well, and what do I care for your character? The devil take it! Surely pretty women need no character! The main things are the eyes, the teeth, the arms and legs. . . . If you knew the combination of repulsion and respect I feel for your husband. O Goddess that you are! Send down the gout upon him! The gout, I say! Yes, the gout! It is my only hope!" And then he writes:

> A wondrous moment I remember:
> Your face before me did appear.
>
> I know no finer poem.

Combining one with the other is what made the true, the living Pushkin. < . . . >

9 March.

Turgenev's letters to Flaubert. Nothing interesting. Kamensky states in the preface that Turgenev and Flaubert were close friends, all but in love with each other. Perhaps. But there is nothing warm or intimate in the letters. [. . .] They are no more than brief notes with Turgenev's somewhat annoying, somewhat tactless lisping quality.

< . . . > Have been reading Belinsky. I don't like his articles. [. . .] If you read ten or fifteen pages of the blah blah blah, it all sounds pretty enough, but try to put it in your own words. Impossible! He couldn't do it himself! In a letter to Annenkov he admitted he was lucky when it came to friends. No sooner did he die than they started writing about him, and, certain like all graybeards that things were much better "in their day," they made a mythical figure out of him. Nekrasov, who wrote an epitaph just after his death, called him a "friend" and a "naive and passionate soul," but by several years later he had grown in his eyes into a "teacher" to whose memory he "genuflected."[4] [. . .]

---

4. Quotations from two poems by Nekrasov: "In Memory of a Friend" (1853) and "The Bear Hunt" (1867).

27 March.

< . . . > I read *The Kreutzer Sonata* today.[5] It is a crushing experience. I feel horror, pure horror (pure and simple, you might say). One can raise all kinds of objections, of course, one can even dismiss it entirely, but the horror remains. A model of the power of art.

I am crying. My heart is heavy. Why I cannot say—who am I to know?—but I have the feeling that it's wrong, off the mark, that I've been had, and it makes me want to rant and rave.

< . . . >

27 November.

Novosti has published a long feuilleton of mine, "A Perennial Issue" signed Kornei Chukovsky.[6] The editors identify me as "a young journalist with paradoxical but highly interesting opinions."

I feel not the slightest elation. My soul is empty. I can't squeeze a line out of myself.

10 December.

< . . . > Read Chekhov's *Sisters* today. It did not make the impression I'd expected. What's wrong? Either I've changed or he has! A year ago I would read a Chekhov story and find it so plain, powerful, and true that I'd wander about in a daze for a week, and now I feel he's lost his objectivity: I can see his hand guiding the sisters; it feels forced, calculated (calculating?). [. . .]

By the way, I'm supposed to write a Christmas story. I'm going to call it "The Crocodile" (and it won't be at all Christmassy). < . . . >

5. *The Kreutzer Sonata* (1887–89) is one of Tolstoy's late narratives. Cast in the form of a monologue of a landowner who has just been acquitted, on grounds of temporary insanity, of the murder of his wife, it is a strident diatribe against carnal love and what passes for "normal" marriage. (V.E.)

6. It was Chukovsky's first publication and bore the subtitle "Art for Art's Sake." It appeared in *Odesskie novosti* on 27 November 1901.

1902

8 January.

I'm dying of boredom. I can't get down to anything.

It is generally held that the sixties were the populist years, an opinion that has been bandied about even more so lately as it is the fortieth anniversary of the death of (the senior representative of the sixties) Dobrolyubov. I believe I share many traits with the men of the sixties. There was no particular idea predominating at the time; all people had in common was the freedom of the individual. It was wrong to mete out punishments, to call a Jew a Yid, to look on peasants as "cattle," such things being of the same order, but it was a long way to "systematic" populism. Besides, the teachers of the times, Dobrolyubov and Chernyshevsky, were not exclusively partial to the people. As Podarsky shows in the twelfth issue of *Russkoe bogatstvo,* they were not afraid to call the people "dim-witted," "ignorant," and "indolent" from time to time and even—*horrible dictu*— deemed a parliament harmful, and so on. Their rationalism, as Podarsky is correct in noting, kept them from placing the people's instincts in the forefront of organizing history. [. . .]

1903

Masha is my wife.

Today for the first time I've been able to look back over my life and emerge from the tumult of words, facts, thoughts, and events surrounding me, created by me, and apparently belonging to me, but in fact completely alien to me. It's frightening—that's the only word for it—frightening to live, frightening to die. I am frightened by what I have been, frightened of what I shall be. My work is worthless. I am absolutely certain I have no artistic talent. I'm too much of a poseur for that. I lack spontaneity. I am inconsequential. Life's events have no influence on me. My marriage is not my own; it seems an outsider's. I came to London to absorb the local spirit, but am unable to. I am making no spiritual progress. I see nothing and nobody. I am ashamed to be such a failure, but I can't seem to give myself up to London. I've bought a bowler hat, but made no further steps in that direction. Lethargy of the soul. A vacuum. Where am I going and why? Where am I? I have a wonderful wife, she couldn't be better, but she knows what it is to love and hate, and I know nothing. I love and envy and worship her, but nothing really unites us. Nothing spiritual, of course. I hide as much from her as from others. She takes pleasure in each day-to-day bit of unity. Fine. I like to see her happy.

1904

>->->->->->->->->-

18 April.

What nonsense I've been talking. I'm in London and feeling perfectly fine. I've given myself up to its influence, I feel a great deal of unity with my wife, and I've any number of new feelings. Life is easy.

2 June.

Thursday. Today is the kind of day worthy of starting a diary: it is unique. Yesterday I took my bed apart and lay on the floor. I read Shakespeare late into the night. Masha never left my thoughts. I got up in the morning, made a gift of the rest of my things to the neighbors, took my basket to Upper Bedford Place myself, came to an agreement with the porter, took my **breakfast** in the **boarding-house** and went back to Gloucester Street for some other things. The bell rang. Mrs. Noble handed me a telegram.[7]

Suddenly my whole being broke into a song of joy. I started pacing the empty room, where only a rolled up piece of oilcloth and the tied-up bed remained, taking huge steps, a stride totally new for me. I do not know—

7. The telegram announced the birth of Chukovsky's first-born, Nikolai, to whom he refers as Kolya throughout the diary. (M.H.H.)

nor do I wish to know—what went through my head. I felt too good without that. Then I started thinking that he would outlive me and see things I'd not see, then I decided to write a poem on the subject, then I thought of Masha's suffering, then I realized the following motif was running through my head:

> I am healthy and my wife
> Has brought a son, Yan, to my life.[8] [. . .]

20 June.

I am learning vocabulary from Browning. I have decided to do it daily. I am waiting for newspapers and letters. When they come, I'll go to the free reading room. Browning is to my taste. We're going to be friends; I'll be with him for a long time. I like the way he justifies everything, his positivistic mysticism, even his nervous dialogue with the reader. But his language is difficult, and it will take much time to master it. < . . . >

10 July.

I am reading Renan's *Life of Jesus*. I've decided to copy out everything I can use for my fanciful book on aimlessness. My hypotheses are the following: lacking goals is more attractive than having them; aimlessness is the only way to achieve goals. I shall set aside a few pages for notes on the subject. < . . . >

1 August.

I am writing a preface for my *Onegin*.[9] If I were a critic and had to review this novel in verse, I'd write the following: We never expected so imperfect a work from Mr. Chukovsky. Why did he write it? It is too long to be a joke, too short to be serious. The characters are wooden, there is no action, and, most important, the tone that conveys his relation to the subject matter is that of a feuilleton or light comedy and highly frivolous. Choosing the title of Pushkin's masterpiece for such a work is nothing short of blasphemy.

---

8. An approximate quotation from Pushkin's *Songs of the Western Slavs* (1834). Pushkin has the protagonist's landlady, not his wife, bear him the son.

9. Chukovsky's *A Contemporary Eugene Onegin: A Novel in Four Cantos* appeared in *Odesskie novosti* (25 December 1904, 1 January 1905), though with no preface.

The verse is generally light, clear, concise . . . Fine for "train literature" but nothing more. < . . . >

29 August.

I am not doing anything. Literally. For the last three weeks I haven't held a book in my hands. I haven't written an article for a month. I don't know what the future will bring, but if this keeps up I'm a goner. [. . .] My latest nightmare is neither chess nor the boat nor Kew Gardens—it's photography. I've acquired a twenty-three-ruble camera for the wholesale price of fifteen rubles, and I'm on a picture-taking binge. [. . .] Oddly enough, the only things I'm taking pictures of are the things Masha saw when she was in England, the things we experienced together. The rest is worthless in my eyes. [. . .]

1905

9 April.

Am translating Byron for Vengerov. I don't know how good it will be. Sometimes I like it, sometimes I don't. < . . . >

16 June.

< . . . > The bombing has begun. A battleship is heading toward the Cathedral, where the Cossacks are. Bombs are flying everywhere. The city is in a panic.

   I was an eyewitness to everything that happened on the fifteenth and shall explain it all in detail. At about ten in the morning I went to the boulevard, to Shaevsky's, for a glass of beer. There was a triple-stacked battleship lying at anchor between the lighthouse and the breakwater. People said that it had hoisted the red flag and that the sailors had mutinied and all the officers aboard had been killed, that a sailor who had been killed by an officer—which event set off the mutiny—was lying in state on the shore, and that the battleship could destroy the entire city in an hour, and so on.

I said to the man next to me, a court official, "Why don't we go to the port and see the dead sailor." But he said, "I can't. I'm in uniform." So I went alone.

Down at the port I saw a great swarm of people. They were all heading for the new jetty. No policemen, no soldiers. At the far end of the jetty there was a makeshift tent. It had the sailor's corpse in it. There was a crowd standing around the corpse, and a lively little sailor, a swarthy type, was reciting the proclamation lying on the dead man's chest: "Comrades! The sailor Grigory Kolesnichenko(?) was brutally murdered by an officer just for reporting that the borsch was bad. Take vengeance on the tyrants! Cross yourselves (or if you're Jewish, do whatever you do). Long live liberty!"

At these words the people in the tent shouted "Hurray!" and their cry was taken up by hundreds of voices on the pier. Then the sailor recited the proclamation again. Coins poured into the cup next to the dead man; they are for the funeral. The crowd was teeming with Social Democrats calling out "Comrades! Comrades!" to the down-and-outs. They made a point of telling people not to disperse, to remain in the port until further instructions from the battleship.[10]

1906

➤-➤-➤-➤-➤-➤-➤-➤

5 June.

I can't write a thing—not even the awful, awkward doggerel I mention above. There's not a thought in my head. < . . . > I think I'll write about Rozanov.

Rozanov's little book is very clever. To write a book as clever as that he needed not to know and not to understand a number of things. What

---

10. Chukovsky is describing the aftermath of the mutiny on the battleship *Potemkin*, one of the high points of the Revolution of 1905. His description closely parallels several sequences in part three of Sergei Eisenstein's classic film *Battleship Potemkin* (1925). (M.H.H.)

would Lucretius' verse be worth had he known Darwin? The "good, solid revolutionaries," the "professional revolutionaries" will reject Rozanov's philosophical and psychological interpretations first because good, solid people can't stand philosophy, and second because Rozanov is an onlooker. [. . .]

There are onlookers and onlookers. Some look out of upstairs windows and see everything that happens; they see things "from the outside" and understand more. Others come up and say, "What's going on, gentlemen?"

That's the kind of onlooker Rozanov is. He went up to the revolution when it was at its height—he hadn't noticed it till then—he went up to it and said, "What's going on here?" They tried to explain. But he is a "dreamer," a "visionary," an "independent thinker," an underground man. That's why he writes articles with titles like "In My Corner." Rozanov's great plus is that he is incapable of listening to anyone or anything, incapable of understanding anyone or anything. People explain things to him, and instead of listening he comes up with his own explanations. His own explanations coincide with Marx (certain pages) without his realizing it. And that's what makes his odd (and constant) combination of Khlestakovian superficiality and Dostoevskian depth.[11] Without Khlestakov, Rozanov would have no Dostoevsky.

I've found four kopecks. I'm going out for paper and will put it all down immediately.

7 June.

< . . . > I'm thinking of writing an article about the Goal in Itself. People with symmetrical souls. The great tautologies of life: love for love's sake, art for art's sake, life for life's sake, being for being's sake.

I need to re-feel it all, however, because I can only remember what I once felt. < . . . >

8 June.

Received a letter from Remizov today. A strange man. He is highly perceptive, but his soul is like tinted glass: it lets very little through. And

---

11. Khlestakov is the protagonist of Gogol's comedy *The Inspector General* (1836). His priceless self-definition—"There is an extraordinary lightness about my thoughts"—is an apt evocation of the mindlessness, frivolity, and utter lack of substance at the core of the Khlestakov syndrome. (V.E.)

everything is so lean, so sparse, so terribly difficult. There is no air in what he does. [...]

I've decided to translate one Rossetti sonnet a day (into prose).

A sonnet is a monument to a moment, a monument created by the eternity of the soul to a dead but immortal instant. Do not let it strut its hard-won perfection, be it purifying prayer or evil portent. Mint it from ivory or ebony so that it may resemble day or night. And may time behold its helmet hung with garlands, studded with pearls, and glistening. A sonnet is a coin, the head telling of its soul, the tail—of whom it serves, whether it pays the imperial tribute imposed by life or the exaction by the high court of love or whether, amidst infernal winds in the wharves of the dark, it places the excise of death in the hands of Charon.

Splendid! I began with the clumsy lines:

> O sonnet, monument to a moment,
> To an instant dead but immortal! < ... >

18 June.

< ... > I've become interested in Chatterton. I'm struck by what Rossetti has to say about him [...]

24 June.

< ... > I feel I had no youth. The only freedom I know is the freedom to walk down the street. I don't like the impressions I have, nor do I live by them. I went to the State Duma[12] and was too lazy to enter it in my diary.

1907

17 July.

The most miserable day I've ever had. I received a letter filled with insults I don't deserve from a usurer; I failed to write the Chekhov article I'd

12. The State Duma was a parliament with limited powers instituted after the Revolution of 1905 as a step in the direction of a constitutional monarchy. (V.E.)

promised; there was no sign in *Rech'* of my feuilleton on short-term thoughts. < . . . > Insomnia. It's now one in the morning. Not even Chekhov can cheer me up. What shall I say about him?

People claim that Chekhov hated life, that he was a pessimist, a grumbler. Slander! The bleakest of his stories is harmonious. His world is elegant, perfect, charming in a feminine way. "Gusev" is more perfect than anything Tolstoy ever wrote. Chekhov is the most mellifluous, the most musical of all writers. When you read "Gusev," you can't believe that those few scraps of paper contain . . . and so on. < . . . >

Starting the day after tomorrow I resolve to work as follows: Read until one o'clock. Walk from one until mealtime. Work until six. Then walk until ten—and to bed. In addition, try to see as few people as possible and spread myself less thin in what I read. I'm happier with my latest *Rech'* articles on Chekhov, short-term thoughts, and Kamensky. [. . .]

9 September.

Had a visit from Repin today. He is very polite. His beard is grayish and—you'd never know it from his portraits—grows straight into his mustache. He is unassuming. No sooner did he arrive than he climbed up on the couch and took down Vrubel's portrait of Bryusov. "Good show. That's Bryusov, all right." Somov's portrait of Ivanov. "Good show. That's Ivanov, all right." He called Bakst's portrait of Bely "painstaking." His comments on the engravings of Byron's portraits: "banal" and "clichéd." He approved of Lyubimov's caricature of me. Then he took a seat and we talked about Rossetti (he is too academic) and Leonid Andreev ("Red Laughter"[13] represents the insanity of war today; the governor is a combination of Tolstoy, Gogol, and Andreev). < . . . > When I showed him his Alexei Tolstoy, he said, "That was after his death. It influenced me. Some rotter touched it up. It's terrible!" Then we went downstairs for tea, pears, and plums. < . . . > He had left his coat upstairs and ran up to get it so as not to be thought an old man. I saw him out to the gate and watched him depart, a hunched old man in a cape. [. . .]

13. "Red Laughter" (1904) is an impassioned response to the debacle of the Russo-Japanese War. (V.E.)

21 October.

Everything was white when I woke up today. It felt like the Christmases of my youth. Yesterday Tan and I dug sand as usual down by the river. I'm digging to divert the river bed, building gigantic dams. Someone keeps tearing them down and I put them back up. For a month now. < . . . >

After that I lay in bed a long time thinking about my book on the goal in itself. Will I ever write it—the only book in my life? I came up with the idea at the age of seventeen, when I thought it would refute Darwin, Marx, and Schopenhauer. Now I doubt my ability to refute even Chulkov, and merely pretend to state opinions. What are my opinions?

Repin recently resigned from the Academy.[14] He visited Tolstoy and the Crimea and is now back. I went to see him on Wednesday. It was unpleasant. There was a general there talking about dirty Jews, pillaged estates, and impoverished landowners. Repin nodded away. He showed us pictures of the Tolstoys, count and countess. Pitiful. She is like his impresario, "a walking, talking Lev Tolstoy." Repin reported Tolstoy reading Kuprin's "Night Watch" and weeping at the sad passages.[15] Tolstoy's peasants "confiscated" the oaks, and the countess called the police. Tolstoy got upset, began to cry, and said, "I'm leaving." The public doesn't know this is going on, and obnoxious newspapermen hurl abuse at him. [. . .]

1908

+>-+>-+>-+>-+>-+>-+>

1 June.

"You're 'bedeviled,' Papa," Kolya[16] says.
   I'm translating "Rikki-Tikki-Tavi."

14. In October 1907 Repin relinquished his position at the Imperial Academy of Fine Arts School following serious policy disagreements with the academy's president, Prince Vladimir.

15. Repin's report tallies with a passage in N. N. Gusev's standard Tolstoy biography: "When the reading [of "The Night Watch"] was over, Tolstoy said, 'How true! There's nothing superfluous here. None of our younger writers can match Kuprin.' " (N. N. Gusev, *Letopis' zhizni i tvorchestva L. N. Tolstogo, 1891–1910* [Moscow, 1960], 567).

16. Chukovsky's first child, the future writer Nikolai (Kolya for short), was born in 1904. (V.E.)

29 August.

< . . . > I need to study, but how? If I want to study the cinema, I need to go to the cinema. But where can I find a cinema in Kuokkala? I'm reading Berdyaev. The thing about Berdyaev is that his page twelve is always dull and dreary. That's a bad sign. Anyone can write ten pages; the trick is writing pages eleven and twelve.

11 September.

[. . .]

I have no doctrine, no commitment. The only time I can write is when something emotional grabs me for an instant. If I had an "idea," I'd be a writer. And without commitment I'm practically illiterate, I'm impotent, and I envy reporters who can put ten coherent lines together.

5 November.

I'm getting down to work on Ibsen. Early morning. < . . . > Przybyszewski once told me that he was introduced to Ibsen at a ball (or was it a rout?) in Christiania. Ibsen shook his hand and said, without looking at him, "I've never heard your name, but I can see by your face that you are a fighter. Keep fighting and you will achieve your goal. Good-bye." Przybyszewski was delighted. A week later he saw Ibsen in the street. He caught up with him and said, "Hello! I'm Przybyszewski." And Ibsen shook his hand and said, "I've never heard your name, but I can see by your face that you are a fighter. Keep fighting and you will achieve your goal. Good-bye." < . . . >

1909

20 February.

< . . . > A moonlit evening with much snow and wind. Mama is with us. < . . . > I'm surrounded by Ukrainian books and, oddly enough, as I read

them I start thinking in Ukrainian. And what's even odder, when I've been reading all day I dream in Ukrainian. And even odder than that: the Ukrainian verse I knew as a child but have completely and utterly forgotten—pushed into the background by Blok and Bryusov—is surfacing, coming back to me <. . . . >. And even odder than that: I feel a sort of Ukrainian naïveté, artlessness welling up in me—in my mood, my spirit. So not only does the soul create language; language (in part) creates the soul.

Lida[17] put on Kolya's brown coat today and refused to take it off, even inside. It's odd: her language is developing in an entirely different way from Kolya's. Kolya creates his own words, but retains only a few of them; he increases his vocabulary gradually. Lida can pronounce all words more or less properly and has an enormous vocabulary, but they are not so much words as their shadows. That is because she doesn't create them; she merely repeats what she hears. [. . .]

7 *May*.

Am reading Dostoevsky's *Idiot* for the first time and find it obvious that Myshkin is Christ. The incident with Marie is the story of Mary Magdalene. She loves children, she preaches; the prince comes from an impoverished but ancient line, sets great store by equality (with the concierge), and says "Thou shalt not kill" about executions.

2 *June*.

Masha and I were at Andreev's the day before yesterday. < . . . > "You are necessary," Andreev said about me, "because you show the bottom of every chair. We never even suspected chairs had bottoms, and you show them to us. But you are often in the position of Poe's hero who wanted to take a picture of a man with a pimple and ended up with a picture of a pimple with a man." [. . .]

---

17. Chukovsky's second child, Lidia (Lida for short), was born in 1907. The future author, editor, and human rights activist proved his most celebrated offspring. (V.E.)

1910

-+->-+>-+>-+>-+>-+>-+>

23 January.

Nemirovich-Danchenko came to see me today and told me the following story Chekhov had told him in Nice. Chekhov answered every letter he received. Why? asked Nemirovich-Danchenko. Because, Chekhov said, we had a teacher in Taganrog, a teacher who meant a lot to me. One day I held out my hand to him and he (didn't notice and) failed to respond. I was terribly hurt.

Spent the evening at the Repins'. Repin said that a genius often fails to understand himself.

8 February.

< . . . > Went to see Nemirovich-Danchenko yesterday morning. He told me that Chekhov had been afraid of death and kept saying, "When I die, you must . . ." and so on.

Nemirovich-Danchenko has many kinds of vodka, many books, many Japanese pictures, and close to forty bottles of eau-de-cologne in the bathroom. Multiplicity and vacuous grandiosity are two of his traits. He even has a double-barreled surname. It's a strange disposition the desire to multiply everything around one. < . . . >

20 April.

Repin did my portrait in three sittings. He told me many interesting stories, for instance, about the time Alexander II visited Antokolsky's studio when he was painting *Ivan the Terrible*. He walked in, looked him up and down, and asked, "What religion are you?"

"I'm a Jew."

"From where?"

"From Vilna, Your Majesty."

"Just as I suspected."[18]

18. Antokol was a predominantly Jewish section of Vilna. The Tsar seems to have been aware that many Jewish family names derive from place-names. (V.E.)

And he left the room without another word.

He told the following story about Musorgsky. Stasov wanted Musorgsky to be treated at the Military Hospital, but of course Musorgsky was no military man. Then call him an orderly, said Stasov. And when Repin went to the hospital to do his portrait, he found the sign "Orderly" above his bed.

Repin came to see us yesterday. His memory is failing: he forgets what happened to him the day before. Gessen clearly made a bad impression on him. When Repin showed him his canvas *18 October*, which is meant to show the apotheosis of the revolution, Gessen said, "Now I see why the Russian revolution failed." It's a caricature of the Russian revolution.

29 *April.*

[. . .]

Kolya and his friend Yegor were having a talk over dinner, and Yegor was lying shamelessly. I said, "Don't lie like that, Yegor, or God will punish you." To which Kolya replied, "But He's the one who makes people lie. He makes them lie, then punishes them."

Determinism and free will. I wouldn't have believed it if I hadn't heard it with my own ears. [. . .]

15 *July.*

Went out on a boat with Korolenko. < . . . > Here is what he said about Leskov: "When I was a proofreader for *Novosti*, we heard a rumor that our paper, which had never been subject to censorship, was going to be visited by a censor. I was on my guard. We were running Leskov's *Items from the Diocese*. One day an official-looking man came in and said, 'Let me have a look at Leskov's *Items*.'

'I will not.'

'And how will you keep me from seeing them?'

'Simple. I'll tell the typesetters not to give them to you.'

'But why?'

'Because our paper has never submitted to censorship, and censors . . . '

'But I'm not a censor. I'm Leskov!' [. . .]

"The shift in his views toward radicalism was influenced by a Jewish student. I would see her when I worked at *Novosti*. She would bring articles and was quite full of herself."

5 October.

Spent yesterday evening at Rozanov's. His wife had a stroke three days ago. "She's a simple woman," Rozanov said. "When we were abroad just now, she started using her mind for the first time, wondering why God did this or that. We got back to Saint Petersburg and she had a stroke, and the first words she said were, "It comes from living by the mind and not the heart."
< . . . >

1911

➤-➤-➤-➤-➤-➤-➤-➤-➤

30 January.

< . . . > I'm working on Shevchenko, but now that I've read him carefully I don't know what to do with him. I feel him in my bones, I hear his voice, I see his walk. I couldn't sleep last night so clearly did I picture him plying Nevsky Prospect in the thirties, running after girls and the like. Will I manage to get it all down on paper? Kuokkala is my downfall. There's a shroud of snow covering everything at the moment, and I feel it's covering me as well. I am a man of concrete ideas; I need images. Living in isolation is fine for someone with a logical mind, but instead of images all I see is snow. [. . .]

I've received a letter from Rozanov asking for his books back. A total break, in other words. [. . .]

1912

+>-+>-+>-+>-+>-+>-+>-+>

15 May.

< . . . > Called on Rozanov. Disgusting impression. < . . . > He com-
plained that the Yids were tormenting his children at school. The interesting thing is how: by being likable!

"Is Rosenblum a Jew?" the children ask.

"Yes."

"Oh, he's so nice!"

"And Nabokov?"[19]

"No, Nabokov is Russian."

"The swine!"

That's what makes Jews so awful. < . . . >

He is setting up a library in Kostroma. He showed me the peasant
house where he was born. He kissed me and thanked me when I left—and
turned up at my house the same day. An hour later. [. . .]

Repin has come to see us four or five times; I've gone to see him once.
He's doing a portrait of Andreev and a painting called *Before Sunset* with
a stylized Tolstoy: Tolstoy lit by the setting sun and in a state of spiritual
exaltation, the body melting away leaving only the soul. But I fear the lack
of taste: the branch of the apple tree is tendentious, the shining sun gaudy.
It's like a poem in prose: it seems easy, but few can pull it off. Repin is
waiting for his own apple tree to bloom so he can paint it from life. [. . .]

5 June.

Repin again yesterday, this time for Masha's name day. He gave her an old
photograph of himself. We spoke of literature. It turns out Repin worships
Chernyshevsky: his eyes sparkled as he talked about *What Is to Be Done?*
He detests Turgenev's poems in prose.[20]

19. The future writer Vladimir Nabokov was a student at the school—the prestigious Tenishev School in Saint Petersburg—at the time. (M.H.H.)

20. Nikolai Chernyshevsky's novel-tract *What Is to Be Done?* (1863), with its portrayal of a
totally dedicated revolutionary, was immensely influential among the Russian radical intelligentsia. Some years later its title was echoed in a major programmatic statement by Lenin. (V.E.)

6 July.

< . . . > Repin gave a talk last Sunday that ended: "And God, at the end of each day of Creation, said, 'And it was good!' A great artist praising his own creation!" Many readers of the *Vestnik znaniia* asked me what Repin was doing talking about God. I replied that it was only a metaphor, but the day before yesterday he told me at table, "No, it's no metaphor. It's what I believe. God must have been an artist. Otherwise how can you explain the joy and religious ecstasy you feel in the process of creation and why something as useless as art has been so highly valued?" < . . . >

1913

22 February.

Kolya is writing out words in my study (paying special attention to penmanship): steppe, singing, century. "The worst part of me," he says, "is my desire for revenge. I nearly killed Boba[21] today with a crow bar. And why? Because he didn't put the broom back right, that's all. And when I hit Lida yesterday, do you think I was sorry? Well, later I was. I very much regretted it." Word for word. [. . .]

1914

4 February.

< . . . > Went to Marinetti's reading. A common, dull-witted Italian with expressionless, piglike eyes making primitive, bombastic remarks. < . . . >

---

21. Chukovsky's third child, Boris (Boba for short), was born in 1910. (M.H.H.)

10 February approximately.

[. . .] Yesterday at twelve Chaliapin arrived with his dog and his Chinaman Vasily. Repin took out an enormous canvas and is painting him in a recumbent position. He ogles him the way a cat ogles a piece of lard, with tenderness and love, while Chaliapin looks at Repin like a little old man, kissing him on the forehead, patting him on the head, and telling him bedtime stories. His voice is not the most pleasant: he utters everyday thoughts in a highly sententious tone. [. . .]

He talks about himself ecstatically, admiring himself, naively amazed at what he sees. "How grateful I am to nature. She could have made me smaller or given me a poor memory or a sunken chest. But no, it concentrated all its energy on making me Chaliapin!" The habit of feeling thousands of eyes and opera glasses on him day in and day out has turned him into a flirt. < . . . >

They have confiscated my book, arrested it; I was very worried. But now I'm calm. I can get to work on Chekhov. I worship Chekhov, I dissolve in him, I disappear. That's why I can't write about him or write only trifles.

2 April.

Chaliapin on Chekhov. "I remember once reading Chekhov's stories aloud to him. Bunin and I. I read 'A Dear Dog.' Anton Pavlovich smiled and kept spitting into a paper cone. Consumption."

Lida and I were out for a walk yesterday (she had been crying since morning, unable to understand why her goldfish had died) when she said, "Everybody must get together and decide that there will be no more poor people. Rich people will live in peasant houses and poor people will be rich or, no, rich people can stay rich, but poor people will be a little richer. People are so cruel. How can they kill animals and catch fish? One person should collect a lot of money and give it away to the people who need it. And other things like that."

She hadn't heard it anywhere; she'd come to it on her own and was expressing it all for the first time in a thoughtful voice. I was amazed. For the first time I realized what a pure, poetic soul she is. Where does it come from? Were I to put it in a book, it would sound sugary sweet, forced, but here in nature it sent shivers down my spine. [. . .]

15 July.

< . . . > War. Ben Livshits has been called up. A pity. I'm fond of him. He's got a personality all his own: he's resourceful, strong, witty, sentimental, a good friend, and now he's writing good verse. Yesterday I took him and Mandelshtam, the "marble fly,"[22] home with me, and Repin liked Ben better. [. . .]

26 July.

I was in town yesterday. To get some money: I delivered an article to *Niva*. It's in a bad way. Subscribers owe two hundred thousand rubles, Panin told me. [. . .]

Went to see A. F. Koni. He'd just come from the Winter Palace, where the Emperor had given a speech to the people's representatives. He had a strange story to tell: the Emperor, having received Germany's declaration of war, worked for a while and when at one in the morning he went to take tea with the Empress he was given a telegram from Wilhelm II asking him to postpone mobilization. [. . .]

More about the Emperor: He looks paler, younger, more handsome; he used to be flabby and unsure of himself.

I'm back in the street. The cabbies are asking exorbitant prices. The *Vienna* has taken down its sign. *Leiner's* has done the same. They have been replaced by white canvas ones saying *The Waiters' Society Restaurant* and *I. S. Sokolov's*. The sign for the *St. Petersburger Zeitung* has become *Nemetskaia gazeta*. The streets are full of soldiers with mess tins and shovels. And one man bears the entire weight on his shoulders. Terrible. < . . . > A perfectly good-natured woman (Ukrainian?) reads aloud from the newspaper: "Fifteen thousand Germans have been killed at Liège" and says, "Thank God. Glad to hear it."

[. . .] How are we going to earn our daily bread now that the only theater is the theater of military operations and the only book is the Orange Book.[23] Ganfman and Tatyana Alexandrovna comment on the Winter Palace

---

22. It was the avant-garde poet Velimir Khlebnikov who dubbed Mandelshtam "a marble fly."

23. A collection of diplomatic documents bearing on the events leading up to World War I.

and the Duma in *Sovremennoe slovo*.[24] They find the Poles' declaration very clever, subtle, Kerensky's speech intelligent, and Khaustov's speech silly. [. . .] Rumor has it that Madame Milyukova, who has a dacha in Finland with six thousand books, has locked it up and given the key to a local commanding officer, saying, "You may use it for officers. No soldiers, please." < . . . >

1916

➤-➤-➤-➤-➤-➤-➤-➤

22 September.

Yesterday I met Gorky for the first time. Grzhebin said we'd be going to Repin's at 1:15. I went to the station and didn't find him, but glancing into the window of a first-class compartment I noticed a rough, ungainly face and realized who it was. I went in. He was gloomy and uneasy. Without so much as looking at me, he said to Grzhebin, "What is that man selling on the platform? The cleanly shaved one? I bet he's a Russian trying to pass for an Englishman. I bet he's from Siberia. You don't believe me? I'll go and ask him." I could see it was all an act, he was just uneasy, and I decided to set him at ease with some down-to-earth talk. < . . . > I started talking about Vengrov and Mayakovsky, and his face grew tender, his voice gentle, exaggeratedly so, and he started talking like Mirolyubov: "They should read the Bible . . . the Bible . . . That's right, the Bible. There's something going on in Mayakovsky's soul . . . That's right, his soul."

But he's clearly not a good judge, because Vengrov is neurasthenic and confused, he doesn't exist yet, and Mayakovsky is monotonous and poor. Like urban life in general.

The gig at the station already had two people in it: a man with gray hair and his young wife. Gorky's bad leg kept him from walking, and they graciously let him sit with the coachman, thinking him a poor man. At Repin's Gorky felt constrained. He paced up and down looking depressed.

---

24. Reference to the 26 July 1914 session of the State Duma in response to the declaration of war by Germany and Austria. Khaustov spoke for the Social Democrats, and P. N. Milyukov for the People's Freedom Party, another name for the Constitutional Democratic or Kadet Party.

Repin posed him in profile, but he failed to keep the pose, bobbing his head and looking at Repin when he should have been looking at Grzhebin and me. He told some curious stories, about his dealings with the censor, for example.

GORKY. Your censor is not an intelligent man.
HEAD CENSOR. How dare you say such a thing!
GORKY. Because it is true, sir.
HEAD CENSOR. How dare you call me "sir." I am not "sir"; I am "Your Excellency."
GORKY. Go to hell, Your Excellency.

The censor didn't realize he was dealing with Gorky. "Then we turned out to come from the same part of the country." (And Gorky showed how they shook hands.) < . . . >

He also talked about a prison guard who was known throughout Nizhny Novgorod for his cruelty but who would turn up his collar now and again and go to see his seamstress. "The seamstress lived in the foul house that I happened to be living in at the time. Our rooms were separated only by a partition. And he would sneak into her place and (softly, in almost a whisper) recite Lermontov to her: "The mournful demon, spirit of exile . . ."

At that point Repin's son Yury said timidly, "I'm very sympathetic to your position on the war," and Gorky started in on the war. "So many useful brains going to waste—French, German, English, ours too, we're no fools. The English have seized so and so many acres in the Urals. I remember a merchant in Nizhny Novgorod—Russians are strange people, let me tell you—who'd just come from there and took gold out of one pocket, tungsten out of another, silver out of a third, and so on.

" 'Look, look at it. It all comes from my land. And you think I'll let the English have it? No, no!' he said, cursing the English.

"But then he saw a picture on the table and asked, 'Who's that? An Englishman? What's he doing here?'

" 'Just what you were talking about: buying . . . '

" 'Think you could introduce me? I could get a million out of him for my land.' "

We went to eat. At the end of the meal an officer who had sat there quietly the entire time burst into a tense, convulsive tirade—never glancing at Gorky—about how we will win, our French allies are so valiant, our English allies too, and about how Russia, which has given the world Peter the Great, Pushkin, and Repin, must be defended against German milita-rism. < . . . >

"That man seems to think I'm commander-in-chief of the German army," Gorky said to me.

I went home and didn't sleep a wink.

1917

➤➤➤➤➤➤➤➤➤

1 January.

Lida, Kolya, and Boba are ill. We have no help. Returning from town yesterday evening, I found Lida reading aloud: " 'I swear to God,' said the sultan to the eunuch, 'I own the most beautiful woman in the world together with all the odalisques in my harem . . . ' "

I fled the room in horror. The editor of a children's magazine, and what his own family has come to!

21 February.

Just back from the Merezhkovskys'. I can't get their hungry canine faces out of my mind. They've got a plan: to take over *Niva*. I had no idea. I went simply because Filosofov, who is ill, means a lot to me and I wanted to see him. I phoned and asked if I could. Gippius was unexpectedly gracious: by all means, we'll be only too happy, do come. I went. Dear Dmitry Vladimirovich had put on a little weight and looked healthy, if tired. Tea. They asked what I was up to. I was amazed. Why this sudden interest in me? I brought up *Niva*. They came alive. They listened closely to my "Crocodile." Gippius praised the first part for being silly. "The second part has a plan and is less elemental." Merezhkovsky came in and mentioned *Niva* as well. What was the matter? Why was *Niva* so bad? I told him everything I could. < . . . > Finally, after many significant looks and pregnant pauses, they presented Zinaida as their candidate to take over *Niva*. "Of course!" I responded without thinking. "Zinaida Nikolaevna is an excellent editor!" "Or me," said Merezhkovsky innocently. And I realized I'd been taken for a ride: they'd set up the plan long before. That was why they'd invited me. They didn't care about me and my "Crocodile"; they'd rehearsed the whole thing in advance. It turned my stomach. I felt I'd been involved in something indecent. That was when I noticed their hungry canine look. It was as if they'd been offered a bone.

"We would take the upper rooms for the Religious Philosophical Society," he said.

"My works could be run in the supplement," she said.

"And Bely and Sologub and Bryusov in a supplement next year!"

In short, they were bubbling over with plans designed to send *Niva* to its grave. And what greedy, hungry faces.

4 March.

Revolution.[25] The days burn up like paper. I can't sleep. I walked all the way from Kuokkala to Petersburg. I want to walk the streets, but my legs won't carry me. At Nabokov's.[26] He has been asked to draft an amnesty. [. . .]

30 April.

We've just walked along the water to Repin's: Boba, Kolya, Lida, Manya, Kazik, and I. We hung an empty bucket on a long pole and sang a song composed by the children:

> Two stumps
> Two bumps (we may meet on the way)
> Make sure it doesn't break (the bucket)
> Make sure it doesn't shake
> Splat!

Repin took me to see his pictures. There's a lot that is tasteless and limp, but it's not as bad as I expected. He himself was ashamed of his "sister leading a soldier into the fray" and said, "A buyer came to see it and I advised him against it. I told him it was trash and not worth buying."

25. Refers to the democratic February Revolution, which was triggered by the bread riots and by the soldiers' refusal to fire at the demonstrators, and which led to the Tsar's abdication and the proclamation of the republic. (V.E.)

26. The Nabokov in question is Vladimir Dmitrievich, the writer's father and a prominent liberal politician in the years immediately preceding the Revolution.

About some portrait or other: "You know what Khlebnikov the futurist said: 'A certain Burlyuk did my portrait in the form of a triangle, but it didn't look like me." About *The Church Procession:* "Now the censor will approve it." About his new portrait of Tolstoy: "I've always made Tolstoy too gentle, too meek. He was malicious, he had malicious eyes. I want to make him more truthful."

12 May.

[. . .]

Kolya and Lida confessed to me today while we were out rowing that they are starting to fear death. I reassured them and told them it would pass. < . . . >

The children are playing croquet with Zhenya Sokolov, and I enjoy hearing them laugh. Only now have I understood the joys of fatherhood, only now that I've turned thirty-five. Before that children are clearly an abnormality, a burden. Men should start having children at thirty-five. That's why most men marry at thirty-three.

Am reading Whitman, a new Whitman. Until now I paid no attention to whether I liked him or not, only to whether the public would like him and when I write about him. I tried to please the public rather than myself. Well, now I want only to please myself, so for the first time I'm measuring him by my own standards, and mirabile dictu! he's turned out to be an indispensable, life-saving poet for me. I go out in my boat and take great pleasure in reading:

> Did we think victory great?
> So it is—but now it seems to
> me, when it cannot
> be help'd, that
> defeat is great,
> And that death and dismay are great.[27]

This used to seem mere words and *wanton* formula to me, while now it is full of human meaning.

27. Lines from Walt Whitman's poem "To a Foil'd European Revolutionaire" (1856), which appears in the "Autumn Rivulets" section of *Leaves of Grass.*

16 June.

I nearly drowned yesterday. I jumped into deep water from the boat, swam a bit, and felt myself being pulled down. I couldn't cry out to Kolya, I forgot how to speak; I could only show him with my eyes. (From childhood I was certain I'd die in the water like the Russian critics Pisarev and Valeryan Maikov.) At last Kolya caught on. [. . .]

19 June.

Can't sleep. This is the second night I've been reading Stendhal's *The Red and the Black*, a fascinating novel in two volumes. It robbed my entire morning too. I was so annoyed at being taken away from my work that I tossed it out. Without a heroic gesture I'd never have torn myself from it. Five minutes later Masha told me about a Bolshevik demonstration that took place in Petrograd yesterday. It sounded less interesting to me than the fabricated sufferings of Julien Sorel dating from 1830.

I've written a little play for the children or, rather, the first act. Lida said to me, "Whenever you have a *nonwriting* time (when you can't seem to write), write something for children."

20 June.

Writing a play about Tsar Puzan. The children forced me to. They needed a play to keep them busy, and I've been at it for two days. I'm having great fun, but who knows what will come of it. Being funny isn't easy. Things that don't seem funny to grown-ups can send children into gales of laughter.

10 July.

Masha said to me this morning, "You know we have a dictatorship in Russia." She was upset. Only a month ago I couldn't understand how the bourgeoisie would win over the army and treasury and authorities. Despite all the laws of history it seemed that Russia, after centuries of autocracy, was becoming a socialist state. But no, history will out. With a wave of the hand it took power away from the progressive radical socialist groups and gave it to the moderate socialists.[28] In no less than three weeks it will take it away from the socialists and hand it to the Kadets. Everything goes quickly these days. The historical process has been speeded up.

15 July.

< . . . > Rumanov has the following to say about Lebedev, Kropotkin's son-in-law: He's an inconspicuous little man, always in the background, yet were it not for him Kropotkin and his family would have nothing to eat! Kropotkin is an anarchist, so of course he can't accept money for his works, and this inconspicuous, anonymous little man pays for his servants, his food, and so on.

The last time I saw Kropotkin he spoke of the inevitable rebirth of the working class after the war. "The workers are ready to start a new life," he told an American. "Mr. Thompson of Clarion told me that the transport workers, weavers, and railwaymen are ready to take production into their own hands and **control it**. < . . . >

23 July.

Went to see Kropotkin today. He lives in the House of the Netherlands Consul, Kamenny Ostrov 45, where he has a large, comfortable, two-story flat. [. . .] The Kropotkins' garden was dampish, but comme il faut. Some Dutchmen were playing tennis. A tired-looking Alexandra Petrovna was sitting on the terrace in a long pink sweater trying to smile but not bringing it off. "I'm so tired. The Winter Palace . . . the telephones . . ." We went to have tea. Kropotkin's niece, Katerina Nikolaevna, a woman of about forty-five, was serving some nice old men with false teeth and a military attaché at the British Embassy whose name I don't know. She told about a search of their dacha about two weeks ago to see if they were hoarding food. She asked the soldiers, "Do you know who lives here?" "Who?" "Kropotkin, the revolutionary." "So what?" And they broke down the door to the attic. The Kropotkins then phoned Commissar Nevedomsky (Miklashevsky), and the soldiers left with their tails between their legs. Meanwhile a broad-shouldered, massive, Pickwick-complexioned Kropot-

---

28. By "progressive radical socialist groups" Chukovsky means primarily the Bolsheviks, who seized power some three months after these words were written. (V.E.)

kin was making his way through the adjacent rooms < . . . >, and before long he came up to me, cheerful, beaming. "Well! Well! I never stop reading you. Welcome! Welcome!" Then he sat down next to me and struck up a lively conversation, taking a polite interest in any topic I touched upon. When we came to Nekrasov, he said, "Yes, yes. He lost the manuscript of Chernyshevsky's *What Is to Be Done?*, lost it."[29] Prince Suvorov (the General Governor at the time) had obtained it for him from the Peter-Paul Fortress, and he lost it. Let me recite a poem of Nekrasov's that has never been published." And (with an old man's wink) he recited the well-known:

> I was only four years old
> When by Father I was told,
> "All that counts is bought and sold
> With cash, with capital and gold."

He accompanied his recital with gestures. < . . . >

At this point his wife came up to us and said with cordial indifference, "Shame on you for not coming to see us in England!" and I suddenly realized that they were tired and I was a burden, but that for the past forty years they had humbly submitted to their fate of receiving guests, listening to them attentively, politely, cordially, and with indifference. He asked me where I lived. I gave him a detailed description of our commune and said it was an entirely new environment for me and one that our writers had not yet taken into account. I told him about the workers and young women intellectuals, how little they earned, how modestly yet honorably they lived, without ambiguous relationships. "What about unambiguous relationships," he asked with an old man's snicker. "Watch out you don't fall in love!"

Had I not known that the man sitting in front of me was a great prophet, a brilliant champion of a higher ideal for mankind, I'd have put him down for a good-natured family man. All domesticity and simplicity. [. . .]

"It's strange that nobody in Russia knows shorthand. When I talked to reporters at the Finland Station, not a single one of them took down the

---

29. On 3 February 1863 the Petersburg police bulletin carried an announcement about the loss of a package containing the first chapters of Chernyshevsky's *What Is to Be Done?* Its author, who was incarcerated in the Peter and Paul Fortress, gave the manuscript to his cousin, who was to convey it to Nekrasov for publication in his journal *Sovremennik*. Nekrasov mislaid the manuscript en route to the printing shop. After four announcements the package was recovered, and Chernyshevsky's novel started appearing in the March 1863 issue of the journal.

precise words I said. They made everything up because they didn't know shorthand."

The conversation turned to Dostoevsky, whose wife was a stenographer. "The renegade!" Kropotkin said. "Returning from Siberia and renouncing Fourier and socialism. It's remarkable how all renegades become worthless once they renege on their principles; they lose their talent."

I was amazed, because Dostoevsky's talent took flight after he returned from forced labor, but I sensed that Prince Kropotkin's enormous brain had no aesthetic bump to it. When I told him I liked Mikhailovsky's style, he said, "Yes, but I can never forgive him his political cowardice. I met him in 1867. He was like a pretty little girl—so afraid of me and my brother! < . . . >"

The princess asked whether there was food in Kuokkala. I said I didn't know. "Then there is," said Kropotkin. "By the way, I went to see Kerensky at the Winter Palace today, and four of us were served four slices of bread this big on an enormous plate with crowns and the tsar's monogram . . . And water! (He frowned.) Sasha and I shared one slice and left the rest for Kerensky."

[. . .]

"Give my regards to Repin. I respect him. I know all his painting though (alas!) only from reproductions."

I was under the impression that Kropotkin disapproved of Repin's having done portraits of autocrats and grand princesses, and I sensed again how alien art was to him.

"I dictated *Notes of a Revolutionary* in English. Then Dioneo translated them. After a page or two he would come and see me in Bromley and I would spend the entire day going over the text. He found it insulting. I would completely redo it, rewrite it from scratch. I had no choice. 'Mutual Aid' I wrote in English for *Nineteenth Century*." < . . . >

I had the feeling that Kropotkin was very tired, and I hastened to take my leave. [. . .]

31 July.

Back at Kropotkin's. He had an American with him and was talking about tractors. The American turned out to be an engineer who had brought over trains for the Siberian Railway. "There's no point in bringing us military equipment," Kropotkin said. "What we need are tractors and **crossing** switches." And he used his fingers to show rails crossing. "Everyone tells me we need tractors and crossing switches. I'd like to see the American ambassador and tell him."

"Nothing could be simpler," said the engineer. "And I'd very much like you to come to America."

"America is closed to me, unfortunately."

"Why?"

"Because I'm an anarchist."

"Are you really an anarchist?" the engineer exclaimed.

I looked at the venerable old man and saw the aristocrat, the prince, the courtier in his every feature.

"Yes, I am," he said, almost apologetically.

[. . .]

Kropotkin has the most varied company. It drives his family to distraction. They regard each new arrival as an affliction that must be patiently withstood to the end.

I brought up Walt Whitman.

"I can't say I'm the least bit interested in him. What good is poetry that sounds like prose? Besides, he was a pederast! I told Carpenter—I fairly shouted, 'Really, it's too much! In the Caucasus anyone caught seducing a boy is run through with a dagger!' I know there's degeneracy of the sort going on in our military school. Encouraging onanism among children!"

His anger then ricocheted onto me, as if I were to blame for Whitman's homosexuality.

"Then there's Oscar Wilde. He had such a nice wife. And two children. My wife gave them lessons. He had great talent. Élisée Reclus used to say that his writings on anarchism(?) should be carved in bronze as the Romans did. Every statement was a masterpiece. But the man himself was so fat and disgusting! Ugh! I saw him once. Horrible!"

"In *De Profundis* he called you 'the white Christ from Russia.' "[30]

"Yes, what nonsense. *De Profundis* is insincere."

We said good-bye, and although I agree with his view of *De Profundis*

---

30. Oscar Wilde wrote in *De Profundis:* "Two of the most perfect lives I have come across in my own experience are the lives of Verlaine and of Prince Kropotkin: both of them were men who have passed years in prison: the first, the one Christian poet since Dante; the other, a man with a soul of that beautiful white Christ which seems coming out of Russia" (London, 1905), 96.

I left feeling perplexed and offended. I felt the same when I read his uninspired book on Russian literature.[31] [. . .]

4 October.

[. . .] Dropped in on Repin. < . . . > He showed me some pictures. *The Volga Boatmen:* "Oh, how it's dried out. But I see what I need to do. I'll give the syphilitic (in the very front) a red (not bright red, pale from laundering) calico shirt (instead of blue) and make the red one in the last figure blue; otherwise the background is too loud. [. . .]

10 October.

Have spent days organizing the Anglo-American gift to the Russian people: two million free textbooks. I'm done in, so exhausted I can't sleep. I'm growing old, going gray. I'm ready to drop. And winter's just beginning. There's no rest ahead. So Kornei will perish just like that. And his family? Kolya is growing—into an unthinking egoist; Lida is sickly, green, exhausted.

Lida: "I don't like wasting fairy tales on non-sleepers." [. . .]

1918

➤-➤-➤-➤-➤-➤-➤-➤

14 February.

With Lunacharsky. I see him nearly every day. People ask why I don't try and get something out of him. I answer I'd feel bad taking advantage of such a gentle child. He beams with complacency. There is nothing he likes more than to do somebody a favor. He pictures himself an omnipotent benevolent being, dispensing bliss to all: Be so good, be so kind as to . . . He writes letters of recommendation for everybody, signing each, with a flourish, Lunacharsky. He dearly loves his signature. He can't wait to pick

31. *Ideals and Reality in Russian Literature* (1907), which is based on lectures delivered in the United States in 1901.

up his pen to sign. He lives in a squalid little flat off a nauseating staircase in the Army and Navy House opposite the Muruzi House. There is a sheet of paper (high-quality, English) on the door that says "I receive no one here. You may see me from such-and-such a time to such-and-such a time at the Winter Palace and at such-and-such a time at the Commissariat of Education, etc." But no one pays the slightest attention to it: he is constantly barraged by actors from the imperial theaters, former émigrés, men with harebrained schemes or out for easy money, well-meaning poets from the lower classes, officials, soldiers, and more—to the horror of his irascible servant, who rages each time the bell rings: "Can't you read?" Then Totosha, his spoiled and handsome young son, runs in, shouting something in French—never Russian—or the ministerially unceremonious Madame Lunacharskaya. It is all so chaotic, good-natured, and naive that it seems a comedy act. [. . .]

Lunacharsky is late for his appointments at the Commissariat of Education: he gets involved in a conversation with one person and makes others wait for hours. To show how liberal he is, he has a portrait of the Tsar hanging in his office. He calls in his visitors two by two, seating them on either side of himself, and while he talks to one of them the other can admire the Minister's statesmanlike acumen. It is a naive and harmless bit of swagger. I asked him to write a letter to the Commissar of Post and Telegraph Offices, Proshian, and he willingly picked out a letter on his typewriter to the effect that I was such-and-such a person and he would be delighted if Proshian agreed to reopen *Kosmos*. [. . .]

15 October.

Had a message from Lunacharsky yesterday telling me to come to the Commissariat of Education at three for a meeting. I gathered up Kolya and Lida and off we went. < . . . > No sooner did Lunacharsky arrive than a deputation of mealy-mouthed professors came to see him. Lunacharsky was the picture of humility, and they mealy-mouthed their way into having their living quarters saved from division into communal flats and other such things. The Proletkult poets made boorishly malicious comments like "All they care about is their own skin, that kind" and "Look at him, closing the window. Afraid of the Spanish disease." They paraded around Lunacharsky's office as if they owned it, drinking endless glasses of tea with gigantic pieces of caramel and behaving in a provocatively informal manner (à la Mayakovsky). < . . . > Having dismissed the professors, Lunacharsky invited us to sit around a large table and gave a very witty and pleasantly frivolous speech. [. . .]

He radiated good humor as he spoke. I felt I was in a Pickwickian atmosphere. He appeals to me more and more: his incredible ability to work, his constant good mood, his preterhuman kindness, so angelic and helpless, make any mockery on his account cynical and vulgar. It is as shameful to laugh at him as it is to laugh at a child or someone ill. Only recently have I come to realize what a big heart he has. Amen. I will never laugh at him again.

Zinaida Gippius wrote me a nice letter two weeks ago asking me to pay her a visit. I arrived during the day. Merezhkovsky, groveling in insincere concern over me, asked me to introduce him to Lunacharsky! I can't get over them! First they rake me over the coals for my supposed bolshevism; then they want to worm their way into the Bolsheviks' good graces. Could I get a letter to Lordkepanidze? Could I get them a document that would save their flat from being divided into a communal flat? Could I arrange for the government to buy the cinema rights from him for his *Paul, Alexander*,[32] and so on? I did everything he asked for—it took two whole days— and I'm sure that as soon as the Bolsheviks go to pot Merezhkovsky will be the first to slander me. [. . .]

27 October.

Went to see Eikhvald and buy some English books. She and her daughter live in a luxurious Sergeevskaya Street apartment (she is the widow of the famous doctor and surgeon), but their poverty is evident. They haven't even got potatoes. Apparently the same holds for the residents of all the neighboring streets: Kirochnaya, Shpalernaya, the entire region.

From there I go to the Merezhkovskys'.

Zinaida Gippius is all made up and wearing a wig. She's a bit deaf from her illness, but affable. She's sitting at the samovar, where for the past year she's been reviling the Bolsheviks from morning till night, seeing and hearing nothing but the samovar. < . . . > Then she tells a story about Blok: "I ran into him in a tram. He looked lethargic, rattled.

32. Merezhkovsky's historical drama *Paul I* (1908) and historical novel *Alexander I* (1911–12). (V.E.)

'You refuse to shake my hand, Zinaida Nikolaevna?'

'I shall shake the hand of my friend, but not of Blok.'

"The whole tram heard. They all wondered whether he was my lover!"[33]

28 October.

Tikhonov invited me a fortnight ago to edit Anglo-American literature for the Publishing House of World Literature of the Commissariat of Education headed by Gorky. I've been at it night and day ever since. Putting together the preliminary list was a colossal job, but it makes me so happy to think that I can give readers a decent Stevenson, O. Henry, Samuel Butler, and Carlyle that I work from dawn till dusk and at times the whole night through. The worst part are the meetings chaired by Gorky. I feel stupid and shy, I don't say what I mean, I have trouble looking in his direction. I like him a lot, though he has such a studied way about him. He comes to the meeting in black kid gloves, cleanly shaven, morose, and prefaces everything he says with "May I take the liberty of saying," "May I take the liberty of proposing," and the like. (Once after coming back from a meal next door he took a box out of his pocket and a toothpick out of the box and dug about with it for an entire hour.) When Victor Hugo came up, we discussed how many volumes to include. Gorky was for as few as possible. "May I take the liberty of proposing that we leave out *Les Misérables*. Yes, we don't need *Les Misérables*." (He likes to repeat things with different intonations, a trait I've observed in Chaliapin and Andreev as well.) When I asked what he had against *Les Misérables,* he got upset and said, "At a time when in Samara Province a spool of thread (a tiny spool of thread, this small) costs two poods of flour (and he demonstrated how much two poods is with his arms), yes, a tiny spool of thread . . ."

He cleared his throat, but went on showing how much two poods is with his arms.

"I don't like Hugo."

He doesn't like *Les Misérables* because it preaches patience, submission, and the like.

"What about *Toilers of the Sea?*" I asked.

"I don't like it."

33. Gippius was incensed by Blok's great poem of the Revolution, "The Twelve" (see note 40, below), which she saw as an unequivocal endorsement of the Bolsheviks and thus an unforgivable act of betrayal. (V.E.)

"But it preaches action, man's victory over the elements. It's in a major key." (I was trying to catch him with his own bait.)

"All right, then. And you write the introduction. If that's in the introduction, it will be just fine."

All he cares about is his series for the people. The basic series, which we're doing together, leaves him cold. His fund of information is remarkable. < . . . > The name of a second-rate French writer I've never heard of comes up. All the professors present stare down at the table like schoolboys who haven't done their lessons, and Gorky says, "He's written such-and-such and so-and-so. Such-and-such is a bit weak, but so-and-so (and here he beams) is excellent, a fine piece of work."

The meetings take place in the office of the former *Novaia zhizn'* (at Nevsky Prospect, 64). The help is new and doesn't know Gorky. A boy ran up to Gorky one day and asked, "Where are the glasses? Have you seen where they put the glasses?" (He took Gorky for one of the servants.)

"I'm not the head of that department," Gorky replied.

12 November.

Kolya showed me his diary yesterday. It's very good. He writes perfectly decent poems—and by the dozens. Otherwise he's impossible: he forgets to turn off lights, he's hard on books, he ruins or loses things.

A meeting with Gorky yesterday. He outlined the preface he's going to write for our project, and suddenly he lowered his eyes, gave a wry smile, started playing with his fingers, and said, "Only with a government of workers and peasants are such magnificent editions possible. But we've got to win them over. Right, win them over. So they don't start quibbling, know what I mean? Because they're real schemers, those devils. We've got to win them over, know what I mean?"

I had a run-in with Gumilyov at the meeting. A gifted craftsman, he came up with the idea of creating a "Rules for Translators." To my mind, no rules exist. How can you have rules in literature when one translator ad-libs and the result is top-notch and another conveys the rhythm and everything and it doesn't go anywhere? Where are the rules? Well, he lost his temper and started shouting. Still, he's amusing and I like him.

Gorky looks like an old man when he pulls on his silver-rimmed glasses before reading something. He receives batches of letters and pamphlets (from as far as America these days) and skims them with the eye of a merchant poring over his accounts.

Kolya may not be a poet, but he's poetry personified!

22 *November.*

Our World Literature meetings are in full swing. I sit next to Gorky. He is favorably disposed toward me. Yesterday he told the following story: "I was riding along in a cab—the trams weren't running—and the coachman was whipping his jade and shouting, 'Get along there, you damned Bolshevik, you! You ain't long for this world anyway.' And there just happened to be a convoy of detainees, you know, prisoners walking past." (He showed them with his fingers—his fingers are always in motion when he talks.) Yesterday I first saw Gorky's famous tears. He was telling me about the foreword to the World Literature collection: "Think of all the icons people have created, damn it, great icons. (He gazed upward, to the heavens, and his eyes became moist; he was full of tenderness and ecstasy.) And the fools don't even know how superb their creations are. And all of them, even Negroes, they all have the same divinities. They have, they have. I know. I've been to America. I met Booker Washington. Yes, yes, yes . . ."

I can't say it particularly got to me. It's the Volga in him, the sectarian. There's something abstract and dogmatic about it. I told him I preferred writing about writers not *sub specie* of mankind or as figures of planetary art but in and of themselves, unhindered by schools or trends, as unique individuals, not about what makes them similar to others but what makes them different. However, Gorky is completely taken up by the "people's collective work."

23 *November.*

[. . .]

Saw Sologub at World Lit. < . . . > Blok was there too. He's in the Theater Division of the Commissariat of Education. He complains he not only has no time for poetry, he has no time for decent dreams: he keeps dreaming of work, telephones, official papers, etc. [. . .]

The day before yesterday I wrote the preface to Rider Haggard, yesterday to Twain, today to Wilde.[34] It's a regular factory!

24 November.

Yesterday was the day the translators were to gather and hear Gumilyov's "Declaration," but yesterday was Sunday and World Lit was closed. The translators crowding the stairway decided to descend on Gorky en masse, and off they went to the tram. Gumilyov read out his maximal and minimal programs—superb but unrealizable—after which Gorky made a speech.

Twisting his features into a timid-tender-ecstatic grimace (one he always has at his beck and call), he begged and pleaded with the translators to do a good, honest job. "Because this is an examination. That's right, an examination, the results of which will be sent to writers and journals in Italy and France (though how the great writers of France and England will be able to judge whether the translations are good or bad is Gorky's secret). We live in a time of destruction and disruption. That is why we must create." [. . .]

4 December.

I'm confused. I must think matters through carefully. The thing is, I'm in a highly comfortable financial situation: I've got enough money to last for three months! [. . .] I solemnly vow that as soon as I hand in the most urgent assignments—the foreword to *A Tale of Two Cities*, the foreword to *Salome*, the essay on the principles of prose translation, and the introduction to the history of English literature[35]—I shall seriously bear down on Nekrasov, and the literature most completely accessible to me.

I must see a doctor about my illnesses, buy galoshes and a hat—and return in earnest to Russian literature.

---

34. The works in question are H. Rider Haggard, *King Solomon's Mines* (1885), Mark Twain, *The Adventures of Tom Sawyer* (1876), and Oscar Wilde, *The Happy Prince* (1888). (M.H.H.)

35. The foreword to the Dickens novel appeared in its World Literature edition. The lecture on prose translation appeared in a collection of articles dealing with the principles of literary translation (*Printsipy khudozhestvennogo perevoda* [Petrograd, 1919]). The introduction to English literature apparently never materialized.

1919

→>-→>-→>-→>-→>-→>-→>

Already 1919. [. . .]

Lunacharsky and I visited a transport ship on the Neva. He gave a speech to the prisoners about socialism and how Gorky was with them now and the Red Army was making great inroads. They listened with sullen faces; there was no telling what was behind them. The ship was completely bedecked in red—even the electric bulbs were red—but there was filth everywhere and it was teeming with big-bosomed girls and dull, indifferent faces.

Lunacharsky told me that Lenin sent the following dispatch to the Commissariat of Internal Affairs: "Happy New Year! It is my wish that you commit fewer follies this year than last." [. . .]

13 February.

Yesterday there was a meeting of the editorial board of the Union of the Artists of the Word on Vasilyevsky Island at two o'clock. It included Koni, Gumilyov, Slezkin, Nemirovich-Danchenko, Eizen, Zamyatin, and me. Appalling. Afterward I took the tram with Koni and Nemirovich-Danchenko. Koni forgot he'd told me the contents of his lectures on ethics four times, and told them to me once more using the same intonation, the same vibration in his voice. He opposes the doctor's right to secrecy. "Supposing you're a father and you have a daughter, your pride and joy. A young man is courting her seriously and you go to his doctor and say, 'I know Mr. Such-and-Such is about to propose to my daughter; I also know he is your patient. Please tell me what you are treating him for. Eczema is one thing; eczema isn't catching. But what if it's secondary syphilis?' And the doctor replies, 'I'm sorry. It's a medical secret.' Or, for instance . . ." and he repeated word for word what he had said before in perfectly formed sen tences. He walks with two canes and is completely bent, oozing insincere concern over me. When we were still in the tram, he laughed and said people had begun calling him an old man fifteen years ago. Later he paused to relieve himself in front of Stasyulevich's house, and a policeman came up to him and said, "This isn't the place for that, old man. You should go into the gateway." And two (tipsy) Red Army men said to him not long ago, "Crawling on all fours, old timer? Well, keep it up, keep it up."

5 March.

Had yesterday an unusual gathering of important writers at my place [. . .] In came Gorky, saying, "I practically ripped your bell out, and the door was open." He has two expressions: tender emotion or sullen alienation. He usually opens with the latter. Kuprin ran up to him and asked meekly and lovingly, "How is your health? Are you over your Moscow illness?" "Yes, though without Manukhin I'd be dead. I should spend some time in the sun, but I haven't a moment. I've just come from the Central Paper Board. What a mess! Here's the official document (he went and fetched it from his coat pocket). Damn!" He read out that there was no paper to be had, because "of the 70,000 poods 140,000 poods was earmarked for the Commissariat," and so on. "The illiterate asses! Can't even count. The other day Chaliapin and I were on our way to Kronversky and what do we see but soldiers transporting arms. We ask them where they're going and they say, 'To the Finland Station,' and when we ask what's going on they say, 'Fighting.' They're thrilled: 'Real combat: stabbing, attacking.' 'Who are they attacking?' 'Who? Us!' Chaliapin laughed the whole way."

Then Blok arrived. Then Muizhel. Then Slezkin, and so on. The encounter between Blok and Merezhkovsky was interesting. The Merezhkovskys had declared a Blok boycott: they had been having "down with Blok" conversations all winter. Merezhkovsky kept phoning me and asking, "How am I going to handle meeting Blok?" Well, now they've met and even stood next to each other. Blok was taciturn and lethargic; as for Merezhkovsky, he'd been pestering me over the phone since morning, "What do you do, Kornei Ivanovich, if a cow has a dog's tail?"

"What do you mean?"

"We bought veal and the cook says it's dog meat. We refused to eat it, but Grzhebin bought it from us." [. . .]

Kuprin launched into an account of having his flat searched. "I never thought I'd get into Petersburg today. You needed a pass, and there was a two-hour wait. Suddenly I see the soldier who did the search of my flat.

'You know me, young man! You've been a guest in my house.' 'Right,' he says and gets me the pass in a twinkling."

< . . . > Everybody curses the Bolsheviks, and Gorky the Bolshevik curses the most. Those bastards! Those bureaucrats! No matter what you want it takes fifty illiterate signatures. [. . .]

"I've had a visit from an American, Kornei Ivanovich," said Gorky. "I've sent him to you. A tall man with an interpreter. Shy. He says to me, 'You're going to have a peasant reign of terror. Mark my words. I'm sorry to have to say it, but it's inevitable, and that's a fact.' "

Gumilyov and Blok started billing and cooing. They are both true poets and in charge of poetry for us. Said Gumilyov to Blok: "We have identical tastes, but different temperaments" [. . .]

26 March.

Yesterday at the World Lit meeting Blok gave a talk about the Heine translations he is editing. He was wonderful. He looked like an engraving of a German poet, his face peaceful and wise. Calling Heine an anti-humanist, he said that because the humanistic civilization of the nineteenth century has now come to an end and the bell of anti-humanism is making itself heard, Heine will be understood in a new way. He said that liberalism had attempted to co-opt Heine, that Apollon Grigoryev, plagued by liberalism, and so on.[36]

Gorky was on edge: he banged his large fingers on our black table; he smoked, lighting a new cigarette before finishing the old and lining the butts upright like columns along the table; he tore off strips of paper and turned them into cockerels (his usual activity when he's on edge: he makes no fewer than ten a day); and the moment Blok was through he said, "I'm an ordinary man. You (Blok) and I differ, so you'll be surprised at what I have to say, but I too think that humanism—that's right, humanism in the Christian sense—should disappear off the face of the earth. I feel . . . I . . .

---

36. Ideas related to Blok's lecture-essay "The Collapse of Humanism," which pitted the "spirit of music" against liberal civilization. Blok delivered the lecture on 9 April 1919 at the opening session of the Volfila (an acronym for Free Philosophical Association), a short-lived group that combined overall commitment to the Revolution with "untimely" metaphysical concerns and included Bely, Blok, the freewheeling leftist critic Ivanov-Razumnik, and the cultural historian A. Z. Shteinberg. (V.E.)

I recently attended a congress of poor peasants—ten thousand of them. Country and city will inevitably clash. The countryside harbors a visceral hatred for the city. We'll feel we're on an island. The educated will be under siege. I don't mean there will be a battle; no, this goes deeper: it will be like two races. Humanistic ideas must be taken to their extreme; humanists must become martyrs, Christ-like. And they shall, they shall. I sense much that is prophetic in Blok's words. All we need to do is replace the word humanism with the word nihilism."

How odd Gorky failed to see that Blok was *against* humanism and on the side of the bestial, that he placed Heine with the latter, and that his rancor was aimed at liberalism, whose main representative is none other than Gorky. It is amazing how Gorky can be possessed by a single idea! No matter what he starts in on now it ends up being about the rift between country and city. We had a meeting about children's literature; he talked about the countryside and the city; we had a meeting about a magazine for the provinces: there too—down with the countryside, up with the city. And so on.

He recently invited me to a lecture at the Palace of Labor. I asked him what he would be lecturing about. "About the Russian peasant," he said.

"I bet he's in for it, the Russian peasant," I said.

"There will be some of that," he said. "The reason for the lectures is to give the peasant what for. It can't be helped. He's our enemy, our enemy."
[. . .]

30 March.

A birthday celebration for Gorky at World Literature. I gathered up Boba, Lida, and Kolya, and off we went. On the way I told them all about Gorky, and suddenly there he was, riding past in a gray hat. He took it off and waved it for a long time, then called out to me, "You look awfully funny striding along with the children. Like a crane."

The tributes were banal. The workers from the printing press stood out in this regard: "You are the vanguard of the revolution and of our printing press." "You are the poet of the insulted and the injured." Batyushkov's speech was particularly egregious: he kept harping on words like "humanist, humane, poet of the people" and ended by saying, "And you have recently revealed a living soul to us in the form of a mysterious old man" (a reference to his play *The Old Man*).

Gorky then stood and responded in an unceremonial fashion, plainly and well. "You're all exaggerating, of course, but what I want to say is this: Russians tend to prophesy at the age of twenty, but don't start thinking until they're forty or, perhaps, thirty-five (in other words, he wouldn't have written either his "Chelkash" or "Falcon"). What can you do? That's how it is. That's how it is. I'm not sorry. I don't regret anything. The people who need to understand what I mean will understand. And let me point out to Fyodor Dmitrievich (Batyushkov) that he is wrong: I had no intention of praising the old man. I hate old men. He's like that bastard of a Luka (in the play *Lower Depths*)[37] or the one in *Matvei Kozhemyakin* who, when told that God exists, says, 'Fine, just leave me alone' and when told there is no God, says, 'Fine, just leave me alone.' He cares about nothing but himself, about his own petty revenge, which is often more than petty. Much more." (And he opened his arms to show how much.) [. . .]

1 April.

That is, 19 March,[38] that is, my birthday. Had practically no sleep and now I can feel how drawn and green my face looks. < . . . >

< . . . > Yesterday I had a long talk with Merezhkovsky. < . . . > I praised the structure of his novel *14 December,* which is much more clear-cut and chaste than that of his other novels. "It must be because you were writing about the autocracy and then the autocratic regime fell and you crossed out all your philosophical and religious outpourings." "Right, right," he said, and added, "In the final chapters I hinted that the sovereignty of the people is another form of devilment. I wrote a novel about one thing; it turned out to be wrong, and (here he gave a naive laugh) I had to write the opposite." At that moment in came Boba and Lida blissfully happy. "Close your eyes. Wrinkle your nose. Put the index finger of your left hand on the index finger of your right and what have you got? A watch!" I finally have a watch. In comes Masha and gives me sealing wax,

37. Luka, the chief protagonist of Gorky's best known and most effective play *The Lower Depths* (1902), is a canny but kind old man who seeks to bring solace to the hapless denizens of a night asylum. There is no dearth of evidence that Gorky did not at first view him as a negative character though he eventually took to maligning him. (V.E.)

38. Until the Revolution, Russia adhered to the Julian or Old Style calendar. Conversion to the Gregorian or New Style calendar involved the suppression of thirteen days. As a result, the October Revolution, which is named after the taking of the Winter Palace on 25 October (O.S.), took place on 7 November (N.S.). (M.H.H.)

paper, four penholders, and some pencils—all of which are unavailable now. She also gives me a jar of treacle from Slonimsky with a touching inscription.

2 April.

No sleep again. During yesterday's meeting Gorky came up to me with his blue eyes and told me about a petition he'd received from a prisoner on the occasion of his fiftieth birthday. It had been written with a violet pencil clearly moistened over and over with saliva: "Dear Writer, Will there be an amnesty on the occasion of your birthday? I am in jail for murdering my wife. I murdered her on the fifth day after the wedding because I was impotent and unable to deflower her. I hope you will call for an amnesty."

Gorky was down with a cold yesterday and morose. Lugging his heavy briefcase around tires him out. He has brought (as always) a pile of manuscripts. He has worked so hard on them their authors would not recognize them. When he manages to get so much done and why he does it is beyond me! I pointed to a boat he had unconsciously fashioned out of paper, and he said, "It's all that's left of the Volga fleet," and added in a whisper, "By the way, *they* are making arrests again. They arrested Filipchenko yesterday. Others too." He always refers to the Bolsheviks as "they"! Never once have I heard him say "we." He always speaks of the Bolsheviks as the enemy. < . . . >

18 April, Friday, night.

This is the second night I haven't slept. We've just moved to a new flat. It's awful: that light, those big windows. I'll be wailing when the white nights come.

I've decided to write about Gorky. I spent about five hours with him last week for two days in a row, and he told me a lot about himself. I'd never heard anything like it in my life. It showed ten times as much talent as what he writes. I was under his spell the whole time—what a "musical," all-comprehending talent! I found it particularly odd after his naive, sectarian articles about Tolstoy to hear his complex, highly nuanced memories of the man. It was an entirely different Gorky.

"I was a young man; I'd just written 'Varya Olesova' and 'Twenty-Six Men and a Girl.' I went to see him, and he asked me in simple, peasant language $<\ldots>$ where (on a pile of sacks?) and how the hero of the story 'Twenty-Six Men and a Girl' had taken the girl's virginity. I was so young I didn't see what he was aiming at, and I remember getting angry; now I see and realize: yes, that was the question that most needed asking. Tolstoy spoke of women using the same fiery words as Rozanov. No, he outdid Rozanov! $<\ldots>$ There is a bud of ravishing beauty blossoming in this world, a bud begetting all acathistoi, all legends, all art, all heroism, everything . . . He loved Sofya Andreevna with a *sexual* love and was jealous of Taneev. He hated her, and she, that despicable impresario, she hated him. He understood us all, everyone. All he had to do was glance at you and he'd see everything there was to see. He would crack us like nuts with his tiny predatory teeth: Here you are, how do you like it? You couldn't lie to him: he would see right through you.

" 'You don't like me, do you, Alexei Maksimovich,' he once said to me.

" 'No, I don't, Lev Nikolaevich,' I replied. $<\ldots>$

"He could do as he pleased with people. 'This is where Fet read me his verse,' he said to me once as we were walking through the woods. 'He was a funny one, was Fet!'

" 'Funny?'

" 'Yes, funny. All people are funny. You're funny, Alexei Mikhailovich. I'm funny. We all are.'

"He had his own way of dealing with everybody. Once a varied assortment of people was with him—Balmont, myself, a worker belonging to the Social Democratic Party, the grand prince Nikolai Mikhailovich (replete with jeweled, monogrammed cigarette case), Taneev—and he talked to each of us differently, using the style of the person he was addressing: a princely language with the prince, a democratic language with the worker, and so on. I remember going to visit him in the Crimea—there were tiny clouds in the sky and small waves on the sea—and as I walked along I caught sight of him down by the shore among the rocks, sitting and gazing into the distance, running his fingers through his beard. And I had the feeling that the clouds and the waves—they were all his doing, he was their master, their commander, and it really was so. When you think of it, at this very moment people are pondering him in India, debating him in New York, adoring him in Kineshma. He was once the most famous man in the world and received a pood and a half of letters a day. Yet he was going to die. He feared nothing as he feared death; it tortured him his whole life—death and women.

"Chaliapin once gave him the triple Easter kiss and said the traditional 'Christ is risen.' He was silent for a moment, then instead of the standard 'Verily He is risen' said, 'Christ did *not* rise, Fyodor Ivanovich.' "

Putting these remarks on paper, I realize that what gave them their power was Gorky's ability to mimic, reproduce the intonations and pauses: in and of themselves they are rather simple-minded, flat even. The next day we talked about Chekhov.

"Chekhov . . . My *Reminiscences* of him are bad. I should have written about other things: he kept asking me whether he should marry Knipper."

The second time I visited him he invited me to stay for lunch. Commissar Marya Fyodorovna Andreeva—dressed to the nines, hat and all—rushed into the study and said, "Yes, yes. I'll take care of it. You'll be served immediately," but we had to wait two hours, and I'm afraid my extended visit wore him out.

As we talked, I noticed a special trait of his: he kept hundreds of names—first names, patronymics, and surnames, names of cities, titles of books—in his head. The stories he told had to go like this: "< . . . > At the factory belonging to the Kudashin brothers, Stepan Stepanovich and Mitrofan Stepanovich, there was a bookkeeper by the name of Alexander Ivanovich Korenev. It was at his house that I saw Mikhailovsky's book *On Shchedrin,* published in 1889." I suspect that all his vast and amazing erudition can be summed up in this ability of his to name. He believes in appellations, in proper names, in titles, in lists and catalogues.

Easter. April. Night.

I haven't slept for four nights. I don't see how I can stand it. I should be exhibited for money: the man who hasn't slept for four nights and hasn't yet slit his throat. I'm reading Gorky's "Yermalash." My eyes hurt. I have the feeling I've aged three years.

27 April.

I've just returned from a reading at the Petrograd Municipal League with Gorky, Blok, and Gumilyov. Oddly—and embarrassingly—enough, mine was the only successful one. What can it mean? Blok recited his verse in a lackluster voice, and while the audience enjoyed it, it was not overwhelmed

or intoxicated as it was in 1907 or 1908. Gorky had forgotten his glasses
and borrowed a pince-nez from somebody in the audience (it was the wrong
prescription). He then mumbled his way through "Strasti-Mordasti," ruining what is an excellent story. The response was more respectful than
enthusiastic. But when I appeared, they gave me an ovation worthy of a
Chaliapin. I don't say this to puff myself up—I know it is due to my
voice—but still it makes me feel good. They followed my Mayakovsky
piece very, very closely and called for more. I read a passage about Nekrasov
and they called for more. Then they gave us ham sandwiches (!), little
rounds of sweet cheese, tea, and chocolate. I was so grateful and thrilled I
practically flew home. I want to go back to Nekrasov and I've got proofs
to read and the translation of *Bleak House* to correct < . . . >

28 April.

< . . . > Gorky has given me some material about himself: a number of
articles, letters, and drafts. They make me realize that every great writer is
also to some extent a graphomaniac. A writer needs to write even if it's
drivel. In the hope of becoming a great writer I vow to put my pen to
paper on every possible occasion. Rozanov once told me, "When I'm not
eating or sleeping, I'm writing." [. . .]

7 June.

Tikhonov, Zamyatin, and I have founded a journal called *Zavtra*.[39] Gorky
likes it a lot. He's drafted a number of articles—some he's read to us,
others he's just told us about—all anti-Bolshevik. I went to Smolny for
permission from Lisovsky, and he gave it to me, but said, "I must ask you
to submit each issue for review. We are not sure of Gorky."

   Gorky is a member of their executive committee and they want to
censor him. Unbelievable! < . . . >

39. Chukovsky's archive contains the plans for "a non-Party monthly, *Zavtra*, dealing with
problems of literature, science, technology, education, and contemporary life." The journal, which
was to be edited by Gorky and published by Zinovy Grzhebin, was to "promote culture, defend
cultural achievements and values, marshal the country's intellectual resources, restore the spiritual
ties with the West broken during the World War, and further Russia's access to the great
international of the Spirit that will unfailingly come about in the transformed Europe of tomorrow." The journal never materialized.

5 July.

Gumilyov gave a lecture about Blok yesterday at the Zubov Art Institute.
I talked Blok into going. [. . .] I looked over at him: his face, though
drenched in perspiration, looked majestic: a combination of Goethe and
Dante. When it was over, he made the following pronouncement with
solemnity and long pauses: "I don't care for the end of 'The Twelve' either,
but it is not tacked on; it is of a piece with the rest. When I finished it, I
remember wondering, 'Why Christ?' But I immediately wrote myself a
note: 'It is Christ, unfortunately. Christ and no one else.' "[40]

It's curious, but when we were having our soup Blok took my spoon
and used it. I asked him whether it didn't bother him, and he said, "Not
in the least. I was squeamish before the war, but not after it." This has
merged in my mind with "The Twelve." He wouldn't have written "The
Twelve" if he'd still been squeamish. < . . . >

9 July.

Went to see Merezhkovsky. He took me into a dark room, sat me down on
a sofa and said, "You've got to send Lunacharsky a telegram saying that
Merezhkovsky is starving to death and demands that his works be published. He is in dire need of the money."

Yet only two weeks ago I gave him fifty-six thousand rubles from the
Bolsheviks for *Alexander I* and twenty thousand to Gippius. In other words,
they received a total of seventy-six thousand rubles two weeks ago, and
now he's sunk to simulating poverty to scratch up another hundred thousand.

Shklovsky published an article about me today. It deals with my talk
on "The Technique of Nekrasov's Lyrical Poetry,"[41] but I can't bring myself
to open the newspaper: there's too much hunger and death.

40. In the closing lines of "The Twelve" (1918) no less a figure than Jesus Christ appears at
the head of a relentless march through the chaotic Petrograd of January 1918. It is Christ who,
floating high above the snowstorm, leads the ragged Red militiamen—without their knowledge
and perhaps against their will—toward what a prose companion piece of the poem calls a
"beautiful life." The strange alliance of Christ with the October Revolution displeased nearly
everyone. Blok's own uneasiness over the unexpected finale has elicited frequent commentary.
(V.E.)

41. "Tekhnika nekrasovskogo stikha," *Zhizn' iskusstva* 9 (10 July 1919).

4 September.

I've just seen Gorky crying. "They've arrested Sergei Fyodorovich Olden-burg!" he shouted, running into Grzhebin's publishing house on his way to Stroev's office. I followed him to ask for his help with Maria Benkendorf (my assistant at the Studio), who has also been arrested. He started in on a long reply, but it disintegrated into gesticulations. "What can I do?" he finally managed to come out with. "I told the bastards—I mean, the bas-tard—that if Oldenburg wasn't released this very minute I'd make a scan-dal. I'd break with them, with the Communists, for good, damn them!" His eyes were moist.

The day before yesterday Blok told about having nearly been arrested, drunk and out late, with a friend at Alkanost. "What are you doing in somebody else's flat after twelve o'clock? Show me your papers. It is my duty to detain you."

Luckily, the head of the House Committee turned out to be Azov, who announced to the man doing the arresting, "Don't you realize he's the famous poet Alexander Blok?" and they were released.

Blok is morbidly neat. He stuffs his pockets with notebooks and makes neat little jottings of everything he needs. He reads all decrees with even the most indirect bearing on him, then cuts them out, sorts them, and carries them everywhere in his pockets. It is impossible to imagine a scrap of refuse to say nothing of a mess on his desk or couch. Each line of what he writes is neat and clean. [. . .]

28 October.

There was supposed to be a meeting of the Historical Paintings Section, but it didn't take place (Tikhonov got into a conversation with a woman and lost track of time), and Gorky told all kinds of stories. We sat there mesmerized. He jumbled things up at first, but when he got going he told us about the time he and Chaliapin had gone to the circus and seen an ape eating and smoking and the like. "And all of a sudden there is Chaliapin aping the ape—scratching behind his ear and so on—right there in public. Amazing!"

Then he told us how a herring "walks." An island appears in the (opal greenish) Caspian Sea and starts moving. The herring layer is so thick that an oar will stand in it. The ones on the surface, exposed to the air, get drowsy. It's a beautiful sight. Some smart alecs (people) dive in and can't surface. It's like diving under ice. They keep sinking."

"Have you ever sunk like that?" Oldenburg asked.

"Five or six times. Once at Nizhny. My leg got caught in an anchor cable (the anchor was in the water) and I couldn't work it free. I'd have drowned if a coachman riding along the slope hadn't seen me, seen me go down, and rushed in after me. I was unconscious, of course, and the skin on my leg had come off like a sock. Anyway, to revive me they dragged me along the rocks and boards—my body was all splinters and bruises—but I opened my eyes and thought, 'Good show!' even though they'd flung me around as if I were dead. And the moment I came to, I lit into the policeman, who wanted to haul me off to the station. I kept at it, but I ended up there anyway.

"Another time a barge I was on was swept into the Caspian Sea. There were a hundred of us. The women took it in their stride; the men made a mess of things. Two of them went out of their minds. We were on the waves for sixty-two hours . . .

"Then there were the women in the fisheries. You should have seen them. They would stand at a table twice as long as this one with a three-pood fish going from hand to hand, never stopping for a minute, slicing out the roe and all (he came up with ten or so more technical terms) so fast you wondered how they do it. Bare arms, big muscles, and bosoms like this (he showed what they were like). It's handed down from mother to daughter and goes back to Catherine's day. They're fantastic, those women."

Then he told about how he'd run across the tracks right in front of a locomotive. Scary and fun. Strel [the rest of the name is torn off], a shockheaded friend of his, had done it a thousand times, and Gorky envied him. As I say, we were mesmerized, Blok in particular. [. . .]

1 November.

Volynsky expressed a desire to protest against Gorky's attack on Zhukovsky.

There is a dead horse lying near our street. It's been there for more than a week. Someone has hacked about ten pounds out of its croup—for sale, I hope, not for himself.

Was at the Writers' House yesterday. Everyone's clothes were crumpled, hanging loose: people are obviously sleeping in them and covering themselves with their overcoats. The women are as crumpled as their clothes; they look as though someone had chewed them up and spit them out. [. . .]

4 November.

< . . . > Grzhebin came to see me in the evening and walked around the kitchen, recalling Andreev's drinking habits. One group after the other would join him in the tavern, and he'd outdrink them all. "I once drew a bath for him, but he refused to get in, so we took him up to it fully dressed and made believe we were going to throw him in, and he finally had to undress and bathe. He fell asleep immediately afterward."

5 November.

< . . . > Gorky told me yesterday that he had a note from the Kremlin reproaching us for being too "talkative" during our meetings. He was very upset. He said a woman had come to see him—a woman wearing four pounds of silver and two of gold—about interceding on behalf of two men in Gorokhovaya Prison. " 'They are both my husbands,' she said, and when I promised to do what I could she asked what I charged." [. . .]

< . . . > Otsup read me his sonnet about Gorky. It begins "with his cunning smile." Gorky cunning? He's not cunning; he's simple to the point of irresponsibility. He understands nothing of real life, or his understanding of it is infantile. If the people around him (people he likes) are well disposed toward a person, he loves that person instinctively, without thinking; if any of his intimates < . . . > takes a disliking to a person, that's the end. < . . . > Now (after a year and a half of working with him) I have a clear picture of the man; I see how he was drawn into *Novaia zhizn'*, Bolshevism, World Literature—everything. Tricking Gorky is as easy as pie; Boba could trick him. Among friends he is trusting and docile. Just because a speculator by the name of Makhlin happens to live next door to Tikhonov, he had him released from Cheka[42] custody and saved from the firing squad.

42. The Cheka (abbreviation for the All-Russian Extraordinary Commission for Fighting Counter-Revolution and Sabotage) was the Soviet secret police from 1917 to 1922. It was the main vehicle for the policy of Red Terror, instituted by Lenin and implemented by Felix Dzerzhinsky. A *chekist* works for the Cheka, or, more broadly, the Soviet security organs. (Al-

6 November.

The first wintry (sunny) day. This is the kind of day when smoke coming out of chimneys is particularly attractive. But there's no smoke now: no one has anything to burn. Merezhkovsky came to see me. For the second time. He wants me to get Ionov to buy the *Trilogy* he's already sold to Grzhebin.[43] For once he made a good impression on me. I read him my Andreev piece, which he didn't like and had interesting things to say about. He said that Andreev was no chaff, that he had a certain darkness in him and darkness is more solid than granite. He tried to get me to write that Andreev was a metaphysical writer, a bad lot, but a metaphysician. < . . . > He placed him much higher than Gorky, because "Gorky doesn't feel the world, doesn't feel eternity, doesn't feel God. Gorky is supreme and frightening kitsch."

7 November.

I've just recalled that after receiving an advance from Tseitlin for his complete works Andreev went out and bought himself a donkey. "Why a donkey?"

"It was absolutely essential. It reminded me of Tseitlin. As soon as I forgot how lucky I was, the animal would bray and I'd remember."

[. . .]

Today is the second anniversary of Soviet rule. Photographers have been taking pictures of schoolchildren and telling them, "Toss your caps in the air and look happy!"

9 November.

No sleep again. I keep thinking about yesterday's reading in honor of Andreev. I can't get it out of my mind. It was a failure, an embarrassment. [. . .] I was nervous when I read my piece—I kept standing up and sitting down (and leaving a lot out)—but I read it in a loud voice and in a way

---

though the Soviet secret police was renamed several times, the term *chekist* survived in common parlance.) (V.E.)

43. *Christ and Antichrist* (1896–1905) is the overall title of Merezhkovsky's metaphysical and historical trilogy, which comprises *The Death of the Gods: Julian the Apostate, The Resurrection of the Gods: Leonardo da Vinci,* and *Antichrist: Peter and Aleksei.* (V.E.)

that showed how much I loved Andreev. I was hard on him, occasionally even caustic, but in the end I showed how much he meant to me. < . . . > I put a lot of myself in the event—I even put up the posters—which is what keeps me awake. I have a feeling that Gorky is a mediocrity, dull inside, and that we've got what we deserve. The former cultural milieu is gone, dead, and it will take a century to re-create it. Nobody understands anything the least bit complex these days. I love Andreev for his irony, but that's inaccessible now. Irony can be grasped only by the sophisticated, not by commissars or Otsup's mother. The reason why Gorky has become today's icon is that he is neither psychological nor complex; he is elementary. < . . . >

11 November.

< . . . > A meeting of World Lit. The issue of feeding members of the literary community was brought up on my initiative. Money will do no good; we need bread. We need to come together and work out what to do. Gorky responded with gusto: "Right! Right! *They* damned well better feed us or else—if they're so weak they can't keep us warm and fed—let us go abroad. Why, the way things are now it's better to be in jail than free. I've just been working on behalf of the prisoners at Shpalernaya, and they didn't want to go when they were released: they were warmer and fuller inside! < . . . >

13 November.

Ran into Volynsky yesterday at World Lit. We talked about drafting something about the writers' disastrous situation.

Volynsky: "It's better to keep quiet, more dignified. I'm no politician or diplomat."

"Is Gorky a diplomat?"

"You bet he is! I have it from reliable sources that he says one thing here to us and something else there to *them*." I told Volynsky I'd witnessed that myself: I'd heard him talking pure Bolshevik with Comrade Zarin. I couldn't believe my ears. I realized I was intruding and left. But I put it down to Gorky's artistic impressionability rather than a premeditated plan. It's just like Nekrasov: he too had to cover two fronts as an artist. < . . . >

    [. . .]

14 November.

Had lunch at Smolny. Sardine soup and kasha. We had to pay a hundred-ruble deposit for a spoon. Took the tram to World Lit. We had a Picture Section meeting. One story after the next. Gorky had been at a meeting yesterday. < . . . > "Somebody mentioned that the young of a rhinoceros had died in the zoo, and I asked, 'What do you feed the animals anyway?' 'The bourgeoisie,' Zinovyev answered."

Then they started discussing the issue of whether or not to slaughter the bourgeoisie . . . I'm serious . . . It makes you wonder: When were these people sincere? When they pretended to be decent or now? I talked to Lenin today over the phone about the decree dealing with scholars. He laughed. The man is always laughing. He promised to take care of everything but asked, "How come you haven't been arrested?" < . . . >

It occurs to me that Andreev once had this to say about Gorky: "Have you noticed that while Gorky may be a proletarian he's always playing up to the rich. < . . . > I once tried taking the train with him in Italy. Forget it! It nearly ruined me. No, really, the man travels like a prince!" [. . .]

16 November.

Blok is pathologically neat. This is not at all in keeping with the poetry of madness and destruction he does so well. He enjoys wrapping everything in a piece of paper, binding it with a string. He loves all kinds of little cases and boxes. The most dog-eared book looks less soiled, less mangled. Now that I've pointed it out to him, we exchange knowing glances each time he manifests his "mania." Everything he hears he records in a notebook; he takes it out twenty times a meeting and jots things down (what? I wonder), then, closing it neatly and all but blowing on it, calmly returns it to its specially designated pocket.

17 November.

[. . .]

Merezhkovsky came to see me. He is all complaints. He wants to leave Petersburg. He was wearing a magnificent fur coat, high boots, a sable hat. We talked about Gorky. "Gorky's a double dealer < . . . >, but he's sincere about it: when he's with you, he's on your side; when he's with them, he's all theirs. It's a Russian talent, talking sincerely out of both sides of your mouth." Merezhkovsky and I went to the Kolos, where Blok was giving his talk on musicality and civilization. I'd heard it before. It was a pitiful sight: everybody's nose red, the room freezing, Blok wearing a sweater, steam coming out of his mouth with every word. Poor, rawboned people listening to him go on about having too much civilization, civilization having caused our downfall. [. . .] I went from there to a doctor's (I forget his name), where Zhirmunsky was giving a talk on Shklovsky's *Poetics*. Among those present were Eikhenbaum wearing a scarf that went down to the floor, Shklovsky wearing puttees, Sergei Bondi, Bakhta the actor, Veksler, Chudovsky, Gumilyov, Polonskaya and her brother, et al. Zhirmunsky gives the impression of being bright and well-educated but trivial: he never calls anything into question, he understands and accepts everything and he runs his ideas into the ground. Shklovsky brought up difficult, spirited, very clever objections. Veksler recalled Zhirmunsky's having spoken of "the writer's soul" somewhere, and she gave him a scolding: What do you mean by "the soul of the writer"? Where does it get us? We need the principles of composition, not a soul. All the young women trained by Shklovsky fear nothing more than—saints preserve us!—the word soul.[44] The slightest allusion to psychology in literary criticism elicits a chorus of:

> Oh, how vulgar he is and how callow!
> He's nothing if not obsolescent. [. . .]

19 November.

Three meetings in a row yesterday: the first of the Historical Paintings Section, the second of World Lit, the third—at Grzhebin's—of the Hundred Best Russian Books. [. . .] Blok surprised us by stating lugubriously that nineteenth-century literature was not representative of Russia, that all

---

44. This entry echoes Chukovsky's disagreements with the Formalist movement, of which Shklovsky was one of the principal exponents. In 1920 Chukovsky wrote to Gorky: "One is expected to apply formal approaches to the material to construct what was previously known as the poet's soul. . . . As long as the critic is engaged in analysis, he is a scholar, but when he shifts to synthesis, he becomes an artist, because from small, seemingly inconsequential details he constructs an artistic image of a man." He returned to this theme in 1924: "I know it is improper to speak about [the poet's] soul as long as we have at our disposal such safe categories as Symbolism, Classicism, Romanticism, Byronism, Neo-Romanticism and the like. . . . The soul will elude eunuch classifiers and will reveal itself only to another soul" (*Aleksandr Blok kak chelovek i poet* [Petrograd, 1924], 78–79).

Europe (together with Russia) had gone crazy in the nineteenth century, and that Gogol, Tolstoy, and Dostoevsky were mad. Gumilyov said that Maikov had no gift for poetry and Ivanov-Razumnik was a rotten critic. Grzhebin jokingly called me a scoundrel, and I threw Gumilyov's brief-case at him and broke his fountain pen. We had a heated discussion about money, from which it became clear that we were all paupers and that writers today have passionate and disparate views on money. [. . .]

27 November.

A meeting at World Lit the day before yesterday. < . . . > Then Blok, Gumilyov, Zamyatin, Lerner, and I went off to the "room with the sink"—the typists' room—and discussed the program for the hundred best writers. Gumilyov presented the impressionist program, excluding Denis Davydov (because he was a hussar) and Nikitin. Zamyatin backed Gumilyov. Blok's platform is a historical one, his program ideal: it is fresh, stimulating, never vulgar, and scholarly. We argued on and on. Gumilyov says my program is a provincial museum: it displays the cigarette Tolstoy smoked but not Tolstoy himself. I made fun of Gumilyov's, but deep down I respect him greatly: he is a whole man. Indeed, the entire discussion bore the stamp of his purity and naïveté. Blok with his love for systematization set up a number of tables: how many poets, how many prose writers, what per-centage of humorists, etc. I included the modernists in my program. "What do you want all those young people for?" Blok wanted to know. I put Sologub down for two volumes. Blok: "Don't tell me you think Sologub is 1/50 of Russian literature!"

Next day (yesterday) we met for a House of the Arts meeting. "Gum-ilyov wants only the good, the absolute," said Blok, "in which case we must have Pushkin, Lermontov, Tolstoy, Dostoevsky."

"What about Tyutchev?" I said.

"Tyutchev? Everything he wrote is so short; it's all fragments. Besides, he's a German, too abstract."

I've agreed to organize the Studio, the Library, and the Children's Theater for the House of the Arts. It wears me out just to think of them. I didn't sleep a wink last night. < . . . >

3 December.

< . . . > Meetings all day yesterday starting at one sharp with the program for Grzhebin. Ivanov-Razumnik was present again. Gorky got there before me.

When Sleptsov came up, Gorky told us that Tolstoy had once said about a Sleptsov story: "The scene on the stove is like my 'Polikushka,' only better." The only thing that bothered him was an incorrect verb form. Tolstoy really gave it to him for that.

When we got to Zagoskin and Lazhechnikov, Gorky said, "I don't like them. They're second-rate Walter Scotts." Once more he amazed me with his thorough knowledge of Russian literature. When we got to Veltman, he said, "Have you read Sofya Veltman, his wife? She had a fine novel in *Otechestvennye zapiski* in the fifties. It showed an excellent knowledge of the times."

Blok presented a highly detailed list complete with dates of birth and didn't balk when, for instance, Delvig was moved from the second to the first category. An incident occurred when Ivanov-Razumnik, reading out his program, said, "One book of the former Acmeists . . ." and Gumilyov requested the floor for a point of personal information and asked haughtily whom Ivanov-Razumnik meant by "former Acmeists."

"You, Gorodetsky, and a few others," he replied.

"No, we're not 'former,' " Gumilyov said, "we're . . ."

I managed to allay the skirmish. < . . . >

4 December.

Gorky's memory surpasses all his other mental abilities: his ability to reason logically is pitiful, his ability to make scholarly generalization less than that of a fourteen-year-old. [. . .]

7 December.

< . . . >

The day before yesterday Blok and Gumilyov were sitting opposite each other in the meeting room and broke into an argument about Symbolism and Acmeism. It was very profound. I admired both of them. Gumilyov said most Symbolists were speculators, specialists in insights into the beyond. They took a dumbbell and wrote "10 poods" on it, but hollowed out the insides. Then they tossed it here and there, but it was empty.

Blok responded in a cautious monotone, as if monitoring something inside himself. "That's what the followers and imitators of all schools do. But there's something wrong in what you say. It doesn't sound Russian to me. It's the kind of thing that sounds very good in French. You're too much of a literary man. I look at things through the prism of politics and social import."

The more I observe Blok, the more clearly I see that by the time he's fifty he'll forget about poetry and start writing artistically prophetic journalism (in the spirit of *The Diary of a Writer*).[45]

[...]

Gorky brought some of his own people to the theater meeting. < ... > The commissar of the Red Army theaters was there too and, smoking away, completely oblivious to Gorky's presence, he delivered a speech about the ignorant mass of soldiers it is our job to enlighten. Each and every sentence had a few "I mean" 's in it: "I mean, comrades, we'll show them Kant and Laplace, their world views, I mean." Clearly he had once been a telegraph operator who read nothing more than *Vestnik znaniia*. He reminded me of another such propagandist who stood up before a performance of *The Robbers* in the Bolshoi Theater and said, "Comrades, the Russian writer, comrades, Gogol, comrades, once said that Russian is a troika, comrades.[46] Russia is a troika, comrades, and you know who pulls that troika, comrades? The peasants who feed the revolutionary cities, comrades, the workers who made the revolution, comrades, and comrades—you, my dear Red Army men, comrades. Anyway, Gogol, comrades, the great Russian revolutionary writer of the Russian land (he went on without a pause), comrades, smoking in the theater is strictly prohibited, and if you want to smoke, comrades, go out into the corridor."

[...]

45. *The Diary of a Writer* (1873–81) is a series of articles published by Dostoevsky, many of which are imbued with a nationalist bias. (V.E.)

46. A clumsily politicized version of the much quoted finale of part one of Gogol's *Dead Souls* (1842), where Russia is portrayed as a troika hurtling toward an unfathomable future. (V.E.)

9 *December.*

Have just been to ten meetings in a row. Yesterday I received Blok's charming "Verses on the Rose, the Cabbage, and Bryusov."[47] It really raised my spirits.

Gorky brought the humor magazine *Shut* to the picture meeting. "Russians haven't got much humor," Zamyatin said.

GORKY. "What do you mean? Russians are great humorists!" < . . . >

I noticed for the first time today that Blok is "favorably disposed" toward me. When I said at the picture meeting that iambic pentameter is unsuitable for a tragedy dealing with Jewish life, that iambic pentameter is Esperanto, he said, "A wise remark." He told me his wife made up the line about Bryusov in the humorous epistle he wrote for me, "the best line, actually." She has a line in *The Twelve* as well:

Wolfed down tons of chocolate.[48]

"What was it like before?" I asked. "It was bad," he said.

Swept the street up with her skirt.

And *they* had short skirts.
My financial situation is disastrous. Only a miracle can save me.

11 *December.*

This is the second night I haven't slept a wink, but my mind is working perfectly. I've made a discovery (?) about the dactylization of Russian words, and it's cleared up a lot for me in my work on Nekrasov.[49] [. . .]

47. "Blok's Verses on the Rose, the Cabbage, and Bryusov" were a response to a lighthearted ditty by Chukovsky: "Can it be you, Blok? / Shame on you! / Now it's no longer a rose or a garden of nightingales [title of Blok's lyrical cycle] but the meager offerings [rations] provided by the Sovnarkhoz that beckon to you!" In *Chukokkala* Blok's poem is entitled "To Chukovsky"; in Blok's collected works it appears under the title "Verses on Items of Prime Necessity."

48. The line in "The Twelve," allegedly contributed by Blok's wife, occurs in the context of the bitter ruminations of the Red militiaman Petka over the "good times" had by his former lover Katka while gallivanting with an army officer. (V.E.)

49. Chukovsky's "discovery" may be a variant of the notion that, given the high incidence of long words in Russian, Russian verse is especially suited to trisyllabic meters—the amphibrach, anapest, and dactyl. (V.E.)

15 December.

< . . . > Went to the Conference of Proletarian Poets yesterday. I wish them well in the abstract, God knows, but in the flesh it was so vulgar, so utterly brazen that I made a show of leaving, even though I had to give up the meal, the bread and tea, that went with it. A numbskull came out on the stage (the kind who make good bouncers, but also turn up as copy-readers and rural statisticians) and started going on about how "a bourgeois actor don't understand how we suffer, he don't know our sorrows and joys, he don't want to help us. We got to make our own actors. Me, for instance, comrades." Not a drop of talent. And all those nobodies, those vulgar phrasemongers, those scribblers of official clichés—they applauded him. It was just what they wanted to hear. < . . . >

1920

)►·}►·}·─·}·─·}·─·}·─·}·─·}►·}►

2 January.

Have been semi-ill and only semi-sleeping for two weeks now. My life is unreal. Since neither writing nor going to meetings provides means enough to live, I've become a peripatetic: I run from one commissar to the next in search of rations. Every once in a while someone takes pity on me and gives me a herring, a box of matches, a pound of bread—I have no shame, I'm thrilled with everything—and I fly home to Manezhny like a papa bird to feed the booty to my fledglings. < . . . >

3 January.

The Merezhkovskys have left. Misha Slonimsky saw them off at the station. It was a disaster, he said. First the crowd carried them off in different directions, then they lost their luggage, and they couldn't find their places until the last minute.

"I'm a member of the Soviet," Merezhkovsky kept shouting. "I'm from the Smolny!"[50] But that did him no good. Then he screeched, "My coat!" Somebody had made off with his fur coat in the crowd.

Blok said yesterday, "Sailors used to be Mayakovsky-like. Now they're more like Igor Severyanin." He's absolutely right. There was a discussion about the "art of the future" at the House of the Arts[51] yesterday, but I didn't go: I was exhausted, famished, and unshaven.

Christmas 1920.

That is, 1919, because today is 7 January 1920. < . . . >
    [. . .] The children have done an amazing thing: for an entire month they saved up the scraps of bread they were given at school, dried them, and made them into small white cones and pasted pictures on them. Then they stuffed the cones with biscuits and put them under the Christmas tree as presents *for their parents!* Children surprising their father and mother at Christmas! Next thing you know they'll be telling us it was all **Santa Claus**'s doing. Next year I'll hang up a stocking at my bed! On top of it all, but *à rebours,* our servant Zhenya, whom we can't afford to give a Christmas gift, gave Lida, Kolya, and Boba woolen pen wipers she knitted herself—and pens to go with them.

Second Day of Christmas 1920.

< . . . > At four I went to Gorky's. < . . . > He was fussing with the fire and saying to himself, "Dearest Alexei Maximovich, permit me to inform you that you are about to burn yourself . . . By the way, Kornei Ivanovich, ask Fyodor (Chaliapin) to tell you about the time we bathed a steward in milk. He was lying there reading and we picked up some pitchers and poured them over him. By the time he came to his senses he was covered with it. Then we went for a boat ride and I took out the stoppers in advance and when we got to the middle of the river we began to sink. < . . . > Lunacharsky tells a funny story about some boys in Moscow who ate their friend. Chopped him up and ate him. The chopping went on forever. Finally one of them realized you had to cut behind the ear. So they sliced

---

50. The building that had housed the Smolny Institute, a bastion of higher education for women, served as Bolshevik headquarters during the early years of the Revolution. (M.H.H.)
    51. A refuge for writers and artists in the early 1920s. (V.E.)

the carotid artery and started cooking! Lunacharsky told it with great gusto, great relish. "Oh, and last year a man cut up his wife—now that I can understand. A telegraph operator. Very clever, those telegraph operators. He lived with her for four years, and in the fifth he ate her. 'I'd long thought her body would be delicious,' he said. He hit her on the head and cut off a slice. He ate her for a week, but then she started smelling: the meat had gone bad. When the neighbors came, all they found was bones and spoiled meat. See how bad you women are, Marya Ignatyevna? You go on being spoiled even after you're dead. I think Marya Valentinovna [Chaliapina] is next. It makes me lick my lips just to look at her."

17 January.

Boba ran into the room a while ago brandishing two potatoes. "Papa, here's a poem a boy told me today:

> Oh, there's no flour and there's no bread,
> The Bolsheviks leave us unfed.
> Not only there's no bread about,
> The lights keep going out.

Whereupon he banged the two potatoes together and vanished.

19 January.

< . . . > Called on Anna Akhmatova yesterday. She and Shileiko have one large room with a bed behind a screen. The room is raw and cold, with books on the floor. Akhmatova's voice is harsh and penetrating. I have the feeling she is talking to me over the phone. Her eyes sometimes look blind. She is affectionate with Shileiko, occasionally going over and brushing the hair back off his forehead. He calls her Anichka; she calls him Volodya. She told me proudly that he can translate a whole ballad *à livre ouvert* into verse; he dictates it to her in the final version! And then he has bouts of sleepwalking. I brought up Gumilyov and how awful his translation of Coleridge's "Ancient Mariner" was. Akhmatova: "You mean you didn't know? He's an awful translator." That's not the first time I've heard her say bad things about Gumilyov.

Nikolai Otsup phoned me yesterday morning and asked if I couldn't find out from Gorky whether Pavel (his brother) had been executed. Marya

Ignatyevna answered the phone. "Yes, Kornei Ivanovich, he was." It was very hard for me to tell Nikolai, but I finally did. [. . .]

12 February.

I want to describe my day yesterday, a typical day. Night. Marya Borisovna had a fever, the Spanish influenza, her legs were swollen, and we expected her to go into labor any minute. I got up and worked on the *byliny* lecture I'm giving for the Baltic fleet. I'm reading Speransky's foreword to Sabashnikov's edition. Then I ran to the phone in the cold room and rang Kaplun, the Municipal Police, the Political Department of the Baltic Fleet, and a number of people bearing no resemblance whatsoever to Ilya Muromets.[52] There was no tap water; the wood needed chopping; a bald man (with the face of a black-marketeer) came and asked me to arrange an official trip for him; < . . . > and so on. Then I read what the Studio people have to say about Akhmatova.

I dream of the day, somewhere in the distant future, when I can read a book for myself or simply spend some time with the children. At three I had soup and a potato and ran off to World Lit for a meeting of writers I want to band together in an Itinerant University. Amfiteatrov sporting a beard, Volynsky, Lerner—the whole gang was there. Everything was topsy-turvy, absurd. Gorky turned up for five minutes, and when we asked for his views, he said, "You've got to speak simply. Yes, simply. They're just children, after all: policemen, sailors." Shklovsky said we need literacy schools, we should be teaching literacy. Shtraikh (not all that literate himself) announced that he was an Arabian stallion and had no intention of carrying water. Whereupon they all declared themselves Arabian stallions. Then off to Akhmatova (at top speed) to pick up a copy of *The Rosary*,[53] which I didn't have and wanted to lecture on at the Proletcult.[54] From Akhmatova (at top speed) to the Proletcult. What a wind and what long, merciless staircases the Proletcult has! I gave my Akhmatova talk to a group of down-and-out chambermaids and the like—who seemed quite atten-

52. A hero (*bogatyr'*) featured in one of the Russian folk-epic (*bylina*) cycles. (V.E.)

53. Akhmatova's second collection of verse, it appeared in 1914. (V.E.)

54. The Proletcult (an acronym for Proletarian Culture) was founded in 1917 as a branch of the People's Commissariat of Education, its objective being to create in short order a culture that embodied the proletarian worldview. This monumental enterprise entailed, inter alia, "instituting courses in ancient and modern literatures, Russian and foreign to be given from the standpoint of the working class." (V.E.)

tive!—and from there (at top speed) to Kaplun in Palace Square. I missed him, I was late, he was already at Gorky's. I went to his sister's and ate the bread Samobytnik the proletarian poet gave me, but it had begun to mold and made me nauseous. I asked them to send Kaplun's motorcar over from Gorky's place. Several minutes later a boy appeared and said, "Is there a writer here Kaplun sent for?"

"Yes."

"Well, the driver phoned and left a message that he'd be late because he ran over a woman on the way."

"Again?" said Kaplun's sister.

When the driver showed up several minutes later, I asked, "Is she dead?" He said she was.

We drove to Gorky's place. I'm so hungry my head is spinning; I'm ready to faint. There are meetings going on in two rooms. Gorky goes back and forth like a chess player playing two matches. Later they come together: the professors and us. A short dark man sitting with the professors keeps talking about Narkompros: Narkompros this, Narkompros that, Narkompros, Narkompros, Narkompros. Finally I shout, "To hell with Narkompros!" and start cursing it. Well, it turns out the man *is* the People's Commissariat of Education: he's Zelikson, a man we all fear and want to win over at all costs. Shivers ran up my spine.

I got home at about one in the morning. Marya Borisovna was in a bad way: she was sweating profusely, she hadn't slept for five nights and had a terrible headache. She asked for her woolen kerchief. I went to bed, but couldn't sleep, of course. I jumped out of bed in the morning. Zhenya was exhausted, my fingers were frozen. I went and sawed some wood.

20 *March*.

< . . . > Yesterday, Wednesday, we had a meeting at Grzhebin's. < . . . > Gumilyov had agreed to edit Aleksei Tolstoy and done an awful job of it. He cut up a book, handed it in, and got twenty thousand rubles. Gorky counted as many as forty mistakes and omissions. Blok agreed to edit Lermontov and naturally did a fine job. He made a very good selection of the verse, but the article is not in the popular, lowbrow tone Gorky needs; it's the usual Blok plus forced attempts to sink to the level of the uneducated reader. For Blok Lermontov is a magus, a seer, a dreamer, a rebel against God, whereas for Gorky he's a "cultural force," a "stimulus for progress."

The difference is one of essence, not style. Blok is in a tragic position: the more Gorky tried to persuade him to change his tune—"What matters is not that Lermontov had dreams but that he wrote 'On the Death of the Poet' "[55]—the more downcast, proud, and distant Blok's wonderful, gaunt face became. Zamyatin hasn't finished Chekhov yet, but I, after an enormous effort, have finally handed in my Nekrasov.

When Gorky and I happened to find ourselves in the other room, he said with great disappointment, "What good are writers? They can't do a thing. Not a thing. Scholars are better, Kornei Ivanovich. They were here yesterday and what fine people! < . . . > How they work! You're the only writer who does. I admire you. Really I do."

He'd just received a letter from Wells and some books Wells has written, popular science. Gorky sets great store by popularizations. He simply cannot see that Blok was not made for them, that he was made for free creativity, and that one poem by Blok will do more for the Russian people than any ten popular pamphlets he might write and that could be written by any more or less literate, moderately gifted person—of my vintage, say.

After the meeting I ran (at top speed, absolute top speed) to the Naval Corps, Vasilyevsky Island, Line 11, where I gave a lecture and ran back (at top speed, absolute top speed)—God only knows how far. We're really under the gun, we lecturers. We earn our rations! Oh, if only they'd give me a month off—just once in my life—so I could spend my time writing what *I* care about, what *I* think! Now the only day I'm free is Thursday. Tomorrow I lecture at the House of the Arts, the day after tomorrow at the Board of the Soviets, Kaplun's cronies. Oh! Oh! Oh! Oh!

30 March.

Like Nicholas I, we too have a closed class of officials, office rats with their own language and customs. The "commissar misses" have developed their own jargon. They say, for instance, "I find that *decidedly* to my liking," "he is *decidedly* good," even "I'm *decidedly* going there." Instead of "Goodbye" they say "Bye." < . . . >

The other day Grzhebin phoned Blok and said, "I've bought Akhmatova," by which he meant he'd acquired her poetry. He'd had her sent a

55. The poem, composed in the wake of Pushkin's fatal duel, is an impassioned indictment of Nicholas I, whom Lermontov declares responsible for Pushkin's death. (V.E.)

dress she'd long dreamed of. She immediately went to him and sold him her books for seventy-five thousand rubles.

[. . .]

1 April.

[. . .] I once asked Blok why he dedicated his poem "An Incandescent Gilded Globe" to Boris Sadovsky, with whom he had nothing in common. After a pause he replied, "He asked me to, and I couldn't refuse." Which is Blok's usual passivity: "What must be, must be" and "They had to be put on the table."[56]

10 April.

[. . .] Gumilyov had a reading that evening. It was a success. The poem "Damara: A Hottentot's Cosmogony" received a special ovation. During the break Arsky, a Proletcult poet, called me over and asked in the company of other Proletcult poets, "Did you notice?"

"Notice what?"

"Quit pretending. You know what made them applaud Gumilyov like that."

"His poetry. You write poetry like that and you'll get that kind of applause."

"Quit pretending, Kornei Ivanovich. The reason they clapped was that he had that bird in there."

"What bird?"

"The white one. The *white* one. That's what they liked. The allusion to Denikin."

It was so idiotic it made my head spin.

"And when he says 'the portrait of my sovereign,' what sovereign does he mean? Who has he got in mind?"[57]< . . . >

---

56. Lines from Blok's poems "Conceived at night, I was born at night" and "My Friend's Life."

57. "A Hottentot's Cosmogony" contains the image of a white bird torn in two. "The portrait of my sovereign" is a line from the poem "Galla." Both poems appear in the collection *The Tent* (1922).

19 April.

Today for the first time I saw the magnificent Gorky and thoroughly enjoyed the spectacle. The thing is, there's been a campaign going on against the House of the Arts for a long time now. Why the auction? Why the concentration on the bourgeoisie? Punin, the commissar of fine arts, is particularly indignant. Why don't we submit to them? They give us subsidies. Why do we engage in our own, un-Communist activities? And so on.

Gorky, holding a black, broad-brimmed hat, responded in a supercilious, domineering, cavalier tone. "You've got it all wrong, good sirs. Like all people in power, your goal is concentration, centralization, and we know what centralization led autocracy to. You say the House of the Arts is full of bourgeois elements, but I say they're all your commissars and their wives. And what's so bad about getting dressed up? If people pay attention to what they wear, they'll stop having lice. Everyone should dress well. And why not let people buy pictures at an auction? Put a picture on your wall and your life changes. You'll start working so you can buy another. As for the attacks you have just heard, I refuse to respond to them. They stem from personal animosity: the man who made them was a candidate for the House of the Arts who failed to be elected."

Punin was sitting opposite me. His briefcase lay on the table in front of him. He kept locking it and unlocking it, locking it and unlocking it, his face twitching with a nervous tic. He said he was proud to have been rejected by the House of the Arts because it meant that the bourgeois dregs of society hated him.

Suddenly Gorky stood, nodded good-bye in my direction, and, pulling on his gloves in the middle of the room, said sternly, "So he says he is hated in the House of the Arts. I don't know. But *I* hate him. Him and all his kind. And . . . and I don't believe in their communism." He waited a moment, then left. [. . .]

28 June.

I remember seeing two "proletarians," the former Prince Volkonsky and the former Princess Urusova, greeting each other gallantly in the House of the Arts kitchen as they received their cheap lunches. Their talk was peppered with French and English phrases, but her fingers were still frozen from last winter and both their faces showed the humble melancholy of the dying. When I said to him in jest the other day, "Good day, your highness," he was insulted and corrected me without a bit of humor—"I am your grace, not your highness"—and gave me a detailed account of why his grandfather became his grace. He was carrying a slop bucket.

I can't believe the number of English books I've read for no particular reason. I began with *Pickwick*, whose grandiosity and magnificence I appreciate only now. As you read it, you feel you're undergoing an immortal, joyful infusion of youth. Then Chesterton's wild "Manalive" with its questionable aphorisms and sham but provocative wisdom, then Stevenson's *Kidnapped*, so wonderfully written and exciting, then excerpts from *Barnaby Rudge*, then Conan Doyle—the short pieces (skillfully written, but forgettable and, when all is said and done, inconsequential)—and so on and so forth. And I'm so tired now that I don't think I can read anything else. Getting through any book is a chore. I started *Anna Karenina* and gave up. I started Stevenson's *Catriona* and gave up.

We have a staff of about fifteen in the House of the Arts kitchen—and not one thief! Amazing. I keep an eye on them, and I can't get over how idyllically honest they are! They're the aristocracy of our simple folk. If Russia has been able to produce so many fine, honest, humble people in times like these, Russia is not lost. Take our Zhenya, for instance, our sweet servant, who is utterly devoted to our family. But find me fifteen honest intellectuals! I haven't seen a single one in this whole period.

While reading *Anna Karenina*, I had a sudden feeling it was out of date. When I read it before, it was a contemporary novel; now Kitty, Oblonsky, Lyovin, and Karenin—they're ancient history. < . . . > Today, in the era of Soviet misses, the Baltic Fleet, and female commissars, female police, and female tram conductors, the forms of jealousy, love, betrayal, and marriage portrayed by Tolstoy seem antediluvian. And the way he psychologizes. [. . .]

I was very young when I first "turned up" in Petersburg, but people grew tired of my youth soon enough. Kuprin once said, "Chukovsky is about to celebrate the twenty-fifth anniversary of his seventeenth birthday."

3 October.

The day before yesterday I went to Gorky's Kronverksky place and had a serious talk with him even though Wells was there. < . . . >

"Why don't you like World Lit any longer?" I asked. "Why do you like the House of Scholars?"

"Very simple. Nobody in the House of Scholars informs against me. I've seen four denunciations from the House of the Arts in Moscow (Kamenev showed them to me). [. . .] The whole thing is despicable. And not because I'm involved. I've never wanted to be loved by anyone. I don't care. I know people won't and can't love me. I've made my peace with that; it's my role. I realize I'm often duplicitous. I never used to resort to trickery, but with our regime I've got to, I've got to lie and dissemble. I know there's no other way."

I was stunned.

Now Gorky has quarreled with the regime and set Moscow a number of conditions. If they're not met, he claims he will leave everything: Grzhebin, World Lit, the House of the Arts, everything.

23 November.

In the morning I write by candlelight. I've just finished "Muravyov and Nekrasov"[58] and am going back to Blok, but I seem to have lost my appetite for him. The "Poem About the Lady Fair" that so charmed me in my youth sounds dead to me now, just so many words! [. . .]

Mura is nine months old and makes the most unbelievable faces. The first thing she does when I take her in my arms is to reach for my mustache, my mustache being the feature distinguishing me most clearly from the non-mustachioed people surrounding her. She loves the fan in my room, an armless doll with a cracked head, the light, and the rocking horse. The moment she hears the word "light," she lifts her head. < . . . >

25 November.

Blok came up to me at the Tikhonov meeting (World Lit) yesterday and went on and on about a German writer he'd met while visiting Braz the artist. The man's name is Holitscher and he's come to study Soviet reality.

58. The essay subsequently appeared in *The Poet and the Hangman* (1922). It deals with a low point in Nekrasov's career when to save his liberal journal, *Sovremennik,* from extinction, he demeaned himself at an official function by reciting an ode extolling General Muravyov, who bore the ominous epithet "the Hangman" for his savage suppression of the Polish national uprising in 1863.

"The best you can hope for," he said, "is that all other systems will be worse than the Bolshevik system." (Clearly Blok found those words highly significant.) "Did you agree with him?" I asked. "Not so much with him as with his tone of voice. He spoke in journalistic clichés, but the tone was profound." We also talked about Gorky. "Gorky makes believe he's solved all problems and doesn't believe in God. There's something poetic, something mysterious about him." [. . .]

1 December.

< . . . > Yesterday at the World Lit meeting the ever flowery Levinson said to Blok, "Chukovsky is like a hero out of Dickens." I was surprised at how pertinent I found the remark. I do in fact feel ridiculous, pitiful, very nice, and picturesque in an amusing sort of way. Even the hang of my trousers is Dickensian. But I've no support, nothing. Solitude, penal servitude—that's all. So I go on living, laughing, running like a Dickensian hero, and may the Dickensian God, the Great Humorist in Dickensian heaven, come to my aid. < . . . >

5 December.

The last few days I've been down with my old curse: insomnia. Mayakovsky arrived in Petersburg on the mail train yesterday at my invitation. I enticed him here with all possible enticements when I saw him in Moscow a month ago. For a while he was adamantly against it, but the moment I mentioned that the House of the Arts, which was where he would be living, had its own billiard table, he agreed to come. He arrived with Brik's wife, Lili, Lilia Yuryevna [Lili Brik], who is wonderful with him: friendly, cheerful, and straightforward. It's obvious they're very close—and have been for many years now: since 1915. I'd never have thought that a man like Mayakovsky could keep up a relationship with one woman for so long. But only now do I plainly see what nobody has ever noticed: the thorough, sound, solid quality of everything he does. He is loyal and dependable: all his relations with old friends—Punin, Shklovsky, and the rest—have remained close and warm.

They arrived at the House of the Arts at about two and were taken to the library—which is unheated—near the dining room. I knocked on their door just after three and found him calm—self-confident but simple, not posing in the least. He told me that Moscow calls the Palace of Art the Palace of Slime and the House of the Press the House of Depression and that Shklovsky had a run-in with Kerzhentsev (who was trying to prove that Lunacharsky's works are petty bourgeois) and said, "The reason Lunacharsky is not a proletarian writer is that he is a bad writer." Lunacharsky was present. "Lunacharsky spoke like a God," Lilia Yuryevna interrupted, "but what he said about Volodya [Mayakovsky] was: 'It's a pity Mayakovsky is under the influence of Brik and Shklovsky.' " We ate together, the four of us: Mayakovsky, Lili, Shklovsky, and I. "Do eat our white bread," Mayakovsky said expansively, "though if you don't, Mandelshtam will." < ... >

The members of the House of the Arts had a meeting, but it was so boring I slipped out, and before the Khodynka[59] began—the crowds descending upon Mayakovsky—I went to see him. We had tea and talked about Lurye. [...]

"The bastard," said Mayakovsky. "Him and all those commissar upstarts. But he really gets my goat. The other day we were talking about Blok and gypsies, and he says, 'I know a place where we can go and see gypsies. They'll do all their songs and dances for us: I'm the commissar for music.' " But I said, "That would be like going to a brothel with a police officer." [...]

His introductory talk did not go over well. "The reason there's such a crowd here is you think that 150,000,000 refers to rubles. Well, it doesn't. I submitted the work to the State Publishing House, then asked for it back, and they said, 'Mayakovsky's asking for 150,000,000.' "[60] And so on.

Next came the reading. The poem about Ivan. They were bored by the bombastic section, but he won them over with the second impish part about Chicago. I noticed that everyone enjoyed the passages where Mayakovsky uses the intonations of current-day, 1920 colloquial speech. It sounds new and fresh and daring.

59. Hundreds of people were crushed to death in the Moscow district of Khodynka when an enormous crowd that had been promised Imperial trinkets in conjunction with the coronation of Nicholas II in 1894 got out of hand. (M.H.H.)

60. In his *Hundred and Fifty Million* Mayakovsky casts the epic struggle between the revolutionary masses and world capitalism in the form of the hand-to-hand combat between Woodrow Wilson "swimming in fat" and a Russian superman Ivan, who bears a distinct resemblance to Mayakovsky himself. The bombast of the Ivan section is partly redeemed by the comically hyperbolic portrayal of Chicago. (V.E.)

"You know Adelina Patti? She's the cat's whiskers." When Krylov or Griboedov reproduced the natural intonation of their times, it must have had the same effect. The third section dragged, but the audience clapped like crazy at the end.

Konukhes shrugged his shoulders and said, "It's idiotic." Many people told me, "Now we see how accurate your Mayakovsky article is." The Tenishev corner went wild. < . . . >

"Read some more," I said to Mayakovsky.

"Do you mind if they're revolutionary?" he asked, and the audience laughed. He read on and on, and again I noticed the audience reacted better to the humor than to the bombast. Later the Tenishev students, led by Lida, broke into his room and demanded "A Cloud in Trousers."[61] He recited "The Right Attitude to Horses." I introduced Zamyatin to him. A large group stayed to have tea with Mayakovsky, but I went home to bed with the children. [. . .]

7 December.

< . . . > Spent the whole day—between my morning and evening talks at the Red University—with Mayakovsky. Lilia Yuryevna made an astute observation: "He has only good things to say about people now. He's all praise. Everything's to his liking."

I've noticed it too. It's a big change. "It's because he's sure of himself now," I said.

"No, on the contrary," she said. "He is plagued with self-doubt." < . . . >

All morning Mayakovsky looked for Dumas in our library, and in the afternoon he taught Lili to play billiards. She says she's twenty-nine. He's twenty-seven or twenty-eight. He loves her with a calm, placid love. I jotted down his poem about the sun:[62] it made a great impression on me when he recited it; in written form it made almost none. He says every child in Moscow knows my "Crocodile."

61. "A Cloud in Trousers" (1916) is Mayakovsky's lyrical masterpiece and possibly the most explosive love poem in the language. (V.E.)

62. Chukovsky probably means Mayakovsky's poem featuring a dialogue with the sun, "An Extraordinary Adventure That Befell Vladimir Mayakovsky at His Summer House" (1920). (V.E.)

8 December.

Mayakovsky told a funny story about a visit he'd paid to Blok a long time ago. It was Lili's name day and she'd made *bliny* and told him not to be late, so he decided by what time he wanted to be back. She'd asked him to bring back Blok's books with dedications. "So there I am, with Blok going on and on. I look at the clock and reckon ten minutes more for talk, ten minutes to ask for the books, and three or four minutes for him to sign them. Everything's fine. Blok offers me the books on his own and says he wants to write something in them. He sits down at his desk, picks up his pen, and starts thinking. Five minutes go by, ten, fifteen. I'm horrified, I want to shout, 'Come on! Come on!' But he just sits there. I say politely, 'Don't put yourself out. Write the first thing that comes into your head,' but he sits there, pen in hand, thinking away. Good-bye *bliny!* I pace back and forth like a madman. I'm afraid to look at my watch. He's finally finished. I slam the book shut, smudging the ink a little. I thank him, run, and read: 'To Vladimir Mayakovsky, so often in my thoughts of late.' "
< . . . >

22 December.

At yesterday's meeting of the board of the Writers' Union somebody reported that about eight hundred books will remain in manuscript, unpublished, because of the paper shortage. Blok (cheerfully, to me): Good news! Thank God!

Merezhkovsky's attack on Gorky was read aloud at the World Lit meeting. Blok (in a whisper to me): He's right, Merezhkovsky.

1921

➤-➤-➤-➤-➤-➤-➤-➤

3 January.

I don't know what got into me yesterday, but I went to the Belitskys'. There I met the slender dark-haired Spesivtseva, a dancer and current wife of

Boris Kaplun. Kaplun was there too, in yellow boots. Very nice. He played the piano a bit, but soon grew tired of it; he wanted to do something amusing. "How about going to the crematorium," he said, the way people used to say, "How about going to the Cuba or the Villa Rodè."

"Are there any corpses?" somebody asked.

"Let me find out."

He phoned and we turned out to be in luck: there were nine.

"Let's go!" he cried.

Only he, Spesivtseva, and I went; the rest refused. < . . . > Kaplun drove. In twenty minutes we were at the former baths, now turned by Kaplun into a crematorium. The architect, whom Kaplun had found in a penal battalion (he'd strangled an old man), showed us around the building with great deference. It is not finished yet, but it's a colossally ambitious project. [. . .] We laugh; we feel no reverence, no solemnity whatever. Everything is bare, wide open. Neither religion nor poetry nor simple respect adorns the place of burning. The Revolution has abolished our former rites and rituals and failed to provide its own. People are wearing their hats and smoking; they talk about the corpses as if they were dogs. I went into the morgue with Spesivtseva. We opened one of the coffins and saw an orange-colored man, his feet at our end, completely naked, with no cloth, nothing but a strip of paper on his leg saying, "Popov, died on such-and-such a date."

"It's odd, that note," Kaplun told us later. "Usually they just spit on the heel and write the name with an indelible pencil."

What's the point of formalities, anyway. There are no formalities left, I kept thinking; everything's clear and simple, wide open. Who cares about the name of the useless carrion about to be shoved into the furnace. All that matters is to cremate him as fast as possible. But the carrion refused to burn. The furnace was Soviet, the engineers Soviet, the corpses Soviet, so everything went awry, amiss, astray. < . . . >

In the corner of one of the adjoining rooms Spesivtseva and I came upon a pile of human bones. Several spare coffins were crammed full of bones as well, but as there were not enough coffins to hold them all, the floor was strewn with them. < . . . > We were told there were no urns as yet, though they did have boxes made of sheet iron ("from old shop signs") and it would be a shame to bury urns. "There isn't enough room for all the remains anyway," the head engineer told us. "We'll use it for fertilizer in the spring," he added, rubbing his hands.

The engineer also told us that his children play Crematorium. A chair is the furnace, his girl the corpse. The boy comes running up to the furnace shouting, "Beep! Beep! Beep!" which is Kaplun pulling up in his car.

Yesterday Mura said "papa" for the first time without being prompted: she has learned to keep track of her speech and control it. [. . .]

4 January.

World Literature held its first reading yesterday. Because the government is treating us offhandedly and with suspicion, we've decided to advertise to the public, "appeal to the people." The whole thing, though my doing, was approved by the board, and I was certain that Gorky, who has a lot at stake, knew how to go about it. We decided Gorky would say a few words about the activities of World Literature. But things turned out differently. < . . . >

Dobuzhinsky and I tried to get him to discuss the program of literary talks in the countryside, but he went off on such a dull academic tangent that I put an end to it. For example, he said that Dostoevsky was unnecessary and that instead of introductions to Gogol and Pushkin we should be giving "a brief sketch of the laws of literary development." To peasant women and girls! < . . . > He was in a terrible hurry. It was all I could do to hold him back until seven fifteen. Then, even though people were still coming in, he went out on the podium, sat down at the table, and said, "I'm supposed to be talking about world literature, but I'd prefer to talk about Russian literature. It's closer to you. What has Russian literature been until now? A white spot on a Negro's cheek. And the Negro didn't know if it was good for him or a disease . . . It's been judged on the basis of its political affinities rather than on its merits. Liberals like liberal literature only, conservatives—conservative literature. A fine author like Dostoevsky was unsuccessful because he wasn't a liberal. A daring young critic like Dmitry Pisarev could destroy Pushkin. And that's how it's remained. Writers must be Communists. If they're Communists, they're good; if they're not, they're bad. Then what are non-Communist writers to do? They're forced into silence. Of course every house has a front door and a back door. They could stand at the front door and protest, but would it lead anywhere? That's why writers are not writing now, and those who do are mainly descendants of Smerdyakov.[63] If anyone wishes to object, the floor is open!"

No one wished to object.

"Gorky does love to talk out of both sides of his mouth," Annenkov whispered to me. [. . .]

12 January.

Went to Blok's the day before yesterday. [. . .] About his verse: he wrote "The Unknown Lady" while Bely was spending the day at his place and squealing, "I'll just listen and write a little more."

He showed me the Parisian editions of "The Twelve," but when I talked of his European renown he said, "No. I picture a tiny Jewish book-shop in Paris, one nobody knows, cobbling together 'The Twelve.'"
< . . . >

"What do you mean by 'stars taking revenge'?"

"Oh, nothing. I don't know why I came up with it. It replaced 'thirst and hunger to quench.' And my Christ at the end of 'The Twelve' is half literary, of course, but there's a certain truth to Him. I suddenly saw Christ with them—which I found very unpleasant—and I reluctantly, grudgingly *had* to put Him there."

He showed me the first draft of "The Twelve." It had surprisingly few rejected variants. He wrote the first part—more than half—in one go. Then, starting with "The Neva Tower," "out came the bag of literary tricks." I asked him so many questions about his verse that he said, "You're amazingly like a Cheka investigator," but he enjoyed answering them. [. . .]

2 February.

Gumilyov is a Salieri who doesn't even envy Mozart. Yesterday he tried to prove to Blok, Zamyatin, Tikhonov, and me that Blok achieves perfection *unconsciously*, while he does so consciously. He believes in his dogma of absolute beauty in art like a medieval scholiast. Yesterday he delivered some claptrap about the rules for writing and understanding poetry. < . . . >

Slaving away, doing the work of ten to feed the eight mouths I support

---

63. Smerdyakov is Fyodor Karamazov's repulsive illegitimate son and Ivan Karamazov's understudy in *The Brothers Karamazov*. (V.E.)

on my own, I used to have the morning hours to myself. They were all I lived for. I would go to bed at seven or eight, get up at four, and read or write. Now no sooner do I sit down at my desk than Marya Borisovna brings Murka over to me to hold, and that's the end. I just babble on for two or three hours: kitty, kitty, miaow miaow miaow, the kitty goes miaow miaow; doggy, doggy, bow wow wow, the doggy goes bow wow; giddap, horsy, giddap, giddap—day after day. I'm wildly jealous of anybody who has even four hours a day for writing. Everyone else has; I'm the only one condemned to this. Once I've lulled Murka off to sleep, it's Boba's turn. The whole morning's gone. And at eleven I'm off to the Municipal Council to beg a saw for firewood or to the House of Scholars to see if they've got gloves or to the House of Writers to see if there's any cabbage or to the Petrokomnetr to inquire when they're handing out rations or to Murmanka to find out whether we can get food without cards, and so on. Then there's military service and firewood and semolina for Murka. Coming up with a pound of semolina can take ten or twenty hours.

3 February.

Ran into Akhmatova yesterday in the lobby of the House of Scholars. She looked happy and young; she's put on some weight. "Come to my place today and I'll give you a bottle of milk for your little girl." I did drop in that evening—and she gave it to me! To think that in February 1921 one person offered another a bottle of milk! < . . . >
< . . . >

13 February.

It's one in the morning, and I've just come back from a Pushkin evening at the House of Writers. A historical event. Sitting around the table were Kuzmin, Akhmatova, Khodasevich, Kristi, Koni, Alexander Blok, Kotlyarevsky, Shchogolev, and Ilya Sadofyev (from Proletcult). < . . . > Koni's talk was disappointing: it was cold on the inside, all surface; you could feel the void behind the rhetoric. Kuzmin lisped and minced his way through some unexciting little poems written for the occasion. After Kuzmin came Blok. In a white sweater and jacket. Sitting immobile at the table. (Before the program began, he asked, "Is Ionov coming? Or anyone from official circles?") He went up to the rostrum, unfolded a piece of paper, and started reading in a dull voice about how unlike today's officials Benkendorf did not stifle inspiration and Pushkin could go on writing, while for us (poets) all that remains is death.[64] He said it in so muted a fashion that some people didn't get it. < . . . > But most people did and applauded for a long time. Afterward in the green room Marya Valentinovna Vatson, a fanatic anti-Bolshevik, thanked him over and over, shaking her head and saying he had "made amends" for his "Twelve." < . . . >

Then there was a meeting of the All-Russian Writers' Union to discuss my Wells letter.[65] Thank you, all. Everyone was sympathetic and tried to defend me. Shklovsky, Guber, and Gumilyov spoke with great passion. I didn't expect people to have so passionate a reaction to an offense aimed at another. Guber quickly drafted the text of the resolution, and I walked away from the meeting on air. I walked Misha Slonimsky, Shklovsky, and Otsup home on air, but then couldn't sleep.

We're going through another bread shortage. Oh the anguish of never eating your fill. Bread is now a rare delicacy, and Marya Borisovna has to keep telling Kolya, "Why are you taking a piece before dinner? Put it back." < . . . >

14 February.

Morning, that is, night. I'm reading Maeterlinck's *Treasure of the Humble.* It's all about stars, fates, angels, and mysteries, and I can't help thinking

64. Blok delivered this remarkable speech, "On the Calling of the Poet," at the commemoration of the eighty-fourth anniversary of Pushkin's death. It included the following remarks: "The amiable officials who interfered with the poet's testing hearts by harmony have been stigmatized forever as a mob [a reference to Lermontov's poem "On the Death of the Poet"]. A still worse label may be in store for those officials who set out to guide poetry along particular channels, encroaching upon its secret freedom and hindering it from fulfilling its mysterious mission." (V.E.)

65. When H. G. Wells came to Petrograd, Gorky asked Chukovsky to show him a Petrograd secondary school. Chukovsky took him to the Tenishev School, which was located opposite the World Literature Publishing House and which three of Chukovsky's children happened to attend. The students Wells talked to there vied with one another in naming the books of his they had read. A few days later Wells paid a visit to another school, where no one had heard his name. Upon returning to England, Wells wrote in *Russia in the Shadows* (New York, 1921, 121) that he had been taken to the first school "by a literary friend, Mr. Chukovsky the critic, affectionately anxious to make me feel myself beloved in Russia," thereby implying that Chukovsky had staged the warm reception. Chukovsky was hurt by Wells's accusation: the Tenishev School was known for its excellent teachers and high standards, and many students contributed to its literary journals. For a more detailed treatment of the episode and the relevant evidence, see Kornei Chukovskii, "Fantasmagoriia Gerberta Uellsa," *Literaturnaia Rossiia,* 25 September 1964.

yes, but Maeterlinck had enough to eat. I can't read about anything now without thinking about food. Yesterday I was reading Chekhov's "Teacher of Literature" and I couldn't get over the passage where they go to a dairy, ask for milk, but *don't drink it*. Milk, and they don't drink it!!! When I told the children, it turns out they too had remembered the passage and were as surprised as I was. < . . . >

I've forbidden Kolya to take part in the activities of the Russian Telegraph Agency, because they call every poem he writes counterrevolutionary. When Mayakovsky invited him there, we thought he'd be able to work in an honest, poetic atmosphere. It turns out to be all bureaucracy and death.

Tomorrow I'm going with Dobuzhinsky to Kholomki, the estate of the House of the Arts in Pskov province, to try and save my family and myself from the famine that is approaching ever more menacingly.

18 February.

Kholomki. < . . . > Here I am nearly forty, and for the first time in my life I am seeing the Russian peasant. And I see that he is basically a very real, capable, indestructible specimen, unafraid of any revolution. His main strength is his kindness. I've never seen so many truly kind people as I have in the past three days. A peasant woman gave Princess Gagarina a pair of felt boots, saying, "Take them for the love of Christ." [. . .]

20 February.

[. . .] Saw a country wedding today; a fancy sleigh, well-fed horses; the men and women in the sleigh sitting on cushions; the proxy father leading the bride and groom along the street like children; ribbons, beads, bells—a strong tradition, a strong sense of day-to-day existence. Mother Russia is hale and hearty: the peasant women are giving birth, the priests are remaining priests, the princes—princes; deep down everything is as it was. Only city life has fallen apart, and it can come back together in five minutes. Russia as a nation has never been so invincible. < . . . >

4 March.

< . . . > Gossip about me in the press—I am called a former spy—has shocked the professional Writers' Union, and it has unanimously resolved

to lodge a protest. The protest was sent to *Zhizn' iskusstva* together with my Wells letter, but Marya Fyodorovna Andreeva used her commissarial power to squelch it.

< . . . > It turns out Blok knew nothing about the Kronstadt events,[66] and when he found out he suddenly felt sleepy. "Events like that always make me sleepy. My eyes start closing; I go weak all over. I was sleepy all through the Revolution." And I recalled it was the same with Repin: at the first sign of anxiety he would feel sleepy.

7 March.

[. . .] Yesterday I was summoned by Gorky. < . . . > He was irritated, drumming his fat, powerful fingers on the table, first fast, then slowly, as if playing a long passage on the piano, tearing himself away only to moisten the fingers of his right hand and twist his long, red mustache (a compulsive gesture he repeated over and over). < . . . > People kept bringing him letters, signed them, ran out, ran back, elastic as always. (When he's sitting, you always have the feeling he's about to stand and go off somewhere—to answer the phone, for example, or say a few quick words to a visitor, but he always comes straight back to his post.) "This issue of *Dom iskusstv* is weak. It's got no spirit, as Tolstoy would have said. That's right. No spirit. What's the Blok article doing there? It's as if it were in a void." (He put on a sweet, gentle expression to make it sound less of a reproach.) I told him that the readership saw things differently: there had been much praise for the journal at the Writers' House, I'd received complimentary letters from readers, and Zamyatin's article "I Fear" had earned everyone's favor. At that point, as usual, Gorky changed the subject to politics, and, as usual, he talked tommyrot. Naive people who have had little contact with Gorky tend at first to set great store by what he says about politics. But I know the authoritative, contemplative look with which he's reiterated the most arrant nonsense and tittle-tattle for the past two years. This time he went on about the ultimatum and how shooting could begin at six and the Bolsheviks might really be in for it.
< . . . >

66. Kronstadt was a naval base situated eighteen miles west of Saint Petersburg. During the Revolution it was a major Bolshevik stronghold, yet the sailors staged a mutiny there on 28 February 1921. The uprising, which called for "Soviets without Communists," was promptly and brutally suppressed. It was a symptom of a widespread popular discontent. (V.E.)

30 March.

Tomorrow is my birthday. I spent all morning with the New York *Nation* and the London *Nation and Athenaeum*. They make intoxicating reading. The style is so civilized, the range—world-wide. How witty Bernard Shaw's polemic with Chesterton, how caustic the articles on Lloyd George! New materials on Walt Whitman! And most important, how closely knit the world has become: the English write about the French, the French respond, the Greeks intervene—all nations are inextricably interwoven, civilization is spreading and becoming one. I feel I've been dragged out of a pond and dunked in the ocean!

I've decided to stop writing about Nekrasov and rooting among literary wrangles and to throw in my lot with world literature. I find it easier to write for *The Nation* than *Letopis' Doma literatorov*. And write for *The Nation* I shall. My first piece will be a "Chesterton."

31 March.

I've conjured up a genie I can't get back into the bottle: after an inordinately long interval I've suddenly read *The Times*, and the whole world has gushed forth at me.

1 April.

My birthday. < . . . > Once more I had no sleep. Zamyatin told me there was a rumor making the rounds of the Writers' Union to the effect that I had made a profit on the Repin book. I didn't receive a kopeck for my pains, nor do I expect to. The rumor so upset me it gave me a headache that kept me up all night. < . . . >

Far from the Madding Crowd is a treat, but Hardy doesn't merge with his characters (as Tolstoy does in *Anna Karenina*); he stands off to the side, flaunting the elegance of his diction, his knowledge of the classics, and so on. < . . . >

25 April.

There's a Blok reading tonight. I'm all nerves. I haven't slept for three nights. There's almost nothing to eat: all each of us had today was a crust of bread. Kolya grumbled his disapproval. To make matters worse, I'm highly dissatisfied with my talk. Selecting passages for it from my Blok book, I realize you can't read good material in a theater (and we've rented the Bolshoi Dramatic Theater, the former Suvorinsky, on the Fontanka); you've got to read commonplaces, that is, second-rate things. That's the law of theater talks. The reason many of my articles don't ring true or read well is that I wrote them to be talks, and talks have their own laws, which are related to the laws of drama. They need action, motion, conflict, ex- citement—no subtleties, everything in the open. I called in Kolya yesterday and delivered the talk, headache and all. If he had said "good," I'd have gone to bed and had a good rest, but he said "bad" and glared hostilely at me all the way through it. "It's all wrong," he said. "You're not writing a character reference. It's a bunch of clichés. Blok is not at all like that. And it's so spasmodic. All bits and pieces." I found his criticism so on target that I fortified myself with caffeine and started cutting and pasting from scratch. But again I failed to come up with a real lecture . . . It is now half past six. I've donned my death-cell uniform—shined my shoes, attached *one* cuff, pressed my trousers—and off I go. I feel awful, disgusted with myself. It starts in a half hour. What will I write when I come home? God help me. < . . . >

It was horrible, a bust. Blok treated me solicitously, as if I were ill. [. . .]

Easter Night, 31 March–1 April.

< . . . > Ate practically nothing this morning. Wrote a lot of letters for Gorky to sign, then went to the House of the Arts and dictated them to Kolya to type up. On the way there I thought about what Pilnyak had said the night before: "Gorky is a has-been. He's a good man, but as a writer he's a has-been."

I went straight from the House of the Arts to Gorky. He was gloomy and—because he had a hangover—aloof. He looked through the letters and said, "I'm not going to sign these. No, no." He gave me a penetrating look, and I started going on about starving writers. "Yes, yes, I know," he said. "I've just received this letter," and he picked up a letter and read out loud about peasants bringing back all kinds of things—door curtains, embroi- deries—they had obtained in exchange for food and now wanted to trade for bread and potatoes. I returned to the starving writers, but he remained adamant. < . . . >

1 May.

Trip to Moscow. Blok came for me in a carriage, I carried my suitcase downstairs, and off we went. We gave the cabby three thousand rubles and two pounds of bread. We waited for an hour at the station. Blok has the gout. Two hours before we were due to leave, he had categorically refused to go, but I talked him into it: he's having a bad time of it at home. He knows about his wife's infidelity, and I wanted to get him away from that atmosphere. We sat on my suitcase while the First of May ceremony went on in the square. Speakers. Uhlans. He got up to have a look, but came back because his leg hurt. In the train we talked about his verse.

"Where's the woman you dedicated 'Twelve Years Later'[67] to?"

"Dead by now I hope. How old would she be? Ninety? I was a student then, and she was already fading."

On Akhmatova: "Her poems have never touched me. I found only one poem in her *Plantain* appealing: "When in the Throes of Suicide."[68] He began reciting it from memory. He had scorn for the rest of her verse. Of the line "Your nights [*nochi*] are unclean" he said, "It must be a misprint. What she must have meant was, 'Your feet [*nogi*] are unclean.' I don't know Akhmatova well. She once came to see me on a Sunday (she wrote a poem about it) because she happened to be taking a walk in the neighborhood and was wearing a beautiful scarf, the one she posed in for Altman." < . . . >

He talked about Chaliapin and what Monakhov the actor had told him. Chaliapin was very rude to women singers and would shout dirty words at them. If they were offended, Isaika would tell them, "God grant you earn as many dollars abroad as the number of times Fyodor Ivanovich called me that name." [. . .]

"Do you feel any reaction to your fame?" I asked.

67. Blok's lyrical cycle "Twelve Years Later" was dedicated to Xenia Mikhailovna Sadovskaya.

68. In this, one of Akhmatova's most frequently quoted civic poems, the persona unequivocally scorns the "soothing voice" that urges her to abandon her "wild and sinful country." It was written in 1917. Clearly Blok would have found her stance congenial. (V.E.)

"Fame? What fame? Most of the population has never even heard of me."

We had a serene and enjoyable trip. His leg bothered him, though not all that much. We traveled with Alyansky and a woman partial to the word "maddeningly."[69] It was a maddeningly cold night. I read O. Henry.

3 May.

< . . . > My lecture was a disaster. The house was far from full. Blok was so upset he refused to go on. In the end he agreed, but gave a mechanical, halfhearted recitation of only four poems. The audience reacted with weaker applause than he was accustomed to. He walked off stage, and for a while nothing we could do would make him go back on. Finally, he did read some Fra Filippo Lippi, in Latin and Latin only, looking sullen, though not defiant.

"Why did you do that?" I asked him.

"I saw a Red Army man with a star on his cap. I did it for him." [. . .]

5 May.

The Blok lecture went well: the audience was attentive and asked lots of questions. < . . . > Blok read on and on; he was his good old self and a great success. < . . . >

Mayakovsky came to the lecture wearing a loose artist's jacket that went down to his knees. He found everything we did deadly dull and kept yawning and calling out the rhymes ahead of time.[70] He went home early for a nap: he was leaving for his dacha in Pushkino that night. I had lunch

69. Many years later Alyansky recalled: "En route Alexander Alexandrovich complained of a pain in the leg. To distract him, Kornei Ivanovich entertained him with funny stories. . . . (Blok laughed a lot and apparently forgot the pain.) When Blok returned to Petrograd, the first thing he told Lyubov Dmitrievna [his wife] at the station was that on his way to Moscow Chukovsky had treated his ailing leg with funny anecdotes and extraordinary stories. 'And you know,' he added, 'it worked: I completely forgot about my leg.' The entire journey, as he put it, was in the key of Chukovsky major" (*Vstrechi s Aleksandrom Blokom* [Moscow, 1972], 134).

70. In the article "Alexander Blok Is Dead," published in 1921, Mayakovsky reminisced as follows: "I heard him last May in Moscow in a half-empty hall. It was as still as a grave. Softly and sadly he read his old lines about gypsy songs, love, the Lady Fair [the elusive love object of Blok's early verse]. There was no road ahead, only death" (*Gazeta Agitrosta*, 10 August 1921, reprinted in *Polnoe sobranie sochinenii* 12 [Moscow, 1959], 21–22).

with him today. He was cold to me, but I like him. We talked about *Mystery Bouffe*,[71] which is currently being staged by Meyerhold here. He accused Meyerhold of going a long way toward ruining the play, but had kind and affectionate things to say about him as a person. < . . . > He talked about the trouble he'd had with the text. The day before the production was due to open, he'd been summoned to the Kremlin by two midwives and told they wouldn't let the play go on because they didn't like the verse. "I gave them what for," he said, "but they managed to mess things up. It couldn't open on May Day." < . . . >

6–7–8 May.

The days all run together. I went to see *Mystery Bouffe*. It was a sorry sight. It lacks genuine vulgarity. The rhymed puns sound forced, self-conscious; they straightjacket the action. There's no free-flowing poetic diction, no chance for good declamation, which is an essential part of plays of its kind. And the crazy things Meyerhold came up with! He puts actors up hill and down dale, he brings in circus performers, he has all hell break loose in the audience, but it's all on the surface, trivial and lifeless; it never comes together. The humorous depiction of Lev Tolstoy is particularly nasty. < . . . >

The House of the Press has mounted an anti-Blok campaign. They very much wanted him to come, so he went and recited a few poems. Whereupon a certain dark-haired Comrade Struve came out and said, "Tell me, comrades! Where is the life in all this? The rhythm? It's dead as a doornail, and Comrade Blok is a corpse."

"Right, right," Blok said to me behind the curtain. "I'm a bona fide corpse."

Then P. S. Kogan came on and gave a trite, Marxist argument against Blok's being dead.

"Let's get out of here," I said to Blok. We went to the Italian Society. < . . . > The audience there was different: reverent, cultivated. Muratov, the head of the Society, gave a brief introduction: "I don't know about

71. A revolutionary morality play infused with the biblical motif of the Flood. It was premièred under Meyerhold's direction in the fall of 1918 on the first anniversary of the October Revolution. The performance of a significantly modified second version was synchronized with the Third Congress of the Communist International in Moscow in 1921. (V.E.)

other generations, but for those of us born between 1880 and 1890 Alexander Blok is the dearest of names."

The audience listened rapturously. It was an exhilarating performance. He recited in a rich, long-suffering, mellifluous, measured voice.

The same thing took place the following day at the Writers' Union. < ... >

12 May.

[...] Mayakovsky soaks up all kinds of jokes. Over lunch he told me the following: < ... > A Jew traveling by train and hearing that a new locomotive was being put on asked, "How much did they get for the old one?" Another Jew praised a woman by saying she had a twenty-five carat nose. And a third Jew saw the Tsar and bowed, and when the Tsar asked, "How did you recognize me?" he answered, "You look just like the ruble."

22 May.

< ... > Went to see Gorky. [...] Gone is the playful coquetry Gorky used to use on me, gone the "theater for theater's sake" he'd put on for new people he had reason to want to magnetize. We went in, and he sat down, tired but alert, and listened. < ... > Writers are completely alien to him, though he perked up a bit when Shklovsky mentioned Vsevolod Ivanov. "Is it true he hasn't any trousers? We'll have to get him some. We'll have to get him some." < ... > But he was so exhausted his voice was hoarse. We left, and he didn't try to stop us. [...]

24 May.

Saw Gumilyov at the House of the Arts yesterday with a pale frightened-looking woman. She turned out to be his wife, Anna Nikolaevna, née Engelhardt, the daughter of the amusing *Novoe vremia* literary critic famous for his plagiarisms. Gumilyov treats her like a despot. He packed her—a pretty young woman—and their child off to exile in Bezhetsk, while he led a charmed life here. She grew sickly and pale, so he's called for her and made her put the child in an orphanage in Pargolovo. She is so afraid of him she did as she was told. She's twenty-three and has a washed out look about her. I met them in the library. She kept giving him frightened glances and saying, "She'll be all right there, won't she? Even better than at home. They let her take her bread to bed with her. She has this bad habit of taking bread with her into bed. A very bad habit . . . And then there's the air . . . But I'll go and see her, Kolya, won't I? I'll go and see her . . ." [. . .]

26 May.

Arrived in Pskov in the morning. I went to the lavatory in the first-class waiting room. All the doors were torn off. People were defecating in plain sight and without the slightest shame, some talking, others silent. There was a two-hour wait to leave things in the cloakroom, where an extremely sluggish Ukrainian was in charge. < . . . > "Come back for your things as soon as possible," he told people. "We've got rats and they eat my labels." < . . . >

The third-class waiting room boasts a photograph of Maxim Gorky among those of other dignitaries and next to that of Kalinin. Opposite them I found these lines on the grain tax:

> The Soviets were right when they deplored
> The peasants' bent to live it up and hoard.
> The foe gave Russia not a moment's peace.
> There was no choice but surplus grain to seize.
> The Commissars did everything they could
> To get the peasants to produce more food,
> But they refused and ate all they did grow
> Thus leaving cities to starvation slow.

But now—or so the Telegraph Agency would have it—things will be different:

> The State will not take what you plant and you reap.
> According to law you give only one tenth.
> The rest is all yours; the rest you can keep.
> And no one will snoop round your barns and your pens.
> It makes sense to sow bigger plots than before:
> The State will get something, but you'll get much more.

For May Day the local government put out the following document, which I found pasted all over the station: "World capitalism, sensing in its death throes its inevitable end, reaches out its blood-stained hands to the throat of the burgeoning spring of mankind reborn. Second State Printing Office. Pskov. 400 copies." A perfect example of the bureaucratic imagination: a pack of clichés culled from the press and pasted together any old how by an indifferent hand. Still, we did get "the throat of spring." Clerical decadence! < . . . >

Fool that I am I picked up my gigantic briefcase, struggled into my coat, and set off for town, where I wandered from office to office and met gobs of people. I managed to get a horse for the colony and win back Belskoe Ustye.[72] < . . . >

But why in the world so magnificent a town with its fine churches and fine river should have so drab, undistinguished a population I have no idea. I found not a single remarkable person, not a single truly human individual. The austere lines of the Pogankin Palace, the local museum, are nothing if not noble, but the hand of a Pskov resident has scribbled on the outside door:

> I love you. Is there any hope?
> Let me send you a flea in an envelope.

And here is what recently happened inside: There had been a sudden increase in attendance. People kept flocking to the museum, looking for something, but what? They would move from case to case, scrutinizing everything. At last somebody went to the director and said straight out, "Show us the devil." It turned out there was a rumor that a local woman had spawned a devil by a Communist and had hidden it in a bottle of alcohol, which was now in the museum. That's what they came to the Pogankin Palace for.

3 June.

At Gorky's. < . . . > A young man, announced as Chernyshev, came in. "I am obliged to tell you," Gorky said to him, "that your father is no more." A long silence ensued, during which Gorky drummed on the table with his fingers. Finally the young man said, "Bad news," and was silent again. Then they had a long discussion over when his father had been in

72. In 1921 the Chukovskys, in concert with the painter Dobuzhinsky, set up a literary-artistic colony in the Pskov province, in the environs of Porkhov, in two adjacent manors, one of which was Belskoe Ustye. The colony played host to such Petrograd writers and artists as Zoshchenko, Zamyatin, Dobuzhinsky, and Radlov.

Kronstadt and when in Ladoga, and the young man kept repeating the inappropriate phrase, "Well, what do you know!" On his way out he said, "Well, what do you know! He died a natural death. He'd had stomach troubles." When he was gone, Gorky said, "The Soviet regime is rearing a generation of avengers. That's Dr. Chernyshev's son. And he guessed correctly: his father wasn't executed. He died. He's right. He guessed it."

Then the Serapion Brotherhood[73] was announced, and we went into the dining room, where we found Shklovsky (barefoot), Lev Lunts (his head shaven), a dandified Nikitin, Konstantin Fedin, Misha Slonimsky (wearing white ducks and an open-necked shirt), Kolya (wearing a peasant shirt patched for show), and Gruzdev (with a walking stick).

The talk was trivial. "What's Moscow like?" Gorky asked.

"All bazaar and bureaucracy," Fedin answered.

"It's like landing in a spider's web," said Gorky. "Lenin's supposedly scored a brilliant victory. He says straight out we've got to put off Communism for twenty-five years. You'd think they'd object, but no, they agree. How's Trotsky?"

"Trotsky is seriously ill. On his death bed. It's his heart. Zinovyev has heart trouble too. A lot of them have. They're poisoning themselves. It's the anger. It's physiological. There's less illness among the intellectuals. The former workers, though—they're unaccustomed to all that thinking; they're completely worn out. It's only natural." [. . .]

Gorky then told the following story: "On my way home yesterday I noticed a light on in a window. I looked in and saw a man fixing his typewriter, absorbed in his work, his face brightly lit. A bearded policeman came along, looked into the window, and said, 'What'll they think of next, the swine! Can't write like the rest of us. No, they need a machine for that too, the swine!' "

Then Gorky gave his opinion of the stories of the young writers present. He had edited them for Grzhebin, who was about to bring them out under the title *Nineteen Twenty-One*. "Let me tell you what I think of the collection. For no special reason. I don't want to be didactic. I've never liked preaching to people. I'll begin with a compliment. It's a very interesting collection, a first in the history of literature: a group of unpublished writers putting out a collection of literary merit. As a writer concerned with

73. The Serapion Brotherhood was a lively literary fraternity comprising some of the most gifted and promising young Soviet fiction writers. "Kolya" is apparently Nikolai Tikhonov, the only significant poet in the group. (V.E.)

everyday life I value its overall tone. Looked at superficially, it seems counterrevolutionary. But that's good. That's very good. It's strong, true to life. You can almost feel the history in it. It's alive and palpitating. It's a fine book."

He talked a lot about the unfortunate lack of a hero, the human element, in the book. "Man is sacrificed to fact. I find this belittlement of man an error of sorts. Aren't skin irritations taken for something else? History plays an ironic game, wickedly ironic. With the revolution the idea of collectivism should have triumphed. Well, it hasn't. The role of the individual has proved enormous. Take Lenin or Lloyd George. And you suppress the hero. Not one of the stories pays enough attention to man. Yet man has his human role to play in life."

Having held forth rather tediously on this hobbyhorse of his, he naturally moved on to the peasant. "You'll pardon my saying so, but the peasant is not yet human. That doesn't mean I'm defending the Soviet regime; no, I'm defending the individual. There aren't many heroes, and they're often zoological, but they do exist, even among the peasantry. Peasants have their Bonapartes, village Bonapartes . . .

"I know the Cheka has its heroes. They love mankind to the marrow of their bones, yet are forced to kill. Their faces break out, yet they've got to go through with it. It's Dostoevsky to the nth degree. I recently had a person here who'd heard a Cheka man tell his stories. The man finished boasting about some murder he'd committed and suddenly smiled. That's right, smiled. And the person who'd come to see me said, 'You see? Even a secret policeman smiles, so even he has something human about him.' It's like the onions in *The Brothers Karamazov*.[74] Even onions you have to renounce." (Here, as in all his articles and speeches, he keeps bringing in that tiresome *have to*. And he doesn't think he's didactic!) [. . .]

5 July.

I have now acquired the Belskoe Ustye colony and the orchard in my name. For the orchard I've gone to town four times, for the vegetable garden once, and for the meadows four times (first they gave them to me, then they took them back); I've acquired two horses by myself, with no outside

74. Gorky is speaking of the passage where Grushenka tells Alyosha a story about a "very wicked" peasant woman who has done one good deed in her life: "She once pulled out an onion in her garden and gave it to a beggar woman." (V.E.)

help. < . . . > I've acquired fodder for the horses and, most important, a second ration for all colony members and their families—a ration with sugar and groats.

It's torturous work, much too much for one person. It's taken me to the Kremlin, to Pskov, and to countless Petersburg offices. < . . . > People here regard me as the bailiff and say, "When are we going to have firewood? Have you seen to the firewood, Kornei Ivanovich?" [. . .]

11 August.

Dobuzhinsky has just come in and told me that Blok is dead. I am crying, and what can I [a part of the page is torn off].

12 August.

Never in my life have I been so sad as when leaving Porkhov with Lida in the miller's break. Sad unto death. I felt I'd left for Porkhov young and carefree and was returning an old man, drained, spent, as torpid as that blasted tree sticking up along the road a verst outside Porkhov—gray, dry, the epitome of provincial despondency. Every house in the blasted place seemed made of torpor, and together they made me endlessly despondent in my longing for Blok. Without even thinking about him, I felt the pain of his absence and asked Lida to recite her English words aloud to keep me from crying all the time. Every gray, lopsided house said to me, "Blok is no more. Who needs him anyway? I'm perfectly happy without him. I don't ever want to hear his name again." It was as if all those good-for-nothing houses had devoured him, and I mean that literally: I saw him tan, radiant, resplendent, being smothered by those hovels with their lice and bedbugs, their pickles and moonshine and homemade Porkhovian torpor. Once out in the fields, I stopped crying for Blok, but everything around me cried for him. And not so much for him as for me. "There goes an old man, dead, stifled, not a penny to his name." I thought about the children, and they seemed part of the torpor. I thought about literature and realized I was simply a poseur with nothing real to contribute. It was as if Blok had taken the enchantment of everything with him, the sugar-coated lie, and suddenly the skeletons were out of the closet. I recalled how beautifully he tanned, as only very calm and solid people do, how receptive and lively his face was—for all its seeming stoniness—forever in motion, smiling, absorbing impressions. He hadn't been able to tolerate Gorky or Tikhonov lately, and his face would freeze, but if a person dear to him—Zorgenfrei, say, or Knipovich—turned up in the hustle and bustle of World Literature, that face, though hardly changing, would show in no uncertain terms how happy he was. Still three or four steps away from you, before holding out his hand, he would greet you with his eyes and before greeting you or instead of greeting you in words he would simply state your name and patronymic—"Kornei Ivanovich," "Nikolai Stepanovich"—as if he were saying hello. The same held for 6 12 00. Whenever you dialed it, you would hear a deep, mournful voice—as if from the grave—utter the standard [Russian] salutation, "I am listening" (it never varied), followed by "Kornei Ivanovich" (again, a simple statement). Oddly enough, I recalled more physiology than events, how he always stood while reciting his poems and never held a piece of paper, how his voice was always steady and sad, and how he would shift ever so slightly from one foot to the other and take half a step backward, or how, after Lyubov Dmitrievna had recited "The Twelve" and was sitting in the salon of the House of the Arts, he entered from the auditorium with a loving, enraptured look, < . . . > how on the roof of Vyacheslav Ivanov's Tavricheskaya Street flat he recited "The Unknown Woman," and at Sologub's "The Snow Mask" <. . . . > I recalled that doomed gait of his and his perpetual unintentional stateliness—even when he was just running off to the House of Writers for a quick cup of tea or sandwich—the entire, ineffable Blokian atmosphere, and I was horrified at the thought that it was no more. It was all in the grave: his voice, his handwriting, his amazing cleanliness, his hair *abloom,* his knowledge of Latin and of German, his small elegant ears, his habits, loves, his "decadence," his "realism," his wrinkles—all beneath the earth, in the earth, earth.

What horrified me most of all was that with Blok Russian literature had come to an end. Literature is the work of generations; it never ceases; it is the highly complex relationship between everything printed and what over the centuries has survived, and . . . [The page is unfinished.]

His life had no events. "I went to Bad Nauheim." He did nothing but sing. A never-ending song passed through him in a continuous stream. For twenty years, from 1898 to 1918. Then he ceased—and immediately started dying. His song was his life. Once the song was over, his life was over. [. . .]

6 December.

It makes me very sad not to have made an entry for so long. It's been the usual whirlwind; I never know what will set my head awhirl next. Yesterday my three little books about Nekrasov came out simultaneously—in terribly shabby editions.[75] I'm currently reading the proofs of *A Book About Blok* and find it ghastly. Yesterday there was a celebration of the hundredth anniversary of Nekrasov's birth in the concert hall of the People's House. I fled in horror. < . . . > From the moment we entered, we could feel the vulgar, official, police-station atmosphere associated with the commissars. The weather was awful, worthy of Nekrasov, wet snow lashing at our faces. [. . .]

24 December.

Home from a visit to Akhmatova. She is staying at Fontanka 18 in the flat of Olga Afansyevna Sudeikina. "Olechka is out of town and I'm living here for the time being. I'll have to move when she gets back." The room is tiny, the bed unmade. There is an icon, the Mother of God in a silver raiment, nailed to the left-hand door of the wardrobe. There is a small table next to the bed with butter and black bread on it. An old woman servant opened the door and said, "Our door has a will of its own." Akhmatova has a lap blanket draped over her legs. "I've caught a cold. I keep coughing." We had a long chat. < . . . >

"I've been having a lot of trouble with Petropolis. They owed me nine million rubles, but then they calculated it in foreign currency and paid only four. [. . .] My *Rosary* is coming out soon. Oh, how I detest that book. It's a book for little girls. Have you read the journal *Nachala?*"

"No," I said, "but I noticed it had a review of your work."

"Yes, yes," she said nonchalantly, but came back to the article so often that it was clear how deeply Chukovsky's remarks had wounded her. "I wish Anna Radlova all the success in the world, of course, but why pull everyone else to pieces." (The review contained jabs at Blok, Akhmatova, and Bely.)

75. The books in question are *The Poet and the Hangman, The Poet's Wife,* and *Nekrasov as Artist,* all of which were published by Epokha in a series devoted entirely to Nekrasov.

"Why not face up to it?" I said. "Let's be frank. Chudovsky is a first-class idiot, and Radlova—a big nothing."

"I don't want to malign her," she said. "Maligning people is wrong, but . . ." She was clearly pleased. "I've been asked to go to Moscow, but Shchogolev advises against it. He says I'm hated there and the Imagists[76] will make a scene, and I don't know what to do in that kind of situation. They attacked Blok in Moscow too."

Then the old woman lit the stove and said there wasn't any wood left for the next day.

"It doesn't matter," Akhmatova said. "I'll bring a saw along tomorrow, and you and I can saw some." (I'm sending Kolya to her today.) She lay down on the bed in her coat, reached under the lap blanket, and pulled out some large sheets of rolled up paper. "It's the ballet of Blok's *Snow Mask*.[77] Listen to this, and don't be a stickler for the style. I'm no good at writing prose." And she read me her libretto, which I treasure as a wonderfully subtle commentary on *The Snow Mask*. I don't know if it works as a ballet, but as an analysis of *The Snow Mask* it is excellent.

"I haven't yet come up with the death scene in the third tableau. I'm doing the ballet for Artur Sergeevich [Lurye]. He asked me to. Diaghilev may put it on in Paris." [. . .]

1922

✦➤➤➤➤➤➤➤

1 January.

I celebrated New Year's Eve at the Writers' House. I didn't think I would—I didn't reserve a table—I went on the spur of the moment, because I couldn't sleep. Oh, the melancholy of all those old people, all that loneliness. I'd ban everyone forty and over from New Year's celebrations. I sat at a table with Fedin, Zamyatin, Khodasevich, and their ladies, surrounded

76. Imagism was a branch of the literary avant-garde lasting from 1919 to 1927 and headed by Vadim Shershenevich. It called for a *"vers libre* of images." (M.H.H.)

77. A 1910 lyrical cycle by Blok. According to Akhmatova, "the manuscript of the libretto has not survived. All we have is the cover." See Dmitrii Maksimov, "Akhmatova o Bloke," *Zvezda* 12 (1967): 190.

on all sides by unfamiliar bald pates. M. V. Vatson came up and said she'd made her peace with me. Then she said Gumilyov had been "gunned down like an animal."[78] What a battleaxe! What hatred! Three months ago she'd said to me, "Tell me, did your comrades help you to save Gumilyov?"

"What comrades?" I asked.

"The Bolsheviks."

"Why, you bitch, you!" I screamed at the seventy-year-old woman, and everyone who heard me approved and said my response to her insult was the only one possible. Of course I felt terrible about calling an elderly woman and a writer a bitch, and now she comes and says, "Don't be angry . . ."

There were speeches, each of which began: "It is now four years since . . ." after which they made it more or less plain that we need freedom of the press. Then Fedin came out and said that critics should stop frowning, that Russian literature has a future as well as a past. I found that offensive, because I kept thinking of Blok, Gumilyov, and others like them. So I went up and said (too neurasthenically, it would appear) yes, Russian literature did have a future, because the Russian people had inexhaustible reserves of talent, but "the grass, though growing green again, is growing on graves." And we all stood in silence to honor the memory of the departed. [. . .]

14 February.

Called on Akhmatova yesterday. There was no light in the stairwell. I made my way to the door and knocked, and the door opened immediately. It was Akhmatova herself. She'd been in the kitchen chatting with "grandma," her cook, Olga Sudeikina.

"Have a seat," she said. "It's the only warm room."

Today I noticed for the first time what a sunken "chestless" chest she has. You can't see it when she wears a shawl. I told her I found her "Slander" poem cold and overly classical.

"That's what Volodya (Shileiko) says. He says that if Pushkin had lived another ten years he would have written verse like that. Nasty, don't you think?"

She gave me some sardines and some bread. We spent a long time

78. Gumilyov was executed in 1921 for alleged counterrevolutionary activities. (M.H.H.)

talking about Anna Nikolaevna, Gumilyov's widow. "How can she fail to realize that people's relationship to her is based on sympathy for her grief. Without grief there is no sympathy." Then in a feminine vein: "Why did Kolya take a wife like that? His mother says he told her the last time he saw her, 'If Anya doesn't change, I'm getting a divorce.'

"I can imagine her petty concerns getting on his nerves. But Kolya was unhappy in general. He was tormented by the idea that my poems were better than his. Once we had the kind of argument everybody has, and I said to him—I'd found a note from another woman in his jacket pocket—'If nothing else, my poems are better than yours!' God, you should have seen the expression on his face! Why did I say it? The poor thing! He did so want to be a good poet.

"The Nappelbaums have asked me to take over leadership of the Re-sounding Shell.[79] I refused."

"You're in a difficult position," I told her. "You are Gorky and Tolstoy and Leonid Andreev and Igor Severyanin all rolled into one. It's awful."

It's true. Her fame is at its height. Yesterday the Free Philosophical Association devoted an evening session to her poetry, and the journal editors phone her morning, noon, and night begging for anything she may have.

"Lucky Sologub," she said. "All his published verse is in alphabetical order and numbered. And he writes so much: several poems a day."

19 February.

Annenkov is always so late! He came to see me one morning (three days ago) and stayed until three, saying all the time, "I have to be at Duncan's[80] at one." (He calls her Dunka the Communist.) < . . . >

25 February.

Yesterday was Murochka's birthday, a sacred day for me, but packed with guests. It's sickening. I hate organized inactivity. < . . . > And I was con-

79. A literary circle headed by Gumilyov until his death. The meetings were held in the Nevsky Prospect attic of the famous photographer M. S. Nappelbaum. Nappelbaum's daughters, Ida and Frederika, were members.

80. The American dancer Isadora Duncan enjoyed great popularity in Soviet Russia and was married to the poet Sergei Yesenin for two years (1922–23). (M.H.H.)

stantly afraid that yet another guest would bring her yet another elephant.
[. . .]

12 March.

I have just now, at twelve midnight, finished Henry James's *Roderick Hudson* and am bowled over by its wise, extraordinarily subtle, irresistible artistry. Other writers—Dostoevsky, for instance—put their characters on stage, whereas here you are in their room and have the feeling you have been living with them for years. I know his Mary Garland and Christina as I know my wife. He is impatient, petty, always aloof, always peering into the microscope, always foppish and cold-blooded in his sentence structure, yet he charms and excites you and you can't put the book down. There's nothing like it in Russian literature. And what a brilliant connoisseur of human nature, what daring portraits, what a sure, firm hand he uses to portray genius. His sculptor Roderick is not the banal genius of novels for women; he is his own man, a capricious egotist, blind to the psychology of others, a man who treats himself, his ego, as a sacred object, and is actually of another world. Then Christina Light, a beauty with the same relationship to her ego—a coquette, a good-for-nothing, a bad lot, yet sacred. And Rowland, the perfect gentleman, attentive to his duty, very noble (but no mannequin), yet doomed to fall on his face—how delicately and unobtrusively James shows his moral bankruptcy, shows that each time Rowland tries to help he does ill, that in life we must run wild, go berserk, rather than proffer moral precepts. **Fancy such a theme in an American novel! It was written (as I found in a dictionary) in 1875.** Premonitions of Nietzsche, Wilde, and the general theme of **disquiet** in literature and thought. **I wonder whether this extraordinary novel had a good reception on its native soil.** There is a lot of the French about it, a lot of Flaubert. Occasionally his sublime analysis seems in vain, **to no purpose.** You read it and think, "So what?" That is what I felt when I finished "International Episode." But *Washington Square* and *Roderick Hudson* are something else again. In *Washington Square* too he shows the moral victory of the strong, intact, elemental spirit *over* the concocted trifle.

It is now a quarter to one. The electricity will be turned off soon. < . . . > I've lighted the oil lamp and found another book by James: *Confidence*. I hope it will distract me however slightly from the despondency I feel when I have insomnia . . . No, I've read twenty pages and given up.

What's bad about James is that every piece of a story is equal to every other piece: everywhere the same high-quality material, the same rich, weighty language and ironic intonations—and often the same plot. In *Confidence* it is Rome again, artist and girl again, Love again, **brilliant dialogue** again, and most of all the idle rich again, people living only for pleasure, **making nothing but love.**

15 March.

Night. I don't know how many nights I haven't slept. The moon is shining. I went out for the first time yesterday. **Dizziness**. But no major problems.

I am reading Thomas Hardy's *Far from the Madding Crowd*. It's wonderful!

It has just now come back to me how politely Gumilyov used to greet Nemirovich-Danchenko. He would even pay his respects to him on holidays. When I asked him why, he answered, "It's like this. I'm an officer and respect subordination. In literature I'm a captain and he's a colonel."

"I see. That's why you're so respectful to Gorky."

"Right. Gorky's a general!"

It was in his blood. He could never forget his own rank or anyone else's.

And he so hated my "Crocodile"! There too he had a reason of his own. "You make fun of animals—elephants, lions, giraffes." He didn't like making fun; he did not like humor. He attacked it with all his might in his studio classes[81] and considered every insult to an animal a personal affront. There was a kind of adolescent sweetness to it all. < . . . >

It is six a.m. I'm going to put out the oil lamp and lie down. Maybe I'll get some sleep. Clearly I'm fated to die from insomnia. It's ruined my life. Between twenty-five and thirty-five—my best years—I led the life of an invalid: I wrote practically nothing and shunned human company. My head was a constant muddle. It's all starting up again, and I don't know how to deal with it. [. . .]

81. The House of the Arts employed a number of writers to teach creative writing in what were called studio classes. (M.H.H.)

16 March.

Six a.m. < . . . > I read over my sketch of Leonid Andreev yesterday. I'm afraid I haven't quite conveyed his good-natured, open-hearted, childlike quality. He was basically a good man, and if I hadn't been a critic we'd have been on the best of terms. But he had a unique and inexplicable quality: he feared critics, hated them. I remember once walking twelve versts (barefoot) with Oldor to see him. He was very warm with me, as always, but he practically ignored Oldor. Oldor is in fact a boring fool of a wag, and when I asked Andreev, "Why are you so cool to your guest?" he replied, "To hell with him! He did a parody of me in 1908." [. . .]

17 March.

It's freezing. Bookshops are opening all over the place, but they have no customers. < . . . > Spend an hour in a bookshop and you'll see two or three people come in and ask, "Have you got any Blok?"

"No."

"Not even 'The Twelve'?"

"Not even 'The Twelve.' "

Pause.

"Then give me Akhmatova."

I just remembered (I don't know whether I've put it down anywhere) that Mayakovsky said an awful thing about "The Twelve" last year: "Ugh, what weak rhymes!"

18 March.

Went to a Whitman Society meeting yesterday and came back ashamed of myself. True, there wasn't much Whitman-like about it—it was mostly quarreling, yelling, and mutual accusations of insincerity—but what a thirst for all-concerning "religion," what reserves of fanaticism. I've become far too literary in the past few years: I can't conceive of Whitman in terms other than literary. And now, thanks to my purely literary efforts, these young people sit up till all hours, eyes burning, deliberating *how to live.* One of them—from Kostroma, I believe—kept assailing me with the words, "That's aesthetics!," "aesthetics" being a term of abuse. They have no use for aesthetics; they are passionately involved in morality. Whitman interests them as a prophet and teacher. They want to kiss and work and die "according to Whitman." Instinctively sensing the "literatus" in me, they recoiled. No, I thought as I left them, Russia is still intact. And what makes her strong is that she is basically young, naive, and "religious." No irony, no skepticism, no humor—everything serious, **in earnest**. < . . . > Exhausted by lack of bread, lack of heat, and lack of money, these girls and adolescent students longed for faith rather than firewood or aesthetic pleasures. I felt like a beggar in comparison and left them dispirited. Now I'll start rewriting my Mayakovsky article. Yesterday at the World Literature meeting they told some pretty good censorship stories.

Zamyatin has written a story called "The Cave"[82] about the terrible destruction of the intelligentsia in Petersburg. It's dense, the ending is false, and as usual you feel him winking at you, but it's still good. It was published in the January issue of *Zapiski mechtatelei*. Zamyatin is putting out a book of stories with Grzhebin, "The Cave" included, and suddenly a "warrant" turns up at the press and the type is destroyed. The story has been banned! So off he goes to the military censor, where they shower him with compliments: We thought it was wonderful! It's not us; it's Political Education. So on he goes to Bystryansky on the Fontanka. Bystryansky is sitting in a large room all by himself. High as the ceiling is, it seems to be pressing down on his head; clear as his glasses are, they seem to have blue lenses.

"See this?" Zamyatin says to him. "It's the January issue of *Zapiski mechtatelei*. The censor passed it. Two months go by and it's considered unprintable. You may have noticed that the Soviet Republic has not dissolved. The story has done it no harm."

Bystryansky was embarrassed and approved publication without reading the story. It turns out the story was banned by a Comrade Grishanin and he and Bystryansky are at loggerheads!

19 March.

< . . . > The new censorship stories are, alas, true to life. Aikhenvald submitted an article saying that the youth of today is being murdered, perverted, and so on. The censor banned it. Aikhenvald assumed it was

82. A poignant story about the plight of an intellectual couple clutching at the residues of civilized existence in cold and hungry Petrograd of 1918. (V.E.)

banned because of the passage about the youth and went to Polyansky (the censor) and said, "I'm willing to cut those lines."

"Those lines aren't the problem."

"Then what is?"

"It's your mysticism."

"What mysticism?"

"Here: 'to sleep, to dream.' You can't say that. It's mysticism."

"But it's a quotation from *Hamlet*!"

"It is?"

"I swear."

"Just a second. Let me talk it over with my colleagues."

He left the room, and when he came back he said, embarrassed, "We'll let it go this time."

I have it from Zamyatin, who loves these kinds of stories and tells them slowly, smoking, and with the expression of a cat being stroked. He's a most pleasant fellow, all shiny, clean, and easygoing, the kind who knows the score and how to get on swimmingly with everybody, to please everybody, cautious, yet nice. At least I'm always sincerely happy to see his sated face. < . . . > He cleverly and cautiously sulks against the authorities, that is, enough to please the émigrés. His style is modest, without panache, with the little inventions of the little man. He plays the Englishman, but speaks no English and knows amazingly little of English literature and life. But even that makes you want to like him, because basically he's such a nice chap: he never gets in your way, he's a good conversation partner, a good drinking partner. < . . . >

20 March.

< . . . > *Far from the Madding Crowd* is about a farmer named Oak who falls in love. I keep wondering, What's it to me? By the time we reach forty shouldn't our receptivity to the artistic reproduction of the psychology of a total stranger be on the decline? But no, it's superb. The depiction of the matchmaking is classic—so terse, so fresh and vivid.

21 March.

< . . . > I think I've been privy to the birth of a religious cult. Next to my couch there is a box I used for writing while I was ill. (Lida has this

to say about it: "You have eight tables in your room, and, eccentric that you are, you write on a box.") The box has a little hole in it. We've told Murka the box is where Boo lives. She believes fervently in Boo and comes in every morning to feed him. What? Paper. She crumples up scraps of paper and sticks them into the hole. If we forget, she reminds us: "Boo, eat-eat." With a little development the myth will give us new Euripides, Sophocles, liturgies, icons . . .

23 March.

Took opium for sleep. Woke with a heavy head. Read *The Wisdom of Father Brown* by Chesterton. **A wisdom rather stupid and Chesterton seems to me the most commonplace genius I ever read of.**

Mura pointed to the ventilator, and I sang:

> Ventilator, ventilator
> Ventilator, ventila.

She immediately picked up the **tune** and sang:

> Pappa papa papa papa
> Pappapapapapapa.

She's very sensitive to rhythm.

24 March.

I'm flat broke. I'm reading Chesterton's *Innocence of Father Brown*—**the most stupid thing I ever read.**
< . . . >

26 March.

< . . . > I stupidly made an appointment with Akhmatova for four today. I buy a roll (with my last kopeck!) and set off for the Fontanka. She is expecting me: the kitchen is neat and Olga Afanasyevna's old cook is sitting on the stove, mending one of Akhmatova's black stockings with white thread.

"Light the stove," Akhmatova tells her, and we go into her narrow room, three quarters of which is taken up by a double bed covered with a big blanket. It's terribly cold. We sit by the window, and with the gesture of a hostess entertaining a member of high society she hands me the journal *Novaia Rossiia,* which has just come out under the editorship of Adrianov, Tan, Muizhel, and other Bolshevik sympathizers. < . . . > I point out a funny passage in Vishnyak's article, < . . . > but I can tell she isn't the least interested in what I think of the journal's orientation. She has something else in mind. As soon as I come to the end of my liberal remarks, she says, "Have you read the reviews? The review about me? They tear me to pieces!"

I picked up the journal again and found a very respectful but less than enthusiastic article by Gollerbakh. Poor Anna Andreevna! If she only knew the reviews awaiting her!

"This Gollerbakh sent me some very laudatory poems, but wait till you see what he wrote in his book on Tsarskoe Selo. Here, look!"

It turns out he had presumed to mention that Akhmatova's maiden name was Gorenko!

"How dare he! Who gave him permission? I've asked Lerner to let him know I find it an abomination!"

I could tell that this was the emotional core of her life, what she basically lived for.

"The fool!" she said about Gollerbakh. "His father had a bakery, and I bought rolls from him when I went to school there. But that doesn't mean he can call me Gorenko."

I tested my hypothesis by telling her that there was a schism in my studio class between those for and those against her. "And actually there are some refined and intelligent people among the opponents. One of the students, for example, a girl with a poker face and no gesticulations, upped and gave a paper about you last Thursday. It was devastating. She argued that you'd taken your aesthetic from 'the old years' and Kurbatov's history of Petersburg, that your Florence and your Venice were just a fad, and that your poses were just that—poses."

This so unnerved her that she felt the need to affect indifference and, looking in the mirror and adjusting her bangs, she said superciliously, "Interesting, very interesting! Please bring me the paper, and I'll have a look at it."

I felt terribly sorry for her. Her life is hard, and she focuses entirely on herself and her fame, having little else to live for. She showed me the notebook, large and square, she used for her new poems. "See? Enough for a new book. But the critics will say, 'Akhmatova is repeating herself.' So I'd rather have them published in Paris. They can send me a little something from there."

The critics abroad are much kinder, she says. "*Novaia russkaia kniga*[83] that has just come out in Berlin writes in the most glowing terms about me and about all of us. I'm a genius. Remizov is a genius. Andrei Bely is a genius."

"Have you got enough money now?" I asked.

"Oh, yes. Plenty. I got a hundred and fifty million for *The White Flock*[84] and had a dress made for myself, sent some money to Lyovushka, and mean to send some to Mother in the Crimea. I'm in a terrible way. I am one of four sisters and the third is dying of consumption. That's what Mother writes: "dying." In a hospital. I know they need the money badly, but I can't send it. "Don't send it by mail," Mother writes.

We then began talking about the famine. I told her about my idea of writing a children's book for Europe and America. She was very enthusiastic.

It was hot in the room by then. She made me some coffee, setting the table herself and coping marvelously with the dampers on the stove. It wasn't until then that I noticed how becoming her new dress was.

"The material comes from the House of the Scholars!"

I took the roll out of my pocket and tucked in. It was my lunch.

< . . . > Then she asked, "Would you like to hear some poetry?" and read me her "Judith," which is similar in meter to "Three Palms."[85] "I wrote it on the train, on my way to see Lyovushka. I'd begun it in Petersburg by opening the Bible (at random), and that was the episode I came up with. < . . . >

27 March.

Up all night. Read Hardy and Chesterton. I'm as taken with Hardy as I was before. The book is full of humor. The humor doesn't come from one

83. The journal was a critical and bibliographical monthly launched in 1922 in Berlin. Its first issue included reviews of works by Remizov (*City Noises* and *Fiery Russia*) and Akhmatova (*Anno Domini*). Remizov is called "a splendid artist." The Akhmatova review concludes as follows: "Akhmatova's poetry is one of the finest flowers of our culture."

84. *The White Flock* (1917) is the third collection of Akhmatova's verse. (V.E.)

85. There is no such poem by Akhmatova. Chukovsky must have had in mind "Rachel" from the cycle "Biblical Verse." "Three Palms" is a well-known poem by Lermontov.

page or another; it comes from the entire work, the feeling of life in the work. There's something attractive about Chesterton in the end. True, he's a non-entity, but cultured people in Europe know how to be non-entities, which is something we Russians are completely incapable of. If you're a non-entity in Russia, you write about Pushkin or you join the Poets' Guild or you publish *Capital and Country Seat*. In England you have so much clothing and other cover that the naked truth remains invisible; besides, Chesterton has so distinguished a gait that there seems to be an important personage beneath the clothing. < . . . >

29 March.

[. . .] Went to the House of the Arts for an evening meeting. I wasted six hours on nonsense. It turns out the House of the Arts has no money. It has come up with the following ways to raise funds: set up a club and introduce dominos, lotto, billiards, and the like. That's what our lofty, noble enterprise has come to. With a fervor not at all like me (I don't like flights of lyricism) I said that it was all perfectly possible but in the name of what? Not for forty or fifty layabouts and drones to receive (for reasons unknown to anyone) some easy money and live in clover but for there to be effective cultural activities—a journal, a lecture series, living art, music, and so on and so forth.

On the way home Tikhonov told me an interesting thing about Chekhov: Tikhonov admired Gorky greatly when he was a student, and Chekhov said to him, "How can you praise trash like 'The Song of the Falcon'? Wait till you're older. You'll be ashamed of yourself."

"And I am," said Tikhonov. < . . . >

Nabokov has been murdered.[86] God, so many deaths! [. . .]

2 April.

< . . . > This is the end of my diary, the end of forty-year-old Chukovsky. We shall see what is yet to come. **It's rather interesting what Life has in store for me. Through all my youth and middle age I was laden**

---

86. V. D. Nabokov, the writer's father, was shot in Berlin by a right-wing fanatic. He was shielding the actual target of the assassin's bullet, the Kadet Party leader P. N. Milyukov.

with such a heavy burden and bore it unfailingly, bore it like a slave. I can't go on!

4 *April.*

< . . . > Am editing a Sinclair translation with great antipathy. It's a totally illiterate rendition of crass American trash.[87] Comparing Sinclair's style to Hardy's is like comparing a monkey to a man.

7 *April.*

World Literature held a Whitman celebration on Tuesday the fourth. The Whitmanites arrived while a meeting of the Writers' Union was going on and had to wait. None of the writers and professors was in favor of the celebration. They all behaved as if it had been imposed upon them—Lerner actually took off!—yet it turned out to be quite interesting. I read several passages from *Democratic Vistas,* and Volynsky gave a splendid talk on it which I enjoyed immensely, though it was based on a major misconception. Latching onto the words "transcendental social structure," Volynsky claimed that Whitman negated what is in favor of what should be, that is, the metaphysical; in other words, he made Whitman a kind of spiritualist. < . . . > I wrote to Zamyatin that Volynsky was wrong about many things. [The following note in Zamyatin's hand is glued into the diary.]

> His religion is not the least bit rationalistic or cerebral; it is corporeal. His iconostasis has no curves or transcendental geometry; it is all stones, locomotives, policemen, thieves, wires, grain, and worms.

He always thinks in truisms like that. At the celebration he said what is written here and then the Whitmanites took the floor. They are all savages compared with us; they are naive, but their naïveté is their strength. One of them had this to say about their group. "At first we thought of calling our society 'The Society of Genuine People,' but when we came to know Whitman we realized he was perfect for us. These are hard times, and we have no criteria, no sense of purpose. Our institute has some twenty clubs

---

87. The translation of the novel, *100%: The Story of a Patriot,* was eventually published and Chukovsky's contribution as editor acknowledged.

and organizations; they are all falling apart. We need a teacher and guide like Whitman."

I haven't got a kopeck. I'll have to find something to sell tomorrow. The sun came out early today, but I haven't been outside; I sweated over Nat Pinkerton. Lida has taken on the Houseman Sinclair translation and is doing a brilliant editing job. Imagine that! A fifteen-year-old correcting the work of an experienced middle-aged translator.

8 April.

Amazing! English writers don't know how to end their works. The best of them turn to the most shameful commonplaces. They start off brilliantly, all fresh energy and muscles, but the ending is trivial, cobbled together from clichés. I've just finished *Far from the Madding Crowd*. Who would have expected Thomas Hardy to turn into such a vulgarian! Everything is perfectly predictable: one villain ends up in prison, another in the grave, and the third, the hero, after the requisite anxieties and impediments ends up in the arms of Bathsheba, the woman he was meant to marry. Why do all novelists seem to think that getting married is the best thing in the world? Why—by whose command—do they save all marriages till the end? I'd like to write an article called "Endings in Dickens." I would get hold of all the endings of his novels and comment on their biological, sociological, and aesthetic value in it.
< ... >

11 April.

Saw the *Nekrasov Miscellany*, which contains many attacks on me, in a bookshop today, but had no money to buy it! Boba has developed a passion for windmills and is putting one together with great ingenuity. There is no firewood. I scratched my hand smashing a bookcase, but it doesn't matter. For some reason I'm in a good, even cheerful mood. I was so hungry yesterday I went to the Basseinaya Street student hostel, where each girl had received eight pounds of peas. They soak them in water and eat them raw and without bread. It's not so bad. I'm back at work on Akhmatova. You have to finish what you start. The Futurism manuscript I sold to Livshits will probably go unpublished.

25 April.

< . . . > Saw Sologub on Saturday. He seems much better: he's put on weight; his eyes are clear and bright. He looks like an engraving. "That's a venomous little book you've written about Blok," he said to me in front of the Tenishev School. "Oh, it's an excellent book, elegant, masterful. You could send it off to Paris. But what venom. Blok was no Russian—you've shown that very well yourself—he was a German, and his 'Twelve' is German. I've only just read it. It's horrible. You consider him a great national poet. Well, in my opinion his nationalism is nothing but a construct based on Dostoevsky. There's nothing of him in it. He didn't know Russia, he didn't know the Russian people; he was an upper-class student." < . . . >

He had a playful way of talking about his plagiarisms. "Redko found a passage I'd plagiarized from a trashy French novel and printed it *en regard*. All that proves is that he reads trashy French novels. What he didn't notice was that at nearly the same spot I'd cribbed five or so pages from George Eliot. Which proves that he doesn't read serious literature." < . . . >

I set out at ten this morning looking for three million. I walked all over town and couldn't come up with it. Akhmatova had only a million, but she gave it to me. She's getting four million from the Institute of Agronomy in three or four days. After handing over the million, she impulsively grabbed a tin of milk from the cupboard and gave it to me. "For the baby!" [. . .]

26 May.

Had a wonderful talk with Misha Slonimsky. "We are *Soviet* writers," he said, "and fortunate to be so. All the squabbling, the trouble with censorship and so on—it's just incidental, temporary; it's not typical of the Soviet regime. We'll soon have the kind of freedom bourgeois writers have never dreamt of. We may sneer, mock, and complain, but our basic attitude is one of love and trust. We must be worthy of our country and our times." And he said it in intimate tones, the way you talk to friends, not the way you talk at a rally. < . . . > Put it into a novel and it would sound false and cloying, but in life it was perfectly natural. [. . .]

1 June.

< . . . > It's been raining all day. While translating O. Henry, I came up with an idea for a long article about contemporary world literature: a bill of indictment. O. Henry is enormously gifted, but how external he is: all his protagonists are on stage, all his effects—purely theatrical; each story is an operetta, a farce, etc. Most are about money and financial operations. He has an interesting biography, but that's part of literature's decline: writers' lives have become more interesting than their works.

It's night now, and I'm reading *A Chronicle of the Conquest of Granada* by Washington Irving, a soporific piece, but how well written. Why have I since childhood been so sensitive to literary style? Why can't I stand Pokrovsky the historian and am so enthralled by the flow of words in Irving? < . . . >

July.

Saw Akhmatova. She walks as if her shoes were too tight. She started in on the Change of Landmarks group.[88] She'd been at the Writers' House and attended a talk by the editors of *Nakanune.* "Disgusting! I told Volkovysky I wanted to meet the editor-in-chief. I said to him, 'Why did you publish my verse?'

" 'We got it from Moscow.'

" 'But I haven't been to Moscow for seven years.'

" 'I don't know. I'll find out in Berlin and write to you.'

These people always land on their feet." [. . .]

5 September.

Met Charskaya for the first time yesterday.[89] Goodness, what a pitiful creature. She gave me two just as pitiful manuscripts. It's interesting how

88. The Change of Landmarks group consisted of intellectuals who despite their anti-Bolshevik sentiments chose to accept the regime, construing it as the bulwark of a strong imperial Russia. The Berlin-based *Nakanune* was their mouthpiece. (V.E.)

89. Lidia Charskaya enjoyed considerable popularity at the beginning of the century as a purveyor of flamboyant yarns verging on kitsch and designed primarily for a female adolescent audience. Chukovsky wrote a devastating review of her oeuvre in 1907. (V.E.)

illiterate she is; she uses commas in the wrong places, for instance. Or maybe she's too hungry to care. She hasn't received a single ration yet. It's disgraceful. The author of 160 novels and she gets nothing. But she does tend to go on, and she hasn't a clue about what makes her so famous.

20 September.

When they asked the pupils at the Tenishev School where their parents worked, most answered, "Maltsevsky Market," because most of their parents spend their time selling whatever they can.

29 September.

< . . . > Called on Annenkov yesterday. He was painting Pilnyak. Pilnyak is about thirty-five and has the elongated face of a Volga German.[90] He is sober, but his tongue is as sluggish as a drunkard's. He mutters indistinctly if he talks a lot, but his eyes are sly and—even when he's drunk—quite penetrating. He's a scoundrel through and through: he told us about how in Berlin he made up to Gessen and the Soviets and Chernov and the *Nakanune* people—mostly while under the influence. But he's very, very crafty about it: when you're under the influence, you have an easier time getting to the people you need and they soften easily. He makes the rounds of the drinking establishments with the men in the leather jackets[91] and they sign the papers he needs. He thinks of himself as a winner, super smart, always on top of things. "Me and the publishers—we're thick as thieves!" [. . .]

30 September.

Took Boba to the Children's Theater to see *The Hunchback Horse.*[92] It opened the season. Who should be sitting in front of me but Zinovyev and Lilina with a bald, pink, healthy pastor of a man between them. Lilina introduced him to me. He was Andersen Nexø, fresh from Denmark. The play went well: the production was meticulous and inventive. The text was practically undistorted, and the action took place in a frame that provided

90. Pilnyak's real name was Vogau. He was descended from German colonists. (V.E.)
91. Cheka agents were known by their leather jackets. (M.H.H.)
92. A famous nineteenth-century fairy tale in verse by P. P. Yershov. (V.E.)

a border for the stage. I was transfixed. It was the first time in my life I had ever seen original theater for children, and I kept thinking of the hard, lackluster life of the play's luckless author. How bright, how dazzling he is on stage, how much happiness he gave to others—to the younger generations—and all he got for it was hostility. I made this point to the pointy-nosed man sitting next me, who turned out to be a high-ranking official. Then Pilnyak and Vsevolod Ivanov came for the Dane and took him to the House of the Arts. It was a Serapion Saturday, and there was debate about art going on. Andersen was banal and insipid, and Pilnyak tried to expound a convoluted credo. Pilnyak spoke Russian, and the interpreters did not do too accurate a job. He used the terms matter and spirit (*Stoff und Geist*), and each time he heard the word *Stoff* Pilnyak would nod to show he understood.[93] Zamyatin took part as well, spouting liberal thoughts. When people began talking about writers, he said that we so loved writers that we even exported them for foreign consumption.

Pilnyak has gone to Zinovyev to intercede on Zamyatin's behalf. I've seen a note handwritten by Zinovyev to Messing authorizing Zamyatin to travel to Moscow. When Annenkov saw the note, he had a long talk with me. If Zamyatin is such an enemy of the Soviet regime, he said, why does he beg notes and indulgences from them? Zamyatin's opposition is all sham, window dressing. < . . . >

27 November.

Have been in Moscow for three weeks. I'm leaving tomorrow. I've been staying at the Art Theater's First Studio in Sovetskaya Square, where I have a fine room (with the purple couch that was used in Andreev's *Katerina Ivanovna*) and a lamp of three hundred candle power. I've grown quite accustomed to this curious existence and quite fond of many of the people. I've seen little of Moscow, because I've been working day and night on a rush translation of *Playboy*.[94] But when I did run out to buy some bread at Filippov's or apples at a stand, I noticed happiness on everybody's faces. The men are happy that there are cards, horseraces, wine, and women; the women press their breasts against the Kuznetsky shop windows and gaze

93. Russian has borrowed the German word *Stoff* (matter, material), but in Russian it designates a particular kind of material: damask or brocade. (M.H.H.)

94. *The Playboy of the Western World* by John Millington Synge. The play was translated by Chukovsky and published with his introduction in 1923. Its Russian title was *A Hero*.

at the silks and jewels. There is beautiful female flesh by the wagon-load at every turn. The passion for goods and pleasures is prodigious. Dancing is so popular that I know families who gather at seven and are still drinking tea and tripping the light fantastic at two in the morning—good people, actors, writers, doing the dixie, the fox-trot, the one-step. Zoology and physiology is what people live by. < . . . > The life of the soul has suffered, and the theaters are full of shooting and clowning and slapstick. But it all has one splendid thing in common: vitality. The women are strapping, the men have necks like oaks. These oaks are everywhere now, and they make fine material for history. When you look at an oak, you have no qualms about the future. You can turn an oak into anything. Well, not a Dostoevsky, not for the time being. But for rough work it's a treasure. [. . .]
< . . . >

15 December.

I've frittered away all my time since Moscow. I can't put my mind to anything. We're getting "Wash 'Em Clean" and "The Giant Cockroach"[95] ready for print, and I go back and forth between the typesetters and the lithographers and hang around the machines. The censors have recently cut the line "Oh my God" from "Wash 'Em Clean" and I went to have it out with them.

I dropped in on Anna Akhmatova yesterday. < . . . > She had just been to see a Kamerny Theater actress by the name of Kaminskaya who has a cold and no money and is nine months pregnant. I promised to ask the Americans to give her medical assistance. < . . . > Akhmatova is currently in her third hypostasis: the daughter. I have seen her as the starving nun who has renounced the world (when she lived in the Liteiny flat in 1919), as the society lady (about three months ago), and now she is simply the daughter of a petty official, a girl from a petty bourgeois family. Cramped rooms, entrance through the kitchen, mother, maid of all work. Who would have thought that this is the Anna Akhmatova who all by herself has replaced Gorky and Lev Tolstoy and Leonid Andreev (in fame),

95. These are two of Chukovsky's most popular children's poems. The lines banned by the censor were "Oh God! Oh God! What has happened? Why is everything topsy-turvy?" The ban and the campaign against the heretical passage lasted for decades: as late as 1967 Chukovsky wrote to his publisher: "Some odd people send me letters excoriating the new edition of *Wash 'Em Clean* because it contains this terrible line: 'Oh God! Oh God! What happened?' "

who is the subject of dozens of articles and books, and who is known by heart in the provinces. Now she is sitting on the couch "entertaining guests." The conversation turns to Moscow. Akhmatova very much wants to go to Moscow, but is afraid of a scandal, afraid her Moscow confrères will stage a demonstration against her. [. . .]

We also talked about critics. "Have you read what Aikhenvald wrote about me?" Akhmatova asks. "I think he copied it all from you. Then there's Vinogradov. His article about me in *Literaturnaia mysl'* was so boring that even I couldn't get through it. Shchogolev told his wife, 'If Akhmatova can't read it, God doesn't want us to read it either.' Eikhenbaum is writing a book as well."

I departed in high spirits: I could tell the true Anna Akhmatova behind all the nonsense. She seemed uncomfortable showing her true self in public and out of shyness couldn't help putting on the most trivial of exteriors. I noticed it when we were at Shchogolev's. "I'm like everybody else. I even like a drink now and again. Have you heard the latest gossip about Annen-kov?" That was the tone she used with friends. Her admirers would have been amazed to hear it. Yet it is only a shield to keep intact what is near and dear to her. Tyutchev, for example, used the same tone. < . . . >

20 December.

< . . . > I've given my winter coat to a tailor named Slonimsky for mending, so I'm sporting my summer one. I wound a scarf around my neck and hopped, skipped, and jumped my way down Nevsky Prospect, like Mr. Scrooge's clerk, to the American doctor, Gantt, to give him a letter requesting assistance for Kaminskaya, the unfortunate actress Akhmatova spoke of. He agreed to help, but asked who the child's father was. "There is no father," I said. He frowned. He obviously found helping an unwed mother problematic. That was yesterday. Today we're due to go and see Kaminskaya at five, I'm still without an overcoat, it's freezing, I have a cold, and my stomach bothered me all night. [. . .]

23 December.

< . . . > Here is what is happening with my "Giant Cockroach": Klyachko is so intoxicated with it he's set a price of ten million and refuses to budge. Show it to the booksellers and they'll say it's a piece of trash. Give me four

lemons and maybe I'll take one or two off your hands. Well, that's fine with me. I hate the book. The book trade has never been in such a shambles. There are any number of new books and no buyers. The only items selling are textbooks. Yesterday I bought a deluxe edition of *Peter Pan* with Bedford's illustration for one and a half million, in other words, ten kopecks! (A tram ticket costs 750,000.) < . . . >

30 December.

Yesterday was the most unpleasant day in my life: I had a visit in the morning from a man wearing a greasy military uniform and covered with sweat, but handsome, elegant, and burning to say something to me, a few words, he'd never done anything like this before, he'd come all the way from Moscow—and I refused to see him. At first I thought, I'm too busy, I'm in a rush, but that was nonsense: I simply didn't want to open the cracks I'd hastily puttied and expose myself to major human concerns. And that's what I told him. I said, "You should have come ten years ago, when I was still alive. Now I'm a literary man and lifeless, of all the people you see on the street the last you should go up to."

"But you don't understand," he said softly. "I'm not the one who'll be the loser. You are. You, not me." And off he went.

All day I felt shame and pain and true loss. I gave him a letter to Olshansky asking Olshansky to help him (he needed psychiatric treatment). I offered him money, but he refused.

1923

➤-➤-➤-➤-➤-➤-➤-➤

Well, well. It's New Year's. 12:00.

[. . .] 1922 was a terrible year for me, a year of insolvencies, failures, humiliations, affronts, and illnesses. I could feel myself growing callous, losing faith in life. I thought my only salvation was work, and how I worked! How I slaved! I was so stricken I nearly cried as I wrote "Wash 'Em Clean." Then, still crushed, I turned to "The Giant Cockroach." I completely and utterly reworked my Nekrasov books as well as the ones on the Futurists, Wilde, and Whitman. I founded the journal *Sovremennyi Zapad*,[96] wrote nearly the entire current events page for the first issue, obtained the pertinent newspapers and journals, translated *Cabbages and Kings*, translated Synge—but oh, the energy wasted for want of a goal or a plan! And not a single friend! Not even a well-wisher! All claws and fangs and horns! And yet I enjoyed 1922 somehow. I got close to Murka, I had fewer insomnia problems, I had an easier time working. So thank you, 1922!

Now I'm seeing the new year in alone, pen in hand, but I'm not sad: I love my pen, my lamp, my inkwell; I dearly love my *Encyclopedia Britannica* sitting here on the desk so affectionate and reassuring. The knowledge it has given me. But now I must get on with my Synge article!

Now I know what it is to be forty: when I have a visitor, I can't wait for him to leave. I've lost all curiosity for people. I used to be like a puppy: I'd sniff each passerby and lift my leg at each tree.

Now I know what it is to have children and a large family: the moment you put a pencil down it disappears into a deep hole. Someone is always losing something: "Have you seen the scissors, children?" "Where's my ribbon, Papa?" "Was it you who took my eraser, Kolya?"

< . . . >

5 January.

Man is born to wear out four children's coats and six or seven adult ones. What is man but ten coats.

Got a telegram from the Studio of the Art Theater today. They want me to change *Playboy* to *Hero*.

Yesterday afternoon I told Murka she was a kitten. She jumped up with unusual energy, flung herself on the floor, and grabbed something in her mouth. "Mousy eat!" (I'm eating a mouse.) She did this about fifty times. There was nothing I could do to stop her. She kept saying, "Where more mousy?" (Where's another mouse?) as if possessed, darting here and there and grabbing, grabbing, grabbing. I was frightened. The tempo alone was frightening. < . . . > "It's time for the cat to rest, to sleep," I said. < . . . > I tried showing her pictures. But she kept shouting, "Me meow!" [. . .]

96. Publication of the journal, which was meant to introduce the reader to contemporary trends in Western literature and thought, was halted by the regime after several issues. (M.H.H.)

8 January.

Called on Koni. < . . . > The only new story he told was this: In an article he is writing about suicide he quotes the suicide note of a worker. The note was written in 1884. The worker wrote: "Life is hard and so on." The censor has demanded that Koni change it to: "Life is hard under the capitalist system. Long live the commune!" < . . . >

14 January.

< . . . > Reading the silliest novel, Arnold Bennett's *The Gates of Wrath.* I didn't realize he had sinned so grievously. [. . .]

17 January.

< . . . > Called on Mr. Kinney and his wife the day before yesterday. She is a redhead from the southern state of Georgia; he is the only American interested in art and literature. They gave me Mencken's controversial book *Prejudices.* It's nothing special. I did better in my day. < . . . >

Murka is so imaginative in her play that when asked to catch a fish for the bear on the floor she asked me to take off her shoes. Now she's a bird, flying from room to room, flapping her arms for hours.

20 January.

Called on the Americans and stayed for dinner. They might well have stepped out of a novel: Brown of Brooklyn, Renshaw wearing dark glasses, and Dr. Gantt, endearingly gauche. We sat in the **parlour** talking about literature. Brown gave me a marvelous novel, *Babbitt* by Sinclair Lewis.

< . . . > Yesterday was Epiphany. All of us at World Literature—Volynsky, Oldenburg, Vladimirtsev, Tikhonov, and I—agreed to listen to Zamyatin read his play. Oldenburg fell asleep and even snored from time to time. Vladimirtsev kept jerking his head, as if his collar were too tight. Tikhonov corrected proofs. Volynsky, a little old man, sat there impassively (you can see what he'll look like in the coffin—I suddenly noticed that until he opens his mouth he looks like a corpse). Oh, how boring and pretentious and paltry the play was. Not a passage with any life to it. Not even by accident. He uses the same device over and over: the characters

speak like neurasthenics, in unfinished sentences. He wants to sound edgy, but he's just dull. He also tries to make things sound outlandish, give them a naive twist: "a smile was glued to her face." He thinks that's sophisticated. He's forever posing, putting on airs; he is for anarchy at all costs, praises freedom in the raw, and condemns authority, norms, order of any kind. Yet he himself is a philistine from top to toe. He hates timetables (he mocks his character Dewly in *The Islanders* for kissing his wife according to a timetable), yet he himself writes according to a timetable.[97] And how poor and petty the writing is. An impressionism in bad taste. Dash, dash, dash plus silly cerebralisms: he keeps trying to breathe through his ears instead of his nose or mouth. Some call him a *maître*. Well, I call him a *centimaître*.[98]
[. . .]

13 February.

[. . .] Many of the people at the American Relief Administration[99] are very nice. Kinney is the best of the lot. I've never met anyone like him. He has such an easygoing, cheerful way of dealing with life and acquiring knowledge that at times he seems quite brilliant, though he's just an ordinary Yankee. He has a degree from Oxford and is writing a dissertation on the authors who wrote for the *Retrospective Review* (early nineteenth century). When he learned about the famine among Russian students, he

97. *The Islanders* (1916) was a starkly satirical portrayal of the staid philistinism and self-righteousness of an English provincial backwater. One of the protagonists, the Vicar Dewly, is the epitome of sexual repressiveness. (V.E.)

98. After Alexei Tolstoy published a private letter from Chukovsky containing unflattering remarks about Zamyatin among other confrères, relations between Chukovsky and Zamyatin soured. The pertinent passage in the letter, which appeared on 4 June 1922 in the Russian émigré newspaper *Nakanune*, runs as follows: "Zamyatin is a very pleasant man, very, very, but he is a fastidious, cautious man who has never had any feelings." Three weeks later Zamyatin wrote to Chukovsky, apparently in response to his apologies and explanations: "It would be wrong to say that I am angry with you. After your letter to Tolstoy I had the feeling you were both a friend and a comrade, but a prickly and rather unreliable one. I know that if I land in jail tomorrow or in a month (for there is no writer in the Soviet Union less cautious than I), Chukovsky will be among the first to intercede on my behalf. But under less dire circumstances, for rhetorical effect or I don't know what, Chukovsky is apt to throw me to Tolstoy or God knows whom else. Nonetheless, you are still Chukovsky, that is, one of the five or ten people who truly care about the word and about verbal art. (And these, I suppose, are the five or ten people for whom I write.)"

99. The American Relief Administration, an organization set up to help famine victims in Russia.

collected considerable contributions from members of the YMCA, to which he added a small sum from the YMHA, and set off for Russia, where he singlehandedly put together a splendid program of aid for Russian professors and students. He has been here only eight months, yet he has an excellent knowledge of Russian life—its art, history, and literature. He's a small man, twenty-eight or so, with calm, cheerful eyes; he looks like a student himself. He's selected fine people to work with and knows how to keep discipline: they obey him, but are not intimidated by him; they love him. He has asked me to help distribute the rations. < . . . > The most needy of all is my wife, Marya Borisovna. She hasn't had a warm coat for six winters now, but I'm embarrassed to ask and don't know what to do.

A few days ago I took Kinney to World Literature. Tikhonov gave a talk about expanding our offerings. He wants to include Shakespeare and Swift and the Roman and Greek classics. But because we have to get everything past the Gosizdat Editorial Division, we have to give each author the appropriate tags, for example:

Boccaccio—opposes the clergy
Vasari—brings art to the masses
Petronius—satirizes the merchant class

When it came to *The Divine Comedy* we were stumped.

On the way home from the meeting, Kinney asked, **"What about copyright?"** I, well, **blushed**, because *we* consider copyright an outmoded institution. Kinney advised us to publish Benvenuto Cellini. [. . .]

15 February.

< . . . > Gave a talk on Synge at the House of the Press, but it went poorly. Nobody cares about Synge, and anyway Moscow's new NEP[100] audience goes to lectures not so much for knowledge as for scandal. < . . . >

I'm terribly depressed: I feel hemmed in on all sides by the NEP mentality: nobody needs my books, my psychology, my outlook on life. The theater is all slapstick. I went to *Playboy* on the twentieth, and oh the red and blue wigs, the hopping and jumping clowns, the screeching, the

100. The New Economic Policy (NEP) was adopted by the Soviet government in 1921–22 to restore the economy by making concessions to private enterprise in agriculture, trade, and industry. The changes it brought about in the country's cultural life are also evident in the entry for 27 November. (V.E.)

grunting, the circus tricks! A play full of psychological subtlety is doomed to failure. Kinney tells me that Synge's language has been called redolent of nuts, but nuts in America can mean crazy. I didn't laugh; I nearly cried. < ... >

Saw Strindberg's *Eric XIV* yesterday. They tried hard, but failed. Why do actors nowadays refuse to do a play in the style in which it was written? Why must they turn it upside down? The actor Smyshlyaev is directing *The Taming of the Shrew* with the most preposterous tricks: Sly has a dream about himself, so there are two Slys, one moving about on stage, the other in the audience.

At Gosizdat I overheard Meshcheryakov say, "I think I'll tell Chukovsky he's wrong and at the same time give the censor a dressing down." < ... > Meshcheryakov is much nicer to me now: he's fallen in love with "Wash 'Em Clean." [...]

Moscow is terribly overcrowded. A characteristic Moscow smell has settled into flats here; it comes from the concentration of human bodies. You can hear the toilet flushing every minute in every flat: the toilets are continually in use. And the door to each flat has a note that says: one ring is for such-and-such a person, two for such-and-such, three for such-and-such, and so on.[101]

27 February.

Was at Gosizdat from eleven till half past four yesterday and finally signed a contract, but oh, what a headache, running up and down the stairs. They rewrote it twice. < ... > I also went to see Pilnyak at Krug Publishers. They have a tiny office with two tiny rooms and four secretaries, one with flaming red hair. < ... > They also have their own motor car, which Pilnyak rides around in more than anyone. I've come to know him better. He may give the impression of being giddy and muddleheaded, but he's perfectly businesslike and serious. He has a grave air about him and is likely to go off in the middle of a conversation to a pub or somebody's place to make a telephone call, and the transition from conversation to telephone call is imperceptible, effortless. He's on the phone to Krasin a

101. Because of the acute housing shortage the room rather than the apartment became the typical urban living space. The result was a system of communal apartments, that is, whole families squeezed into single rooms and forced to share one set of kitchen and sanitary facilities with the rest of the residents. (V.E.)

lot, because he wants to go to London with Foreign Trade. He cuts a comic figure with his long torso and short legs, his red hair and spectacles. He's always with friends, always has some business to take care of, hoping for something. < . . . >

Spent the evening at Mayakovsky's. < . . . > Pastry and cognac. He waited a while for McKay, but then started reciting. He does it well. He pronounced *w* for *v* as Ukrainians do and drawled the *o*: Mayako-o-o-wsky. There were snippets of true poetry and the subject matter was broad, but on the whole it was tedious. He stood by the stove, looking out at us with his intelligent eyes, and it was clear he was emotionally involved. The audience consisted of the artist Rodchenko, Lilia Brik, and two young ladies, who hung on his every word. I told him my honest opinion, but he wasn't particularly interested. He also recited quite a funny propaganda piece he had written for the journal *Zhurnalist*, an article in verse about what it means to be a journalist.[102] In the hallway on my way out (McKay never came) I told him in Lilia Brik's presence that the mention he made of us in his autobiography was shameless, that he didn't come to our place for the food, etc.[103] He promised to change it in the next edition. When I told him Annenkov wanted to do a portrait of him, he agreed to pose for it, but Lili Brik immediately intervened: "You ought to be ashamed of yourself, Volodya. You, a constructivist, posing for a painter! If you want a portrait, go to a photographer. Vasserman will make two hundred portraits free of charge."[104]

19 March.

Have been home for a week and can't get down to work. I read my memoirs of Leonid Andreev yesterday at a celebration of his work, but left before it was over. It's terrible to be at loose ends. I have no refuge, no friends, no ideas, either acquired or of my own. At first I saw this as a position of

102. Reference to "A Newspaper Day," published in *Zhurnalist* (March–April 1923).

103. Mayakovsky's pithy autobiography *I Myself* contains the following passage: "Seven-day-cycle system, seven dining acquaintances; on Sunday I 'eat' Chukovsky, on Monday Yevreinov, and so on. On Thursday things are worse: I eat Repin greens!" (The Russian word for turnip is *repa*.)

104. Lili Brik's phrasing is imprecise: in 1923 Mayakovsky was a "neo-Futurist" rather than a "Constructivist." Yet he presumably shared the disdain of the latter for representational painting such as portraiture. (V.E.)

strength and daring, but now it means nothing but total isolation and gloom. The journals and newspapers all reproach me for being alien. I can stand the reproaches, but I can't stand being alien.

Went to see Akhmatova. She is very nice to me. She keeps complaining about Eikhenbaum. "We had a falling out after his book about me."[105] We looked through Nekrasov, whom we'll be editing together. She eliminated the same poems I had eliminated in the Grzhebin edition. Total agreement. Reading "Masha," she recalled an argument she'd had with Gumilyov, when she had to stay in bed for a long time and he, working at his desk, quoted the line: Only the pale-faced husband labored < . . . >

29 March.

< . . . > At Akhmatova's with Shchogolev. Making the Nekrasov selection. When we came to the lines:

> Toiling and moiling to harvest the crops in time—
> Such is your fate, Russian women, your destiny.
> Nor do I know a fate crueler than yours

Akhmatova said, "I always say that about myself." And when we came to the lines about Dobrolyubov:

> If people of his stamp
> Were not sent down from heaven,
> The lea of life would wither

Shchogolev said, "I always say that about myself."

Then Akhmatova said, "There's one line I don't understand."

"Which is that?" we asked.

"The one that goes: 'On a red velvet pillow a first-degree Anna is lying.' "

We all laughed. [. . .]

1 April.

I am now forty-one. Only forty-one. How envious I'll be when I reread this page at the age of fifty. I should be happy! When I turned nineteen, twenty-two years ago, I wrote, "Is it possible I'm *already* nineteen?" Now

105. *Anna Akhmatova: Opyt analiza* (Petrograd, 1923).

I write, "Is it possible I'm *only* forty-one?" Bad as things are, I'll have to put a brave face on them. [. . .]

24 April.

McKay the Negro is back. He's put on weight, but claims that it's the cold, that his cheeks are frozen. He laughs a lot, but is serious by nature and cannot talk about the position of Negroes in America without getting upset. Fool that I am, I took him to see Klyachko: I was amazed to learn that Klyachko had no idea Negroes in America are oppressed by Whites. "What do you mean?" he said. "America's a free country. Three cheers for the Americans!" McKay is expecting a visit from a **wine merchant,** whose doctor, he says, is Blok's cousin. The wine merchant keeps him in wine free of charge.

I was walking with Akhmatova along Nevsky Prospect—she was accompanying me to Gosizdat—when she told me there was another farewell party for Zamyatin this Saturday. I couldn't get over it: he's been going away for a year now, and each Saturday somebody gives him a going away party. It's not as if he were being sent away. He made all the rounds, kowtowed to all the Communists, and now he's playing the political martyr.[106]

7 May.

[. . .] Went to Akhmatova's yesterday. She was lying on the couch, bundled up in a fur coat. She had Olenka Sudeikina with her. They've no money, no husbands—I felt sorry for them. Olga Afanasyevna told me she'd sold everything and had no prospects. Akhmatova had a fever, she said. It was particularly high in the morning. I was so sorry for them I took them to *The Miracle of Saint Anthony*. I'll have to ask the Americans to do something for Sudeikina.

106. Recent research sheds some light on the circumstances that occasioned Chukovsky's snide comment. In 1922 Zamyatin, along with a number of heterodox intellectuals, was slated for deportation—a decision rescinded at the last moment due to the apparently unsolicited intercession of friends. Shortly thereafter he applied for and eventually obtained permission to visit Western Europe, but chose to remain in Russia, possibly as a result of friendly gestures on the part of the Soviet literary establishment. Thus, he was twice on the verge of going abroad. (See John Malmstad and Lazar Fleishman, "Iz bibliografii Zamiatina [po novym materialam]," *Stanford Slavic Studies* 1 [1987]: 103–53.) (V.E.)

McKay came to call tonight. He's written some verse for May Day and wants me to translate it. He had bad things to say about the American Relief Administration, I defended it, and we quarreled. I have a feeling that what he writes about Russia will include a lot of the slander he picks up from all kinds of riff-raff. [. . .]

10 May.

< . . . > Went to Blok's yesterday. I just had to see the apartment. [. . .] I ring the bell. The cook opens the door. To the left I see the telephone with a list of numbers—World Literature, Gorky, etc.—in Blok's hand-writing < . . . > I sit down at a table by the window and leaf through *Vestnik*, a journal Blok published in his childhood. Oh, what a brilliant job of pasting and basting and binding, and what a bevy of grannies, aunties, and nannies. The handwriting is completely different, and everything is happy and gay. Only the pictures are tragic. Especially the one in which Blok has turned away from the table and everyone at it—à la Lermontov— and is looking straight ahead with terror in his eyes. Even as a child he looked like a rebel in the pictures.

His aunt, Marya Andreevna Beketova, read me excerpts from her man-uscript, which of course contains not a clue about who Blok was. [. . .] You keep feeling she's passing things over in silence—the role of his wife, Lyubov Dmitrievna, the weight the family placed on him. [. . .]

From there I went to see Olga Forsh. She was by herself. She sat me down and started talking about Blok. About his mother, too, she spoke wisely and well and full of emotion. "It was she who did him in. I went to see her after Blok died, and she said to me, 'We both killed him, Lyuba and I. She killed half and I killed half.' " < . . . >

14 May.

< . . . > Kolya, a young sculptor friend of his, and I went to the Hermitage. We spent a long time going through the sculpture rooms, then looked at the Germans, Dutch, and English. I went into raptures over Rembrandt's *Danaë:* I heard music, I thought I was seeing a picture for the first time in my life. Other pictures are good or bad; the *Danaë* is absolute, for all time. I was also struck by a small (relatively speaking) canvas of Titian's: the portrait of a woman in a round room—and nothing more. The rest is

literature. The Hermitage is full. Interest in art among the masses has grown considerably. But the poor museumgoers. They wander about aimlessly, bored, not knowing where to look, and the guides talk utter nonsense—and in such loud voices that you can hardly enjoy the paintings. < . . . >

Called on Akhmatova. She showed me her pictures of Blok and a letter from him, all crumpled and pin-scratched. The letter is about her poem "Down by the Sea." Whether he praises or scolds, how true he remains to himself.[107]

I showed her my emendations to her Nekrasov commentaries. I think they are terrible. Akhmatova, like Gumilyov, doesn't know how to write prose. Gumilyov couldn't even translate prose, and when asked to write an introduction to a World Literature book he said, "I'd prefer to write it in verse." It's the same with Akhmatova. Almost every comment is misleading and semi-literate. For instance, "Nikolai Alexandrovich Dobrolyubov (1836–1861) is a contemporary of Nekrasov and *more or less shared his views.*" Or "Kleinmikhel is the main figure in *constructing* . . ." Or "Byron had a strong influence on both Pushkin and Lermontov." To say nothing of substantive errors. The elegy is "a form of lyric poetry" and so on. At one point she changed my "they staged plays" to "they acted plays."

I didn't hide my opinion of her work; I said it must have been a man who wrote it instead of her.

"What makes you think that?" she asked. "The only thing you need a man for is to make children." < . . . >

7 October.

Just back from the Crimea. I've brought some pebbles for Mura. She picks out the green ones and runs through all four rooms to ask "Is it green?" about each. I brought back three poods [one hundred pounds] of grapes. We strung them up, and by the fifth day there was nothing left. The pears I brought haven't ripened yet; they're lying on the windowsill. I'm completely black. The sun really got to me. I feel refreshed but drowsy. I'm not doing anything, nor do I want to see anyone or anything. I've

---

107. Blok's letter was subsequently published. After some critical remarks he concluded: "But all these things are trifles. The poem is real and you are real."

never been so sluggish. And I have reason to be. I had a wild time during my month in the Crimea. I arrived in Koktebel on 3 September after an excruciating journey. I was barely alive and ready to take the same train back. By Sunday at four I'd managed to drag myself to Max's [Voloshin].

Koktebel is an idyllic spot, unspoiled as yet by tourists, its manners naive, and I felt as if Max and I and all the residents of Koktebel were ancient, prehistoric people about whom books would eventually be written. [. . .] The evening I arrived Zamyatin read from his novel *We*. [. . .] I find Zamyatin's *We* despicable. You'd have to be a eunuch not to see the roots of today's socialism. He directs all his biting remarks about the system of the future against Fourier's utopian socialism, which he mistakenly takes for communism. Besides, Fourierism has been "blasted" by talents much greater than Zamyatin's: there is more intellect and wrath in one line of Dostoevsky than in Zamyatin's whole novel.[108]

13 October.

Called on Akhmatova yesterday. < . . . > I found her lying down, elegant, fragile, racked with fever. She'd had a cyst removed under a local anesthetic and was still running a high temperature and losing blood. She went on delightfully about the operation: "As the anesthetic wore off, I began to feel the knives and scissors running along the wound, and writhed in pain." < . . . > She showed me a plaster mold of her hand. "This is my left hand, slightly larger than nature, though just like it. They're going to do it in porcelain, and I'm going to write 'my left hand' here and send it to someone I know in Paris."

The conversation turned to Guber's *Pushkin's Don Juan List* (which she hasn't yet read). "Whenever I read about Pushkin's amorous intrigues," she said, "I think how little our Pushkin scholars know of love. All their commentaries show a total lack of understanding." (And she blushed.) < . . . >

---

108. The blueprint for an ideal society, the doctrine propounded by the nineteenth-century French social thinker Charles Fourier features elaborate domestic arrangements supplanting the "obsolete" institution of marriage. This may have suggested to Zamyatin an essential aspect of his collectivist nightmare—the bureaucratic regulation of love-making. (V.E.)

14 October.

Sunday. "The wind is more stifling than normal."[109] I read despair on people's faces. It will be a hard autumn. The intelligent proletarians are in a bad way. Droves of people with crazed faces are rushing around the city with letters of recommendation in search of employment. [. . .] Gosizdat isn't paying anybody; it's gone bankrupt. Nobody buys anything in the bookshops but textbooks. It's terrible. My future is grim: I have no suit, no bread. The house committee is on my back, so I've spent all week running from office to office, trying to get the documents they want and not getting them. And here I sit, a near wreck. < . . . >

21 October.

On Monday I made the mistake of going to Sologub's. < . . . > He said that a writer doesn't learn to write until he's a hundred. "Everything till then is just an exercise. Take Tolstoy. *War and Peace* is full of mistakes, *Anna Karenina* is better, but *Resurrection* is very good." < . . . >

24 October.

< . . . > We told Murka she would come down with something if she ate so little. She immediately drank a glass of milk and said, "Now I won't die?" < . . . >

7 November.

The anniversary of the Revolution. I have just finished an article about Gorky and am about to take it to the copyist. Yesterday morning I gave a children's reading at Gosizdat. I read "The Chatterbox Fly" and "The Wonder Tree." < . . . > Now I'm reading proofs of *Murka's Book*. Some of Konashevich's drawings have already been lithographed. I took Murka to Klyachko's yesterday to show her *Murka's Book* in the making. Everyone there gathered round her, and Konashevich asked her to open her mouth. (He needs to draw a piece of bread and butter flying into her mouth. He's

109. A line from Nekrasov's poem "About the Weather."

done a drawing, but it's not right.) She was so excited she turned bright red, but couldn't open her mouth. When I asked her later why, she said, "I was just being silly." < . . . >

Mura and I were once in a dark bathroom when she shouted, "Out, out!" When I asked her who she was chasing, she said, "Night. Out out, night!"

Murka is crying. "You can't say, 'The cloud walks through the sky.' Clouds have no legs. You can't. You mustn't." She cries and cries.

She sings a song Kolya has brought for her:

> Vanya loves his Manya.
> Vanya says to Manya,
> I'm in love with you.
> I'll buy wood for you.
> But the wood he buys
> Will not burn no wise.
> He strikes matches one two three
> Lansa dransa hee hee hee.

"He doesn't love her," she says. "He gave her bad wood." < . . . >

14 November.

Called on Akhmatova yesterday. < . . . > She has no warm coat, so she wears a sweater "underneath," which means under a light blouse. I was there to check the text of a letter Blok wrote to her against the original. She rummaged through her dresser drawers, which were overflowing with pictures of Gumilyov, books, documents, and so on. "Here's something unusual," she said, showing me a contract Gumilyov had drafted in French to purchase some horses from a French officer in Africa. < . . . >

She had to go to a meeting at the Writers' Union, so we took the tram. I bought some apples and offered her one. She said, "I won't eat it in the street < . . . >, but let me have it and I'll eat it at the meeting." She didn't have enough money for the fare. (It costs fifty million and she had only fifteen.) "I thought I'd taken a hundred million banknote, but it was only ten."

"Taking a tram makes me feel generous," I said. "I'll treat you to a ticket."

"You remind me of an American I met in Paris," she said. "It was raining, and I was standing in an arcade waiting for it to stop when an

American came up to me and whispered, Come to a cafe with me, Mamzelle, and I'll buy you a beer.' When I gave him a haughty look, he said, 'I will treat you to a glass of beer but it doesn't put you under any obligation.' " < . . . >

18 November.

We've just discovered that all our underclothes have been stolen from the attic: mine, the children's—everything. We haven't a stitch for the winter. I am very disappointed in Konashevich's drawing for *Murka's Book*.

20 November.

Wet snow, slush. < . . . > I'm editing Swift to earn enough to replace the underclothes. [. . .]

24 November.

< . . . > Went to Gosizdat. There I learned from Belitsky that Zamirailo had been arrested. Belitsky says it's serious. I asked Zhitkov to ask Misha Kobetsky to intervene. During the search at Zamirailo's they confiscated some manuscripts of my tales[110] and the Blok tale I found among his papers.

From there to Akhmatova's. The dear girl is sick in bed: neurosis of the solar plexus. Punin was with her. She was upset at having learned that the *Critical Miscellany* volume Ivanov-Razumnik was editing for Mysl' would include an article by Blok with a number of attacks on Gumilyov. "You know I didn't care for Gumilyov's verse, but to attack him after he was executed. . . . Go to the publishers and tell them not to print it. Ivanov-Razumnik chose it on purpose." < . . . >

25 November.

< . . . > The weather is beastly: the sky is releasing enormous quantities of muck that forms a mush when it hits the ground and—instead of running off like water or piling up like snow—turns the streets into one

---

110. Chukovsky consistently uses the word "tale" (*skazka*) to designate the children's poems that made him famous. (M.H.H.)

big puddle. And the fog. Anybody who went outside yesterday is doomed to influenza and typhoid fever. < . . . > I dropped in on Akhmatova. She's still in bed—with Stendhal's *De l'amour* beside her. This is the first time I felt she was really glad to see me. "I used to be terribly afraid of you," she said. "When Annenkov told me you were writing about me, I trembled and said to myself, 'Heaven help us!' " She had a lot to say about Blok. "Many people in Moscow think I wrote my poetry for him. That's not true. I couldn't have loved him as one loves a man. Besides, he didn't care for my early verse. I knew. He didn't hide it. Once the two of us gave a reading at the Bestuzhev Courses[111] < . . . > and in the green room he decided to talk to me about my poetry. 'I've been having a correspondence with a young woman about your poetry,' he began. And I was brazen enough to respond, 'I know your opinion. Tell me hers.' " < . . . >

27 November.

Called on Sologub. He told me his memory was failing. "I can remember things that happened long ago, but what happened yesterday flies out of my head."

"That means you should write your memoirs," I said.

"Memoirs? I've thought of it. But in the life of every person there are times that seem fantastic and false the moment they are put into words in a biography. Were I to describe my life truthfully, everyone would say I had lied. [. . .] I won't write a biography, though, because it's best to die without one. I have some diaries, but as soon as I feel the moment of death approaching I'll have them destroyed. It's better not to have a biography. The reason I want to live to a hundred and twenty is to outlive any contemporary who might include me in his memoirs." [. . .]

3 December.

Went to Kinney's yesterday to plead for Orbeli, Muizhel, Sologub, and Akhmatova. Sitting by the fire was a man short on talent and long on mustachios, a certain Vladimirov, for whom they'd brought brushes and paint from Warsaw. He was telling them stories about contemporary life.

---

111. A free university for women in Saint Petersburg, the Bestuzhev Courses were founded in 1878 and named after an eminent Russian historian. (V.E.)

Art collectors are taking their canvases down from the walls, rolling them up, and stashing them away: they're afraid of tax inspectors demanding taxes on them. One gentleman who owns an Aivazovsky original of very large dimensions asked Vladimirov to cover Aivazovsky's signature with gum arabic and paint "copy of Aivazovsky" over it to fool the tax inspector. Time was when they'd do the opposite: paint "Aivazovsky" on copies. [. . .]

4 December.

Accompanied Kinney yesterday on his rounds. We made our first stop at Akhmatova's. We were given the royal treatment: tea and biscuits, all very serious and ceremonial. < . . . > Embarrassed as she was, Akhmatova gladly accepted thirty rubles. She asked Kinney to help Shileiko. Kinney agreed.

From there we went to Sologub's. He looks bad. He began panting heavily after climbing one flight of stairs and adjusted the curtains to give himself time to recover. (He'd arrived a few minutes after us.) When I said I hoped he didn't find it awkward to take money from the American, he replied at length in a firm singsong voice, as if having thought it all out in advance, "One cannot find it awkward to accept money from an American, because that great country has always lived in harmony with the great ideals of Christianity. Everything that comes from America is imbued with high moral values."

Very naive, but nice in its provincial way. From Sologub's we went down the same staircase to Alexei Tolstoy's. Tolstoy was self-important: he complained that Liveright, his American publisher, hadn't paid him the money they owed him, and showed us some children's poems he had written "because I'm so hard up." His poems were bad, but his flat was sensational—in the best of taste and luxurious—with a magnificent antique couch, paintings and engravings on shiny wallpaper, etc. [. . .]

10 December.

Called on Tolstoy. < . . . > He read me excerpts from his play *The Revolt of the Machines*. I liked them a lot. The Philistine is a terribly funny, lively, contemporary character, very Russian, and, as always in Tolstoy, a likable fool. Tolstoy sets great store by showing how all the great events in the play are reflected in the fool's mind. The fool is the litmus paper he uses to test everything. He even sends the idiot to Mars . . . < . . . >

I'm writing this in the morning in bed. All at once I hear steps. It's Boba with Murka. Murka never gets up so early.

"What's the matter?"

"Where's *Murka's Book?*"

Suddenly I remembered that three days ago, when Murka was pestering me about whether *Murka's Book* would be out soon, I'd told her that the cover was drying and the book would be ready the day after tomorrow. "You'll go to bed tonight and get up tomorrow, then go to bed again and get up again, and then the book will be ready."

She had remembered what I said and came to see me the moment she woke up.

11 December.

Had a talk with the actors at the Bolshoi about Blok. They adored him, but apparently didn't read him. Komarovskaya recalled that Blok loved the gypsy romance "Gray Morning" and had been thrilled to hear it in Moscow at Kachalov's, but when I pointed out that Blok himself had written a poem called "Gray Morning" it was obviously completely new to her. < . . . >

I have sent Valery Bryusov the following letter:

Dear Valery Yakovlevich:

No writer has done so much for me as you, and I should be the most ingrate of ingrates were I not to congratulate you on this special day. It is not your fault if I, your disciple, have failed to justify your efforts on my behalf, but I shall never forget the scrupulous and persistent care with which you guided my first steps.

12 December.

Today is one of the most important days in my life: early this morning Mura finally received her long-awaited copy of *Murka's Book.* < . . . > She examined each picture for a long, long time and noticed something that not one in a hundred thousand grown-ups would have noticed: "Why does Mura have two shoes here?" (on the last page—one in the pig's mouth, the other underneath the bed).

I didn't understand the question. She told me what she meant: "Mura *buried* one of the shoes!" (on a previous page).

14 December.

< . . . > We have no money—not enough to buy bread—yet "The Crocodile" and "Wash 'Em Clean" are doing very well. Yesterday Alyansky said to me, "I thought you'd be a rich man by now."

16 December.

< . . . > Spent yesterday and the day before at the censorship office. A funny place: in the outer office a morose elephantine Communist with a bass voice and no sense of humor, an ugly mug with a jutting jaw, bellows more than speaks; in the next office Comrade Bystrova all naive and twittery; and finally the censors, her charges. You can't imagine a more pathetic bunch of degenerates. A few came out into the waiting room—ghastly caricatures all. One old woman wearing scuffed shoes, woozy from nonstop reading, reeking nicotine, dirty, slovenly, and sallow, a cross between a shrew and a whipped cur, came out and whispered, "When are they going to pay us, damn them! They take forever." And she was the fool who had read my *Two Souls of Maxim Gorky* and cut a lot of harmless material while leaving what could be considered harmful.

Besides her I saw two students, oriental in appearance, from the Caucasus, without a glimmer of intelligence on their faces, and two trainees, still in sheepskin military caps. One of them said to Bystrova, "I'm boning up on my French now, and soon I'll know the whole language by heart."

"Come back when you do," she said. "We need foreign censors."

"I'm memorizing English," the other one boasted.

"Good for you," she said.

< . . . >

20 December.

The Tolstoys came to call on Sunday. Alexei Nikolaevich said Gorky had been nice to him at first, but then turned against him. "And just think, when Bunin learned that the *Figaro* wanted to publish my *Road to Calvary*, he showed up at their offices and started going on in his awful French about how I'm not related to Lev Tolstoy and I'm a bad writer and nobody pays any attention to me in Russia."[112] [. . .]

20 December.

The day before yesterday I visited Abram Yarmolinsky and Babette Deutsch. He is head of the Slavonic Division of the New York Public Library. < . . . > They are very nice. She has an indisputable gift for poetry, he—a selfless love of literature. He's writing a book on Turgenev, which is partly why he's come. I believe it will be a good book. Apparently he'd been looking all over for me to talk about—Panaeva. So New York is interested in Panaeva! [. . .]

27 December.

"Go and drink your cocoa, Murochka!"

"Stop pestering the life out of me!"

Murochka has been dying for Christmas to come. Ten days before the big day Boba put ten pebbles in the cupboard, and Murochka has been taking one out every day. On Christmas morning she got dressed very early and ran to the Christmas tree. "Look what Grandfather Frost brought me," she cried, crawling under the tree on her belly. (It is in a corner and laden with candles.) She found a car (a truck), a horsy, and a fife. She was so excited she could hardly speak. Once more I observed what a bad influence toys have on children. She was so wrought up by the exhilaration of it all that she kept bursting into tears at the slightest trifle. < . . . >

30 December.

On the night after Christmas Mura was afraid Grandfather Frost would come and take the tree away. < . . . >

I've managed to get some money from Kinney for Anna Ivanovna Khodasevich, for Nekrasov's sister, and for Anna Akhmatova. [. . .]

112. Tolstoy's *Road to Calvary* (1921–40) is an attempt at a panoramic treatment of Russia in the throes of war and revolution. The presentation of the Civil War, where ambivalence increasingly yields to a pronounced pro-Bolshevik bias, was totally unacceptable to Ivan Bunin, a bitter opponent of the Soviet regime. (V.E.)

1924

→>-→>-→>-→>-→>-→>-→>

18 January.

Akhmatova is remarkably egocentric. Kinney has asked me to work with her and Zamyatin to put together a list of needy Russian writers. I went to see her the day before yesterday—she is still in bed—and she thought and thought and couldn't come up with a single name! < . . . >

15 April.

Lakhta, a small tourist town. The shelf above my head has jars on it labeled "Common viper," "Lacerta vivipara" (Viviparous lizard), etc. I've just finished a whole pile of work: 1) writing an article about Alexei Tolstoy, 2) translating Chesterton's *Manalive*, 3) editing Jack London's *Valley of the Moon*, 4) editing the first issue of *Russkii sovremennik*, and so on. I'm enjoying the privacy here. One thing is entirely superfluous: the museum. The boys and girls who come here on outings take no interest in it; they spend their nights playing cards. The soldiers make off with the jars containing frogs to drink the alcohol and formalin mixture. Three times a day a scientist by the name of Taisia Lvovna measures the depth of the snow, the direction and force of the wind, and the quantity of precipitation. She is very conscientious, taking readings in three places, two of which she can reach only on skis; she even gets down on her stomach to make sure she's getting the number right. But once a few of us were discussing what the weather was going to be like, and when somebody said we were in for rain the next day I, believing as I do in science, asked, "How do you know?" and he said, "Taisia Lvovna dreamed of a corpse last night, and dreaming of a corpse means rain." What's the point of getting down on your stomach?

16 April.

Off to Moscow today to give a talk on Alexei Tolstoy. < . . . > I've enjoyed my stay here. I needed to be away from people. It's not that I don't like people; it's that I don't like myself when I have to be with them. I don't sound like myself, I don't sound right.

Unfortunately I had to make frequent trips to Petersburg for *Sovremennik* meetings. We worked for days on end from morning till night—me, Zamyatin, Tikhonov, and Efros. Tikhonov was once so exhausted that instead of Dostoevsky and Tolstoy he said Tolstoevsky and Dostoy. And in the first issue we're running some poems by Tyutchev, but Tikhonov said, "We're running poems by Fet."

"Not Fet," I said. "Tyutchev."

"Oh, I got them mixed up. They both start with F." [. . .]

17 April.

Arrived today. Am lying on my bed in the Hotel Hermitage. In a half hour I'll be giving my talk at the Literature Today event sponsored by our journal. < . . . > Zamyatin and Akhmatova are staying at the Hermitage as well. I saw Akhmatova for a second. "I can't go out for a walk," she said. "My posters are so awful." And in fact the whole town is covered with posters saying "Here from Leningrad for an Exclusive Engagement." I'm going to fetch her and take her to the Conservatory. She's getting dressed. Efros is very unhappy with the way things are turning out: he says there's been too much of a fuss made over the journal. It would be particularly bad if people took our program to be counterrevolutionary. That would be a shameless juggling of the facts. Before the journal began, Tikhonov asked us all, "Let me ask you straight out whether you intend to attack the Soviet regime in secret, in part, in any shape or form. If so, there's no point in starting it." We all answered "No," Zamyatin included, though his no was not so energetic as, say, Efros's. < . . . >

5 May.

Sunday. Kolya is getting married. [. . .] Yesterday I paid a visit to Marina's mother, and I was surprised to find the lower story of their house inhabited by a whole colony of robbers known to everybody in the house by that name. Two of the robbers sat at the gate, cracking walnuts with their teeth. A robber grandma sat at an open window watching her robber grandson walk along the street. A robber wife looked out of another window, exhibiting the white breasts in her low neckline by leaning on the windowsill. In a word, the perfect idyll. Room number six in the same house is apparently inhabited by another band of robbers, one (unlike the downstairs band) known to commit murders. They were extremely accommodating and helped me to find where Marina lives. Marina's mother tells me nobody turns them in because they keep the house free from other robbers. I think what keeps the house free from robbers is its poverty.

Five o'clock. My son will be my son for two more hours; then he'll become Marina's husband. Ten to six. Kolya is going to be married. Yesterday he washed and shaved—making ready. I found something unpleasant in that *making ready.* "Poor Kolya," Maria Nikolaevna said yesterday with a laugh, "he's all worn out." That jarred on me too, the female triumph over the complacency of the lingam: We can wear out anyone. That and the mamas' winks and whisperings, speculations, observations—it's all wrong. I'm glad I left the wedding. < . . . >

Alexei Tolstoy's *Revolt of the Machines.* I went twice and left in the middle both times: I couldn't force myself to sit through it. The second time Tolstoy turned up with Isadora Duncan. Monakhov spied them, and just before the play began he announced to the audience, "A special personage has sneaked into the theater tonight: Alexei Nikolaevich Tolstoy, author of the play you are about to see. A round of applause, please." Everyone applauded. "No, no," he said. "More organized." The audience clapped in cadence. But that was before the play. There wasn't a single clap at the end of the first act. < . . . >

6 May.

Eight a.m. Well, Kolya has spent his first night with Marina. I slept, but the moment I woke up I was plagued by thoughts about Kolya as a little boy in Kuokkala and, even before that, in Odessa. I sailed back to Odessa from London in 1904 and went straight to oleander-lined Bazarnaya Street, where my mother and bittersweet oleander wife were living. There we sat, happy, when suddenly my wife said, "Don't you want to see Kolenka?" I had completely forgotten about him.

They brought out a little black-haired boy with a round face, and I looked at him as my enemy. I had no use for him then. I didn't start loving him until we'd moved to number 11 Kolomenskaya. He was a real dreamer at the time. "How about building a house, Kolya," I'd say. And he'd build one out of air. "Window, window, window, window," he'd say, jumping up and down. He couldn't stop. He put windows everywhere, windows without end. He would draw a window in the air with his finger and jump for joy.

Again and again. He loved the Pushkin Street Pushkin monument: the "momment." He would climb up on a chair, fold his arms, and say, "I'm a momment." "And what does a monument do when it rains?" "A momment goes here," he would say and crawl underneath the chair. Kuokkala was where he came up with his first verse ("Hear how yellow I can talk"), made friends with Lida, and daydreamed. He would actually say, "I'm going to the rocks to dream" (the rocks being blocks of granite dragged to the shore to prevent breakers from hitting the dacha of a rich German). Back and forth, back and forth he'd walk like a bird on a perch, following the rhythm of his thoughts, thinking up flying machines, telling himself fairy tales, making up journeys and adventures with Redskins. He had a round, naive face and a passive mind that, while failing to take the initiative, instinctively safeguarded its spiritual life from alien incursions. I remember his passion for Darwin, his doubts in God, his skis, his boat, and his English. I tried to get him interested in English; he resisted loyally: he refused to learn vocabulary words and forgot everything two days later. Lida was always a model for him, though she would claim out of loyalty that he knew much more than she did. His life was lazy, lethargic: he drifted through the Revolution and the Tenishev School with ease, half asleep, head in the clouds, never making a splash or even a place for himself. Now he's at the university and letting scholarship and events pass him by, stumbling his way along the street mumbling poetry. He fell in love with Marina without warning and immediately set to learning English so he could earn enough to get married. He translated Longfellow's *Evangeline* (quite poorly), *The Son of Tarzan* (with Lida, a sloppy job, hit-or-miss, harum-scarum), *The Chess of Mars* (better), *Valley of the Moon* (even better), and he is currently translating *The House of Gerdlestone* at the speed of an express train. And all for Marina. Which means Marina has been good for him so far. His relationship to me is excellent: I wouldn't say he respects me, but he has a great filial affection for me. And yet—I don't know why—I didn't want him to marry and I pity him now. [. . .]

The sun came out at noon. After lolling blissfully on the balcony, I decided to go out to the water. Two men on white horses rode up and asked for my pass. "I haven't got one," I said.

"Then you have no business walking here."

If people have no business walking along a sun-drenched seashore, they have no business walking anywhere on this earth.

Akhmatova has moved to a new apartment on the Fontanka. I went to see her there about three weeks ago. It's an enormous building: it used to house the imperial laundry. She was sitting in front of the fireplace, and a candle was burning on the mantelpiece in broad daylight. Why? She had no matches. She would have to light the stove and wouldn't be able to. I snuffed out the candle and ran next door and bought some matches from the painters working there. [. . .]

12 May.

The sun is out. < . . . > I've been having a run of bad luck lately: I've twice been denied permission to give a talk about Gorky. [. . .] At present the subject of Maxim Gorky cannot be discussed in public from any perspective whatever. < . . . >

The first issue of *Russkii sovremennik* has aroused the indignation of official circles: "It fairly reeks of Tsarist spirit." "No wonder they chose a yellow cover."

When Efros asked Lunacharsky whether he liked it, Lunacharsky said, "Yes, yes. It's very good."

"Would you agree to collaborate?"

"No, no. I'd be afraid to."

Trotsky said, "I didn't want to attack them, but I have to. They are smart people doing stupid things."

Mayakovsky: "What can I say! It's a fine journal. It's got Tolstoy and Dostoevsky working for it." [. . .]

14 May.

I met Demyan Bedny for the first time at Gosizdat today and chatted with him for an hour or so. A clever man. I bet he reads a lot too. He loves telling stories.

"I decided to play a joke on a driver I have, and told him my daughter's real father was Chaliapin. The driver was embarrassed at first, but then pulled himself together and said, 'So that's what gives the young lady her rich voice.'" [. . .]

7 June.

"You're a sly one," Akhmatova said about me today, "but I believe what you write. You can't lie. I'm convinced of it."

She was ill, in bed, all curled up, with the teapot bubbling away on the kitchen primus.

10 June.

Rain. What a loathsome man that Zinovyev is. I saw him at Gorky's today. He doesn't shake hands with writers. Fedin and I were there. He was on the couch and didn't even stand to greet us.

    Gorky is either terribly sullen or totally heart-to-heart when he talks on the phone. There is no middle ground. < . . . >

17 June.

Night. < . . . > Yesterday it was twenty-two degrees [Celsius] in my room behind the wardrobe. Toward morning I made my bed on the floor and fell asleep. I slept for two hours, grateful for a chance to call it quits for a spell. The awful thing about insomnia is that you stay in your own company longer than you should. You get terribly bored with yourself, so much so that you start thinking of death. You want to strangle that hateful conversation partner, smother him, snuff him out. You yearn terribly for your ego to be snuffed out. I was desperate last night: I thought I'd never make it. You rest your head on the pillow, you doze off, but you don't go all the way. There's always a tiny scrap of something. You've nearly sunk into oblivion, but there's still that tiny scrap. Your powers of observation are heightened: Am I asleep or not? Will I fall asleep or not? You track that tiny scrap: Is it growing? Is it shrinking? And the tracking process itself keeps you awake. Things got so bad last night I took to pounding my skull with my fists! Pounded the stupid skull black and blue! If only I could turn it in. < . . . >

22 June.

Alexei Tolstoy paid me a visit today at the *Sovremennik* Mokhovaya Street offices. It's Monday, we're open to the public, and there was a large crowd. The corpulent Tolstoy, wearing an unbecoming *tolstovka* [a stylized peasant blouse popularized by Tolstoy], stood around for a while looking lost. < . . . > Then he came up to me and said, "So you think I'm an idiot." (He was referring to my article about him in the journal.) I mumbled something in reply and we started talking like friends again. He is very worried about the upcoming trial in connection with *The Revolt of the Machines*.[113] I tried to calm him by telling him about an introduction to *The Taming of the Shrew* which claims that Shakespeare had borrowed most of the play from Čapek. That made him very happy, and he went to my office to get the book. [. . .]

Tikhonov was at the Pechatkin Paper Factory on Saturday. The Moscow Gosizdat House will now be using it for its own needs. Otto Yulyevich Shmidt and other notables came to the ceremony. There were the usual speeches: "This factory is a nail in the coffin of capitalism." "The opening of this factory is an important international event." Everything was proceeding as planned, in the prescribed grandiloquent manner, when suddenly who should appear in the crowd but the former owner, the very person whose coffin had just had a nail hammered into it. The women were overjoyed to see him. They kissed his hands and greeted him warmly. Many people wept. He was very moved. He is a fine man. His workers always loved him.

Dreiden is training to be a guide at Tsarskoe Selo. The guides are taught to give the economic basis for all works of art. The instructor told them that the Zinovyevites had recently asked his supervisor about the economic basis for "Comrade Murillo's *Madonna*." He was unable to reply. "We don't need people like him!" And right he is.

27 June.

In Sestroretsk. Yemelyanova's empty dacha on the other side of the river. < . . . > Five hundred workers are taking the cure at the spa here. They are provided with baths and excellent food (six meals a day of the highest

113. In the preface to *The Revolt of the Machines* (in *Zvezda* 2 [1924]) Tolstoy noted: "Before writing this play, I familiarized myself with *RUR*, a play by the Czech writer Karel Čapek. [*RUR* introduced the word *robot*—from the Czech *robota* "corvée"—into the English language. The play was an early warning against the dangers of a machine civilization. (M.H.H.)] I made use of its subject matter, which in turn was borrowed from the English and the French. My decision to use someone else's subject matter was encouraged by the examples of great playwrights." On 15 July 1924 the journal *Novyi zritel'* reported: "On 31 June the People's Court considered the case of a revision by A. N. Tolstoy of Karel Čapek's play *RUR*. Last year Kroll, the translator of *RUR*, gave Tolstoy the translation for editing. Their contract stipulated that Tolstoy was obligated to pay to Kroll half the royalties should the play be performed. Kroll maintains that Tolstoy's *Revolt of the Machines* is simply a revised version of his translation, and requests royalties from Tolstoy according to the contract."

quality). Everything is as orderly as can be: the grounds are replete with receptacles for cigarette butts, the patients all wear officially issued striped garb. At last workers too can take the waters. (There are some two hundred attendants.) True, after a while one's enthusiasm wanes. Most of the patients have dull or angry looks on their faces: they are dissatisfied with the diet, they complain there's not enough food (they're given twice the number of calories necessary for normal people, but the quantity is not large), they throw their cigarette butts on the ground rather than in the receptacles and run off to the pub at every opportunity, though it's against the rules. Yet all this is piddling compared with the fact that these people used to gasp their way through life in filth, fumes, and disease, and now they can breathe like humans.

Lida and I called on Khanka Beluga, head of the school district, a big wheel. We had an argument about fairy tales. She hates them and says, "We gave children fairy tales when we couldn't tell them the truth."

I've been reading Freud. I'm not wild about him.

Mura says, "The big ball met the little ball under the table."

Looking at the children's homes and workers' sanatoriums makes me an enthusiastic supporter of the Soviet regime. A regime that puts the happiness of children and workers first is worthy of the highest praise.

11 July.

Today is dear Bobobchka's birthday. He came to see me this morning and tidied up my room here at the spa. [. . .] He is very loving and unpretentious. < . . . >

I can't get over the phenomenal ignorance of my neighbor, the twenty-four-year-old Yelizaveta Ivanovna Nekrasova. She is the wife of a professor and comes from the town of Luga. When I quoted Pushkin's line "Here on earth there's a town named Luga," she said, "Oh yes, I know that poem. I read it *in the newspaper*." She is surprised to learn that Max Voloshin is a poet. "I knew a Max Voloshin; he was one of my suitors. I have a friend named Alexander Blok; he's not a writer though." But she has her nails done once a week. [. . .]

12 July.

Lida is leaving for Odessa today; she's going to see her grandmother. She's a charming creature, full of energy but lacking an outlet for it. She has a colossal, all-consuming passion for constructive activity. She had no desire to go to the Crimea because there's nothing to do there, whereas in Odessa she can help her grandmother prepare for the trip to Petersburg.

15 July.

< . . . > I am very much upset by household matters: our telephone gets switched off, our electric wires get cut; the rent is colossal and the fines . . . **Oh, bother.** < . . . >

On the terrace this evening I told Mura "The Golden Goose" in my own words, and each time a new character appeared she'd ask, "Is he good?" She needs to know whether to sympathize with him or not, expend her love on him. < . . . >

27 July.

< . . . > I spent yesterday at a sanatorium for child cripples—children suffering from bone tuberculosis. It is on a sandy slope in the dunes. < . . . > I went up to a red hut with twenty-five to thirty monstrosities of all kinds lying next to it. They were overjoyed when they learned they were going to be read to, and rushed off to call the others. It was the most awful sight: some on one leg, others on all fours, still others slithering along the ground they gathered round me—and with amazing speed. One had his nose all bandaged, another had terribly spindly legs and a gigantic head; the most fortunate were on crutches. I read "Wash 'Em Clean" and "The Giant Cockroach" and then chatted with them. Some have to be tied to their beds they writhe so. < . . . >

30 July.

Yesterday's sunset was magnificent. I walked longer than usual above the sea. Evenings such as these would seem to come once in a thousand years, and one is afraid of wasting or spoiling them. People walk along quietly, under a spell, as if accompanied by a serene music. The solitary figures are especially moving: they seem ever on the verge of soaring into the sky or breaking into some extraordinary song. I caught up with a couple that looked the epitome of poetry, and what I heard was:

SHE. Absolutely not!
HE. Well, *I* say yes!
SHE. And *I* say no! < . . . >

1 August.

< . . . > Yesterday I visited an orphanage a stone's throw from the spa.
I'd not been there before. It seemed splendid from far off: I heard A. K.
Tolstoy's "There Is No Month More Vibrant Than the Merry Month of
May" ringing out over the terrace. I introduced myself, and the director
showed me a small museum of the children's drawings and figurines—
autumn, winter, summer, etc.—and the Lenin Corner, where next to and
just below the portrait of Lenin I saw my "Crocodile," "Blue Grandpa,"
and "Giant Cockroach," Marshak's "Kids in a Cage," and so on. It's all
quite gloomy, dull, and official. Looking through some notebooks containing the minutes of the children's meetings, I found the following:

Dear Boss,
　　We love you more and more every day.

"Who is your boss?" I asked the children.
"The GPU," they answered. It's a special department.
All they get to eat is boiled millet. [. . .]

6 August.

Three days ago Boba felt offended to the core: after he'd passed his French
exam on the second try, I gave him French vocabulary to learn. With his
customary obstinacy he defended his right to do nothing. He went so far
as to announce a hunger strike and didn't eat a thing for twenty-four hours.
[. . .]

22 August.

< . . . > Kolya seems to have had a sudden breakthrough: he is writing
several things at once. [. . .] He read the poems and the novel out loud to
me one after the other, and I liked them all. They're all full of life. But
the novel was what surprised and gratified me most. I have a feeling that

Kolya has a harder time not writing it than writing it and that he takes immense pleasure in it. < . . . >

26 August.

< . . . > Chatting with Lida is my only relaxation. Her intellectual vitality is even scary. You can feel a steel spring in her just waiting to uncoil. She is currently reading up on politics and has gone through dozens of books about Marxism, breaking them down, digesting and assimilating them, calling for more and more. She's mad about economic theory. [. . .] The life she leads is unbelievable: never a second wasted, everything planned in advance, reading from morning till night, swotting, going to the library, and so on. She told me more about Odessa. She talks about my mother with great tenderness.

3 September.

[. . .] I am doing nothing but proofreading: I am proofreading Kolya's translation of *The Prospector*, the miscellany *Satire*, the page proofs of *Sovremennyi Zapad*, and the page proofs of *Sovremennik*.

For the first time in my life I feel healthy and, funny as it sounds, young.

Called on Akhmatova yesterday. She looked so sad when she saw me that I asked, "Aren't you glad I've come?"

"Olenka wants to go abroad," she said. "She's trying to arrange it. She had appendicitis and peritonitis and was in bed for fifty-eight days. (I think that's what it was.) I took care of her, so I didn't write a line. Anything I write I'll give you immediately for *Russkii sovremennik*. It's the only place left. I've received fifteen dollars from Kinney in America. I'm grateful to them."

She obviously couldn't wait for me to go. And she's always been so friendly. "I have a feeling you've got someone hiding in the wardrobe and you can't wait for me to go," I said.

"No, stay, please," she said (but lamely).

I said nothing; she said nothing.

Then: "I saw Lidochka the other day. My, how she's grown."

On my way out I said, "Where do you think Punin's swing to the right will end?"

"In Solovki,"[114] she said with a sardonic smile and closed the door after me.

She had two home-made strips of **tangle-foot** paper hanging from the mantelpiece, but they attracted hardly any flies. < . . . >

23 September.

< . . . > *Russkii sovremennik* is in trouble. Five or six days ago the Literary Division made me cool my heels in the antechamber, and I barged in and talked to Bystrova without permission. On my way out I was bawled out by Petrov, the man sitting at the entrance.

"Who let you in?"

"I let myself in."

"Weren't you told Bystrova was in a meeting?"

"She wasn't in a meeting. I was misinformed."

"Well, I'll never let you in to see her again."

"Oh, yes you will."

Then I was stupid enough to shout that there are many bureaucrats and few writers and our time is more valuable than yours. He was fit to be tied. And today the Literary Division rang and told me to deliver a complete list of the writers working for *Sovremennik* so they can dismiss them all. And of course the list goes to Petrov. Is this life worth living?

< . . . >

9 November.

I'm having trouble with my "Barmalei." I don't like it at all. I wrote it for Dobuzhinsky, in the style of his drawings. Klyachko and Marshak don't like it either, but Marya Borisovna, Kolya, and Lida do. A lot.

Kolya is coming to the end of his first novel.[115] "I'm on Chapter Nineteen!" (There will be twenty in all.) Each time I see him he tells me what chapter he's on. I remember hearing him say, "I'm bogged down on Six," "Thirteen drags," and the like, but for the most part he has a sure and easy touch and is passionately involved, running back and forth between the *Encyclopedia Britannica* and his desk. [. . .]

---

114. A labor camp for political prisoners on an island in the White Sea. (M.H.H.)
115. The novel, *Tantalene,* was published in 1925 by Raduga.

Zamyatin has rung to say that there's a *vile* article about us (that is, about *Sovremennik*) in *Pravda*.[116] He's working on a historical novel about Atilla.[117] "At first I thought it would be just a story, but no, it's turned out to be an exciting topic. When I started doing background reading, I found it much more interesting than I'd expected."

"Are you drawing any parallels with the present?"

"Definitely. You know who they were, the Huns? They were our Russian louts and savages. Yes, yes, I'm sure of it. Atilla was Russian too. Atilla is one of the names for the Volga." [. . .]

13 November.

They are coming down so hard on us (*Sovremennik*) that I told Zamyatin he should write an article entitled "What Would Have Happened Had Pushkin's 'A Wondrous Moment I Remember' Been Published in *Sovremennik*."

> A wondrous moment I remember
> (*An imperial gala, no doubt*)
> Before mine eyes *thou* didst appear,
> (*Probably refers to the Princess Xenia Alexandrovna*)
> A fleeting vision rich in splendor
> The essence of a beauty pure.
> (*Pure beauty! A courtly aesthetic ideal*)
> Years passed. The mighty blasts of tempests
> (*The October Revolution*)
> Have scattered all my dreams . . .
> (*Of restoring the monarchy*)

and so on. Because that's just what our critics do.

I'm having trouble with the other journal, *Sovremennyi Zapad*. The board has criticized it severely, and I've decided to hand in my resignation. < . . . >

---

116. Reference to an attack in *Pravda* (5 November 1924) on the first two issues of *Russkii sovremennik*. The author, a certain Rozental, maintains that "NEP literature showed its real face" in the journal, and concludes: "The Nepman [the entrepreneurial type spawned by NEP] and the bourgeois intellectual who yearns for the 'values' of the bourgeois world and dreams of returning to them have found expression in *Russkii sovremennik*."

117. Apparently *The Scourge of God*, a novel to which Zamyatin was to return in his late years. The fourth issue of *Russkii sovremennik* announced its forthcoming publication, but the journal was shut down before the fifth issue could appear.

16 November.

[. . .] The day before yesterday a proofreader at the Leningrad Gosizdat House showed me—in strictest confidence—the proofs of Trotsky's article about me. He is critical again.[118] Very. If the publishing house accepts my Nekrasov book, I'll make sure to rework it. Now I'm going through Kolya's novel. He's got imagination but not the slightest sense of reality. In one chapter he describes a cannonball "flying slowly over the square and disappearing in a nearby lane." That's not a word-for-word quotation, but it's close. Still, his energy is amazing. He's barely finished the novel and already he's planning a poem for children—about a chimney sweep. < . . . >

17 November.

Grandma looks hale and hearty if a lot older. Her voice doesn't sound the same. She brought a cup for me, a sugar bowl and tongs for Kolya, Christmas tree decorations for Mura, and so on, but most of all she brought whole handfuls of the past, a past that touched me, moved me to tears yesterday. She brought a darling picture of Kolya in which helpless, naive, and frightened that he is he appears to be looking ardently into the future. Apparently he once stood up for his sister, when an outsider affectionately referred to "our Lida," by saying, "No, Lida's ours. We're the ones who gave birth to her." < . . . >

Am coming to the end of Adams's *Success*. It's typically American: dark, false, but exciting.

24 November.

[. . .] It's been a week full of flaring and flickering passions, the first of which was the Moscow writers' letter, a protest against the current literary

---

118. Trotsky's first article against Chukovsky appeared in February 1914. He called Chukovsky "totally incoherent theoretically" and maintained that "he led a purely parasitical existence in the methodological sense." The chapter on Blok in Trotsky's *Literature and Revolution* (1924) contains a savage attack on Chukovsky's discussion of "The Twelve": "What charlatanism, what moral vacuity, what cheap and mean and shameful jabber!" (V.E.).

situation. Exactly a week ago, on Monday at four, Tikhonov showed it to Zamyatin and me. "What a bungler that Tolstoy is! He's just sent me this letter he got from Moscow, and now it's too late: they're delivering it to the authorities in Moscow at three, so none of the Petersburg writers will have time to sign it." I took it to *Sovremennik* anyway, and there Eikhenbaum, Vsevolod Rozhdestvensky, and I signed. On Tuesday Zamyatin got Sologub's signature. Then in my presence he gave it to Misha Slonimsky, who took it to Gosizdat. There a whole bunch of proletarian and semi-proletarian writers declared it "insufficiently strong" and put together a "stronger" version. Tynyanov showed me the "stronger" version on Saturday at the Vremia Publishing House. Skimming it, I saw that this "stronger" version was at the same time more servile and that it contained the monstrous phrase "the recruitment of censors from among writers"! Tynyanov (who turns out to be a babe in the woods when it comes to these things) agreed with me and removed his signature, and the two of us went to the Writers' Union. I didn't go in—it was full of smoke, and I don't like noisy mobs in the evening—but Tynyanov spent about an hour there and said the Union was planning to write a third letter of its own. < . . . >

Event Number Two: Zamyatin and I wrote a response to our detractors.[119] The idea was mine. It was to take a poem by Pushkin and tear it apart à la Rodov, likening the latter to Peregud in Leskov's "Rabbit Warren." I made major revisions in what Zamyatin wrote, but he acts as if it was his and his alone. The same holds for the Panopticum column[120] in the *Sovremennik*. Something similar happened when he wrote the article "I Am Afraid." I had just read, in Gorky's presence, an outline for a protest containing the words, "If Chekhov were alive today, he would be carrying a briefcase," and so on. Zamyatin took them over without realizing it.[121]
[. . .]

---

119. Chukovsky is speaking of the article "To the Pereguds from the Editors of *Russkii sovremennik*," a polemic with the campaign unleashed by Rozental (see note 116) and several others.

120. The department of literary satire featured in *Russkii sovremennik*.

121. Zamyatin's essay "I Am Afraid" was published in the journal *Dom iskusstva* 1 (1921). The sentence, presumably coined by Chukovsky, does appear in the essay without attribution. (Would Chukovsky have wished to be quoted by name in the article containing the oft-cited assertion: "True literature can exist only when it is created not by diligent and trustworthy officials, but by madmen, hermits, heretics, dreamers, rebels and skeptics"?) (V.E.)

26 November.

The Trotsky portraits hanging in almost every office of Gosizdat are being taken down. [...]

Volynsky read us the introduction to his Rembrandt book at last Tuesday's World Literature meeting. Sologub's reaction was both playful and scathing. "Your book is dangerous. You call upon the Jews to cut our throats. You defend Judaism, but it doesn't need your defense. And why do you call Christianity stonelike and desertlike?"

During the break people joked that Volynsky called Christianity stonelike to please Kamenev [*kamen'* "stone"]. [...]

12 December.

Went to the censors yesterday to see about some reviews and the Panopticum. One hundred and sixty pages are ready, and we're rushing to get the issue out by the holidays. It was rather late by the time I arrived. Petrov was sitting there idly, looking languid.

"Can we have the material today?" I say. "We're in a rush."

He doesn't respond at first, then says, "We won't be giving you the material, because *Sovremennik* has been banned." [...]

15 December.

Well, Tikhonov and I went to the Literature Division. The head censor is Ostretsov, his assistant—Bystrova. When Tikhonov talked to Bystrova, he merged the names into Bystretsova. We pointed out to her that we ourselves had cut passages from Poletika's reviews; we told her that none other than Kamenev had promised Tikhonov that the authorities would not be hostile to the journal; we argued that it was absurd to ban a whole issue when the individual parts had been passed by the censors, and so on.

Bystrova lowered her eyes and said, "Your journal is harmful as a whole. It's not the individual articles. The whole thing, everything needs to be cut. Don't you realize the harm it can do the workers and Red Army men?"

But she did promise to think about whether to allow the fourth issue to appear.

I went back the next day. They will allow it to appear. "Yours isn't the only journal we need to close down," she said. We're examining a lot of military journals as well." (They're obviously trying to eradicate Trotsky-ism!) [. . .]

16 December.

Had a dream about a "widowed empress" whom I'd never seen and never thought about. It was very clear. She was a little old woman with a face the size of a fist. She was sitting on the couch with Marya Borisovna. The two of them were whispering together. I handed her my Chukokkala album and said, "May I have your autograph, Your Highness?" It was summer. A sunny day at the dacha. How silly and completely unrelated to what is going on.

And what is going on is the following: Tikhonov and I went back to the Literature Division. Ostretsov was in. He told us he'd been raked over the coals on account of *Sovremennik* and had gone to Moscow to see Polyansky about it. Polyansky suggested he make a summary of the material for the fourth issue. The fate of the *Sovremennik* would be decided once the summary had been discussed first in Petersburg, then in Moscow. [. . .]

Lunacharsky's portrait is now prominently displayed at World Litera-ture. There is a Lenin Corner, too.

17 December.

[. . .] I gave my lecture on Eikhenbaum at the university yesterday. During the question-and-answer period the audience proved itself a pack of num-skulls stuffed with Marxism: of the myriad issues I raised the only one they cared about was "the social approach." [. . .]

18 December.

I had an absolutely awful day yesterday and am having an absolutely awful night now.

In the afternoon I learned that because the Literature Division has decided to close Adolf Marx's publishing house, an official showed up at the press where my "Fifty Piglets" is being printed, and demanded it be set aside. That was an idiotic move if there ever was one. Doesn't the work of the author, the copyreader, the typesetter, and so on count for anything? But no, they set it aside, which, because it won't come out in time for

Christmas, is tantamount to bankrupting the publisher. In addition, they took a hundred and fifty rubles away from me and so on and so forth.

Next I learned that Kolya's book *Tantalene* had been alloted a run of five instead of ten thousand. Why? Because it's not an industrial novel and the Literature Division is waging a campaign against adventure novels.

I've been so upset I can't sleep and am reading Eikhenbaum on Lermontov, which is good if a bit shabby: Lermontov without Lermontov. I'm editing Lida's translation of Jack London's *Smoke Bellew* and rewriting my Eikhenbaum article. < . . . >

Two new books came out yesterday: Nikolai Chukovsky's *Fugitives* and Kornei Chukovsky's *Doctor Ouch-It-Hurts.*

Our children and their children soon
Will push us out to make them room.

< . . . >

19 December.

Went to see Eikhenbaum yesterday. A tiny room, tidy, with lots of books and a slantwise desk. Sit at it and you're in a nice cozy corner. Most of the books are very old and have morocco leather bindings. There is a portrait of Shklovsky behind glass in one bookcase; there are some works by Annenkov and a portrait of Akhmatova below them. Eikhenbaum told me about a meeting he had attended the day before at the Institute, where Inspector Karpov, who had come from Moscow for the purpose, urged all the scholars and professors to swear allegiance to the social method. They then passed a resolution to the effect that all students and teachers were only too glad to take social approaches to literature. (Passing the resolution was essential for the survival of the Institute.) Once they had voted, unanimously, Eikhenbaum raised a lone—heroic—hand against the "social method."

Now he's worried he has hurt the Institute. I sensed great spiritual purity and a love for what he does. [. . .]

21 December.

Collapsed yesterday after the nineteenth. Took great pleasure in reading Wycherley, Saltykov's letters, Moore on Byron, rereading Nekrasov, and so on and so forth. Called on Ionov at Gosizdat. He is helping me with his connections to get permission to go to Finland. He was very nice to me and showed me a letter from Gorky, an odd letter. The content was more or less as follows: "< . . . > Regards to Zinovyev. Send me the works of Professor Pavlov and any other book you want to boast about. Fedin's novel is very good;[122] he's obviously going to be a serious writer. Oh, how sad this Trotsky business is![123] People here are overjoyed, exulting in *our* misfortune." < . . . >

22 December.

Yesterday was a day of great tribulations. We gathered at eleven in Tikhonov's office at World Literature. As I walked up to the building where I had felt so at home, I saw three carts, carts filled with all our bookshelves, everything that had meant so much to us. Tikhonov's office was still intact. The gold-green cloth on the ornate table we sat around at meetings had not yet been removed. Oldenburg, Lozinsky, Volynsky, Tikhonov, Smirnov, Vera Alexandrovna, Zamyatin, and Zhirmunsky were all there; Lerner and Sologub had promised to come, but after waiting for a while we started the meeting without them. We got embroiled in a long discussion, Volynsky for some reason having proposed that we examine the situation *sub specie aeternitatis*. < . . . > We finally phoned Ionov, asked if he would see us, and set off—Oldenburg and I, Volynsky (slightly cowed) and Kashtelyan, the latter trying to bring the former back from eternity to real events. We had splendid weather on our way to Gosizdat: crisp air and light snow. We took back streets: it was Sunday. Ionov's chauffeur was in the waiting room. We went into his office. He was wearing a European suit and a shirt made abroad. Very nervous, he asked us to sit and said, "I meant to inform you personally about what I plan to do with you, but postponed our talk till January. I could have been much more specific then. But since you've come, I'm willing to talk to you now. You are aware that the Moscow Gosizdat has failed to accomplish what it was meant to. I have been asked to undertake a major reorganization of Gosizdat, using our experience here in Leningrad as a basis, that is, not resorting to state funds. Looking at the operations of the Moscow Gosizdat, I found a number of growths, some

122. Gorky is referring to Fedin's first novel *Cities and Years* (1924).

123. In November and December 1924 *Pravda* published a number of hostile responses to Trotsky's latest book *1917*.

healthy, some harmful. The ones that hindered operations—the art and poster studios, for instance—I removed. Gosizdat was also home to World Literature. A year ago I offered you the possibility of working openly and freely and you snubbed me. What can I do? To pull the whole cart, I've got to cut expenses. As it is, I have to plug up the Moscow gaps with the pitiful resources of the Leningrad branch. If I live like a lord, those resources will dry up by January and I won't be able to publish anything. I've got to take things in stages. What do I plan to do with World Literature? I have a Foreign Literature series as well. It is run by A. N. Gorlin. < . . . > I think it would be a good idea to combine the two and reduce the personnel involved. You know my point of view. We can't do things on a grand scale. The plan you at World Literature came up with seemed excellent for a while, but it has proved unpopular with the public." < . . . >

1925

+>-+>-+>-+>-+>-+>-+>-+>

< . . . >

10 January.

I'm suffocating . . . Poor Fedin is terribly disconcerted; he keeps blushing and hemming and hawing. The thing is, he is the chief administrator for *Zvezda*, and *Zvezda* is publishing a harsh philippic against the *Sovremennik*, to which he is a contributor.[124] "I'll leave," he says. "I'll ask Ionov to transfer me; I can't work here any more. Maisky, who edits *Zvezda*, is a former Menshevik, and like any former Menshevik does everything he can to out-Bolshevik the Bolsheviks. Gorbachov's article is said to be highly denunciatory."

124. "An Open Letter to the Editors of *Zvezda*" by Georgy Gorbachov appeared in the journal's January 1925 issue. Gorbachov takes Alexander Voronsky to task for "literary Trotskyism," accusing him of "organizational affiliation with the chief contributors to the arch-reactionary *Russkii sovremennik*." He is speaking on behalf of the All-Russian Association of Proletarian Writers (VAPP). A kindred organization, the Russian Association of Proletarian Writers (RAPP), was founded in 1925 and eventually became the main vehicle of proletarian cultural zealotry. From 1929 to 1932 it exercised dictatorial powers over literature.

I'm suffocating! . . . Things have come to such a pass that I spend my time between one and five running from office to office, and all I see is woe and more woe. Apparently Ionov is under a lot of pressure in Moscow; his position is quite shaky. Stalin is against him, Zinovyev for him. To placate the former, he's had two series of Stalin portraits printed. They're the first things he's published in Moscow. At least that's what Tikhonov says. < . . . >

11 January.

Saw Ionov. "When can a deputation from the World Literature board come and see you?" I asked.

"Board?" he screamed. I could tell that the very word offended him. "Board? Your board has been disbanded! < . . . > Your Tikhonov wants to set Gorky against me. Well, Gorky has sent me a telegram informing me that you say in your meetings you refuse to be part of Ionov's *gang*. I know everything. One of your colleagues tells me your every word." < . . . >

14 January.

Yesterday we held the last meeting of the board. When Ionov refused to accept Tikhonov as a member, it had to be dissolved. It was a very solemn occasion. Volynsky called us the flower of art and the intelligentsia. < . . . >

16 January.

The most amazing thing about it all is that it's not the readers who want freedom of the press; it's only a bunch of writers nobody cares about. The readers even find it more convenient not to know the truth. And not only more convenient but also more to their advantage. So it's not clear what we're fighting for or whose interests we represent. < . . . >

I haven't left for Finland yet, and already I miss Petersburg, the children, Marya Borisovna. I'm homesick in spades! I miss my cozy room, the desk I'm writing at now, etc.

Mura is playing with a ball and saying, "The armchair can play ball, the wall can, the stove can." We've made her some paper money: three, two, and one kopecks. She uses it to play at shopping, unaware that it is helping her to learn arithmetic.

21 January.

I'm in Kuokkala. < . . . > I called on Repin. The minute I saw his feet (from afar—he was in a downstairs room), I burst into tears. We embraced. "I can't stand effusive sentiments," he said. "Do you want tea or coffee?" I brought up the Russian Museum. "As long as Petersburg is called Leningrad," he said, "I will have nothing to do with the place." [. . .]

I read him excerpts from Gorky's essay on Tolstoy's wife. "He can write, the rascal," he said, "but he's left out the most important thing, namely, that that villain of a Chertkov hoodwinked Tolstoy into handing over Yasnaya Polyana to your blankety-blank proletariat."

24 January.

Poor Ilya Yefimovich! < . . . > He may look young, but it's an illusion; in fact, he is hopelessly decrepit. <. . . .>

At first he was willing to have his memoirs published, but now his retinue claim to have uncovered some monkey business and are telling him I ruined the book during the editing process. Though politely beating about the bush, he hinted as much today. I reminded him that I had done my work in his presence, that he had unfailingly, even uncritically praised it and admired the devices I used, and that I had respected and preserved the intonations of his speech. But he stubbornly if quite civilly refused: "No, the book is not to be. It must not be published until ten years after my death."

28 January.

[. . .] I parted with Repin on less than warm terms. "I've turned aristocrat," were his parting words, and "I refuse to publish any book whatever with Gosizdat. As long as Bolshevism exists, I don't want to hear about Russia and I consider everyone who lives there a Bolshevik."

"Strange," I said. "Your daughter lives there; your granddaughter is an employee of the Soviet state, and your pictures are exhibited in Soviet museums. Why do you refuse to give your book to a Soviet publisher?"

He was not at all pleased with my response.

29 January.

For the first time in ages I've been able to sleep. How could one fail to sleep in such magnificent conditions? < . . . >

Went to the University Russian Library, where my papers are kept. It's a fine library, a quiet, staid place with portraits of Gogol, Tolstoy, Chekhov, and Mickiewicz on the walls. < . . . > There I found Professor Igelström at a small table reading an old journal with Leskov's *Cathedral Folk* in it. [. . .] Besides old man Igelström I found Professor von Schulz, who is giving a course on Dostoevsky and looks like Kipling: black eyebrows, gray mustache, and bald pate. [. . .]

I was struck by the sympathy both Igelström and Schulz have for the current situation in Russia. Neither believes the tales the émigrés use to console one another. Without lauding all the measures taken by the government, they realize it is a veritable renewal of Russia, not just the whim of a band of evildoers. Igelström says that the monarchist propaganda here is so repugnant and stupid that it should be disseminated freely throughout Russia to give the peasants an idea of who wants to rule them.

I invited Schulz and Shaikovich to a restaurant. Schulz was hungry for what I had to say about Tolstoy and literature; I was hungry for food, not having had a bite to eat since morning and it being half past four. I was amazed to learn that neither of these literature professors had heard a thing about the Formalist method or the works of Eikhenbaum, Tynyanov, and Shklovsky. I gave them a complete lecture right there at the table. [. . .]

I am writing these last lines on Friday morning, 30 January 1925. It's after eight. Time to get dressed.

3 February.

I've been going through papers for five days now, my correspondence dating from 1898 to 1917. I've stumbled upon some terrible, long forgotten things. It was especially grueling to read the letters from the time I spent in Odessa just before leaving for London. I've torn them all up and would have been glad to wipe out the period itself. I was terribly restless and unsettled.

< . . . > As an illegitimate child, deprived even of a nationality (What am I? A Jew? A Russian? A Ukrainian?) I felt I was the most unfinished, unfathomable being on earth. And the main thing was, I was unbearably ashamed of saying at the time that I was illegitimate. We had a horrible word for it, *baistruk*, the equivalent of **bastard**. Admitting you were a *baistruk* meant first and foremost disgracing your mother. I thought of it as something monstrous: I was the only one; everyone else was "legitimate." I thought that everybody was whispering behind my back and that when I showed my papers to people (porters or gatekeepers) they would mentally spit at me. And they probably did. I remember the tortures I went through:

"Your social origins?"

"I'm a peasant."

"Your documents?"

And the documents contained the terrible words: son of a peasant woman by the name of so-and-so. I was so afraid of them I never even read them.[125] I was afraid of seeing them with my own eyes. I recall the stigma, the mockery I felt my sister Marusya's school-leaving certificate to be. She was the best pupil in our diocese school, and the certificate read: Maria (no patronymic) Korneichukova, daughter of a peasant woman, made excellent progress. I can still remember that the absence of a patronymic made the line for the pupil's name and social origins shorter than normal, than other pupils', and that it plagued me with shame. "We're not like others; we're worse; we're the lowest of the low." And when children talked about their fathers or grandfathers or grandmothers, all I could do was blush, hem and haw, fib, lie. I never had the luxury of a father or even a grandfather. The lies of that period are the source of all the falsifications and lies of the following period. Whenever I see a letter I wrote then to anyone, I can tell it was the letter of an illegitimate, a *baistruk*. All my letters (with the exception of some to my wife), the letters I wrote to everyone, are false, fabricated, insincere—and that is why. My "self-honor" was shattered in my youth. I had a particularly hard time of it at the age of sixteen or seventeen, when people begin calling you by your name and patronymic rather than your name alone. I remember the clownish figure I cut trying to tell even people I'd just met, "Just call me Kolya" or "My name's Kolya" and the like, though I had a mustache at the time. I tried

125. One such document, found at the Saint Petersburg Church of Saint Vladimir, is the birth certificate of one "Nikolai, son of the Ukrainian maiden from Gumbarova village Yekaterina Osipovna Korneichukova, illegitimate."

to make a joke of it, but it was painful. That's where I get the tendency to confuse pain, clowning, and lies and never show people my true face; that's where that and everything else comes from. And only now do I realize it.

As for Helsinki, I walk all over, eat kasha, peer at shop windows, pore through my letters and manuscripts—and long to go home. Oh, how hard it is to do nothing. [. . .]

15 February.

Things are happening! All kinds of things. Tikhonov has been arrested. For what nobody knows. The wildest rumors have been circulating. Some say it was on Ionov's orders and for embezzling World Literature funds. But the people at Gosizdat deny it. They say not only did Ionov have nothing to do with his arrest, he tried to get him released: he went to see Messing and took it upon himself to seek out Zinovyev in Moscow. I too believe he was not involved, but when I tried to say something to that effect at *Sovremennik,* they looked at me as if I were an Ionov agent. Yet I really do feel that the coming together of Ionov's threats and Tikhonov's arrest may be nothing but a fateful coincidence. [. . .]

16 February.

[. . .] Went to see Ionov yesterday. Just as I thought, he has nothing to do with Tikhonov's arrest. "I may get annoyed with someone," he said, "but I'm incapable of writing a denunciation." He is offended that anyone could even suspect him of such a thing. I told him that one way of setting the rumors to rest was to put in a good word for Tikhonov, and he said, "What do I care about their rumors? I despise the lot of them. (He means the board.) I've been to the GPU—and not to rehabilitate myself—but they just told me to get lost. On Thursday, as soon as I get back from Moscow, I'll do what I can—in secret, so no one will know—to make things easier for him, have food sent to him, that kind of thing. As a Communist I naturally accept responsibility for everything done by the Communist Party, but you know that I have never sent anyone to jail and have got a lot of people out." And he said it all with such dignity that I believed him. I couldn't help believing him. < . . . >

21 February.

Had visits from Zhenya Shvarts and Yury Tynyanov yesterday. < . . . >
Tynyanov came to talk about his *Kyukhlya,* a novel for young adults I've
commissioned to inaugurate the Children's Section of Kubuch, the Commission for the Improvement of Scholars' Living Conditions. He is very
much in need of money. The outline he brought is charming. Even if the
novel is ten times worse than the outline, I told him, it will be a fine novel.
He himself is charming: he enhances the intellectual and moral atmosphere
of wherever he happens to be. He read his virtuoso verse translations of
Heine. [. . .]

    Gosizdat are reviving *Sovremennyi Zapad.* I'm trying to get Eikhen-
baum and Tynyanov involved. I can't let them die in the street, can I? But
I can't work for the journal. It would be like crossing a picket line. < . . . >

    Poor Anna Ivanovna Khodasevich is so hungry she's taken to writing
film reviews. She recently saw a very interesting American film and wrote:
"Yet another trashy American product in which decadent bourgeois morality etc."

    "It's the only way to get published," she says, "and get my three rubles."
< . . . >

    Zamyatin and his wife are thrilled with the success of his *Flea* on the
Art Theater's second stage. It's a well-deserved hit. He says he's gone out
drinking with the cast six nights in a row. < . . . >

    I've got all kinds of "new toys": Marya Borisovna has bought me a
calendar, an inkwell, a blotter (made of marble), and more. I always love
getting new things. It's a trait left over from my childhood. A new penknife
is a source of bliss for me to this day.

23 February.

Tomorrow is Murka's birthday. She'll soon be coming in to confirm the
fact on the calendar.

    Yesterday I had a visit from the most talkative man on earth: the poet
Nikolai Tikhonov. He spoke in a hoarse bass and was very elegantly dressed.
Lean, calm, strong, he moved his hands while his body remained immobile
in the chair. He rose at four as fresh as when he sat at twelve. We began
by talking about children's literature. He told me Kipling's *Jungle Books*

had been banned because they have animals speaking in them. "You'd think our leaders were a pack of nannies," he said. < . . . > When he talked about the Caucasus, where he'd been last summer, he gave the precise Tatar, Turkish, Armenian, and Georgian names for the mountains, gorges, villages, and inns he passed through and the names of all the people he encountered. At first it was fresh and exhilarating, like a new carpet; then it began to pall. And the erudition may not have been so sound as it seemed. [. . .] Which makes his passion for names and dates all the more remarkable. Gorky has the same tendency, as does Korolenko. But in Korolenko they hold up the story he's telling unnecessarily, while in Tikhonov they are almost always poetic, a matter of exotic ornamentation. Everything about him is exotic, in fact. He comes into a room, and an air of exoticism seems to waft in with him. Something southern and exciting. You can't have a chat about everyday affairs with Tikhonov; he's always absorbed in peculiar books with peculiar subject matter, anecdotes, and verse. Even when he talks about his Petersburg friends, they sound like extraordinary heroes—travelers to outlandish places, possessors of recondite knowledge. < . . . > One thing he has in common with our times is that he is all facts. He has no connection to psychology or spiritual life. He has no soul and no spirit, but he loves life more than a thousand Greeks. That is why he is so well received in contemporary literature. He hasn't got a trace of the curiosity about the human personality so characteristic of Tolstoy, Chekhov, Bryusov, Blok, and Gumilyov. He finds an individual interesting only insofar as he is interesting, that is, insofar as he has seen and experienced interesting things, interesting places. Nothing else exists for him. I saw something similar in England, but Tikhonov goes farther. I must say I enjoyed those four hours. < . . . >

24 February.

The big day has arrived: Mura's birthday. Last night I washed my hair, and now I'm putting on my dressy *tolstovka* and semi-new trousers—and waiting. Marya Borisovna is giving her a chair, Grandmother a cradle, a doll, and toy plates and food, Boba a horse, Lida toy cups, and yours truly a little doodad of my own making. None of it cost very much, but she'll be thrilled with it all. < . . . >

3 March.

Saw Lyubov Dmitrievna Blok yesterday. Either she is feigning poverty or she's in a bad way. There she stood in the Kubuch doorway, a moth-eaten fur coat on her back and a gap in her teeth, trying to sell her translations from the French. The widow of one of the most famous Russian poets, his "lady fair," and Mendeleev's daughter! < . . . >

22 March.

Had an idea for an article on the use of fantastic tales, which are so under attack nowadays. It goes like this:

> A pregnant woman learns that in such and such a month her future child has grown fins. "Woe is me!" she cries. "I don't want a fish baby!" A month or two later the child grows a tail. "Woe is me!" she cries. "I don't want a dog baby!"
>
> "Don't worry, woman! You won't have a fish baby. You won't have a dog baby. You'll have a human baby. All babies in the womb have to be a little like a fish and a little like a dog. That's how they grow into people. Lev Tolstoy, Thomas Alva Edison, and Karl Marx—they all went through it. Nature makes lots of sketches before she gets us right. At three we're all visionaries, at four—warriors, and so on. There's nothing to fear. They're sketches, that's all. Just temporary. The most sober nation of all, the English, has the most noted visionaries. Why shouldn't animals talk to four-year-olds? All things talk to four-year-olds."

I'm having a rough time with "The Samovar Revolt." I end up with two lines after working five hours nonstop. It's a pity I didn't start writing children's poetry when I was young and rhymes fairly spouted from me.

Five days ago I had a visit from the choreographers who are adapting my "Wash 'Em Clean" into a ballet for children. They told me that after the first performance some Komsomol representatives came and protested against the line "shame on the dirty chimney sweeps" because sweeping chimneys is an honest profession and it was wrong to insult the proletariat. Now the narrator reads "shame on the dirty and impure," which makes them sound like devils.

No sooner do I set foot outside with Mura than it starts snowing. She's convinced I've arranged it on purpose. Now she's hiding in the wardrobe. [. . .]

26 March.

Mother is going back to Odessa tomorrow. I hear her coughing—and trying to hide it from everybody. She is intelligent, reserved, reticent, observant, and hardworking. She did a lot around the house without calling attention to herself—read to Murochka, washed the laundry, cleared the table—she was almost never idle. Her eyes have improved. < . . . >

Kolya is back from Moscow. < . . . > He saw Meyerhold. He says that Pasternak the poet is destitute. His *Tantalène* is sold out. Klyachko had a run of two thousand printed clandestinely and sold it too. < . . . >

Am reading Shevchenko's diary. It's remarkable. < . . . >

< . . . >

1 April.

I'm grateful for having lived another year. I used to say, "Am I as old as eighteen?" Now I say, "I'm glad to be forty-three and not eighty and glad to have lived to such a ripe old age." [. . .]

This is the year of new things: I dip a new pen into a new inkwell; I hear the ticking of a new clock; I have a new suit in the wardrobe, a new overcoat on the coatrack, and a new couch in the corner of the room. New things make you feel younger; they keep the elderly from thinking of death. Put on a new shirt and you feel revived.

I've just had a letter from Repin—a love letter. It makes me feel uncomfortable somehow. So much so that I didn't finish it and have left it for the time being.

I can't find the right ending for "Fedora's Misfortune."

< . . . >

8 April.

Called on Sologub at one. < . . . > The first thing he talked about was Shevchenko. "Shevchenko was a boor and an ignoramus. A crude man. All his satires fall flat, they've no bite, they're too long. He had no knowledge of the human soul; he didn't understand himself or others or nature.

Compare him with Mistral. Mistral has so many plants and flowers and the like. All Shevchenko has are roses and two or three more. Shevchenko saw nothing; he didn't know how to look, but he did know how to sing. He's a boor and an ignoramus, but what a musical instrument!" < . . . >

10 April.

I forget to mention that oddly enough Sologub had very positive things to say about Pioneers and Komsomol members. "Everything that's bad about them comes from age-old Russian traditions, and everything new about them is good. I like what I see in Tsarskoe Selo: discipline, friendship, high spirits—and they know how to work." < . . . >

Sologub also paid me an unexpected compliment: "No one in Russia knows children as you do." Is that true? I don't think so. I know women in the same way, that is, I know instinctively how to behave with them in a given situation, but I'm no good at putting what I think about them into words. I can play with children—romp and walk and talk with them—but I have trouble writing about them without sounding unnatural and affected. Incidentally, I've calculated that I wrote three lines of "Fedora's Misfortune" a day, and some days I worked as many as seven hours. Three lines in seven hours. And even that's not so bad. In fact, though, things happen differently. Once a month I'll suddenly have a blissful day when I write fifty lines with ease and almost no erasures, fifty deft, pithy, ringing lines perfectly conveying the vitality and spirit I'm after—and the next day I'm a failure again, scribbling away, writing absolute rubbish, waiting for "inspiration." And I go on waiting, day in and day out, agonizing, hating myself, but pen in hand, filling page after page with rubbish. Then in two or three weeks I'm suddenly able to come up with something on the basis of that rubbish, *using* that rubbish, as if it were the simplest thing in the world, a joke. [. . .]

13 April.

Isaak Babel was here on Sunday. When I last saw him, he was a red-cheeked student successfully imitating enthusiasm and naïveté. The imitation is harder to accept now, but now as then I believe in him and love him.

"Have you still got the same name and patronymic?" I asked him.

"Yes, but I don't use them."

He had very amusing things to say about his adventures in Kislovodsk, where he'd been sent with Rykov, Kamenev, Zinovyev, and Trotsky. He wears his fame with humor: "Let me tell you a funny thing that happened to me," he says all the time. He complained about the censors' having cut the following sentence of his: "He looked at her the way a girl desiring the discomforts of conception looks at a popular professor." He said that Pyotr Storitsyn was spreading terrible gossip about him, and when he heard that Storitsyn was hard-up he decided to give him ten rubles, but with the following proviso: "Money always comes with strings attached. You can go on saying bad things about me, but only up to a point. Let's settle on that point."

Lida didn't like Babel: "I don't care for famous writers." [. . .]

11 May.

Extraneous circumstances have kept me from writing.

Mura and I went for a walk one Sunday, and she said she was bored with everything around her and wanted to go to "a new country." So I took her past the Summer Garden to Trinity Bridge and told her that a new country began on the other side of the bridge. She set off almost at a run and stared at everything with the greatest of curiosity, feeling *romantic*. < . . . >

13 May.

[. . .] Nestor Kotlyarevsky is dead. < . . . > I went to the funeral service yesterday. It was stuffy and strange. Members of the intelligentsia never used to cross themselves at funeral services—by way of protest. Now they do cross themselves—again by way of protest. When are you going to live for life itself and not for protest? < . . . >
< . . . >

23 May.

Mura found a worm on a willow branch and has fallen in love with it. It's a greenish little creature, and she's put it in a box, where it crawls about and eats leaves. She can't take her eyes off it. When it fell asleep—curled itself up in a leaf and dozed off—she started walking on tiptoes and talking in a whisper. < ... >

Tynyanov was here yesterday and read part of his novel to me. I liked it a lot. < ... > He's struck a wonderful balance between psycho-physiology, history, and fantasy. I told him the opening was weaker than the rest. He agreed and promised to cut it. I walked home with him at ten—the dead of night for me. His study is filled with books: books on the floor, on the couch, on the chairs. All of them full of Kyukhelbeker and *Russkaia starina*, the journal that published him. < ... >

4 June.

< ... > Yesterday Sapir rang to say that Ostretsov the censor had given my Nekrasov the go-ahead and that Kubuch would see to having it published. Can it be? It's too good to be true: publishing about something you love. [...]

Mura in June 1925: "The moment Mama gave birth to me I guessed you were my papa!" < ... >

The day before yesterday we tied a kerchief with two little knots in it around her head. The knots looked like bunny ears, ergo she was a bunny rabbit. Ergo the grass growing around her was cabbage. She immediately invented other rabbits—Twitchytail, Squintyeye, etc.—and started carrying on endless conversations with them. Gradually the dialogues turned rhythmic: the rabbits were speaking in verse. The verse was rhymed, and any rhyme would do. I stopped listening, but suddenly, fifteen minutes later, I heard:

> Up hopped the fairest rabbit I'd e'er seen
> And right behind her . . . magazine.

"Magazine?" I said. Which meant she had to come up with a motivation for the rhyme.

"Magazine," she said with aplomb. "That's a rabbit. He reads magazines, so they call him Magazine." (She paused, then took the myth a bit farther.) "He has insomnia like you. He has trouble sleeping, so he reads magazines at night." Whereupon Magazine joined the rabbit clan and thrived for the rest of the day.

But when we started playing rabbit on the following day, she told me,

"No, there are no rabbits like that. Rabbits never read magazines." And she absolutely refused to go back to the myth. < . . . >

7 July.

A glorious day. Hot. I took the children to the lake. Lida and Boba rowed for two hours. I stripped to the waist. I felt somewhat less depressed. Boba was tan. Lida and I swam for the first time. Everything was glorious. But when we got home, Nadezhda Georgievna handed me a telegram saying I was a grandfather. So that's what caused the constriction in my chest yesterday. I have a granddaughter. I lay down and haven't got up. Strange. I have a granddaughter. So I'm no longer the person I've always felt myself to be, the child with everything ahead of him.
< . . . >

10 July.

There is serenading along the river, a general exhilaration. Even a grandpa like me leaped out of bed with the flush of an eighteen-year-old. Subduing the flesh, I run naked into the garden and—cough, cough, cough—catch cold, so I stretch out in my cabin, my solarium, and commune with the beauty of immortality: the moon, trees bewitched, the breathtaking pattern of the clouds, a bat flying past, a nightingale in the wood, and the wondrous rustlings, swishings, whisperings, quiverings of the wild and magical moonlit night. And even if the devil comes and takes me—touch wood—even if I'm a doddering, tottering old grandpa, I'm happy to be experiencing this night. Life has taken on the proportions of the universe; I can't say whether I'm outside history or prior to it, and for some reason I pictured— no, I can't go on, I'm ashamed. As I write, the birds sing as if they had something interesting to tell. < . . . >

17 July.

[. . .] Lida and I have become close friends. During our intimate evening talks I see more and more clearly the terrible fate she has in store. She has an amazingly noble character that does not bend and can only break. [. . .]

1 August.

Had to go into the city yesterday. Klyachko called me in: my "Chatterbox
Fly" has been banned by Gublit. "The Giant Cockroach" was hanging by
a thread, but they saved it; they couldn't save "The Fly." My most happy-
go-lucky, my most musical, my most successful work has been destroyed
because it mentions a name-day celebration! Comrade Bystrova explained
to me in dulcet tones that the Mosquito is a prince and the Fly a princess.
That really got my dander up. If that's the case, then Karl Marx is a prince
in disguise! I argued with her for an hour, but she stood her ground.
Klyachko came and tried to put pressure on her, but she wouldn't budge.
She even started going on about how the drawings were indecent: the
Mosquito is too close to the fly; they're flirting. As if there were a child so
dissolute as to think salacious thoughts when he sees a mosquito and a fly
close together. < . . . >

6 August.

[. . .] The other day I sent Ostretsov the following letter about "The Fly's
Wedding":

> I have been informed by the Regional Department of Literature that
> the Fly is a princess in disguise and the Mosquito a prince! I hope this
> is meant as a joke, because there are no grounds whatever for such a
> suspicion. It is tantamount to saying that the Crocodile is a Chamberlain
> in disguise and Wash 'Em Clean a Milyukov.
>   I have also been informed that the Fly stands too close to the
> Mosquito in one drawing and that her smile is too coquettish! Maybe
> that is so (the drawings as a whole are abominable!), but luckily co-
> quettish smiles are not particularly dangerous for three-year-olds.
>   There is also an objection to the word *wedding*. That is more serious.
> But let me assure you that the Fly had a civil ceremony. Even civil
> weddings have a ceremony attached. Besides, what does a wedding
> mean to a child? Food, music, and dancing. No child has salacious
> associations with weddings.
>   If you are looking for people in disguise in my book, what is to
> keep you from identifying the spider as a bourgeois in disguise? "The
> repulsive spider is a symbol of the New Economic Policy." I may find
> that every bit as arbitrary, but I will not protest. "The Fly's Wedding"
> is my best work. I expected it to redound to my credit; instead, I'm

being blamed and cruelly punished. Suddenly, without warning, my best book is destroyed, and only six months ago it was passed by the selfsame Regional Department of Literature without undermining the foundations of the Soviet regime.

Some works are trash, others are art. Be strict and uncompromising with the former, but do not destroy the latter just because the word "name-day" happens to appear in one of them. The Soviet regime does not even destroy monuments to the tsars if they are works of art.

I was advised to rewrite "The Fly." I have tried. But every change I make only makes it worse. I spent two years writing it; it cannot be rewritten in a few days. Why rewrite it in the first place? To satisfy arbitrary and biased demands? And who is to prevent the Regional Department of Literature from deciding the next time round that a bedbug is Rasputin in disguise and a bee—Vyrubova?

I should like to give the book a simpler reading: the spider is evil and cruel; it wants to enslave a defenseless fly and would have done her in had it not been for our selfless hero the mosquito. It is a book that promotes hatred for evildoers and despots and sympathy for the underdog. What is harmful about it—even from the point of view of pedagogues who do not understand poetry?

Kornei Chukovsky

< . . . >

11 August.

No aging man of another generation has ever seen as clearly as I that life is passing him by and that no one needs him any longer. The reason why it is so obvious to me is that along with the shift in generation there has been a shift in the social structure. There are different people sailing past the window, different people lying on the beach, and they laugh and dance and kiss differently. It's not only that they're younger; they're different. I try to love them, but can I? [. . .]

15 August.

Night. Summer lightning. Lena, the maid, woke me up at two on the way back from a dance, and I can't get back to sleep. I'm thinking of my trip into town the day before yesterday to talk to Ostretsov. He was drunk. I met him in the street. He was eating an apple. He face was all red and fleshy, and he was wearing a Central Asian skullcap. He claimed not to have received the letter I sent to him via Boba: Sapir never gave it to him. I told him in so many words that he should stop making up stories. "Do you know what people abroad are saying about you? That you've banned *Hamlet*."

"And we will!" he said. "What does a workers' theater need with *Hamlet*?"

I bit my tongue and changed the subject to "The Fly."

"Can't you see?" he said. "It's not a matter of this or that book or one phrase or another. Moscow has simply decided to cut Chukovsky down to size and have him write books with a social purpose. They'll lower the boom on you one way or another. The Regional Department of Literature has received a review of all your children's books showing all your short-comings . . ."

"A review or a memorandum?"

"A review, but . . . of course pretty much like a memorandum."

He promised to help, but I don't have much faith in him. And I'm so disgusted with the whole thing I feel sick. [. . .]

24 August.

[. . .] Tynyanov had breakfast with us. He was all manners and stories.

About Shklovsky. Shklovsky gave Tynyanov a tie. "Here, take it. Yours is awful. Let me tie it for you." Which he did, and off they went to see Jacques Izrailevich. "Yury Nikolaevich," Jacques said after they'd been sitting and talking a while, "I have a tie remarkably like yours." But when he called out to his wife to bring it, Shklovsky said, "Don't bother. It *is* yours."

One day Shklovsky went to Ignatka to see about a payment. When Shklovsky learned Ignatka was to have given the payment to his mother and had failed to do so for six months, he was so furious that he snatched his gold watch from the table and shouted, "I won't give it back till you pay up." [. . .]

About Vengerov. On his death bed he begged Tynyanov and Toma-shevsky, "Talk about the formal method while you're here." [. . .]

Then he recited several of his Heine translations. They were excellent, though he's in trouble as soon as anything the least bit romantic comes up.

Mura loves Pushkin. "He's dead? I'll dig him out of his grave and ask him to write some more. What about Lenin? Is he dead too? What a shame. All the good people are dying."

4 September.

Went into town yesterday. I'd received some new summonses from the tax collector. Ran into Sologub at Gosizdat. He and Fedin and some other writers had been to see Ionov to make arrangements for the festivities at the Academy of Sciences on Saturday. I said one thing they could do to celebrate the two-hundredth anniversary of the Academy was to remove the burden of the title "liberal profession" from the writers' shoulders. Liberal professions are none too respectable in contemporary Russian life. A witness in a court case reported in the press a few days ago turns out to be a colleague of ours:

> Lelya of Kazanskaya Street, a young woman wearing a modest blue suit, answered the question "What do you do for a living?" in a loud, clear voice, even with a certain bravado, "I practice a liberal profession."
> "Which one?"
> "I'm a prostitute."

We need to see to it that we are recognized as at least as useful as shoe-makers, glaziers, and the like. [. . .]

4 November.

Yesenin has come to Petersburg. He is completely and utterly knackered. When I told Tynyanov that Yesenin has a Balmont-like logorrhea, a gra-phomaniacal talent that will dry up any day now, he said, "Right, he's Balmont before Mexico."

My "Crocodile" is still banned. My furniture is still in the hands of the tax collector. I'm still up in the air with Klyachko. My novel *KKK* isn't finished yet. I'm still working on the Nekrasov book. I'm still in bed (anemia), but all these tribulations seem to be on the point of taking care of themselves. The two months preceding the move to the dacha were the worst months in my life: my furniture was carted off with nothing to replace it, I was duped by that scoundrel Klyachko (he never came up with the money he'd promised), I fell ill, Lida fell ill, Boba fell ill, I kept being dunned for the rent, for the taxes—I really don't know how I withstood all the misfortunes coming down on my head.

Now there's a ray of hope. Things seem to be going better. The day before yesterday, Sunday 1 November, I was sitting here with Sapir when suddenly—suddenly there was a ring at the door and a man with a mustache asked to see me. I was frightened. Men with mustaches had brought me all kinds of catastrophes! Well, this one brought me $250 from Lomonosova. To pay for or buy what I have no idea. But I'm saved. < . . . > < . . . >

17 December.

I've just written the words "End of Part Five" in my *Borodulia*. [. . .]

Lying in bed felt good. I gave my study to Kolya during the day and to Boba at night and took over the tiny room where Mura was born for myself, setting up a stool and two tables around my bed and scribbling with a pencil from morning till night. What makes things so difficult is that I can't write a single line off the cuff. I've never known anyone to have such trouble with the technical aspect of writing. I recast each sentence seven or eight times before it even starts to look decent. There isn't a line in *Borodulia* I haven't crossed out. So the way I worked was as follows: I wrote any old thing on random scraps of paper and corrected and reworked it the next day. Then Boba took that messy manuscript and typed it up, I messed it up again, Boba typed it up again, I messed it up again and then had the young lady at *Krasnaia gazeta* type it up. That is why it took me a hundred days to write ninety pages, in other words, less than a page a day of daily and day-long concentrated labor. I am clearly ill. I have inertia of the brain. But what to do about it I have no idea.

25 December.

I'm in bed with influenza. I've had a fever since the twentieth and haven't done a thing. I had two days of work left on *Borodulia* and on the Nekrasov book proofs when suddenly

Infirmity, that hurricane, o'ercame me. [. . .]

When my Gorky book came out last year, there wasn't a review anywhere, though hacks pilfered its ideas right and left in their articles. I'm forced into silence as a critic, because RAPP has taken over criticism and they judge by Party card rather than talent. They've made me a children's writer. But the shameful way they've treated my children's books—the persecution, the mockery, the suppression, and finally the censors' determination to ban them—has forced me to abandon that arena as well. So now I've found a last refuge: a burlesque novel in installments written under a pseudonym. They have forced me—now that I have stopped being a critic and stopped being a poet—to become a novelist. But I, Kornei Chukovsky, am *not* a novelist; I'm a former critic, a former person, and so on. < . . . >

31 December.

I can't get enough of the newspapers, though the Congress holds no surprises for me.[126] Ever since working on Sleptsov and Uspensky I've seen how hard it will be to put a socialist glove on the hand of a petty bourgeois or muzhik. I expected the glove to split, and split it has in many places. But hardheaded geniuses, determined to make mankind happy at any cost, keep tugging away. The human, psychological stakes involved in the fray are immense. And what a tragic turn things have taken: it's the owners of private property who are keeping the country alive, and every one—or practically every one—of its 150,000,000 inhabitants thinks only of *my* chicken, *my* goat, *my* saddle girth, *my* cow or *my* career, *my* business trip, *my* perquisites, and an economy of "consistent socialist" variety is supposed to result. It will, but the opposition of private elements is enormous and makes itself felt every step of the way.

Yesenin is dead.[127] I used to see him at Repin's and Gessen's. Some day I'll write my memoirs of him.

I'm translating *Rain*,[128] and I'm surprised I've taken so long to think of it. It's very powerful. I get caught up in it even as I work on it. My temperature hovers around 37° [Celsius], but it can leap up like a rabbit, and I'm working on my back again the way I did with *Cabbages and Kings.*

126. Reference to the Fourteenth Congress of the Soviet Communist Party, which laid down the policy of industrialization.

127. A muted reference to Sergei Yesenin's suicide. The wayward poet hanged himself in a Leningrad hotel. He left a suicide note in the form of a poem written in his own blood. The poem, "Till We Meet Again, Friend, Till We Meet," closed with the following lines: "In this life there's nothing new to dying / And yet surely living's nothing newer." (V.E.)

128. A play by John Colton based on Somerset Maugham's story "Rain."

Tomorrow is New Year's Day, and if my health continues as it is going I'll never make it to 1927. But this does not matter. I have more the feeling of being *still* in 1926 than of being *already* in 1926. I regard us as ancients. I don't think the true history of mankind will begin until the year 2000. I look upon myself and all my contemporaries as characters in a book, a historical novel set in the long distant past. [. . .]

1926

->->->->->->->->->

24 January.

This Wednesday was a day of catastrophes. They all came down on me at once. This is what happened: *Krasnaia gazeta* decided to start running my novel on 25 January. They wanted me to write a foreword, which I did— a very journalistic, very petulant one—and since I hadn't written any feuilletons for the past eight years I found it all rather perturbing. I took the piece in to Iona Kugel, who found some passages likely to be cut by the censors: irony vis-à-vis the young proletarian poets, pornography (because of the word "member" in a quotation from Dostoevsky!), etc.[129] To make a long story short, I spent five days fiddling with the thing. They said they'd run the foreword on the twentieth. I phone the morning of the twentieth, and Iona says, "Your foreword's the last thing on our minds! The whole paper's in trouble!" So of course I rush down there. Iona's all upset. He didn't sleep all night. Leningrad is apparently in the throes of a paper crisis. There is no newsprint. An emergency commission for reducing paper consumption has been set up, and after closing down one of the evening papers altogether it has decided to limit each paper not to six or eight but to *four* pages! As a result, there's no room for my novel. Publication is postponed indefinitely.

It was a blow, because I was really counting on the twenty-fifth. I was especially disappointed that the foreword wouldn't be coming out. But that wasn't the end of it.

---

129. The word *chlen* (member, limb) appears in a line of verse by the character Lebyadkin in *Demons* (Part Two, Chapter Two): "The beauty of beauties has broken a limb." (M.H.H.)

The same day I got a call from Kubuch telling me that owing to the paper shortage the publication of my *Nekrasov* was postponed indefinitely. I nearly screamed. [. . .]

But even that wasn't the end of it. It turns out the Leningrad Children's Division had sent a list of its projected books to Moscow for approval, and the Moscow Gosizdat crossed off my "White Mouse," not even knowing what it was about. "Just because it's Chukovsky."

So in one day I was kicked out of literature!

What makes it all the worse is that because my works age quickly they are losing their only charm: their novelty. That's how Epokha ruined my *Book About Blok*. I wrote it while Blok was alive, and they let it sit so long in the printer's office that Blok was dead by the time it appeared and books about Blok were crawling out of the woodwork. It will be the same with the Nekrasov. < . . . > My approach to Nekrasov is fresh and new, but who will realize that if the book comes out seven years from now—if it comes out at all. To deal with the depression that came over me, I went back to *Rain* with a vengeance, drugging myself by translating one page after the other. [. . .]

Today Mura spoke on the phone by herself for the first time.

25 January.

< . . . > Boba is now living side by side with me, and I can observe him up close. He's a pure and artless lad and, alas, as much of a workhorse as Lida. But he doesn't work at things that increase his spiritual capital; he works at things as utterly trivial as the school cooperative! [. . .]

Called on Meyerhold a week ago at his invitation. He's filled out a bit; he's finally "grown up" and "satiated." He's lost the hungry look—the eaglet-fallen-from-the-nest look—he used to have. He walks with more confidence, more authority, and the boots he wears, the likes of which I've seen only on Gorky, reach above the knees, the kind of trim, smart felt boots, made specially for bigwigs, that allow you to slip your hand down the top. He greeted me with open arms and called in his wife, who turned out to be Yesenin's wife[130] and who reminded me that Yesenin had intro-

---

130. The actress Zinaida Raikh, wife of the noted stage and film director Vsevolod Meyerhold, was previously married to Sergei Yesenin.

duced me to her when he was giving a "recital" at the Tenishev School. I don't remember. The Meyerholds apparently know my children's books by heart, and when I told them about my misadventures with the censors he said, "Why didn't you write to me? I'd have had a talk with Rykov and he would have settled everything in no time."

Meyerhold had come to look over the Leningrad crop of writers and to commission plays. He commissioned plays from Fedin and Slonimsky but not Zoshchenko. Zoshchenko (whom Meyerhold very much admires as a writer) refused to talk to him or even make his acquaintance, pleading illness. I was so upset that I went to see him immediately, and he is, in fact, in a bad way. He is living all alone at the House of the Arts, shut off from the world, long-faced. His wife is living elsewhere; he hasn't been to see her for several days. He cooks for himself on a kerosene stove, does all his own housework, and looks upon everything with a jaundiced eye. "What good is my 'fame'? It's nothing but a burden! People keep phoning, writing letters! What for? The letters have to be answered. It's such a bore!" He's about to go off on a tour of the provinces—Moscow, Kiev, Odessa (I believe)—to give readings of his stories (he'll be accompanied by either Larisa Reisner or Seifullina). He thinks of it as sheer torture. I suggested he come and spend the winter with us at the Sestroretsk Spa, and he accepted with great enthusiasm. [. . .]

27 January.

Had a visit yesterday from Golichnikov of the Comedy Theater. When I gave him my translation of *Rain*, he said in passing, "Did you know there's a similar play with the title *Cloud Burst*? It's been translated and even published."

Unfortunately, it's not a "similar" play; it's one and the same. Alas and alack! Another piece of work gone to the devil! < . . . >

28 January.

Received the first 272 pages of the Nekrasov to proofread. Tikhonov has arrived from Moscow and is staying at the Hotel Europe. I have to see him about "The Crocodile." I also have to go to the Tax Bureau. Damn all these "petty daily nuisances."

29 January.

[. . .] I'm editing Kolya's translation of the play *The Apostles*. It's abominable: he translates *slate* [aspidnaia doska] as *salfetka* [table napkin] and *snore* [khrapet'] as *fyrkat'* [snort]. I'm going to have to redo large chunks of it.

1 February.

Called on Tikhonov again. Read him excerpts from *Borodulia*. "Shallow and thin" was his response, and I had to agree. [. . .]

17 February.

Things have been going so badly that I haven't felt like entering them in the diary. It would be like reopening the wounds and reliving what I want to forget. I had five works ready to go, and each has ended in a catastrophe.

   1) *Borodulia.* The very day the first installment was due to appear, the length of *Krasnaia gazeta* was halved. The first and second installments were set and are now hanging on my wall—from a nail.

   2) "The Crocodile." It is no longer available. At the Zemlia i fabrika and Gosizdat Houses I've heard bookshop salesmen say they're sick and tired of customers asking them for "The Crocodile." But Tikhonov left without allotting the paper.

   3) *A Book About Nekrasov* is growing old and out of date, but Kubuch has no funds, so it can't come out. And if that weren't enough . . .

   4) *Sadie*,[131] a play I translated, practically did me in. Here is what happened. Nadezhdin approved it, and Granovskaya consented to play the leading role. I was thrilled. It was scheduled to open on the twenty-sixth and there would be at least thirty performances. But it was not to be. The posters were up, Levin was working on the sets, I had been offered a two-hundred-ruble advance when somebody discovered the play was about to open in another translation at the Academic Theater! I was so upset and depressed I felt sick. I was in desperate need of those two hundred rubles—

---

131. The alternate title of Colton's *Rain*. (M.H.H.)

I wanted to buy Marya Borisovna a coat. [. . .] To forget my misfortunes, I translated *The Apostles* with Kolya and submitted it to the Bolshoi Dramatic Theater and started work on an article in defense of the fairy tale. But after going to the Pedagogical Institute and talking to Lilina and reading up on the topic, I realized I was only in for more misfortune, because the petty bureaucrat mentality reigning at RAPP has decreed fairy tales to be harmful.

Such was the fifth blow that I, a déclassé intellectual, received from a regime which, though still in its formative years, has no need for me. The most annoying thing is that none of them is definitive, that there is a ray of hope attached to each, so I am doomed to make the daily rounds from Kubuch to Gosizdat (in connection with "The Crocodile") to Glavprosvet (in connection with the play) and back to Kubuch and Gosizdat.

The unrelieved misery of it all dulls the sensibilities. I feel life passing me by. I look at myself and say ruefully, "Another writer who thought writing and publishing possible in Russia and therefore spends all his time going from office to office, pours out his life's blood, sleeps on the pavement, dies . . ." For the Nekrasov book to come out I had to go to Kubuch *every day* and keep track of whether the paper had arrived, make sure it didn't go for something else, etc. For the play I had to go and see Avlov in Repertory and so on *every day*. The reason I don't get to my diary is that these travels (in officeland) are more arduous than the travels of Shackleton, Stanley, and Magellan put together. [. . .]

I'm beginning to understand why people drown their sorrows, but I'll go on fighting for the right to create cultural values. In the current situation one tenth of one's energy goes to creative activity and nine tenths to defending the right to create. I went to see Yulia Fausek the other day. She told me that her Montessori system is under attack again: they won't give her funds to maintain the school. She had to sell a piano to pay her employees. It's the only way to do things; anything less is hackwork, prostitution of the spirit, death. Only by fighting can you get results: Kubuch will in fact start printing my *Nekrasov* in a few days; Tikhonov did in fact come up with the paper for "The Crocodile"; Paparigopulo phoned last night to say we've been given the go-ahead for *Sadie* in spite of everything. And even though I still don't believe all these beautiful dreams will come true, I feel relieved enough to go back to my diary.
< . . . >

18 February.

Went to the pictures yesterday with Marya Borisovna for the first time in ages and saw Pat and Patachon.[132] It was wonderful—suave and human. [. . .]

Went to see Bystrova and got her to restore a chunk of text cut by the censor. Went to the Tax Bureau. Went to the Bolshoi twice in connection with *The Apostles.* < . . . > I'm also trying to come up with the document that will exempt me from paying two hundred rubles rent. Oh, what a bore! [. . .]

19 February.

Yesterday was a black day. Nothing to recommend it. Felt rotten, had a pain in my eyes, couldn't sleep, read *Not at Night,* a collection of asinine English horror stories.

Now I'm reading *Juno and the Paycock.* < . . . > I've decided to translate it.

An incident from my childhood has suddenly come back to me, one I'd never thought of before. I liked to play truant. I would put on my satchel and instead of going to school I would go to Alexandrovsky Park. It's a foggy day—it must be October. There's a big pit in the park, and down in the pit the fog is more concentrated. I'm sitting there reading Ovid, and the *rhythm* of it moves me to tears. < . . . >

22 February.

I hope this diary isn't going to turn into a list of my failures! It began with the post office. I went there to pick up a doll Lomonosova had sent Murka. I found a crowd of a hundred or so piled up in the back right-hand corner at five or six windows watching the slow, clumsy people behind the bars open all the miserable, pitiful parcels and weigh each rag on their scales. I waited about three and a half hours! To get the doll. But I didn't get it. When they opened the box it was in, they saw the doll had a lace ribbon in its hair, and lace is subject to horrendous duty: for one small doll they

132. Pat and Patachon were a Danish comedy team (their real names were Harald Madsen and Carl Schenstrøm) featured in a series of films popular during the twenties and thirties throughout Europe and America. (In America they were known as Long and Short.) (M.H.H.)

wanted twenty-five rubles. I cursed and went home, and the doll stayed at the post office.

24 February.

Went back to the post office yesterday and got the doll for twenty-five rubles and fifty-seven kopecks. < ... >

26 February.

< ... > Yesterday Iona offered to make me the American correspondent for *Krasnaia gazeta*. Four hundred rubles a month for eight articles. I said I'd think it over. When I got home, Lida said to me, "I dreamt you were in America." I was astounded.

Phoned Gosizdat and learned that "The Crocodile" is now in pages and has been sent to me for proofreading.

Then phoned Kubuch and what I learned practically made me faint: "It has been decided not to publish your *Nekrasov*."

"What do you mean?"

"The Kubuch board have found it unsuitable."

I was terribly upset and rushed over to *Krasnaia gazeta* for advice. Iona said he'd try to find me another publisher. Mak advised me to ask Bukharin. I rushed back to Kubuch—on foot, I was low on funds—but they had all gone. Still terribly distressed, I went to see Neradovsky at the Russian Museum, and there I realized the enormous influence art can have on a person. First we walked through rooms hung with Vrubels, Serovs, and Nesterovs; then suddenly he moved a wall and we entered a magnificent room of old portraits with a long table and fantastically beautiful chairs. I don't know what style they were, but their sense of proportion, their harmony, balance, and austerity suddenly calmed me. I even felt ashamed of having been so dismayed and overwrought. [...]

Having settled with Neradovsky that my lecture would take place on the 17th, I left calm and collected for Kubuch. I was so calm that instead of waving my arms and screaming when I went into the office of Comrade Kuznetsov, Kubuch's executive secretary and the man who held the fate of my *Nekrasov* in his hands, I simply sat down, took out my lunch, and ate it slowly while he talked to other people who had come to see him. My first impression of the place was that it felt like a police station: smoky, official, and uncomfortable, especially compared with the museum. But after observing Kuznetsov in action, I came to like him. He gave clear, simple, sensible answers to everyone, spoke well on the telephone, seemed to know what he was talking about, and showed no trace of boorishness. I had a perfectly straightforward talk with him. I told him that I'd been working on the book for eight years, that it was not a piece of hackwork, that I was willing to forgo royalties, etc. "Your book," he said, "is the only one we felt sorry about destroying. Our predecessors left us with a number of worthless books. We paid 12,500 rubles for them and can't publish a single one. That puts a great strain on our budget. But if you are willing to give up your royalties, we will consent to publish it." I nearly cried for joy. < . . . >

1 March.

The last two days have been graced by the presence of Olga Ieronimovna Kapitsa. On Saturday I attended her lecture on children's folklore at the Writers' Union. It was a banal lecture and uninteresting. She used the traditional classification of folklore based entirely on content. Not a word about the form of the remarkable verse. Besides, the examples were chosen at random and were not the most expressive; the variants were bad. She spoke with enthusiasm, but it seemed unfounded and was not catching. The talk went on for about two hours in a poorly heated and poorly lit room with a parody of a poster—"Comrade Writers, Unite!"—on the wall. But an outsider might well have thought it was the Old Ladies' Almshouse rather than the Writers' Union, because all the seats were occupied by boring, half-dead, sheep-like biddies who were as far removed from liter-ature, creativity, or any ideas whatever as Alexandra Tutinas or Klyachko. No matter what you said to those living corpses, they would sit there like bumps on a log. And sure enough, when Vera Pavlovna Kalitskaya asked after the lecture, "Are there any questions?" there were no questions. It had made no impression on any of them. [. . .]

Had a letter from Tikhonov yesterday saying that everybody at the Art Theater likes my *Sadie*, but they can't put it on because Mikhail Chekhov opposes it (on religious grounds). < . . . >

3 March.

Mura: Papa, I have something to tell you, but I'm ashamed to. It's a big secret. (Running around the room, excited.) I won't tell you for anything. I can't! I can't! No, I will. But let me whisper it. Put your ear next to my mouth. (Blushing with excitement.) You're a great writer!

I told her there was only one great writer now, and he was Maxim Gorky, and she seemed pleased to learn that I wasn't a famous writer.

"Oh, how freezy it is," she says playfully. "That's a children's word. Write it down." (Marya Borisovna has read her my article on children's words.)

"You mean you think you're a child? Why, you're all of six." And so on.

Saw Babel the day before yesterday at *Krasnaia gazeta*. He was picking up a three-hundred-ruble advance from Iona. He was nice to me, as always. < . . . > He still has that nice Jewish-student face. A combination of cynicism and lyricism. "Oh, I see you've got your lunch in your briefcase. It's probably God awful. Let's go to the Hotel Europe and I'll treat you to a real meal." But I never did get my meal, because Babel ran into the State Bank to wire his wife in Paris a hundred rubles. "I'll only be a minute," he said, but half an hour later he ran out saying, "Not ready yet. The red tape!" and dragged me in. I took my lunch out of my briefcase and had a bite or two while Babel stood waiting. "Sorry, but I took you for a ride," he said to me after we left the bank. "I had two wires to send, not one. One to my wife in Paris, the other to my sister in Brussels."

All dimples. [. . .]

7 March.

< . . . > The day before yesterday I met the "lady fair,"[133] Lyubov Dmitrievna Blok, on the stairs of Gosizdat. She is working there as a proofreader. A big, podgy, forty-five-year-old woman, she had come out onto the landing for a smoke. She is slit-eyed. She wears her hair banged. She was chatting with the other proofreaders.

"Have you been working here long?"

---

133. The idealized heroine of Blok's first major lyrical cycle, "Verses About the Lady Fair." For a while he cast his real-life love object, Lyubov Mendeleeva, in an equally exalted role. (V.E.)

"Very long."

"Who got you the job? Belitsky?"

"No, Rykov. Rykov wrote to Lunacharsky, Lunacharsky to Gekht, and for a while I had no more worries. In the summer I earned as much as two hundred rubles a month. But now that we've merged with Moscow I'm down to half that amount."

One would never know she had been "immortalized in verse," and nothing about the conditions in which she lives would promote any such nonsense. [. . .]

Yesterday I received a note from Krug Publishing House informing me that "The Crocodile" has been passed by the Glavlit censors. I was over-joyed, though the note has no official stamp and is signed by Voronsky (an editor at Krug). The Nekrasov book seems to be on the right track as well: it will go to press tomorrow.

The Tax Office tells me I not only paid my 1924–25 taxes but overpaid by thirty-six rubles. The thirty-six rubles will be applied to my 1925–26 taxes.

In other words, my problems are gradually taking care of themselves. It feels odd not to have a wall to beat my head against. [. . .]

I am reading Bühler's *Spiritual Development of the Child*. It is systematic in its Germanic way, but a far cry from the wise and gifted Sully. < . . . >

10 March.

My hands are still trembling. I've just unmasked Ruvim Lazarevich Mel-man, Klyachko's right-hand man. He's been leading me on for two weeks now, the rotter, promising day after day the money he owes me. That Raduga scum is exploiting me with might and main. Klyachko has grown so brazen-faced as to answer my "Hello" on the phone with "Yes, yes," in other words, "Get on with it, will you."

Melman promised me thirty rubles yesterday. Without it I can't pay my Writers' Union dues and get the document I so urgently need. I rang him at Raduga today, and when they learned who was speaking they said, "He's gone home." So I asked Lida to phone and say she was from the State Bank. Suddenly he was back in the office.

"Chukovsky speaking," I screamed, "the man you weren't in for just now. Don't lie," and hung up.

That is how my day began. It got much worse. "As the reader will recall," Tikhonov arranged for my "Crocodile" to pass the Moscow censors. < . . . > I made the changes they required and received a "note" from Tikhonov in Moscow on Glavlit stationery stating the work had been "passed by the censors." Signed Voronsky. I was jubilant. All I had to do was trade the Glavlit note for a Gublit note and everything would be fine. I went to the Regional Department. Karpov looked at the note and laughed. "Where's the stamp?" he asked. There was no stamp. So it was invalid.

"Let us look over the book," said Bystrova (with great sympathy). "We can look it over by Saturday."

They can look it over, but they'll ban it. *I know it for a fact.* That is, they'll cut a number of important passages and my **ordeal**—getting Bystrova to reinstate them—will commence.

< . . . > Called on Klyachko in the evening. He was wearing round (American) spectacles and laying out a peaceful game of patience. The room, furnished "luxuriously," was lit *a giorno* though there was no one else in it. He pretended not to hear my request for money and told me jokes—dirty jokes—about Russian prostitutes, whose way of life he has studied in detail. And about censorship, with which he is equally well acquainted. < . . . >

14 March.

Went to Gublit yesterday morning to see about "The Crocodile." Looking at the sign on the door, I realized it should be called the Ruinous Department of Literature! Yet nothing was ruined. On the contrary. "The Crocodile" got through without a scratch. I was sorry to have been so nervous the past two days. < . . . >

17 March.

< . . . > Went to see Tynyanov on Sunday. The dear man read me excerpts from his new novel *The Death of Griboedov*.[134] They were well written— too well written. He overdoes the archaic style. There isn't a line left unstylized. The result is overly concentrated, lacking in inner truth, smack-

---

134. The novel, a re-creation of the plight of the remarkable early nineteenth-century playwright and diplomat Alexander Griboedov, eventually appeared as *The Death of Vazir Mukhtar* (1927–28). It has been translated into English under the title *Death and Diplomacy in Persia*. (M.H.H.)

ing of "literature." I told him so, and he agreed and said he would rework it. [. . .]

Then something happened that still rankles. We were talking about Kyukhelbeker, and I mentioned that Kubuch had offered me three hundred rubles to edit his *Kyukhlya,* which I of course refused: I think the three hundred rubles should go to him. But he said, "Oh no! I think it should go to you. You did such a thorough job, especially on that one chapter . . ."

I don't know why, but that hurt me. How could I take money from a writer I loved for having read his work and made a few friendly remarks about his (very minor) failings. And I burst into tears like a perfect idiot. He threw his arms around me and kissed me. < . . . >

24 March.

< . . . > "The Crocodile" is in press, but wouldn't you know that some control commission or other has called attention to its subversive nature, obviously on the basis of a denunciation. It has caused a big scandal, and they've pulled the book from the printing press, compiled a report, and so on. They'd somehow got the idea I still needed permission from Gublit, and when it came out I had permission from both Gublit and Glavlit they decided to give them both a good dressing-down.

Things are even worse with the Nekrasov. < . . . > All my hopes that the book would come out before summer were in vain. And summer publication for a book like that is disastrous. Those swine, those petty bureaucrats, sitting on our literature, smothering it, thwarting it at every turn, wearing us to a frazzle, making us graybeards at forty. [. . .]

29 March.

< . . . > Called on Koni, who told me some anecdotes I hadn't heard before, anecdotes about Nicholas I and his decrees. One of them goes like this. A Russian officer had taken up with a Frenchwoman, and she wanted him to marry her. They went to a church, where a wedding took place. Everything was as it should be: the bride was given flowers, and so on. Two years later it came out that the officer had deceived her, that it had been an ordinary service, not a wedding, which meant the Frenchwoman's children were illegitimate. She took him to court, but the court hadn't the right to legitimate the children or force the officer into marriage. The case

reached the Tsar, who resolved it by decreeing the "service to have been a wedding."

The second anecdote was about a drunken peasant who was using foul language in a tavern. "Can't you see there's a portrait of the Tsar hanging here?" he was told, and he replied, "I don't give a damn." So they arrested him, charged him with treason, and sentenced him to forced labor. But when the case reached Nicholas, he decreed, "Close the case. Ban my portrait from taverns and tell Nikolai Petrov that if he doesn't give a damn about me I don't give a damn about him." A less than plausible anecdote. [. . .]

1 April.

Today is my birthday.

> Having learned that Universal Library has published several books of my O. Henry translations without considering it necessary to inform me or bothering to send me a single copy, and assuming that this results from an oversight, I suggested that Universal Library pay me an honorarium for the material and requested only thirty rubles per sixteen pages of printed text. A month has now passed, and the editors have not deemed it necessary to respond.
>
> I shall wait for a response and for the requested honorarium until the fifth inst., after which time I shall seek other means of defending my rights as an author.
> Kornei Chukovsky

5 April.

[. . .] I'm under a terrible strain: I've promised the Writers' Union to give a lecture in defense of the fairy tale, I've collected a lot of material, I'm raring to go, and—I can't squeeze a line out of myself. I'll have to go back on my word: shameful as it is, I have no choice. Oh dear, oh dear. There's no other way. [. . .]

"Call her all you like. She won't come!" said Mura, bursting into tears. She meant her fairy. Mura was picking the raisins out of my raisin cake. But I waved the magic wand, and she appeared. "Tell Mura to stop eating my raisins," I said. But not only did she fail to do my bidding; she ate one of my raisins. "What good is your magic wand?" I said and tossed it onto the couch. Mura was terribly hurt.

13 April.

Sadie opens tonight. Why am I so excited? I've no idea. But I didn't shut my eyes all night; I roamed the streets under a magnificent starry sky. I feel closer to the theater. I've caught the bug of excitement from the merry band called the Comedy. < . . . >

Granovskaya is amazing. Ungainly, exhausted, half-dead, her legs pure pain. Hounded, harassed to such an extent she looks as if she'd fall apart the moment she let herself lie down. You can't look at her without thinking "What can bring a person to such a pass?" She rehearses from ten to five, rushes home for a minute, and is back for the performance. She performs every day, every single day. She alone keeps the theater going with her nerves and her personality. [. . .] One feels a colossal sense of observation at work, a penetrating eye that sees all of life as a resource for art. Not that I have any illusions about *Sadie*. < . . . > When Granovskaya leaves the stage, there's nothing to see. < . . . >

And flop it did. No one clapped at the end. It didn't bother me all that much, though I'm sorry it will keep me away from the theater. < . . . >

19 April.

< . . . > The Union of Workers in Education has suddenly hurled all writers overboard, which puts me outside the law. To be a full-fledged citizen, I have to be gainfully employed, and the only gainful employment available to me is at the *Krasnaia gazeta*. It's loathsome work, because what I really want to do is write about children, but I have no choice. So for the past two weeks I've been beating down the doors of their repulsive evening supplement, begging them to take me on at the lowest salary. Kugel would be glad to oblige, but the evening supplement has just initiated an "economy phase." Even though they have shown a net profit of ninety thousand rubles this year, they have decided to cut reporters' fees and abolish the institution of staff writers. At the very time when I need to become just such a staff writer. They're stringing me along, putting me off from day to day, making me cool my heels three and four hours at a time and then promising they'll let me know tomorrow. < . . . >

24 April.

Tinyakov came to see me. He brought a book of his poems and asked me to buy it for a ruble.

"What are you writing these days?" I asked him.

"I'm not writing; I'm begging."

"Begging?"

"That's right. Begging for alms. Liteiny is my beat. I earn about two and a half rubles a day. The only problem is, my legs get cold. I have a sign that says WRITER. If I sat there the whole day, I could earn five rubles. It's a lot better than literature. I've written three articles for *Krasnaia nov'*—one on Nekrasov, one on Yesenin, and another on something else— and they haven't paid me a kopeck. But out there in the street I can keep myself in food and drink."

And in fact he's put on weight. < . . . >

Called on Ben Livshits. Once more he struck me as a man of spiritual purity and total commitment to literature. He can talk about poetry for ten hours running. He feels that if there are any remarkable people in Russia today they are Pasternak, Kuzmin, Mandelshtam, and Konstantin Vaginov. Vaginov in particular. He's even written a manifesto-like article for presentation to the Union of Poets—and he presented it to me. He praises Vaginov for his metaphysical insights. Strange: Livshits is the picture of a middle-aged Jew beginning to fill out, someone you'd think of as a practical person with a head for business, but no, he's been a literary person of the highest order all his life.

We also reminisced about the war, and he said, "Only two of us, Gumilyov and I, took an honorable stance, joining the army and fighting. The rest of them were a bunch of double dealers. Even Blok got a cushy post somewhere. As for Mayakovsky . . . Well, Mayakovsky never summoned anyone to battle."

"Oh yes he did," I objected. "He wasn't always a pacifist. Before writing 'War and Peace,' he would sing the most bellicose songs.

> Our allies the valiant French
> Shoot the *Boches* from trench to trench,
> While our brothers the bold Brits
> Shoot it out with evil Fritz." [. . .]

10 July.

There is an unusual trial under way today. The defendant is a Doctor Lebedev who (along with another doctor) has written a letter to the editor denying that a woman doctor in their hospital was rude to a nurse and made her bring her her coat. As a result of this letter, which is a response to an item that had appeared in the paper, the two doctors are being sued for perjury *even though the letter itself never appeared in the paper*. The paper didn't print the letter, but took its authors to court. Can there be any more monstrous mockery of freedom of the press? I went to see Lebedev last night. He's putting up a good front, but he's a terrible bundle of nerves.

Simultaneous with this hard line, landowners are experiencing a sudden rebirth. It's all NEP's doing. Karnovich, who works as an engineer for the Agricultural Department, has had his dacha returned—a large house over-looking the river (near where Marshak, Lugovoi, and other writers live). Then there is the one belonging to Fride (a former singer), which is so huge you can hardly walk around it, and the one belonging to the Kolbasovs (luxurious!), where the Abramovs' pension is: both have been restored to their owners to turn to good account. They have rented them out and are raking in an enormous income from their capital. Popovka, a magnificent place, is being returned to the Popovs. It is currently a holiday home for workers accommodating more than a hundred people. Once it reverts to the owners, the holiday home will apparently close and the Popovs will return to their family nest. Dmitry Kolbasov says that whenever he saw the Agricultural Department big shots in charge of returning dachas he'd race into town and bring back a sackful of bottled beer so they could sit around in his gazebo and get drunk.

12 July.

I am trying to write a little book called *Porcupines Laughing*, but it hasn't got any oomph to it. I'm in good health and sleeping well at night, but my writing isn't going anywhere.

Dr. Lebedev has been acquitted. What happened is more or less the following. The dental clinic has a dentist by the name of Oppel, a thirty-year-old woman who is perfectly nice and does a good job. But one of the nurses, a certain Katya, took a disliking to her, and this Katya's husband published an article entitled "The Officer's Wife and Unhappy Katyas," in which he naturally wrote that it was time for the "red broom" to sweep clean, that is, get rid of the officer's wife (Madame Oppel) who was bossing his wife around, shouting, "Katya, get me a chair. Katya, get me my coat." He also implied that the care she gave the patients varied according who they were: if you're an ordinary worker, don't go to her. Dr. Lebedev wrote a letter to *Krasnaia pravda* stating that the article didn't correspond to reality, but instead of publishing the letter *Krasnaia pravda* took him to court for "perjury." The trial took place on 15 June, I believe, and Lebedev was acquitted. < . . . >

1927

+>-+>-+>-+>-+>-+>-+>-+>

20 February.

The report on my *Nekrasov* by Lebedev-Polyansky has finally come. It is presumptuous and full of undistinguished caviling, but the main thing is that it ends with the words: "In spite of the above, I must state that this is an important and interesting work. In any event, it deserves to be published." [. . .]

The results are as follows: "An essay based on the Marxist view of literary history is obligatory." Who will write it is clear: Lebedev-Polyansky!

24 February.

Mura is our birthday girl today. I gave her a lotto game, Boba—a set of nesting dolls, Marya Borisovna—dominoes. [. . .]

Mura, Dora, and I went to the Summer Garden. She remembered the bench where we'd seen a centipede—two years ago. They imitated the way "goosies" walk, just as children's dear sweet legs did in 1127, 1327, 1427, 1527, 1627, 1727, 1827 and will go on doing in 2027 and 20027. < . . . >

4 March.

< . . . > Things seem to have sorted themselves out with the Nekrasov edition. Yesterday I signed the twenty-fifth printer's sheet of his poems

over to the printer and delivered all the galley proofs. < . . . > The question now is whether I'll be able to finish my own *Nekrasov*. There are clouds on the horizon once more: Olminsky has come down on me again in *Na literaturnom postu*, calling the 1919 edition everything under the sun.[135] No one has "squelched" him, as the current saying goes. I thought of responding, but I haven't the time. I'd rather spend it on improving the new Nekrasov edition. < . . . >

Spent this morning at Pushkin House. What a pleasant place to work. You're not cramped, they bring you your books instantaneously, there's none of the flurry you find in the Russian Division of the Public Library, where all the employees are exhausted, overworked with myriad demands from the reading room. This year the number of users has increased dramatically. The assistants who deliver material from the stacks are weighed down with books and manuscripts. You feel guilty asking them for anything. [. . .]

26 April.

Called on Tynyanov yesterday. His tiny room is so crammed with bookshelves that they obstruct even the windows. Poor Inna is emaciated—from learning. He was explaining a homework exercise to her when I came in. The couch had all kinds of manuscripts on it—parts of the Griboedov novel, a scholarly article about the evolution of prose fiction, Heine translations. < . . . >

Tynyanov is very happy that the people at *Na literaturnom postu* are beating a retreat and beating the living daylights out of the Marxist critics (see the latest issue). He is enthusiastic about Dos Passos's novel *Manhattan Transfer*. "American literature is flourishing like never before. All the O. Henrys and Jack Londons are starting to seem as old fashioned as Cooper." His enchanting energy, his ready response to everything cultural, his thoughtful forehead and youthful smile—I can see why poor Varkovitskaya has fallen head over heels in love with him. The brilliant things he says about Turgenev! The letters.

135. Mikhail Olminsky, "Kak ispravlen Nekrasov," *Na literaturnom postu* 2 (1927): 30–32.

21 May.

Ivanov-Razumnik came to call yesterday. I have the deepest respect for
him. His spiritual constitution makes him the heir of Belinsky, Dobrolyubov, and the like, that is, of the finest and by now legendary representatives
of the Russian intelligentsia. I know he is living in dire poverty (I also know
he dislikes me heartily), but when I asked him to proofread my *Nekrasov*
and mentioned that Gosizdat would pay him for his pains, he cried out,
"Why should they? Absolutely not! It's a favor to a friend!"

"A favor to a friend" that will take no less than a week!

His clothes are a fright: a tattered overcoat, a dirty, crumpled jacket
(but not rags, no, clothing worn with dignity). His face is gaunt, his hair
still black but very sparse. He is shabby all over, willfully unattractive, yet
everything about him radiates an "inner beauty," and every word he pro-
nounces is permeated with it. It is genuine, modest, and unaffected. He
refused the food and drink I proffered, took a seat, and lighted up (he
smoked the whole time). He knows the seventies inside and out and made
a number of minute points. His voice showed no trace of weakness or
lamentation; on the contrary, it was full of a gleeful curiosity about literature, about things, about Mura's cat, Mura, Chernyshevsky, and, most of
all, Saltykov-Shchedrin, whom he is currently editing for Gosizdat.

Trouble with Nekrasov again: there was a telegram from Frumkina in
Moscow asking for an immediate run of five thousand copies *without my
notes.*

23 May

[. . .] I am starting to feel less positive about Voitolovsky. He has been
appointed censor of my Nekrasov annotations. This is how it goes. Every
morning I go to Red Dawns Street and read him my annotations one after
the other. He sits on his couch and listens. We come to "A Bargain."

"Moved by the misfortune of a young woman forced to sell her
dowry . . ."

"Come now! We can't have that! Dowries are a bourgeois custom.
Wasn't she from a working-class background?"

"No, she wasn't."

"Then we'll cut the part about his being moved."

"I can't . . ."

We argue for half an hour and leave the note as is, but in the course of the discussion I realize he's never read the poem. When I come to a note about how during the Sebastopol campaign Nekrasov longed to go to war, he cries, "That we have to cut! Nekrasov could never have wanted to fight an imperialist war." This time I yield.

The most amazing thing is how ignorant a RAPP literary historian can be. He has never heard of Iakov Butkov, he has never read Nekrasov's best poems, and the only time a work of literature comes alive for him is when the word *worker* comes up or if by wildly stretching a point you can argue it has some connection to a worker, though the worker was for him, who had never seen one much less had anything to do with one, a purely metaphysical substance, something he loved at the bidding of a higher power and worshipped like a god in the name of the future blessings that the Voitolovskys of fifty years ago expected from the equally mystical "people." But faith in the salutary strength of the "people," though likewise idolatrous, was nobler: the blessings it promised were not material, whereas Voitolovsky believes what his bosses tell him to believe and gets a fat salary for it. Back then the believers *went* among the people, to huts teeming with cockroaches, while now they *sit* among their own, in posh flats, paying homage to abstract and transcendental "workers" instead of mingling with them. And ten years from now, of course, a new "teacher" will arise and argue we shouldn't be bowing to the worker, we should be bowing to somebody else—and then people will start bowing to that somebody. After all, as soon as the *obshchina* [traditional Russian commune] and the Russian peasant's penchant for socialism were pronounced myths, all your pseudo-Marxist, quasi-Social Democrat Voitolovskys changed their tune.

14 June.

< . . . > Mura has been ill for ten days. Appendicitis. The first attack lasted a week, and a new one started up two days ago. The causes are unknown. We had two doctors in yesterday, Bichunsky and Bush. They prescribed fasting and ice. She just lies there, thin as a rail, red from the fever (38.5), and sad. But her head is constantly at work.

"I will never marry and for three reasons: 1) I don't want to change my name, 2) having a baby is painful, and 3) I don't want to leave this house."

"So you'd be sorry to leave us?"

"I'd be sorry to leave you . . . and, most of all, Mama."

I read her *Tom Sawyer* and *Huckleberry Finn* and she said, "I like Tom Sawyer better than Huckleberry Finn for *four* reasons . . ."

Everything she says is the result of a long and lonely thought process. She is taking the illness like a hero. Yesterday I was frightened by a ghastly vision: I saw two black women moving stealthily but confidently and quickly in the direction of Mura's room. I was stunned. They turned out to be Tatyana Alexandrovna and Yevgenia Is., but the symbolism of it makes my heart stop. It couldn't have come at a worse time: I've just started some cheery children's verse and need peace of mind.

15 June.

< . . . > Mura is in a terrible state. She has a temperature of 39. She hasn't eaten for ten days. She feels worse. She can't get any weaker. "No more doctors," she says in delirium. < . . . > Yesterday I read her Hector Malot's *Without a Family*. Instead of listening enrapt, she lay there like a corpse. The flies are bothering her. Two doctors, Konukhes and Bush, will come this morning at nine to decide whether to operate. < . . . >

I had a phone call from *Krasnaia gazeta*. Jerome K. Jerome has died. I dictated a statement to them.

By four Mura's temperature was up to 39.2. I brought her some books from Gosizdat: *Little Swiss, Little Dutchmen, Tyoma's Childhood,* and *Prov the Fisherman*. I ate some chopped meat in her room. "Oh, how good that smells," she said. Marya Borisovna has a headache. I'm now going to run through the *Huckleberry Finn* proofs a second time.

The day before yesterday she said, "You're terribly funny, Papa." She no longer has it in her to joke.

16 June.

< . . . > Mura constantly seems on the point of saying, "What makes you look at me like that, all sad and solemn? I'm the Mura I've always been, just plain Mura; nothing special has happened to me."

But she's not the Mura she was. Yesterday I had to pick her up twice. I was horrified. She's so light as to be not thin but *spare;* I've never seen so spare a child. < . . . >

I've bought her two white mice and a terrarium. She immediately fell in love with them and stares at them endlessly, whispering, "If it weren't for those mice, I'd be dead by now."

17 June.

Morning. Five o'clock. I've lost all hope somehow. I no longer chase thoughts of death from my mind; they fill my days and nights. She's still fighting it, but her eyes lose luster by the day. I'm afraid to go into her room now. The human heart isn't made for the kind of grief I feel when I gaze on the former Mura turned into a semi-corpse. < . . . > So as not to talk about the disease gnawing away at her, she talks about the mice: one picked up a wafer in its paws and ate it; the other must have something wrong with it: it isn't drinking its water. And so on.

18 June.

Three o'clock in the morning. I went in to see Mura. Marya Borisovna was crying: "Mura is no more." But Mura woke up and said, "Why are you talking so softly?"

This was the first time Marya Borisovna let herself think that Mura would die. "She has the nose of a corpse," she said. "She's stopped eating entirely."

It's true. I avoid her face so as to keep from crying.

27 June.

Mura is all better. Her temperature is down to 36.6. She's playing with "Thumbelina": she cut a little girl with wings out of paper, put her in a walnut shell, and put the shell in a vat of water; she spends hours looking at her. < . . . >

5 August.

< . . . > Zoshchenko has been to see me twice. He has recovered and is looking handsome. Suddenly you notice his black Ukrainian eyebrows[136]

---

136. Zoshchenko's father was a Ukrainian landowner. (V.E.)

and a calm that has come over his face, as if he had discovered a great truth. And he has, in a book by Jaroslaw Marcinowski entitled *The Struggle for Healthy Nerves*, which he brought me from town. "Fighting disease only causes disease," he preaches in dulcet, ingratiating tones. "Be an idealist, renounce ambition, rise above petty squabbles, and the disease will take care of itself. I've experienced it myself. I feel fine now." He forces a smile. But as the conversation proceeds I can tell that he finds people as repellent as before, that his day-to-day environment turns his stomach as before, that he has reduced his circle of acquaintances to three < . . . >, that he leaves Sestroretsk for town on Sundays to avoid the crowds. On the press: "You'd never believe the world had so many crooks." Everyone who works for *Krasnaia gazeta* is a snake in the grass, even Radlov (who is now the editor of *Begemot*). On Fedin: "Our Rabindranath Tagore. He was terribly insulted when he learned I'd called him that." On L.: "I saw his wife yesterday. Beautiful, but brazen!" On himself: "I was surrounded the last time I was at Sestroretsk, and why? 'There's a man who gets five hundred rubles!' "

I've been reading the book he brought me from town. It's full of truisms in the Christian Science mold, yet Zoshchenko underlines them and jots appreciative notes in the margins. He underlines maxims like: "The road to healing lies within ourselves, in our personal behavior. Our fate is in our own hands," and writes notes like: "Literature should be beautiful as well! (English literature.)"

Called on Lunacharsky yesterday at Sestroretsk. He's staying in the enormous room above the restaurant with three windows facing the sea. He was reclining on the couch when I knocked (barefoot). He'd just finished my book on "the Panaeva woman."[137]

"You certainly are hard on Turgenev!" he said. < . . . >

We moved on to children's books.

He: It's an idiotic policy, but unfortunately I can do nothing about it. Lilina is in charge now . . .

I: And things will get worse, because both Lilina and Natan Vengrov have extreme rightist views on children's literature.

---

137. Avdotya Panaeva, a contemporary of Turgenev's, whose memoirs appeared in 1927 under Chukovsky's editorship.

He: Yes, but now GUS[138] will take over children's literature, and there is some hope it will be more flexible.

I: I'd be surprised.

He: We'll call a meeting in the autumn.

6 August.

Saturday. Zoshchenko came to see me this morning with three of his books: *What the Nightingale Sang, Nervous People,* and *Dear Citizens.* He complained that Gorokhov had distorted the *Nightingale* preface. He clearly wanted to stay and talk about the works, but I was in a hurry to see Lunacharsky, so we set off together. He had many bad things to say about contemporary life, but we both agreed in the end that there was no other way of handling Russians—at least we couldn't come up with anything— and it wasn't the Communists who were to blame for everything, it was the Russian man in the street the Communists wanted to remake. The weather was superb. I was wearing my white suit, Zoshchenko—shoes without socks. We barely managed to squeeze onto the grounds (entrance fee: forty kopecks) and went straight to the restaurant, which was the only way to Lunacharsky's room. Zoshchenko kept insisting he didn't want to come along, but I could tell he was really only timid, and in the end I talked him into it.

"Vsevolod Ivanov says that the reason Lunacharsky is here at the resort is that he wasn't given foreign currency or permission to take Soviet currency abroad. Vsevolod was given permission and took 1500 rubles with him. Vsevolod writes well. Very well. He is the only good writer."

We sighted Lunacharsky the moment we entered the restaurant. He was sitting at a table drinking seltzer water. I introduced him to Zoshchenko, and we went up to his room, he leading the way and not looking back at us. We went in. His assistant started showing him stills from motion picture footage brought from Moscow: "Lunacharsky in his office at the People's Commissariat of Education." Rozenel, a shapely woman with dyed hair, was there too along with a charming little girl, her daughter, and the girl's grandmother. Lunacharsky introduced everybody and

138. GUS, an acronym for State Learned Council, was a methodological center at the People's Commissariat of Education. From the end of 1927 on, no children's book could be published by Gosizdat without being authorized by GUS.

then turned to the girl with the cliché, "Do you know who that is? That's Chukovsky."

So the Chukovsky infection lies deeply rooted in the very family of the People's Commissar who heads the institution fighting Chukovsky's evil influence.

Rozenel: (To me.) I recognized you immediately from Annenkov's portrait. (To Zoshchenko.) But you don't look like any of your portraits . . . What a pity you have so many male roles in your works and not a single female role. What is it you have against us? < . . . >

Lunacharsky then signed a document authorizing Zoshchenko and me to sail along the coast and announced he was going to play billiards with his assistant. < . . . >

Zoshchenko later told me that his wife's brother had been arrested on charges of espionage and that all the supposed espionage consisted of was giving a bed for a night to an acquaintance who then may have turned out to be a spy. His brother-in-law had been exiled to Kem. Someone should intervene on the young man's behalf, he said; he was only twenty. It would make his mother-in-law very happy.

"Why don't *you* intervene?" I asked.

"I'm not good at it."

"Nonsense! Write a petition and send to Komarov or Kirov."

"All right. I'll do it."

But as it turns out, it isn't so easy for him. "I'll think about nothing else for three days, torture myself with having to write the letter, with having taken on the burden of writing it. I'm impossible."

"Remember what Marcinowski said."

"To hell with Marcinowski!"

When we got back to my place, we sat under a tree and he read me his favorite stories—"The Monastery," "Big Matryona," "A Historical Story," "Firewood"—and complained about his publishers: Zemlia i fabrika had paid him only half of what they promised for *Dear Citizens,* Proletarii had cheated him hook, line, and sinker. In the end, he earned only enough to keep working.

Zoshchenko is very cautious I would even say timorous. Ten days ago the children and I went sailing in the sea. It was an intoxicating experience. The sail was rigged by Zhenya Shteinman, a very skillful mechanic. We had a wonderful time, but when we docked we were told that sailing vessels are prohibited by the coast guard. So I wrote a petition in my name and Zoshchenko's asking the coast guard for permission to sail, and Lunacharsky signed it to certify we could be trusted. Then Zoshchenko started thinking and got scared and asked me to cross out his name: he's afraid "something may come of it." It's given him quite a turn. < . . . >

A week ago he told me he was on good terms with a Cheka officer by the name of Agranov. "I was introduced to him in Moscow, and he was apparently so taken with me that he phoned me when he came to Petersburg, and asked me if there was anything he could do for me." When I suggested he ask the officer to intervene, he immediately said that he didn't know Agranov well, that Agranov wasn't likely to do anything, and so on and so forth. I saw fear written all over his face. < . . . >

8 August.

At one o'clock today we received permission from the GPU to sail in the bay here. We rowed out to sea, heading into the wind, and hoisted our sail in the lee of another boat. During the hour it took Zhenya to get the mast and sail ready, we rode the other boat's waves—warm, broad, benevolent waves. Once the sail was up, off we sped—the bliss of it!—straight to Sestroretsk. < . . . >

23 August.

Already. Time flies, and I am doing *absolutely nothing*—neither working nor relaxing. Now I realize I'm not meant to relax; I need the drug of work to keep me from noticing the utter horror of my life. Without it I see all my frenzied flitting from one thing to another. < . . . >

My one and only consolation at this time is Zoshchenko, who often comes and spends whole days with me. He is very worried about his book *What the Nightingale Sang*. He is outraged by a review, published by some idiot in *Izvestiia*, that treats *Nightingale* as a petit bourgeois encomium to petit bourgeois life.[139] In response to the review he has written a hilarious note to the preface for the second edition, claiming that the author of the

---

139. This work consists of a cluster of novellas that reappeared under the deliberately misleading title *Sentimental Tales*. The review in question is "Obyvatel'skii nabat," *Izvestiia* (14 August 1927).

book is in fact Kolenkorov, one of his characters.[140] Since he is so worried about the book, he was very happy when I told him that I read it as poetry, that the amalgamation of styles he achieves with such virtuosity does not prevent me from sensing the work's lofty—biblical—lyrical qualities. He has nothing but scorn for other writers (with the exception of Vsevolod Ivanov). Passing the house where Fedin lives, he said, "They ought to put up a plaque saying 'Fedin lived here.'" Seifullina he calls "a stupid, spiteful peasant woman," Zamyatin "very bad."

It's amazing how old he looks today—he seems to have aged ten years—and the reason, in his own words, is that he's succumbed again to the devil in him. The devil in question consists of a lack of the will to live, a melancholy distancing of himself from the world, an absence of strong desires, and so on. "There is almost nothing I want," he says. "If I felt like, say, going abroad, spending some time in Berlin or Paris, I'd be there in a week. But I can easily picture myself holed up in my hotel room, so repelled by things foreign that I can't move. This summer I wanted to go to Batum. I took the ship, but got only as far as Tuapse (I think) before I turned back out of sheer boredom. The nausea will not let me live or, what is more important, write. I am supposed to be writing a new book, something different from *Sentimental Tales,* life-affirming, full of love for mankind, but before I can start I must remake myself. I must become like a person, like other people.[141] That's why I play the horses, for example. I get excited, it even looks like the real thing, as if I were really excited, and only occasionally do I despond and see it's all a fake. I've studied Gogol's biography and can tell what made him go off his head. I've read a number of medical books and know how to turn myself into the author of a positive, life-affirming book. I have to go into training, and the first step is to disbelieve in my disease. I have a heart defect and used to tell myself, 'That pain—it's your heart, so you can't do this, you can't do that.' Well, just now in Yalta I had an attack, but I said to myself, 'Don't be silly. You're

140. In a facetious and unmistakably parodic preface to *Sentimental Tales,* Zoshchenko draws a distinction between Kolenkorov, whose narrative voice is characterized by "neurasthenia, ideological wavering, gross contradictions and melancholia," and the "real" author, the writer Zoshchenko, who "has left all this far behind and is perfectly free of contradictions at the moment." (V.E.)

141. Zoshchenko's determination to write a life-affirming book was soon to produce a half-novel, half-tract—*Youth Restored* (1933)—dominated by the notion that the scientific management of one's body will enable one to conquer seemingly serious ailments and postpone senescence all but indefinitely. (V.E.)

making it up,' and kept walking as if nothing had happened—and I con-
quered it. I have psychasthenia, and I force myself to pay no attention to
noise and write in an office where there is a racket going on at all times.
I'll even start answering letters soon. God, the letters I get! One man, from
the provinces, offers to be my partner—'I'll do the writing, you'll do the
selling, and we'll share the profits fifty fifty'—and signs his name 'with
Communist greetings.' It would be a good idea to publish a collection of
authentic letters I have received together with brief annotations. It would
make a very funny book."

Zoshchenko had brought the slip of paper on which he'd jotted down
the note to *Nightingale* about Kolenkorov being the author rather than
himself. We started talking about the work, and I read it aloud to him. He
listened and said, "How well you read. It's clear you understand *everything*." I was so nonplussed by his praise that from then on I read terribly.

From my flat we went to Academia Press to look at Blok's letters. They
also showed Zoshchenko the book about him currently in preparation.[142] It
has one article by Shklovsky, another by somebody else, and an introduction
by himself. I read the introduction and wasn't too happy with it: it comes
across as very provocative, and although it's basically accurate it could
cause him needless trouble. Besides, it's very short. I didn't think the name
Karamzinovsky worked; Karamzinsky would have been more precise.
"Right you are!" he said and changed it, but then he thought a bit more
and said, "No, given the style Karamzinovsky is better."

They also told him Zamyatin was writing an article. He was silent the
whole time; he just frowned. When we left the office, he said, "How lucky
you are to be fearless with everybody."

He borrowed my copy of Fet's memoirs. It wasn't a random choice.
He's searching for an explanation of some kind, the answer to a question
of the soul. He's a man very much involved with his soul. < . . . >

Had a letter from Repin. It was upsetting. He is clearly in a bad way.
I felt a new wave of love for him.

Am reading Blok's letters to his family, volume one, and don't feel the
thrill I expected: they show Blok "the fashionable poet," a rich man and
spoiled, indulging his mystique. And they have a fragmentary feel to them,
they don't flow, they lack "juice," as he puts it.

< . . . >

---

142. *Mastera sovremennoi literatury. Mikhail Zoshchenko. Stat'i i materialy* (Leningrad, 1928)
contained contributions by Shklovsky, Vinogradov, and other major critics.

11 September.

[. . .] The dialectics of history: "A base soul emerging from oppression will oppress others." Dostoevsky[143]

< . . . > Went to Gosizdat. They have the corrected version of *Ouch-It-Hurts*. It has been there, awaiting a new edition, since I completed it last summer, and has just gone through censorship with Gorokhov. Gorokhov is the "editor-in-chief" of Lengiz. Handsome, quite smart, long-haired, but long-winded and slimy as a bog. He goes on coquettishly about nothing at all, and what he's implying is: "Even though I'm the boss, the chief censor, I can have a simple, human, man-to-man talk with you. I even crack jokes." He makes a show of being liberal: "Personally, I'm fond of *Ouch-It-Hurts*. I've read it aloud to my son. A fine piece of work, highly original. But as editor-in-chief I cannot recommend it for publication. No, that's out of the question at present. We're going through a hard patch. GUS is in power and we must do as they say."

If they'd accepted *Ouch-It-Hurts*, I'd have had the money I'm so desperately trying to come up with. Dear me! The things I have to waste my heart and soul on!

11 September.

< . . . > I forgot to mention the following about Gosizdat: Galaktionov did such a bad job on my *Nekrasov* that they had to reprint a large section: stanzas in "The Barrel Organ" were reversed, page numbers were wrong, and poems written by Nekrasov were preceded by the heading "Poems Ascribed to Nekrasov." Gessen and Cherkesov mangled my Chronological Index, and Cherkesov managed all by himself to introduce an error on the errata page: "to the Tsar's great joy" for "to the Tsar's great sorrow."

"That's nothing!" Kashtelyan responded impassively to my complaint. "When we were publishing Lenin's works, we vowed not to let a single typo through. We did everything possible. But the Lenin Institute found approximately fifty serious ones, so in all ten thousand copies of the already published books we had to scrape letters out with a knife and print others in!"

---

143. This is Dostoevsky's comment on Foma Opiskin, the ponderous bully at the center of his novella *The Village of Stepanchikovo and Its Inhabitants* (1859).

Of course people used to methods like those will think nothing of making a mess of Nekrasov. [. . .]

13 September.

[. . .] From Academia went to *Krasnaia gazeta* to see Chagin. < . . . > Kuznetsov said with his usual stammer, "I m-m-must t-t-tell you, Pyotr Ivanych, the following, namely, that Radlov and I found that Meyerhold's *Inspector General* had a good deal of mysticism and a blunted satirical sting. It is Gogol of the fifties. He has destroyed the play's social message. We will be writing about this." [. . .]

Called on Slonimsky to pay off my debt. He has his mother-in-law and someone named Anna Nikolaevna staying with him, so he can use the money. He told me the story of his trip to Paris, where his family consists of Zina, a Bolshevik; Minsky, a Bolshevik; his sister, a monarchist; his brother, a counterrevolutionary; Isabella, a counterrevolutionary. Their get-togethers can be very funny, especially as his immortal mother (he immortalized her in *The Lavrovs*) changes sides from one minute to the next depending on her conversation partner. "You should call on Milyukov," she said to Misha. "He's a Communist too."

"Milyukov a Communist?"

"Well, if he's not, he's a sympathizer."

She assured Misha that the slogan "Proletarians of the world, unite" comes from a poem by Minsky. [. . .]

15 September.

Didn't sleep a wink. Am waiting for Lida. The cannons started going off at three in the morning: there was a flood. But the morning is sunny and clear, no wind.

Zoshchenko came to see me yesterday in a sporty yellow leather cap and a light raincoat, all elegance and calm. [. . .]

He has a new book coming out with ZIF. It's called *Who Are You Laughing At?* "People seem to think that I'm not laughing at peasants or workers or Soviet officials, that there's a special Zoshchenko class." [. . .]

20 September.

The Nekrasov book (*Complete Works*) came out four or five days ago. I was not thrilled: it has typos (that are not my fault) and a gray cover reminiscent of the former edition and giving it a calm, official appearance that belies the agitation, the pulsation in the poetry. It's more tombstone than monument, damn it. I wish I hadn't wasted so much time on it. < . . . >

22 September.

Early morning. Boba has tried reading me to sleep with Klyuchevsky's history of the Tatar yoke. I can't shut my eyes. At half past ten I went to the pharmacy and, after begging and pleading for a while, got them to promise me a sleeping draft by half past eleven. I went to Marshak's, but he wasn't in. On the way home I stopped outside a few of the taverns (serving beer) that have sprung up all over. What I saw coming out of them were unhappy people in filthy, tattered clothes, cursing and falling. Sometimes I think this city has more drunk people than sober. "And this is the material they're using to build our Crystal Palace!" says Klyuev, who knows his Dostoevsky backward.[144] < . . . > Yet "everyone has a foreboding of disaster. What kind of disaster isn't clear. Not political or military. Something more grandiose and horrifying."
< . . . >

25 September.

Rozenblyum phoned at eleven a.m. "Your 'Barmalei' has been banned," he said. "Go and see if you can get anywhere with Engel" (the head of Gublit). I did as told. Engel is a man of about thirty-five with a high forehead. "You ought to be ashamed of yourselves, you stupid idiots!" I screamed. "What are these stories I've been hearing?" And so on. He informed me that

---

144. The image first appears in Dostoevsky's travel sketches *Winter Notes on Summer Impressions* (1863) in conjunction with the Great Exhibition of 1851 in London. The building known as the Crystal Palace, meant to exemplify the triumph of Western science and technology, was to Dostoevsky "nothing but the triumph of materialism over the spiritual principle." It recurs in *Notes from Underground* (1864) in the context of a polemic with Chernyshevsky, who extolled it in *What Is to Be Done?* (1863). (V.E.)

Gublit had nothing to do with it: the Social Education division had banned it, finding that while "the book was written in melodious verse," children would not understand its irony. So just because Social Education presumes that children don't understand irony it is obliterating Dobuzhinsky's charming drawings and blithely dismissing a book of verse. Instead of fighting alcoholism, syphilis, and all the horrors of the child corruption so characteristic of our times, Social Education fights books with illustrations by Dobuzhinsky and verse by Chukovsky. And how arbitrary can you be! Nobody said a word against the first three editions; they came out without a hitch. And all at once the fourth edition is subversive. Not only that, Gublit authorized the fourth edition—Noevich has the authorization number—and then retracted it! And on the basis of that authorization (given in camera) Raduga printed several thousand copies of "Barmalei," which are now lying in the basement.

26 September.

Tears come to my eyes every time I read the Shevchenko poem:

> Lulee, lulee, my dear one,
> All night, all day
> You roam the Ukrainian land, my son,
> Cursing us twain.
> Do not—o my boy!—curse your father!
> Leave your wrath unsaid.
> Curse me, your accursèd mother,
> Curse me instead.

I've had the same reaction since childhood. I came upon it looking for some lines from Shevchenko just now, and felt the tears well up. < . . . > < . . . >

11 October.

Called on Tynyanov with Lida yesterday. < . . . > He was reading my *Nekrasov* when we arrived. "Oh what a wonderful poem 'Despondency' is. This is the first time I've read the revised version." He avoids mentioning the notes, though: clearly he doesn't like them. His professorial courtesy requires him to say only pleasant things to a colleague's face.

He read his *Lieutenant Kizhe*.[145] The opening sounds like Leskov, the middle like Gogol, and the end is Dostoevsky. He doesn't quite convey the horror of Kizhe's nonbeing, but his Meletsky and Emperor Paul are marvelous, the language is magnificent, and the work as a whole is a good deal more airy than the Griboedov novel he's slaving away at now. He read me an excerpt from the latter—about how Griboedov was plagued by his own *Wit Works Woe*—the emptiness, the soullessness, the absence of a knack for fertile foolishness.[146] As I see it, the two subjects—Kizhe and Griboedov—are one, and both are about Tynyanov. To some extent he himself is a Kizhe, as is evidenced by his Heine translation: it lacks the "fluid," "lyric," "melodic" qualities that come only to fools. He's got everything else in spades: he is charming in his tiny book-lined flat at his bazaar-stand of a desk amidst pads covered with notes of plans for future works such as novellas about Maiboroda and the dying Heine (Maiboroda is to some extent a Kizhe character too); he is charged with creative energy; he's got thousands of themes in his head; he goes on about Sapir and Nekrasov's influence on Polonsky and the film version of *Poet and Tsar*. ("There's a man by the name of Gardin, a dyed-in-the-wool director type, who doesn't give a damn about Pushkin and is as vulgar as [gap in the original], and I said to him, 'Go and have a look at Mikhailovskoe [Pushkin's estate],' which he did, but the horrors he came back with! 'If Pushkin hobnobbed with bastards like Benkendorf, he was a bastard himself. Why did he stick around a court that only wanted to boot him out?' ") < . . . >

27 October.

< . . . > Have just had a letter from Voronsky. "GUS is now holding up 'The Crocodile,' because starting 1 November all books have to go through GUS." < . . . > And yesterday Gublit put a hold on all my Raduga books, including "The Crocodile." **Oh, bother!** [. . .]

---

145. *Lieutenant Kizhe* (1927) is a satirical novella that later provided the basis for Sergei Prokofiev's comic opera of the same name. Set in the late eighteenth century, it chronicles a nonperson born of a misprint: Lieutenant Kizhe owes his existence to a scribe who neglected to leave a space between "ki," a plural ending, and "zhe," a particle meaning "and." (V.E.)

146. *Wit Works Woe* (1822–24) is Griboedov's classical comedy of manners in verse. (V.E.)

Russian criticism is a disgrace. I made four errors while editing Panaeva, and no one has noticed them, the ignoramuses! All critics can do is write reviews paraphrasing my introduction. Not one has had a thing of his own to say.

30 October.

Going through the children's language letters I'd received in the past year, I came across a very serious one from a woman by the name of Suzanna Eduardovna Lagerkvist-Volfson about her two children, Tulenka and Lilenka. She had interesting things to say about Annenkov, Konashevich, and Chekhonin and appended the following: "Are you really the author of *Borodulia*? How can you waste your talents on such rubbish?" I'd long since meant to pay her a visit and have a look at her children. I found their very names intriguing. Today—it had snowed a bit and the air was pure and brisk—I went to 25 Grechesky Prospect and asked for Suzanna Volfson. The responses were evasive. I rang the bell—the entrance was through a fairly dirty kitchen—and a bald man, hard of hearing, came out to meet me. For a long time he couldn't understand a thing, but in the end he told me that Suzanna Eduardovna had recently thrown herself out of the window and been smashed to death, though the children didn't know yet. I gave the orphans my books. They are very nice (Suzanna was a Frenchwoman), but I've no hope of getting new words from them: their deaf father can't hear what they sing or say. I looked at her picture: she has a demented look. [. . .]

I'm tired, doing nothing; I want to work, but can't. I detest our writers' attitude toward the Revolution. Not one poster designed by the Writers' Union has anything but officially sanctioned content. The very lines, straight and scant, evince official, servile minds, the kind that hang out flags and garlands without inspiration, on command. I went to the House of the Press for a meeting of writers. < . . . > The only ones there were the functionaries, the ones obliged to come. On the other hand, Gosizdat was present in full force: Gosizdat consists of officials who will get it hot and strong if they don't show up, so to save their bread baskets the Brethren of the Bureaucracy called for a world revolution.

< . . . >

Bought some chocolate for Kolya, Lida, and Mura with my last kopecks. Kolya looked as if he were listening to poetry as he ate it.

Called on Zoshchenko in his six-room Sergievskaya Street flat. Black-browed, handsome, and tan, he has just come back from the Caucasus. "As luck would have it, I happened upon a group of writers. I lived in the same boarding house as Tolstoy, Zamyatin, and Tikhonov. What you write about Tolstoy is true: he's a marvelous fool." What about Zamyatin? "He's unhappy. He has a vague feeling his career has ended in smoke, and it plagues him, he can't sleep. We traveled home together and had to draw the curtains at night to keep the light out. He's adapting *Wit Works Woe* for Meyerhold."

"What about you?"

"Oh, I'm fine. I'm organizing my self to live a normal life. One should be able to lead a decent third-rate existence. I purposely took the room next to the servants' quarters in my Moscow hotel so I could practice staying asleep while hearing the bells going off at night. You and Zamyatin never wanted to live like other people. Well, now if I write a poor story I publish it anyway. And I drink vodka. I got home at two yesterday. I was at Jacques Izrailevich's. Jacques has taken a young wife (she's already started making snide remarks about him and will soon have him twisted round her little finger). The other people there were Shklovsky, Tynyanov, and Ei-khenbaum—all Jews; I was the only member of the Orthodox Church. No, that's wrong: Vsevolod Ivanov was there too. It was very boring. Shklovsky has put on weight and looks older. He'd like to write a good book, but he won't. And Vsevolod Ivanov does nothing but drink. As for me, I'm in a normal writing mode, like all healthy people. At eleven in the morning I go to my desk and work until two or three. Oh, what a wonderful story I'm writing now. You have no idea. It will go into the second volume of *Sentimental Tales* along with 'Notes of an Officer.'"

We went outside, and he kept talking with genuine enthusiasm about the story. "I've finished the opening. Did you know that Osip Mandelshtam knows many passages from my stories by heart? Maybe because they're like verse. He recited them to me at Gosizdat. The hero will be Zabezhkin or somebody like him, but the plot. Oh, the plot!"

"What is the plot?" I asked.

"I can't tell you yet, but once it's ready I'll read to you before anybody else." And he went back to the subject of organizing a healthy life: "I exercise daily. I'm boxing." [. . .]

9 November.

Called on Tynyanov yesterday and whom did I find there but Viktor Shklovsky. Tynyanov was embarrassed because he remembered Shklovsky's unkind words about me in *The Third Factory*, so he joked (thinking I wouldn't shake his hand), "Have you met?"

"Of course!" I said, and we greeted each other cordially.

"Your *Panaeva* is doing splendidly in Moscow," Shklovsky said by way of amicable gambit. "People are queuing up for it. And you haven't changed a bit."

"The publishers held on to it for eight years," I said.

"They even took their time putting out your O. Henry," said Tynyanov, echoing Shklovsky's amicability. "And look what a hit it's been."

"But he appears to have lost some of his attraction," I said.

"True," said Tynyanov. "America is publishing boring books nowadays."

"But Yury Nikolaevich," I said reproachfully, "didn't you used to praise American literature?"

"I *am* praising it," he replied. "I love boring books."

From then on the conversation took a more natural turn. Shklovsky has put on weight, but is not flabby. He is gathering material for a book on Lev Tolstoy.[147] "I've convinced Gosizdat that a new book on Tolstoy is essential and that I'm the one to write it." < . . . >

Then we had one of those wonderful talks about literature that flourished during the golden hungry days of Formalism—all quips and aphorisms. "What does Alexei Tolstoy call hackwork? One day he was reading from his boring documentary novel and Kaverin said to him, 'Why have you stopped writing in the way you wrote "Ibicus"—the free-and-easy adventure mode?' And Tolstoy answered, ' "Ibicus" is hackwork and here I'm a serious writer: I've done my homework.' " But that's just the problem: what he considers hackwork is creative work, and the moment he starts doing his homework he creates hackwork. [. . .]

11 November.

Yesterday a butterfly I had long thought dead and simply forgotten to get rid of woke up and flew out of my desk drawer. It is fluttering about still, beating against the frozen windows.

147. Viktor Shklovskii, *Mater'ial i stil' v romane L'va Tolstogo "Voina i mir"* (Moscow, 1928). (V.E.)

The whole family had its picture taken at Nappelbaum's yesterday. It gave me a foot-in-the-grave feeling.

Zilbershtein suddenly announced at Academia that Shilov had a Chernyshevsky letter to Panaeva about her memoirs. I set off immediately, as did he—to buy it for himself. I took a cab; he ran. We burst into the shop at the same moment. I got the letter, but am forty rubles the poorer.

13 November.

Mura kisses her mother. "You might give *me* a kiss now and again!" I said.
"I'm not in the habit of kissing men," she said earnestly. < . . . >

26 November.

< . . . > Mura is giving a loud, uneven reading of *Tom Sawyer* and *Huckleberry Finn* to Lyuba in the kitchen. Boba is reading to me from Klein's *Astronomical Evenings* while fashioning a model boat (he is very handy with an ax and a plane). Lida is writing about Shevchenko. I have found Kolya a job translating *Ackridge* for *Krasnaia gazeta.* I am putting together remarks on Nekrasov for his anniversary celebration. I hope to go to Moscow and sell them: I keep trying to get enough money to relax for a week or two.

I was walking along Nevsky Prospect the day before yesterday when I spied a man in front of a wine shop window, sadly studying the bottles. He seemed familiar. I went up close and saw it was Zoshchenko: dressed to the nines and looking young, handsome, and slightly haughty. "It recently occurred to me," I said to him, "that you are the happiest man in the USSR. You've got youth, talent, beauty—and money. The rest of the population of 150,000,000 should be wildly jealous of you."

"And I'm so depressed," he said mournfully, "that I haven't touched a pen in three weeks. I just lie in bed reading Gogol's letters and can't bear to see a soul."

"How so?" I cried. "Aren't you the one who taught me we have to live 'as others do' and not alienate ourselves from people? Haven't you just moved into a flat, bought a radio? Haven't you proclaimed how good it is to wake up early, do your exercises, and sit at your desk writing delightful works like 'Notes of an Officer'?"

"Yes, I have seven or eight excellent ideas in mind," but it's ages since

I've worked with them. As for people, I run away from them, and if they come and visit me I put on my coat instantly and leave. My wife and I have an agreement that the moment anybody arrives she comes in and says, 'Don't forget, dear. You've got to be on your way.' "

"So you hate everybody? You can't stand a single person?"

"No, there's one person I can stand: Misha Slonimsky. But only if I'm at his place, not if he's at mine."

It was a snowy day, but mild. He had come to Raduga with me and waited while I settled my affairs there. Then I walked him home. He never did buy his wine. On the way he talked about prevailing over his health, organizing it; he was just suffering a temporary setback. I found his high spirits eerie. "Should a writer be kind?" he asked me, and we started examining individual cases: Tolstoy and Dostoevsky were vicious; Chekhov forced himself to be kind; Gogol was a heartless egocentric. There was always Korolenko—but he fizzled out as a poet. "No, kindness does an artist no good," Zoshchenko concluded. "An artist must be indifferent to everything." I could tell he was terribly concerned about the issue. Generally speaking, he thinks of himself as a tool he wants to make the best use of; he sees himself as a machine for the manufacture of good or bad books and takes every possible measure to improve production quality. [. . .]

28 November.

Monday. In Moscow. < . . . > At last I'll learn the fate of my "Crocodile." I rush bleary-eyed to Tikhonov's office, where I find him looking fresh and rejuvenated from his recent stay in the Caucasus, as amiable and blameless as ever.

"Kornei Ivanovich! What brings you here?"

"I've come to learn the fate of my 'Crocodile.' "

"Oh, yes. So sorry, so sorry. GUS won't authorize publication. There's no help for it. We're doing all we can."

It turns out the book has been typeset, but is under review by the GUS textbook division, which purposely takes three months to examine a book so as to wear the author down. < . . . >

I go to see Vengrov. He keeps me waiting a full hour, then comes out and won't look me in the eye. He equivocates and prevaricates. I find him physically repulsive. He is excruciatingly jealous of me: the very mention of my name makes him twitch, and when we talk he summons all his bureaucratic majesty: "As an officer of GUS . . . ," "Krupskaya tells me . . . ," "Pokrovsky and I . . . ," "Under no circumstances can we . . ." All I learn is that my "Crocodile" is currently with Krupskaya.

I go to see Krupskaya. She gives me an amiable reception and tells me that Ilyich [Lenin] himself smiled when he read my "Wash 'Em Clean" to his nephews. I told her that pedagogues are no judges of literature, that the red tape surrounding "The Crocodile" proves they have no firm opinion or established criteria, and that on the basis of mere supposition and individual taste they were doing in a book that had sold half a million copies and was supporting a family of nine.

Krupskaya was scandalized by what I said. She is so far from art, so inveterate a "pedagogue," that my words, the words of a literary man, sounded insolent to her. I later learned she wrote Vengrov a note saying: "I had a visit from Chukovsky, who was insolent with me."

I then went to see Demyan [Bedny]. He promised to do what he could. He is reading Gershenzon's letters to his brother; they get his dander up. He told me that Trotsky has quarreled with Zinovyev and that the opposition is done for. "Have you noticed that the opposition is 1) all Jews and 2) émigrés: Kamenev, Zinovyev, Trotsky. Trotsky will announce any day now, 'I'm going abroad,' but we Russians have nowhere to go. This is our country, our spiritual property."

I went to see the Koltsovs. Dear Lizaveta Nikolaevna and her cook Matryona Nikiforovna danced attendance on me—fed me, had me lie down on the couch, asked me whether I felt like a bath. Lizaveta Nikolaevna, the daughter of an Englishwoman, is very ugly—buck-toothed and skinny— but she dearly loves her **Michael**, Misha Koltsov, and has made him a cozy nest of a flat (Dmitrovka Boulevard) filled with elegant things. He is short, wears round spectacles, has a staid way of talking, and smokes a lot, yet he seems a child playing the grown-up. His face is quite youthful looking, he is actually very young: no more than twenty-nine. Yet there is a four-volume edition of his work coming out, and Academia is publishing a work about him; he is the editor of *Ogonek* and *Smekhach* and one of *Pravda*'s top reporters; he is an intimate of Chicherin's and has just made a grand tour of Europe with a false passport. He is experienced, worldly wise, yet oddly modest. When I saw him and his brother, Yefimov the artist, at the Moscow Art Theater three or four years ago, I failed to recognize them. They were so young and respectful that I thought they must be cub reporters or aspiring writers, and when I finally asked their names, one of them said shyly, "Boris Yefimov" and the other, "Mikhail Koltsov."

It was odd to see Koltsov pacing his study, dictating his feuilletons. You'd think it was a play for children. Especially as there were brightly colored toys on the shelves. He writes with amazing ease, dictating in the presence of others and even talking about unrelated issues the while. [. . .]

Two or three days after my arrival in Moscow I gave a talk at the Institute for Children's Literature (Maly Uspensky Lane). The talk was entitled "Sensical Nonsense." I had a large audience, and once more I saw how shaky and tenuous the opinions of pedagogues can be. Sitting near me was a degenerate-looking girl, Myakina by name, who kept glaring at me. When I finished, she launched into a fiery diatribe (practically weeping with indignation), calling my books poison for proletarian children: all they do is give children insomnia, their rhythm is neurasthenic, they are un-adulterated products of the intelligentsia, and so on. Despite the constant, spite-induced twitches she spoke well; I even admired her passionate con-viction. After the discussion I went up to her and said gently, "You rail against the intelligentsia, yet you're a dyed-in-the-wool member of the intelligentsia. And if you're so against neurasthenic verse, couldn't it be because you yourself have neurasthenic tendencies."

Instead of the objections and insults I anticipated, I got a shake of the head and the following confession: "Yes, you're right. Deep down I'm on your side. I love Blok:

> Little girls and little boys,
> Little candles, willow boughs.

I expect inner revelations from literature. I am a dyed-in-the-wool member of the intelligentsia."

This sudden about-turn is typical of the pedagogues' petty shabbiness. In the discussion nearly all of them caviled about particulars, minutiae while praising the whole. < . . . > In the end, they all pretty much paid me compliments (even Lilina), and what I found before me was no pack of enemies but a flock of well-meaning philistines who know not what they do. They repeat what they've been told, and the moment they go off the track they are lost and talk rubbish. It never occurred to anybody that "Sensical Nonsense"< . . . > refutes the philistine approach pedagogues are now taking to children's literature, that is, it refutes current pedagogical policy with respect to the fairy tale.

A feeling of self-preservation kept me from opening their eyes all the way. I was sweet, even sugary the whole evening. Now I see I was wrong. The past few days have shown the official pedagogues to be more offensive and obtuse than they seemed at the time.

1928

➤-➤-➤-➤-➤-➤-➤-➤

17 January.

What will GUS do with my children's books? Judging by all the GUS reports Raduga receives, GUS consists of benighted blockheads, philistines usurping the name of scholar. < . . . > Their reviews are so arbitrary, provincial, and unconvincing that our worst opinions of them have proved milder than reality. They have no criteria whatever, their only cover being the word "anthropomorphism." If things were so simple and all that needed to be done was to banish anthropomorphism, it could be taken care of by the guard who sits at the entry to the Narkompros. It would be automatic: If an animal talks, out it goes! If an animal wears clothes, out it goes! They think children can't handle anthropomorphic books, whereas in fact they orient children in the universe: anthropomorphism enables children to come to an awareness of reality *on their own.* Now there's a topic for a new article: In Defense of the Fairy Tale. When adults claim that anthropomorphism is distracting, they are thinking of themselves, not of children. Adults do find it distracting; children find it helpful. Subject matter for a short story.

Gave a talk about Gorky at the Central House of the Arts the day before yesterday. The talk was full of irony, but everyone took it for fervor. You can't expect subtlety from a brutish crowd like that.

Saw Slonimsky; he's looking greenish-yellow again. He has a new novel out, *Central Prospect,* with a GPU agent in it. Gublit authorized it, GIZ printed it, and the GPU confiscated it. It's become standard practice:

they're in the process of removing a book by Grabar from the bookshops. That's why Chagin is being extra careful with my *Small Children*, which Gublit authorized on the fifteenth. He's cut a number of passages from the authorized book—"just in case." < . . . >

21 January.

Slonimsky called on me yesterday. His *Central Prospect* has been passed by the censors and he brought me a copy, but he has sinister tales to tell. Glavlit held up Selvinsky's *Notes of a Poet,* then let it through. Grabar's book has been held up as well. They don't hold them up for all that long, but the wait is nerve-racking. They are not even holding up that much, because we have all grown so corrupt—we've all "adapted" so—that we are no longer capable of writing anything unofficial, sincere. "I am now writing one piece for the soul," Misha told me, "a piece that will never be passed by the censors and will end up in my desk drawer, and another, perfectly horrendous, for publication."

[. . .] Slonimsky says that some undesirable books are not distributed on purpose for reasons of political control. He cites Kaverin's *The End of the Gang.* He says the entire stock is being kept in the warehouse so the reader can't get to it. I don't think that's true. *The End of the Gang* might fail to reach the reader for reasons of its own. But what is beyond doubt is that we are in the grips of a censorship the likes of which Russia has never known: every editorial board, every publishing house has its censor, and their goal is a ritualized glorification of officialdom.

Yet even after talking over these topics, we decided we are still Soviet writers, because we can easily imagine a Soviet system in which these delays do not take place. What is more, we are certain it is the Soviet system that will enable us to overcome them. < . . . >

22 January.

Received two copies of the new "Crocodile" from Moscow last night. The paper is bad, and it costs one ruble and fifty kopecks. I don't know what the story is: there was no letter enclosed.

Spent two or three hours at the Pushkin House Manuscript Division looking through Nikolai Uspensky's letters. What a relief from the likes of

Klyachko, Gosizdat, and *Krasnaia gazeta*. [. . .] The patriarchal order has disappeared from Pushkin House, and bureaucratic ways have taken root, but the staff, closely knit by love for their work and long years of service together, still meet over tea. Regulars include Dostoevsky's nephew, Ostrovsky's son, Pypin's son, Stasov's daughter, Annenkov's son, Modzalevsky's son, and so on. They drink delicious tea from beautiful old cups, and they enjoy it in a way we seem incapable of now; they drink their tea "historically," à la Pushkin.

Spent the evening at Academia with Frankovsky, who was shaken by Loks's review of his Proust translation. Frankovsky read out his reply to Loks. It is magnificent. Krolenko and I discussed it, and Krolenko made a number of subtle and practical remarks. "You're doing a fine job," I said to him, "but why don't you pay your authors? Why don't you give me my two hundred rubles?"

"Believe it or not," he replied, as ingenuous as you please, "even though business is booming and our books sell like hotcakes, we haven't a kopeck in our current account: we're in debt up to our ears. We're still paying for our former policy of publishing scholars—Balukhaty and Zhirmunsky. Believe it or not, the publishing house owes *me* two thousand rubles, and I can't get it back for anything." < . . . >

The Soviet regime takes advantage of fanatics like Krolenko. It harasses them, it puts constant obstacles in their way, but in spite of it all they work their heads off. < . . . >

22 January.

Went to get *The Young Tolstoy*[148] from Zoshchenko. He wasn't in, but his wife says he is "a human being again": he goes skating, has guests . . . There is (still!) a Christmas tree in his dining room. < . . . >

I've got a lot on my plate at the moment: I'm writing about Nikolai Uspensky and getting ready to write about Tolstoy and Nekrasov, I've got an assignment to write about Gorky (memoirs for Gruzdev), I want to edit Fet, < . . . > to say nothing of the fairy tale and reworking the second edition of Nekrasov's complete works.

148. The work in question, *Molodoi Tolstoi* (Petrograd, 1922), constitutes the first volume of Eikhenbaum's Tolstoy trilogy, which also includes *Lev Tolstoi* (Leningrad, 1928–31) and *Lev Tolstoi: Semidesiatye gody* (Leningrad, 1960). (M.H.H.)

23 January.

Storm clouds overhead again. Chagin has lost my typeset, copyread *Young Children,* so it can't go to press. < . . . > We've spent twelve days looking for it, and now I'll have to copyread it again. The times I trudged up the stairs to *Krasnaia gazeta* in search of it; the number of morning hours I let it steal from my work! And those dirty swine, they never even helped me.

A two-ruble Nekrasov-minus-notes came out yesterday. It makes me very happy. Lida's Shevchenko novel won't come out in the first issue of *Ezh,* though she doesn't know it yet. I've been given the first proofs and will get to them shortly. The day before yesterday I proofread Kolya's nice book of verse.[149]

Yesterday I handed in my tax statement: I made 9,800 rubles last year, nearly ten thousand, but where did it all go and what pleasure did it give me?

I've now proofread Lida's Shevchenko piece, and once more I see what a fine piece it is. Now I'm getting to work on Kolya's awful translation of *Ackridge.* It's so dull and uninspired that if he weren't my son I'd never do it. I don't know how to explain the dull streak, but he does have one and it comes out most clearly in his translations of comic works, which are void of all sensitivity.

Had a visit from Piskarev yesterday. He's a former foundry worker and sailor with the Baltic Fleet and also a very funny poet with curly hair and a marvelously engaging voice, his favorite phrase being "Cross my heart and hope to die!" He's a follower of Gapon and took part in the 9 January march,[150] but he is so disillusioned with the current political line that he has gone into business for himself: he makes felt. He has his own workshop and earned twenty thousand rubles cash last year. Now he wants to buy a painting by Repin—for two thousand rubles. "Many famous men this path have trod," he tells me.[151]

He also tells me stories about workers returning from abroad firmly

149. *Skvoz' dikii rai* (Through a Wild Paradise) (1928).
150. G. A. Gapon, a politically aware priest, founded a workers association in 1903 not without a certain official encouragement, but when on 9 January 1905 he led a march of workers to the Tsar with a rather provocative petition, the Tsar's troops opened fire on them. The event, which became known as Bloody Sunday, helped to trigger the Revolution of 1905. (V.E.)
151. A line from Nekrasov's poem "A Schoolboy."

convinced that "margarine Communism" is doomed to isolation and that America's "bourgeois" system is superior, of a higher order. I think he's mistaken. I've never seen the workers he's talking about.
< . . . >

1 February.

< . . . > Had a phone call from Marshak in the evening: "I spent four days fighting for you in Moscow, and you refuse to come and see me!" How can I tell him that if I go and see him I can be certain of a sleepless night. But I went, and found him beaming: all his books have been passed by the censor. He made his way swimmingly through the rocks, reefs, and shallows of Moscow officialdom and has returned triumphant, while I— his father, his progenitor—am crushed. Not all my books have gone through the process yet, but "The Muddle," "Piglets," "The Wonder Tree," and "The Slipper" are already murdered. < . . . > In Moscow Marshak learned that his "Yesterday and Today," "Ice Cream," "Little Mouse," and "The Circus" were cut, so he phoned Menzhinskaya at the Kremlin. And Menzhinskaya said to him with her guttural *r,* "Are you the Marshak I met at Stasov's, a student who wrote divine verse?"

"I am. Why have you banned my books? I protest."

"Don't get so excited. Nothing is final."

"And why don't you pass Chukovsky's books?"

"That's a more serious matter. How about coming to see me?"

So Marshak went to the Kremlin and charmed Menzhinskaya, who told him that "Chatterbox Fly" and "Barmalei" (my favorite works) will definitely be cut. They all consider me an odious figure. "*The Poet and the Executioner* did you a lot of harm. They say you belittled Nekrasov in it."
< . . . >

3 February.

[. . .] My current woes:

1) Yevgenyev-Maximov is trying to drag me before the Writers' Union Conflict Committee, and although I have in no way wronged him it will be a long, drawn-out process and cause me many a sleepless night.

2) Out of envy and petty spite Yevgenyev-Maximov has managed to get Gosizdat in Moscow to do a collectively edited complete works of

Nekrasov, thus obliterating the collection I edited and placing everything in Maximov's hands. In other words, eight years of work down the drain.

3) Gosizdat is no longer publishing Chesterton, which means that my translation of *Manalive* will not be reprinted.

But oddly enough, despite all these woes, *I slept*. Vasilyev brought me a pair of high felt boots yesterday; they cost thirty rubles. I'm getting to work on the Gorky memoirs.

I've just been told about the Krupskaya article.[152] Poor me, poor me! So it's poverty again?

I'm writing a response to Krupskaya.[153] My hands are trembling. I can't sit on my chair; I have to lie down. < . . . >

I met Zoshchenko walking along Liteiny. He'd just read my "Friends of the Poet" and said, "It makes me see yet again that you're a good poet." Left-handed compliment though it was, it made me happy. [. . .]

Tynyanov phoned to report that Yevgenyev-Maximov has made a bee-line for Gosizdat to offer his services instead of Chukovsky. ("I warn you I won't work with Chukovsky. I have taken him to court over a matter of honor." And so on.) When Eikhenbaum asked him, "Can you state that he is a bad editor?" he mumbled, "N-no." And the reason he can't is that he's praised my work in reviews. < . . . >

I'm beginning to feel that January 1928 marked a watershed in my life: the Krupskaya article, the new bookshelves Marya Borisovna ordered, serious heart trouble, the onset of a mortal illness. < . . . > I'm taking on new projects and leaving old books and topics behind.

If only my *Small Children* would come out now. It contains an indirect response to all the attacks.

9 February.

Finished my Gorky memoirs yesterday. I wrote them to forget the shock Krupskaya caused me. It worked. I threw myself into it, body and soul— I wrote warmly and lovingly. I gave it one last read and took it to Gosizdat.

---

152. On 1 February 1928 *Pravda* published an article by Lenin's widow, Nadezhda Krupskaya, characterizing "The Crocodile" as "bourgeois muddle." She also took a dim view of Chukovsky's studies of Nekrasov, going so far as to maintain that "Chukovsky hated Nekrasov." As a direct consequence of the article, all Chukovsky's works for children were summarily banned: Krupskaya was head of the GUS Commission on Children's Books at the time.

153. The reply was published only sixty years later in *Detskaia literatura* 5 (1988): 32.

In the Literary Section I found Slonimsky, Varkovitskaya, and, fortunately, Voitolovsky. I was particularly happy to see Voitolovsky because he is 1) so vulgar and 2) so stupid. I needed just such a reader, a representative of the contemporary reading public. If he accepts it, everything will be fine. But he rejected a number of passages, for example, the one where Gorky talks about the harm of preaching endurance. "Gorky couldn't have said that after the Revolution. *Before* the Revolution—that's another story. But now that the Soviet regime has gained a firm hold, we must endure it no matter what."

I crossed the passage out.

"Then you say that Gorky describes Chaliapin giving Tolstoy the triple Easter kiss. That's impossible."

"But it happened. I took it down word for word. From Gorky's mouth."

"Well, cross it out. A great writer like Tolstoy wouldn't clown around like that. Besides, Chaliapin wouldn't dare go up and greet Tolstoy."

I crossed it out.

"Then you write that in 1916 people sent Gorky nooses. Officers! Well, I don't believe it. I was at the front, and I know that to a man they hated the bloodbath."

"How can you say such a thing!" Slonimsky broke in. "I was in the war too, and I know there were many patriots in favor of fighting to the end. Especially among the officers. Besides, I saw the envelope where Gorky kept the nooses the readers of *Letopis'* and *Novaia zhizn'* sent him. Most readers hated him."

"Nonsense! They worshipped him!"

"The readers of *Rech'* and *Russkaia volia,* etc., etc. hated him, I tell you."

"Well, they were rear-guard patriots. At the front everybody worshipped him."

I crossed that passage out.

"Then you write that a noblewoman who came to see Gorky in 1919 was wearing four pounds of silver. There were no such women left."

But Varkovitskaya objected that there were such women, so the passage was saved.

I left Gosizdat with Marshak and Slonimsky, and met Gaik Adonts, the censor, on the way.

"You're a lucky man, Chukovsky!" he said, exultant.

"I am?" I asked innocently.

"A lucky man!"

"What are you talking about?"

"The Krupskaya article."

"Oh, very lucky," I said, and added, "I felt like a birthday boy the day I read it," proving yet again what a past master I am at putting my foot in my mouth. [...]

14 March.

Had a phone call from the Telegraph Agency. "Kornei Ivanovich, we have just received a telephonically transmitted letter written by Gorky, a response to Krupskaya's article about 'The Crocodile' and Nekrasov."[154] I was writing a letter, but after hearing those words I couldn't write another line. I went to see M. in a sort of trance. I didn't feel a weight had been lifted from my shoulders; I felt a new weight had descended on them, one of unbearable happiness. Yes, happiness can be unbearable. < . . . >

Somewhat calmer, I moved on to Gosizdat. There Osip Mandelshtam called me ceremoniously over to a couch and made a marvelous speech about the merits of my Nekrasov book, which he had just finished. He hadn't shaved, and his chin and cheeks were covered with a gray stubble. He has an unnatural way of talking: after every three or four words he says, "Mmm, mmm" or even "Em, em, em," but the words he chooses are so ingenious, so unusual, so profound that his presence aroused in me the feeling I had as a child when the priest came out onto the altar bearing the sacraments. Now that the novel is undergoing a hero crisis, he said, the hero has overflowed the bounds of the novel into my book, mine being a true hero, the kind who suffers, the kind we love, a hero I don't judge by the official criteria novelists use for heroes nowadays. And more in that vein. < . . . >

I went outside and couldn't find a paper, so I set off for *Krasnaia gazeta*, but I bought one for ten kopecks on the way, and there it was—the Gorky letter. Very restrained, the proper tone. Yet for some reason I saw it as a misfortune. < . . . >

154. In a letter to the editor of *Pravda* (14 March 1928), Gorky took issue with Krupskaya's strictures and recalled Lenin's favorable opinion of Chukovsky as a Nekrasov scholar. (According to Gorky, Lenin called Chukovsky's book on Nekrasov "good and sensible.") Gorky's letter halted the baiting of Chukovsky's Nekrasov books and articles, but "the battle over the children's tale" went on for years.

22 March.

< . . . > Went to see Demyan [Bedny]. His study is solid books, from floor to ceiling. There are even bookcases in the middle of the room. It's a magnificent collection with many rare items. "I spend three quarters of what I earn on it." His verdict on the Vyrubova diary: "A forgery! < . . . > I immediately sensed it was written by Olga Nikolaevna Broshniovskaya! I recognized her style. < . . . > She was wrong to make Vyrubova sound so intelligent. Vyrubova was a fool. < . . . > And Olga Nikolaevna is smart enough to write anybody's diary. She's bragging now she has Rasputin's diary! Rasputin, who couldn't even write 'Jesus Christ our Lord' without making a mistake. When the Tsar and his family were shot, all their belongings were thrown into trunks and taken to the Kremlin. The commission set up to look into the contents consisted of Pokrovsky, Sosnovsky, and me, and I found a letter from the Grand Princess Tatyana about how she'd lived with Rasputin."

"What else was in the trunks?"

"Stockings, jewels . . . Many jewels. Notebooks, blank notebooks, with gilt-edged pages, and cigarette holders, unused, ten or so of them. Who took the jewels I don't know, but I so coveted those notebooks and most of all the cigarette holders (no, I didn't take any) that it made me sick, literally, and I had to ask to be excused from the commission."

At that point the telephone rang. "A public debate on 2 April? Thanks, but no, I won't take part. I'll attend, though." It was Meyerhold.

"He's a brave man, that Meyerhold. Have you heard? They threw him out of the auditorium of the State Academy of the Arts the other day. And to their 'Get out!' he responded with Chatsky's closing line in *Wit Works Woe*: 'A carriage. Call me a carriage!' But I can tell you what will get him in the end. Know how much his production of *Wit Works Woe* cost? 135,000 rubles! Quite a sum."

"But the hall is always packed. It will pay for itself before long."

"No it won't. < . . . > When the scandal surrounding the production dies down, the same thing will happen as happened to his *Inspector General:* nobody goes to it, nobody cares. You can't stage *Wit Works Woe* as if it were a Jewish joke: 'So Sophia calls Chatskin on the phone and she says to him she says, "Hello there, Chatskin." ' 'But she can't call Chatskin on the phone. The phone wasn't invented yet.' 'What do you know? If they was rich enough, they had a phone.' Well, that's the whole basis for Meyerhold's production."

Demyan is very good at telling Jewish jokes: he gets the intonation right. < . . . >

When it comes to Gorky, he's quite hostile. "Rumor has it," he said, "that when our ambassador went to Mussolini to get permission for Gorky to enter Italy, Mussolini (a crafty fellow) asked him, 'What does this Gorky write?'

" 'Memoirs.'

" 'Well, if it's memoirs, I give my permission. Anyone who writes memoirs is finished as a writer.' " [. . .]

1 April.

I am forty-six. Need I say more? But instead of sentimentalizing, let me write about my children's books, that is, about the GUS fight over them. Marshak stood up for me. On that fatal Tuesday—in other words, five days ago—we set off bright and early to see Rudneva, a sweet, fragile-looking old woman who has been very sympathetic to my cause, and she advised us to see Epshtein at Narkompros. I'd just got over the grippe. I was green, dead tired from lack of sleep, and listless, and I refused to go, but she said my fate depended on him, so I went. Epshtein—a high official, the head of Sotsvos—turned out to be candid, unceremonious, and liberal. "I can't keep proletarian children from reading 'The Crocodile,' if I give it to my son," he said. "They're no worse than my son."

I gave him the protest the writers had signed,[155] my response to Krupskaya, and (while I was at it) the letter from Nekrasov's sister. The protest so upset him that he went to see Yakovleva, the head of Narkompros. What he said to her I don't know, but it obviously had an impact, because from that moment on things started going right. Marshak went to see Menzhinskaya, who told him to come back in an hour and warned him, "If it's Chukovsky you want to talk about, don't bother. I've already made up my mind," but Rudneva also got him an appointment with Krupskaya. His first impression of Krupskaya was of a total wreck, so he began by talking

155. A number of writers—including Fedin, Forsh, Marshak, Tikhonov, Alexei Tolstoy, and Zoshchenko—wrote to Lunacharsky, the People's Commissar of Education, protesting against the ban on Chukovsky's books for children. Their letter may be found in *Detskaia literatura* 5 (1988): 39.

down to her as befitted her age. Then he realized she had boundless energy and sharp claws. Their conversation went more or less as follows (according to Marshak): he told her that writers were dissatisfied with GUS, that it had turned into a kind of pan-Russian editorial board lacking in knowledge and authority, and that if you want to have a man shot then have him shot by the person who owns the gun. What he said about me was that she had miscalculated: she had meant to make a quiet statement and the whole country took note. She responded that "The Crocodile" was a parody of Nekrasov's "The Unfortunates" (!) rather than Lermontov's "The Novice" and that I was hanging out Nekrasov's dirty laundry by arguing that he had had nine wives.

"Chukovsky wouldn't have devoted fifteen years of his life to Nekrasov if he'd hated him," Marshak said.

"What makes you say that?" she objected in stentorian tones. "We don't love the tsarist regime, yet we've been studying the tsarist archives for ten years."

"The parallel is not entirely valid," said Marshak. "You don't study Beethoven's sonatas out of a hatred for Beethoven."

He then moved on to "The Crocodile," arguing that it was about freeing animals from the yoke.

"You don't expect me to believe that," she replied. "No, you haven't changed my mind about Chukovsky."

Yet she clearly took to Marshak. Shortly after his visit he was deluged by her stooges: once they learned she was favorably disposed toward him, they fawned all over him.

Menzhinskaya immediately treated him differently once she heard he had been to see Krupskaya: she talked to him for a whole hour about me. So by the time the commission reconvened at six o'clock she was 1) intimidated by the rumors about the writers' protest, 2) intimidated by Gorky's letter, and 3) intimidated by the influence my protector Marshak had gained over Krupskaya—and the fate of the works was sealed. Overcoming my illness, I put together a (perfectly civil) statement defending them, and luckily for me < . . . >, as Marshak put it, "Vengrov was absent and the air was cleaner." The battle took place in this clean air. At first the commission's Black Hundreds elements[156] refused to look at the works, but

---

156. The Black Hundreds comprised a group of extreme rightist organizations that emerged after the Revolution of 1905. They had names like the Council of the United Nobility and the League of the Russian People and pursued anti-revolutionary and anti-Semitic policies. Chukov-

they were overruled by the majority. Then they said, "We must go through
everything he has written," but Marshak replied that the affair had been
dragging on for months and it was time to put an end to it. From defendant
Marshak had suddenly become the commission's inspiration. When Menzhinskaya was called away for a phone call, Marshak took over her place as
chairman. With Frumkina's assistance both "The Muddle" and "The Giant
Cockroach" passed muster. The worst fight was over "Chatterbox Fly." It
was called a bourgeois book full of philistine elements: jam, the merchants'
way of life, a wedding, a name-day party, a mosquito dressed in a hussar
uniform . . . But it passed too (though Prushitskaya wrote a dissenting
opinion), as did "Wash 'Em Clean."

Not until "The Wonder Tree" did things grind to a halt. "Many
families have no boots," said a certain Shenkman, "and look at the frivolous
solution Chukovsky offers for so complex a social problem." But the real
reason they banned "The Wonder Tree" was that they had to ban something: it would have been embarrassing to replace a blanket ban with blanket
authorization! Marshak gave the following brief speech at the end of the
"battle for Chukovsky": "I must be frank and tell you I have no sympathy
for the prohibitory activities of your commission. Your reports have been
weak and unconvincing. Your job is to guard the gates of children's literature and keep out rowdies and drunks. It has been decided to
bring Veresaev, Pasternak, Aseev, and Lev Bruni onto the commission."
[. . .]

31 August.

Heard at Gosizdat yesterday morning that Gorky was in town. Incognito,
because this morning's *Krasnaia* had announced his arrival for 3 or 4
September. Marshak and I went to the Hotel Europe to see him. [. . .]

We were called into room number seven, and there he was. He came
up to us in a gray jacket, very informal, all droopy red mustache, and gave
us a warm greeting. (He even kissed Marshak, who told me later that he
kisses like a woman—right on the mouth.) Sitting at a table were 1) Stetsky
(from Propaganda), 2) a tall sullen-looking man (who turned out to be a

---

sky uses the term here and elsewhere figuratively to refer to reactionary, nationalist elements
within the Party, elements opposed to liberal reform. (M.H.H.)

driver), 3) Gorky's son Maxim (balding, well-built), and 4) Gorky himself, on the couch. The table was spread with appetizers, vodka, and wine, and Gorky ate a lot and drank. He talked exclusively to us, Marshak and me (though mostly Marshak, whom he hadn't seen in twenty-two years!). What I recall from their conversation is that Gorky was still in Petersburg when Marshak first went there from Krasnodar to start his career. Marshak had hoped to publish his Blake translations with World Literature, and Gorky had rejected them (because of their mysticism), but now he greeted Marshak as a long-lost friend and launched into a lively tale about how he, Gorky, had fooled everybody and managed to slip into Petersburg without being noticed: he hadn't even been recognized on the train, and there wasn't a soul at the station. "You get sick and tired of it. Every town, every station seems to have the same people waiting, saying the same things in the same words. A peasant woman with a red kerchief and vacant eyes. Horrible! One of them once said, 'Look, comrades! It's Demyan Bedny, the proletarian poet!' So I had to tell her I was rich, not poor. [The pseudonym Bedny means 'poor.'] And somebody corrected her: 'Don't you know your literature, you fool? Bedny is fat and Gorky is skinny.' "

Gorky *is* thin. His shoulders are much narrower than before, but he still has his youthful build: you always have the feeling he's about to leap up and run off somewhere. As usual Maxim takes an ironic stance vis-à-vis his father in public, as if he didn't take his pronouncements seriously and had something funny to say about him. < . . . >

Gorky pointed out that biographical novels like Tynyanov's *Kyukhlya*, novels about great figures and their successes, are appearing all over Europe. He cited dozens of French and German works and even a Spanish one about Tirso de Molina, though he pronounced the author's name as if it were French. He also mentioned Olga Forsh in this connection, then moved on to Zamyatin. "Do you like his 'Attila'?" In other words, he had decided to talk to Petersburg writers about Petersburg literature. He had also adopted a slightly ironic attitude to the ovations he was being given. Scifullina told me he said this to her in Moscow: "Everywhere I go they make me an honorary this or that: I'm an honorary baker, an honorary Pioneer. I'm going to see an insane asylum today, and you watch if they don't make me an honorary lunatic."

He talked about "industrialization" with as much enthusiasm in private as in the papers, but with a large dollop of irony that obliterated the fervor. He seemed uncomfortable in our presence and said things like: "It takes a madman to describe a mammoth undertaking like the Dneprostroy. I mean, building a seaport in the steppes!" You can't tell whether he's saying "what idiots!" or "what heroes!" [. . .]

6 September.

On the way to Kislovodsk. [. . .]

About Gorky. He said to Marshak, "**Our government?** A bunch of do-nothings, card players! You don't catch Briand and Chanteclaire playing cards!" < . . . >

Gorky told the story of a thirteen-year-old made pregnant by a fourteen-year-old schoolboy who was so frightened that he hid her in a shed—that's right, a shed—took her rugs and furniture, and fed her in secret while she swelled. When the whole thing came to light, her mother scolded her for keeping the blessed event to herself. After the birth of a six-pound baby girl mother and father went back to school together.

"But that's the exception rather than the rule," I interposed.

Gorky: "I realize that. I know a penal colony made up of former prostitutes and thieves where the unwritten law is: Hands off your own girls. They're so funny. I had them write autobiographies, and one girl said, 'Slitting the throat of a stranger always shakes me up a little. Maybe you'd like to do it.' "

Somehow the subject of Svyatopolk-Mirsky came up. "What a character he is!" he said. "He doesn't eat, he doesn't drink, all he does is read poetry. French poetry, German poetry, English poetry. He lives and breathes poetry. He's constantly looking for people to read it to."

Then he laid into Merezhkovsky: "He's written an Egyptian novel in which all the Egyptians sound as though they came from Ryazan. It's a riot. We would read four or five pages after lunch for laughs." < . . . >

7 September.

The Ukrainian steppe. A gray, Petersburg sky. I slept tonight. From eight till eleven. And then some. Pumpkin fields. Peasant huts. Poplars. Sunflowers. But unconcealed poverty.

I met an engineer yesterday, a thirty-four-year-old athletic type with

not a hair on his head and the face of a Norwegian. He designs air sleighs
and he's clearly good at it. He's a good storyteller, too—full of fire and get
up and go. He's got a high opinion of himself, and I share it. [. . .]

But what my fellow passenger had to tell me about our industrialization
was horrific rather than funny. He had just come from the Dneprostroi.
Apparently an American company (Clark was the name, I believe) had
offered to build the whole caboodle for X million dollars, and our side said
no, we'd build it ourselves, but brought the Americans in as consultants.
Consultation fees amount to hundreds of thousands of rubles, he says, but
our engineers are too proud to ask for help, so the Americans are playing
tennis and having a grand old time, while construction costs have reached
twice what the Americans had asked for doing the whole thing themselves.
The workers are doing a mediocre job: the good ones are taking their cue
from the bad ones. But the bad ones can't be fired because the local Party
committee won't allow it, the red tape is awful, and so on and so forth. I
listened to him, but didn't believe everything he said: like all gifted people
he is too impressionable. < . . . >

We passed through Tula yesterday. How close Tula landscapes are to
Anna Karenina and *War and Peace*. Looking at them you could be reading
Tolstoy. < . . . >

9 September.

We've arrived. First stop—the Tsekubu [Central Committee for the Improvement of Scholars' Living Conditions]. There are several houses on
the hill, one of which is an enormous dining hall. I immediately find the
tan and blue-eyed Vyacheslav Polonsky, the tall and pleasant Leonid Grossman, < . . . > Stanislavsky, and Kachalov. Stanislavsky didn't recognize
me at first, but when he did he ran after me and gave me a warm welcome.
All the "venerable scholars" worship him with reverential gazes, and I must
say he's made for it. Though more than courteous—amicable, even affectionate—he is not in the least condescending (as is Chaliapin) or servile
(as is Repin); he is majestic and imposing yet on an equal footing with
everyone. The secret of his style will disappear with him, but everyone he
talks to feels blessed. What he said to me was that his six-year-old granddaughter loves my books, that he reads them too, and that he is currently
completing the second volume of *A Life in Art*. Kachalov added the children's word "professoress" to my collection. < . . . > We had a delicious

and filling meal and went off in search of a room. At the Pension Larisa we ran into Alexei Tolstoy. He has lost some weight and looks terrific, but later I learned he'd been spending every night of his month there at the tavern. Our conversation was brief. He said that Pilynak had not been successful, that Talnikov's article had completely done Mayakovsky in[157] and "Mayakovsky would never be the same again," that Nikolai Radlov, who once stayed in the room I was now in, had been robbed of two hundred rubles, etc. Then I walked around (for too long) to get a feel for the place. It made me very tired. At five I went to the station to see off Stanislavsky and Kachalov with the "venerable scholars" and thought to myself for the umpteenth time what past masters the Art Theater crowd were at celebrations and burials, at receiving bouquets, sending congratulatory telegrams, and the like. Stanislavsky must have shaken a hundred hands and had something personal to say to each individual. The touching little scenes might have been staged, for example, the two Armenian shoeshine boys— they looked about eight—who braved the buffers at the last minute to reach the platform where Stanislavsky was standing and give his hand a farewell shake.

Visited the Narzan mineral-water source, then made my way back, with heart palpitations, to bed.

16 September.

Went to see the "Temple of the Air." Sunny and windy. Got a sunburn on my nose. Tikhonov was there when I got back. He'd been given a basement room. He told me that Vasilchenko, the editor of *Pisatel' i chitatel'*, had been dismissed for writing a lampoon of a novel featuring Rykov, Stalin, et al. < . . . >

Tikhonov had traveled from Nizhni Novogorod to Astrakhan. He says Russia looks awful: it's all beggars, benighted and forlorn. He had intended to get off at Tsaritsyn, but when he saw the crowd standing on the pier he couldn't bring himself to do it.

157. The critic Talnikov brands Mayakovsky's poem "My Discovery of America" "a narrative in his characteristic vulgar, brash, gazetteer-like tone" and—quoting the Constructivist poet Ilya Selvinsky—"a polka-dot drum à la LEF" ("Literary Notes," *Krasnaia nov'* 8 [1928]). Mayakovsky protested to the journal's editors in the following terms: "I am amazed by the brash tone of the all but illiterate people who write for *Krasnaia nov'* under the pen name 'Talnikov.'" He also published a versified reply to Talnikov in the newspaper *Chitatel' i pisatel'* 36 (1928).

Gorky is in bad hands: Kryuchkov can't advise him on the position to take in various minor matters. (Gorky can handle the major ones himself.) Kryuchkov doesn't know how to deal with the details necessary to put Gorky in a positive light. < . . . >

Tikhonov went off for a game of tennis and returned with Mikhail Koltsov. Koltsov had arrived the day before yesterday in white ducks and a crew cut, full of interesting Moscow news and opinions. He had this to say about a review by Gorky entitled "Two Books":[158] "Gorky doesn't know what an impact his voice has. He has no business writing reviews. A person who is met at the station by the Politburo in full array and has triumphal arches raised wherever he goes should not point out typos in the writings of second-rate authors." < . . . >

"But he loves people who attack him," said Tikhonov.

Koltsov laughed. "That's true. When Bryusov, who'd always hounded Gorky, visited him on Capri and started praising him, Gorky was terribly disappointed: he'd lost a good enemy."

Then we talked about Lili Brik. < . . . > "An intelligent woman like Lili Brik is important," Tikhonov said. "Once, just after he'd come back from America, Mayakovsky started reading her a poem of his and she gave him a line-by-line critique that was so intelligent, so subtle and biting that he burst into tears, threw the poem away, and ran off to Leningrad for three weeks."

Then we talked about Babel. Koltsov: "I remember him in the days just after he'd come to Petersburg with three stories for Zozulya to read. 'Are they publishable?' 'They are.' 'Where?' 'Anywhere.' He took them to Gorky.

"The three of us lived together like brothers. It was during the famine. We would eat nuts and wash them down with tea. Sometimes a tin of sardines turned up and Babel shared it with us fairly. One day Zozulya came up to me and said, 'Peep through the crack and see what Babel is eating.' He was standing there chewing a piece of bread. Later he came out and said, 'Oh youth, youth! I haven't seen a scrap of bread in three days.' And so on." < . . . >

Then we talked about Alexei Tolstoy. All three of us praised his talent,

<hr>

158. The review in question appeared in *Izvestiia* on 11 September 1928. One of the books Gorky reviews was entitled *Writers of the Contemporary Period*.

his character, and his Natalya Vasilyevna, then went our separate ways—
they to their dreams, I to my insomnia.

22 *September.*

The evenings are cold, the days hot. I moved to the Tsekubu today. What
bliss. I have a desk at last, a cupboard for my things. I can work. And I
don't have to see the nasty, sham-sentimental face of that Larisa.

For three days I'd been waiting anxiously for a telegram about Boba,
and today Mikhail Skobko, an engineer, brought me the following telegram
at lunch: ACCEPTED POLYTECHNIC CIVIL ENGINEERING LOVE MAMA. I was
terribly happy. I even cried. Boba has a vast new vista opening before him.
Gone forever is the funny little black-haired boy with the guttural *r*'s . . .
< . . . >

I've just had a visit from four Armenians, one of whom, Avetik Isaakyan,
is a well-known poet. I can't tell you what a nice man he is: modest, quiet,
completely unaffected. He spent a fortnight here without anyone's knowing
who he was. Yet his fame is such that when I mentioned him to our
Armenian barber, he immediately beamed and started reciting his poetry
in Armenian. The shoeshine man had the same reaction: "Avetik! Avetik!"
He has a sad, absent look about him. They say the regime (which pays him
a small pension) won't let him visit his family abroad. I was surprised to
find that he was unable to recite even four lines of his verse in Armenian
when I asked him to: he's forgotten everything. And when we had an
Armenian evening and his poems were read from the podium he just sat
there in the audience, hunched forward, his hands over his face. He refused
to go out on the podium or utter a single word. The Armenians stick so
close together that he had his shoes shined by the Armenian shoeshine
man and his hair cut by the Armenian barber, took the cab with the
Armenian cabby and tea with the Armenian architect Khadzhaev, and so
on and so forth. He seems to have taken a liking to me. He tells me the
Armenian translations of my children's books are very good.

5 *November.*

< . . . > I've met dozens of engineers since I've been here. They all agree:
you can't do a decent job; you can only do what you're told. [. . .] Engineers like Zhdanov, Krug, Kutsky, and Piolunkovsky—famous experts—

tell story after story about the bureaucratization of the industrialization process and how it ties them hand and foot. < . . . >

6 *November.*

Here I am on the marvelous balcony again, coatless, facing the sun. The sky is covered with tiny white clouds, the balcony with poplar leaves. I'm alone. < . . . >

The state of our verse culture has plummeted disastrously! I recited Mandelshtam's magnificent "Rose Muffled in Fur"[159] at V. I. Popov's, and *after that* Mandzhosikha asked me to read Vyatkin's awful, barrel-organ, Nadson-like doggerel! Then Pazukhin read a Balmont poem about fairies that was all banal posturing. And when I yell at them, wracked with anger and anguish, they say I'm neurasthenic. Well, maybe they're right. You can't upbraid people for being banal. [. . .]

10 November.

Approaching Petersburg. Passed through Lyuban. Haven't slept for three nights. Called on Koltsov yesterday in Moscow. Both he and his wife were down with the grippe. She was in bed. He told me the news: LEF has fallen apart because of Shklovsky.[160] Lili criticized Shklovsky at a meeting of the editorial board, and Shklovsky said, "I cannot speak if the mistress of the house interferes in editorial discussions." Lili thought he'd said "housewife" and took offense. That's how it got started.

Chekhov has been banned from *Ogonek*'s supplement. Koltsov went to see Lebedev-Polyansky about it the day before yesterday.

"Hello, there, columnist!" Lebedev said to him.

"Hello, there, bureaucrat!" Koltsov said back.

Koltsov's wife told me there are rumors to the effect that Gorky is behind the effort to keep Chekhov off the pages of *Ogonek*. I don't believe them, though Gorky could say straight out somewhere that "Chekhov is not in keeping with the times."

159. "A rose muffled in fur" is not the opening line of the poem Chukovsky clearly has in mind. It occurs in the second stanza of "the wonderful poem," which begins "A ghostly scene scarcely glimmers" and comes from *Tristia* (1922). (V.E.)

160. LEF (Left Front of the Arts) was a neo-Futurist group launched in 1922 to combine commitment to artistic innovation with blatant political instrumentalism. (V.E.)

"Why isn't [*Nashi dostizheniia* (Our Achievements)] coming out?" I asked Koltsov.

"Because of the paper shortage," he replied.

"Now there's an achievement." [. . .]

Forty-five minutes to Petersburg. I'm all aflutter. I've never been away from the family for so long.

Muromtsev has told me in confidence that Zhdanov has been arrested. There was a call from Pyatigorsk, and he was picked up by a *chekist* and taken to an unknown destination. He is said to be a top-notch worker, to have restored our metal industry; he is to metallurgy what Kutsky is to mechanical engineering. But his ideology smacks of reaction: he's an anti-Semite, spurns the "rabble," and so on. Kutsky is completely different: during the Kishinyov pogrom both his brothers worked with Jewish self-defense; he himself was a Social Democrat, and so on.

All I see through the windows is poverty and dreariness. When I think of the oxen, the maize fields, the splendid haystacks I saw three days ago in the mountains . . .

Muromtsev talks a lot about Bunin. When Bunin writes, he eats no meals: he just ducks into the dining room from his study and munches mechanically on something, then back he goes to write. Day in and day out. He finds the Revolution hateful. He wouldn't last a day under our conditions. [. . .]

1929

➤-➤-➤-➤-➤-➤-➤-➤

2 February.

I feel better. My temperature is down to 36.9. Marshak and Lebedenko came straight from the train. Marshak has gained weight and had a new cap on. He can't decide whether to accept the job of heading children's literature for Moscow and Leningrad. He is asking them to appoint Lebedev as the equivalent dictator of art. He brought his Blake in the suitcase (Gorky has promised to publish it) and, forgetting everything else, held forth passionately on the "Songs of Innocence," which he has translated. He left with his fists clenched, ready for action. < . . . >

Marshak is the kind of person with whom a conversation is always a monologue: he leads the discussion and countenances only modest responses; he is always the one to establish the topic. All in all, he is a **pushing and dominating personality,** and his **push** is colossal. The only topics that can be discussed in his presence are those he finds engaging. He was happy this morning because his old friend Alexinsky from MONO phoned to say he would side with him in the battle for the Marshak line of literature. That means that Kasatkina of the Central Children's Library will submit to him and GUS (or whatever succeeds it) will be in his hands. He's in ecstasy. He read me his new story (about Ireland) over tea, then we carried on enthusiastically about Blake, who really is amazing, and then he went to see Ioffe and Khanin to draw up the conditions for his dictatorship of children's literature. [. . .]

29 September.

Have been away from home for a week, and can't imagine anything more awful than the week in question. I couldn't get a room at the Tsekubu: everything was taken. I had to put up at the desolate Red Dagestan, where the entire staff consisted of an old Tatar porter who reluctantly let me into a cold, damp room and handed me a bunch of keys without indicating which was mine. And so I started trudging to the Tsekubu four times a day—for food. I wouldn't have minded had it not rained the whole week without letup—which made the roads one deep swamp—and had I not left my galoshes at home. My shoes had holes in them, and after each foray I spent *hours* getting them back into shape—scraping the mud off with a knife, wiping them inside and out with cotton wool, changing socks and pulling the wet shoes on over them because I have no others. How I kept from catching pneumonia I'll never know.

The guests are a dreary lot, mostly provincial teachers with cotton wool in their ears and galoshes on their feet. I find their presence oppressive. But then there's Sergei Gorodetsky, who recently lost his son-in-law, Reti the chess player, and whom the press has hauled over the coals for his latest volume, *The Tsar's Candlemas.* I share a table with him and an engineer by the name of Gonzal. This Gonzal, a remnant of the past, recounts his adventures in Nabokovian tones. Most are frivolous and sound like tales from Boccaccio along the lines of: "How a Reluctance to Shave Earned Me a Great Fortune." And suddenly among the stories he told today there was one that nearly made me weep.

Gonzal had two children, a boy and a girl. He loved the boy more. The boy was nine. One day when they were all together, he called the boy "my shining sun."

"And what am I," the girl asked, jealous.

"You're the moon."

Six months passed. Gonzal had been away. Coming home, he made straight for the bedroom to regale the boy with the gifts he had bought. He found the boy dead, lying in state. It was so horrible and unexpected he nearly went out of his mind. And just then his daughter said, "I'm glad he died. Now *I'll* be your sun and not your moon."

She was five at the time.

30 September.

Took my first Narzan bath yesterday. Today the sky is blue for the first time and the sun is out, but it's windy and there are clouds coming from Mount Elbrus again. < . . . > Going in to supper, I found a new fourth at table: Kozlov, the famous traveler. He is sixty or so, but you don't notice his age because he has such a youthful, lively, brilliant way of talking— and never stops: in the space of a quarter of an hour I learned that the foals of a Przewalski horse can be reared only by killing the foal of an ordinary mare and covering the Przewalski-horse foal with the ordinary foal's hide, that the horns of (certain) rams prevent them from eating young grass, and that in Ascania a Caucasian goat, homesick for the mountains, climbed the stairs to a tower and starved to death when the door slammed shut. < . . . >

3 October.

When I asked a doctor here—a healthy specimen from Irkutsk with good teeth—what he was being treated for, he said, "I'm being treated for the 'policy of economy.' Three years ago when we got word of Dzerzhinsky's famous decree,[161] they gathered up the chloroform in all the warehouses

161. On 6–9 April 1926 the Central Committee met to discuss the economic situation. On 20 April *Pravda* featured an article by Felix Dzerzhinsky, "Struggle Against Waste and the Press," calling for draconian measures to counteract the high prices of manufactured goods. "Our current production costs are twice what they were before the war," he wrote. "Superfluous organizations

and distributed it to the hospitals. It was a disaster! After the very first operation I felt nauseous, my hands trembled: I was poisoned."

"What about your patients?"

"Twelve of them died. Twelve women. I have only women patients."

"You mean you didn't stop using it until twelve women had died?"

"Yes, but I had problems too."

"What kind of problems?"

"With their husbands." < . . . >

The same doctor told me that during tsarist times the governor once inquired of an Irkutsk village whether its inhabitants were involved in prostitution. The villagers called a meeting and made the following statement: Since we have so long been involved in agriculture, we have no desire to be involved in prostitution.

10 October.

Have been down with the grippe for four days. Sonya Korolenko brought me my food. Her kindness is not for effect, for show: she showed me no compassion; she merely brought me the food and returned for the dirty dishes. Only once did I have a genuine conversation with her, and I was fascinated by her intimate insights into Tolstoy. Tolstoy, in her words, was a very kind man (that he was ill-natured is a lie), worshipped nature, and so valued the truth that if he wrote "I was very glad to receive your letter," he would cross out the *very* when he read it over because he didn't wish to lie even when it came to formulas of etiquette.

Meshcheryakov has shown his true colors here. The sanatorium keeps two dogs and a cat named Murka. He has declared war on them, demanding that the cat be poisoned and the dogs be sent packing. He keeps exhaling cigarette smoke into their noses, which has provoked general consternation. He is one of the overlords of the place and is (partly) in charge of assignments. People court him, he was given the best room, but he threatens to write a negative report if the cat is not destroyed. His wife glares at everyone with extraordinarily malevolent eyes. She is a true harridan. On 30 September the woman who runs the dining room presented a guest with a telegram and congratulated her on her saint's day. Meshcheryakova threw

have been created, institutional personnel is bloated; the state apparatus suffers from over-bureaucratization."

a fit: "How dare you use the word 'saint's day' in a Soviet institution!" She is forever snooping about, seeing if people are doing the foxtrot or flirting or saying bad things about the regime. < . . . >

12 October.

I can't sleep. I was very upset by Gorodetsky's poetry reading this evening. I've known him for twenty-two years, and I found it painful to see what he's come to. He read from his book called *The Verge,* and each poem filled me with pity for him. There are a few fine passages, but the whole lacks character and style—it is impoverished. The more he vows allegiance to the new regime, the more distant he is from it, the more alien it is to him. He has nothing to hold on to. His verse ignites no sparks; it is shoddy, poorly constructed, approximate. In bad taste even. The poem "Dostoevsky," for instance, in which he juxtaposes Dostoevsky and the five-year plan. What makes me so disappointed and is keeping me awake is that he is my coeval and has written poems about Blok, Gumilyov, Nekrasov, and Pushkin. I went out into the garden. The stars are unbelievably magnificent, the night is quiet, I wet my head under the tap, and yet writing these lines I still can't calm down. [. . .]

1930

→>-→>-→>-→>-→>-→>-→>

14 April.

It's been a terrible year, 1930. I meant to start the diary in January, but didn't want to open it with unhappy events and kept waiting for a happy day, but then Mura began to have problems, first with her leg, then with her eye, next I had trouble with my *Kolkhozia,* next my children's books were banned, next there was the crazy bureaucratic mess with the Housing Rental Cooperative Society, so there have been no happy days to choose from. And now Tager phones and tells me that Mayakovsky has shot himself. Some happy day! Alone in the flat, I pace up and down, weeping and saying, "Dear Vladimir Vladimirovich," recalling the "Mayako-o-o-wsky"[162] who was so close to me—for only a second, but still—< . . . > whom I was foolish enough to think I "championed," who played croquet as if it were billiards, < . . . > who, when he fell in love with Lili [Brik] and visited her, took my overcoat, who went to Dr. Dobry for his teeth and would say to Lili, "I kiss your **body** and all that sort of thing" and go to my talks in a yellow sweater, who went his own way thumbing his nose at us, and instead of "Dear Vladimir Vladimirovich" I found myself saying, "Take care of your writers, you rotters!" The last time we met he was walking down Stoleshnikov Lane as if it belonged to him, and he put his arm around my waist and said I must come and see him, but then (it would seem) refused to see me, which was clearly the work of a third party: I phoned and said I couldn't come, and he promised to find another day, but never did. Still, how I loved his poems. I sensed the depth beneath the surface, the lyricism, the great spirituality . . . Oh God, to think I'll never have the joy, the moment's respite, of looking forward to meeting him, having a chat, "picking up where we left off," of telling him how holy he is for me and why. I feel that as a writer he had said what he had to say. He was the sort of writer who has one BIG thing to say, but only one. Why did such a giant have to have all those petty bosses trailing after him? In my very first articles about him I saw him as a mad and tragic figure, a suicide by vocation, but I thought it was pure literature (as it was in Kukolnik and Leonid Andreev). Now literature has become reality. The lines

> Tell his sisters Lyuda and Olya
> He has nowhere to turn any longer[163]

will have a different ring from now on, as will all his catastrophic verse of the time—including the lines to Yesenin.[164] How clearly he must have foreseen everything that is now going on at his grave, the whole brouhaha. < . . . >

---

162. See the 27 February 1923 entry for a description of Mayakovsky's pronunciation of his name. (V.E.)

163. From one of Mayakovsky's signature pieces, "A Cloud in Trousers." (V.E.)

164. Reference to Mayakovsky's 1925 poem on the death of his fellow poet Sergei Yesenin. (V.E.)

22 April.

In the tram. My myopic eyes make out a very sad figure, and its sad way of walking identifies it as or, rather, gives me to believe it is—Zoshchenko. I jumped off the tram (at Basseinaya) and went up to him. His face looked troubled, grim, complex; his cheeks were unshaven, his eyes tired. [. . .]

"I'm having all kinds of trouble with the theater: the actors don't understand a thing, they're using a raked stage." (There is anguish in his voice.) "They asked me to go to the Bolshoi Dramatic today and give a reading of my 'Comrade.' I promised I would, and didn't sleep all night as a result. In the end I phoned and said I wouldn't do it. And they had all gathered by then."

He is very depressed. I told him he was the luckiest man in the USSR: he was known and loved by millions of people, his talent had matured unusually well, and that very day I'd read his "Lilacs" to some friends and we'd laughed our heads off. That bucked him up a bit, and he walked me to GIZ. He was glad to hear something that happened to come up in another connection, namely, that Gogol was also criticized roundly, his work called "Little Russian burlesques."[165] It is a long time since I've seen him so misanthropic. He says he doesn't feel like seeing anybody and is bored with Stenich, but can't do without people either. I suggested he go to Sestroretsk Spa and finish the novella he's writing, *Michel Sinyagin.* "But I wouldn't last a day there without people," he said, frightened at the thought. "I feel better when they flash by."

He last saw Mayakovsky after *The Bathhouse* flopped at the People's House. Mayakovsky was gloomy, distracted, disheartened. "I'd never seen him like that. 'You're always so triumphant,' I told him." < . . . >

My *Tales About Nekrasov* is out, not that I'm happy about it. Not at all. On the contrary. It will affect my position as Nekrasov's editor. I sense disaster.

Everybody at GIZ was saying that Osip Mandelshtam had committed suicide.[166]

I met Misha Slonimsky at *Zvezda.* I enjoy *Zvezda* because it has preserved its Bohemian spirit. [. . .] The rest of the GIZ offices have a

165. The term "Little Russian" is an obsolete chauvinistic name for Ukrainian, the Russians who used it referring to themselves as "Great Russians." (M.H.H.)

166. The rumors about Mandelshtam's suicide proved false. (V.E.)

graveyard-like order to them, a morgue-like discipline, whereas here you feel a modicum of literary life.

Slonimsky told me that the source for Zoshchenko's Soviet language (apart from what came from the front) was the communal apartment of the House of the Arts, where Zoshchenko and he lived after the House of the Arts was liquidated. He was so impregnated with it that he could use no other. Slonimsky also reminisced about Mayakovsky: in December 1920, he said, Gumilyov organized a séance at the House of the Arts so as to undermine interest in Mayakovsky.

7 May.

About Mura. I can hardly bring myself to write the following: Mura has lost her left eye, and there is little hope of saving the right one. One leg is apparently doomed as well. < . . . > I read Pushkin's letters at night, and "Kozlov *the blind man*"[167] and the like jumped out at me. I then read Lermontov's "The Blind Man Inspired by Suffering." < . . . > Marya Borisovna has been weeping, tearing at her clothes, pulling her hair. < . . . >

11 May.

Tynyanov phoned. "How are you, old chap? I'm off to Peterhof tomorrow for a few days. Can I come and see you?" He was exhausted, but spent a whole hour with Mura, learning what he could about her illness and giving this, that, and the other kind of advice. < . . . > [. . .]

12 May.

< . . . > Kopylov says Mura's leg is healing. "If all goes well, we'll take off the cast in two weeks and give your leg a nice tan in the sun."

25 May.

< . . . > Mura was in a very cheerful mood yesterday. I read her Schiller's *William Tell*, and she laughed at the line "the Baron, dying in his easy

167. A minor Romantic poet, Ivan Kozlov (1779–1840) began to write after discovering almost overnight that he was blind. His appeal was enhanced by the success with which he overcame his disability. (V.E.)

chair." We also read *The Little Humpbacked Horse* and *The Storm Child*.
< . . . >

1 June.

< . . . > Now let me write about what has been engaging me most lately
(after Mura's illness): Populism. I've been doing scrupulous research into
the writings of Nikolai Uspensky, Sleptsov, Zlatovratsky, and Gleb Uspensky to find out what they offered the peasant. How did the Populists intend
to save their beloved "folk"? By the most idiotic, sentimental, and home-
opathic of means. In their view the peasant would still carry a staff at the
century's end, but the staff would be lacquered; he would still live in a
hut, but the hut would have a brick chimney; he would still be a peasant,
but he would wear a velveteen version of his rags. Mikhailovsky's view of
progress has us all turning into peasants in terms of our spiritual makeup. When you read it all carefully, when you study it from A to Z, what
you see is that the kolkhoz [collective farm] is Russia's sole salvation, the
only solution to the country's peasant question! It is remarkable that not
one among the wisest of the Populists—not even Shchedrin or Chernyshevsky—came even close to imagining a kolkhoz. Within ten years a
millennium of Russian peasant culture will be completely different: it will
undergo a magic transformation, and life will be happier than the Populists
could ever have imagined—all because of kolkhozes. Nekrasov was wrong
when he wrote:

> To make men out of slaves it takes blood, sweat and tears
> And yes, centuries, centuries, hundreds of years.[168]

It hasn't taken centuries. By 1950 the productivity of the kolkhoz village
will have increased fourfold.

5 June.

[. . .] Called on Tynyanov in the evening. When I told him my thoughts
about the kolkhoz, he said, "I agree. I'm a historian and it is the historian
in me that admires Stalin. As the author of the kolkhoz, Stalin is, historically speaking, the greatest of geniuses to reshape the world. If he

---

168. Lines from Nekrasov's narrative poem *Sasha*.

accomplished nothing but the kolkhoz, he would deserve to be called the most brilliant man of the age. But please don't tell anyone I said so."

"Why not?"

"Well, you know. All kinds of scoundrels are praising him now in self-protection, and if *we* start praising him too loudly we'll be identified with them."

Tynyanov is very devoted to the regime, but out of a certain respect for it refuses to make a show of his devotion. Saying good-bye to him, I mentioned how much I admire the works of Lenin.

"Sh!" he said. "What if somebody hears!" And he laughed.

I understand. I love children, but when people say, "You certainly do love children," I respond, "No, not really. No more than anyone." [. . .]

19 July.

Have been going through the letters about children that come to me from all over the country. I receive no fewer than five hundred a year. I've turned into a kind of "countrywide mother figure": no sooner does something happen to a child than I get a letter about it.

Seven or eight days ago I was in my room with dust and rubbish everywhere, unshaven, ashamed to look at myself in the mirror, and the doorbell rings. I see two smartly dressed, intelligent-looking men—a submarine navigator and his friend. They stood at attention while one of them said with a heavy Ukrainian accent, "We've come to thank you for your book about children. My friend here had no intention of marrying, but after reading your book he went and got married and now he has a little girl." The other man said not a word; he just smiled blissfully. Then they saluted, clicked their heels, and—though I asked them in—left. < . . . >

6 September.

We are in Sebastopol. It took us three nights and two and a half days to get here. Mura was very uncomfortable the whole way. There were five people in the compartment and a clutter of luggage, dust, dirt, and drafts. She caught a back cold, her temperature soared to thirty-nine, she started complaining of a pain in the *other* leg, and the knee of the sick leg began to hurt. < . . . > By the time we arrived, her temperature was up to nearly forty. From what? What from? Nobody knows. We rushed to the pharmacy to order iodoform candles, but they haven't got the spices it takes! < . . . >

7 September.

We are in Alupka. The drive from Sebastopol was incredibly hard. < . . . > The pain in Mura's heel was so excruciating that she grabbed me with her burning hand and begged me to tell her a story or read her something to help her forget it. I said the first things that came into my head < . . . >, and she did forget the pain and even smiled from time to time, but no sooner did I stop to think than she would shout, "Go on! Go on!" The pain seemed the result of my having stopped. < . . . > Every pothole, every pebble, every turn made her cry out in pain, and her pain made the three of us suffer so that I look upon the fantastically beautiful road as the most repulsive place I have ever been to. < . . . >

11 September.

Mura is doing as poorly as ever. We took her to Izergin on the seventh, and her temperature has not gone down since. The poor thing just lies there in the empty, drafty room, staring into space, bored to death. Yesterday he gave her three injections in the wound; he thinks it got infected on the road. She tells me that everything has turned out the way she foresaw in her diary. Before the trip she had joked about all the horrors awaiting her, and I made a list of them as a joke so we could laugh about them when it was over. And now she says they've all come true. < . . . > Marya Borisovna is suffering terribly.
< . . . >

13 September.

Visited a kolkhoz in the Tatar village of Kikeneiz in the mountains twelve kilometers from Alupka yesterday. [. . .] The kolkhoz was founded on 19 November 1929. It incorporated one hundred and six farms (of which fifty-eight had been worked by poor peasants and forty-nine by average peasants and farm laborers). It has three members who do not work the soil: a teacher, a librarian, and a culture officer. There was a fierce battle against the kulaks: 10 percent of the population were arrested as political prisoners (though some of them have returned and had their rights restored). It has tilled much formerly uncultivated land and currently has 27.5 hectares [68 acres] of tobacco, 35.5 hectares [88 acres] of grapes, 15.5 hectares [42.5 acres] of fruit trees, and 10 hectares [25 acres] of vegetables. It has opened a new, earthquake-proof school and set up a new clinic (which cannot yet serve as a hospital) and a canteen reserved for the school and kolkhoz.

Bobrishchev noted sadly that work on the kolkhoz was lackadaisical, that peasants put in less effort for the commune than for themselves, and that kolkhoz members cheated one another, taking twice as many meal tickets as they were entitled to, but he immediately pointed out that these shortcomings were gradually being dealt with. The kolkhoz members were especially upset at having to sell their grapes at seventy-five kopecks a kilo, when the private farmers sneaked their grapes down to the market at night and sold them for two rubles fifty, but now that it has been decided to sue the private farmers for failing to respect the official price scale things will be better. They have no tractors: their crops aren't right for them. < . . . >

I went to the school. < . . . > When they abolished the Arabic alphabet in 1924 and introduced the Latin one, the Tatar elders were so furious that the teacher had to run for his life. The school has approximately one hundred and ten pupils, nearly 100 percent of the school-age population. The teacher, Aladinov, played a major role in the dekulakization campaign in Kikeneiz, and he often had to hide out in cellars because kulaks wrote him anonymous letters saying they would kill him. After three such letters he complained to the GPU and apparently established the identity of the authors on the basis of their handwriting. But he speaks such a broken Russian that it's hard to grasp the full meaning of his stories. < . . . >

Getting the Tatars to expose their bodies to the sun is considered part of educational efforts here. Despite the magnificent nature surrounding them they keep them covered. Women wind their thighs round with kerchiefs and wear skirts to their waists [sic] in summer and winter. Teachers are forced to advocate shorts as a sign of culture. The Tatar teacher taking his charges on an outing has them take off their clothes in secret once they are out of the parents' range.

Storm clouds were gathering, fog swirling down the mountains—grippe weather, angina weather. We drove our nag down the road, and in two hours we were in Bobrovka. We found Murochka weeping from the agony in *both* legs. It was painful to see her suffer so. I tried to distract her, but they chased me away, and Marya Borisovna and I set off for Alupka distraught.

14 September.

The western part of Alupka is now covered in a deep purple hue, and a piece of glass is sparkling from the rising sun, which I, standing on the balcony, cannot see. The sky is a glassy blue. I find it hard to believe that the people sleeping at dawn in cypress-lined houses painted a dignified white are the dim-witted, boorish, uninspired people crowding the beaches and dining halls. What a pleasure to walk along the shore to Simeiz and breathe in the scent of the warm, pungent sea! How delightful each path underfoot!

Mura was better yesterday: 36.9 in the morning, 37.3 in the evening. Her spirits are slightly higher. < . . . >

17 September.

We are spending a fortune on hotel bills and will be bankrupt in two months, so I've decided to move into the sanatorium, for which I need the permission of the spa authorities in Yalta. Marya Borisovna and I are going there today. < . . . >

I found Yalta repugnant: vulgar little houses, petty little people, and a quay where you're bored from the word go. Everything about the architecture is puny, busy, clumsy, contrived. It's like the shell boxes made by the local artisans. You'd think it would all be redeemed by an abundance of the fruits of the earth—pears, grapes, apples—but the local markets are a disaster: a few women with two or three tomatoes to sell, just waiting to be chased away by the authorities. We bought some sausages and two kilos of grapes and found a decent tearoom. < . . . >

21 September.

I witnessed the strangest meeting yesterday. Everyone was in bed, even the chairman with his bell; in fact, he was tied firmly to his bed and had a heavy bag attached to his chin. The meeting was in full swing by the time I arrived. There was a contest to see who could speak the least, eat the most, and lie the stillest. Some of the children signed up to be shock workers: "We pledge to sleep during nap time, to eat everything put before us, to refrain from shouting, to take good care of our books and things, to tell the truth, and to lie still."

About fifty children lay on wooden beds under an awning, looking out at a warm, kind sea with the Ai-Petri at their backs. Some are hunchbacked, legless, and have been strapped to the beds for four years; many have casts on their legs, on their whole bodies, and they lie there without crying or whining, they laugh out loud, they read, they play ball—and hold meetings. < . . . >

27 September.

The storm is over. The air is clear. Alupka has been washed clean by the rain. I went to see the Simeiz children yesterday. They hugged me and fed me and gave me postcards. And asked for fairy tales. More, more! I didn't see Murochka: I was consumed by my Uspensky proofs.

30 September.

The day before yesterday Marya Borisovna and I < . . . > visited Vanda Stanislavovna in Yalta. She was in bed in her bonnet with Mikhail Chekhov, an old man of sixty-six, sitting next to her. I took an immediate dislike to him because he makes himself up to look like his uncle. He looks disgustingly like him as it is, which only underscores the difference. He said the authorities had demanded that the icon be removed from Anton Pavlovich's room even though it figures in the inventory, and so on. < . . . >

10 October.

[. . .] To see Mura I had to walk seventeen versts [eleven miles]—eight and a half each way. Mura is working on her arithmetic. < . . . > She asked me to bring her some Jules Verne, and when she learned that one of the children had a snail she said, "Find me a snail, and I'll make a little couch for it." I got her eight snails and handed out about ten more to other children. Then I picked oak leaves for them and gave one to each child.

Mura told me, laughing, that Marina had asked her, "Did your papa write *The Little Humpbacked Horse*?"

"No, it was Yershov."

"Then did your papa write Pushkin?"

It's amazing how underdeveloped the children here are.

I've also met a poet, a man by the name of Nikitin, who doesn't know about meter. I tried to show him iambs, trochees, and the like, and lo and behold, he'd never heard of stress! He writes poetry, but can't grasp what syllable the stress falls on. < . . . >

Mura is very much involved in preparations for the anniversary of the Revolution. She joins the entire sanatorium in the lines:

> Aroused by their initiative,
> The world will follow suit . . .

but then asks me, "What's 'initiative'?"

She's had another haircut. [. . .]

19 November.

Have been in Moscow since the fifteenth < . . . >. Yesterday I was at Zemlia i fabrika talking to Chernyak about Pasternak, and suddenly somebody flings himself on me and gives me a wet, noisy kiss, somebody so full of energy you'd think he had a thousand springs wound up inside him. "How young you are," he said. "You're the same age as Kolya. Do you like music? Come and see me. I'll send you my *Spektorsky*. You'll be the first. After all, you sent me Lomonosova, and what a wonderful person she is. True, I've never seen her, but my wife says . . ."[169] It turns out I told Pasternak about Lomonosova about five years ago, before her husband had officially been declared a swindler, and that was what he was thanking me for in so waterfall-fountainous a fashion. I'll be going to see him today. [. . .]

There is something ponderous about Shklovsky; he seems to be made

169. In a letter to Raisa Nikolaevna Lomonosova, the wife of a prominent railway engineer, Chukovsky wrote: "I would like to get Pasternak in touch with you and have given him your address. I consider him one of the most outstanding Russian poets, and it grieves me no end that he is in such dire straits. Could you help him?" In 1930 Pasternak wrote to the eminent literary critic D. S. Mirsky: "I wonder if Kornei Ivanovich realizes what a priceless gift I received from him. I have acquired a friend who is the more marvelous, that is, improbable, as Raisa Nikolaevna is not a literary person." Pasternak corresponded with Raisa Nikolaevna for many years. The correspondence continued even after the Lomonosovs chose to emigrate. At Pasternak's request Raisa Nikolaevna began to help Marina Tsvetaeva and soon engaged in an exchange of letters with her.

of cast iron and moves like a monument. He shows me his overly ordered books in that suitcase of a room he so identifies with. < ... > His wife is ill; his sister-in-law does the honors: meat, sweets, honey. The doorbell rings. It's Ilya Gruzdev. Though only thirty-two, he is quite portly and talks about politics like a forty-eight-year-old. Will there be war? Rightist deviation, leftist deviation, who will win, etc.

Shklovsky: In case of war I'll move the family to a city where the five-year plan has had no results. If the city is worth only two thousand and a bomb costs eight thousand, they won't waste their money on it.

The next topic of conversation was the proliferation of panicky rumors making the rounds. The other day I heard that XY had been executed. I go to Herzen House, and there he is drinking tea. "Sh!" I say. "He doesn't know yet."

Gruzdev assured everyone that the West has no desire to fight us, and I said there would be no war, but Shklovsky pointed out that on the eve of the Imperialist War I was certain there was no chance of war and he, Shklovsky, had believed me. < ... >

We talked about the upcoming trial of the counterrevolutionary saboteurs. < ... > Then Gruzdev asked whether we authors would lose copyright protection, and Shklovsky said, "No, because Marx was apparently in favor of copyright." There is an obviously much-read copy of Marx's *Kapital* on the desk in the library among the eighteenth-century volumes. < ... >

The conversation turned to Voronsky—"He's been exiled to the classics"—and Kamenev—"They've let him edit *The Marriage*, but don't trust him with *The Inspector General*."[170] He's clearly repeating choice witticisms he's picked up here and there, and if you let him go on he starts sounding like a marvelous feuilleton full of juicy bits. But there's a human quality to him, a warm undercurrent, and I left with a good feeling inside. < ... >

2 December.

[...] Turned to literature yesterday, and the first thing I did was to go and see Lidia Filippovna Maklakova, Sleptsov's former wife. [...] I found

170. Shklovsky may be a bit facetious here. At any rate, the implication is that Kamenev, who by 1930 was under a cloud, could not be trusted with a proper Marxist interpretation of Gogol's comic masterpiece, *The Inspector General*, which Soviet criticism was duty-bound to view as an unsparing indictment of tsarist bureaucracy. (V.E.)

her in the old-age section of the House of Scholars. The Soviet regime takes excellent care of these "oldsters." Each of them is well fed and has a room of her own with all the necessary services; in a word, they live in clover. To enter this amusing and slightly unsettling establishment is to enter a world where to be sixty is to be young, where talking about 1873 is like talking about last Friday, and where no one has heard of five-year plans, shock workers, and accelerated work tempos, where everything is ancient portraits, souvenirs, and gossip. [. . .] The ever so tiny, half-deaf old woman, moved here against her will from Moscow, looked over my lanky frame with fear and aversion and was none too happy to let me into her room. On her desk she had *Faust* in German, Marcel Prévost's *Les Demi-Vierges* in French, and the 1861 edition of Nekrasov. There was a draft coming from the window.

"You want to know about Sleptsov?" she asked with a frown. "What is it you want to know?"

But gradually she softened up. < . . . > "Here is a letter Sleptsov wrote about my novella *Lida, a Girl*." She showed me a letter addressed to Lidia Filippovna Lomovskaya, Petrovskaya Academy, a letter written by a man in love, an enthusiastic response to the novella. < . . . > "He so loved life that he had no time left to write: he kept dissipating his energies, falling in love." She showed me a portrait of Sleptsov in middle age, a semi-profile. "He had dark hair, but not black. Beautiful hair. To have an excuse to meet we put on an amateur play at the house of some common friends."

A bell rang. It was half past eight. Time for the pensioners' supper.

1931

➤➤➤➤➤➤➤➤

20 April.

Went to see Mura yesterday. A terrible thing has happened: her other leg has gone bad at the knee. Her temperature is up, her weight down.

There is a wild wind blowing in the courtyard; everything is flying into the air. The children are constantly shouting, "Catch it! Catch it! It's flying away!" Even books fly into the air. Stamps, scraps of paper, postcards, notebooks, and pictures sweep across the courtyard; sheets and the smocks of the orderlies and nurses flutter wildly. Mura's face is badly chapped; her hands are red and trembling.

She recited Lermontov for me by heart. < . . . >

June.

I've been reading Hugo's *Toilers of the Sea* to Mura, and when I read a page over again five days later I happened to leave out a sentence of no importance. "What happened to 'He looked askance at him'?" she asked.

2 September.

< . . . > Mura does her best to be cheerful, but there is no hope left for a cure. The pulmonary tuberculosis is spreading. < . . . > Her face has shrunk to nothing, her color is terrible—an earth-like gray. And for all that her memory is keen, her understanding of poetry astute. < . . . >

7 September.

I am gripped by periods of anguish. It is not a steady stream; they come and go. The day before yesterday I could still talk about extraneous matters, remember things, and suddenly I grab for my heart. Maybe it's because I so nourished her with literature—with poetry, with Zhukovsky, Pushkin, and Alexei Tolstoy—that I feel so close to her and look upon her as a friend who understands everything; maybe it's because she has such a good sense of humor and laughs so easily. Why, just yesterday she laughed at Zhukovsky's lines about the general and the Armenian. Parents do learn that their children are sentenced to death, but it usually happens within a few days and the shock, though powerful, is short, instantaneous. But it has been our lot to witness her being quartered: an eye put out, a leg chopped off, then another, then a reprieve, then back to the knife: kidneys, lungs, stomach. She's been here for a year now . . . (In the middle of the night I heard her moan and rushed in, and she said nothing but, "Don't worry, don't worry. Go back to sleep.") And all this against the backdrop of sublime, gentle, salutary nature, beneath the marvelous southern stars, where pain seems so unnatural.

Leonid Nikolaevich was here yesterday and said the process in the lungs was progressing. He sees no hope. < . . . >

8 September.

< . . . > Mura is reading my "Sunny Girl" and smiling. "When I was little," she says, "I dreamed they banned 'The Crocodile.' He was walking a tightrope, and suddenly they said, 'Stop. You can't go any farther.' But then they let it be published, and he started walking the tightrope again." < . . . >

5 November.

< . . . > Yesterday we had a letter from Kolya saying that Lida has scarlet fever. I'll never forget how shaken Marya Borisovna was. She stood stock still in the middle of the kitchen, her back hunched, her hand out as if begging for alms, and asked imploringly, "What will become of the child? What will become of the child?"

Nothing could be more desperate than our current situation, nothing even in books. We are riveted to the bed of the dying Mura, condemned to witness her death agonies, while our other daughter is in mortal danger thousands of versts away. And we can do nothing for either one or the other. I sent Boba a telegram from Yalta yesterday, but things are evidently so bad that he is afraid to telegraph back the truth.

And to make matters worse, I was running up the stairs to the Vorontsovsky Palace four or five days ago and fell flat on my spine. There was damage to the internal tissues, but absorbed as we are in Mura's illness I did nothing about it. Now there's swelling and pain and partial atrophy in my left leg. < . . . >

11 November.

Night. Mura died two and a half hours ago, at eleven o'clock sharp. I had sat at her bedside the whole night. "Go and lie down," she said. "You're tired. You're just back from Yalta." She had smiled during the day. It was strange to see a smile on a face so wan. < . . . > She never got to finish telling me her dream. She is lying on her back. She looks serious and very different from herself, but her hands are elegant, noble, spiritual. I have never seen hands like those before. < . . . > Fyodor Ilyich Budnikov, a carpenter from Tsustrakha, has made a coffin out of Olga Nikolaevna Ovsyannikova's cypress trunk (which Mura had once lain on), and now, after sending Marya Borisovna off to the cemetery to make arrangements with the gravediggers, I have placed Murochka in it with my own hands. She is so light. < . . . >

13 November.

< . . . > Visited the grave site. It is deep. The soil is rocky. It is like Sestroretsk. She would have liked it. < . . . > There was no one to hammer the coffin shut. I hammered in a nail above her head. It went in crooked and I had a hard time with it. L.N. hammered in the second nail. We picked up the coffin and carried it down one staircase and the next past the bells (Mura enjoyed lying under them and watching the sow that came there) along the row of cypresses to the pit. Marya Borisovna walked behind the coffin, but did not lead the others and shocked the old women by talking about extraneous matters. She had decided not to solace the on-lookers by weeping and wailing. As soon as we got there, we lowered the coffin into the grave. At the sound of the earth hitting the coffin Marya Borisovna let out a cry, but then fell silent. The burial ran its course. People dispersed quietly after strewing flowers on the grave. We stood there for a while, but eventually realized there was no reason to stay, there being no longer the slightest possibility of communicating with Mura, so we took the magnificent road to Gaspra, paused by a waterfall, and read and talked, feeling with all our being that the funeral was nothing compared with the torments of watching her die for two years, seeing the blood abandon her talented, joyous, loving body drop by drop.

22 November.

Arrived in Moscow yesterday second class, which means hard seats and feeling like beggars, orphans, torture victims. I couldn't sleep, but stayed away from drugs, because the pontapon and veronal I had been taking made my hands shake and my head ache. Moscow fell upon us like a wild beast. < . . . >

After Alupka I was bowled over by the luxury Koltsov lives in: dozens of appetizers on the table, four large rooms, and the highest degree of comfort imaginable even in Moscow: a pleasantly empty study, with four or five things where there is room for thirty. Koltsov has just returned from some Ukrainian sovkhoz or other. "They've frittered away umpteen quintals of grain. They had to replace the entire leadership. Here are some samples of the bread they used to feed the kolkhoz members." He opened an envelope and showed me a disgusting mess. < . . . >

24 November.

All Moscow writers seem to have been promoted: they've all acquired high-class flats, fur coats, and mistresses and gone in for a luxurious life. A private residence for writers has gone up just opposite the Moscow Art Theater. < . . . >

27 November.

Yesterday a Pilnyak full of affection, life, and self-confidence came to Koltsov's in a black beret to fetch me. He has an oddly shaped Ford he drives brilliantly, with great finesse. [. . .]

"I've almost nothing to do with writers," he said as he drove. "They're scum. And *Literaturnaia gazeta* is no newspaper. Averbakh is no writer." He pulls up to a fancy food shop, again with great skill and confidence, and runs out with a bottle. He has two writers at his place, Platonov and a friend of Platonov's, and he says they are the best writers in the USSR and "very fine people." Platonov's friend is a Communist ("You've never seen Communists like him before"), and in fact this unusual Party member immediately announced, "I don't give a damn about machines and kolkhozes (!); what matters to me is man (?)."

We sat down to dinner forthwith: Olga Sergeevna, an American woman and her husband who had just arrived, Yeva Pilnyak, and we three guests. We had goose with apples. To console the three of us writers who have been abused by the times, Pilnyak told the following legend:

There once was a town so crippled by tribute that its inhabitants decided to protest. When they confronted their oppressor with tears in their eyes, he said, "Double the tribute!"

They returned home in horror and decided to beg for mercy. So they went back and fell on their knees, but again he said, "Double the tribute!" They had nothing left, and all he would say was, "Double the tribute!"

Suddenly they burst out laughing. "What?" he said. "They're laughing? Then we've nothing more to take from them."

Clearly they have something more to take from us, because we did not laugh very hard.

Platonov told the plot of a novel of his, *Chevengur*, about a commune of fourteen true Communists who have chased all non-Communists, non-revolutionaries, from the town and about how the commune flourishes. And for all the piety with which he treats the Revolution, the novel—all four hundred pages of it—has been banned.[171] [. . .]

To console us again, Pilnyak repeated that we live in a world of shadows, that the Federation of Proletarian Writers is utterly useless and remains alive only because of the privileges it dispenses to its members, that there are no writers by the name of Fadeev and Averbakh and no newspaper by the name of *Literaturnaia gazeta*. The officials running literature want it to run smoothly; they want as little trouble as possible. Kanatchikov best conveyed these administrators' ideal when he said, "Instead of writing, let us edit." But writers go on writing; they've just stopped publishing. Platonov has a novel lying there waiting. Vsevolod Ivanov has one too (called *The Kremlin*, though it's not about the Moscow Kremlin).

To change the subject, I told the story of the bookkeeper at Molodaia gvardiia who, after paying me, told me there was no such writer as Chukovsky: she had never heard of him, nor had five or six other people working there. [. . .]

Suddenly Pilnyak felt feverish. It was his malaria. They gave him quinine, which he refused to take until Olga Sergeevna licked it off the paper. We moved into the study, where there was a couch. Pilnyak's teeth started chattering. He wrapped himself up in a blanket. There is a portrait of Pasternak hanging in the study. It has a tender dedication—"To a friend whose friendship makes me proud"—which is followed by the poem that has the following line in it:

And do I not measure up against the five-year plan?

171. Since the 1980s Andrei Platonov has been considered among the most significant prose writers of the Soviet period, but in his lifetime he was under constant attack by official critics and intermittently silenced. His first full-length novel, *Chevengur*, was not published in the Soviet Union until the advent of glasnost. The synopsis offered by Platonov is not entirely accurate: the commune of true believers does not thrive; it is about to be subverted by creeping bureaucratism when it succumbs to external attack. (V.E.)

It turns out Pasternak dedicated the poem to Pilnyak, but *Novyi mir* published it under the title "To a Friend."[172]

Now that the conversation had turned to Pasternak, Pilnyak made a fiery speech in praise of him. It was very precise and formally brilliant: it had been thought out long before. Pasternak was a man of great culture . . . No, I won't try to paraphrase it; I would just spoil it. It was the first time I'd heard Pilnyak make such wise and incisive comments. Everyone listened spellbound. They all felt Pilnyak to be a good, warm, pure man, and that was something new to me. It was also clear he enjoyed radiating the warmth. He was very friendly to me, giving me a tie when I turned up, distracted as I was, without one. I left in bliss, the Americans having made me a present of some recent issues of American magazines and Pilnyak's niece having seen to my every want. < . . . >

28 November.

[. . .] I went to Ionov's in the evening. He's just moved to a new house: Government House. He has four rooms, three of which are enormous. The place is still a mess; he hasn't put things away yet. < . . . > He wasn't there when I arrived, but as soon as he came in, coated with hoar frost, we sat down and decided on the spot that he would purchase four of my books for export and give me a five-hundred-ruble advance. [. . .]

It came out during the conversation that Koltsov had written a book about Stalin commissioned by Derevenskaia gazeta. When he finished it, he wanted to show it to Stalin, but no one could bring himself to give it to him. "He'll give me a beating and you a lashing," said Sergo,[173] so nothing happened with it until it got sent as a matter of course to Glavlit and from Glavlit to Stalin's office.

Stalin read it and told Koltsov over the phone, "I've read your book about Stalin. You praise him too much. You shouldn't. Come and see me in the summer, and I'll tell you what you need to add." Publication was postponed.

172. Pasternak's poem "To a Friend" appeared in *Novyi mir* (1931, 4, 63) and was later included in his *Verse from Various Years*. It confronts the problem of the poet's role in an era of major social upheavals and contains the much-quoted lines about the calling of the poet in Soviet Russia: "It is imprudent when a higher passion / Takes over at the Soviets' congress hall. / To leave the poet's seat empty, vacant / Is dangerous." (V.E.)

173. "Sergo" was the Party pseudonym of Grigory Ordzhonikidze, an influential Georgian official close to Stalin. (V.E.)

Now Lyadova is eager to have Molodaia gvardiia put it out. Koltsov obviously has nothing against it. "All I have to do is stick the word 'uncle' in everywhere. 'Uncle Lenin told Uncle Stalin that Uncle [illegible] < . . . >" And so they decided to bring the Pioneers into it. A group of them is coming to see Lyadova today, and they can go to Stalin as a delegation and beg him to have a book about himself published, because the Pioneers are dying to find out about his life and there are no books about it. They started formulating the text they would need to reach Stalin. It would have to be in writing. That didn't make Koltsov happy: it meant Stalin could commission the book from somebody else, and after we had gone over the plan for quite some time he said modestly, even timidly, "Wouldn't it be better to send the delegation to me? You could tell the Pioneers to write that they want me to do the Stalin book. Then I could go to the Old Man and say, 'They keep pestering me day and night. What shall I do?' "

Lyadova nodded yes, yes, yes. "That's a terrific idea, Misha. I'll plant it in their heads in such a way that they'll think they came up with it themselves."

The papers announced today that the head of the colossal Association of Grain sovkhozes, Comrade Gerchikov, had been dismissed and demoted for incompetence. Gerchikov lives in the same building as Koltsov, and Koltsov went to see him. He was phenomenally calm. On the morning of the day when the directive signed by Stalin and Molotov appeared in the press, he woke up at nine, read the papers in bed, saw the terrible news, and put it aside, saying, "There's plenty of time to get upset." Then he went back to sleep and didn't wake up for three hours.

Koltsov says there will be a grisly editorial about him in *Pravda* tomorrow. [. . .]

3 December.

< . . . > I had an hour and a half before lunch and went to see Seifullina, but she was out. What to do with an hour and a half? I went down the corridor to Marietta Shaginyan. The visit I had with her gave me more pleasure than any other I had in Moscow. She kissed me at the door, put her arm around me, and showed me with great sympathy to the couch. I realized her sympathy had to do with Murochka, and I burst into tears. She was the first person I told about Murochka, about what a gentle,

proud, pure, unique soul she was. She understood: her mother had just died of cancer in terrible pain. In fact, I found everything she said on that couch to be imbued with a profound humanity and spiritual serenity. "I've given up literature. I'm studying. In the Planning Institute (I think). I'm having trouble with the mathematics part. I'm forty-three, after all. Besides, mathematics has changed: there's a new Marxist method. But how I love being among students. They're such simple, enthusiastic, selfless, decent people. Not like our literary crowd, which I've broken with completely. I've been living here since October, and the only writers I've seen are you and Seifullina. Seifullina is a fine woman; I have no use for the others. I'm tired of literature: it's too irritating, too aggravating. For the first time in my forty-three years I'm enjoying life because I'm free of its heavy yoke. After finishing *Hydrocentral,* I took a look at myself and said, "What am I anyway? An unattractive, half-deaf, half-blind woman with a very bad character," so I decided to change my life, and I'm glad. I've divided the fee I got for the second edition of *Hydrocentral* into twelve parts and will live on it for the whole year."

There is a bookcase on the wall crammed with Goethe and other Germans, and portraits of Lenin and Stalin on the desk. The couch is untrustworthy: if you sit on one end, the other end tips up.

"My biggest worry now is keeping my name off the student blacklist. The blacklist is worse than all your reviews put together. I was on it the day before yesterday, because I was late to the first lecture. I really let my family have it!"

Everything she says rings true; there's not a drop of posturing or pretense. The conversation turned to Gorky. She hates him with a foolish passion.

"I've seen the contract stipulating that Gorky is to receive his fees in hard currency, seen it with my own eyes. Every day, holidays included, he gets paid so and so many dollars. Shame on him! Funneling hard currency out of the country at a time like this! Besides, I think he's an empty writer, the way a glass is empty and becomes whatever you fill it with. Now he's railing against all non-Marxists, but once I went up to him in Leningrad, wanting to talk about Marxism, and he said scornfully, 'Fine, but let me warn you: I'm no Marxist,'" and so on, and so forth. The same old attacks on Gorky. [. . .]

From there I went to see Zelinsky. He pointed out which passages in Kolya's novel he found the most sensitive and gave me concrete advice about how to make them ideologically acceptable. There has been a crack in his calm and collected gentleman-like exterior. "It wasn't easy," he said frankly, "to go through a crisis like that, to be a leader of the Constructivists and suddenly . . . They'll never let me forget it, and now I've got to prove my loyalty, my break with the past (which I very much love), over and over. So I hope you won't be too hard on me. We're not completely responsible for the 'social masks' we're forced to wear."[174] < . . . >

8 December.

< . . . > There's an ancient parchment about two arshins [four and a half feet] long hanging in the Koltsovs' lavatory with the following text in Church Slavonic lettering:

> DECREE
> Upon the most gracious authorization of the living Church, the Soviet of the People's Commissars do herewith decree that all State Registry Offices in the Parish of Father Yevlampy shall be abolished; that all those not yet baptized shall be baptized; that all those not yet married shall be married; and that all those not yet divorced shall be divorced. And all this shall be done with shock-work speed. Amen.

The word "decree" was illuminated in vermilion and gold as if in a fifteenth-century manuscript.

Yelizaveta Nikolaevna says it comes from a film that was banned. Koltsov says the lavatory exhibit changes regularly. "Here is what was there before." He gave me a sheet of paper with portraits of White generals, the heroes of the Intervention: Yudenich, Kolchak, Vrangel, et al. "We took it down when a lady visitor protested." < . . . >
< . . . >

10 December.

Soon after my arrival in Leningrad, when I was in bed with the grippe, Tynyanov came to call and tried to entertain me with his stories. He did a

174. From 1924 to 1930 Kornely Zelinsky belonged to the avant-garde group known as the Constructivists. At the peak of the campaign against its members Zelinsky published an article entitled "The End of Constructivism" in the hard-line journal *Na literaturnom postu* 20 (1930), seeking to prove his right-mindedness by assailing his erstwhile fellow Constructivists Selvinsky, Bagritsky, and Lugovsky.

marvelous imitation of Pasternak wrapped in a felt-like material and never quite catching your words. He listens but does not hear, mumbling a sympathetic "Yes yes yes" until—two or three minutes later, when he finally understands what you've been saying—out comes a trenchant "No." In other words, Pasternak's responses run as follows: "Yes . . . Yes . . . Yes . . . Yes . . . NO!"

Tynyanov's imitation captures Pasternak's sonambulistic quality, his isolation from the outer world, and his verbal energy. Tynyanov showed how Pasternak killed a book—Vostokov's *Essays*—at a meeting of the Biblioteka poeta [Poets' Library] with Gorky. Initially he nodded energetically and muttered, "Yes, yes, yes," then ended the series of yes's with an abrupt and incisive "No." He imitated Alexei Tolstoy, who had come to another of Gorky's meetings dead drunk, < . . . > Tynyanov called Gorky "a charmer—and a menace." [. . .]

28 December.

< . . . > Went to the Turner Institute for the Physical Rehabilitation of Crippled Children < . . . > and from there to see Zhitkov. [. . .] Zhitkov is all upset about the self flagellation going on among critics at the Writers' Union. He says that at the meeting where Eikhenbaum was asked to practice self-criticism, Eikhenbaum responded, "Self-criticism should be practiced before one writes, not after."

[. . .] Zhitkov's interpretation of the now famous meeting runs as follows: "We're all just so many sons of bitches, so let's pull down our pants and let ourselves be whipped."

[. . .]

1932

-✦-✦-✦-✦-✦-✦-✦-✦-✦-✦

25 January.

Went to see Olga Forsh yesterday. She has put on weight and is looking hale and hearty. She is writing about Novikov and the Martinists and working at the Svetlana Factory. She told an amusing story. They've put up her portrait in Pushkin House with the caption "Writer of the Petit Bourgeois Camp," and now she's ashamed to show her face there. [. . .]

Went to *Krasnaia gazeta,* where I saw the following announcement on the wall:

> For political errors made in editing non-periodical materials, N. N. Glebov-Putilovsky, non-periodical editor, requests dismissal on his own initiative.

24 February.

Moscow. Freezing cold. Clear sky. Stars. Today is Mura's birthday. She would have been twelve. How well I remember the gentle, greenish, glassy Petersburg sky in 1920 on the day she was born, born to suffer. I'm glad I can't see that February pre-spring sky here. It is too closely connected with the days of her birth. I can imagine what Marya Borisovna is feeling. [. . .]

Went to see Shaginyan. There was a bottle of cognac on the table. She had company: David Vygotsky. He had come from the Izdatel'stvo pisatelei to ask her to withdraw all passages from her diary—which was being published in Leningrad—having to do with Shklovsky and his flight.[175] When I showed her my *Chukokkala* album, which she fairly devoured, I noticed for the first time what a fine, childlike, naive laugh she has. Maybe it's because she's deaf and has limited resources: she can't laugh at what she is told, so the supply of laughter we use up on other things she retains. It's a pity she's deaf. She'd be an excellent writer if she could hear human speech. Deafness plays the nastiest tricks on her. A month ago her neighbors came and said to her, "We've heard you through the wall complaining about the cost of food. Please have some of our sausage. Our rations are so large we can't finish what we have." "When I asked how it was they rated such luxurious rations, they told me they were 'writers' rations.' I was the only one not getting them."

By the same token Marietta is cut off from the world of our literary circles, it being a world where people whisper. She cannot hear rumors or

---

175. Apparently Shaginyan honored Vygotsky's request: her *1917–1931* (1937) contains no reference to Shklovsky's involvement with the anti-Bolshevik Socialist Revolutionary Party. Venyamin Kaverin relates the attempts to arrest him in *Epilog* (1989).

grasp shades of meaning. It is very hard to establish the kind of relations with her that are established in a whisper.

Once I saw her carrying firewood and an ax into her room at the House of the Arts. Feeling sorry for her, I said, "Give it to me. Let me help." She thought I wanted to take the wood away from her and waved the ax at me!

She showed me a letter Stalin had written to her about *Hydrocentral*. Stalin had intended to write an introduction to the novel, but was too busy to make time for it and asked her to let him know whom he should contact to make sure the novel was published with no changes. It was a nice letter, in red ink, very friendly. [. . .] The telling part was that Shaginyan never risked having an audience with Stalin, meeting him face to face, though there was nothing she'd have liked more: she was embarrassed at not being able to hear. [. . .]

Next day I went to see Kornely Zelinsky. Pasternak and his new wife, Zinaida Nikolaevna, came as well. His arrival raised the temperature by a hundred degrees. You can't have banal talks when Pasternak is in the room. He is highly strung, full of joy; he radiates light. He recited his poem "Waves"—which he himself was obviously very taken with—laughing when he came to successful passages. He performed with frenzied energy, as if laying siege to each stanza, and I so enjoyed it that I didn't want it to end, I wanted to go on listening forever—not "over the barriers"[176] but "through the walls." Could this new surge of creative energy have come from the sweet-looking woman with him? Clearly it had, because every three or four minutes he would look over at her, his face transmogrified, beaming with love, with gratitude for her very existence. The last time we met he seemed lost; now he was firm and inwardly calm. He didn't know his collected works had been banned in Leningrad. I mentioned it, thinking that he did, and he was upset. She asked why; he said, "Because of Polonsky's death." But she said, "And because of the books themselves." He nodded.

< . . . >

4 March.

< . . . > I'll be going back to *Literaturnaia gazeta* today to beg for what they owe me. How tired I am of this endless running from one editorial

176. The title of an early collection of Pasternak's verse. (V.E.)

office to the next. But how can I ask Marya Borisovna, after what she's been through, to make the rounds of the tax commissions and finance departments?

You'd think we wouldn't need much: there are only two of us, after all. Yet we both work like mad, and in the past three months I haven't been able to put three hundred rubles in our savings account. I've sold some of my library, and I'm still in debt. < . . . >

Yesterday I took tram A to *Literaturnaia gazeta* to get my money and looked at Moscow through the window. During the entire stretch of several kilometers I noticed one thing: 95 percent of the women are weighed down by kerosene cans, baskets, purses, bags—the older the woman the heavier the load. Only young women turn up occasionally with free hands, but they are in the minority. Food purchasing is so poorly organized that every "housewife" has turned into a camel. Their bags and bundles have made the trams a national disaster. [. . .]

11 March.

An excruciating headache, unlike any I've had before. And heart trouble. I had so much pain last night that my left arm swelled up the way Slonimsky's used to do. And no matter how hard I try, I can't help thinking of Murochka. It is now four months from the day of her death, but my very blood is saturated with her.

[. . .] Yesterday I had to go to the building where Gosizdat used to be. I'd been there before to see Voronsky when he was head of it. Voronsky told me that Lenin had liked my one-volume edition of Nekrasov, and his secretary, Galina Konstantinovna, ferreted out a small sheet of paper with his remarks and gave it to him, and on the basis of that scrap of paper he was kinder to me than when we first met. But what happened to the scrap of paper I do not know. [. . .]

18 March.

Yesterday morning Marya Borisovna and I went to the Tretyakov Gallery. The first thing I wanted to see was the portrait Repin had done of me. [. . .] It was repulsive. A flabbily done face, a tasteless tie, a vulgar background. It certainly wasn't the way I'd pictured it all these years. The original background was a small raspberry-colored couch, beautifully painted, its shiny yellow silk exquisitely rendered, and what in the world was this? It made me sick to look at it. That nasty bright shirt and green tie.

Then we went through the gallery. It gains a lot from being cramped for space, because now it has only first-class paintings. I was as charmed now as in my youth by Serov, Bakst (the Rozanov portrait!), Levitan, Gué, Somov, Repin (Musorgsky and Pisemsky). < . . . >

19 March.

An illiterate, crazy, morally despicable engineer by the name of Avdeev has proposed a grandiose plan to the authorities: to bring the Volga to Moscow from Syzran, thereby "changing the face of the land in Bolshevik fashion." The Communists like the idea and have set up a project they call the Moscanal. < . . . > Do we need the Volga in Moscow? Not particularly, reply the skeptics. First, because until you get to Nizhny the Volga is not the Volga, it's small potatoes, and second, because water transport is practically nonexistent here. True, we lack sufficient water for drinking purposes and for the various other needs of the Moscow population, but we can get it by building a small canal at a quarter the price and faster. < . . . >

20 March.

< . . . > Only now have I had a chance to look at the translation of my "Crocodile" done by Babette Deutsch. The woman has made mincemeat of me. It's the kind of hackneyed verse nice ladies by the hundreds write for children. Everything I wrote it for is gone. The drivel she came up with for "a thousand portions of ice-cream"!

23 March.

You see Goethe everywhere and in all possible misspellings.[177] "Who is this Goethe fellow anyway?" a Komsomol girl asks.

A good question. Nobody has ever mentioned Goethe to them before, they've done perfectly well without him, and all of a sudden the papers devote page after page to this unknown shock worker as though he were

---

177. Much was made of the centenary of Goethe's death. (M.H.H.)

breaking all production records at some factory. It's sick, really. Everybody's trying to outdo everybody else in their praise of Goethe. Sitting in Khalatov's waiting room, I hear nothing but "Have you got a ticket to the Goethe?" and each time with a different pronunciation. < . . . >

I went to see the head censor today—Volin at Narkompros. He's turned gray since I saw him last. He gave me a friendly welcome and immediately started telling me about his daughter Tolya, who at the age of eleven has completely mastered the art of censorship.

"Take the latest issue of *Zateinik*, for instance. I noticed nothing and gave my authorization, but Tonya said, 'You can't pass this.' And when I asked why, she said, 'Just have a look at the cover. It shows a May Day parade with foreign workers and Soviet workers together. But if you look closely, you'll see that the foreigners have all the red flags and there's a big crowd of them and only one Soviet worker, and even though he's big he has no flag of his own. That's why, Papa."

Papa was in ecstasy. < . . . >

25 March.

Went to the Moscow Automobile Factory.[178] A brief visit unfortunately. < . . . > The pediment of one of the buildings has a cloth sign that reads:
STALINITES!
STORM THE HEIGHTS OF MODERN TECHNOLOGY

And although I often read such slogans with less than piety—I find them monotonous, jargon-ridden, and banal—here they are perfectly appropriate. < . . . > What in the bureaucratic system of, say, GIKhL is a senseless overstatement is absolutely essential here at Amo.

26 March.

[. . .] The rubbish heap where the Church of Christ the Savior once stood has not yet been removed. There are people milling all over it, carting away bits and pieces, but it hasn't gone down after a whole month. It's surrounded by a fence, and passersby peer eagerly through the cracks. < . . . >

178. Writers were often taken to factories, collective farms, and construction sites and encouraged to incorporate scenes from them into their works. (M.H.H.)

27 March.

Called on Zhanna Matveevna Bryusova, Valery Bryusov's wife, yesterday.
[. . .] I came in to find Zhanna Matveevna deciphering the draft of a letter
Bryusov wrote to Gorky in 1901 to distance himself from all political
commitment and convey his lack of sympathy for the rioting students. "I
perceive every phenomenon sub specie aeternitatis, and as far as I'm concerned political parties are a game, but my verse is destructive and serves
the revolution, because 'eternity' does not prevent me from feeling my link
to a given segment of time." Such is the sense of the letter. Zhanna
Matveevna is retouching it in the spirit of the Revolution, removing all
Bryusov's but's. She is working for Academia, which intends to put out a
two-volume edition of Bryusov's works. < . . . > She praised Postupalsky,
who is writing a long article on Bryusov ("and is apparently going to include
Comrade Stalin's 'six conditions' "),[179] and just before I left she confessed
to having inserted a number of corrections and new lines (the song of the
Halb-Hexen, the half-witches, for example) in Bryusov's translation of *Faust*
(which he considered a rough draft) and his translation of the *Aeneid*. "Of
course I told Gabrichevsky that I found the lines in Valery Yakovlevich's
papers. You won't betray me, will you?" < . . . >

30 March.

[. . .] Pasternak phoned in the evening and said, "Come and bring your
Chukokkala. Yevgenia Vladimirovna is looking forward to seeing you."
[. . .] At the entrance to Pasternak's former flat I saw the figure of a tall
woman wearing a fashionable coat, which still looks strange after last year's
dumpy models. She called me by name. I recognized her as Pasternak's
former wife, though I'd seen her only once before. She too was going to
Boris Leonidovich's. She was waiting for a Georgian to accompany her,
but he was late, so we went in together. I could tell she was terribly nervous.
"It's the first time I've been there," was all she said. "You don't know how
my son adores you. When you came to see us, he said to me, 'I so wanted

179. The "six conditions" were formulated by Stalin in a speech on 23 June 1931 dealing
with "new tasks for economic construction." Among them were better organization of the
workforce and improved economic cost accounting, matters that were less than germane to
Bryusov's legacy. The clear implication was that the author of the article was casting his net a
bit too wide. (V.E.)

you to have a chance to meet Chukovsky that I prayed for it,' and see? It worked." Pasternak was sitting at a long table with Loks, Pilnyak and Olga Sergeevna, Zinaida Nikolaevna (his new wife), Alexander Gabrichevsky, his wife Natasha (to whom I am related through Marina), Pasternak's brother and his wife, etc. No sooner had Yevgenia Vladimirovna entered the room than it was clear she shouldn't have come. Zinaida Nikolaevna said not a word to her. Boris Leonidovich was highly distracted; he kept coming out with irrelevant remarks and clearly feared throwing Yevgenia Vladimirovna a kind or affectionate glance. The Pilnyaks made a show of boycotting her. She had only one recourse: vodka. She started downing jigger after jigger. Emboldened, she joined the conversation. Gabrichevsky was drunk by then as well and began to court her in a way reserved for "unattached women." Zinaida Nikolaevna's beautiful face maintained a majestic expression through it all. The talk was trivial. < . . . > I had no contact with Pasternak whatsoever, and Zinaida Nikolaevna gave me hostile looks as if I were responsible for bringing Yevgenia Vladimirovna into her house. Gabrichevsky fell asleep, and Natasha poured cold water over him. Pasternak was terribly worn out. Loks, Yevgenia Vladimirovna, and I finally left. Yevgenia Vladimirovna told me that Pasternak did not wish to break off relations with her and whenever he was in a bad way he would phone and come and see her for consolation ("not when things are going well, he doesn't give me a thought"). < . . . >

2 April.

Pilnyak stopped off to see me yesterday < . . . >. I was in bed: my heart had been giving me trouble after a sleepless night. Pilnyak said he had no desire to go to Japan. "I was all set to slip off to the country and work on a novel. I was sure I could pull it off in two months flat. But Stalin and Karakhan want to send me. I'm sorry Borya (Pasternak) isn't coming. I could have obtained a passport for him too, but he insisted on bringing Zinaida Nikolaevna along, and she would have been a burden on the two of us, so I refused even to ask. That set Borya sulking. She's turned him against me. She's worse than the last, let me tell you. The last one was a gem: he was always doing her bidding, setting up the samovar, etc. And this one . . ."

Pilnyak received a payment of five thousand rubles at OGIZ today for no reason whatever. He had told Karakhan modestly enough that he did not want any money for the Japan trip but that he had ten volumes he'd like to see published as his collected works. Karakhan—with Stalin's support—rang Khalatov, and Khalatov sent Pilnyak to Solovyov, who said, "We're not going to publish you. We've no paper. But you'll get your money. Money is no problem."

And he gave him five thousand rubles.

"Not bad," said Pilnyak. "A publishing house that pays an author five thousand rubles not to publish him."

< . . . >

5 April.

Khalatov has fallen. Tomsky seems to have been named in his place.

Am returning to Leningrad today. My accomplishments here are as follows: Volin authorized a four-thousand-copy edition of a book of my children's verse for adults; I set my *Walt Whitman* in motion; I saw various aspects of industrialization and modernization; I saw Seifullina, Pasternak, Pilnyak, Koltsov, Marietta Shaginyan, Miss Lee, etc.; I came to know Moscow really well for the first time; I came to hate the Moscow publishing house Molodaia gvardiia along with all the bureaucratic nonsense connected with OGIZ; I recited "Wash 'Em Clean" twice on the radio yesterday to great acclaim. [. . .]

29 May.

Kislovodsk. Yesterday I made the acquaintance of the famous Leningrad educationalist, Olga Syrkina, the author of many scholarly articles that have come in for much official criticism lately. A terrible thing happened to her not long ago: a burglar fell on her at the entrance to her house and cracked her skull open with a crowbar. When three days later she finally regained consciousness, her first reaction was, "Thank goodness. They won't be able to drag me over the coals!"

Nowadays people prefer having their skulls cracked open to having their works gone over by a publishing house.

< . . . >

17 June.

< . . . > Literature is on the decline nowadays because there is no demand for originality, inventiveness, verbal magic, or brilliance. Platitudes are all that matter, all that anyone requires. For every phenomenon in life there is a set formula, and the platitudes and formulas are so majestic that nobody tires of repeating them. A Yerevan chemistry teacher I talked to recently here in Kislovodsk told me, "I have two hundred students, and not one of them thinks for himself." A former RAPP member, a literary critic, attacked me here after reading my article on Sleptsov's commune. "Why didn't you say that Chernyshevsky was a utopian socialist?" he asked. "Why didn't you say that Sleptsov's commune was impossible under capitalist conditions?" In other words, he wanted me to repeat the well-known dogmas and to repeat them in the exact form they have come to assume. He took no notice of anything else in my articles—the new materials, the new interpretation of Sleptsov's *Hard Times,* the notes to Ostashkov; all he saw was what I *didn't* say. There are a lot of young people here, and I like them, I like their enthusiasm and willingness to work, but they are all the same, one like the next, and if one of them agreed with me when I said that we mustn't make judgments based on dogma, on preconceived notions, that we must first study the material at hand, the only reason he did so was that Stetsky had written an article along those lines in *Pravda.* He was given an order to think in a certain way, so he did. Had there been no article, no decree, he would have gone by the previous one and punched me in the nose. Though maybe it's all for the best, since we "loners" and "nonconformists" haven't come up with much ourselves.

1 July.

I'm leaving tomorrow. I'm depressed. My health hasn't improved. I didn't get anything done. I've forgotten how to work. I've lost whatever self-respect and will power I once had. I'm fifty years old, and my ideas are trivial and inane. I'm a failure, a loser. After thirty years of keeping my nose to the literary grindstone, I've neither a penny to my name nor any name to speak of. I'm a novice. I'm so depressed I can't sleep. Yesterday on the playground I had my only joyful moment here. The children were kind and trusting: they threw their arms around me, dragged me here and there, showed me rebuses, gave me flowers, and saw me back to my room. I couldn't help feeling they'd taken me for somebody else. The clock is striking six a.m. < . . . >

4 July.

Our trip to Alupka was horrible. Instead of going straight to Novorossiisk, we bought (I was stupid enough to buy) tickets for Tuapse and had to change at Armavir. < . . . > We were tossed out onto the platform of the Armavir station in the middle of the night amidst a pile of unfortunates like ourselves, some of whom had been waiting for trains promised them by the timetables for three whole days. < . . . > It soon became clear that even lying on the platform next to one's suitcase was a boon: every ten minutes a furious, dog-tired official would come and chase us into the third-class "waiting room," where thousands of passengers "of low degree" with small children and bags were patiently, meekly lying in an incredible stench, run down with hunger and lack of sleep—and there was every indication that they found this the rule rather than the exception. Russians, now as always, seemed to be made for waiting days on end for trains, lying side by side in stations and on piers, plagued by porters, speculators, drunkards, and thieves. < . . . > I finally got us tickets by sheer nerve: first, I told the stationmaster I was a member of the Committee of Soviet Scholars, a branch of the Council of People's Commissars, then, a fellow passenger and I pretended to be foreigners. That got us onto a packed train going to Sochi (via Tuapse).

We spent an entire day in Tuapse, because the steamer *Gruziia* didn't leave until ten in the evening. It was hot and dusty. We saw many revolting things and many wonderful things, and we felt that the wonderful things had a solid future ahead of them and the revolting things were temporary, short-lived. (People throughout the USSR have the same feeling.) The wonderful things include oil refineries that did not exist in 1929, a small workers' city, the river, whose course has been diverted to the left (and whose bed has been straightened in a manner that has nothing of the Ugryum-Burcheev to it);[180] the revolting things—dust, high prices, Asiatic ways, and scorn for the individual. We experienced a good deal of both

---

180. Ugryum-Burcheev, a character in Saltykov-Shchedrin's satirical novel *The History of a Town* (1869), attempts to change the course of the river running through the eponymous town. (M.H.H.)

that day. We took our tea (there was no sugar, but there was honey, and the tea was served with painstakingly perforated spoons; when we asked what the holes were for, we were told, "Spoons without holes get stolen") and our ease in a cool, fashionable tea salon in the center of town (ficuses hung with flypaper, *two* portraits of Voroshilov, oleander in bloom, and a poster exhorting citizens to buy state bonds in the spirit of "socialist emulation and shock work"). < . . . >

We made it safe and sound to the *Gruziia* that evening. < . . . > Its first class is actually third class. The entire deck was strewn with bodies, wall-to-wall Russian bodies that, as I say, seem made for railway platforms and ships' holds, while up above, where the great unwashed are not admitted, a few haughty round-spectacled and white-ducked plantation owners whiled away the time. Nobody flushes the toilets in the lavatory, the desk is covered with the shells of sunflower seeds, only one in three hundred faces has a cultured look about it, and the crew are rude: when I asked one flunkey without thinking whether the meal ticket Marya Borisovna had bought for me was valid, his answer was, "You mean you found it on the deck?"

Still, there's nothing I enjoy more than a sea voyage, and I spent the whole day as in a dream even though we were on our way to the grave. And before long there it was, a hazy mountain range, the Crimea, the place of her grave. The very sight of the shore was repulsive to me, and the moment I set foot on it the boundless suffering began again. The grave. It is a suffering aggravated by apathy: I do nothing, have no thoughts, no desires. I am living on credit, with no tomorrow; I am living in anger, immersed in petty cares. I feel I have no right to be so trivial and contemptible in the presence of *her* grave, but *her* death is what made me so. Only now do I see how poetic, serious, and pure I was thanks to *her*. It is gone now, all of it; the only thing left is . . . Well, actually, there is nothing left. So here we are, tied forever to this cursed place, where everything reminds us of her death: the tree opposite the balcony and the brook running through the Ovsyannikovs' property and the bell tower and the road to Bobrovka and the pretty flowers—they looked like berries glued together—I would pick for her when she was lying under the tree with all the weeds near the sanatorium and the stones and the songs of the passing shock workers and the pharmacy and the cabby who took me to Bobrovka. And to make matters worse, Lyadova sent the money to Leningrad rather than to Alupka, where I have been running up debts. < . . . >

8 August.

< . . . > Arrived three days ago. Moscow is having an unprecedented heat wave. I went to see Kamenev at the Concession Commission. He was in his shirtsleeves—good-natured, plump, and hairy. Academia has given me three editing jobs: Nekrasov's collected works, his "Who Lives Well in Russia," and Nikolai Uspensky. It will bring in about twenty thousand rubles altogether, but now I'm so broke I had to borrow twenty rubles from the secretary. Without it I'd literally have died. [. . .]

16 August.

Yesterday was my only more or less worthwhile day in Moscow. In the morning I went to GIKhL and learned that the Whitman had been typeset and would be printed as soon as paper was available. *The Men of the Sixties* was also under way. < . . . > Then I went to Molodaia gvardiia, which was its usual bungling self. Everybody is at meetings, "busy with the plan," no one has time to breathe—or get anything done. [. . .]

So off I go to see Gorky, that is, Kryuchkov. The Moscow Communal Housing Department is remodeling—yet again—the building where Gorky lives, the former Ryabushinsky House. It is uglier than ever, a most repellent example of decadence. There's not one clean line, one right angle. It's a mess of unseemly flourishes, uninspired, unabashed squiggles. The vulgarity is everywhere—in the staircases, the ceilings, the windows—and stands out in all its brazen glory now that it's painted and shiny. That son of a bitch Kryuchkov keeps hemming and hawing and won't let me in to see Gorky. All I really want is to show him "Sunny Girl." I have a feeling he'll take to it. Besides, I worked with him for three and a half years, damn it; I've had a long-standing correspondence with him. I'm entitled to see him once every ten years. "No, I'm sorry. Alexei Mikhailovich regrets he can't see you now, but he *will* have time . . . at noon on the nineteenth." He won't look me in the eye, and his breath reeks of vodka. < . . . >

Then on to Academia at Herzen House for lunch. The Herzen House used to be an unsightly den of thieves where I was afraid to show my face, the shameless proletarian writers clubbing the skulls of anyone who dared to enter. Now liberalism has made a showing even there. A heavy-set woman came up to me and asked, "What is your view on children's literature, Kornei Ivanovich? May I interview you?" I was greeted at *Literaturnaia gazeta* with open arms. "Who do you think could do an article on you?" I was at a loss for words. At that point Shklovsky entered the room and said, "*I* will, and I'll praise you to the skies." Usievich, a *Literaturnaia gazeta* editor, wanted to meet me and phoned to invite me to her office. Another sign of liberalism: I was asked to do an article on Mandelshtam. "It's time to put the master on the pedestal he deserves." Two of the big bosses, Feldman and Tseitlin, are passionate about literature. I ate in the dining room with Abram Efros, who promised to find me an illustrator for my children's books and *Who Lives Well in Russia*. In the dining room I also met Aseev, Bukhov, Bagritsky, Anatoly Vinogradov, Mandelshtam, Kruchonykh, and many more. < . . . >

18 August.

Called on Shklovsky. I enjoyed visiting him most of all, though I had trouble locating his place in the maze of Maryina Woods. [. . .]

"Forget children's literature and the men of the sixties," Shklovsky said. "A critic—that's what you really are. Write about your specialty. You've got enormous talent and influence. I'll write about you in *Litgazeta*, shed a tear for you ("A crocodile tear," Khardzhiev inserted), and you take up Joyce. Yes, you must write about Joyce."

Then all three of them walked me to the bus stop. [. . .]

21 August.

< . . . > It's interesting to follow the life of *Literaturnaia gazeta* now that the people in charge are trying to make it super liberal, commissioning articles on Zoshchenko, Mandelshtam, and my "Crocodile."[181] But its position is tragically tenuous. RAPPovitis is rampant. Yesterday Zhurbina proposed a series of anti-Shklovsky articles to Feldman, who is high in the *Litgazeta* hierarchy. "We've got to show up his reactionary nature," she said. "He's smuggling in Formalism." If, even after the Party has allowed

---

181. A propos of "liberalism": on 23 April 1931 the Soviet press published a resolution of the Central Committee entitled "On Restructuring Literary Organizations." With one stroke of a pen it put an end to the four-year hegemony of the doctrinaire RAPP and announced the founding of an all-inclusive Union of Soviet Writers. Although in the long run the Writers' Union established direct Party control over literature, it was initially welcomed by the Soviet intelligentsia as it offered immediate relief from harassment by RAPP zealots. (V.E.)

us to "breathe at three-quarters capacity" and RAPP has been dethroned, a young writer like her voluntarily joins battle with an already defeated Formalism, then RAPP can't be smoked out by decree.

[. . .]

RAPPovitis has contaminated even the anti-RAPP contingent. Usievich's fifteen-year-old son, the grandson of Felix Kon, has proclaimed, "I can't read Pushkin. I don't like what he writes about. I find *Eugene Onegin* abhorrent. The rubbish Academia publishes! There's nothing with revolutionary spirit."

The Gorky-Marshak paper on children's literature (I was given it yesterday) is too mild and glosses over the errors in literary policy. It fails to deal in so many words with the fairy tale, mentioning only "the development of the imagination." < . . . >

28 September.

The day before yesterday I took part in a celebration honoring Gorky at the Academy Capella. The hall was packed. The people at the table had that gloomy, gray, official look and were presided over by a former *Krasnaia gazeta* editor by the name of Bauze. The writers—there were three of us: Eikhenbaum, Chapygin, and I—felt out of place. The main speaker was a plump, self-confident, agitprop type of orator who launched into a diatribe about how Gorky had always been an unadulterated Bolshevik who despised the petite bourgeoisie, and pounded away for an hour and a half at the hopelessly tedious topic. I must say I was amazed: the truth held no interest whatever for him; his task, as he understood it, was to shuffle the facts in such a manner as to come up with the version of the subject mandated by the authorities. He uttered not one word with any life or humanity in it: it was all on the level of duly authorized platitudes from the provincial press. The audience was in such a stupor from the officialese that when the speaker slipped and said Trotsky instead of Gorky nobody batted an eye. It made no difference!

Then came Eikhenbaum. He had his talk written out, because he hadn't spoken in public for three years. It was hard to follow—he compared the lives of Turgenev and Tolstoy with Gorky's using rather lame arguments—but it got a big hand, because weak as it was it was at least human. Chapygin came next. He played the fool, as is his wont. Once a fool, always a fool, he seemed to be saying. "Me and Gorky, we're good friends," he began, "and of course he thinks the world of me." $<$ . . . $>$ All the "celebrating" made me uneasy: on the one hand, there was the state with its endless and unrelieved officially sanctioned bromides; on the other, there were the writers, the All-Russian Union of Writers, in the persons of a sickly, obscure professor and a buffoon. I wanted to convey as much of Gorky's *human* side as possible; I wanted to show him as a mischievous, cheerful, talented, impassioned, very much alive human being. So I spoke about his witticisms, his jottings in my *Chukokkala* [an album that contained entries, often versified, by Chukovsky's contemporaries], the funny stories people tell about him; I read excerpts from my diary. I gave a picture of Gorky the man; I didn't turn him into an icon. The audience responded with genuine enthusiasm, clapping at various points along the way, and when it was over they expressed their appreciation so warmly that the officials glowered. Then one of their prostitutes got up and read out—in a deadly voice—the text of a telegram that the writers, *Russian writers as a whole*, were sending to Maxim Gorky. Again it strung together the kind of clichés and inanities that have gone out of style even in the provinces. Imputing a message like that to writers and sending it to another writer—and in the city of Pushkin, Shchedrin, and Dostoevsky! And not only did it go on for three hundred lines; the authors seemed to have gone out of their way to avoid expressing an original thought, a genuine, personal feeling. Their Gorky is the Gorky required by the latest memorandum. Worst of all, they gave us no say in the message they were sending in our name. And in general, they treated us very strangely: they scarcely looked at us. It was as if we were the enemy. $<$ . . . $>$

11 October.

$<$ . . . $>$ Nizhny is being renamed Gorky [bitter]. They're going to have a hard time naming other cities after writers what with Mikhail Golodny [hungry] and Demyan Bedny [poor] and Ivan Pribludny [born out of wedlock].

[. . .]

Maria Nikolaevna Reineke paid us a visit yesterday, and just as we were talking about Angert and Raisa Grigoryevna the phone rang: it was Angert himself, risen from the dead. I was so moved I burst into tears and ran off to see him. He hasn't changed a bit; if anything, he looks younger. From one day to the next he stopped being a prisoner with a ten-year sentence and started working for the GPU with a four-hundred-ruble-a-month salary. He is content with his stay at Bear Mountain: he says the system there is excellent "and the project is terribly interesting." (They're building some canal or other.) < . . . >

14 October.

Pasternak scored a great success at the Capella. He spent the night, from twelve until morning, at Kolya's, when Kolya was practically in delirium with a temperature of thirty-nine, no money, and a pregnant wife. A fine time for a drinking bout!

While the barber was shaving me yesterday, he told me he'd fled the Ukraine, leaving his wife and daughter behind. And suddenly he started screaming hysterically. "Exterminating mankind—that's what they're doing there! Ex-ter-min-at-ing man-kind! I know. You work for the GPU. (!) But I don't care. Exterminating mankind—that's what's going on. Oh well, the same thing's going to happen here. And I'll be glad. We deserve it!"[182] And so on.

Academia still hasn't paid up. Ditto Molodaia gvardiia. You can drop dead for all they care. People are queuing up in front of banks. Even savings banks are reluctant to give out money. Marusya has to go to Odessa, but has no money for a ticket. She's been staying with us for two days. < . . . >

Went to the Writers' Congress. A bunch of lickspittles.

17 November.

Ill. Pharynx and palate. Grippe. < . . . > The performance is off. What rotten luck. For five years they've kept me from performing my works for children, and when at last I've received permission and Alanin the Fat plasters the city with posters announcing a reading for children with Kornei Chukovsky on the program, I come down with the worst grippe in history. < . . . >

But no, on the twentieth I pull on my old overcoat and my tattered,

---

182. He is referring to what has come to be called the great famine: during the early thirties millions of Ukrainian peasants starved to death while feeding urban workers. See Robert Conquest, *The Harvest of Sorrow: Soviet Collectivization and the Terror-Famine* (London, 1986). (M.H.H.)

not quite matching galoshes and descend, hoarse and trembling, into the Petersburg November. I keep thinking I'm going to fall, but eventually I make it to the Chamber Music Theater and take my seat next to the stove. < . . . > I get a warm reception, but read three or four times worse than usual, scarcely make it through the second performance, and scarcely make it home. I'm still not myself: I have a headache, I ache all over, I can't do a thing. Two weeks down the drain. Dear me!

21 November.

Went to the Izdatel'stvo pisatelei to hand in my *Small Children*. I still can't believe it will come out in a new edition: I'd long considered it dead and buried. Then a month ago, to my amazement, the censors passed it and Kirnarsky, who is in charge of artistic design at the house, worked up the layout with me.

Ran into Tynyanov there. He left with me and we talked about his work. "I can't bring myself to write the book about Russian participants in the French Revolution. Like it or not, there are bound to be parallels with our Revolution. People will say Anakharsis Klootts is Trotsky, the queues at the *boutiques* are our food queues, etc. It's dangerous. I'd better hold off. I'm doing some writing now for the Moscow Music Hall; I made a special trip there to draw up the contract. My Heine translations are being published by GIKhL. It's the last book I'll publish with them. Shiller is doing the foreword. It's crude and vapid, but no matter. Especially as Berkovsky's notes are impossible—all insolence and ignorance. You'll see.

    [. . .]

    The conversation turned to Shklovsky. "Yes, we've met since his article.[183] We've talked. But it's not like before and never will be. The article was like a stab in the back. He wrote another one to smooth things over, saying I was a master craftsman, but no . . . Forget it. As long as we had a common theoretical ground, we were friends. Now he throws me together

183. In "About People Who Always Follow the Same Path and Don't Know It" (*Literaturnaia gazeta*, 17 July 1932) Shklovsky calls *The Wax Figure* Tynyanov's best work, especially praising the portrayal of Catherine the Great, "whom we see here for the first time." Then, however, he observes that "the people at the tavern don't so much drink wine as talk about various brands of wine and marvel at their odd-sounding names. The novel does not flow out of a swamp—great rivers sometimes flow from swamps—it flows into a swamp and peters out inconclusively. Tynyanov is defined by the cinema, waxworks, and German Expressionism."

with a bunch of writers and Olesha gets a column while I get a few paltry lines. About how I keep reading the same books and don't even own many books. Me! I don't own many books!" Yury Nikolaevich obviously found that remark particularly offensive. [. . .]

22 December.

Went to Moscow with Ilyin and Marshak for the Komsomol meeting at the Kremlin. Gloveless, tattered coat, unmatched galoshes. Pain and humiliation. Insomnia. Gave a preposterous speech in defense of the fairy tale. Old age. Disgrace. < . . . > And now I'm bogged down in Nikolai Uspensky, bound hand and foot by him—it's sheer torture. The editorial work I'm doing for Academia is a heavy yoke and keeps me from writing anything of my own. Now that I'm back at home, there's damned Nekrasov to contend with, the loneliness, the forced labor of day-to-day drudgery.

Called on Fedin five days ago. He'd put on so much weight I barely recognized him. He had a new way of laughing too: mechanical. In fact, everything about his manners and gestures was machinelike. He had strange clothes on: padded shoulders and a patterned sweater. Everyone who came commented on the sweater, then looked through the books from abroad (Romain Rolland, Gorky, etc.), and then asked, "What's your view of the crisis?" And everyone received a response in the same well-rehearsed, mechanical voice. But *what* he said was very straightforward. "I got off the train at Luga with an American woman (I was struck by the sickly green faces), and had to queue for a spoon and then a glass and never got anything. Then I had to run back to the train—it had started— and ended up in a Russian carriage rather than my German one. I was mortified: the filth, the murk, the gloom! I've been spared that kind of thing because the slushy winter has kept me at home (I've been waiting for real snow so I can go to Detskoe: I'm getting a new flat), and suddenly I saw how emaciated people looked. To say nothing of the typhus." Which led to conversations very unlike the interviews he gave to the press upon his arrival. [. . .]

Kornei Chukovsky, Saint Petersburg,
1910s

With wife Marya Borisovna,
Kuokkala, Finland, 1910s

With children, (from left to right) Nikolai
(Kolya), Boris (Boba), and Lidia, Kuokkala,
summer 1913

Portrait by Isaac Brodsky, 1913

In his study, Kuokkala, 1915

With Alexander Blok (left), Petrograd, 25 April 1921

With daughter Mura, Sestroretsk, 1924

Chukovsky, sitting at front, with members of the World Literature Board,
Leningrad, 15 December 1925

With Boris Pasternak (left) at the 10th Komsomol Congress, April 1936
(Photo by B. Ignatovich)

Moscow, 1940s

With wife, Marya Borisovna,
and grandchildren,
Peredelkino, 1947

With daughter Lidia and son Nikolai, Peredelkino, 1957

With Samuil Marshak and Yekaterina Furtseva during the
World Youth Festival, Summer 1957

With Olga and Vadim Andreev, Peredelkino, 1960s

With great-granddaughter Marya (Masha), Peredelkino, 1968
(Photo by Polianovsky)

With Alexander Solzhenitsyn, summer 1969
(Photo by N. Reshetovskaya)

Mid-1960s

1933

25 January.

The celebration for Alexei Tolstoy's fiftieth birthday took place today. I've never seen a more sorry or more official affair. As I entered, a speaker was saying, "Flattery is out of place even at a celebration, so I will be blunt: your description of Kornilov's death is unsatisfactory, unsatisfactory to me and to the Soviet reading public. You have described his death in such a way as to make us sorry for him. That casts a great shadow over your work."[184] < . . . >

I have failed to keep up with my diary for an absurd reason: I've no more notebooks. Once this one runs out, I'm done for. [. . .]

28 January.

I've always detested Trotskyites not so much for their political ideas as for their characters. I hate their phrase-mongering, their posing, their gesticulations, their bombast. I have always found their leader unbearable from an aesthetic viewpoint: his hair, his weak chin, his cheap provincial demonism—he's a combination Mephistopheles and court clerk. There's something of the Kerensky in him as well. I feel a physiological revulsion to him. Interestingly enough, the feeling is mutual: in his *Literature and Revolution* he treats me with the same scorn I have for him![185]

30 January.

A new batch of Nekrasov proofs has piled up. A ghastly sight: 1,280 pages! How will I ever get through them? Yet get through them I must. Otherwise I'll be less a writer than an editor, that is, a paraliterary. < . . . >

184. Reference to a passage in Alexei Tolstoy's *Road to Calvary*. General Kornilov, who became Commander-in-Chief of the Russian Army on 1 July 1917, sought to preempt the Bolshevik threat by staging a conservative coup. Arrested on Kerensky's orders, he escaped and formed one of the first anti-Bolshevik armed units. He fell during one of the early Civil War battles. (V.E.)

185. See note 118.

1 June.

Left my suitcase with Ionov's concierge and went running around Moscow with my briefcase. Yesterday was a busy and eventful day. I first went to Molodaia gvardiia. The doors were freshly painted, and Lyadova's office had new wallpaper and clean windows, though it was as messy as ever. It was office hours, yet no one was in, not a soul: they were all at a Party meeting. After much perturbation I located Rozenko, the head of the publishing house, a simple, open-faced man, a former miner, very likable, straightforward, and untouched by diplomatic machinations. He had taken offense because in a letter to him I said, "You'd have to be an idiot to . . ." He thought I was calling him an idiot. I explained what I meant. He took my *Nekrasov for Children* and asked me to make some additions and changes. I gave him a book of my tales. He promised to let me know within three days whether Molodaia gvardiia would publish a one-volume collection of them. < . . . >

From Molodaia gvardiia I went to the Radio Center. They want me to do two programs for them: my verse and my book *Small Children*. That will earn me two hundred and seventy rubles, enough for a hotel: today I decided to spend the night at a hotel. The people at the Radio Center showed me a letter from somewhere in the provinces saying that the local children had "*resolved* to name Chukovsky their favorite writer." < . . . >

From the Radio Center I went to Academia, where the first person I saw was Kamenev. He was good-natured and cheerful as usual, but gray: he's turned completely gray in the course of a year. < . . . > "I had a good time in Minusinsk," he told me. "Nobody kept me from working. I got nearly two hundred pages written. (He is working on a biography of Chernyshevsky.) It's a pity I was called back to Moscow. I'd have gone on to Nekrasov there, but here I've no time." I think it's a sham; I think he was perfectly glad to be called back to Moscow.

I've been under the weather lately: my head aches, I can hardly sleep, I caught a cold in the train (there was a draft), etc.

I am editing Kolya's translation of *Treasure Island*, poring over each page for hours.

Gorky has fallen ill. He came down with a cold after returning from Italy and Turkey. I can't say I'm surprised: it's freezing cold and cloudy all the time, not a hint of sun. The day before yesterday people feared he was dying. < . . . >

5 June.

Misha Slonimsky was given his last rites at the writers' organization committee today after reading from his latest novel. It must be bad, because
none of his colleagues had a thing to say about it: Olesha kept his lips
sealed; Vera Inber yawned and went home to bed; Vsevolod Ivanov told
me it was a piece of junk and even wrote about it in *Chukokkala.*[186] < . . . >

That evening Slonimsky, Fadeev, Olesha, Stenich, and I went to a
restaurant together. On the way there Olesha said, "You can tell he senses
he's done for. It's like thinking to yourself after a card game, 'Now why
didn't I lead with a nine?' Look at him. He's got the walk of a victim."
But then he said, "No, he has no idea. He's content. And if that's the case,
he's beyond help: he hasn't got a shred of talent."

But Fadeev said he liked the novel. "Vsevolod has written a novel called
Y," he said, "a big bore.[187] When you get down to it, I write in the
straightforward Leningrad way and so does Slonimsky. Vsevolod is all
Moscow—winding alleys, a tangle."

7 June.

< . . . > Called on Olesha and found Stenich, Ilf, and an artist I didn't
know having a grand old time around the table. Olesha is a great one for
table talk and maintains a constant flow of jokes, stories, and wicked remarks. Ilf is also endlessly witty. Looking out of the window, he said, "Oh,
what a well-placed flat you have: you'll have a bird's-eye view of Stanislavsky's funeral!" Which led everyone to imitate Nemirovich-Danchenko and
Stanislavsky wondering which of them would die first. Then he said that
Afinogenov had tried to hide his monthly income (fourteen thousand rubles), but the tax board had discovered it.

I asked Olesha about his *Three Fat Men,*[188] and he said that when
Stanislavsky came back from abroad he decided to stage it differently and
had postponed the production for a while, but he didn't care, because it
was going to be done by the Music Hall, where it would have lots of circus

---

186. *Chukokkala* (Moscow, 1979), 362.

187. *Y* is an experimental novel dealing with the private sphere. It was not published in the
Soviet Union until 1988. (M.H.H.)

188. Reference to the stage adaptation of Olesha's first novel of the same title, a fable about
the class struggle. (V.E.)

acts. Olesha has taken my case to heart and has been ringing a man named Riskind. Then we set off for Pasternak's, that is, I went to Koltsov's to get some sleep, and they—still laughing and skipping from anecdote to anecdote—took Gazetny Lane. As we walked past MOPR,[189] Ilf called the building's architecture prisonlike. That's how the architect won over the political prisoners. "I'll make you a building like a real prison. With real bars." They fell for it. And rejected Le Corbusier.

7 August.

Yevpatoria is as tawdry as Yalta: they take good, honest seashells and decorate them with the most impossible, unnatural patterns. One of the workshops in Yevpatoria where they make the ugly things is called "Gift of the Sea Floor." Vendors cry, "Medicinal young millet kasha!" There's a shoemaker near us who takes his sign down when he goes off to lunch: people steal. The amount people steal in Yevpatoria is astounding. Thieves learn from posters which actors are on when, and go to rob them just as they are nervously making their appearance. < ... >

I met Oistrakh the violinist here. He still has a student look about him and is affable, refined, and modest. I'm disappointed in music-hall bohemianism.

27 August.

Arrived in Yalta on the night of the twenty-sixth. Went to Mura's grave in Alupka on the evening of the twenty-seventh. < ... >

Made the rounds of the Yalta bookshops, which are supplied from Moscow by Soiuzpechat' with titles like: *Fulfilling Heavy Industry's Plan, Malignant Tumors, Guide to Steam Turbines, Problems of China, Road Machines, Restructuring the Local Budget.* There is not a single book about the Crimea. It is all so much dead weight, and the man in the street takes one look and buys—shells. There are also lots of books in Tatar, but the Tatars don't read them. The shop assistant told me that after a while they tear out the pages and roll them into cones to sell to tourists going grape picking. < ... >

189. The International Organization for Aid to Revolutionaries, designed to assist foreign Communist victims of political persecution. (V.E.)

The first thing I did when I got to Tiflis was to take the tram to Plekhanovskaya Street and the Children's Park of Culture and Rest that the papers have made so much of. I was curious to see the only socialist park for children in the USSR. It turned out to be a joke in bad taste, a tiny strip of land sandwiched between large buildings and sullied by nocturnal visitors. By night it was an open stage and drinking bouts, by day— the only socialist park for children in the USSR. < . . . > In fact, the Children's Park of Culture and Rest was a piece of wasteland where young people carried on and behaved like hooligans and stuck around so as to get into the evening performances free of charge. < . . . > I was taken to the children's pool. It was disgusting—a small basin holding eight or nine hundred liters of stagnant water crammed with naked *adult* bodies and two or three children for good measure. When I asked why there were grown-ups in the children's pool, people told me that the pool had been made a commercial enterprise and was now open to anyone wishing to bathe and that the money went to cover their unpaid salaries! Then they admitted that there was actually no photography club or amateur theater, that it was all on paper only, and that all the pictures were fake. The display of articles made by children—a table, a chair, etc.—was likewise fake: they were made by an adult for his own eventual use.

I decided to report all this to the municipal authorities and went to the new offices of the newspaper *Zaria Vostoka*, an obvious parody of *Izvestiia*, where they greeted me with open arms and told me that Pilnyak was in town. It was four o'clock by then, and I hadn't yet had anything to eat or any sleep or found a place to stay. All the hotels were full—I had spent a good fifty rubles on cabs and porters and left my things in the lobby of the Hotel Palace (I believe)—and there was little hope of finding a room. In desperation I went to the Hotel Orient and asked whether Pilnyak was staying there. "He is in the government suite," I was told. I went up and saw a table groaning with delicacies in a spacious dining room and a beaming Pilnyak at the table. Also present were Herzl Bazov, a Georgian Jew who has written a play about a Jewish kolkhoz; Alexander Duduchava, head of art for the Georgian Narkompros; the playwright Grigory Bukhnikhashvili; the film director Lina Gogoberidze; the Vice Minister of Education S. S. Gegenada; Yevgenia Vladimirovna Pasternak, Pasternak's former wife; and several others. Titsian Tabidze, the *tamada* [toastmaster], sat at the head of the table; corpulent and lethargic, he was a born *tamada*. He immediately toasted Marya Borisovna and me (and even mentioned my

Shevchenko article and my book *From Chekhov to Our Times*), and Zhenichka Pasternak immediately ran off and arranged for us to have her room
in the Orient and booked another for herself. < . . . >

The talk was of Gorky and it was all hostile. Pilnyak, hurt by Gorky's
article,[190] was highly gratified by the hostility of certain obtuse literati
toward Alexei Mikhailovich. "What is stronger than Gorky?" he asked in
riddle form.

"Death," an old man answered.

"Right! Right! Hear that, Chukovsky?"

The *tamada*'s toasts were very lofty in style: "Beauty has its obliga-
tions." "Beauty will save the world." "The holy family of *Boris* Pasternak,
Boris Pilnyak, and *Boris* Bugaev"[191] (three writers who had visited Georgia).
I eventually understood the essence of the Georgian feast: the number of
toasts equals the number of people at table multiplied by the number of
glasses. Tabidze drank continually, and the toasts went on for three and a
half hours. [. . .] Tabidze recited Blok, and the poems seemed to gain in
beauty from his Georgian accent. Tabidze is a former symbolist in the
Russo-Gallic vein, a vestige of that great poetic period, and his drunken
poetic wails evoked the spirit of 1908–10. His face resembles Oscar Wilde's
when swollen with absinthe. For ten years now he's been collecting material
for a novel about Shamil.[192] < . . . >

Next day I went to a museum where they show the life of the Khevsurs
and Svans. I saw an exhibit of Khevsur medical instruments—gruesome
pincers and lancets—skis, and beds, luxurious for the men and pitiful for
the women (a basketlike affair that can be carried out by the handles when
the woman is in labor). [. . .]

On the evening of 2 September Pilnyak set up a meeting with local
writers in the Palace of Arts, Machabeli (formerly Sergievskaya) Street 13.
About three hundred people came. The hall couldn't hold them all. There
were people standing in the aisles and the adjoining rooms. They asked

190. In a *Pravda* article published on 10 July 1933 Gorky wrote: "Some tricksters seek to
contrive ultra-sophisticated literature, imitating, say, Dos Passos, an unsuccessful caricature of
Pilnyak, who is himself enough of a caricature."

191. The real name of the prominent Symbolist Andrei Bely. (V.E.)

192. Shamil (1797–1891) was a political and religious leader of the North Caucasian moun-
taineers who resisted Russian conquest. He surrendered to the Russians in 1859. Originally
extolled by the Soviets as a folk hero, he came to be seen as a Turkish and British agent in the
last years of Stalin's regime. (V.E.)

Pilnyak questions, and he responded with a pugnacious wit. "Not everyone can write *Klim Samgin*, after all!"[193] He was asked what he thought of Dos Passos (in connection with the article in which Gorky accused Dos Passos of being a Russian Pilnyak), why he had written *Mahogany*, etc.[194] All at once he called out my name. Because of the crush and the din and distance I failed to hear him, so he went down into the audience and pulled me up on stage. I began to recite my tales, and the audience welcomed me with a warmth I've never experienced before. [. . .]

11 September.

Kislovodsk. [. . .] A. N. Tikhonov is here too. He's been telling us about Gorky. Gorky doesn't feel like going back to Sorrento this winter; he wants to winter in the Crimea, in Foros. A house has been made ready for him. He's working on *Samgin*. It's giving him trouble. Gorky has never before asked anyone for advice, and now he's reading *Samgin* to all kinds of people and asking what they think. < . . . >

Saw Budyonny yesterday.

16 September.

< . . . > People have begun talking about Gorky. Khalatov feels offended by him. "After all, I'm the one most responsible for his rapprochement with the USSR and not only through Ogiz but personally as well. I met Gorky in 1918 and was close to him. After visits to Vladimir Ilyich [Lenin] in the Kremlin he would come and see me at Narkomprod. We were neighbors. 'Why have you taken Rode under your wing?' I asked Gorky. 'Don't you know what a villain he is?' Gorky took offense and turned his back on me. One day Rode turned up with some notes from Gorky. We'd always honored his requests, but this time we had our doubts about them. They were outrageous, out of touch with reality. My secretary noticed that

193. Gorky's *roman fleuve*, *The Life of Klim Samgin*, chronicles the vicissitudes of an allegedly typical intellectual in the first quarter of the twentieth century—vacillating, egotistical, and vacuous. Begun in 1925, the highly ambitious novel remained, not surprisingly, unfinished. (V.E.)

194. *Mahogany* is a somewhat heterodox novella, marked by a sympathetic portrayal of the last Mohicans of revolutionary fundamentalism, including a Trotskyite. In 1930 Pilnyak was bitterly attacked for publishing it in Berlin. (V.E.)

while the signatures at the bottom were Gorky's, the text itself was in Rode's handwriting. Rode had got several dozen blank forms from Gorky and was filling them in as he saw fit. On the basis of those forms he had received trainloads of flour, which he then sold on the black market at outrageous prices. I resolved to take them away from him. We got him drunk and filched twelve or fifteen of the signed forms when he was far gone. Two or three years later I gave them back to Alexei Mikhailovich.

"In 1921 (I believe) Vladimir Ilyich sent me to Berlin to deliver a handwritten letter to Gorky. Gorky had broken with Rode by then, but I didn't know it. Rode met me in Stetin in splendor—he had reserved an entire compartment in the train < . . . >—and went all the way to Fried-richsstrasse with me and then took me to the Russischer Hof, a White Guard nest. I didn't realize what kind of a hotel it was, and there I was with a letter from Lenin and a pile of conspiratorial documents. My room was luxurious. < . . . > I rang the Embassy. 'Why have you put up at that White Guard stronghold?' they asked. 'Stay where you are, don't move, and we'll come and rescue you.' They had to save me from Rode's clutches. When I went and told Gorky, 'Your Rode is at it again,' he said, 'I've broken with him once and for all.'

"I can't tell you how many times he put Gorky in a bad light. Here is an example. One day Vladimir Ilyich did everything Gorky asked in con-nection with his writers' needs. Gorky was so happy he came to my office and sat motionless, beaming, for twenty minutes. My fellow workers were amazed. At last he said, 'Bring Vladimir Ilyich to my place—Mashkov Lane—for tea.' He was waiting at the entrance when we got there, and apologized for the broken lift. We walked up the five flights, and no sooner had we taken our seats at the table than the door to the nursery flew open and out came a Gypsy chorus led by Rode! Ilyich poked me with his thumb as if to say, 'Look what we've got ourselves into.' Gorky frowned and said, 'Sorry,' and took Rode into the nursery. One minute later the chorus was liquidated, and Gorky came back looking sheepish."

Then Khalatov told me the story of Ganetsky, who decided to tell Gorky "the whole truth"—and what came of it. Another curious story he told was about Gorky's relations with Khalatov after Khalatov's fall. "He wrote me a very nasty letter—it had obviously been dictated to him—and when he came back and we met, he invited me into his motor car, sent everyone else away, embraced me, and was much nicer than usual. When

I went to visit him, he was so happy to see me that he jumped up off his stool and would have fallen if I hadn't held on to him."

It was a friendly conversation and lasted about two hours. [. . .]

Tikhonov says that Gorky has changed radically: he's begun to heed the advice of doctors and worry about his health; he's working terribly hard—he's at his desk from morning till night; and at night he plays cards and goes to bed. [. . .]

24 September.

There is a deaf woman among the patients, a Lizaveta Yakovlevna Drabkina, who has been a member of the Party since the age of four. During the Moscow Uprising her mother went to Moscow wound round with Bickford fuse cord, taking her daughter along and dressing up like a society lady as a blind.[195] Her father is S. P. Gusev, her husband—head of the Cheka. Yesterday she told me, Tikhonov, Yadviga Nikolaevna, and Bella Borisovna the story of her adventures in Kamo's unit. They were so horrific they kept me up all night. Kamo took Lizaveta Yakovlevna and a group of young people preparing to assassinate Denikin to a small wood outside Moscow, where a unit of Whites fell upon them and started taking them off one by one to be executed. Lizaveta Yakovlevna, who was twenty-seven at the time, launched into the Internationale the moment they aimed their guns at her, but four of the group caved in and began to renounce their ties to Kamo and betray their comrades. Then it turned out that Kamo had staged the whole thing to test how devoted the members of his organization were to the revolution. Her adventures as a machine gunner were equally exciting. She told them with humor, though they were all drenched in blood, and I had the feeling that if she had it to do over she would approach it again with her wild, Nechaev-like spirit.

1 October.

< . . . > Tikhonov stoked the fire with magazines and *Nashi dostizheniia.*
< . . . >

195. A Moscow-wide general strike in December 1905 turned into an attempted uprising. Its suppression spelled the virtual end of the revolution of 1905. (V.E.)

9 October.

Have been in Moscow for three days now. At the Koltsovs' in Government House. Rain. Many changes, as usual in autumn. < . . . > I went to Molodaia gvardiia.

"May I see Rozenko?"

"Rozenko?"

"The head of the publishing house."

"There's nobody here by that name."

They've forgotten they ever had such a boss.

"Well, where can I find Atsarkin?"

"Atsarkin is gone. He was expelled from the Party and dismissed."

"I see. Can you show me to Sverdlova's office?"

"Klavdia Timofeevna? She doesn't work here any longer."

"Then who does? Shabad?"

"No, he doesn't either."

But Lyadova is still there. Lyadova is in power. She is the assistant director of Detizdat. I went to see her. She is heady with victory and claims her position is as secure as can be. Yet Gorky and Marshak are against her, she and Smirnov are at daggers drawn, and she has no idea of what makes children's literature or of how to work. She hasn't done a thing with any of my books they've bought. < . . . > *Robinson* has been lying there for about a year. My collection of tales is still at the censors'; for four months no one has been able to pinpoint where it's got bogged down. She is good at squabbling, scheming, snaring, and backstage machinations. She is rumored to be under Kaganovich's wing. Even though Gorky and Marshak did everything they could to have Detizdat based in Leningrad, she managed to defend Moscow. She squeezed out the Shabad woman and took over as assistant director. She doesn't read, she doesn't see children; all she does is run from meeting to meeting and from Party organization to Party organization imposing her line under the counter. I saw her in the offices of *Pionerskaia Pravda*. One person brought her a pear, another presented her with some cigarettes, every person passing in the corridor greeted her— she is clearly very much at home here. I caught a glimpse of a gray-haired, energetic Smirnov at Ogiz. But people say he is out of his mind.

19 October.

Unfortunately I had proof today that they are right. I went to see Lyadova at Molodaia gvardiia, where Smirnov has now moved from Ogiz. He is pompous, yet affable. "Kornei Ivanovich! Just the person I was looking for! Tell me the ten best children's books for us to publish immediately." As I spoke, I noticed he was writing the titles on a scrap of paper instead of on a pad and when he had finished he left it lying there amidst a pile of other scraps. < . . . > He agrees with everything you say and makes the most colossal promises only to forget them a minute later. When he saw the drawings Konashevich had done for the Academia edition of my tales, he said, "We'll publish it immediately with all the illustrations."

"But some have as many as eighteen colors," Konashevich said. "It would take three years."

"We'll put it out on quality paper and by the first of January."

"The first of January?"

"Yes!" he said triumphantly. "We'll put out an entire line of quality books!"

He started listing the most pie-in-the-sky projects when he was called away to a meeting. [. . .]

26 October.

Marshak came to call yesterday, bursting with creativity. He's writing a narrative poem about the rivers of the north and an article about children's literature and has reworked *Mister Twister* yet again. He's got all kinds of ambitious plans. He's learned Italian and is much taken with Dante. He says that Gorky stole nearly half of a recent article, "On Plans in Children's Literature," from a letter that he, Marshak, had written to him. < . . . >

10 November.

< . . . > I've heard terrible rumors about our madman Smirnov. They say he's held up publication of all children's books in Moscow—every last one—"until the necessary technical foundation is in place." The idiot! < . . . >

23–24 November.

I'm giving a reading tomorrow at the Chamber Music Theater. Denisova will perform my songs for the first time. The music is by Strelnikov. < . . . > There will also be an exhibit of my (children's) books.

About five days ago I attended a session of Children's Court. I saw a boy who had climbed down into a refuse pit where a friend was sitting and broken the friend's nose; I saw a girl who was a full-fledged thief and professional prostitute at the age of fourteen; I saw a twelve-year-old boy who had attempted to rape a twenty-eight-year-old girl, all of which goes to show how terribly abandoned by the family today's children are: parents work themselves silly, they come home only to sleep and hardly see their children; children go to school on an empty stomach, they roam the streets at night in gangs, and all their fathers say is, "Do your homework. Make something of yourself." [. . .]

26 November.

My reading took place at the Chamber Music Theater on the twenty-fourth. A sellout. There were so many people that Strelnikov, the composer, couldn't push his way through and left. There was a crowd out in the street as well. Everyone is as warm as can be, yet I feel terribly lonely. Why I don't know. Lida, who is so interested in everything having to do with children, didn't even ask me how it went. Nobody seems to realize that I'm more than a children's writer; I'm a grown-up. < . . . >

21 December.

The bells are being removed from our Church of the Savior. In the middle of the night. They're clanging so you'd think they were calling the faithful to mass. < . . . > [. . .]

1934

+>-+>-+>-+>-+>-+>-+>

12 January.

The day before yesterday we were given a new phone. Gone forever 194–75, a number so familiar it was part of me. Also the day before yesterday I delivered *From Two to Five* to the Izdatel'stvo pisatelei for the fourth edition.[196] I want Rudakov to do the illustrations. < . . . >

Saw Zoshchenko. He looked wild, self-satisfied, well-groomed. "Oh what a magnificent book I'm writing, Kornei Ivanovich! A Decameron. About love, intrigue, all sorts of things. It's got fantastic epigraphs, fantastic quotations! By the way, Gorky has put in a good word for my *Youth Restored.*[197] He's an old man, he wants to hold out a few more years, and my book gives the prescription for longevity. That's why he's taken a liking to it. He sent Glavlit an insulting letter, highly insulting—Misha Slonimsky suddenly found the book ever so praiseworthy—and Glavlit restored even the cuts it had forced me to make." < . . . >

13 January.

Morning. Have just completed a brief radio piece on Nekrasov.

Called on Alyansky yesterday. He told me Smirnov had been dismissed. I don't know how or under what circumstances.

I'm finally out from under proofreading the one-volume Nekrasov for GIKhL and the other Nekrasov for Academia (both at the same time!) and my *Sixties* book, etc., etc. I was given a copy of the fine bourgeois scholar Piaget just after I delivered the fourth edition of *From Two to Five*. I am so sorry I was unable to include excerpts from it in my book. < . . . >

196. *From Two to Five* is a pioneering and richly documented study of children's language. (V.E.)

197. See note 141.

15 January.

Called on the Tynyanovs with Marya Borisovna yesterday. They've got a new dining-room set, Swedish, and a new radio. They gave us a sumptuous repast. They are living in clover.

Yelena Alexandrovna is upset by the fate of her Stradivarius book: Muzgiz had commissioned the book from her, she spent a year writing it, and suddenly a decree descends from on high to the effect that "we have our own Stradivariuses and there is no need to praise the Italians," and the plates are destroyed (the proofs were ready).

Yury Nikolaevich was very affectionate with us. He said we were practically the only friends he had left. Everyone else was an enemy. He spoke again about his break with Shklovsky: "Now instead of writing *predannyi vam* [Yours truly or, literally, devoted to you] before my signature I can write *predannyi vami* [betrayed by you]. He told us about his run-in with the Belorussian cinema people, who took it upon themselves to speak about his *Kizhe*[198] (after the film was ready) in less than deferential terms, at which point he had risen and pronounced a majestic "I am Tynyanov; you are small fry."

For the next hour or two he read from his new novel. Just yesterday he had completed the chapter about the four-year-old Pushkin or, rather, the opening of the chapter, and he read us the entire baptism section. The writing is magnificent. It is not two-dimensional, like *Kyukhlya,* or limited to the fourth dimension, like *The Wax Figure;* it is three-dimensional— you sense the characters' "volume."[199] Confident of his success, he is exultant, jubilant, cordial. He harbors an unmitigated hatred for anyone he considers his enemy. Three times within the past two weeks he has told me about attending a *Litsovremennik* meeting and lifting his head to see that "they were all enemies." [. . .]

20 January.

Moscow. Yesterday morning my friend Marshak was getting ready for an important meeting. "Where are you going?" I asked.

198. See note 145.

199. The manuscript he is reading from would eventually become the biographical novel *Pushkin* (1935). *Kyukhlya* (1925) is a fictionalized biography of Pushkin's classmate, the libertarian poet Vilgelm Kyukhelbeker. *The Wax Figure* (1932) deals with the reign of Peter the Great. (V.E.)

"Oh, nowhere important."

It turned out that a meeting of Rabichev's children's book commission was to take place in an hour and my friend was very anxious for me not to attend. "Gorky won't be there. It's nothing interesting," from which I concluded that Gorky would be there and that my presence was imperative. Much to his disappointment, I waited for Alexinsky's car with him. < . . . > I had no idea where the commission was housed, and suddenly the car pulled into the courtyard of Gorky's private residence. < . . . >

Marshak sat opposite Gorky. < . . . > His report was magnificent—serious and beautifully written. Gorky listened as if in love, though making occasional corrections in word choice. < . . . >

Marshak got into hot water by bringing up Dumas. Since he never reads, he was unaware of Gorky's feelings about Dumas and expressed his disapproval of schoolchildren who read him. "I have noticed that young people who loved Dumas in their childhood never amount to anything. *I never thought much of him.*"

"Well, that's your loss," said Gorky. "I loved him as a child. Still do. He's amazingly good at dialogue. Amazingly good. Paradoxical as it sounds, the only other writer who can match him is Balzac."

Marshak faltered a bit, but the rest came off just fine. The report gives a bright and clear picture of the Soviet schoolchild, and once it has been translated Europe will have documentary evidence of the great potential of our educational system.

Gorky also interrupted the report with suggestions: "We need biographies of bourgeois heroes. Coolidge, for instance: president, world leader—and blockhead. Or Cecil Rhodes: a man who had monuments built to him during his lifetime and remained a fool through it all. We should reprint Menzbir's book on birds. Brehm too, though without the nonsense in the Soviet editions: 'on the influence of pregnant women on whaling.' "

I began to notice that Gorky's voice was muffled, his words indistinct, as if coming from a toothless old man. Even though I was sitting right next to him, I couldn't make out much of what he said. All I caught was: "How about a history of arms . . . Or an anatomy book . . . A translation of Olivia Schneider . . . And here's an important issue: the influence of children's books on adults. In villages adults read only their children's books. They have none of their own." < . . . >

Went to Detizdat and asked, "Not one of my books is coming out. Whose head do I bash?"

"Smirnov's," came the unanimous reply.

So I went to see the lunatic.

"Well, well! Kornei Ivanovich. How are your readings going?"

"I'm not here to talk about my readings; I'm here to talk about your maraudings. How dare you hold back my *Robinson* and call it illiterate! How dare you shelve my *Tales*! How dare you deprive children of *Treasure Island*!"

"Why, I've done nothing of the sort!" said Smirnov. "Who's been maligning me like this? I simply forgot."

"Everybody's talking about it. You called my book illiterate."

"Never! Here, you see? It's in production. Give me all your tales. I'll publish them on the spot. Tell me, who of my staff has been maligning me?"

Then I saw Lyadova, who told me she had reported Smirnov insane to the Central Committee on 19 November of last year; she says she accused him of hatching wild schemes and publishing nothing, etc. Smirnov was then called before the Central Committee and told to put the publishing house back on its feet within a month's time. A month went by, he got nothing done, and the Central Committee decided to oust him. But because of the Moscow conference there was no time to draw up the dismissal order, and Smirnov is taking advantage of the situation to make it seem he is still in power. From other things Lyadova said I could tell that she too had been dismissed: she told me she had put in for retirement and *wanted* to withdraw. "I've no desire to go on," she said. "I'm sick of it all."

"Rozenel, Lunacharsky's widow, has a streptococcus infection; Gorky has quarreled with Stalin: 'The honeymoon of their friendship is over'; the government has presented Litvinov with a magnificent house"—I learned these three things from Lizochka Koltsova, who is fresh from Paris. She also brought a globe-shaped lampshade and a set of whiskey glasses-cum-carafe mounted in four antique books with the title *The True Religion* (La Religion vraie) on the spine. Sitting on Koltsov's desk they look absolutely genuine, but when you open them out comes the vodka. They cost two hundred francs. < . . . >

30 January.

From the twenty-fifth until this very minute I've been in bed with three ailments: the grippe (I caught a cold at the Park of Culture and Rest), food poisoning (from beef stroganoff at the Great Moscow), and a broken rib (I fell and injured myself when I fainted from the food poisoning). < . . . > Am reading *Novellas and Stories* by Herzen (in the new Academia edition) and Shevchenko's verse.

Gorky, who caught a cold in Gorki, went to the Congress to hear Stalin,[200] and now he has a very bad case of the grippe.

31 January.

Khalatov came to call yesterday. He is getting me into the Kremlin Hospital. I can't believe my luck, because I'm a total invalid. My temperature is normal today for the first time. I am reading the eighteenth-century volume of *Literaturnoe nasledstvo*.

I was brought here to the Kremlin Hospital in an ambulance. I was given a washing and a smock and put in ward number two. I said I had the grippe, a cough, and kidney and stomach problems. From the ambulance I saw an enormous number of policemen and a huge crowd demonstrating with flags. Light snow, no wind, fog—rotten weather. A few military units in Red Square. Once I was in bed, I turned on the radio. They were broadcasting from Red Square. I was surprised to learn that our Kirov, Kirov from Leningrad, was the only one who had come from the Congress to greet the Muscovites, the workers of Moscow. Something was in the air, something gone wrong. There had been no response to the workers' celebration. I could hear the endless cheering through my window, as sincere and impassioned as always, yet I was struck by the fact that Comrade Kirov made no mention of the flight into the stratosphere. (This morning the mother of Koltsov's wife told me the stratosphere balloon had set down safely in Kolomna.) And as I was slipping the radio under my pillow, I heard the words "sad news" and, quickly pulling the earphones back on, I heard Enukidze announce the deaths of the three *Osoviakhim* heroes.[201] I am so overcome with grief that I can't sleep.

---

200. Stalin spoke at the Eighteenth Party Congress on 26 January 1934.

201. On 30 January 1934 the Soviet stratosphere balloon *Osoviakhim I* broke the world record by climbing to a height of twenty-two kilometers, but it crashed during the descent and the entire crew perished.

2 February.

My temperature is a steady thirty-seven. I am terribly weak. < . . . >

10 February.

Still at the Kremlin Hospital, therapeutics, ward two. Had a visit from Mandelshtam the day before yesterday. He recited poems about poets (Derzhavin and Yazykov), Petrarch translations, and a poem on the death of Andrei Bely. He recites poorly, in a singsong whisper, but it is extremely powerful: no other poet has been vouchsafed his feeling for the physical sweetness of the word. His beard is gray; there is almost nothing left of the "marble fly" I knew in Kuokkala. He praised my Nekrasov book again.

19 February.

So Bagritsky has died. Little did I think when I visited him on 24 January that I was seeing him for the first and last time.

Still at the Kremlin Hospital. I'm allowed to walk on the roof, though I have a hard time getting up there in my fur coat and the hospital's felt boots. I've got an unobstructed view of the site of metro shaft thirty-two. It is directly opposite the hospital in back of the construction site for the Lenin Library. In two or three years everything I now see will seem like ancient history, but what I see is the following: a two-story building put up about forty years ago but full of cracks because the metro tunnel runs too close. As a result, bearded Scythians with axes are hewing logs and fashioning struts to reinforce it. The majority of the workforce on the site is female. They swarm here and there in groups of eight, dressed any which way and shoveling the earth brought up from below into carts and trucks. < . . . > From above much of the activity looks absurd. Once the earth is dug up, why don't the workers shovel it directly onto the trucks instead of leaving it on the ground to freeze so badly that it has to be broken up with crowbars? It makes for twice as much, if not three times as much work, because the piles of earth congest the site and must be moved from place to place in addition to being loaded onto the trucks. There are all sorts of foul-ups, yet the metro *shall* be completed. < . . . >

Kamenev is working on Modzalevsky's notes to Pushkin's letters. He says they consist of such an unmanageable number of facts that he has to redo every page.

21 February.

I thought I could leave tomorrow, but my head suddenly started aching and my temperature is back up to thirty-seven. < . . . >

I've started putting together new material for the fifth edition of *From Two to Five*, even though the fourth isn't out yet. I need to catch up on the latest in psychology, education, and linguistics or else it will be the work of an amateur. I've also got to make my style more limber and appealing. The book is stiff and lifeless. People don't notice it, because the material itself is so heart-warming, but correcting the proofs for the fourth edition I was amazed at how poor the writing was. < . . . >

< . . . >

25 March.

Titsian Tabidze is in Leningrad. I am in his debt: he was very warm to us while we were in Tiflis, and I must pay him back with Leningrad hospitality. He's staying at the Astoria. I went there, but he wasn't in.

When I got home, I found Tynyanov waiting. We embraced. He invited me to a party for Tabidze at his place, and off we went. He is upset by the vulgar screen adaptation of *Lieutenant Kizhe*. "If there's a Lieutenant Kizhe in the film, it's the director; the director is a true Kizhe, because he doesn't exist."[202] I consoled him as much as I could, though the film *is* bad. < . . . >.

Zoshchenko's *Youth Restored* was given a public discussion at the House of Scholars the day before yesterday. Academician Derzhavin lashed out at Zoshchenko for his "petty bourgeois" language; Fedin defended the work. Relating the incident, Tynyanov revealed a strong and unexpected antipathy to Fedin. "Fedin defending Zoshchenko! Fedin patronizing Zoshchenko! That bloated mediocrity!" and so on. He spoke with the same surprising animosity of Mandelshtam and Pasternak. He was very funny about Mandelshtam. There was an act in a Berlin music hall that went as follows: two perfectly nondescript men came out on stage and stood on a gigantic rubber

202. The director in question was Alexander Faintsimmer.

pillow; then they jumped and jumped, higher and higher, until up they flew to the ceiling—and disappeared. About Pasternak he said that his father was a poor [illegible] of the Munich school with woolly brushwork. Like father like son: vague words, vague images . . .

He also talked about Gorky. Gorky couldn't stand the success Alyoshka (Tynyanov never called Alexei Tolstoy anything else) once had with a joke about a chopped-off head, so he immediately came up with a story about a woman with a chopped-off head driving along Nevsky Prospect in a cab on 9 January—just to spite him. (But don't tell a soul, Kornei Ivanovich!)

Nobody had come yet when we got to his place, so he read me his latest Heine translations. He's putting together a book of them. Some are magnificent—the one about Napoleon III (as an ass). He is at his best when Heine is dry, brutal, biting; the lyrical ones are weaker. [. . .]

29 March.

Went to the Raisovet to press for a room for the Club of Children's Writers. The club was originally supposed to be housed in the recently added top floor of the Griboedov Canal building, where the writers are moving soon, but at the last moment the space was redesignated as a flat for Zoshchenko and somebody else and we were told to make a place for ourselves in the Power Cooperative in the same building. < . . . > I climbed the stairs just behind Zoshchenko, who carried himself like an old man with heart trouble. When I asked him why he was exchanging a good flat for a worse one, he said with surprising candor, "I have a nasty shrew for a wife, she's quarreled with all the neighbors, and while I never intervene I've had enough. I don't know how I've made it through these two years with her. It's been a real trial."

He is ecstatic about the success of *Youth Restored*. "It sold out in a day. I get piles of letters from all over," and so on. Mannered, affected, full of himself as he is, he is still a charmer. He gave a copy of the book to the chairman of the Raisovet "on the part of the writers' community." He says Bukharin invited him to his hotel room. "Rang me personally. He's got the grippe. He was in bed naked. Full of energy. 'I'll give you a flat in Moscow and a salary of two and a half thousand a month if you write feuilletons for *Izvestiia*.' I declined. On the basis of ill health. 'Then go to Nalchik.[203]

203. Nalchik is a vacation spot in the Northern Caucasus. "Go to Nalchik" means "go South," "take a holiday." (V.E.)

I'll write you a recommendation on the spot.' Things are bad at home. New tenants have moved in, and my son has a fever all the time." [. . .]

18 June.

Went to Solts's talk on the Party purge at the Writers' Organizational Committee. Solts is seductively intelligent, gray, and good at striking a liberal pose. Marietta [Shaginyan] sat literally at his ear, like Mary at Christ's feet; Seifullina opposite him, stiff, motionless; Fadeev presiding < . . . >. As long as he had the floor to himself, he was not a particularly brilliant speaker, but when people started questioning him about the purge, that is, how it was to be carried out, he sparkled, and the assembled company laughed uproariously. It was a naive laughter, because the basic audience consisted of perfectly simple people, the kind that fill the galleries: empty stares, fleshy peasant-like cheeks. Almost no "intellectual" faces. You'd be hard put to identify them as writers. Solts said that the purge was aimed primarily at "boring" people. "There are people who fought for the Revolution and made great sacrifices and who have very interesting things to say about what happened here before 1917 but are boring when they talk about what came after. That's a bad sign. Are those the people who need to be purged? No, they are not. They need to be pensioned. They are no longer good for anything but pensions."

"How do you go about purging young people?" Lyadova asked.

"I am particularly demanding when it comes to the young, but as a judge I never give young people stiff sentences. I feel no sympathy for the elderly. Or the infirm. Who will do the building if we support the weak, the ailing, and the wretched? I am not interested in a man's origins. People used to brag about being a count; now they brag about having a locksmith for a father, and some even think that pulling off the feat of having a locksmith father is enough. That is something we must fight. I have reinstated all sons of tsarist policemen in my work on the purge commission. After all, they're the same as our police: they come from indigent peasant stock. A peasant with land didn't go into the police. No, I purge the purgers; I purge Party bigwigs."

Then he started in on sex. "Sex has a social character. If you consider sex a natural function of the organism, you are demeaning yourself in that domain, and not merely in that domain. You gain nothing from putting yourself on the level of an animal."

When asked about his attitude toward contemporary Soviet literature, he said, "My memory isn't what it used to be. I forget everything I read. I've just read Sholokhov's *Virgin Soil Upturned* and forgot it immediately."

Seifullina: "Well, I'm glad you forget everything. That means you've forgotten me and forgotten bawling me out."

There were sandwiches with caviar and salmon and tea and sweets. We left with Seifullina, who grumbled, "I'm tired of liberal dignitaries. *He* may have nothing against the son of a tsarist policemen, but when I mentioned in a questionnaire at a Kuznetsk construction site that I had clergymen in my background, the head of operations ran up to me and asked me to cross it out. Why does he say the only people they persecute are the ones who hide their origins when in fact they *force* you to hide them?"

All this sulking has turned Seifullina into one of Solts's bores, and Arkhangelsky and I left her as soon as we could.

20 June.

Middle of the night. They're going to make a recording of my voice in the morning at the Radio Center. A tape recording. I'm so nervous I can't sleep and am plagued by a variety of nocturnal thoughts. This trip to Moscow has confirmed that a directive about loving my children's verse must have come down from on high. People are going overboard, in fact, and that frightens me. I know my worth, but I must say I was more comfortable when they reviled me than I am when they praise me. The way people in Moscow treat me now you'd think I'd never written anything but children's verse, though when it comes to children's verse I'm a classic. I find it all highly offensive.

It rained so hard yesterday I had to stay inside until one; I couldn't even run out for a shave. Then I went to Molodaia gvardiia, where that toothless carrot-top of a Shabad told me yet again that they had decided to remove "Chatterbox Fly" and "Barmalei" from the collection.

7 September.

[. . .] Grabar talked for four hours yesterday about himself, the autobiography he has just completed, a book on Repin he is planning to publish in a deluxe edition, a painting he did in Paris entitled *Portly Women*, and the Hermitage. We have sold 80 percent of the most valuable paintings abroad. Eighty percent! But there's hope that in two or three years we'll start buying them back—and at lower prices, given the economic depression the West is undergoing. I've no doubt this will happen. Rumor has it that none other than Igor Grabar was instrumental in the sale of many of the finest canvases, though to hear him tell it he fought it tooth and nail, wrote memoranda to Kalinin, made phone calls to the Kremlin, and so on. He claims that Benois left the Soviet Union in protest against the sale of Hermitage paintings and has been living abroad with the support of Ida Rubinstein. Chekhonin took a thousand-dollar bill with him; he sewed it into the sole of his boot and is now in America. [. . .]

14 November.

Kamenev is in town. He's staying at the Academy of Sciences with Academician Krzhizhanovsky. Last night Tomashevsky, Tynyanov, Eikhenbaum, Gukovsky, Shvalbe, Sayanov, Oksman, Zhirmunsky, and I gathered in Krzhizhanovsky's beautiful round hall. Good-natured as usual, he took a piece of paper out of his pocket and said, "This is a letter from Alexei Maximovich [Gorky]. He writes that we need a book showing the *literary devices* of the old masters, something young writers can learn from. Exactly what he has in mind I don't know, but I think it is something like a guide to the technique of writing." Whereupon he presented a list of Formalist demands to an audience of former Formalists, a list that would have dazzled Eikhenbaum and Tomashevsky ten or twelve years before. "Less Marxism, more Formalist analysis" the Kamenev-Gorky idea has it. But the Formalists—who are now separated by more than ten years from Formalism and who were upbraided for precisely what they were now being presented so genteelly in Academician Krzhizhanovsky's stylish digs together with tea and biscuits—the Formalists gave this "indulgence" a cold reception.

"We've broken ourselves of the habit of thinking in terms of literary devices over the past ten years," Eikhenbaum said with great dignity, "and we have basically lost interest in them. Theoretically it would be possible to put together a book like that, but . . ."

"It would be a piece of hackwork," Tomashevsky interrupted.

Eikhenbaum: We'd either have to rehash old ideas or come up with new ones. And they wouldn't be a technique of writing but something else (that is, Marxism).

All the responses reminded me of Nekrasov's lines:

Why then, ravens black,
Did you peck my eyes out?

Kamenev immediately grasped the situation. "All right then!" he said. "I can't lock you up in a concentration camp."

Zhirmunsky: We haven't thought about these things lately. And not by chance, no; out of a certain historical necessity.

I went home with Tynyanov. [. . .]

Tynyanov is angry with Gorky. "He founded Biblioteka poeta and played his games with us—we went to his meetings in Moscow—and now he tells us to go packing." [. . .]

1 December.

Worked on *The Art of Translation*. Was completely absorbed. Took some bromide, but could tell I'd not sleep. Went to see Shchepkina-Kupernik, who fed me cherry preserves and told me about her translation of *Much Ado About Nothing*. That made me sleepy. I went home and lay down. I was reading Xenofont Polevoy when all of a sudden Lifshits phoned me from *Pravda:* "Kirov has been murdered!"[204]

My head began to spin. Sleep was out of the question. What a vile and bald-faced act of provocation! Who would do such a thing?

I went out at eight in the morning and roamed the city. Freezing weather, moon in the last quarter, flags of mourning. < . . . > No papers. (They didn't come out until three in the afternoon.) < . . . > Everyone laments the loss of Kirov and has kind things to say about him. Once more I could not sleep or settle down to anything, so I took off for Moscow.

I can't get over how fast Moscow is changing. It's not so long since my last visit, yet I find myself walking along new streets with new multistoried dwellings and can't recall what was there before. < . . . >

5 December.

< . . . > I spent all day yesterday writing; I never left my Moscow hotel room (114 at the National). In the evening I rang up the Kamenevs and

204. The assassination of Sergei Kirov, a charismatic Leningrad Party leader, is now widely assumed to have been authorized by Stalin. In retrospect, it can be seen as a prelude to the Great Terror. (V.E.)

they invited me to supper. Zinovyev was there too. Strange to say, he is writing an article on Pushkin ("Pushkin and the Decembrists"). The versatility of those old Bolsheviks is astounding. I remember the days when Zinovyev wouldn't even nod in my direction, when he was an unapproachable myth (in Leningrad, at least), when he was fat, bloated, physically repulsive. And now he's a lean old man, sprightly, cheerful, laughing an open, spontaneous laugh.

Kamenev said he'd received a letter from a translator of Spanish poetry named Parnokh branding him a "Balkan gendarme" and breaking off all relations with him. And on the same day he received the issue of *Literaturnyi Leningrad* with the article calling him, Kamenev, a self-serving usurper, a despot, etc., etc. in connection with the Biblioteka poeta affair. I stood up for the authors of the article, because Lev Borisovich was wrong to insult the literary pleiad that had provided the series with such valuable monographs. And what kind of a motto is "First we publish Mikhailov and only then Khomyakov"![205] And so on and so forth. < . . . >

Then we walked along the Arbat to Kirov's grave. About forty thousand people were waiting two by two in Theater Square to get into the Hall of Columns. Kamenev's face fell. He didn't know what to do. To my amazement some Red Army guards in the cordon recognized him and let us pass—if halfheartedly, almost reluctantly. Then there was another cordon to get through. But Kamenev's wife, Tatyana Ivanovna, ran up to the man in charge and said, "That is Kamenev," and the man immediately came to life and even accompanied us to the main entrance of the Hall of Columns.

"Why so modest, Lyova?" Tatyana Ivanovna asked. "Why didn't *you* tell them who you are?"

"It wasn't modesty; it was pride. What if the man had said, 'Kamenev? Never heard of him.' "

We were ushered into the Hall of Columns immediately. Even the electric lights were covered with black cloth. People advanced through the hall in an uninterrupted flow, the GPU guards hurrying them along with the words "Faster, faster. Keep moving." Passing the coffin at such breakneck speed, I didn't see a thing, of course. Nor did Kamenev. We paused at the stairs leading to the choir, hoping the commandant would let us have another look at the coffin, but no one could locate him. As the procession

205. Mikhailov (1829–1865) was known as a revolutionary; Khomyakov (1804–1860), though more respected as a poet, represented conservative, Slavophile ideas. (M.H.H.)

made its way past us, many people recognized Kamenev and pointed at him not particularly respectfully. In the end, what Kamenev wanted was not to see the corpse but to be part of the guard of honor. When the commandant finally showed up, he took us to a round "green room" behind the stage. It was full of Cheka officials and very mournful-looking workers. The workers, Stakhanovites from all over the country including the Leningrad Stalin Works, stood in the middle of the room, and every two minutes eight of them were dispatched to the coffin as a guard of honor. Kamenev signed me up along with himself. An extremely well-built Cheka man—cordial and smiling, though terribly exhausted—handed us crepe bands and we went back into the hall. I stood to the left of Kirov's legs and had a clear view of his face. It hadn't changed, but was a horrific green, as if painted green, and it was all the more terrifying because it hadn't changed. Meanwhile the crowd kept coming, endless, boundless—a man with dried-up limbs hobbling tortured and bowlegged on his crutches up the stairs, a woman with a bandaged head who seemed to have come straight from hospital, a blind man, sobbing, led by an old woman. It was all we could do to push our way downstairs against the current. < . . . > I got home at half past two in the morning.

20 December.

< . . . > There are rumors going round Academia that Kamenev was arrested four days ago. No one says anything definite, but what they don't say leads me to believe it is true. Can he really be such a villain? Can he really have had a connection with Kirov's murder? If so, he is a supernatural hypocrite, because when we went up to Kirov's grave he was overcome with grief, indignant at the despicable act. Was he only pretending to be involved exclusively in literature? He worked with professors and academicians like Oksman and Azadovsky from morning till night, discussing Pushkinskii Dom or the journal they wanted to start, and so on; he read my Shakespeare article, which he liked very much, and kept phoning me late at night, telling me how to make it better, asking me about Radlova's *Othello* translation. He seemed totally absorbed in his literary activities. And yet . . . < . . . >

23 December.

Have just had a talk with Glavlit and learned that my "Crocodile" has been banned again. Does that mean the liberalism of 1932 is a thing of the past? Something funny has happened: when they banned "Crocodile" in 1925, they said, "It's got a *gorodovoi* [tsarist policeman] character, and the action takes place in Petrograd, which no longer exists. It's Leningrad now." As a result of these objections I reworked the text so that the Crocodile gobbles up a *militsioner* [Soviet policeman] in Leningrad. It was approved and passed on to the illustrators. Both Konashevich and Konstantin Rotov drew a *militsioner* in today's Leningrad. And now the censors have vetoed it because it has a *militsioner* in today's Leningrad.

< . . . >

28 December.

A new chapter in the "Crocodile" saga today. It began back when everyone at Detgiz told me, "We'll be only too glad to publish it." Semashko too: "Why, of course! It's wonderful. We're going to publish it." Academia too: "We're publishing it with no ifs or buts." < . . . >

On the basis of all this Konashevich did the drawings for the Academia edition < . . . >, Rotov did the drawings for the Detgiz edition, and just when everything was ready, about a month ago, there was a vague rumor that Volin had some objection. Nobody paid much attention to the rumor, because Volin was in hospital. Semashko told me it was all nonsense, and I was certain things would be all right. Since Volin is involved in the trial of Kirov's murderers, he is incredibly busy and getting hold of him on the phone is all but impossible. When I did finally reach him yesterday, he told me that he considered "Crocodile" a political work heralding the February Revolution, that the animals "suffering" all through the work in Leningrad represented the bourgeoisie, and so on and so forth. It was all so absurd that I lost my temper once and for all and decided to clear the air. I rang him again this morning at nine. He'd expressed the desire to have "Crocodile" published in the old edition, and I pointed out that it was impossible, since some idiot or other was bound to think that the lines

> And all at once the policeman proud
> Made an appearance in the crowd

contained a political allusion in the word *gorodovoi* [tsarist policeman]. He agreed and asked me to ring back tomorrow morning.

Thinking he was retreating in the face of my arguments, I made a jubilant call to Obolenskaya. "Have you heard the bad news?" she said in a voice hoarse with a cold. " 'Crocodile' has been cut from your book of *Tales*."

"Who is responsible?"

"Volin."

"But I've just talked to him."

"I don't know anything more. Try Semashko."

I tried Semashko. Semashko was off in Smolensk.

I tried Suvorov. Suvorov said, "Yes, it's true. I do as I'm told, and I've been told to go to the printer's office at once and have 'Crocodile' removed from the book."

"And you're going to do it?"

"I do as I'm told."

It turns out that Semashko had gone to see Stetsky yesterday, but Stetsky had already succumbed to Volin's propaganda and banned "Crocodile" outright.

I finished my Repin article yesterday and submitted it to *Pravda*. *Pravda* accepted it along with "The Art of Translation," which I'd also written in Moscow. I wrote the Repin article from what is the least interesting angle for me but one that is indispensable for his place in the USSR, namely: "Repin Is Ours!" The article will make it possible to glorify Repin, who is still considered illegal.

29 December.

Can't wait to get home. Because of "Crocodile" I've done no work for two days. I tried to reach Stetsky at the Central Committee. "Alexei Ivanovich won't be in today. He's visiting factories. Try his secretary." I phoned Volin and spent an hour making my case, but he wouldn't budge. I'll try and catch him at Narkompros today. I curse that summer in Kuokkala when I wrote "Crocodile." The grief it's caused me. I tried to talk to Epshtein about it not long ago. He had long refused to see me, and I happened to catch him on my way to Bubnov. He brushed me off as if I were an importunate beggar. I went on to Bubnov. "He can't see you. Leave your telephone number, and he'll get back to you." I left my number and have been waiting ever since. Then there are all the earlier slurs, insults, press campaigns, and the like. I don't know what possessed me to write it. < . . . >

Went to see Volin at Narkompros. He made it plain—politely at first, then more and more crudely—that he was doing me a personal favor to talk over the matter with me, that he was very busy and couldn't afford to spend time on such trifles, but if I insisted, he would point out the political follies, the madness of "Crocodile." First of all:

> Up runs an officer of the law.
> "What's this din, this wild uproar?"
> *I'm the one who will determine*
> *Whether or not you may talk in German.*

Can you give me one instance of a Soviet policeman banning anyone from speaking German? It goes against everything we stand for as a nation! (Can he give me one instance of a Soviet policeman carrying on a conversation with a crocodile?)

Next:

> Very glad
> *Leningrad*
> And get the frenzied cad
> Away from *Leningrad*
> They march full force on *Leningrad*
> O poor, misfortunate *Leningrad.*

Leningrad is a historical entity, and every flight of fantasy evoking it will be taken as a political allusion. Especially lines like:

> Our brothers live in hell, they do,
> A hell that humans call the zoo.
> The zoo it is a frightful place
> Which from my thoughts I would erase.
> The masters treat us all like trash
> Suited for nothing but the lash.

A month ago this would all have sounded like an innocent joke, but after Kirov's death it has the ring of a parable. Which is why . . .

Which is why Semashko ordered the elimination of "Crocodile" from the volume of my tales without even informing me.

From Volin's office I went to the Central Committee of the Party. There I was received quite amicably by Comrade Khevinson (I think that's his name), Stetsky's assistant, but . . . But he's in a great rush, he knows nothing, he's never read "Crocodile." Would I leave him the text. He would read it and tell me what he thought.

On to Semashko at Detgiz. Semashko was a bit nonplussed. After all, he assured me he wouldn't let anyone cut a line from "Crocodile." "Yes, yes. It's a great pity. But there was no time to lose, so I told them . . . to remove 'Crocodile' altogether."

"You didn't even try to push it through?"

"You know . . . In times like these . . ."

From Semashko I ran to Yermilov, who promised to talk to somebody, but in what terms he didn't say. Everyone advises me to go to the Writers' Union, but that's only a palliative, of course. The only person capable of defending "Crocodile" is Gorky, and he is currently in Moscow. But Kryuchkov won't let me in to see him. I'm even afraid to ask. < . . . >

The article I gave to *Pravda*, "The Art of Translation," contains praise for Academia. I was told to take it out. You can't praise Academia in *Pravda* now: it was Kamenev's home. Yet on the eve of his arrest *Pravda* was going to print an article by him, a review of some memoirs. It was already typeset. < . . . >

31 December.

Have just had a phone conversation with Semashko. Since I'm longing to go home and am sick and tired of officials and running from office to office, I've decided to make a concession to Volin and ask him to include only the first part of "Crocodile." When I told that to Semashko, he said, "I don't remember 'Crocodile' well enough. Let me run over to Detgiz and look into things." As a result of which . . .

1935

+>-+>-+>-+>-+>-+>-+>-+>

2 January.

"Crocodile" is banned in its entirety. Even the lines

are considered criminal. Semashko suggested I should redo the criminal lines, and someone who happened to be present came up with

Sitting pretty
Our great city.

Exhausted, I bought a train ticket at Intourist and was home for New Year's Day. < . . . >

18 January.

If I haven't been keeping my diary, it's because I've been taken up with *A Lofty Art* and a Repin article that is growing and growing.

I am very nervous about the affair involving Zinovyev, Kamenev, and the others. I read the indictment yesterday. It appears they were using literature as a smoke screen to mask their sorry political goals. And I believed that Kamenev was truly interested in Shakespeare translations, that he cared about the Pushkin celebration, that he was pulling strings for the Pushkinskii Dom journal, and that his life was absolutely transparent. I thought that he himself had realized he was done for in politics and that he had retreated into literature in all sincerity, following Party instructions. Everyone knew that he was to be elected to the Academy of Sciences in February, that he had been proposed by Gorky for head of the All-Union Institute of Literature, and that these perspectives fully satisfied his ambitions. According to Kamenev, Zinovyev had made literature such a part of his life that he was starting to write children's stories. He had in fact shown me an illustrated children's story written by Zinovyev—inept, but touching. We writers respected Kamenev: he had made considerable progress in literature recently, his book on Chernyshevsky and his edition of Herzen's *My Past and Thoughts* representing quite a high level of scholarship. The pleasant way he had of putting all writers on an equal footing meant that he had won over 1) all the scholars connected with Pushkinskii Dom, 2) all the translators connected with Academia, and so on. He was gradually acquiring a certain moral authority in literary circles, and all that, it turns out, was merely a screen for his political adventurism, his attempt to scale the country's cultural heights as a means of regaining the political power he had lost.

Is it true? I don't know. It seems to be. I recall something that happened during the Writers' Congress. Kamenev spent the whole time at his dacha outside Moscow. His wife, Tatyana Ivanovna, whom I met in the Hall of Columns, told me about it in a whisper, because everyone thought he was off in the Caucasus. He was in hiding and so cautious that he didn't go out of the dacha for days on end, no matter how beautiful the weather. The reason he was in hiding is that it had originally been announced he would give a talk at the Congress and, generally speaking, play a major role in the proceedings. Clearly the Central Committee later decided against his playing that role, and he had to pretend he wasn't there. I had never been to his dacha and put the whole incident out of my mind, but while in Kislovodsk I received a letter from Tatyana Ivanovna saying, "I apologize for being so rude when I spoke to you at the Writers' Congress, but I was terribly upset that Lev Borisovich couldn't give his talk there." I don't know a thing about his political career, but I liked him as a literary man (though what he said about Mandelshtam and what he wrote about Pole-zhaev, Andrei Bely, and some others makes it clear he had no understanding of poetry whatsoever).[206]

I've made my peace with having "Crocodile" removed from the book. "Crocodile" can go to hell for all I care.

I'm writing about Repin again and cursing my ineptitude: there he is, standing before me in all his complexity, large as life, and I can't get him down on paper. I've been going through the letters he wrote to me. Some are remarkable. But the unfounded ferocity of his hatred for everything Soviet will put people off.

27 January.

< . . . > Gave a talk on Repin at the Artist Collective Society on the twenty-fourth. It was a great success: I made the entire audience fall in love with him. There was a large, lifelike portrait of Ilya Yefimovich on the

206. After Kamenev's arrest and demise his name ceased to be mentioned. Not until 1988 did *Soviet Bibliography* publish a list of his articles. In connection with Kamenev's introduction to Bely's *Beginning of the Century* (1932, the second volume of Bely's autobiographical trilogy) the poet and critic Vladislav Khodasevich writes in the Paris-based Russian-émigré weekly *Vozrozhdenie* (28 June 1934), "One would not call Kamenev a wise man, but neither is he stupid. Despite his Marxist obtuseness he has written an introduction that touches on many issues germane to Bely's book."

podium, and I had the feeling he was watching me and smiling his approval.
< ... >

Next day, the twenty-fifth, I ate at the National and met Prince Mirsky there. He is all the rage now. Gorky has written about him in the most glowing terms in two successive *Pravda* articles ("Literary Games").[207]

"Are you happy?" I asked him.

"Remember Polycrates' ring?" he replied.[208]

I liked him enormously: the vast erudition, the sincerity, the literary talent, the ludicrous beard and ludicrous bald spot, the suit which, though made in England, hung loosely on him, shabby and threadbare, the way he had of coming out with a sympathetic ee-ee-ee (like a guttural piglet squeal) after each sentence you uttered—it was all so amusing and endearing. Though he had very little money—he's a staunch democrat—he did inherit his well-born ancestors' gourmandise. His stomach will be the ruin of him. Every day he leaves his wretched excuse for a cap and overcoat with the concierge and goes into the luxurious restaurant, spending no less than forty rubles on a meal (since he drinks as well as eats) plus four to tip the waiter and one to tip the concierge.

There are many factual errors in Gorky's "Literary Games" and his polemic with Zaslavsky.[209] For instance, Gorky calls Belinsky the son of a

207. In one of his articles on contemporary literature serialized in *Pravda*, "Literary Games," Gorky praised D. S. Mirsky, an eminent historian of Russian literature who was of aristocratic lineage and had spent many years in emigration. "Dmitry Mirsky had the audacity to be born into a noble family, and that was enough to justify the outcry: 'How dare this man of incorrect birth criticize a book by a Communist!' [a reference to Mirsky's unfavorable review of Alexander Fadeev's *The Last of the Udeges*]. Let me remind you that Belinsky, Chernyshevsky, and Dobrolyubov [the founders of Russian radical criticism] were sons of priests and that sons and daughters of the bourgeoisie entered the history of the Russian Revolution as staunch fighters and faithful comrades of V. I. Lenin."

208. A ballad by Schiller, "The Ring of Polycrates" is based on an episode told by Herodotus. The Egyptian king Amasides was envious of his contemporary, Polycrates of Samos (sixth century B.C.), whose life was an unbroken string of successes. He advised Polycrates to divest himself of the object he treasured most, and Polycrates cast his favorite ring into the sea. A week later a fisherman found it in the abdomen of a fish and promptly returned it to its owner. This apparent windfall proved the prelude to a disaster: shortly thereafter a Persian satrap lured Polycrates to his realm and had him hanged by his feet. Since Mirsky was soon to perish in the Great Terror, his reaction to Gorky's praise acquires the force of an ominous prophecy.

209. The exchange between Gorky and Zaslavsky was prompted by an announcement in *Literaturnaia gazeta* that the publishing house Academia was about to reprint Dostoevsky's *Demons*. In an article entitled "Literary Rot" (*Pravda*, 20 January 1937) Zaslavsky assailed the notion that *Demons* was a major work of art, stigmatizing it as a "filthy counterrevolutionary

priest and so on. But on one point in the polemic Gorky is absolutely right: *Demons* is a brilliant, yes, brilliant work. "Next thing you know you'll be calling for publication of White Guard writers," says Zaslavsky. Well, why not? Lenin called for the publication of Arkady Averchenko's *Seven Knives in the Back of the Revolution,* didn't he? < . . . >

I talked it over with Mirsky. He had the same objection and promised to bring up the matter with Gorky.

After the meal we went to Academia for the first meeting of the editorial board since Kamenev's departure. We arrived to find an empty room. The reason? "Kuibyshev is dead."[210] Kuibyshev is dead! Dear me, dear me! [. . .]

31 January.

I'm leaving Moscow devastated and morally blemished. < . . . > I took the same train as Yuryev. < . . . > He told me that Mekhlis—personally, on his own—had initiated a campaign against Gorky: the article by Zaslavsky, an article by Panfyorov.[211] Koltsov toned down Zaslavsky's article, while Mekhlis made Panfyorov's more pointed, inserting a number of his own formulations. His actions were sanctioned from above *post factum.* < . . . >

12 February.

On the ninth we attended a Georgian Evening at the Mayakovsky Club. < . . . > [. . .] The Georgians are past masters at reciting their poetry. People were particularly impressed with the performances by Grishashvili

---

lampoon." Gorky offered a prompt rebuttal: "It is essential to know your enemy, to know his ideology. . . . Comrade Zaslavsky has given aid and comfort to our enemies, particularly the White émigrés. Thanks to Comrade Zaslavsky, they can now shout, 'The Bolsheviks are banning Dostoevsky!' "

210. Valerian Kuibyshev was Deputy Chairman of the Council of People's Commissars, a head of the Central Control Commission, which supervised Party discipline, and a member of the Politburo from 1917. In 1930 he took Stalin's side in the struggle for power. Chukovsky is clearly upset by his death, perhaps suspecting foul play or serious repercussions. (E.C./V.E.)

211. Fyodor Panfyorov, a mediocre Socialist-Realist novelist, inveighed against Gorky in *Pravda* on 28 January. Irked by Gorky's "Literary Games," he denigrated writers singled out for praise by the grand old man: "You praise Mirsky to the skies and come down on Fadeev!" In concluding, Panfyorov reminded Gorky of "Comrade Stalin's injunction to nurture the cadres as affectionately as a gardener nurtures a fruit tree."

and Tabidze, their highly effective oriental gestures from the upper abdomen to the shoulders. Pasternak received so much applause when he came out that he (rather coquettishly) tried to wave it off. Then he sat down energetically and recited his verse in a quiet voice that said, "I'm perfectly aware that this is worthless and my poetry has nothing to recommend it, but what can I do if you're foolish enough to listen." He swallowed words, threw away rhymes, and obliterated phrasing. He didn't recite much, though. < . . . >

15 March.

Igor Grabar is doing my portrait. It's not easy, sitting for him three to four hours a day. I find the portrait superficial and inane, and Grabar himself—a hardworking mediocrity with a great talent for self-promotion—terribly disappointing.[212] During the sittings we've been reading *The History of a Town*, and he keeps exclaiming mechanically, "Just listen to that! Well done!" Or he tells me how much a certain lunch cost or a dinner or tries to wheedle information about Repin out of me.

We were jabbering away—he couldn't quite get my mouth right—when I was suddenly called to the phone and told < . . . > that Moscow had ordered publication of the fifth edition of *From Two to Five* to be held up because it includes "Crocodile."[213] The book has been printed and is due out on the seventeenth. Volin had read in the papers that "Crocodile" was included and, without seeing the book himself, ordered the publication delayed. Hearing the news, I turned white of course and began to shake. All I could think of was racing off to the publishing house for details, but Grabar insisted I go on with the sitting and "give him a nice cheerful smile." I was certain there had been a misunderstanding and they would eventually let the book come out, but I had as much trouble smiling as if I were sitting on a frying pan. < . . . >
< . . . >

212. Grabar characterizes the portrait as follows: "It turned out rather well, I think, in terms of both the horizontal composition and the color scheme: the green background, the red book cover, the silver hair and gray jacket." *The History of a Town* referred to in the following sentence is a satirical novel by Mikhail Saltykov-Shchedrin (1826–1889).
213. The only components of "The Crocodile" left in the fifth edition of *From Two to Five* (1935) were fragments from its first part.

1 April.

I'm fifty-three today, but, fool that I am, I'm not so much upset at teetering on the brink of old age as at learning that yesterday, after three days of bureaucratic machinations, Koltsov refused to publish my Vengrov article: a woman named Lerner (who works with Vengrov) persuaded him not to.[214] We've decided to get Mekhlis to adjudicate in the matter. I went to *Pravda* to see him and found him downstairs in the *Pravda* screening room watching a film called *Kolyma*.[215] The head of Kolyma—a Latvian, I think—was there. I sat between Levin and Gerasimova. The film was very long. Mekhlis didn't stay till the end. "Let's run after him," I said to Koltsov, but he held me back. When it was over, I sat outside Mekhlis's office for two hours and he wouldn't see me. That's what upset me more than being fifty-three. < . . . >

For some reason Koltsov has advised me not to see Pilnyak. Pilnyak has a strange reputation: he lives high off the hog—he has two motorcars and a butler—and spends money like water, though where the money comes from is not clear: his works are not being published. < . . . >

26 April.

Went to the Petergof Hotel International for a gathering of Tynyanov, Tikhonov, and Slonimsky, the cream of our literary crop. Tynyanov greeted me warmly, and I immediately asked, "How old is Pushkin now?"

"Eleven," he responded with a guilty look. (Tynyanov is working on his *Pushkin,* and the last time I saw him Pushkin was seven.) [. . .]

6 May.

Gave a reading at the Herzen Pedagogical Institute as part of a program on children's writers. There was an audience of about fifteen hundred. I

214. The article was a review of Vengrov's *Little Ditties with Little Pictures for Little Children* (1935). Vengrov threatened to commit suicide if the article appeared. He died in 1962.

215. Kolyma is a vast region in northern Siberia where some three million prisoners died in forced-labor camps ostensibly mining for gold. See Robert Conquest, *Kolyma: The Arctic Death Camps* (London, 1978), for a study of the camps and Varlaam Shalamov, *Kolyma Tales* (New York, 1980), for a fictionalized view by a man who spent seventeen years there. The film in question, a silent ethnographic documentary, was commissioned by the NKVD. Although it contained no hint of the labor camp, it does not appear to have been released. (M.H.H.)

was greeted by such wild applause I couldn't start for a long time. They made me read four tales—clapping after each—plus excerpts from *From Two to Five,* and I remembered having given a talk in defense of fairy tales in that very hall eight years before and being hissed by the same sort of people for the same words. And not only did they hiss; they shouted "Enough!" and "Down with him!" The dirt those educators flung at me— the very people now ogling me lovingly. < . . . >

12 May.

Had a visit from Khardzhiev and Akhmatova yesterday. Akhmatova said she had sold a volume of selected poems to Sovetskaia literatura, which demanded there should be:

1. no mysticism,
2. no pessimism,
3. no politics.

"All that was left was fornication," she said. < . . . >

19 December.

Went to see Tynyanov. It was odd to see the following on the door of so famous a writer:

For Tynyanov ring once
For Yampolsky ring twice
For X ring three times
For Y ring four times

He lives in a communal apartment! You have to go through the kitchen to get to his room. His face is emaciated. We hugged. Things are very bad. Yelena Alexandrovna is ill: both her spinal column and her duodenum are affected. The poor woman has been in bed, immobile, for several months now. Tynyanov is her nurse. She needed a special soft mattress, and Tynyanov bought two and a bedstead. They turned out to be worthless, and he had to throw them out. "And it's hard to get the specialists to come. They're all so busy." Doctors, pharmacies, consultations, prescriptions— it's all so oppressive he can't get any writing done. "And then there are the Yampolskys, the perfect triumphant philistines!" To say nothing of the wailing baby next door, who keeps them up at night. Yury Nikolaevich is doing what he can to get permission and money to go to Paris, where there's a clinic that treats his illness with a special serum. "Either my leg goes numb or I start going blind." < . . . >

On Marshak: "What kind of Talmudic nonsense is

> What do we plant
> When we plant a forest?

That's just the kind of thing they tell cheder children: 'When we plant a forest, we are actually planting.'

"And how illiterate he can be:

> Masts and yards to hold the sails.

Why 'to hold'? And wouldn't a finite verb be preferable? Read Marshak and you think you're reading exceptions to Latin grammar:

> Aec
> Int
> ar ur us
> *Are* nertrius." < . . . >

He also talked about meeting Romain Rolland at Gorky's. "Rolland pretended to be ill, but he's not ill; he's a corpse." Rolland had a magic presence, though. "Is your style more like Balzac's or Zola's?" he asked Tynyanov, and Tynyanov replied, "My stories are in the spirit of Voltaire, my novels in the spirit of Rousseau." Rolland found this very moving and, pressing his hand to his water bottle (he no longer had a stomach, only a water bottle), said that as a young man he himself had < . . . > and so on. He spoke with great feeling.

"There's nothing vulgar about him. He objected strenuously to the way we turn our children into *Wunderkinder,* spoiling them with fulsome praise in the press, calling them 'young geniuses' and the like. He's deep, *genuine.*"

His wife complained that Arosev, who had invited the Rollands to stay with him, didn't bother to clean the bed, and the bedbugs kept poor Rolland from sleeping for the first two nights. Rolland not only refrained from complaining; he tried to change the subject. And Gorky said, "Arosev is a perfect idiot" in such a way that it sounded like praise.

Seeing me home, Tynyanov came to life: he did his Marshak, Gorky, and Oksman imitations. He was the old Tynyanov again for a time. He jumped at my suggestion that he go to Moscow. He had a lot to say about

Shklovsky: "We're friends again. He's sent me two remarkable letters. Wait till you see them. They're out of this world. If his correspondence were published, everyone would see what a fine writer he is." < . . . >

1936

➤➤➤➤➤➤➤➤➤➤

1 January.

Went to bed yesterday at seven. Got up at three and am sweating over that awful *Prince and the Pauper*. Kolya and I are doing a new translation of it, Kolya the second half, I the first. The first half has ninety-six pages and has gone very slowly, but at least I've got eighty-two and a half over with. A page can sometimes take as much as an hour and a half or more. And what am I doing it for? I really can't say. I so want to write my own things. My head is bursting with ideas, and I have to spend my days on this back-breaking unskilled labor. There's so much of it too. The moment I finish *The Prince and the Pauper* I'll have to take on the Nekrasov editing job and the Shakespeare editing job and the Repin editing job. When can I write, damn it all? Why has the writer turned into a day laborer? I am making a new year's resolution to accept no more paraliterary jobs to my dying day, to write nothing but stories, articles, and verse. Why, it's absurd: my tales are enormously successful, and for the past five years I haven't had a free second to write a new one. I envy everyone with the opportunity to write as he pleases, even drivel. < . . . >

7 January.

Tynyanov came to call yesterday with Veniamin Kaverin. He brought me a collection of his stories and a volume of his Heine translations (1935) He signed the Heine "Rejected candidate for the Translators Section [of the Writers' Union]": he had been viciously attacked at the recent translators' conference in Moscow, he told me, and he kept imagining a band of enemies waging a secret campaign against him. I put it down to his illness. His face was haggard, lined with grief. Things at home are as bad as ever.

He did imitations of all the doctors treating Yelena Alexandrovna. < . . . >
Kaverin reproached him for not giving him any of his books, and he said,
"I give the doctors all my books. And you should see the inscriptions I
write!" < . . . >

Then he cheered up and acted out amusing scenes from the lives of
various friends. Once he and Mirsky were in a tavern in Kislovodsk and
who should turn up but Alexei Tolstoy. Tynyanov had considered Mirsky
high-principled, but Tolstoy made such an imposing entrance, casting his
aristocratic glance over all and sundry, that Mirsky jumped up and said,
"Allow me to introduce myself," whereupon Tolstoy gave him only two
fingers to shake. Now Tynyanov has only bad things to say about Tolstoy
and claims he won't greet him in public.

We talked about poets too. "There are none," he said. "Pasternak is in
ruins. Look at the drivel he's writing for *Izvestiia*.[216] [. . .] He had a lot
to say about Gorky, who charmed him from the outset. "Gorky has no will
of his own and is thus susceptible to the influence of others, but he is
delightful, poetic, and a marvelous artist (in life as well as art)."

Everything Tynyanov says he says with gusto. As a writer he is fascinated by life as expressed in human relations, careers, and everyday details.
We talked until half past twelve. Marya Borisovna and I saw them out. I
haven't been able to sleep all night.
< . . . >

17 January.

At the Children's Writers' conference sponsored by the Central Committee
of the VLKSM. It has been on for two days now. Left for Moscow on the
fourteenth. < . . . >

216. Tynyanov is referring to two poems from the cycle "The Artist" that appeared in the
January 1936 issue of *Izvestiia:* "I Realized Everything Is Alive" and "I Like the Recalcitrant
Temper." The former concludes with the persona listing a number of things that will resound
in him forever, including: "Both Lenin and Stalin, and these verses too." Two months later at a
meeting of the Soviet Writers' Union, Pasternak voiced an equally critical view of the poems:
"For some time yet I shall write badly . . . until I come to terms with the novelty of themes and
theses I wish to treat. . . . Two poems I published in the January issue of *Izvestiia* are written in
haste, carelessly, with a facility permissible in purely lyric poetry, but inadmissible in dealing
with subjects that require serious artistic thought." In 1957 Pasternak wrote that in the poem
beginning "I like the recalcitrant temper of the artist at the peak of his powers" he had in mind
both Stalin and himself: "It was a genuine attempt (one of the last in that period) to live by the
ideas of the age and fall into step with it."

Lili gave me a detailed account of how she wrote a letter to Stalin about the cowardly treatment of Mayakovsky at the hands of Gosizdat and its attempt to keep him down, keep him quiet.[217] She let three weeks pass before handing it on, but two days after she did she had a phone call (in Leningrad) from Comrade Yezhov asking her to come to Moscow. "I told him I'd be there on the fourth, but he said, 'Can't you make it earlier?' so I booked a ticket for the third. He saw me immediately and asked, 'Why did you wait so long to write to the Central Committee?' and I said I'd written to Stetsky, but had received no answer. 'I love Mayakovsky,' Yezhov said, 'but look at how they publish him, the paper they use. It's disgusting.' 'That's just the point I'm trying to make,' I said.

"I knew Stalin loved Mayakovsky. Mayakovsky used to read his poem *Lenin* at the Bolshoi, and Stalin would clap and make loud comments about how much he liked it. I knew that. But I was still frightened." < . . . >

Ilyin came up to us and told the following story: A doctor friend of his had recently had a patient by the name of Marie-Antoinette. When he asked her mother why she had called her Marie-Antoinette, the woman said, "There was this day in my calendar that said 'Marie-Antoinette executed,' so I reckoned she was a revolutionary.' " < . . . >

For some time now I've had a splendid idea for a children's book. It would give me a way to convey my love for Soviet children and—through them—for our times. I've been collecting material for the book for four years, and only now, after talking to Kosarev, have I been able to formulate the point behind it to my satisfaction.

Kosarev is a delightful person. He speaks with a charming French *r* and has a youthful-looking haircut. You feel compelled to believe his every word. His every move, his every smile comes straight from the heart. He cannot tolerate anything false, bureaucratic, or banal. I'm so glad children's literature is finally in his hands. And in the hands of the Komsomol. You can feel the fresh air already; it's as though a door had been flung open. Children's literature used to be in a fetid cellar, and the VLKSM has brought it out into the open. Many unearned reputations will founder, but for the first time true creativity will find a firm foundation here.

217. Lili Brik's letter to Stalin as well as his directive, jotted down on that letter, are now published in full. Stalin's injunction addressed to Yezhov, head of the NKVD, contains the much-quoted statement: "Mayakovsky was and remains the best and the most talented poet of the Soviet era. Indifference to his memory is a crime." This obiter dictum provided the basis for the subsequent canonization of a poet often criticized and slighted in his lifetime.

It makes me want to do ten times as much for children's literature than I've done so far. I have set a new goal for myself, namely, to provide Detizdat with fourteen books, and I'll do so even if it kills me.

I haven't put anything about the conference down on paper because I remember every word. Everything I've been fighting for all these years has now come to pass. Soviet children will have excellent books. And soon < . . . >

27 January.

The second meeting of the editorial board for the Academy edition of Nekrasov was supposed to take place today. The first meeting—with Lebedev-Polyansky, Meshcheryakov, Kirpotin, Lepeshinsky, and Essen— took place the day before yesterday at Essen's flat. Yevgenyev-Maximov was summoned specially from Leningrad. Oh, and Zaslavsky was there too. They all care about one thing and one thing only: to make sure that Nekrasov does not—God forbid—come out a Populist, because, according to the interpretations of the powers that be, the Populists are not so close to our times as was once thought. The fact that Nekrasov was a poet was of no interest to them whatsoever. They had no time to bother with poetry. I made a speech saying I felt the odd man out since for me Nekrasov was first and foremost a poet, a man who owed his greatness to his talent as an artist, and had Nekrasov expressed his convictions in prose I would never have studied and loved him as I do. I called for this aspect of his work, which they had ignored, to figure in all our prefaces and critical articles. No one attacked me, though I detected a certain coolness in our relations. Yevgenyev-Maximov, Essen, and I formed a subcommittee to discuss the number of volumes, their makeup, and so on. We met yesterday in my room and worked long and hard. And today it turns out that 1) Kirpotin has vanished into thin air, 2) Lebedev-Polyansky is busy, 3) Meshcheryakov is busy, 4) Lepeshinsky is out of town, and today's meeting has been postponed. < . . . >

Tynyanov is here in Moscow and has phoned twice (once to invite me to the theater). He came to see me this evening. He had a lot to say about his family troubles. "You're the only one I can tell this to: I feel so sorry for Lenochka I sometimes feel like weeping. Poor thing! All her hopes for recovering are dashed: now the upper half of her spinal cord is affected as well."

In a fortnight Tynyanov is going for a two-month stay in Paris. Everything is set, though there is still a problem with the hard currency. He has no desire to go ("I'm afraid to leave Lenochka alone"), but he must: his disease is getting worse. [. . .]

He moved on from there to his favorite subject: Alexei Tolstoy. "Alexei Tolstoy is a great writer, because only great writers have the right to write so poorly, as poorly as he does. < . . . > He has tried his hand at several 'yellow' genres: he tried yellow science fiction (*Engineer Garin's Hyperboloid*) and failed; he tried the yellow adventure novel (*Ibicus*) and failed; he tried the yellow historical novel (*Peter the Great*) and succeeded—which makes him a genius!" < . . . >

Lida's speech was published in today's *Komsomolka* and mine in *Literaturka*.[218] I'm jumping with paternal joy.

My health is very bad. It's been a hard winter. [. . .]

2 February.

Had a phone call yesterday from the office of the head of the political police, wanting to know when he could pay me a visit. The tone was quite menacing. It made me terribly nervous. Could Lida have done something wrong, had a falling out with Detizdat? The things that ran through my head! I proofread *From Two to Five* (the sixth edition) all night to calm down. I got through 224 pages. I didn't close my eyes for a second all day today, and then at six I learned that what the man wanted was for me to—write a children's book about the militia. < . . . >

17 February.

Alyansky phoned yesterday to tell me that *Komsomol'skaia Pravda* had lashed out at my "Robin Bobin Barabek." It so upset me that I didn't sleep all night.

21 February.

Tsypin descended on me yesterday with a nice, sweet proposal: to eliminate several of my books from his list. "There's nothing I can do about it. It's

218. The articles in question are Lidia Chukovskaya, "On Rude Words and Impersonal Language" (*Komsomol'skaia Pravda*, 27 January 1936), and Kornei Chukovsky, "Childish Matters" (*Literaturnaia gazeta*, 26 January 1936).

by order of the Central Committee." He expected me to put up resistance, but I said, "Be my guest." < ... >

Then Safonova arrived with her *Ouch-It-Hurts* drawings. She's done a fine job. There's a lot of *literary* inventiveness to them: they don't stick out, they're an integral part of the book, and they give it feminine intimacy and warmth. But what Tsypin liked most was their currently fashionable realism. "That's what we need!" he said (because the Central Committee demands it of him). He was so happy that he doubled her fee on the spot, giving her a hundred rubles per drawing instead of fifty—and there will be about a hundred in all. < ... >

25 February.

< ... > Had a wonderful proposal from Detizdat: to do an anthology of love poems of the romantic type for adolescents so they'll stop going to the mawkish Gypsy stuff. I am having a fine time going through Fet, Polonsky, Anna Akhmatova, Boris Kornilov—all the lyric poets. Mei yielded nothing, even though I perused him line by line.
< ... >

10 April.

The day before yesterday I received an invitation, signed by Bubnov, to appear at the Kremlin for a discussion of the upcoming Pushkin celebration.[219] It hit me like a ton of bricks: I was working on Repin, finishing off my "Bear," putting together the poetry anthology, editing the second Nekrasov volume—all under time pressure—and suddenly this! < ... >

There we were, sitting in the long meeting room of the Council of People's Commissars. Comfortable and majestic. With portraits of Lenin and other leaders: Budyonny, Kuibyshev < ... > and Pushkin. There were all sorts of genuine Pushkin reliquaries along the walls. [...]

The Leningrad contingent gave rather a weak defense of their right to hold the celebration in Leningrad.[220] "But that's where he was killed!" Demyan [Bedny] shouted, and set forth his Pantheon project. The idea

219. The centenary of Pushkin's death—he died from a duel wound in 1837—was the occasion for lavish, officially sponsored tributes throughout the country. (M.H.H.)

220. Though born in Moscow and exiled to the south for several years, Pushkin spent the major part of his life in Saint Petersburg. (M.H.H.)

was to transfer Pushkin's remains to Moscow and form a Pantheon of Russian Writers around them.

"Yes, yes!" Meyerhold chimed in unexpectedly (till then he had been attacked mercilessly by Demyan). "A Pantheon, a Pantheon. Demyan's idea is magnificent. A Pantheon is just what we need." < . . . >

22 April.

Sat in the sixth or seventh row at the Komsomol meeting yesterday, and whom did I see, when I happened to turn my head, but Pasternak. I went over to him and brought him up to the front (there was a seat free next to me). All at once Kaganovich, Voroshilov, Andreev, Zhdanov, and Stalin appeared. The hall was in an uproar! But HE simply stood there, looking slightly weary, thoughtful, and grandiose. You could feel how accustomed to power and how powerful he was, yet at the same time there was something soft and feminine about him. I looked around and saw nothing but loving, tender, inspired, and smiling faces. Seeing him—just seeing him—was a delight for all of us. Demchenko kept turning to him and making conversation, and oh, how envious we were of her, how jealous. We followed his every move with veneration. I never thought myself capable of such feelings. While we were applauding him, he took out his watch (a silver watch) and held it up to the audience with a charming smile, and we all whispered, "His watch, his watch! He's showing us his watch!" Later, going our separate ways at the cloakroom, we brought the watch up again. Pasternak kept whispering enthusiastic things to me about him, and we both said at one point, "That Demchenko. She's blocking our view!" I walked home with Pasternak. The two of us were exhilarated, intoxicated . . .

Krupskaya has been at the Congress every day. Our seats were nearby, and we chatted. She has invited me to her place for a talk. She obviously wants to made amends for her old article about my "Crocodile." And I want to tell her all the things bubbling up inside me about teaching literature in school. Krupskaya and Bubnov think certain "methods" are at fault. No, it's Bubnov and dear Nadezhda Konstantinovna herself who are at fault; they're at fault because they have no real inborn love of poetry or art. < . . . >

June.

Whatever made me go to the Sestroretsk Spa! The roof of my room is red hot; I can't stick it out for five minutes there to say nothing of getting any work done.

A heavily made-up "lady" ("I'm an admirer") said to me at table, "You must love children so! The wonderful things you write about them!"

I was so repulsed by her mincing ways that I responded, "No, I can't abide children. The very sight of them turns my stomach!"

"How can you say such a thing?"

"It's the truth."

"Then why do you write about them?"

"For the money.

"The money?"

"That's right."

And she *believed* me and is telling everybody on the beach, "Chukovsky is a terrible cynic."

By the way, the children here are amazing. The children of the Ukrainian—he's got a half dozen or so, maybe more—they're very poor, but on no account will they take any food from us: they've got their pride. I bought some raspberries and told them, "Whoever cleans the raspberries for me will get half of them as a reward." They cleaned them all right, but refused their due. Even the smallest of them: try and give her a pastry and she'll say, "Thank you. I'm not hungry." All six (or seven? or eight?) of them are holed up in a tiny shed with no windows, but they're happy, neat, full of Ukrainian affability and Soviet self-respect. And not a jot of servility.

Ever since I met those children (and the cook's daughter and the spa director's sweet, slender, bookworm of a daughter), the adults have faded into the distance. Strange as it seems, I can relax only in the presence of the children. < . . . >

I have just heard that Gorky is dead. It is night. I am walking back and forth in the garden, crying. I can't write a word. I've given up trying to work. I wanted to work on some Doctor Ouch-It-Hurts poems, and nothing came. How often I misunderstood him. He was so full of contradictions. He stood above all his writings as a man.

< . . . >

7 August.

Went to Vorzel yesterday for the opening of a new Pioneer camp. I also saw the Institution for the Protection of Mothers and Children. The 1933 famine made many foundlings. The police would pick them up by the dozens along the Kreshchatik [Kiev's main thoroughfare]. In January it was decided to establish something along the lines of a shelter for them. Dr. Gorodetsky was given two months to set it up. He requisitioned twelve buildings, and on 26 March they moved in five hundred children with bloated stomachs, crooked legs, worms in their mouths, and dropsy. Many died on the spot. It seemed unlikely even one would survive. Some had measles, others whooping cough, still others diphtheria. "You wanted to turn and run," Gorodetsky says. And now they're so chubby you'd think they were from bourgeois backgrounds, all neatly dressed and with ribbons in their hair. < . . . >

Nobody tells them they're in a foundling shelter. They all think they're in a sanatorium and "Mama will come and take me home." Well, mamas do in fact appear. Within six months thirty children have been adopted. I've seen several men and "wives of responsible workers"—Sapova, for example, who has a boy but wants a girl—come from Kiev to take "their" children home from the Institution. They spend a long time sizing them up, gazing into their eyes, picking them up. The children size up the parents as well. If someone who looks poor wishes to adopt them, they say, "I won't go. He didn't come by car." When a shabbily dressed mother went up to Zhenya Vetrova, she hid, saying, "I want another mama."

Adoptions take place in secret. When a woman brings a child home from the Institution, she tells people, "My husband committed a sin in his youth, and this is the result." Or she makes it look as if she had brought a niece back from the country. Not only healthy, good-looking children find homes. You are likely to be picked if you look like the foster parents. And your chances go up if you're affectionate. Then you can even be ugly. Anichka Kostenko went up to a visitor and laid her head in her lap. And snuggled up to her. Weak and plain as she was, the woman said, "She's the one!"

There are usually long consultations with a doctor to find out whether the child is healthy. The doctor examines the kidneys, liver, heart, and blood. < . . . > Foundlings can remain in Narkomzdrav homes until the age of nine, at which time they are moved into homes run by Narkompros. [. . .]

7 September.

Arrived in Odessa yesterday. My first visit since 1908. The time before that was in 1905, when I saw the *Potemkin* uprising.[221] But I spent my whole childhood here, my whole youth. And now I've come as an old man and am reminiscing, reminiscing . . . There is the Stock Exchange with its Moorish architecture. Here is where I stood in 1903 with a volume of Chekhov (published by Niva) that I couldn't wait to take home, and opened to read in the snow. There is the lighthouse where Zhitkov and I performed heroic feats. There is the school I went to, the Pro–Gymnasium No. 2. It was what I wanted to see more than anything else. It is now the Lenin Printing Works. There was an old man pottering about at the entrance. "My name is Chukovsky. I'm a writer. You print my books here. I'd like to go into the courtyard. I went to school here forty-five years ago. It was a school then."

"You can't."

"Why not?"

"You can't, I say. It's closed, and I'm in charge."

He refused to yield. His name is Gutov.

I then went to Novo–Rybnaya Street, where I spent my early childhood. Novo–Rybnaya, 6. The columns are still there, the stone columns at the gate. I stood next to them. They used to be taller than I was, and now . . . The wicket door Savely used to open is still there. And the courtyard. Even the dovecote. And the remarkable hovels overgrown with grapevines. There are children playing in the garden, just as Marusya and I used to do. It's not a garden, actually, just a place where some grapevines climbed up a wall near the house and made a kind of bower. Marusya and I played "travelers" there, turning it into Asia, Africa, and Europe. < . . . > The past has returned and won't let me be. Two houses away was Maria Gold-feld's Tarnopolsky "mansion," which turns out to be a fright. Times change: where the statue of Empress Elizabeth once stood there is now a statue of Marx; the synagogue is now a workers club; the infamous Gymnasium No. 5 is a research institute; Saint Michael's Monastery is now NKVD headquarters; and the disorderly, half-starving waifs have turned into top pupils, happy, round-cheeked youngsters. I visited School No. 39 (Chicherin Street, 20) and was delighted with the way the children

221. See note 10.

looked—how much they knew, how neat their copybooks were—and with the teacher, Yekaterina Trofimovna Boguslavskaya, who has been teaching since 1886. But then I went to the eighth form, which was taught by Sofya Yakovlevna Gasko, and asked what an iamb was and what a trochee was. Nobody knew. Nobody had so much as heard of an amphibrach. The year they gave me for Pushkin's birth was the year in which he died. They thought that Catherine ruled after Paul. They said that Nekrasov and Gogol had lived at different times and could not have met. And the name Tyutchev meant nothing to anybody.

Unfortunately I did not get to Kanatny Lane, scene of my murky, erratic youth. Barshman House! I'd have wept at the mere sight of it. Polishchuk, Roza, and Betya lived across the road. How I loved them and everyone who went to see them. Then there was the sweets factory downstairs. You could look through the window and see the women wrapping caramels with their dirty hands for twelve hours straight. It was there I read Buckle, Darwin, Marx, and Mikhailovsky, there I wrote my first verse, there I started to be what I am today. I read poetry (Pushkin, Nekrasov) with tears in my eyes and thought and thought, elaborating a philosophy of the end in itself or self-constraint and filling one copybook after another with it. Had my life been less arduous (numerous offspring, penury, the necessity to earn a living by writing), I should definitely have become a philosopher. I remember having the burning sensation that I alone knew the truth about the world and was obliged to reveal that truth to a world engulfed in delusion. But I was also aware of how helpless I was for want of an education, of a knowledge of physics and psychology, my weak scientific background in general. Oh, the trouble I had writing my feuilletons! During those Barshman House years I learned everything I know now. More even. It was there I learned my English.

I am sitting on the bridge of the *Adzharistan* as we sail out of Sebastopol. The seagulls fly a short distance against the wind, then hover in the air, which carries them back. They seem to enjoy it. At the sight of the Crimean mountains I can't help thinking of Mura.

What intelligent black eyes seagulls have. They keep turning their heads—to the right, to the left—and cocking them. They're looking after one another.

15 September.

Alupka. Murochka's grave. The inscription Prosovetskaya made on the gravestone

MUROCHKA CHUKOVSKAYA

24 FEBRUARY 1920–10 NOVEMBER 1931

has begun to rust and fade. And I still make believe I'm alive. The same thorns surround the poor victim. The same two silly pipes and goat-nibbled trees. < . . . >

I can't get down to work on my story. My life is trivial and vain. I really want to write my memoirs—for children. I keep trying. Nothing comes of it.

My material situation has improved fourfold over the past five years. < . . . >

29 September.

Aboard the steamer *Krym,* sailing from Yalta to Sochi. The children < . . . > gave me an amazing send-off. Each insisted on carrying something: one took my umbrella, the second my hat, the third my briefcase. The one left without anything wept bitterly. They ran off after I got into the **pick-up,** and suddenly I saw them lugging my largest suitcase—it was too heavy for me to lift—all four of them together! The dears! And to see them waving their handkerchiefs . . . < . . . >

26 November.

Arrived in Leningrad. Heard Stalin's speech over the radio yesterday in Moscow, a speech that will go down in history.[222]

28 November.

Visited two new schools yesterday. One is right near us, in Manezhny Street. There I went to a third-form class. It was awful. The children know

222. On 26 November *Pravda* reported: "The Extraordinary Congress of the Soviets opened yesterday. A speech about the proposal for the Constitution of the USSR was delivered by the leader of the peoples of the USSR and all the workers of mankind, Comrade Stalin."

nothing; their copybooks are in tatters. The teacher herself is illiterate and gives marks for *distsiplina* [discipline, conduct], which her pupils spell *disteplina, destsyplina,* and so on. She finds children abhorrent and looks upon them as convicts.

At the other school, which is in Kirchnaya Street opposite the church, I happened on a Pushkin assembly. A man from the Russian Museum had organized a small exhibition and was going on about Benois' mysticism. The children could barely keep their eyes open. There were a few photographs of Benois and Vrubel drawings on the wall, but they were of such poor quality and hung so high that no one could make anything of them. Then their teacher, a man named Skryabin, came out and announced that Pushkin was a revolutionary who paved the way for Stalin's Constitution: he was a realist and wrote a poem called "The Cherry Tree." In other words, all the Narkompros Pushkin clichés in concentrated form. The children paid no attention, squirming in their seats and whispering to one another, but when their teacher finished they gave him a hearty round of applause! < . . . >

1937

➤-➤-➤-➤-➤-➤-➤-➤

1 April.

Turned fifty-five today. I have sciatica, something wrong with my stomach—and more work than ever. I had one illness or another and insomnia all winter. Yet I'm in a calm, holiday mood, thinking of Murochka, Mama, Marya Borisovna . . . [. . .]

29 April.

A gold watch was stolen from my room at the Krasnaya Hotel tonight. I'd gone to the restaurant for half an hour and left my pocket watch and gold chain on the bedside table. The thief, noticing I wasn't in, entered and took "only" the watch.

6 May.

Am leaving Odessa tomorrow with practically nothing for my pains. I'm taking a plane. I'm terribly homesick for Moscow and Leningrad. Leningrad life seems quite noble and productive in comparison with what I've been going through in this squalid town! Only now do I realize how repulsive it is to me. The only thing good about it is the children. But what are they doing to them?

23 May.

< . . . > Arrived in Petergof today. I was promised room nine, and when I got there who did I find but Tynyanov. We hugged and kissed and sat out on the terrace for a long time. He'd been in the sun and was looking much better. "I'm not doing any writing," he said, "or any reading for that matter." But his room was full of books. "Parny over there—a fine writer he was. Intelligent—that's the main thing. < . . . > And you know who Nekrasov's 'Contemporaries' reminds me of? Mayakovsky!" About Slonimsky: "He's done for. Any writer's relatives can write better than he does."

I gave him *Russian Poets in the Age of Pushkin* and he said, "Let's see which of Pushkin's contemporaries most feared death."

24 May.

"Fame?" Tynyanov says. "Do you think I feel famous? I was recently in Yaroslavl visiting my brother, a respected man there, when a doctor friend of his said he was proud to know *Tynyanov's brother*. Well, that was the only time I ever felt famous." < . . . >

[. . .] We talked a lot about his future Pushkin book. "Engelgardt, the lycée director, was someone to be reckoned with, and the school itself, well, it was damned good! It gave us Matyushkin, a fine seaman, Delvig, Gorchakov, Kyukhelbeker. Not bad, eh? And when Pushkin lay dying, the only people he wanted to see were his lycée classmates. I can't wait to get to his death. I'm also looking forward to doing something with the period immediately preceding the Revolution (1909–16): it's a natural for a big, juicy novel!" < . . . >

Kuprin has come to the USSR (or so the papers say). I could fill ten copybooks with him. I remember him from Odessa in 1903; I remember him in 1905 (when he hid in Bolshoi Fontan during the *Potemkin* incident); I remember him young, with broad shoulders and the highly intelligent, charming face of an alcoholic; I remember him with Utochkin (he was in love with Knut Hamsun and would climb up on a table in the Cabaret Capernaum and declaim him); I remember him when he'd just married Maria Karlovna; I remember seeing him play ball in Odessa—he was an excellent ballplayer, very athletic; I remember the night I fell asleep in a chair at Yablochkin's and he came up to me and cut an A into my hair ("in honor of Her Majesty the Empress, it being her name-day"); I can see him with Leonid Andreev, with Gorky . . . The last time I saw him was in my own flat. He had come with Gorky and Blok. He was forty-eight, and he seemed impossibly old to me. He's sixty-eight now, and I hear he's gone soft in the head.

I am at a Pioneer camp. It is late. Eleven o'clock. The Pioneers are not yet asleep. There is no discipline: there aren't enough leaders. A second-floor window in hut five opens onto the white night.

"Are you really the one who wrote 'The Telephone'?"

"I am."

"Then would you tell them we're all crying. We're so sorry for him."

"Who is it you're sorry for?"

"Gypsy."

"There are Gypsies here?"

"Gypsy the dog. Tell them not to kill him. We love him. That's why we're crying."

They've been here all of one day and they're in love with that dog. The boys were playing with him, grabbing the caps off one another's heads and tossing them to him. But running after a cap, Gypsy had played havoc with a flower bed and the guard said in jest, "He ought to be shot." They took him literally—hence the tears.

4 June

It's been raining for three days. The poor Pioneers. There are no leaders. The Smolny people failed to provide them. They're all hoarse; they can only bark and whistle. < . . . >

15 June.

The day before yesterday the children took my suggestion—or, rather, a fleeting remark—and set up a library. I had organized some races for them and given books to the winners, and now they're contributing the prizes plus any books they may have to the library. < . . . >

13 July.

< . . . > Put Manya Shmakova in charge of the library. She is a fourteen-year-old with a past: she has been convicted of pilfering underwear and stealing two hundred rubles from her neighbors. The reason I dared put her at the head of the library was that she had done such a good job of checking in and out books, putting together the catalogue, establishing fines, and working with the readers. There were objections, but Manya has turned out to be a marvelous worker. < . . . >
< . . . >

16 August.

Went to Sestroretsk; saw Zoshchenko. We had a two-hour conversation that convinced me he is a great man, but mad, and his mania consists in his self-cure. < . . . >

29 August.

This is a month I shall long remember. I had a very vivid dream of Boba drowning in the Moscow Canal. I awoke in tears. < . . . > Lida's tragedy.[223] Although I disagree with her on every point, although I feel she is doing the wrong thing when it comes to the interests of Soviet children and children's literature (in other words, I think she should write rather than edit), I admire her dignity, energy, and candor. < . . . >
< . . . >

---

223. Reference to the arrest on 6 August in Kiev of Lidia Chukovskaya's husband, the theoretical physicist Matvei Bronshtein. See G. E. Gorelich and V. K. Frankel', *Matvei Petrovich Bronshtein* (Moscow, 1989). (V.E.)

26 September.

Kislovodsk. [. . .] Gorky's sister-in-law, Vera Alexeevna Gromova, has been sitting at our table. She is forty-seven, plump, and always laughing. She calls Gorky a despot(!) and petty tyrant(!) and says he had no knowledge of life(?). Living at Gorki (or in the Nikitskaya Street flat) was hard to bear; no one could stick it out more than three days. He spoiled one granddaughter and made the other one's life miserable. < . . . >

Utyosov was here on the 27th and told Lezhnev, Kirpotin, and two or three other men a number of jokes. The jokes were so artful and psychologically nuanced that I went and gathered a larger group. . . . But after we left him, I felt sated with jokes and even unfavorably disposed toward him. What a difficult, ignoble, and internally flawed genre the joke is: it excludes all poetry, lyricism, and tenderness and drags you into tawdry relationships with people, making you feel smaller and much worse than you actually are.

13 November.

< . . . > I'm concerned about my place in children's literature. Will my *Tales* come out? Will my verse? And what about Nekrasov? And my memoirs about Repin? My novella is moving slowly: I still haven't finished the Drakondidi chapter and the hardest part is yet to come. I am terribly dissatisfied with myself.

1939

26 November.

Slaving away over *The Art of Translation*. I could have done a decent job on the fifth edition if I hadn't fallen ill. < . . . >

My Radlova piece came out in *Pravda* yesterday, and *Krasnaia nov'* will soon be publishing a long article by me, "Desdemona's Asthma," on the same subject.[224] The same issue will contain the novella Lida is writing. It's about Chernyshevsky and Mikhailov. I'm glad: the topic is tailor-made for her.[225]

< . . . >

30 November.

Just back from the television station (Shabolovka, 53), where I gave a reading. They rouged my cheeks and blackened my mustache. Disgusting! Nobody seemed surprised that a person at 53 Shabolovka Street could be seen tens of kilometers away. < . . . >

5 December.

We received a letter from Marina the day before yesterday. About nothing special, trivialities. But Kolya added a note at the bottom: he's going into the navy tomorrow, a captain. < . . . >

12 December.

The day before yesterday I gave a reading from *A High Art* at the Library of Foreign Literature in the presence of Anna Radlova and her husband, who had come to Moscow expressly to muddy the waters surrounding my article on her *Othello* translation. And muddy the waters they did: yesterday Fadeev cut the article from *Krasnaia nov'*. I had a letter today from Lida saying that the Radlovs have started an all-out campaign against me full of slander. I wrote to her about Matvei Petrovich.[226] < . . . >

---

224. "Shakespeare Mangled" (*Pravda*, 25 November 1939) and "Desdemona's Asthma" (*Teatr* 2 [1940]: 98–109) deal with Anna Radlova's new translation of *Othello*.

225. "History of an Uprising" (*Krasnaia nov'* 10–11 [1939]: 27–71). The novel about Chernyshevsky and his contemporary, poet and journalist Mikhail Mikhailov, never materialized. See Lydia Chukovskaya, *The Akhmatova Journals*, vol. 1, translated by Milena Michalski and Sylva Rubashova (London, 1993), 58.

226. This single line hints at the fate of Matvei Bronshtein. After strenuous efforts Chukovsky was granted an audience with the Chairman of the Military College of the USSR Supreme Court, V. V. Ulrikh, only to learn of his son-in-law's death. In a letter to his daughter from Moscow to Leningrad he wrote, "It is painful for me to write about this to you, but I have now learnt for certain that Matvei Petrovich is no longer alive. My hands are shaking, I can't write any more" (Lydia Chukovskaya, *The Akhmatova Journals,* vol. 1, 47).

1940

< . . . >

26 April.

Peredelkino. Akhmatova came to see me today, all majestic and slow. Ninochka Fedina brought her. She sat on the terrace and talked about the war: "Every day the war is working for us. But the English and the French are turning into savages. They're not the English we once knew. I've put it in my diary: 'Savage Germans are dropping bombs on savage Englishmen.' " She had the following to say about Pertsov: "I've kept a 1925 clipping from *Teatr i iskusstvo* in which he writes, 'Who needs the amorous sighs of this aging woman who has forgotten to die?' "[227] And about my Lida: "She's wonderful and so talented." She was particularly enthusiastic about Lida's Olesha article. She believes Lida has put the loss of Mitya behind her. She also had a lot to say about Lida's operation. "My second book is not to be. No paper, they say, but they're just trying to be polite. I met Dora Sergeevna on the train on my way here from Leningrad yesterday, and she brought me to Peredelkino bypassing Moscow. It's Fadeev I came to see. I've already seen him. He's promised to phone around for information about Lyovushka. I'm on my way back to find out the results."[228]

I walked her there; she was very nervous. "I remind myself of that grande dame in *War and Peace*," she said.

"You mean the one who is 'all tears'?"

---

227. Akhmatova is referring to an article by Viktor Pertsov, "Along Literary Watersheds" (*Zhizn' iskusstva*, 27 October 1926), which contains the following passage: "New, living people are now and will remain cold and unmoved by the moans of a woman who was born too late or failed to die in time." "Lidia's article about Olesha" is her review of Olesha's *Three Fat Men* (*Detskaia literatura* 8 [1940]: 44–48).

228. Akhmatova asked Fadeev, one of the most influential figures in the Soviet Writers' Union, to intervene on behalf of her son, Lev Gumilyov. According to Lidia Chukovskaya, Fadeev promised to help. "Anna Andreevna told me . . . that when she got to Fadeev's villa in Peredelkino she was amazed and of course encouraged by the fact that he received her cordially and promptly did all he could. (In the preceding few days she had kept saying, 'He will not even let me in.') She was also astounded to hear that Fadeev and Pasternak had nominated her book for a Stalin prize." See Lydia Chukovskaya, *The Akhmatova Journals*, vol. 1, 150.

"Why, yes. How did you guess?"

"I was struck by the expression as a child."

"I was struck by another as well: 'a ceremonial face.' "

27 April.

A.A. is downstairs. Fadeev sent her a long letter yesterday saying that he'd reached the person she needs and that if she rang him the following morning he would bring her together with the man.

21 November.

On the way to Leningrad. Almost there. Had a murderous bout of insomnia all night.

2 December.

Called on Tynyanov the day before yesterday. He'd come back to town from Detskoe Selo (that is, Pushkin) to read for the actors his new play based on *Kyukhlya.* His legs are in terrible shape: he gets up to greet someone and falls, then smiles as if it were an accident. His face is all wrinkled. "Thank you for your letter, Kornei Ivanovich. I wasn't able to answer it because I can't write letters anymore. Oh, the letters I used to write! I can't work on my Pushkin either. I'm in an unusual position: I can observe how people will relate to me after my death because I'm dead already." His words lack their former brilliance; he mostly grumbles about imaginary insults. < . . . >

Called on Akhmatova. She was lying down, looking after the neighbors' children. We hadn't anything to talk about really. We talked about John Keats and Pasternak's new book of translations. "What an awful writer that Kleist is!" she said.

1941

+>–+>–+>–+>–+>–+>–+>–+>

4 January.

Met yesterday Sholokhov for the first time. He is at the Supreme Soviet sanatorium. < . . . > He left his quarters with a firm gait (reminiscent of Leonid Andreev) and girded by a magnificent leather belt. < . . . > He has his family with him: "Maria Mikhailovna" (who turned three yesterday), his son Alik, another son, his mother-in-law, and his wife—fine people all, serious, not in the least scattered, organic. They make a charming impression, and he is an integral part of it. He is one with them; to understand him you have to see him with the family. His Alik is already at ten a "Voroshilov marksman" (he won a three-ruble prize at the shooting gallery in the park here), a somewhat somber boy, highly reserved, sincere, naive. I read the Sherlock Holmes story "The Red-Headed League" to him and Lyova Zbarsky yesterday. At first he was afraid of not understanding it, but then he got so involved, emotionally involved, that reading to him was a pleasure.

Sholokhov had the following to say about "Sasha Fadeev": "If Sasha had creative ambitions, he wouldn't go poking his nose in all the writers' squabbles. But no, he enjoys having people wait for him in antechambers, he enjoys being a member of the Central Committee, etc. And if he were just Fadeev, what good would he be?"

"Fadeev is a charming man and a good writer," I said by way of defense. He didn't argue; he told me about hunting pheasants in Kabardino-Balkaria and the moonshine the peasants there had treated him to.

6 January.

Had a letter from Semynin today. He spent the whole evening with Sholokhov yesterday. Their main topic of conversation was what to do with the Writers' Union. Semynin's idea is "the Union should be disbanded. Let the writers write. All that needs to remain is a professional organization."

31 January.

We're leaving today. Just as I arrived, bam! *Pravda* came out with the article on *Literaturnaia ucheba,* and just as I leave, pow! *Litgazeta* attacks me as well.[229] The former was on 29 December, the latter on 30 January. Once a month. I'm lucky it's not more often.

2 February.

Back in Moscow. < . . . >

11 February.

Sholokhov phoned four or five days ago and asked me to come immediately. I did. In a tiny, smoke-filled room (440) at the National I found Lezhnev drunk, Lida Lezhneva half-drunk, and Sholokhov drunk. His mother was downstairs in room 217: he had brought her to Moscow to have the Kremlin doctors look at her, which they had done. But it was painful to see Sholokhov drunk, and I left.

This morning I went back. He's in 217 now. I knocked at 440, where his mother is, but she couldn't open the door, so he got a key and opened it from the outside. He gave me a warm reception. We talked about children's literature. He reads everything, it turns out: *Murzilka, Chizh, Kolkhoznye rebiata.*[230] He came down hard on a tale about a pinecone that climbed a lamp. "Ridiculous." He agreed to write about hunting and the Civil War for our textbooks.

Lida is due today.

< . . . >

229. On 29 November 1940 *Pravda* published an attack by one A. Shtein on the journal *Literaturnaia ucheba.* One of his targets was Chukovsky's article "The Social Nature of a Translator's Work." Stein called the article "an example of vulgar sociology," a pejorative label reserved for Soviet literary criticism allegedly guilty of crude, "nondialectical" treatment of the relationship between literature and society. A month later *Literaturnaia gazeta* featured an unfavorable review of an anthology of children's poetry Chukovsky had compiled. The review is especially critical of the selection from contemporary "adult" poetry.

230. Titles of journals for children. (V.E.)

1 April.

Turned fifty-nine today. I never thought I'd live so long. I got up at four in the morning. I'm writing about Semynin: I'm giving a talk on him the day after tomorrow. I've just finished a new translation of *Robinson Crusoe*. Two days ago the book with all my children's tales, *Wonder Tree*, went off to the printer's. It snowed yesterday. Fine winter weather.

19 October.

Buzuluk, en route to Tashkent.[231] A compartment in international train No. 22. It is snowing. We waited for a long time yesterday just before Kuibyshev. Five trains passed, and the semaphore kept us standing. One of the trains ended up next to us in the Kuibyshev station, and what did I see looking out of the middle (green, armored) carriage but the sad face of Mikhail Kalinin. I bowed my head; he drew the curtain. The five trains were clearly government trains. That is why they had planes flying over them and anti-aircraft guns on the back platforms. So from 18 October 1941 on, what used to be Samara is our capital.

< . . . > On 15 October we packed and went to the station, and suddenly, three minutes before the train was due to leave (it actually left later) Afinogenov showed up terribly upset. "Everyone is ordered to report to the Central Committee by five," he said. "We writers are being evacuated with the government." I was on the list of writers, but getting to the Central Committee building was out of the question: the square around the station was jammed with people. No fewer than fifteen thousand people were advancing on the station, and I would have trouble making it to the proper train to say nothing of the Central Committee. Had it not been for Nikolai Virta, I'd have got stuck in the crowd and never left. Marya Borisovna had had our luggage brought to the station by car, and I couldn't locate the luggage or the car. But luckily in his youth Virta had been a reporter and the manager of a traveling provincial theater company: his drive, his ingenuity, his get-up-and-go bordered on the brilliant. He pinned a medal on his chest, made his way to the stationmaster, and said that he was in charge of a high government official whose name he was not at

---

231. Many civilians were evacuated from Moscow to Central Asia during the early years of the war. (M.H.H.)

liberty to reveal and that he would have to let us all through no questions asked. I knew nothing of this—I had no idea he'd passed me off as a "high government official "—and I was amazed to see all doors open before me and my porters. Virta is as wily as they come. Once we were a thousand or so versts from Moscow, he added another stripe to his collar, thereby promoting himself to lieutenant colonel. Unaware that all writers would be told on the evening of 14 October they could leave Moscow, he tried—in my presence and on the premises of the Central Committee—to talk Afinogenov into helping him to slip out of Moscow (he was eligible for conscription). "You must understand, Kolya," Afinogenov told him, "You could be called up any moment now. You've been put on the Informburo list."

"Come on, Sasha. You can find a way. And if you do, I promise to take care of Antonina Vasilyevna and Jenny [Afinogenov's mother and wife] en route. All you have to do is say my wife is pregnant and I need to be with her." (His wife isn't the least bit pregnant.)

At the stations along the way he managed to get bread for the mysterious official he was supposedly accompanying. But morally suspect as he is, there is something endearing about him: he hasn't read a thing and doesn't care for poetry, music, or nature, yet he is hardworking, tireless in his machinations (and not only when they're for his own good), not without literary ability (some of his newspaper reports are very well written). It's just that he's a predatory type by nature. He adores things—fancy clothes, fine furniture, rich food—and power.

These days have been awful for me. I don't know where Boba is. Nine chances out of ten he's been killed. Where is Kolya? What will happen to Lida? How will Marina survive the hunger and cold? Those are my four wounds.

Practically nowhere along the way have we seen fields harvested. Grain is rotting in ricks over an area of a thousand versts. True, there are piles of grain—millet and wheat—lying in the stations, but they are unprotected and collecting dust and soot. An occasional station will have one or another kind of food for sale: potato pancakes at a ruble apiece, camel's milk, yogurt. Hundreds of passengers descend on the food, crushing one another and the women selling it, crazed with hunger. Trains stand in stations for two or three hours. The supplies we brought from Moscow are dwindling.

21 October.

We have entered Asia. The day before yesterday we saw some Polish troops at a station in Chkalov (Orenburg) District—gaunt but impressive men in pitifully thin overcoats getting out of the train and saluting one another theatrically. They crowded up to a hut with "Stantsia 1" [Station 1] written on it. Their caps, sewn with silver thread, and coats, once quite stately, were tattered and torn by now, yet they still had a look of purpose about them. And several of the officers were dressed impeccably.

"Where are you going?" I asked one of them.

"To Buzuluk. To meet our army."

"I hear the climate there is very good."

"It's better in Poland."

22 October.

Kozalinsk. The Aral Sea. The trees are still green. The lucky ones are buying pike. If you have an evacuation certificate, you're entitled to bread. I tried queuing up a few times, but got nothing. When I went to the commander to ask for a ticket that would enable me to buy some bread, he said, "Leave the room immediately!"

Am giving the Virtas English lessons.

23 October.

Tashkent. The Hotel National. We've just arrived. We were met by local writers and a representative of the Sovnarkom, Kovalenko. They provided four cars for us.

24 October.

The barber has a fan: he squirts you with cologne and fans you. The bootblack has a bell: when he's finished with one shoe, he rings it and you give him the other. Rows of poplars, unusually tall, lend the city a special poetic, musical air. Walking the streets, I seem to be hearing music, and it's all the poplars' doing. Irrigation ditches and the thousands of different little bridges spanning them, a panorama of one-storied houses looking even squatter than they are under the tall poplars, southern street life and the kind and gracious Uzbeks, the bazaars with their nuts and raisins, the bounteous sun—how is it I've never been here before? Why didn't I come before the war? I'm in a terrible state—I have the grippe and dysentery, three of my false teeth have fallen out, I have a fever sore on my lip, I miss Boba terribly, my life is in total chaos—and still I'm happy to have had the chance to see Tashkent in my old age.

The strangest, most unexpected thing about the place is the laughing children. All the way from Moscow to Tashkent I saw sad, weeping children with emaciated, old people's faces, orphaned, abandoned. And here what do I see in every boulevard, in every courtyard but carefree, perfectly normal children running about, fighting, waving their arms in the air. I went outside early this morning and saw janitors, Uzbeks mostly, pouring buckets of water from the irrigation ditches over the streets—an ancient custom, obviously, passed down from generation to generation—and schoolchildren hurrying off to school, something I hadn't seen this year in Moscow. It seemed odd that there were still places in the Soviet Union where children go to school. < . . . >

29 October.

The woman at the pharmacy told a polyclinic patient by the name of Iosif Afanasyevich Kogan that I was here and that the hotel where I was staying had no kerosene for me. Well, early this morning a thin, middle-aged man with a patch over one eye presented me with—a tin of kerosene! I was so moved by his act of kindness after all the malice I'd seen on the road that I dedicated the following improvisation to him:

> I thought the world bereft in its blindness
> Of solace, sympathy, and love;
> I thought the roots of human kindness
> Had long since choked and drowned in blood.
> But then with neither cant nor slogan,
> All of a sudden, out of the blue—
> My God, how touching—dearest Kogan,
> Before me who appeared but you.

30 October.

Tashkent's kindness knows no bounds. The former People's Commissar of Education here, Comrade Yuldashev, *offered me a room,* a wonderful furnished room in the heart of town, the perfect neighborhood—a Ukrainian colleague of his had to move away—and it comes complete with telephone, record player, and desk for only fifty-eight rubles a month! It's a miracle! And I didn't need to bow down to Kovalenko or deprive any of my writer brethren of a roof over their heads. Now Marya Borisovna and I can live far from all the squabbles and enjoy a bit of privacy!

Early November.

Lida is here. Marya Borisovna and I went to fetch her at the station. < . . . > I've been ill and had to spend about ten days in hospital, after which I took on a lot of work: I gave a course on children's poets at the Pedagogical Institute, started writing for *Pravda Vostoka,* and made a number of appearances in theaters and schools. < . . . >

1942

14 January.

Spent the morning with Vladimirova at Narkompros. We had a long queue of people wishing to take in evacuated children. Lyudmila Stepanovna Zaitseva of the Film Distribution Board (she and her husband have a combined monthly income of 1,180 rubles) said, "I don't care what nationality the child is, but my husband told me, 'No lame girls, please!' "
< . . . >
    [   ]

21 January.

Saw yesterday Alexei Tolstoy riding along Pervomaiskaya Street. He's been living at the Abdurakhmanovs' dacha, but I run into him quite often in town. He's never cared much about me, and although we've known each other for thirty years he has little idea of what I write, what I like, and what I want. Now he appears to have taken notice of me and is showing some interest. I've always treated him with great respect, though I am aware of his weak points, the most striking of which is that he has no knowledge of life. He's a real workhorse, writing from dawn till dusk, completely devoted to the paper in front of him; not until six does he break away. That is what his whole life has been like. Then where do his images come from? From within. From his own, inner, genuinely Russian being. He has an amazing eye and magnificent Russian, he is enormously inventive, but he has seen very little life. For example, he gives excellent descriptions of eight or nine battles in his works, but he's never experienced one; he frequently depicts the down-and-out, but associates exclusively with the well-to-do. His artistic intuition is stupendous; it's the only thing that saves him. < . . . >

< . . . >

1 April.

My birthday. I'm exactly sixty. Tashkent. The apricot trees are in bloom. It is cool out. Early morning. The birds are chirping. It will be a hot day.

My birthday presents are the following: Boba has disappeared without a trace. Our last letter from him was from near Vyazma and was dated 4 October 1941. Kolya is in Leningrad, the most dangerous front; he has a wounded leg and is homeless: his flat has been bombed. I am certain my Peredelkino dacha has burned down and with it my entire library, which I have been assembling all my life. And that is the material I am supposed to fashion into a joyous tale of victory.[232]

I am living in a room that has nothing in it but two maps, a broken washstand, a wobbly bed, some books and old clothes on the windowsill—and a yearning to see my children. The windows face the courtyard, and the courtyard has a hundred or so children shouting in a southern fashion from morn till night.

Lida is still working on *The Children Have the Word.*

---

232. A reference to Chukovsky's antiwar tale "We Shall Overcome Barmalei."

2 September.

For the past four and a half hours I've been flying in an eight-seater (a Douglas bomber) to Moscow. < ... > I am reading a good but easily forgettable novella by Vasily Grossman in *Krasnaia zvezda* entitled *The People Is Immortal.*[233]

We stopped in Turkestan to refuel. We are traveling with melons, watermelons, apples, and grapes.

Grossman writes very well. Every line is a gem, but the whole is pale and banal, even rhetorical in places. < ... >

1943

26 January.

Last night Marya Borisovna, Zhenichka, and I set off for Moscow. Farewell to dear Tashkent! To the room with the silly green curtains, the wobbly wardrobe, the broken stove, the rusty, lopsided washstand, the two maps covering holes in the wall, the bashed door that didn't need to be prized open, the child's drawing between the windows, the broken pane in the left window, that wondrous little ventilation window. It was useless as an office in summer when thirty or so of Odessa's loudest outdid themselves from morn to night just outside the windows.

5 March.

< ... > Am reading Carlyle's *History of Frederick the Great.* How instructive! Therein lie the roots of the Prussian mentality, of jingoism and fascism, of mechanical Germanic thickheadedness.

---

233. Four years after publishing a series of sketches and stories entitled *The People Is Immortal,* Vasily Grossman wrote a war novel entitled *In a Good Cause* (1942). While the first part was well received, the second part was suppressed as ideologically flawed. A significantly toned-down 1954 version won Grossman a prestigious decoration, yet its panoramic sequel, *Life and Fate,* was too openly critical of the Soviet regime to warrant publication in the Soviet Union until the advent of glasnost. It appeared in the West in 1980 to much acclaim. (V.E.)

10 March.

Had a phone call yesterday: "Detgiz for Kornei Chukovsky." Then Golenkina's voice: "It is my duty to inform you, Kornei Ivanovich, that we have received instructions not to publish your tale." I hung up without responding. So Naumova has prevailed, and Soviet children will have no tale of victory.

11 March.

Kolya has arrived. He's talking to Misha Slonimsky on the phone.

22 March.

Marina, Tata, and Gulka have arrived. We went for their things. I've started writing about Chekhov.

29 March.

Spoke at the Writers' Union meeting on the 26th. It was very bad. I sounded like a provincial old man. Ehrenburg was terrific. Yesterday I read my memoirs of Gorky in Tchaikovsky Hall (on the occasion of the seventy-fifth anniversary of his birth). Fadeev, Fedin, Surkov, and Vsevolod Ivanov spoke as well. Fadeev, the chairman, threw the tritest of journalistic clichés into the pot, stirred well, and out came a speech that sounded like a parody. And a parody it was, seeing that its whole purpose was to please the authorities rather than the audience or himself. Which is a pity, because the man does have a soul. Fedin told me that when the Central Committee phoned Fadeev and told him to write an encomium to Wanda Wasilewska, Fadeev shouted blue murder and told him point blank, "I won't do it. I won't do it. I won't write a word." But the next day he wrote what they wanted and rang Fedin to say, "You know, her *Rainbow* isn't so bad after all." Even if in the end they didn't take it, he did write what they wanted. And yet there's something strong and poetic about him. < . . . >
< . . . >

2 June.

No word about the tale yet. I don't know what to do. The Presidium of the Writers' Union is meeting at six tomorrow to discuss it. I went to see Tolstoy today. He's having the same problem with *Ivan the Terrible*. Nobody is willing to say whether the play can be put on or not. < . . . > He finally wrote a letter to Iosif Vissarionovich [Stalin] today.

From there, on to Sholokhov. He's flying off to the Don tomorrow morning and is staying at the National. I found him looking sober and sad. "I'm surprised at how frivolous the Muscovites are. The way they behave you'd think there wasn't a war going on. It's very strange when you come from the front."

From there—it was evening by then—on to Marshak. Once more Marshak showed himself the great hypocrite and schemer he is. I didn't ask him to praise my tale, only to protect it from the sordid Detgiz intrigues, and all he did was to tell me "openly, as a friend" and "because you mean so much to me" that my tale was no good and I'd be better off not publishing it. He also refused to sign the document Tolstoy and Sholokhov signed. The tale *is* weak, but that's not the point: the point is a show of solidarity on the part of a colleague.

3 June.

The Presidium met today to discuss my tale. Fedin and Zoshchenko had promised to come but did not [. . .]. Where would I have been without the Tolstoy and Sholokhov signatures I got yesterday? Everybody behaved well: they closed ranks and came out unanimously in favor of the tale. < . . . >

The weather is wonderful. Tverskoy Boulevard is completely green. The barrage balloon has a gentle silver sheen to it. The streets are full of bustle and laughter. Moscow wants to be frivolous. "Moscow has so many superfluous people," Sholokhov said yesterday.

15 June.

< . . . > G. F. Alexandrov has authorized publication of the tale. Why were the evil crows so intent on clawing my eyes out? < . . . >

24 July.

Went to Peredelkino for the first time all summer. To my utter horror I found my entire library pillaged. The few remaining books had their bindings torn off. The following are dispersed or destroyed: my Nekrasoviana collection, the collected works of Johnson, *all* my children's books, thousands of English titles (**British theatre**), my library of essayists, the children's letters, Marya Borisovna's letters to me, mine to her . . . They form a crust on the floor, a path to walk on. On my way out I noticed a campfire in the woods, a campfire with children around it. I started off in their direction, but they saw me. "Stop, where are you going?" I cried, but they ran away. What I saw when I got there were my English books in flames (including my favorite American book, *Think of It*) and some issues of *Detskaia literatura*. And I thought, How grotesque! What do I see before my very eyes but the children I've loved so dearly burning the books I'd have used to serve them.

Our troops captured Kharkov yesterday. I heard about it at the Lenin Library, where I was studying. < . . . >

I've just received *We Shall Overcome Barmalei* published by the Uzbek State Publishing House in Tashkent. < . . . >

23 September.

Poltava is ours!

Tata is back from the Labor Front[234] and is spending her first night in the parental home. She falls asleep, but suddenly cries out.

"What's wrong?" I ask.

"I dreamt the Germans had loaded me into a Katyusha to shoot at the Russians."

7 November.

Kiev is ours. Stalin's speech. Received a telegram saying that Lida and Lyusha[235] had left Tashkent. < . . . >

234. The Labor Front consisted of a network of behind-the-lines civilian work camps. Tata is Chukovsky's granddaughter Natalya Nikolaevna Chukovskaya.

235. Lyusha is Chukovsky's granddaughter Yelena (Elena) Tsezarevna Chukovskaya, who edited the Russian edition of the *Diary*. (V.E.)

1944

➤-➤-➤-➤-➤-➤-➤-➤-➤

1 January.

< . . . > Called on Mikhalkov yesterday. He had spent the whole night with Iosif Vissarionovich [Stalin] and came home in a state of utter exaltation. He recited many poems to Stalin, humorous ones included, and told him, "I have little education, Iosif Vissarionovich, and my poems are often bad." About his text for the national anthem Mikhalkov had this to say: "What do you expect? An anthem is an anthem. Artistic criteria don't apply. But wait till you see the things I'm going to write!" And he *has* written some wonderful poems. I especially like the one about the old man who sold his cow. < . . . >

1 March.

Philistines try to console me by saying, "Beating determines consciousness."[236] < . . . >

The *Pravda* article.[237] < . . . >

236. A melancholy pun on the Marxist formula "Being determines consciousness" (the Russian for "being" is *byt'e*, for "beating" is *bit'e*). (V.E.)

237. On 1 March 1944 one Pavel Yudin published a savage review of "We Shall Overcome Barmalei": "A Vulgar and Harmful Concoction by Kornei Chukovsky" (*Pravda*, 1 March 1944). The attack was prompted by a political denunciation. The neighbor-informer was a painter, Pyotr Vasilyev, known for his depictions of Lenin's life. His most popular work, "Lenin and Stalin in Razliv," was repeatedly reproduced in the Soviet press. Shortly before denouncing Chukovsky, Vasilyev paid him a neighborly visit. A newspaper featuring the painting lay on the table. "Why did you put Stalin next to Lenin?" Chukovsky asked his guest. "Everybody knows Lenin was hiding at Zinovyev's." (Razliv was a summer resort near Saint Petersburg, and Lenin spent some time there in August 1917 after going underground.) Vasilyev lost no time in reporting the conversation to the authorities, and Chukovsky was summoned to the Central Committee and summarily chastised. Chukovsky's archive contains a postcard reproduction of another work by Vasilyev, "Lenin as a Child." At the bottom of the card Chukovsky wrote: "This is Pyotr Vasilyev the informer. He reported to the Central Committee what I said about Stalin, and it nearly did me in." In 1952 the house in which Chukovsky and Vasilyev were living at the time was provided with a commemorative plaque honoring Vasilyev.

Dostoevsky (for my Chekhov article): " 'Nothing is strong unless blood runs beneath it.' What the villains forget, though, is that strength is the property of those whose blood is shed, not of those who do the blood-shedding. Such is the true law of blood on earth."

Am reading Dostoevsky's "The Eternal Husband," Voltaire's *Candide*, Maupassant, Polonsky's verse, Strakhov's biography of Dostoevsky, Dostoevsky's letters, and Heine. < . . . >

28 June.

Night. < . . . > For six months after the blows I suffered on account of my Barmalei tale—and they were legion—I was given to understand that Iskusstvo would put out my Repin, and all at once, five days ago, I was told, "Publication canceled: your portrait of Repin is belittling"! I withstood the torture, firm in the belief that I had Chekhov to fall back on. But now my Chekhov manuscript has fallen into the hands of ruddy-cheeked Yermilov, who, for his pamphlet on the fortieth anniversary of Chekhov's death, has stolen everything I wrote about Chekhov in 1914 on the eve of the First World War and now, during the Second, everything I came up with working in blissful Lenin Library isolation, and much as I should be used to suchlike thefts—my Blok book was stolen, my Nekrasov, and my Mayakovsky article, and Yevdokimov stole my Repin article—I still find it terribly painful. Were I a drinking man, I'd go on a binge, but since I'm not I've gone on a reading binge, I'm reading indiscriminately: *The Eustace Diamonds* and *Barchester Towers* by Trollope, *The Black Tulip* by Alexandre Dumas, *Passage to India* by Forster, and even Aldington, even Thackeray's *The Newcomes,* and I'm shocked by the petty sorrows—microscopic in comparison with mine, with ours—the nineteenth-century novel deals with. I even hurled Trollope to the floor when he tried to make me indignant over the fact that a rich widow, a clergyman's daughter, had received a letter—a perfectly correct letter—from a *bachelor,* Mr. Slope, which episode occupies twenty pages, to say nothing of the hundreds of pages the author devotes to the equally earthshaking problem of whether a priest should remain at the head of an old-age home till the end of his days or be replaced. To us, Russians living in the year 1944, such problems appear ant-like, even bug-like. The other day I read Henry James's "International Episode" and *Washington Square* without the slightest interest. I enjoyed them once, but this time I was insulted by the register of the most paltry feelings of every ant, no, every microbe! Had James spent a single day in my shoes, he wouldn't have written those vibrionic sagas. < ... >

29 June.

Gave a talk on Chekhov at the House of Scholars. < ... > M. F. Andreeva [Gorky's mistress] said that Gorky didn't believe Knipper [Chekhov's wife] when she said his dying words were "Ich sterbe" [I am dying (German)]; what Gorky thought he said, "Akh ty sterva!" [Oh, you bitch (Russian)]. Maria Fyodorovna didn't like Chekhov. She said she couldn't forgive the way he treated Sofya Bonnier, with whom she claims Chekhov lived for twenty years. She is amazingly youthful, lively, and harmonious. < ... >

17 July.

Have just had my last Chekhov talk. It was at Tchaikovsky Hall. I ran all the way in a pair of pockmarked slippers I should have thrown out long ago—and *sockless*. The man in charge of the hall lent me his socks. < ... >

5 October.

My Repin article was cut from *Novyi mir*. < ... >

21 November.

< ... > Am reading Thomas Hardy's *Far from the Madding Crowd*. The narrative texture is amazingly subtle and sumptuous, but what he makes of it is the tritest of hackwork. His subject matter is much inferior to his craftsmanship, his technique. < ... >
< ... >

1945

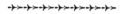

< . . . >

6 July.

The whole family has moved to Peredelkino. In a lorry. It's wonderful here. Lyusha has put up a new hammock. I've started a tale about Bibigon. It will be the last I ever write. < . . . >

15 October.

Moved back to town from the dacha. Two sleepless nights. Was at the Hall of Columns yesterday. Horrible. I've been waiting ten hours to learn whether they'll broadcast "Bibigon." I'm afraid they won't.

Read *Pickwick* and the Blok-Bely correspondence all night. I'm at loose ends. I wish I could get over this . . . or die.

1946

31 March.

< . . . > 1 a.m. Took medinal. Still couldn't sleep. In *The Seagull* Chekhov has:

> "Medical attention at sixty!"
> "Even sixty-year-olds want to live."
> "Going to a spa at sixty? Complaining you didn't live it up when you were young? I'm sorry, that's just plain frivolous."

Well, frivolity is my main salvation.

How marvelous it is that on the very eve of my death I can still read Chekhov with such excitement and pleasure.

1 April.

My birthday. Despite not having slept last night, despite having nothing to look forward to, despite bitter disappointments and deaths in the past and to come, I'm in a fine, perfectly birthday mood. The weather has been clear since morning.

My first present: a splendid paper from V. V. Vinogradov! < . . . >

Here is what I found in *The Seagull* for my sixty-fourth birthday:

DORN. You must admit, though. It's not very magnanimous—all this talk of how badly life has treated you. And at sixty-two.
SORIN. Stubborn, aren't you? Can't you see? I want to live! [. . .]

3 April.

Depressed and completely debilitated. Numbing myself with various medicines. < . . . >

Reading Vinogradov's "The Style of Lermontov's Prose." An exhaustive study, basic, but the end of Lermontov as a living writer. < . . . >

8 May.

Spent the morning at the Lenin Library going through critical articles on Nekrasov in *Moskvitianin* and so on, the afternoon at the *Murzilka* office, the evening at Tvardovsky's. It was my first visit. I was very much impressed by Olga, his six-year-old, by his wife, who *understands,* by his many books, and by his profound involvement with literature. < . . . >

25 June.

The day before yesterday Alyansky came to Peredelkino to tell me there was a big campaign being waged against "Bibigon." < . . . > "Bibigon" is completely defenseless. All some idiot has to do is proclaim it contains political allusions and it's done for: Detgiz won't touch it; *Murzilka* will stop publishing it. That made me nervous, so I went to see Fadeev and laid out my concerns. Kaverin happened to be there and, fine person that he is, he took my concerns so to heart that I decided to go to the Central Committee of the Komsomol the very next day and try to ward off the blows aimed at "Bibigon." < . . . > Nobody at the Central Committee had a sensible thing to say, but nobody tore into it either; on the contrary, they said "children love it" and "lightweight it may be, but it's entertaining," and so on. Kaverin stood up for it bravely: he said I had the "knack" of attracting children and "Bibigon" was full of energy and dynamism, and so on.

Basically things went well, but the main battle was put off until Thursday. < . . . > Stalin has expressed dissatisfaction with the level of the journals being published in the USSR and demanded they raise their standards. The Central Committee of the Komsomol has decided to examine all its journals and make suggestions to each. < . . . > So there will be another chance to rake "Bibigon" over the coals on Thursday. < . . . >

21 August.

< . . . > Ran into Konstantin Simonov on the street. He's just back from Paris and told me about Bunin, Teffi, and Remizov. The Merezhkovskys were apparently dyed-in-the-wool Nazis and received handouts from Mussolini as well. Then again, these God-seekers were always selling themselves to somebody.[238] < . . . >

I've been seeing a lot of Leonid Leonov and admire his splendid character. He's a strong man, well armed for life. He visits once or twice a week and talks nonstop, but never brings up his own plans, projects, or triumphs. The Maly is premiering a play of his tomorrow, say, or he had a book come out yesterday—he'll talk for three hours and never breathe a word of it. Not only is there no hint of the braggart in him, he goes on and on about his failures and defeats. He can do anything with his hands: he makes lampshades, tables, and chairs; he molds faces out of clay; he has fashioned a magnificent cigarette lighter out of bronze—he has all kinds of instruments and tools. Watch the way he handles seeds or berries and you know he's got a green thumb. Simple as he looks, he plays his cards close to the chest. He is well-bred and well-organized, oddly lacking in kindness but a throughbred, and he has a poetic nature. In short, he's a typical Russian.

Called on Pasternak the day before yesterday. He is writing a novel.

238. The God-seekers were a group of intellectuals who wished to build social reform on a religious base and were especially attracted to the ideas of Vladimir Solovyov. They were most active during the years following the 1905 Revolution. (M.H.H.)

His creative juices are flowing, but as usual his speech is a jumble of enchanting obscurities. [. . .]

26 August.

Thought all week about Akhmatova and Zoshchenko.[239] They're not the issue, of course; the issue is educating the young. And there all of us are to blame, though mostly out of ignorance. Why didn't our leaders—Fadeev, Tikhonov—make it clear that peacetime moods are out of place, that the postwar period is not a breathing space, that *all* our literature without exception must be militant and educational? < . . . >

At Fedin's < . . . > Zoshchenko and Akhmatova were on everybody's lips. I do my best to steer clear of such conversations: they keep me from working.

29 August.

Today's *Pravda* carries a nasty article about my "Bibigon" and Kolya's *Silver Island.*[240] In other words, I've got another lean year ahead of me in my old age, and Kolya is in a dreadful situation: he's got three children to

239. A muted reference to the onslaught on Akhmatova and Zoshchenko in the Soviet press in the wake of Andrei Zhdanov's speech "On the Journals *Zvezda* and *Leningrad*" and the resolution of the Central Committee under the same title. In his infamous harangue, which triggered a large-scale cultural purge, Zhdanov characterized Akhmatova as "half-harlot, half-nun" and accused Zoshchenko of slandering Soviet reality in what was a totally innocuous story ("Adventures of a Monkey"). Chukovsky's initial response is characteristically inhibited. Though well aware of the ramifications of the speech (see the entry for 13 October 1946), he did not find the words for Zhdanov's obscene performance until considerably later (see the entry for 19 February 1964). (V.E.)

240. The harassment began a week after the publication of the Central Committee's resolution. On 23 August 1946 a *Pravda* article inveighed against the children's magazine *Murzilka* and Chukovsky's "Bibigon" in the following terms: "It is intolerable for seasoned writers to drag utter nonsense into children's magazines under the guise of a tale, but utter nonsense under the guise of a tale is just what the writer Kornei Chukovsky has offered the children's magazine *Murzilka.* Bizarre and absurd events follow one another. Bad prose alternates with bad verse. Naturalism, primitivism. There is no real fantasy in this 'tale,' nothing but fancy tricks." The author of the article was somewhat less scurrilous in dealing with Nikolai Chukovsky's novel *Silver Island,* though he called it "a tribute to bad models—to the genre of the Western detective story," and concluded: "It is wrong for a journal to publish a poem, story, or sketch that runs counter to the aims and methods of the Communist education of children."

feed, a new flat to pay for, and here he works like a dog without a penny for his pains. < . . . >

Pasternak came to see me in high spirits, his voice booming. He gave me his Shakespeare article.

5 September.

It's been raining nonstop all day. < . . . >

Yesterday's *Pravda* tears Vasily Grossman to shreds.[241]

Leonov was here the day before yesterday. "Why does Pasternak prevent his friends from standing up for him?" he asked. "Why does he say such odd things?" < . . . >

I see no ray of hope for my old age—no friends, no inspiration. Pen and paper have been my life basically, and children my only respite. Now I've been made a villain in their eyes and nobody needs the things I know. < . . . > I am not particularly concerned about the fates of individual writers, my own included, but is it my lot to see the fate of the whole world as I prepare to leave it? I must get the better of my depression, smother it with relentless work. I am going back to the Nekrasov manuscript, which is as much a patchwork as the rest of my life at present. < . . . >

Zoshchenko and Akhmatova have been expelled from the Writers' Union. Zoshchenko has apparently stated that he has enough to live on for two years and that during those two years he will write a novel that will make amends for everything he has written thus far.

Leonov on the Grossman play reviled in *Pravda:* "Grossman is very inexperienced. He should put the ideas near and dear to him in the mouth of a moron, a notorious imbecile. Then if they start picking on them, he can say, 'But the man's an idiot!' "

8 September.

The sun is out. Worked in the strawberry patch. Wrote about Belinsky for the Nekrasov book.

241. In an article entitled "A Harmful Play" (*Pravda*, 4 September 1946) the influential literary hatchetman Vladimir Yermilov offered the following description of Grossman's play *If One Is to Believe the Pythagoreans:* "He has written an ambiguous and harmful play, a malicious lampoon on our reality, our people. Only utter political irresponsibility on the part of *Znamia*'s editors can account for the appearance of Vasily Grossman's reactionary, decadent, anti-artistic play on its pages."

10 September.

The Leonovs came last night, but I was at Pasternak's. He has long since been meaning to read me passages from the novel he is writing. He has read parts to Fedin and Pogodin and wants me to hear them too. The day before yesterday he told Kolya there would be a reading on Sunday, and invited both Kolya and Marina. But as luck would have it, that was the day *Pravda* printed the resolution of the Presidium of the Writers' Union calling Pasternak "an author lacking in ideology and removed from Soviet reality." I was certain that being branded an outcast would be hard on him and that he would put off the reading. But as it turned out, he had invited a number of other guests for that day. < . . . >

It was hard for me to get a handle on the novel, because I have trouble listening well in the evening—I am tired by eight o'clock—but for all the charm of certain passages, most of which were nature descriptions or had to do with childhood—it struck me as alien, confusing, and removed from my life, and much of it failed to involve me. It is the story of a girl debauched by an older man, a lawyer; the lawyer's mistress, who is the girl's mother; some boys named Yura, Nika, and Misha; and a certain Nikolai Nikolaevich, who, deeply affected by the Sermon on the Mount, propagates the eternal vitality of the Gospel truths. Later Yura, a young man by then, starts writing poetry, and his poems will be integrated into the novel. They are highly Pasternakian—about Indian summer and the March thaw—and notable for their impressionism, but they do not in the least convey the characters' "psychic makeup."

After the reading Pasternak invited everyone to supper, but I was so worn out by the novel and found the "feast" so out of place—a show of bravado—that I left immediately. I think Zoshchenko's conduct much more fitting: people say he has accepted many of the accusations as valid and promised to write a work in the next two years that will make amends for everything he has written until now. < . . . >

I've just learned that Pasternak didn't know last night what had been said about him in *Pravda!* Zinaida Nikolaevna had hidden the paper from him. But somebody let it slip out during the supper (Marina told me), and he was shaken. I can't understand why Zinaida Nikolaevna didn't cancel the reading.

16 September.

We called on Vera Inber last night. She talked about Mayakovsky. Mayak-
ovsky happened to go to a cabaret just after Yesenin had taken up with
Isadora Duncan, and when the master of ceremonies—Garkavi I think it
was—said, "And there we have another famous poet. Let's wish him an
Isadora of his own," Mayakovsky replied, "An Isadora maybe, but no
Dizzydora." < . . . >
< . . . >

13 October.

We had some snow last night, and even though the sun has come out the
snow is sticking stubbornly to the trees and the bright green grass.

   This week I had an awful scare and several sleepless nights: I received
an invitation signed by Golovenchenko (head of Goslitizdat) to a meeting
of the editorial board with the following agenda:

> Resolution of the Central Committee of All-Union Communist Party
> on the journals *Zvezda* and *Leningrad* and the task of Goslitizdat.
>   Discussion of the selection for the anthologies of works by N. N.
> Aseev and I. L. Selvinsky and of the third volume of V. I. Kostylyov's
> novel *Ivan the Terrible*.
>   Discussion of the plan for the complete works of Nekrasov.

So my work on Nekrasov is going to be discussed as an illustration of
Comrade Zhdanov's speech about Zoshchenko, Akhmatova, et al. I was
terrified. I could just see them denigrating me, pillorying me and concluding that I was to be removed from the project; I could just hear the gloating
echo resounding from paper to paper: "What an excuse for an editor!
Ruining Nekrasov's verse." It was a perfectly possible reward for thirty-
five years of research and viable spadework for the upcoming Nekrasov
anniversary. My insomnia had never been worse. Not only was I unable to
sleep, I was unable to lie down. I paced the room for hours, wailing. I wrote
Fadeev a desperate letter, and showed up at Goslitizdat—half-dead, ill, and
aged by ten years—to run the gauntlet. The meeting took place in the
large downstairs hall. The first person I saw was Lyudmila Dubrovina, the
head of Detizdat, who last week had my work on Nekrasov returned to

me with no explanation, work she herself had commissioned. Fortunately everything turned out fine. It was just a hallucination brought on by fear. I am still the editor of Nekrasov's verse, and Dubrovina is out in the cold.

12 November.

We're moving to town today. I'll think of this room with fond memories and gratitude. I worked here daily from three to four in the morning till five in the afternoon. Of all the rooms I've ever lived in it is my favorite. The armchair, the round table, the slow and grueling but infinitely satisfying work—how they helped me to go on living. < . . . >

Fadeev is being amazingly good to me. After listening to excerpts from my future book, he wrote four letters—two to me, one to Simonov at *Novyi mir,* and one to Panfyorov at *Oktiabr'*—in praise of it; moreover, he praised it *in glowing terms* to the *Litgazeta* editorial board and claims to have written a long letter to the effect that the time has come to call a halt to the campaign against me.[242]

He is overtired and has insomnia, overworked and has piles of manuscripts to read—his duties at the Writers' Union alone take up hours and hours—yet he puffs out his chest and does everything with the greatest of energy, his every gesture precise, clear-cut, and to the point. < . . . >

13 November.

Zhenya ran into my room this morning shouting, "Look! Look!" He showed me the latest issue of *Murzilka,* the first without a Bibigon installment! They've cut it off at the most interesting point and just when Konashevich's drawings were improving! But most important they kept it going as long as evil had the upper hand, and now that the happy ending is in sight they hold it back, hide it, deprive the children of the moral satisfaction that comes from the triumph of good over evil.

242. Fadeev's letters to the editors of two major Soviet literary journals, *Novyi mir* and *Oktiabr',* were of considerable assistance to the harassed writer. In a letter to Konstantin Simonov he wrote: "Chukovsky has produced a very fine study of Nekrasov. It is written very simply, effectively and persuasively." It was most likely Fadeev's intervention that led to the publication of Chukovsky's article on the 125th anniversary of Nekrasov's birth in the December 1946 issue of *Novyi mir.*

18 November.

The leaders of the Writers' Union have very inert faces. Blank expressions. Tikhonov is the best example: he can listen to you for hours without registering anything. Sobolev is another example. And Fadeev and Simonov. It must come from having to run meetings. Though I've noticed that in our ominous times Russians' faces are less inclined to expressivity than before. My face, for example, is too demonstrative for today's public meetings: it keeps changing, and that alienates people from me, makes me look flighty. [. . .]

23 November.

< . . . > I've submitted the Nekrasov poem I discovered to *Ogonek:*

> When lo! a high official stumbles,
> Hurrah! the jubilant polis cheers.
> But when a well-known writer bumbles,
> It is the greatest fête in years . . .

Stupniker returned it to me, saying, "People might find parallels"! That of a poem written in 1867.

 Litgazeta will carry my "Belinsky on Nekrasov's *Unfortunates*" tomorrow. It's my first foray into print since "Bibigon"!

29 November.

Friday. The list of the Nekrasov Committee members was made public today. Fadeev didn't learn of it until last night. "The government has obviously decided not to celebrate his hundred-and-twenty-fifth anniversary, only his hundred-and-fiftieth," he told me. But this morning he rang to say, "An anniversary committee exists, and you are on it." < . . . >

 Yermilov, the new editor of *Novyi mir,* initiated his term of office today. < . . . > "Are you interested in your article?" he asked me. "Well, we're running it. A fine piece of work." In fact, it's rather weak, and the poems by Nekrasov I've uncovered are poor—first drafts clearly. I had a phone call from *Izvestiia* asking me for a short piece on Nekrasov. < . . . >

15 December.

Lida is having trouble with her eyes. It's a broken blood vessel. Simonov has nominated her as the *Novyi mir* poetry editor. < . . . >

20 December.

Went to the Zbarskys' in the evening. He's just back from Paris. [. . .] He talked about how the French love us, how Königsberg is destroyed and Berlin in ruins—and promised to get me into the oncological institute for an operation. All at once I was glad I had cancer and would soon be departing this world. I realized I was a miserable creature with nothing to live for, a loser from the word go, but completely innocent. I thought back on the hard life I'd lived and the love I'd had for children, books, poetry, and people, on the people—Tynyanov, Leonid Andreev, Koni—who'd loved me and the millions of children who felt close to me, and I saw a lonely, pitiful old man on a stage in an empty hall, slandered for reasons he could not fathom. < . . . >

1947

→>-→>-→>-→>-→>-→>-→>

1 January.

Went to bed at nine in the evening and slept until eleven forty-five. I was awakened by the neighbors' New Year's howling. Marya Borisovna and I had some tea, and I set to work proofreading Nekrasov's frightfully silly plays. This morning I'm expecting a visit from Yulian Oksman, who has just returned from exile. [. . .]

17 March.

Litgazeta recently published an account of a meeting of children's writers that I attended. The article listed the participants as Marshak, Mikhalkov,

Barto, Kassil, *and others*. I was the "and others." The amazing thing is, it didn't bother me a bit. They used to write "Chukovsky, Marshak, and others," then "Marshak, Chukovsky, and others," and now "Marshak, Mikhalkov, Barto, Kassil, and others," the latter meaning me. And while I couldn't care less about what they write, I *am* bothered, terribly so, by the fact that I feel I have lost all my talent, that the gift for verse that enabled me to write the comic "Chatterbox Fly" and "Wash 'Em Clean" and the like has completely dried up, so I have in fact become "and others."
< . . . >

10 June.

< . . . > Saw Pasternak. He's in top form—chest out, head back. He read me his Petőfi translations. They're very good—at times. At other times they're careless, slapdash, any old how. < . . . >

16 July.

There was a fire at the Fedins' yesterday. Their house burned to the ground like a box of matches. He remained dignified and calm; he didn't lose his head. Dora Sergeevna was in tears, distraught. Lida, Katya, and I rushed over with buckets of water: there isn't a drop of water in the vicinity. [. . .]

1948

➤-➤-➤-➤-➤-➤-➤-➤

1 January.

Night. I've spent the whole night—from one till five—reading *Hard Times* by Sleptsov. It's a fine, charming work, the only work of the sixties that has charm. The characters are not two-dimensional, as was the case in fiction at the time, and even though the overall plot is trite it has not a single trite line. Sleptsov is a genuine precursor of Chekhov.

Because Detizdat has ruined me and I need to supplement my income, I've been appearing at children's holiday celebrations on a daily basis. But

I'm sixty-six years old, and I have a right to take it easy. How sick I am of this woeful, doleful life. [. . .]

1949

-»->-»->-»->-»->-»->-»-»

1 January.

I am working on an article about Anglo-American literature. < . . . >
Sitting here at my desk, I've been thinking that the combination 1882 and 1949 is quite an enviable one and no occasion to grumble and that it is in the nature of things for the latter date to be the last.

1948 is not a year to look back upon. It was a year of mechanical, mind-deadening scribbling of one (dull) note after the other for the three-volume Ogiz edition of Nekrasov, the two-volume Detgiz edition, the two-volume Biblioteka poeta edition, the one-volume Moskovskii rabochii edition, the one-volume Ogiz edition, for the Avdotya Panaeva book, for the Sleptsov, and so on and so forth. Not a single line of my own did I write, not a single original word, as if I weren't Chukovsky. < . . . >

9 May.

Moved back to Peredelkino. A magnificent hot day. I'm wearing a new gray suit with no overcoat. Today Viktor Petrovich Dorofeev, a Goslitizdat editor with—as he himself likes to put it—an "unbending character," tore my poor little "Pushkin and Nekrasov" to pieces. [. . .]

10 May.

From three to eight—five full hours—Dorofeev and I wrangled and cursed over every line, and I retreated and retreated and retreated. We were at Goslitizdat. I had L.F. come with a typewriter, and she typed up all the changes on the spot. Also involved in the arguments was a baby-faced young man by the name of Cheryomin, who was bright and knowledge-able—in his field. Two against one. I. V. Sergievsky sat wordless at his desk, smiling a wry smile. He was exhausted: he'd spent the entire day hunched over a manuscript, leaving one line on one page, two on another, and drawing line after line through all the rest. There were also three women in the room: Vyacheslav Polonsky's sister Klavdia Pavlovna, a redhead by the name of Felitsiata Alexandrovna, and a mute unknown quantity. The latter two spend every minute from dawn till dusk cutting other people's manuscripts down to size—their size—so that nothing of the author's individuality remains, no personal opinions, emotions, etc. Everything that leaves their workshop is absolutely uniform in thought, style, and ideological orientation.

11 May.

It's cold out. Cloudy. I'm afraid Marya Borisovna has caught a cold.

18 May.

Four a.m. A splendid morning. The birds are chirping away. The two cherry trees in front of the balcony are in full bloom. The greenery is of a brilliance I've never seen before. "The east, seditious, holds its tongue," but "the worldwide church bells, the sun's rays"[243] are beginning to make themselves felt. Yet deep down I'm sad and depressed. My "Pushkin and Nekrasov" article is in pages. I've just spent two days at the printer's, shielding it from further disfigurement, though it's so disfigured as it is that I find it painful to hold it in my hands.

For several days now I've been devouring *Tom Jones*. I have an 1824 edition of Fielding's complete works, but had never read that novel. [. . .] And now I happen to pick up one volume and I'm wild with joy. Why in the world should I care whether the good-for-nothing rake of a Jones will have his way with the ever so chaste Sophia, but for three days the author made me want nothing more than for it to happen. Every obstacle on his path to bliss was so upsetting that I took it as a personal blow and even had to lay aside the book at times, and the whole sugarcoated ending, when all the positive heroes get what they desire and all the negative ones what they deserve, gave me the greatest of pleasure. Perhaps old and

---

243. Both lines are from an untitled poem by Tyutchev written in 1865. (M.H.H.)

unhappy people like me, demoralized and debilitated by life, are so en-
amored of happy endings in novels because the endings of their own
biographies are so cruel, pitiful, and tragic. < . . . >

16 June.

< . . . > The Nekrasov book is going nowhere. I'd like to write something
for children, but I'm stymied by the memory of "Bibigon." [. . .]

29 June.

An awful fog. It's been pouring cats and dogs for three days running.
< . . . >

Lyusha has received a gold medal: she got top marks in all her exams.
But my joy is tempered by sadness: her generation has no use whatever for
the likes of me, no interest in what I have devoted my life to, no knowledge
of who I am, my passions, my aspirations. I don't deny that her generation
is sound and has great strengths of its own, but so *alien* is she to me that
we have nothing to talk about.

> And our grandchildren one fine day
> Will push us out and have their way.[244]

And right they are, though what their grandchildren will be like not even
the greatest wise man can imagine.

1950

-➤--➤--➤--➤--➤--➤--➤--➤-

28 February.

I'm sweating over Aesopian language. Yesterday I handed in the final
version of the annotated one-volume Nekrasov. < . . . >

---

244. A line from Pushkin's *Eugene Onegin* (canto 2, stanza 38). (V.E.)

11 March.

This morning I finally finished the "Nekrasov and Folklore" chapter I've been struggling with for ages. The trouble is, I set forth so many of my thoughts on the subject in highly condensed form in the commentary to *Who Lives Well in Russia* that they have now become generally accepted and the folklore chapter is considerably less innovative that it would otherwise have been. < . . . >

1 April.

Turned sixty-eight today. I feel like a man being dragged in ropes to the gallows. I dressed with particular care and spent a long time washing, a long time brushing my hair. The condemned man's last ablutions. Sixty-eight! I remember the day Repin turned sixty-eight. I thought of him as a prisoner condemned to death. < . . . >

10 April.

< . . . > I've turned beggar in my old age: I haven't got a kopeck. The car and Peredelkino eat up all my money. Tomorrow I'll have to start earning my keep. Back to the grindstone at sixty-eight. Although as the folk song has it:

> A soldier's lot is plenty hard,
> Although at times not all that bad!

12 April.

Then again there's the variant that goes:

> A soldier's lot's not all that bad,
> Although at times it's plenty hard.

My main problem is the Nekrasov book. I make no headway no matter how hard I try. Everything sounds off-putting, trivial, banal, inept. It all boils down to my lack of a philosophical background—and my age. I work, I slave, and nothing comes of it.
< . . . >

10 June.

< . . . > Kolya and I went to see Kaverin. Vinogradov's Marr article held the stage. And the following lines on the discussion surrounding Soviet linguistics initiated in _Pravda_ by Professor Chikobava's speech:[245]

> Once Marr was wise, once Marr was great.
> Up there with Marx he seemed to rate.
> But then along came Chikobava,
> And that the end of great, wise Marr was.

which are from a long student song. Vinogradov's article is brilliant. < . . . >

1951

→>-→>-→>-→>-→>-→>-

7 January.

Got up at one a.m. Went straight to my desk. [. . .]

From one until eleven—that is, ten hours straight—I worked on the proofs, then went to the Lenin Library, where I checked all the references

---

245. The previous month _Pravda_ had declared, "In view of the unsatisfactory state of Soviet linguistics, the editors deem it necessary to organize a free discussion on the pages of this newspaper so as to overcome, through criticism and self-criticism, the current stagnation in the development of Soviet linguistics." The discussion opened with a long article by Professor A. S. Chikobava of Stalin University, Tiflis, "Some Problems of Soviet Linguistics." Chikobava took issue with the fundamental propositions of the general linguistic theory of Academician Nikolai Marr, an eminent but increasingly erratic authority on Caucasian languages. Marr had created havoc in Soviet linguistics by foisting a bizarre theory of the origin of language on it and making an ill-starred attempt at applying Marxist class-based analysis to grammatical categories. In the wake of Chikobava's article, _Pravda_ took to allotting extensive space to articles on linguistics. Among them was the article by V. V. Vinogradov—"Let Us Develop Soviet Linguistics on the Basis of Marxist-Leninist Theory"—that so impressed Chukovsky. The editors' interest in linguistics became especially keen after Stalin entered the fray with his "On Marxism and Linguistics." Not unpredictably, Stalin's occasionally platitudinous repudiation of "Marrism" (published in the English edition of Stalin's writings as "Marxism and Problems of Language," _Works_, vol. 3, 199) was hailed as a major intellectual breakthrough and such propositions as "language consists of words" were frequently quoted.

to the 1931 Nekrasov edition, then on to Detizdat (for my riddles) and Goslitizdat to talk over the proofs of the third volume with Mina Yakovlevna. I come home. Marya Borisovna is nowhere to be found. She's lying down, someone says. Yes, there she is, lying on the couch, all curled up. She seems asleep. I go up to her. Say a few words. No response. She's angry, I think. I try again. Same thing. The fingers of her left hand move one by one. She is in an uncomfortable position. I stick a pencil in her left hand. It falls out. Her expression is calm, her face frozen. I rush out to fetch the doctor. Sergei Nikolaevich. He comes carrying two instrument cases. He finds cerebral hemorrhaging and paralysis of the right side. [. . .]

16 May.

About three days ago the pounding rains so swelled the lake that the dam burst. I went out to survey the damage today. The whole region is unrecognizable. What was lake is now dry land, but gradated instead of smooth and with a waterfall beating down from the highest gradation. The boats that were in the water are now perched on that peak. One of the age-old trees—they date from the days of Yury Samarin, whose estate this was—was uprooted, swept thirty meters, and is now lying on the ground. Another tree landed in the river with its roots in the air. But more interesting than the particulars is the general colorful, even picturesque chaos in the midst of which a gaping abyss has replaced the devastated dam. It all happened only three days ago, yet already a set and stable routine has established itself such that we seem to have been living in the chaos for decades: a ladder has been lowered into the clayey precipice, and people have grown accustomed to climbing down it to the shaky boards laid yesterday over the river; girls gather flowers along the landslide; boys splash in the waterfall; the wheels of a lorry spin in the mud above the precipice. < . . . >

18 May.

Went to the Choboty school at twelve to give a reading. All the grownups seemed nonentities: a Pioneer leader with professional enthusiasm painted all over her, a female Peredonov with cheerless, cold, condemning eyes,

and so on and so forth.[246] But the children . . . Can these grownups ever have been children? < . . . >
< . . . >

30 June.

Leonov has just come up with:

> And they mowed him down like tractors
> Did Chukovsky's malefactors. [. . .]

31 August.

Mist in the morning, tropical heat by afternoon. Butterflies have stopped flying in at night, and only a week ago they were legion. I work on my strawberries daily, cutting back the older plants, tying the shoots. < . . . > Pasternak came to see me yesterday looking happy, youthful, magnetic, and very healthy. He talked about how Gorky had published his translation of a Kleist play (in *Sovremennik,* I believe) and made some emendations in the verse while it was in proofs. He didn't know it was Gorky who had made the emendations and wrote a nasty letter to Gorky: "It's downright barbaric! What vandal has ruined my work?" Gorky was favorably inclined toward Pasternak and they carried on a correspondence—Pasternak wrote him an enthusiastic letter about *Klim Samgin*—but Gorky knew that Pasternak also admired Andrei Bely; moreover, Gorky disliked Sobakin and Zoya Tsvetaeva, whom he considered Pasternak's friend, and he broke off their correspondence after a very confused, convoluted letter from Boris Leonidovich.[247]

Pasternak also talked about Gogol—with great enthusiasm—and Lermontov. To say that Lermontov is a great poet is tantamount to saying that he had arms and legs. They weren't prostheses now, were they? Ha, ha, ha. He put Chekhov on the level of Pushkin for his vitality, moderation, and unmediated relation to reality. He considered Gorky a titan, an oceanic personality.

246. Peredonov, a paranoid provincial schoolmaster, is the protagonist of Fyodor Sologub's novel *The Petty Demon* (1905). (M.H.H.)

247. Now that the correspondence between Pasternak and Gorky has been published, we know that Pasternak actually spoke of Zubakin and Anastasia Tsvetaeva (Marina Tsvetaeva's sister), who visited Gorky in Sorrento in the summer of 1927.

1952

21 March.

Seven degrees below freezing. Went out for half an hour and came back: my heart was acting up again. I'm sweating over volume twelve. < . . . > There are notes I've written five or six times. The only thing that makes me happy is that Marya Borisovna seems to be in a more stable, positive mood. I'm reading an American book about shamans: the extraneous subject matter helps to take my mind off things. I find the newspaper reports about bacteriological warfare terribly disturbing: so this is what has become of a culture that began with Schiller and culminated in Chekhov. < . . . >

1 April.

Twelve a.m. on the dot. I am seventy. I am calm as a grave. I have a trying, highly frustrating, unsuccessful life behind me, fifty years of drudgery, thousands of fumbles, bungles, and failures. I've not inspired much love: not a single friend, no intimates. Lida tries to love me and even believes she does, but she doesn't. Kolya with his poetic nature is full of compassion for me, but I bore him after two minutes of talk, and I can see why. As for Lyusha . . . Well, when has a twenty-year-old girl ever really loved her grandfather? Only in Dickens, only in melodramas. A grandfather is a strange kind of being that doesn't understand you and is only around when you're young, so there's no point in setting up a long-term relationship with him. Have I ever had friends? I once had Tatyana Bogdanovich, Yury Tynyanov, and two or three more, but now there is no one whose greeting I look forward to and find indispensable. It's like living on another planet. I can't get over the fact that I'm still alive. Marya Borisovna is the only person I feel close to. I'm glad to be spending today with her. She's been ill lately; she'll be better tomorrow, I hope. < . . . >

What happened this afternoon has turned everything around and invalidated the earlier part of this entry. Lyusha and Gulya turned up with a chestload of *papeterie*, a gigantic box of sweets, and a magnificent picture entitled "A Review of the Chukovsky Family." Then Viktor Vinogradov came, bearing a letter from Irakly,[248] and there was a stack of telegrams < . . . > And just when I thought it was over, in came Kassil with letters from the Sobinovs, an oration from the Writers' Union, and a huge box of sweets, and Simonov phoned with the most cordial of greetings. It's a third-class funeral, of course. I understand. But in all honesty I deserve no better.

Rereading my Whitman translations, I am moved by much of what moved me in my youth, when I first read *Leaves of Grass.* < . . . >

1953

➤>-➤>-➤>-➤>-➤>-➤>

[. . .]

13 April.

Amazing things have been happening! The amnesty decree and the review of the doctors' plot have filled my days with joy.[249]

Dora Sergeevna Fedina is dead. I had known her since 1919. Fedin looks emaciated, disconsolate. < . . . > He claims that Dora Sergeevna knew long ago she had cancer, but hid it from him and pretended to believe the things he made up to console her. Why? Because she loved him, he says, because she didn't want to pain him, even though she knew they knew. I think it was something else. If people are ashamed of being old (and I know they are from my own experience), how much more ashamed must they be of dying. She knew she was dying and hid it, just as proud people hide their poverty or defeats. < . . . >

26 April.

< . . . > I'm sorry I didn't jot down my conversation with Pasternak in the charming room where he is proofreading his *Faust* translation. What

248. Irakly is the often-mentioned actor-impersonator Irakly Andronikov.

249. Shortly after Stalin's death—an event which, curiously enough, is not reflected in the *Diary*—the group of Jewish doctors accused by Stalin's henchmen of plotting to poison the Party leaders was declared innocent. (V.E.)

makes the room so charming is its uncommon simplicity, its noble artlessness—pine shelves with books in three or four languages (and only those
books he needs for his work), plain pine tables, and a bed. How much more
elegant, artistic, aesthetically pleasing it is than, say, the oriental furnish-
ings—the Buddhas, elephants, Chinese boxes, etc.—in Vsevolod Ivanov's
office.

Bondi's wife called at the house yesterday, bubbling over with news
about "the new order." The Kremlin will be open to one and all; Stalin
Prizes will be abolished; there will be no more state bonds; kolkhoz conditions will be improved; the Writers' Union will be disbanded; Fadeev
has been removed from office; the militia will be slashed to nearly a fifth
of its present size, and so on and so forth. Everything the philistines want
is being touted as governmental policy. < . . . >

1 May.

[. . .] Strolling through Peredelkino, we came upon Kataev, who was here
for the May Day celebrations. He talked about his play, *Soviet Power:* it
has had a hundred rehearsals and < . . . > could open tomorrow were not
all the actors involved in Vsevolod's *Lomonosov,* which has a hundred and
two characters. Besides, there's some anti-American play that has to be put
on lickety-split. Kataev has nothing but respect for Ponomarenko, the
minister of culture. "We went to Belorussia in the same car not long ago,
and he said to me, 'Pushkin's *Kirdzhali* is a wonderful piece.' I didn't
remember it, so I looked it up and it *is* wonderful. Ponomarenko saved
Yanka Kupala, Yakub Kolas, and others from arrest in 1937. He's a very
refined and intelligent man." Yet for all that Kataev doesn't believe that
literature can recover. "Too many nonentities have latched on to it, and no
reforms will make them let go." < . . . >

2 May.

< . . . > Met General Vasily Stepanovich Popov, who told the story of a
tribute to Comrade Budyonny. "< . . . > Over supper someone pointed
out that the Red Cavalry had yet to receive its due in literature. And not
only that: it had been slandered by Babel. To which Budyonny replied, 'I
went to Gorky, but he didn't help. He stood up for Babel. I went to Lenin,

but he said, "Gorky is in charge of literature. We leave these matters up to him. There's no point in arguing with him." ' " < . . . >

6 June.

Had a long letter from Zhitkov's sister praising my memoirs of him. I was afraid she wouldn't like them. The sisters of great men are very persnickety. In my Mayakovsky memoirs I wrote that there was a period in his life when he did not always have a decent meal to sit down to. His sister Lyudmila was offended by these lines. "We were living in Moscow at the time, Mama and I. He could always have come and eaten with us." Could have, but didn't. He had quarreled with them and was too busy, but he would call at Filippov's and eat five or six *pirozhki* instead of a meal. But Lyudmila refused to hear of it: he did not go to Filippov's and did not eat *pirozhki*. < . . . >

Zoshchenko is very depressed: the Writers' Union advised him to write a petition to the authorities asking for reinstatement in the organization, but he has received no answer. And Leningrad is gloating: they know what he's asked for and the result, which has only worsened his situation. [. . .]

Saw Pasternak. He is absorbed in the second part of *Faust*.

27 June.

< . . . > Had a visit from Leonov. We talked about the currency reform, the Minister of Culture Ponomarenko (everyone in literary circles is talking about Ponomarenko these days), and the *Ogonek* affair. For the first time in its existence the magazine had to cut a number of pages and replace them with others. What happened was that Alexandrov wrote an article about some new films, praising one that Ponomarenko had praised. But it turned out that, Ponomarenko's praise notwithstanding, the film had been banned, and so the article had to be removed. < . . . >

You can't get into any savings bank. The currency reform has set off a panic. I wanted to pick up my pension, but it was out of the question· there were queues of four or five thousand people. People are buying up everything: rugs, horse collars, pots. "We can't sell three pianos to one person, for heaven's sake!" a salesman shouts. All silver has disappeared. (It's tantamount to hard currency!) Nobody gives change—not in the metro or on trams or in shops. It's mass hysteria here in Moscow. The end of the world. You can't get near the Hotel National: people have laid siege to the tables so as to have one last feast from their doomed savings. Leonov, a master raconteur, has come up with the following situation:

"What's that stomping noise? Your upstairs neighbors are jumping and dancing and pounding from morning till night. The plaster is falling, the whole flat is shaking. Are they having a wedding up there or something?"

"No, they've bought a horse and have nowhere to keep it." [. . .]

The shops are completely empty. Somebody saw a man buying six chamber pots. People are buying bicycle parts—a wheel here, a handlebar there. There is no other topic of conversation.

Fedin was at Leonov's, looking aged and unkempt. "What is going on?" he asked. "Why are factories suddenly organizing rallies against the Berlin uprising? Two weeks late. And the currency panic. What kind of faith does the people have in its government if it's so scared of being gypped by it?"

That gave rise to an extraordinarily artistic (because of the imagery) and passionate argument over Russia's destiny. Fedin initiated it with a picturesque description of a trip to the depths of Saratov he had taken as a seven-year-old with his father: every peasant they met bowed at the waist to him. Leonov said that the men of the sixties *overstated* the peasants' sufferings, that the peasants didn't have it that bad under serfdom, that Saltychikha was an exception, etc.[250]

Leonov is in every way an organic Russian. When he has stomach troubles, he goes not only to his Kremlin doctor, Neznamov-Ivanov, but also to a village witchdoctor. His wife, Tatyana Mikhailovna, says they hadn't been able to care for their daughter Lena properly because "when the doctors' plot was revealed we lost our faith in pharmacies, particularly the Kremlin pharmacy. What if all the drugs were poisoned!" In other words, even in literary circles there were people who believed in the doctors' plot! < . . . >

10 July.

Gudzy came today with the July issue of *Znamia*, which has a review of *Nekrasov's Craft*. We went to Selvinsky's and with Selvinsky to Irakly's,

---

250. The term "men of the sixties" refers to political activists of the 1860s who tried to better the lot of the common man. Daria Ivanovna Saltychikha (1730–1801) was a landowner infamous for the mistreatment of her serfs. (V.E.)

where people were talking about Beria, guessing about Beria, heaping curses on Beria, voicing their horror of Beria, and in the end I was as bored as a child in church.[251] Fortunately, Irakly (cautious as always) skirted the topic entirely, doing a marvelous imitation of Fadeev: he closed his eyelids the way Fadeev does, and even seemed to turn as gray as Fadeev. He catches the rhythm that typifies each person's speech and creates each person's atmosphere. All his effects depend on nuance and tonality, and when he's on stage they disappear and his talent does not come across well. < . . . >

12 July.

< . . . > I remember Beria's son Sergo: handsome, porcelainlike, well-groomed, taciturn, arrogant, calm. I saw him on 29 March at the banquet in memory of Gorky given by Nadezhda Alexeevna [Gorky's daughter-in-law]. Tamara Vladimirovna (Vsevolod's wife) raised her glass to "Gorky's grandchildren," that is, to Sergo Beria [husband of Gorky's older grand-daughter, Marfa] and Darya's [Gorky's younger granddaughter] husband. I wonder what's become of his arrogance, looks, and calm and where he is now. People say Marfa is pregnant; they say Yekaterina Pavlovna [Gorky's wife] has been trying hard to reach her by phone. There seems to be a curse upon the house of Gorky. From Yagoda to Beria. Why are they attracted to the GPU with its corrupt mentality, to careerists, degenerates, and crooks? What makes such nice—simple—women like Yekaterina Pavlovna and Nadezhda Alexeevna gravitate toward this bloody business?

18–26 July.

Have been down with the grippe and stomach troubles. I've lost a lot of weight and grown terribly old. < . . . >

Kaverin called at the house and told me Zoshchenko had been accepted back into the Writers' Union and an editor of *Krokodil* had asked him for some stories and said he would buy anything Zoshchenko had, finished or not. It's a great fortune that Zoshchenko is still alive; he could easily have had a fatal stroke or even starved to death, since there was a time when the

---

251. The rumors about Beria, the dreaded NKVD chief, were triggered by a dramatic development: when his attempt to seize power fizzled, he was arrested and shot. (V.E.)

most honest and talented of Soviet writers had to live on two hundred rubles a month! At least that won't happen anymore! $<$ . . . $>$
$<$ . . . $>$

18 September.

$<$ . . . $>$ I'm ill, I have a cold. I'm not seeing anybody, though Nilin called at the house and went on and on about Malenkov with great enthusiasm.[252] "Appearing at the Central Committee, Malenkov was greeted by the usual applause and said, 'This isn't the Bolshoi Theater, and I'm not Kozlov-sky.' "

Spent the whole day indoors working—to no avail, it seems—on an article about textology.

20 September.

A beautiful hot day. $<$ . . . $>$ Called on Kataev. He's reading Gorky. "What a playwright the man is! *Yegor Bulychev* is brilliant![253] By the way, Kornei Ivanovich, would you happen to have Marx, volume one? I need it for my seminar." He's teaching at the University of Marxism-Leninism and preparing his lessons.

13 October.

A beautiful sunny day. $<$ . . . $>$ A Bashkir student came up to me, hatless, and we fell into conversation. He had strong white teeth and a nice smile. Spiritual purity, a noble character, an inquisitive mind. He knows Pushkin well and is translating Lermontov into Bashkir. Simple, calm, thoughtful—he made me feel at peace. He's at the Literary Institute and taking Bondi's course. For some reason I consider our meeting an event.

---

252. In his speech to the Nineteenth Congress of the Russian Communist Party the Secretary of the Central Committee G. E. Malenkov stated: "Our artists and writers . . . should constantly keep in mind that the typical [which Soviet writers were duty-bound to portray] is not what occurs most frequently but what expresses most fully and vividly the essence of the given social phenomenon. The Marxist-Leninist concept of the typical is not a statistical mean. . . . The typical is the essential expression of Party spirit in Realistic art. The problem of the typical is always a political problem" (*Pravda,* 6 October 1952). For some time this formula was a necessary ingredient in every attempt at literary theorizing.

253. *Yegor Bulychev and Others* (1932) is one of Gorky's more effective plays. (V.E.)

Have finished proofreading Whitman, written a short poem for the Fielding play, and completed that awful article on textology and Nekrasov. Even I find my **versatility** rather formidable. And now I have my memoirs of Zhitkov and yet other genres to attend to. < . . . >

20 October.

Called on Fedin. He says that spring has come again for literature. First, Ehrenburg has published an article in *Znamia* in which he goes so far as to praise André Gide (well, not Gide but Knut Hamsun and, of course, Picasso and Matisse).[254] Second, they're going to print a small volume of Akhmatova (it was Surkov's doing and will contain some old and some new work). Third, Borya Pasternak shouted to me over the fence (Varya, Fedin's granddaughter, has scarlet fever, and Tamara Vladimirovna [Ivanova] is afraid Anton will catch it and has warned everybody), "A new age is beginning: they want to publish *me!*" Oh, if only they would publish my "Crocodile" and "Bibigon"! When I reread "We Shall Defeat Barmalei," I couldn't stand it.
[. . .]

25 October.

Called on Fedin. < . . . > He is ecstatic over Pasternak's poem "August," which is in fact magnificent. "It may be about death and a funeral, but it's full of life, a hymn to life." < . . . >

5 December.

Called on Ponomarenko with Fedin. He spent more than an hour explaining his program, playing the naive liberal. "Igor Moiseev asked me to 'inspect' his new production, and I said to him, 'You have mortally offended me.' 'How?' he asked. 'I am no inspector. You are an artist, a master. The only criticism your work is subject to is the free criticism of your audience. No

254. Fedin is speaking of Ilya Ehrenburg's article "About the Writer's Job" (*Znamia*, 1953, no. 10). Among the "writers of bourgeois society who created excellent works" Ehrenburg mentions Knut Hamsun. There is also a reference to Matisse. André Gide's name was not likely to appear on Ehrenburg's list: though a longtime friend of the Soviet Union, Gide was branded a renegade after publishing a highly critical travelogue, *Back from the USSR* (1936).

inspectors needed.' " < . . . > We thanked him for receiving us, and he said, "Oh, don't mention it. It's my job" and so on.

21 December.

It's ten degrees below freezing in Peredelkino. Mild weather, too mild perhaps.

Because Goslit treacherously refused to issue a second edition of *Nekrasov's Craft*, I've been left to my own devices this year and taken on a lot of smaller jobs: (1) revising *Robinson Crusoe* yet again, (2) translating Fielding's *Judge*, (3) revising *Doctor Ouch-It-Hurts*, (4) retranslating a few Whitman poems from scratch and revising the old translations (during which I discovered that Kashkin is a scoundrel and Mendelson an imbecile), (5) revising "Bibigon," (6) writing my memoirs of Zhitkov and Tynyanov, (7) writing an article about the principles of textology on which I based my Nekrasov editions, (8) editing the three-volume Nekrasov for Gosizdat, (9) editing the three-volume Nekrasov for *Ogonek*, (10) writing a fifty-page introduction for the Ogonek edition, (11) editing Nekrasov for Detgiz, (12) writing short articles for *Litgazeta* and *Ogonek*. A lot of "stuff and nonsense," as Zoshchenko used to say. I call it suicide. Starting 1 January, if I'm still alive, I'm going to take on two big projects: the revision of *From Two to Five* on the basis of Pavlovian principles and a radical revision of my *Memoirs of Repin*. Especially as I've got a wonderful secretary, diligent and intelligent, in Klara Izrailevna Lozovskaya.

The day before yesterday we celebrated the tenth anniversary of Tynyanov's death. There were three large boards covered with photographs and his works. The hall was packed, though the Writers' Union staged a bit of indirect sabotage: neither Simonov nor Leonov nor Fedin nor Fadeev was present. The master of ceremonies was the ineffectual (from the point of view of the authorities) Vsevolod Ivanov. Ehrenburg did not put in an appearance, but did send an article or, rather, a three-page letter in praise of Yury Nikolaevich. The celebration was basically masterminded by Yury Nikolaevich's sister—Kaverin's wife—and Kaverin himself. If Tynyanov hadn't had relatives in the Writers' Union, the whole thing would have been even more modest. I spent four days writing my brief talk and can now see I didn't say a tenth of what I could have said: about his pride— he never cast his pearls before swine—his high moral character, his loyalty to his friends, and so on.

I'm sorry that having to hurry back to Peredelkino I didn't get to hear either Shklovsky or Andronikov, who were after me on the program.

The *Litgazeta* editorial board was so pleased with Lida's "A Rotten Tooth" (about lispers in children's literature) that they put it on the front page, an unheard-of honor for an article dealing with children's literature. < . . . >

22 December.

< . . . > Dreamt about Chekhov all night. I had a conversation with him and he made corrections (I even remember his handwriting) in the Goslit edition of his works. When I woke up, I even remembered what the corrections were, but now, an hour later, I've forgotten them.

1954

➤-➤-➤-➤-➤-➤-➤-➤

5 January.

Marya Borisovna gave me an astounding piece of news yesterday, something truly worth celebrating: *Zbarsky has been released!* His wife too. I was so happy my hands started shaking. Not a day passed but that I thought grief-stricken about that fine family—Lyova, Vitya—I was powerless to help. I was tormented by a feeling of guilt: all through the months when they suffered the most I lay ill, barely alive, and later I was no longer needed. Even so, I would think of all the things both Boris Ilyich and Yevgenia Borisovna had done for me and agonize over not being able to do anything for them. < . . . >

Went to *Novyi mir*. Dementyev told me he was thrilled with Lida's article about children's literature and had asked her to do something along the same lines for *Novyi mir*.

11 January.

Twenty-two degrees below freezing. Spent the whole day in town "correcting," that is, ruining my article "From Dilettantism to Science." Dementyev proposed a number of changes, which I accepted at first without giving them much thought, but at night I decided to restore the *status quo ante* in many places. As a result, I proofread it twice, first when it was "à la Dementyev," then when it was "back to Chukovsky."

< . . . >

29 January.

Great joy! I called on the Zbarskys and saw Yevgenia Borisovna and Boris Ilyich. Yevgenia Borisovna is transformed by her suffering—radiant. Boris Ilyich is so emaciated he looks as if he'd come through a mortal illness. There are some *pirozhki* and a pie ("Your favorite," Yevgenia Borisovna says, "with cream") on the round table in Lyova's tiny room. Yevgenia Borisovna had served out her camp sentence in Moldavia, while Boris Ilyich, whose case was still at the inquest stage, was in solitary confinement at the Lubyanka.[255] He didn't even know that Stalin had died; he didn't know about Beria's treachery. When they came to shave him and asked for the receipts he had been given upon being committed, he thought, "This is it." But when they took him to Rudenko, the head investigating magistrate, and Rudenko said, "Have a seat, *Comrade* Zbarsky!" his eyes filled with tears: the moment he heard the word "comrade," he knew a miracle had occurred. They gave him back all his medals, all his titles (and now his chemistry textbook has been nominated again for a Stalin Prize). He had had about two hundred thousand in bonds, and the clerk noted the number of each as she returned it to him: 0.03759, series 612, etc. They were in small denominations, and it took an hour. He was so yearning to be free that he said to the clerk, "I wish to donate them to the State."

"No," she said. "Wait. 0.0971216, series 314 . . ."

Riding home, liberated and exculpated, longing to see his wife and children—it is moments like those that make life worth living. < . . . >

6 February.

Met Kataev yesterday evening at the post office. < . . . > He told me I'd been put up for the prize *unanimously;* there were no objections. < . . . > He also said, "I was the one who brought Mayakovsky to children's liter-

---

255. The much feared Lubyanka was the NKVD prison in Moscow. (M.H.H.)

ature. I'd sold some children's poems to Lev Klyachko, and when Mayakovsky found out about it he asked me to introduce him to Klyachko. So
we went to Raduga, and Mayakovsky became a children's writer." [. . .]

20 February.

Fadeev came to see me yesterday morning and stayed, talking continuously
for nine hours. "I've just finished reading your book, and the reason why
I've come is to tell you how fine it is. After all, I'm a Russian writer, am I
not?"

We embraced, and he asked me all about Kuprin and Gorky and 1905,
after which he spoke frankly about himself. "It was vile of me to attack
Grossman's splendid, magnificent novel.[256] I've had many a sleepless night
on account of it. It was all Pospelov's doing: he forced me to make the
speech. And why did I come down on the kind and venerable Gudzy as
well?"

He spent a long time bemoaning the ignorance of young, contemporary
writers. [. . .]

The visit ended with our reading some Isakovsky and Tvardovsky's
Distance Beyond Distance.[257] We enjoyed the poetry immensely. < . . . >

22 February.

Called on Fedin yesterday with Kolya. Again he talked about the "hide-
bound" elements who have gained the upper hand in the Writers' Union
and are calling the "Ponomarenko period" an ideological NEP. He went
into the ordeals Tvardovsky and Sholokhov have been through. When
Tvardovsky presented the next part of *Distance Beyond Distance* to the
authorities (for the third issue of *Novyi mir*), he was told that two passages
would be excised. The entire second part of Sholokhov's *Virgin Soil Upturned*, the whole story, is in trouble. < . . . >

8 March.

At Vsevolod Ivanov's. (We had *bliny.*) I met Akhmatova there for the first
time since her catastrophe:[258] a self-possessed, gray-haired woman, very

256. See note 233.
257. An epic poem dealing with the injustices of the Stalinist period. (M.H.H.)
258. See note 239.

stout, very simple, nothing at all like the highly stylized, timid yet at the same time haughty woman with banged hair, the slender poetess Gumilyov brought to see me in 1912, forty-two years ago. Of the catastrophe she speaks calmly and with humor: "I was very famous and became even more infamous, and I saw that the two conditions are essentially one."

"The other day I told Yevgeny Shvarts that I hadn't been to the theater in ages, to which he replied, 'Yes, Zoshchenko is the only theatergoing member of your organization.' " (Theirs is a two-member organization.) "Zoshchenko was recently offered a trip abroad. When I asked him to what country, he said, 'I was so scared I didn't ask.' "

She asked about Lida and Lyusha. I experienced the same excitement from her presence as I had in my youth. One can't help feeling her grandeur, her nobility, the immensity of her gift and her fate. Yet our conversation was perfectly banal. "Can you have forgotten that I brought my friend Zhitkov to see you?" (He had turned up one day with a pile of his poems—it was before his career as a writer had begun—and asked me to introduce him to her.)

"You probably did. I'm sure you did. But I was so famous at the time that people brought me poems by the hundreds. Yes, I've forgotten."

We had a visit from Fedin. He'd been in town, rushing through a mountain of Estonian books to prepare for a festival of Estonian literature: he came round for a minute or two—and stayed. Akhmatova had brought along her translations from the Chinese and read a narrative poem written two thousand years ago. She had translated it into crystal-clear Pushkinian verse, noble in its simplicity. How fortunate the Chinese are to have her as a translator: we have had not a single decent translation from the Chinese to date. "My Leningrad editor" (I forget his name) "is an important Sinologist. He spent two years as a lama in Tibet, and nobody knew he was a Soviet spy." Fedin brought up a Sinologist by the name of Fedorenko who was supposed to be Stalin's interpreter with Mao Tse-tung, but Mao was forced to write out what he had to say in characters because while the writing system is standard the pronunciation varies from tribe to tribe. < . . . >

19 March.

Leonov came to see me. Rosy-cheeked, hale and hearty. He stayed for three or four hours, going on about the days when he was out of favor. Once his wife went to intercede on his behalf with Fadeev and Fadeev wouldn't receive her and would talk to her only through a second-floor window with Yermilov's ruddy physiognomy peering out from the side. Leonov has woven the incident into his latest novel.

The Virta affair is at the center of literary gossip these days (see *Komsomol'skaia pravda*, 16 March). The Litfond has passed a resolution to evict Virta's first wife, Irina Ivanovna, from her Peredelkino dacha. It's a short hop from Virta to Surov, who after cracking open his driver's skull, heaped filthy abuse on the doctor, a woman, who came to treat him. He's been expelled from both the Party and the Writers' Union. < . . . >

21 March.

Apparently that fool of a Virta built his estate near the church where his father had been a priest. Then he submitted a request to the local authorities to have the cemetery moved away from his house, because his father was buried there and the view of the cemetery "got on his nerves." He's put triple frames on his windows to keep out the lowing of the very kolkhoz cows he is supposed to describe. (All this comes from Fedin, whom I dragged out for an evening stroll.) < . . . >
< . . . >

5 April.

Yesterday I translated O. Henry's "The Shorn Wolf" in one go. Toward evening I made a discovery about the connection between Nekrasov's folkloric verse and Ryleev's. < . . . >

25 April.

Easter. Since yesterday I've been housed in a phenomenally clean isolation cubicle—all glass and tile. < . . . > I'm reading O. Henry. I find him more congenial than before. [. . .] What is striking is not so much the endings as the texture of the narrative: not a single line is the result of inertia; each is a new discovery. O. Henry constantly takes the path of greatest resistance. We foreigners are specially sensitive to the inventiveness of his vocabulary. < . . . > O. Henry is excruciatingly boring. Even his variety has something monotonous about it. < . . . >

26 April.

< . . . > Read Hall Cain's *Memoirs of Rossetti*. I can't stand Cain, but the memoirs seem interesting: the enormous house in Cheyne Walk where poor Rossetti lived completely cut off from the world, suffering from insomnia, for which he took nightly doses of chloral, and from the delusion that his enemies were plotting against him. According to Cain, Rossetti did not love the woman he married and immortalized in his canvases, the woman in whose coffin he buried a manuscript of poems. He died suddenly of Brant's disease at the age of fifty-four in the spring of 1882, almost on the day I was born.

Cain ends with a platitude: "His insomnia finally over, he fell into an endless sleep." Soon the same will apply to me. < . . . >

13 June.

Leonov called at the house. He says Yermilov will take over *Novyi mir* from Tvardovsky. [. . .]

18 June.

< . . . > Called on Fedin today. < . . . > We talked about Ehrenburg. "I was at a Kremlin reception celebrating the end of the war," he said, "and when Stalin got up and gave his famous toast to the Russian people Ehrenburg burst into tears. He found something insulting about it." Fedin also said he had heard a writer in the corridors of the Writers' Union call Ehrenburg "the patriarch of the cosmopolitans."[259] < . . . >

15 July.

Today is the fiftieth anniversary of Chekhov's death. Exactly fifty years ago, while I was living in London, I read the announcement of it in the *Daily News* and spent the whole night walking round and round the Bedford Square fence weeping—sobbing—like a madman. It was the greatest

---

259. During the large-scale cultural purge unleashed by Andrei Zhdanov in 1946 (see note 239) "cosmopolitan," often accompanied by "rootless," stood for "Jew." (M.H.H.)

loss of my life. I sat down and wrote a bad but deeply felt poem in which I said, "You delighted in life in all its diversity," in other words, I said in verse the same thing I said (today) in *Litgazeta*. Fifty years have passed, yet my love for him—for his face, for his work—remains constant. < . . . >

4 November.

I'm depressed, exhausted. There is no one I would care to exchange so much as a word with. What to do about it? To escape the depression, the proofreading, and the restlessness, I dragged myself off to the village of Barvikh to see Yekaterina Pavlovna Peshkova at her dacha (where she lived with Gorky). How old is she? About seventy-eight, but full of energy, ebullient, emotional, impetuous. She went to a reading of the letters of Stanislavsky to Chekhov at the Literary Museum recently. "They were so wonderful—both high-minded and congenial—that I was moved to the brink of tears. And what beautiful memoirs Olga Leonardovna [Knipper] wrote about Chekhov's death: there he is, lying in his hotel room, freezing, while a marvelous summer morning wafts through the window—the nature he so loved. And then they read the speech Stanislavsky made at the unveiling of the monument to Chekhov in Badenweiler, a splendid speech, youthful, stirring. I was so excited that when Darya came to fetch me in the car she said, 'Grandma, what's wrong?' as I climbed in."

Next she talked about Sergo.[260] "I'm working hard on his behalf. I keep trying to get to Rudenko, but he won't see me, and Sergo had nothing to do with his father, though they were wonderful together and loved each other. (She ran and showed me a picture of them.) We can't live high on the hog any longer: we've stopped receiving royalties for Alexei Mikhailovich's books. The time limit has passed. We've been living beyond our means, it seems. We have to get rid of the dacha and live in town . . . I'm sorry for the great-grandchildren. Country life is so good for them."

Leaving aside personal matters, she went on to talk about the edition of Gorky's letters to her. "The edition of Marya Chekhova's letters that's just come out—she's done the annotations herself. They won't let me."
< . . . >

260. "Sergo" is Sergo Beria, husband of Gorky's granddaughter Marfa and son of Lavrenty Beria.

11 November.

It's warm. What bliss. Klara has brought me the proofs of *Nekrasov's Craft* with the idiotic demands of a very dense editor. I got through about a hundred and fifty pages and was ready to drop. The only pleasant thing was that I had strict orders from the censor not to praise Russian literature at the expense of foreign literature. They crossed out the passage containing Chernyshevsky's statement that "Fielding is good, but he is not Gogol." War has been declared on chauvinism in general. I hear that the Rome and Paris they are showing in films consist not of squalid slums but of fine buildings, monuments, and the like. That too is a pleasant development. < . . . >

14 November.

Lida phoned to say that Katya Boronina has just returned from exile. With a completely clear record. This is the second time I've worked hard for her release. < . . . >

15 November.

Went to the Hall of Columns yesterday to take part in a children's program. I sat next to a congenial Mikhalkov. He told me that when his son Andron was six they had a visit from Rakhil Baumvol and Andron said:

> Rakhil has come to see us
> To make a splash she tries;
> A shame we cannot see her:
> The splash gets in our eyes.

< . . . > Stopping at our flat for a moment, I saw Katya Boronina. She looked as though she had just been run over by a lorry. She was in rags, she had a bad eye and a hoarse voice, and she is wasting away with a goiter—one of hundreds of thousands of Beria's victims. I'm glad I managed to pull her out of hell. She said that Yevgenia Zbarskaya behaved splendidly in the camp.
< . . . >

15 December.

Yesterday there was a meeting of the Moscow delegates.[261] Surkov's speech was superb (in form). It was about the new journals that would be coming out—journals like *Krasnaia nov'* and *Iunost'*—and about how delegates should not leave the room whenever an Azerbaijani or Tatar got up to speak. After the meeting, which was very brief, Surkov was elected leader of the Moscow delegation, and Kataev came up to me and asked me to be on the staff of *Iunost'*.

A major article Fedin wrote for *Pravda* has been returned to him for emendations. He gave me a lift home and worked on the article the whole way. The whole town is talking about the Ehrenburg-Sholokhov conflict. Sholokhov has been using Black Hundreds rhetoric.[262] < . . . >

Have just returned from the Writers' Union. It makes a terrible impression. It isn't a literature congress, it's an anti-literature congress.

19 December.

Haven't slept for many nights now. It's the congress. I thought of driving with Pasternak. He's not going. "Say hello to Anna Andreevna [Akhmatova] for me," he says by way of expressing his attitude toward the congress. < . . . >

261. The Second Congress of Soviet Writers, held on 15–25 December, was preceded by an encounter of the writers with Party and government leaders. Tvardovsky commented in his notebook on Sholokhov's Congress speech as follows: "A pity about Sholokhov. His speech was disgraceful. There was an echo of the attacks on cosmopolitans [see note 259] in his reference to Ehrenberg's early writings, in which he allegedly downgraded Russians and extolled Jews. . . . And then that hoarse, at times barely audible voice, which left no doubt about the origin of its hoarseness." Sholokhov also called Ehrenberg's *Thaw*—a mediocre but relatively candid novel which helped trigger, and gave the name to, the liberalization process in post-Stalinist culture—"a step backward" and accused him of being unable to take the slightest criticism.

262. See note 156.

1955

-+->-+->-+->-+->-+->-+->-

1 January

Zhenya and Lyonya, Borya, Valya, and a few others brought a beautiful large fir tree back from the woods yesterday and decorated it in silence, because I was working in the room next door. < . . . > I was touched by the way Zhenya showed me the ornaments passed on to him by his father— a little cook, a ball, a crocodile, a chain—and I suddenly recalled holding his father in my arms when he was three and watching him stare gleefully at the lighted Christmas tree. [. . .]

4 January.

< . . . > Went all the way to Golitsino to see Lida yesterday. She showed me a volume called *Works of Leningrad Authors for Children.* It is phenomenally illiterate and disgusting. *Novyi mir* has commissioned a review, and for that measly review she will read about thirty books (which she has borrowed from the Children's Book House), work a month and a half, receive no more than three hundred rubles, and make a score of new enemies.

10 January.

< . . . > Leonov said yesterday that Fadeev came out in favor of reducing writers' fees during a Central Committee meeting devoted to the issue. "I don't know what to do with all my money," he said. "When somebody asked me recently for seven thousand rubles, I handed them over and I shouldn't have. I only did it because I didn't need them."

Smirnov opposed him, saying, "Alexander Alexandrovich has lost touch with the average writer." < . . . >

21 January.

Went to town to see about the new collection of my tales, because there was talk of including "The Crocodile." Suddenly Klara phoned,[263] saying "Marya Borisovna has taken a turn for the worse. Call for Alexei Vasilyevich." Her heart had given up completely, her left arm was extremely painful, she had no appetite, and her lips were blue, yet her head was clear and her speech no worse than usual. There was nothing for me to do but rush home and leave my petty affairs behind. < . . . >

22 January.

I am choked with tears by the unrelenting feeling that a person dear to me is about to die. Hoping to distract her from her agonizing thoughts, I tried reading her the "Bibigon" manuscript, but I was constantly afraid of breaking into sobs, and although she listened carefully and pointed out where it dragged and faded, I soon realized it was too onerous a task for her weary brain: I was wearing her out. The only things keeping her going are black coffee and the doctors' poisons. < . . . >

21 February.

Lida came in and said, "She is gone." Olga Ivanovna and Anastasy Ivanovich washed and dressed her, and the doctor came and confirmed her death. < . . . >

23 February.

The funeral was today. < . . . > Looking at the face in the coffin, a face I adored, all pink and spotted with the tiny blemishes I'd kissed so often, I felt I was being taken to the gallows. Knowing that I wasn't alone—that Shtein, Pogodina, the Leonovs, Fedin, Kaverin, and the children and grandchildren were walking behind me—made me feel better, and as I looked at that face and watched the light snow fall on it I thought I saw a kind of stern reverence and calm. < . . . > Looking at the coffin on the mound, I felt I was attending a funeral for the first time, and for the first

263. Klara Lazovskaya, Chukovsky's personal secretary.

time I understood what death is. We had trudged our slippery way along the bumpy snow to the magnificent place under three pine trees I had chosen for her and me, and there I underwent the torture of watching the nails hammered into the coffin, hearing the thump of the frozen earth against the lid, waiting for the slow, excruciatingly slow work of the shovels to finish. Prokopych had fashioned a cross, Zhenya had written a splendid inscription for the plaque, and we sprinkled the mound with flowers and wreaths. I don't remember how I made it home. Sergei Nikolaevich, our former driver, touched me more than anybody. < . . . >

28 February.

Went to the grave again yesterday. Zhenya and Katya Luri came too. Splendid weather: freezing, clear. The ribbons and flowers are intact. Prokopych put wire around them. Saw the Ivanovs—Koma and Tamara Vladimirovna; they walked me back to Pasternak's house. Pasternak has been phoning and visiting me. He has finished his novel and is in the process of making a fair copy for the typist. It is five hundred pages long. < . . . >

Am reading Boswell's *Life of Johnson*. How antiquated! It sounds three thousand years old. The devotion to king and religion! The bombast! I was fascinated by Johnson's reaction to Richardson and Fielding. Richardson knows how clocks are made, he knows every cog of the mechanism, while Fielding looks at a clock and tells you what time it is. < . . . >

Went to see my great-granddaughter yesterday and played lotto with her and Mitya. "I've heard what happened to Gramsie," she said to me (in a see-what-a-good-girl-am-I voice), "and I cried yesterday and today too a little." And then: "You'll be dying soon too. But do try and hang on a bit longer." < . . . >

7 March.

Went back to the grave this morning. Light snow. Took the ribbons off the wreaths. Very few were left. Marshak's, the children's. Some blighter is stealing ribbons from grave sites.

Never before have I felt so clearly the fragility of the concepts "mine" and "yours." Marya Borisovna always had a childlike attachment to her things, so I feel strange taking her suitcase, opening her desk drawers, < . . . > or simply moving things about in her room.

And how acutely I feel the changes going on in the world in her absence. < ... > Sima Dreiden is working temporarily at Obraztsov's puppet theater. Marya Borisovna would have found his situation interesting. He came back from the camps rehabilitated and says that Dembo was one of the people who gave false evidence against him, < ... > accused him of making anti-Soviet statements, accused him to his face. When Dreiden turned up at the theater, Dembo went over to him and said, "Hello there, Simochka! Good to see you back!" and Dreiden walked right past the villain without even glancing at him. Marya Borisovna would have found that very interesting. [...]

When you lose the friend and companion of a lifetime, you look at yourself in amazement and ask yourself for the first time, "Who are you anyway?" And you come to some rather distressing conclusions. < ... > One more thing: when the wife you have spent half a century with dies, you suddenly forget the later years and picture her in the blush of youth, at her most feminine—as a bride and young mother. You forget the gray hair and realize what nonsense time is, what flimsy tommyrot. < ... >

10 March.

< ... > Am reading Stevenson's *Men and Books*.[264] The article "Some Aspects of Robert Burns" is all about me. To my mind, Stevenson is a great writer and *Men and Books* is a thousand times better than *Treasure Island*.

11 March.

Met Kornely Zelinsky and Pertsov in the street. They told me a sensational piece of news: Alexandrov, the minister of culture, has been accused of debauchery. He, Petrov, Kruzhkov, and (perhaps) Yegolin. Petrov, head of the Literary Institute, would apparently procure girl-students for Alexandrov, and Alexandrov would stage his own private orgies. What a sensation! I'd observed Alexandrov in person at Uskoe: he'd get drunk every evening and make his way to X's room, from which (or so the staff maintained) he would emerge at dawn. But that's not what matters. What matters is that

264. Robert Louis Stevenson's *Familiar Studies of Men and Books* (London, 1912) can still be found in Chukovsky's Peredelkino library.

he is a nonentity, an ignoramus, a boor, dense, vulgar, and petty. Since he and a group of "philosophers" were throwing together a philosophy textbook (or history of philosophy) at Uskoe, I spent a lot of time with him. Though a historian of philosophy, he had never heard of Nikolai Yakovlevich Grot, he didn't know that Vladimir Solovyov was a poet, he mixed up Fyodor Sologub and Vladimir Sologub, and so on. You had only to watch him for five minutes to know the man was a pen-pushing careerist with no feeling whatever for culture. And he was *minister* of culture!

It reminds me of the case of Anna Radlova. Her Shakespeare translations were awful. I wrote about them, making my points with mathematical precision. A child could have told the translations were worthless. But she flourished, and they kept being staged. Not until she went over to Hitler was she acknowledged to be the poor translator she was.

Alexandrov's speech at the Writers' Congress came right after mine. I talked about the bureaucratization of our Soviet literary style. Alexandrov's speech was a magnificent illustration of my thesis. The audience couldn't help laughing. I received several notes lampooning his speech as an example of the style I had derided. *Everybody* could see what a Derzhimorda and lickspittle he was.[265] But—it was the Beria story all over again—the authorities turned a blind eye to it, and Alexandrov was made the head of all Soviet culture. < . . . >

Kolya came and told the story of the Surov affair. Surov had taken advantage of the campaign against the cosmopolitans to frighten two Jewish writers into writing a play for him, and for that play he, Surov, received two Stalin prizes! Corruption, lies, lack of talent, careerism. < . . . >

There are all kinds of Alexandrov jokes making the rounds in town. For example, on 8 March he receives a phone call wishing him a Happy Women's Day. "Why are you wishing *me* a Happy Women's Day?" he asks.

"Because you're our most famous prostitute."

Or: Three ministers were arguing over which ministry was created first.

"Mine," said the minister of energy, "because God said, 'Let there be light.'"

"Mine," said the minister of agriculture, "because in the beginning God created the earth."

"No, mine," said Alexandrov, "because before that there was chaos."

265. Derzhimorda is the name of a policeman in Gogol's comedy *The Inspector General.* The name literally means "shut your trap." (M.H.H.)

Apparently Yegolin really did take part in the orgies. Are they going to prosecute him for that and not for, parasite that he is, "editing" Ushinsky, Chekhov, and Nekrasov without doing a thing, making others work for him, and earning more for his nominal editorial services than Ushinsky, Chekhov, and Nekrasov ever earned for their works? Zilbershtein and Makashin work their fingers to the bone, and parasites like Belchikov and Yegolin put their names on the results and get paid for them! < . . . >

14 March.

Am retranslating Whitman's "Song of Joys." It is not going well. [. . .]

15 March.

[. . .] Every day I go to the grave, thinking of her on the way: we are at the Cherkasskys' Magner House flat, she is wearing a velvet blouse, and I am in love with the scent of it, or we are meeting behind the station at Kulikovo Field and she says, "Kind sir," and so on, or there we are at Lanzheron walking home at daybreak, or there is her father reading *L'Aurore,* and now we are in Kolomenskaya Street and I keep saying "Darling" and I run to the grave as if we had a tryst there. < . . . >

24 March.

< . . . > Spent all day reading Tolstoy's diary from 1854 to 1857. I can't get over how much he managed to do with his time: in a day he would see the people and things others see in a month. And his capacity for work! Every day he read and wrote a prodigious amount while accusing himself of sloth and inactivity and the like. And the sheer physicality of the man! Not a week would go by without intercourse with a woman, or if it did he would have nocturnal emissions (which he would prudishly indicate by initial only). Such insatiable virility is in itself evidence of a tremendous vital force. < . . . >

31 March.

[. . .] Had a visit from Yelizaveta Petrovna, the wife of G. N. Speransky. < . . . > She's been married for fifty-seven years and "still can't get used to Georgy Nesterovich's phenomenal goodness." She told me that when they were arresting doctors as perpetrators of the "doctors' plot," some scoundrel from the Medical Academy got up at a meeting and branded them as criminals. "Then he asked for 'an opinion about their crimes from the eldest in our ranks, Dr. Speransky.' So Georgy Nesterovich stood and said, 'I have been working with them for decades and consider them splendid physicians, the noblest of men, etc.' and people burst into applause." [. . .]

Lida brought me a letter that Zaslavsky included with three small books. I wrote him a friendly note without reading the books. Now I'm reading them and find them terribly distasteful. Especially the one about Kierkegaard. It is vulgar and inaccurate, even judging by the quotations he himself gives. Kierkegaard was a deep and gifted thinker. Then there are Zaslavsky's attacks on Huxley and the American philosophers, which are both banal and imbued with the official line. Even if Huxley is as Zaslavsky depicts him, he is not the be-all and the end-all of Anglo-American culture, and Zaslavsky makes it seem as if it had nothing but Huxley to offer.

The same thing happened with a long article I wrote pointing out that alongside the great achievements of Anglo-American children's literature there was the awful phenomenon of the comics, but at the last moment they cut everything about the positive aspects of the literature and left only the part about the comics. Readers were completely disoriented. But Zaslavsky? Doesn't he realize his articles are a harmful distortion of reality? < . . . >

Yelizaveta Petrovna came to see me again today. She gave me a detailed account of how Stalin died. One night Tretyakov, the minister of health, rang Dr. Konovalov and said, "I want you to come this minute. I have a patient in grave danger for you to look at."

"I can't," said Konovalov. "I'm too tired."

"I order you to come. A car will fetch you immediately."

The car took Konovalov to the ministry, where two or three other doctors were waiting. They all drove out of the city and pulled up at a green fence. "Your papers." Another green fence. "Your papers" again. In they go, and what do they see but Iosif Vissarionovich [Stalin] lying before them unconscious. A hopeless case. They can tell immediately. But all the members of the government are in attendance, and medication is administered with much ado. "Let me know tomorrow if the patient's condition improves," Beria says to Konovalov. It was a threat as much as a statement.

"The patient is worse," says Konovalov the next day.

"Why didn't you tell me yesterday?" says Beria.

He was taken to the morgue (near the zoo) for an autopsy. They had to make an incision in his brain. Professor X (I forget his name, a pupil of Abrikosov's), a specialist in the field, was paralyzed, terrified. But again Tretyakov said, "I order you to," and it was done. He turned out to have had a cerebral hemorrhage.

Am reading Twain's *A Tramp Abroad,* a book I first read fifty years ago while awaiting trial in the Shpalernaya Street lock-up.[266] I laughed so hard I started hiccuping and the guard kept running up to the Judas hole because he thought he heard sobs. Fifty years later the book is just as fresh and muscular. It is not only shot through with humor; it is poetic. [. . .]

Reading Stevenson on Pepys's diary, I found a striking passage about Marya Borisovna and myself (page 226).

I feel drawn to Marya Borisovna's grave, drawn even to enter it. It is as though a hand had come out of the coffin and were pulling me, pulling me more and more each day, and I don't resist, have no desire to resist, no will to live, and instead of all the books I once wanted to write what I really want to write is my last will and testament.

I'm trying to get back to my "Bibigon" and *From Two to Five,* but in fact I'm an electrified corpse. < . . . >

1 April.

Well, well, Kornei! You're seventy-three!

Until now I have been writing this diary for myself or, rather, for a Kornei Chukovsky unknown to me, the one I'd become later in life. Now I have no more "later in life." Who is my audience now? Posterity? If I were writing for posterity, I'd write differently, more elegantly, about other things, and I'd use twenty-five or thirty words instead of the two I sometimes use, given that I see myself as the only future reader of these lines. In other words, there's no point in keeping a diary any longer, since no one who knows what a grave is thinks of keeping a diary for posterity

Went back to reading *A Tramp Abroad* yesterday and enjoyed "The Awful German Language" as much as before. I consider it one of Twain's best pieces. No article about philology has ever made people laugh so hard.

---

266. Chukovsky was imprisoned briefly during the 1905 Revolution. (M.H.H.)

Writing a *cheerful* article about linguistics, making grammar hilariously funny—it would seem unthinkable, yet fifty years after reading it for the first time I found it as hilarious as ever. It made me sick to think of Mendelson and the book he published on Twain. That leech looked at the whole man and all he saw were his "oppositional ideas." Instead of a full-length portrait he gave an ear or maybe only an eyebrow, and then blew it up way out of proportion. He's done the same with Whitman. The reader is less concerned with the political convictions of the young Whitman than Mendelson imagines, and political convictions are no more than Whitman's eyebrow in any case. Who would be idiotic enough to characterize, say, Fet's poetry in terms of his political convictions? < . . . >

5 May.

Tamara Ivanova came to see me yesterday. < . . . > She said there had been something of a plot against Vsevolod at the Writers' Union. Back when they gave out their first awards, Vsevolod was supposed to get the Order of Lenin, but Pavlenko had intervened and said, "A medal of honor is enough." Whereupon Stalin said, "If not a Lenin, then at least a Red Flag." Tamara claims there's a closely knit group of bigwigs (Simonov, Surkov, and so on) trying to frighten the authorities by pointing to purported counterrevolutionary activities of a number of writers. It sounded like pure fabulation to me, but before the day was out I received confirmation of the group's machinations. Emmanuil Kazakevich, who was visiting Kolya, broached the subject without any prompting on my part. He claims that Surkov maintains his position by taking every opportunity to point to the (supposed) anti-Soviet line of writers like himself, Nikolai Chukovsky, Leonid Grossman, Vsevolod Ivanov, etc.

I met Kazakevich for the first time yesterday. He fairly radiates talent. Everything he says has an extraordinary energy to it. He has put together a very funny Table of Ranks or, as he puts it, "pecking order" for writers made up of eighty-four (or is it seventy-six?) categories starting with "unrivaled" and "brilliant" and ending with "class enemy." They also include "rightly forgotten" and "wrongly forgotten" and "not unknown" and "interesting" and "outstanding" and "well-known" and "great" and "truly great" and such descriptive epithets as "children's." He says the Litfond bureaucrats would find it quite useful. "Supposing I, Kazakevich, request an allocation of five thousand rubles. Rudyansky has a look at the 'pecking order,' sees 'interesting writer,' and says, 'Sorry, I can give you only two thousand.' "

10 May.

Irakly, who is recently back from Vienna, called at the house just now. He filled me in on the Alexandrov witticisms currently making the rounds: 1) The Alexandrov Philosophical Ensemble of Dance and Romance, 2) Alexandrov has proved the unity of form and content. Give him the right form and he is content. < . . . >

While out walking, we met Pasternak. He has been working so hard all day, every day that he looks sallow. He has finished the rough draft of his novel, and it has clearly driven him to exhaustion. For years he maintained a youthful, student-like appearance, and now he's a gray-haired old man with an ashen complexion to match. "The novel is banal, it's turning out badly, but I've got to finish it." And so on. When I asked him whether he was working on a book of poetry, he said, "As soon as I finish the novel, I want to put together a one-volume edition of my verse. I do so want to rework everything. The only decent thing about the cycle *My Sister Life*, for instance, is the title." And so on. Tired as he is, his face radiates great creative and spiritual activity. < . . . >

30 June.

< . . . > Akhmatova came for a visit on the day Nehru arrived in the USSR. Since the Mozhaiskoe Highway was crowded with people greeting him, no traffic was allowed in the direction of Peredelkino. We were faced with a wall of cops constantly repeating the word "back." But I had a tired, an exhausted Akhmatova in my car, and my only thought was to get her out of the sweltering heat and into nature. In despair we set off for Sparrow Hills, but there a raisonneur of a policeman told us, "You can't go any farther. Go back to town. And throwing a tantrum will get you nowhere: everyone's enjoying the event." (By "the event" he meant the welcome for Nehru. He wasn't the only one. Before long everything connected with honoring the man was referred to as a "Nehru event.")

As usual Akhmatova was simple and good-natured, while at the same time regal. I soon realized she hadn't come for the fresh air, she'd come because of her poem.[267] The poem was clearly the only ray of light, the only illusion of happiness in her tragic, harrowing existence. She had come to talk about the poem, hear praise for the poem, live the poem. She was loath to think the content of the poem would escape many readers; she insisted it was perfectly comprehensible, though for most people it was gibberish. She divides the world into two unequal parts: those who understand the poem and those who do not. < . . . >

17 July.

Called on Kaverin. Lidia Nikolaevna showed me a letter from Zoshchenko's wife. It is terrible. "During his last stay at Sestroretsk he said straight out they were trying to do him in and he didn't expect to last out the year. He was especially shaken by a statement from the Leningrad Writers' Union 'authorities' to the effect that everything he wrote would be banned regardless of quality. To tell the truth, I don't believe they told him that, but he claims those were their very words. He feels that by depriving him of the possibility of working they are depriving him of his profession, which is something he cannot survive. He looks simply awful. His legs are terribly swollen every morning." And so on.

Immediately after reading the letter, I rushed to the Union to talk to Polikarpov, but he was on holiday, so I saw Vasily Alexandrovich Smirnov, his deputy. Smirnov expressed great sympathy and promised to talk it over with Surkov. I rang him up two days later: he had spoken to Surkov and told me in an unofficial tone of voice, "Surkov often makes promises he doesn't keep. I'll make sure he keeps this one." The measures taken by the Union in the Zoshchenko case amount to the following: a call was made to Khrapchenko to find out why the editorial board of *Oktiabr'* had returned ten stories to Zoshchenko, a letter was sent to Zoshchenko asking for the stories Khrapchenko had rejected, a letter of general encouragement was sent to him, etc.

I talked to Lidin, a member of the Litfond. Lidin will try and find five thousand rubles for Zoshchenko. For my part, I sent him five hundred

267. The Akhmatova poem in question is the richly allusive *Poem Without a Hero*, which captures the feverish atmosphere of pre-1914 literary Petersburg and which took her twenty years to complete. (V.E.)

rubles and an invitation to come and stay with us in Peredelkino. How he will respond I don't know. < . . . >

No, Zoshchenko won't be coming. I've received a letter from him, a proud and tragic letter: he has neither the moral nor the physical strength for it. < . . . >

21 July.

It is exactly five months since Marya Borisovna died. I visited her grave today. I must have a railing put around our common grave and a monument made. < . . . >

The Zoshchenko affair has taken a turn for the worse. I tried to get the Litfond to give him five thousand rubles, but as soon as Polikarpov, who had been on holiday, found out the Union was going to provide him with some assistance, he said, "Zoshchenko hasn't taken a step in our direction. Why should we take seven or eight in his?" Whereupon everything came to a halt.

I hear that the tenth edition of *From Two to Five* came out today. Abridged and anemic. < . . . >

1 August.

< . . . > Here is Lida's letter from Leningrad about her meeting with Zoshchenko:

Dear Father,
I visited Mikhail Mikhailovich the night before last. It wasn't easy to find him because he spends most of his time at Sestroretsk, but we met at last. He reminds me of Gogol just before his death, though he is as intelligent, refined, and wonderful as always. < . . . > He says he'll come—if he comes at all—in the autumn, not now. He's ill: he didn't eat a thing for a month; he couldn't bring himself to. Now he's learning how again. He is very, very grateful to you and promises to send you the new edition of *Going for Matches*.[268] He's terribly thin, as thin as Zhenya. "I'd give up completely, but I have to earn a living. I can't get used to the humiliation of it all." < . . . >

268. *Going for Matches* is a Finnish novel by Main Lassila. Zoshchenko was the translator.

20 October.

Kolya is off to Finland, where he spent his entire childhood. Marya Borisovna and I went to Helsinki with him in 1914 before the war (or in 1913).
While we were there, he stopped in the street to stare at something and a
coach ran into him. Horrified and thinking his leg broken, we took him to
a surgeon. The doctor, a Finn, examined the Russian boy's leg with antipathy: to his disappointment there wasn't even a bruise, and Kolya fell
asleep in a trice from all the excitement. To take his mind off things on
the train, I made up a story about a crocodile that went "There once was
a crocodile" to the rhythm of the wheels. The improvisation went on and
on, and the cast of characters included a Doctor Ouch-It-Hurts, though at
the time his name was Ow-It-Hurts. I introduced him to mitigate the
disagreeable impression the Finnish surgeon had made on Kolya. < . . . >

13 December.

Have finally delivered the new, eleventh edition of *From Two to Five* to the
publisher. < . . . > I'd be so happy if they put it out immediately and got
it off my back. I've been meaning to work on Chekhov, Blok, Bunin, and
Sleptsov, but felt *drawn* to that illegitimate little book the way novels
describe a man being drawn to a mistress from a wife.

Last week I gave a talk on Blok at a posh Tchaikovsky Hall celebration
in his memory. Fedin delivered a weighty, pregnant opening speech in an
orotund voice like the Lord of Sabaoth on Mount Sinai. Then all hell
broke loose. Antokolsky shouted his way through a hopelessly empty talk
with false energy—he even began with a shout ("Blok is a realist! Blok
loved the Revolution!"), as if issuing a public challenge with his rancid,
Party-line conception. When he took his seat, Tvardovsky, whom I was
sitting next to, turned to me and said, "You'd think he was shouting from
a plane." Tvardovsky had prepared a few words, but after Kirsanov's
shamanlike contortions and Gorodetsky's canonical mumblings he refused
to take the floor. By the time Fedin called on me, the audience was exhausted, yet mine was the only talk the audience found moving (according
to Fedin, Tvardovsky, and Kazakevich) and it was less moving than it could
have been.

While putting it together, I went back to my old Blok book and was
chagrined to find that it has been completely robbed, pillaged, and de-

spoiled by today's Blok scholars, especially "Volodya" Orlov. When I wrote it, every word was new, every thought my own find, but because the book was banned my finds have been taken over by clever rogues and rotters and now my priority is completely forgotten. The same thing happened with *From Two to Five:* while it was banned, its ideas were purloined right and left. As for me, I can't write anything but "finds," thoughts no one else has put into words. Nothing else is of interest to me. I am incapable of setting forth other people's thoughts. [. . .]

1956

➤-➤-➤-➤-➤-➤-➤-➤

2 January.

I spend my days in a stupor, getting nothing done, botching everything. I'm seventy-four, I could die tomorrow. What's the point of trying something or even wanting something? My solitude is absolute: yesterday was the first of the year and not a soul came to see me.
< . . . >

28 February.

< . . . > The day before yesterday Bek brought me *Literaturnaia Moskva* with my awful, despicable Blok article. Having no idea of what I was in for, I started in on Tvardovsky's verse and when I came to "Meeting with a Friend"—about an exile who had spent seventeen years at hard labor for no reason whatsoever—I burst into tears. Everything about the volume makes it a major literary event. It is an attempt to bring together material of great diversity, to represent literary Moscow from all angles, especially from those it was out of the question to show under Stalin. Kazakevich's novel about the Soviet Army gives portraits of rotters, careerists, and thieves as well as heroes, and so on.[269] < . . . >

---

269. Kazakevich's *A House on the Square* (1956) deals with the Soviet occupying forces in East Germany. (M.H.H.)

4 March.

Kazakevich was here this evening along with Oksman and Kolya. He spent the whole time spouting jokes and witticisms, clowning, and making up funny situations, encouraging us to join in all the while. [. . .]

Now for a joke: A man in a train asks the name of the man in the couchette opposite him. "The first syllable of my name is what Lenin promised us," the man replies, "and the second syllable—what Stalin gave us." Whereupon a voice from the couchette above him says, "You're under arrest, Comrade Goldstone." < . . . >

All the portraits of Stalin painted by toady artists have been removed from the Tretyakov Gallery. When removing his bust whole from the Frunze Military Academy proved impossible, it was smashed to smithereens and taken out bit by bit.[270]

What good timing for the appearance of *Literaturnaia Moskva.* Kazakevich's novel is perceived as a protest against Stalinism and Stalin's "morose mistrust of people." < . . . >

6 March.

Called on the Ivanovs yesterday. < . . . > Vsevolod claims, on Koma's authority, that all books with Stalin's name in them are being removed from libraries. Millions of calendars with the national anthem have been destroyed. All verse collections by Surkov, Simonov, and Co. are reputed to have been mercilessly destroyed.

Work on the *Great Soviet Encyclopedia* has been suspended. It had reached the letter S. The next volume was to be given over entirely to Stalin, the Stalin prizes, the Stalin Constitution, Stalin as the leading light in science, etc. The editor of *Voprosy istorii* said at an editorial board meeting, "Here is a letter by that scoundrel Stalin to Comrade Trotsky."[271] < . . . >

Vsevolod also reports that Frunze was murdered by Stalin! And that the photograph showing Stalin sitting on a bench next to Lenin is an

270. Trotsky had been a nonperson since Stalin took over. (M.H.H.)

271. There were persistent rumors that Stalin was responsible for the death of the popular Civil War hero M. V. Frunze by virtually forcing him to undergo an unnecessary and risky operation in 1925. (V.E.)

unscrupulous fake: Krupskaya claims they never had their picture taken together. < . . . >

9 March.

When I told Kazakevich that in spite of everything I had once loved Stalin very much even if I'd written less about him than others had, he said, "What about 'The Giant Cockroach'? That's all about Stalin!"

Much as I protested—I had written "The Giant Cockroach" in 1921, and it developed naturally out of "The Crocodile"—he would have none of it and gave me brilliant textual illustrations of his thesis. All at once I remembered that Stalin himself had quoted "The Giant Cockroach"— during the Fourteenth Party Congress, I believe. He opened his plagiarism with the line "Somewhere a cockroach rustled" and proceeded to retell the whole story without referring to the author.

The "simple people" are shocked by the revelations showing Stalin to be an incompetent commander-in-chief, a raving mad administrator who violated all the articles of his own constitution. "So *Pravda* [Truth] should have been called *Lozh'* [Lie]," a fourteen-year-old said to me today. < . . . >

13 May.

Fadeev has shot himself.

I heard about it at the House of Creation and immediately thought of one of his widows, Margarita Aliger, the one who loved him most. I went to her flat, but she wasn't in. I was told she was at the Libedinskys'. I went there. Things were in a terrible state: Libedinsky looked as though he were about to have a heart attack; Fadeev's first wife, Valeria Gerasimova, was sobbing upstairs; and Aliger was sitting like a statue in the side room. I put her in the car and drove her home. < . . . > All the writers I meet < . . . > are trudging along with funereal faces, filling one another in on the dolorous details of the affair. Unable to fall asleep, Fadeev had taken ten nembutals and said he would not be having breakfast but should be called for lunch: he wanted to have a good sleep. When the time came for lunch, his wife said, "Misha, call your father," and Misha went upstairs and came back with the words "Papa's shot himself." He had taken off his shirt and shot straight into the left nipple. The doctor from Nazim Hikmet's dacha who was the first to be summoned told me that his body showed spotting as early as half past three, which means he fired the shot at about one. No one in the family heard a thing. The Libedinskys had been visiting the night before, and they say there were no signs whatever of what was to come. Zinaida Nikolaevna (Pasternak's wife) says Fadeev saw her on her way into town the day before yesterday, stopped his car, and called out cheerfully, "Hop in, Olga Vsevolodovna, and I'll give you a lift to Moscow."

I feel very sorry for dear Alexander Alexandrovich: one could sense a man of stature, a Russian brand of natural genius under all the layers—but, good lord, what layers there were! All the lies of the Stalinist era, all its idiotic atrocities, all its horrific bureaucracy, all its corruption and red tape found a willing accessory in him. An essentially decent human being who loved literature "to tears" had ended by steering the ship of literature into the most perilous, most shameful of waters and attempting to combine humaneness with the secret-police mentality. Hence the zigzags in his behavior, hence the tortured CONSCIENCE of his final years. He wasn't born to be a loser; he was so accustomed to being a leader, the arbiter of writers' fates, that having to withdraw from the position of literary marshal was agony for him. None of his friends was willing to tell him that his *Metallurgy* was worthless, that the articles he had been writing during the past few years—cowardly, turbid, and full of normative pretensions—could only lower him in the eyes of the reading public, that reworking *The Young Guard* to suit the powers-that-be was shameful.[272] Conscientious, talented, and sensitive as he was, he was floundering in oozy, putrid mud and drowning his conscience in wine.[273] [. . .]

272. Fadeev's novel about heroic young partisans during World War II received the Stalin Prize when it appeared in 1945. Two years later, however, it was roundly criticized for underplaying the role of the Party in the war effort, and Fadeev reworked it accordingly. The revised version came out in 1951. (M.H.H.)

273. It was common knowledge in Peredelkino that Fadeev had left behind a letter to the Central Committee. The content of the letter remained a mystery until it was published in *Izvestiia* and *Literaturnaia gazeta* in the autumn of 1990. Significantly, some of Chukovsky's reflections coincide with what Fadeev says about himself there.

23 June.

I now see once and for all that I have written these notes into a void and that they are what one might call over and done with, so I am officially bringing them to a close. But as I have not yet died and am still interested in who comes to see me and when (I forget about people the moment they leave), I have decided to turn my diary into a record of visitors and practical details. < . . . >

< . . . >

3 August.

< . . . > Have read a stenogram of a speech given by Oksman < . . . > decrying "belligerent and grossly pretentious ignorance hatched in the capital's incubators and nurtured there for years, reckless opportunistic lying and disgraceful mockery made of historical truth." A stunning speech—brave and splendidly worded. < . . . >

Akhmatova and Lida have just left. Akhmatova has seen Fedin, who told her a volume of her verse edited by Surkov would be coming out soon. < . . . > She talked about the American resonance of her article about "The Golden Cockerel," which is based on Washington Irving's novella. < . . . >

< . . . >

1 September.

Called on Fedin yesterday. He told me in confidence that Pasternak had put his novel, *Doctor Zhivago,* in the hands of an Italian who plans to publish it abroad. It will cause a great scandal, of course: "Pasternak's Novel Banned by the Bolsheviks." Just what the White Guard ordered: they can take isolated passages out of context and concoct a "counterrevolutionary novel by Pasternak."[274]

274. In the preface to the first Russian edition of *Doctor Zhivago* to see the light of day in Pasternak's homeland, his son Yevgeny wrote: "In the summer [of 1956] Pasternak played host to Sergio D'Angelo, an Italian Communist associated with the Italian-language radio broadcasts in Moscow. D'Angelo asked for an opportunity to familiarize himself with the manuscript, and his request was officially granted. He never returned the manuscript; instead, he conveyed it to the leftist Italian publisher Giorgio Feltrinelli, who notified Pasternak that he intended to publish it in Italian. On 30 June 1956 Pasternak replied that he would be glad to see the novel translated,

There is much ado about the novel even now: Pasternak submitted it to *Literaturnaia Moskva*. Kazakevich read it and said, "Judging by the novel, the October Revolution was a misunderstanding and ought never to have occurred." They rejected the manuscript. He submitted it to *Novyi mir* together with the preface he had written for a collection of his verse. Krivitsky was in favor of publishing the preface with minor cuts, but when Simonov read the novel he refused to publish even the preface, saying, "We must not give Pasternak the floor!"

The current plan is as follows: to stem all nasty rumors (both here and abroad) by putting the novel out in three thousand copies—thereby making it inaccessible to the masses—and at the same time proclaiming that we are placing no obstacles in Pasternak's path.

As for the novel itself, Fedin calls it "brilliant": extremely egocentric, satanically arrogant, elegantly simple yet literary through and through—an autobiography of the great Pasternak. Fedin—pacing the room, waving his arms—gave an inspired account of the work, subtle and penetrating. I admire his fiery spirit. He was also highly positive about Pasternak's *Faust* translation, its rich and supple use of common parlance: "You'd think he'd learned the whole of Dal' by heart." Then we went for a walk, and I came away with a more favorable impression of Fedin than I'd had in a long time.

Am reading Pisarev and feel fourteen again.

The new edition of *From Two to Five* came out the day before yesterday. It is now serious, precise, and well balanced. I did not copy a single thought from anywhere: it is all *mine*. The book should have been made to look serious, austere, plain, but they've made it ornate and fussy and added bad children's drawings. [...]

A funny thing has happened with *Literaturnaia Moskva:* I submitted an essay on Chekhov, Kolya a story entitled "The Tramp," and Lida an article. The whole family in one book! It was awkward. Kazakevich and Aliger came to me on bended knee and said, "Please let us put your essay in the next volume; otherwise we'll end up with *Chukovskaia Moskva*." I agreed. [...]

---

but warned: "If publication here, which has been promised by a number of journals, is delayed and you bring the novel out first, I shall be in a tragically difficult situation."

Yesterday Serov the imposter (V. A. Serov) published an article in *Pravda* defending the Black Hundreds view of art.[275]

2 September.

< . . . > An Oxford professor by the name of Berlin came to see me the day before yesterday, an unusually well-educated man. He told me that a wonderful new translation of *My Past and Thoughts* had appeared in England, and the English are thrilled with it. It is the first time that the name of the brilliant Herzen has attracted a broad audience. (He says the British Museum has the Herzen-Herwegh correspondence.) He gave a radio talk on Herzen in London and got a sympathetic response from Herzen's huge family, which now lives in Switzerland. He is currently working on Belinsky. He is well acquainted with my work, even *Nekrasov's Craft*. < . . . >

14 September.

On the way here to Uskoe I learned of an amazing event: Tatka has given birth to twin boys. So from this day on I have *three* great-grandchildren. < . . . >

    Tom Sawyer is a very impertinent book. Twain doesn't even know how old Tom is. Judging by Tom's drawing (the one he makes for Becky) he is no more than four; judging by his relationship to his aunt he is seven. But he steals the gold from Indian Joe as an eighteen-year-old. Artists can never draw him: they can't get a handle on him. The artistic truth of the work lies in the details of everyday life and depiction of the child psyche—Twain is brilliant there (and at capturing his characters' colloquial speech)—but all the **adventures** are unadulterated, crowd-pleasing poppycock. Twain's desire to please goes so far that he has the heroes of both books—*Tom Sawyer* and *Huckleberry Finn*—find heaps of money.

17 October.

I should be writing about Blok and instead, idiot that I am, I'm retranslating *Tom Sawyer* and can't seem to extricate myself from the odious task. < . . . >

---

275. Vladimir Serov was president of the Academy of Fine Arts at the time. Chukovsky calls the fatuous bureaucrat an impostor because Vladimir Serov was also the name of an eminent nineteenth-century painter. (V.E.)

Kaverin called at the house and told me that Khrushchev's secretary had phoned Tvardovsky and said, "Nikolai Sergeevich wants to know how you are, whether you need anything, what you're working on, etc." To which Tvardovsky replied, "I'm fine and need nothing."

"And how is *Vasily Tyorkin in the Other World* coming along?[276] What do you plan to do with it?"

"I plan to publish it."

"Good, this is the time for it."

Tvardovsky has "emended" the poem a bit, but it is basically the same as before, when none other than Khrushchev bawled him out for it. These are **new times**.

Kaverin also told me that at a meeting of playwrights N. N. Mikhailov upped and asked as if it were the most natural thing in the world why Bulgakov's plays weren't being staged—that wonderful play *The Flight*, for instance. And it just so happens that Kaverin has recently had an article about *The Flight* published in *Teatr*, an article that took the editorial board six months to approve. Kaverin looks upon all this as "symptoms."[277]

< . . . >

25 December.

< . . . > Am reading Samuel Butler's *Erewhon*, a satirical utopia that has made a big splash in the English press. It never rises above mediocrity: the language is good, but the images are schematic and the imagination behind them not particularly rich, timid, in fact. I wonder what caused the English press to make so much of it.

Have also read Estelle Stead's book, *My Father*, about William Stead, a journalist who made a name for himself in my day as the editor of *Review of Reviews*. Stead gave of his empty soul to all the stupidities and mirages

276. Tvardovsky's *Vasily Tyorkin* (1942–45) is an epic poem featuring the adventures of a feisty Russian soldier during the Second World War. It was immensely popular, as was its satirical sequel, *Vasily Tyorkin in the Other World* (1963), which depicts hell as very much like Soviet reality. (V.E.)

277. Bulgakov's *Flight* (1927) was passed for production on 11 October 1928 only to be banned on 24 October. Although the play had the support of several powerful figures, RAPP zealots prevailed. In fact, *Flight* is on the face of it less objectionable than Bulgakov's more resonant play *The Days of the Turbins*, which was Stalin's favorite. It features a rather unattractive group of characters who, thrown together by the Civil War, decide that emigration is preferable to the fate awaiting them under the Bolsheviks. (V.E.)

of the nineteenth century: the Salvation Army, spiritualism, jingoism, the Hague peace conferences; he is the epitome of the superstitions of that great and petty era. A sensationalist and self-promoter, he went out with an appropriate bang: on the *Titanic*.

Am writing about Blok. Our relations were quite strained for a time. I did not care for many of the people whose company he kept. < . . . > I attacked Georgy Chulkov in *Vesy* as the embodiment of the "symbolscum" that compromised the symbolist movement. In 1904–5 the article roused Blok's ire; in 1919 he told me he completely agreed with it. < . . . > On the very day the article appeared we happened to be sitting side by side in the theater. He didn't say a word to me. When I asked him what he thought of the article, he said, "It shows talent" with such reprehension and distaste that it sounded like the worst thing he could possibly have come up with. < . . . >

26 December.

I am ill: sore throat, cough; I am weak: cupping glasses.
< . . . >

I must write about Blok and how he loved me during his last years, latched on to me, dedicated poems to me, wrote extraordinarily warm letters to me—and how he *despised* me in 1908–10.
< . . . >

30 December.

< . . . > I learned from Frida Vigdorova that at a meeting Furtseva held for writers Smirnov called Simonov a Trotskyite, *Novyi mir* a Trotskyite journal, Paustovsky a counterrevolutionary, and so on, and concluded by stating he was willing to go on his knees and beg for flats to be allotted to writers. When Fedin took the floor just after him, he said that he too was willing to beg for flats to be allotted to writers, but he couldn't agree with anything else Smirnov had said: Paustovsky was an honest Soviet writer, Simonov happened to be out of the country, representing Soviet interests in India, and it would be unethical to condemn him in his absence; as for *Novyi mir* and the Dudintsev novel it had published, he found much truth and noble-mindedness in the stance it had taken and he stood solidly behind it, though he considered the novel itself immature. Punishing writers would

get you nowhere; educating writers with cudgels was impossible. It was one thing to do a delicate eye operation; it was quite another to go around cudgeling people.

"Are you saying we go around cudgeling people?" Furtseva asked.

Fedin assured her he was not, but after his speech the resolution that had been prepared was rejected; in other words, the cudgel was set aside this time round. Furtseva referred to Fedin several times—"as Konstantin Alexandrovich said"—in the discussion that followed. < . . . > Frida is jubilant.[278]

Margarita Aliger came to see me and brought *Literaturnaia Moskva* as a gift. Kolya's story is wonderful (just a wee bit long in the middle): it's a very solid sketch with scant colors applied just so and an excellent plot; only the title, "The Vagabond," is wrong. The jewel in the crown is Zabolotsky's verse: "The Old Actress" is a marvel of emotion and technique. Pogodin's play is well conceived, but doesn't quite come off: it is the story of two informers, Klara and O., both of whom turn out to be nice people. Olesha's jottings are pretentious. Tsvetaeva is sometimes very good, sometimes frightfully bad. Generally speaking, the volume wants editing: there are no rigorous selection criteria. < . . . > The most intelligent article in *Literaturnaia Moskva* is Alexander Kron's about theater: it is caustic and full of incontrovertible syllogisms.[279] Olesha's flimsy, feeble, lame, pretentious article seems even more pitiful in comparison.

Have been reading Shaw's *Widowers' Houses*, etc.—cold products of the mind without a whit of inspiration or life to them. And so I've made it all the way to . . .

1957

➤-➤-➤-➤-➤-➤-➤-➤

which I never thought I'd live to see. I spent all last year on idiotic chores, wasted two months editing Conan Doyle, one month translating *Tom Sawyer*. Why? What for? When there was no time left for Blok, Sleptsov, or memoirs. Idiot. Assassin. [. . .]

278. Reference to Frida Vigdorova, a writer who later played a major role in defending Joseph Brodsky.

279. Alexander Kron, "Zapiski pisatelia," *Literaturnaia Moskva*, 2 (Moscow, 1956), 789–90.

4 January.

I'm disconsolate, sick to my stomach. I've made an irreparable mistake and it tormented me all night. Yesterday I went to Goslit, to the production department, and asked when they thought the third volume of *Literaturnaia Moskva* would be coming out. March, perhaps? Roars of laughter. "Not a chance! Absolutely not! May if you're lucky, probably not even then." It made me so furious I raced off like a fool for the office of *Moskva* and said, "Take my Chekhov. I refuse to let *Literaturnaia Moskva* have it." Then I went to *Literaturnaia Moskva* and said, "Give me back my Chekhov," and the moment I did so I realized I had committed a vile and treacherous act. I suddenly saw how much I loved Aliger and Kazakevich and, most of all, *Literaturnaia Moskva*, the only *noble* literary organ in these awful, vulgar times. It's too late now, but I shall never forgive myself for handling my Chekhov in so un-Chekhovian a manner. [. . .]

6 January.

I have a special way of curing myself of depression and dismay: I invite a group of children and spend five, six, seven hours with them. To take my mind off the Chekhov affair, I invited Seryozha, Varya (Fedin's grand-daughter), Ira (Kassil's daughter), and Masha and Vera (Tanya's children) and played various games with them. By seven they had completely worn me out, but my heart was light and I went to bed blissfully calm. Then suddenly I heard someone calling from downstairs, "You've a letter from Margarita Aliger!" and that was the end of my sleep. It was like a stab in the heart. < . . . > This business will take a year off my life at least.

8 January.

Two letters: one from Zoshchenko, the other from Sergeev-Tsensky. Zosh-chenko's is modest and touching: he asks me to show him which stories to remove from the new edition of his book and advise him about certain delicate expressions; Sergeev-Tsensky wants me to help him get a review of his *Valya* into *Komsomol'skaia Pravda*. The determination of the man! Nonagenarian that he is, deaf and practically blind, he still has his hopes and desires.

What an intoxicating writer Trollope is! I am reading his *John Caldigate* and find it so exciting that I have to put it down in the tragic parts: I can't go on, I'm too "involved." Then there is the sure hand with which he draws the characters, his knowledge of life and the very depths of the human soul, and the modesty of it all—you feel he has no idea how brilliant he is. [. . .]

21 February.

Marya Borisovna has been dead for two years. Dear Mashenka! You stood for truth and candor, and I was always so perfidious with you. Even in literature I can't recall your ever giving me the ladylike advice to dissemble or ignore the truth. < . . . >

Lida and Kolya paid me a visit today. Lida has roused the ire of Detgiz with her article "Talking About Work."[280] They call it anti-Party (!?) propaganda. Kolya stood up against Wanda Wasilewska in the Presidium and then had a conversation with her. Wanda says Russians are being persecuted in Warsaw, forced to walk in the roadway, Soviets are being boycotted, and so on. The response to his novel *The Baltic Sky* has been enormous.[281] < . . . >

Marshak is in town. We talked for three hours the day before yesterday and spent two hours together yesterday. < . . . > He is a magician. While here (literally before my eyes), he translated a poem by Yeats and a poem by Galkin (from the Yiddish), both of which were finished products on the first try. True, he repeats himself—he said three times (in different contexts) that Dante was the cock's call to a new poetry, that Russian writers are the supermen of literature, that aesthetics needs to be ethical—but he is bursting with talent. Listening to records of Mozart and Bach at Semyonov's yesterday, he reacted to each new phrase with his entire being. The intensity of every aspect of his spiritual life is amazing. Even though he appears ill—he is constantly taking ephedrine and coughing—his head is unusually clear and ready for work. He had interesting things to say about Fadeev and Tvardovsky yesterday: apparently Tvardovsky wrote

280. "Rabochii razgovor. Zametki o redaktirovanii khudozhestvennoi prozy," *Literaturnaia Moskva*, 2 (Moscow, 1956), 752–79.

281. The novel, published in 1955, deals with the defense of Leningrad during the German army's nine-hundred-day blockade (1941–44). (M.H.H.)

Fadeev a biting letter condemning his metallurgical novel and mocking his recent speeches.[282] Fadeev was very upset. [. . .]

7 March.

< . . . > Lida made one of her feather-ruffling speeches at the plenum for fiction writers the day before yesterday. There was thunderous applause. I'm making what feeble effort I can to do the Wilde piece, while thinking (much more seriously) about my will.

Am still reading Faulkner. I very much like his characteristic style. I've found a sentence in *Light in August* directly relating to the people at the resort here: [They] "had a generally *identical* authoritative air, like a policeman in disguise and not especially caring if the disguise hid the policeman or not." Nearly all of them, the great majority, are terribly alike: they've got prominent cheekbones, thick necks, and tactless, monotone voices, and they're loud, healthy, and capable of watching the same film five times, playing cards eight hours a day, and so on.

But to get back to Faulkner. He is wordy and strains credulity here and there, but he is a marvelous psychologist who registers people's hidden, unconscious acts. Moreover, "there are no culprits" for him: he makes you pity even Christmas, a beast who murders a woman who trusts him implicitly, even Brown, who turns in his friend Christmas for the price on his head. His characters speak the rich language of the people; his every epithet is fresh, striking, to the point; the plot is such that you can't tear yourself away. Yet for all his talent he's a *repugnant* writer, nauseating and turbid. < . . . >

---

282. Reference to Fadeev's novel *Black Metallurgy* (1954). The correspondence between Tvardovsky and Fadeev has not yet been published, but echoes of disagreements between the two occur in Tvardovsky's notebook: "I thought of looking up Fadeev's last letter to me . . . , but changed my mind: it's all in the past now. The break announced in the letter occurred much earlier, . . . and much as I pity him in purely human terms, I have nothing to reproach myself for. How could I ring him up and seek a clarification after a letter saying 'I break off all relations with you'? Of course, had I been able to anticipate his end, I'd have done anything to save him, but it wouldn't have been a spontaneous moral impulse" (*Znamia* 7 [1989]: 81–82).

21 March.

< . . . > Called on Fedin yesterday. He waxed enthusiastic over the story "Levers" in *Literaturnaia Moskva.*[283] "What happens in 'Levers' is happening all over the country," he said. "At the Writers' Union too. No one ranted and raved more than Shaginyan during the discussion of my subversive book, *Gorky in Our Midst.* Her speech was all thunder. Then in the lobby she told me what a splendid book it was. If that's not 'leverage,' what is?" [. . .]

27 May.

My life is full of events I haven't registered in my diary. Several dozen of my diaries having disappeared, I've lost my taste for the enterprise. The main event was the party on 30 March for my seventy-fifth birthday!

> That is quite a chunk of time,
> And although I still love living,
> When I think of seventy-five,
> It is not without misgiving.

I was amazed how nice and kind people were at the party and at the quantity and quality of the greetings. Who was congratulating me—me!—but the University, the Gorky Institute, the Academy of Sciences, and *Krokodil* and *Znamia* and *Novyi mir* and Pushkin House and hundreds of orphanages, schools, kindergartens. I felt like an imposter with no right to their love. I realized of course that it was more of a funeral, but a funeral de luxe, first-class. The Writers' Union people thought I'd get the third-class treatment (that was meet and fitting), but there were *so* many people (at Writers House), *so* many delegations, and speeches by *such* dignitaries (Fedin, Leonov, Obraztsov, Vsevolod Ivanov, and so on) that it turned out to be first-class. Ambitious corpse that I was, I felt honored and happy.

---

283. The story, by Alexander Yashin, caused a considerable stir. As Venyamin Kaverin argues in his *Epilogue* (1989), Yashin was the first writer to reveal one of the most characteristic phenomena of Soviet society: the "double life." "Levers" is an account of a meeting of village Party activists. Before the gavel sounds, the assembled chat in a sensible and realistic fashion about the difficulties confronting them. No sooner is the meeting called to order, however, than the likable and sober peasants turn into "Party levers," that is, automatons mouthing meaningless clichés with no bearing on the realities of kolkhoz life. (V.E.)

The second event was receiving the Order of Lenin in the Kremlin from Khrushchev. Voroshilov is a dear soul, not at all as I'd pictured him. He is worldly and very quick on the uptake, witty, brilliant in a way. Khrushchev had the following to say about me: "At last I meet the villain who has tormented me so. The times I've had to read you to my grand-children!" I responded to their congratulations with a silly speech that showed them immediately what an idiot I am.

The third event was an outdoor banquet hosted by the government for writers, artists, and composers. It was held at a government dacha in a nature preserve. Khrushchev gave a four-and-a-half-hour speech. [. . .]

30 July.

Called on Kazakevich, who was as witty and caustic as ever. We talked about Fedin and his plenum speech. Fedin had spoken to me about *Litera-turnaia Moskva* with great sympathy, saying that the only merit of the Moscow branch of the Writers' Union—which was under his leadership— was that it had published two volumes of *Literaturnaia Moskva,* and here he was at the plenum coming down on it, claiming that he had warned Kazakevich, admonished him, but to no avail, etc. I was inclined to see a kind of nobility in it (perhaps he was trying to divert heavier artillery from *Literaturnaia Moskva*), but Kazakevich called it animal fear: immediately after delivering his "disgraceful" speech, Fedin claimed in a paroxysm of repentance that he would "break all ties with the Union" and "leave," that he had been "forced into it." He was on the brink of tears. It wasn't until later that he came up with the idea that by repudiating *Literaturnaia Moskva,* Aliger, and Kazakevich he had saved them, rescued them. Then his conscience was clear. "But what it all boils down to," says Kazakevich, "is that he's been writing badly, he's lost the knack, he's at sea and was trying to put them off the scent." And he told the following joke:

A madman thought he was a grain of corn. He was cured. Then one day he happened upon a chicken, lost his composure, and ran to hide. When a friend ran after him and said, "You know you're not a grain of corn," he replied, "*I* know, but does the chicken?"

Fedin knows *Literaturnaia Moskva* is good, but do the authorities? [. . .]

He has the following to say about the third volume of *Literaturnaia*

Moskva: "We'll take only the strongest artistic works. We've got a wonderful Paustovsky and a marvelous Tendryakov—a magnificent novella. We won't have any criticism: miscellanies don't necessarily include criticism."

He is energetic, very smart, well-educated, sincere.

"I don't know what to do when I see Fedin next. Refusing to shake hands would be silly."

We paid a sick visit to Kaverin. He's lost weight and complains of headaches. It's an inflammation of the brain membranes, a disease with a Greco-Latin name. He's written a poem about it, cleverly incorporating the accusations he's suffered at the hands of the critics into its symptoms. < . . . >

23 July.

Who is Filatov? I've never seen him. All I know is that he's the head of the Interdistrict Office of the Forestry Trade Organization and that his name and patronymic are Alexander Konstantinovich. About a week ago I sent him a handwritten note requesting that I be allotted a "Finnish hut" for my children's library.

Apparently I can indulge in my dreams: they are about to come true. By autumn I should have a spacious construction behind the garage. It will not only house books but have a reading room as well; it will be a children's book center. As soon as the walls start going up, I'll send out a notice to all the writers—Kassil, Marshak, Barto, Mikhalkov—asking them to send me their pictures so the children can see what the writers whose books they're reading look like.

24 July.

< . . . > I wonder why the Litfond considers me its enemy. You'd think they'd have every reason to help a writer who has been actively working with worker and collective farm children for three years, but Lyashkevich makes a show of turning his back on what I've been doing and leaves me struggling to keep my head above water.

25 July.

< . . . > Yesterday the children and I gathered brushwood for a bonfire. A storm had left many broken branches in its wake.

Today is a red-letter day: I sent Klara and P. G. Medvedev to the Odintsovo warehouse to look for huts. While they were there, Filatov phoned the manager, and he gave us permission to come tomorrow and pay for the hut. The hut itself costs 20,500 rubles, but various extras add five thousand to the price.

An article in *Sovetskaia kul'tura* says the Litfond is helping me to build the library. Nonsense! The Litfond has done nothing so far but stand in my way and hold things up. < . . . >

26 *July*.

Medvedev and I went to the warehouse to pay for the hut (taking along seven-year-old Zinochka, the housekeeper's daughter). Ivan Sergeevich Boldyrev flatly refused the money: "I've had no word from Filatov. Filatov spoke to the chief bookkeeper, and he is at the bank."

I was furious, but couldn't do anything about it, because Ivan Sergeevich was called to the phone and yelled at somebody for at least half an hour. < . . . > Then Yelizaveta Samsonovna, Filatov's deputy, took pity on me: she quickly processed the 20,500 rubles and guided me around the warehouse courtyard, an ungodly mess of barrels, vats, and boxes lying out in the open. Seeing the walls of my future library, I nearly wept for joy. There are plenty of walls, the "hut" being actually twice as big as I expected, but the work that remains to be done! The foundation will call for five and a half thousand bricks, and the Litfond has refused to give me even two thousand. Where can I turn? Whom can I importune? Where can I find the masons? How can I protect the parts of the hut delivered to me from the rain? They're out to line their pockets at the warehouse, the lot of them, starting with the gatekeeper and the storeman. < . . . >

29 *July*.

The "hut" is now on my land. Medvedev has deposited a number of boards, doors, ceilings, walls, and roof tiles under the trees, and I am so thrilled with what is going to be my library building that I gave the men twice as much as they asked for. Some library regulars—ten-, eleven- and twelve-year-old children—came and helped the men lay a tarpaulin over the wood.

Yesterday I went to see Lidin in the best of moods, and suddenly I was informed that although the Litfond would consider my petition (petition!)

to build a library on rented land it would in all likelihood reject it, since renters have no right to build anything on the land they rent. Oh no! What do I do now?

30 July.

The Litfond officials are against the library. They couldn't care less that more than seventy children used it yesterday. I took Leonov to the site yesterday. He looked over the building material and pronounced it "junk," which is true of course: compared with its German and Finnish counterparts our hut is knobbly, catch-as-catch-can, thrown together with no respect whatever for the job at hand, a boorish, careless piece of work. And what am I building the library for if not to put an end to such disgraceful, dishonest workmanship. I didn't invite him for his opinion of the building material, of course; I wanted him to stand up for my right to build the library. But he hedged, saying, "I'm on holiday. I'll talk to Surkov. Yes, Surkov," and left.

< . . . >

3 August.

I have decided to deliver the following note to the Litfond:

> Two years ago I opened a small children's library on the ground floor of my Peredelkino dacha. It now serves approximately four hundred children, most of whom are the offspring of collective farmers, workers, and officials, and receives an average of between forty and fifty children daily. It is registered in both Moscow and Kuntsevo and enjoys the support of the Ministry of Culture and the Kuntsevo District Party Committee. The library keeps a strict record of its users and the books they check out. It is run by a librarian with twenty years of experience. Inasmuch as the library fills a burning need among the local inhabitants, I have decided to set aside sixty thousand rubles of my savings for the construction of a library building on Litfond property and present it as a gift to the state.
>
> After many ordeals I managed to obtain a three-story hut in Odintsovo and have had it moved to my land. I naively promised the children that they would have their own club there in two or three weeks. I was naturally certain that the Litfond would lend its enthusiastic support to the project. But as soon as it learned of the modest undertaking, it started putting the most bureaucratic of spokes in my wheel.

Its tactics are the following: "We welcome your noble initiative from the bottom of our hearts, but ask you to hold off until we send a committee and think things over."

I awaited the committee with great trepidation, but of course it failed to show up on the appointed day.

Then I was told: "We would be only too glad to give you permission, but you need permission from the Kuntsevo District Soviet."

When I went to the Kuntsevo District Soviet, they told me, "We would be only too glad to give you permission, but you need permission from the Litfond."

So I rang up the Litfond, and they told me, "Comrade Lyashkevich will come and see you today. He will explain everything."

So I waited all day for Comrade Lyashkevich, and of course he never came.

Meanwhile parts of the hut are warping in the rain, and I can't look the children in the eye. Every day I tell the workers I have hired to come back the next day. I have no idea whether I should buy bricks for the foundation or shut up shop and close the library for good.

This has been going on for three weeks now, and if it keeps up for even three more days I shall fall ill and end up in a hospital bed. The main problem is that the Litfond refuses to say either yes or no. Meanwhile the building season is coming to an end, and the hut will rot in the rain once and for all.

Kornei Chukovsky

< . . . >

22 *August.*

< . . . > The Litfond has refused to provide a single lamppost. < . . . >

Klara Izrailevna brought me today's *Literaturnaia gazeta* with an article entitled "Bonfire at Chukovsky's." I wrote a letter to Druzin asking him not to publish sketches about my private life, especially about the library. People will say I am doing it for purposes of self-aggrandizement.

< . . . >

12 *November.*

Tvardovsky called at the house today with Kazakevich. I had the feeling I was in the presence of Nekrasov. I was as timid as a schoolboy. His *Muravia* and *Tyorkin* mean a great deal to me, and it felt strange having a POET like him sitting and talking to me in Peredelkino like an ordinary person.[284] I read him part of my Marshak article or, rather, bumbled my way through it, and was thrilled when he praised it. He couldn't have been nicer: he brought me the two-volume edition of his works and talked openly about many things. On Ehrenburg, for instance: "He does terrible translations of French poets, and when I read that drivel I lose confidence in his novels to say nothing of his poetry. You can always tell a man by his verse. A doctor who came to examine me—I had a serious sprain—said to me after writing out the prescription, 'I'm glad to meet you. I write poetry too.' Well, he came out with the most God-awful rubbish that I couldn't help wondering how an idiot like that could cure anybody, and suddenly I realized he was as disastrous a doctor as he was a poet."

On children's literature: "It has flourished and all that, but it's an urban literature. The countryside still lacks its children's poet."

On Mayakovsky: "They've hushed up Lenin's views on *150,000,000* and trumpeted his praise of 'To Bureaucrats with Endless Meetings.' For twenty-five years now we've been *forced* to love Mayakovsky. You could be sent to jail for being less than enthusiastic about him. Yes, that's right. I have a friend who was arrested because he didn't consider him the greatest poet . . ." < . . . >

2 December.

< . . . > Today is Marshak's seventieth birthday. I am giving a speech. That is as Tvardovsky wished and as Marshak wishes as well. Yesterday I had the feeling both Alyansky and Konashevich thought that I was taking part in the festivities for tactical reasons, that I was insincere. For some reason they refuse to believe that despite his colossal faults I love his talent and his love of poetry, his humor, and everything he has done for children, and have nothing whatever to say about the nasty tricks he played on me. He is a writer through and through. There is nothing else to him. But that is quite a bit, after all. < . . . >

---

284. Like Nekrasov, Tvardovsky was very much the civic poet, and both *The Land of Muravia,* in which the hero refuses to join a collective farm, and *Vasily Tyorkin,* which depicts a footsoldier's view of the Second World War, reflect his concern for the common man. (M.H.H.)

3 December.

Tvardovsky has really pulled a fast one on me. First he prevails upon me to give a twenty- to twenty-five-minute talk about Marshak, and I spend two weeks studying Burns and Blake and Shakespeare's sonnets; then he goes on such a bender that he doesn't even show up at the celebration (which took place yesterday) and Surkov takes over and tells me I have no more than eight minutes. I made a disgusting hash of it and took to my heels in disgrace, certain of failure. But today I had calls from Paperny, Aliger, and Marshak himself complimenting me on a brilliant talk. I liked Nazim Hikmet best: he appeared for a second like a ray of the sun and said ten clever words. < . . . >

7 December.

< . . . > How I hate our writers' get-togethers. People never talk about what is really on their minds, what really matters to them. They are feasts in a time of plague—all laughter and jokes, anything to fend off serious talk.

27 December.

Well, Kornei, dear friend, the last year of your life may be on its way, so be decent this year at least.

Last year I betrayed myself over and over: I retranslated *Tom Sawyer,* edited Sleptsov, and, heaven knows why, wrote a long article—unnecessary, dull, and still unpublished—about Marshak. My *Books and People* is causing trouble: the editors keep picking at it. My editor, Sofya Petrovna Krasnova, came to see me the other day and lit into me: you're too lovey-dovey with Bakunin, too frivolous with Tolstoy, your Turgenev is too rueful. I've submitted my memoirs to Sovetskii pisatel'. I want to call it *Yes, It Was Was Was* or just *How It Was.* I *should* write what I remember about Alexei Tolstoy and Korolenko, but what I *will* write, damn it, is what I think about Chekhov, because that's what I promised Marya Borisovna on her death bed.

[. . .] The more meetings we have, the worse we write. < . . . >

29 December.

[. . .] Although I did everything possible to prevent it, I've been elected to the Board of the Moscow Section of the Writers' Union. Heaven knows why. The details are being announced today with great fanfare, as if it had anything to do with literature. < . . . >

30 December.

Called on dear Fedin. He's exhausted and depressed. He says the work he's been doing for the Writers' Union has completely done him in. He spent an hour and a half trying to convince Furtseva he can't stay on as head of the Moscow Section because he's ill, burnt out, etc. < . . . >

1958

2 January.

< . . . > Started writing about Bryusov and gave up. Ditto Alexei Tolstoy. Ditto Oscar Wilde. I need to be doing Chekhov, Chekhov, and more Chekhov. I began going through his notebooks yesterday. < . . . >

14 January.

Have been walking a lot with Fedin. He's relaxed a bit since the conference, though he still looks peaked. [. . .]

"I've been having a very interesting correspondence with Pasternak lately," he told me. "I've told the authorities not to sic me on him. I won't do it." He's seen the Italian edition of Boris Leonidovich's novel with a picture and a statement to the effect that the book was published without his consent. [. . .]

1 February.

Pasternak is ill. He cannot excrete the urine in his bladder and needs a catheter. None of us has a driver today—not Kaverin or Vsevolod Ivanov or I. Tamara Vladimirovna phoned me, and I phoned the All-Union Central Trade Union Council, but there was nobody there because it was Saturday. Our only hope is for Kolya to come and drive me there to fetch a doctor. Poor Boris Leonidovich! Last year's malady has returned. Tamara Vladimirovna phoned Lidia Nikolaevna Kaverina in town, and she will buy the catheter, but where can we find a doctor? We'll just have to try the Trade Union Council.

I went to see Pasternak. He had been given a shot of pantopone and was sleeping. Zinaida Nikolaevna is beside herself. No help appears to be forthcoming. She has asked us to concentrate on writing a letter to the government about having Boris Leonidovich hospitalized. Lidia Nikolaevna has brought the catheter, and a nurse (Lidia Timofeevna) will do the operation. I thought of phoning an acquaintance, Mikoyan's secretary, and he promised to phone someone at the Department of Health. Then Kazakevich's wife rang and suggested we have an ambulance sent to the Department of Health. But an ambulance from the Department of Health is not allowed to leave the city. So a famous poet's life is in danger, and no help is forthcoming.

Last year the Writers' Union said straight out: "Pasternak is unworthy of a bed in the Kremlin Hospital." And Zinaida Nikolaevna says, "Pasternak has forbidden us to ask the Writers' Union for anything."

3 February.

Called on Pasternak. He is exhausted, but in good spirits. There is a book by Henry James beside him. He was happy to see me ("I've been reading you and listening to you speak on the radio about Chekhov . . . and Nekrasov. You mean so much to me . . . so much . . ."), and all at once he seized my hand and kissed it. There was terror in his eyes. "I can feel the pain coming back. It makes me think how good it would be to . . ." (He didn't pronounce the word "die.") "I've done everything I meant to in my life. It would be so good."

The whole visit lasted three minutes. Epshtein said he didn't need an operation (for the time being, at least). The main thing is the nerve in the backbone. The neurologist is coming tomorrow.

Called on Fedin. He is proofreading his correspondence with Gorky (for Zilbershtein). "How strange to read your own letters years after the fact." [. . .]

We went out for a stroll, and he talked about the Germans. A number of leading lights in their Writers' Union are coming out with penitential statements meant to distance themselves from their liberal fervor ("We misunderstood the events in Hungary"). In other words, they're going through the same thing we are.

With Pasternak yesterday. His treatment has been all wrong. The doctors who came (Rappoport and one more—Landa?) told Zinaida Nikolaevna that the mustard baths she'd been giving him only aggravated his condition. ("He could have died from them.") Enemas were also counter-indicated. Not a single blood or urine analysis has been done yet. He has no nurse. < . . . > Today and tomorrow I'll look into hospital possibilities. The Kremlin Hospital is out of the question. He needs a private room, and with the authorities still fulminating against him he'll never get one. It's awful. A nobody like Yegolin, a lickspittle scorned by one and all, can command luxurious treatment at the drop of a hat, while Pasternak lies there lacking the most basic care.

7 February.

Couldn't get to sleep yesterday even with nembutal, so I started working on the review of that awful Yegolin at three. At twelve I went into town to look for a hospital for Pasternak. Building Seven of the Botkin was packed—there were patients in the halls—and at the Kremlin Hospital you had to wait your turn. I tried three times to see Mikhail Fyodorovich Vlasov at the Council of Ministers of the Russian Republic. They wouldn't let me in because I had no pass, but I did talk to him on the phone. < . . . > He gave me to believe there was little hope. But when I got home, what did I hear but that he had phoned to say he had found a place in the Central Committee clinic, the best in Moscow. Zhenya will take Tamara Ivanovna into town tomorrow to fetch the necessary papers. I was overjoyed and ran to Pasternak with the news. He now (at last!) has a nurse. He is running a fever. The results of the blood analysis are very bad. A doctor came to see him yesterday. Vovsi's assistant. She's afraid it's cancer (judging by the blood analysis). All my joy went up in smoke. He is restless, feverish. He asked me all about the children's library. Zinaida Nikolaevna can't stop talking about the expenses involved and was not happy to see the nurse: more expenses. < . . . >

8 February.

Yesterday Tamara Vladimirovna (driven by Zhenya in my car) went to the Ministry of Health of the Russian Republic (Vadkovsky Lane 18/20, Butyrki District) to fetch the hospital documents from an official by the name of Nadezhda Vasilyevna Tikhomirova. From there she went to the Central Committee Hospital to see Boris Leonidovich's room and the lay of the land in general. She didn't like what she saw: the head of the hospital is a boor, there's no private room free, he'll be in urology. But things will work themselves out. It's a good thing Vovsi and Epshtein are there. Zhenya came back at three and gave Boris Leonidovich a full report. He is willing to go anywhere—the illness has worn him down—and he thanked me and Tamara Vladimirovna. He took my advice and signed a copy of his *Faust* for Vlasov, expressing gratitude for everything he had done. Zinaida Nikolaevna pulled his fur hat over his head and put on his fur coat. Meanwhile some workers had cleared the snow from the path to the front door. They then carried him to the car on a stretcher. He blew us kisses on the way.

17 February.

The last ten days have been days of insanity, misery, and despair. Bonetsky, whom I like very much, has given me Yegolin's *Nekrasov* manuscript to review. It is full of stupidities, audacities, and lies. I've also read through Yegolin's entire oeuvre. It's the work of a petty crook, a thick-headed idiot, and a repulsive nit of a careerist. Though ill and suffering from acute insomnia, I worked on the review for ten to twelve hours a day, but the more I wrote the more I realized how impotent I was: the combination of villain and vulgarian is too much for me. < . . . >

The library is driving me to despair. I put my heart and soul into it, cared for it like a toy, contributed an enormous amount of money to it when I had little enough for myself—but the children seem crass, dim, dull, no better than their parents. < . . . >

28 February.

I'm idling away the days, though I've so much to do I can't make time for the most urgent, pressing letters. I keep poring over my Chekhov materials and going through old notes, but have nothing *new* to say about him. There's been so much silly claptrap published, childlike babble, primer-level platitudes. The thing to do now is to talk about his *complexity*, and I curse my impotence. < . . . >

What I should really do is forget about literature and devote all my time to children—reading to them, talking to them, bringing them out, challenging them to lead a life of dignity. Without that, lending books is pointless. < . . . >

16 March.

Didn't sleep all night. Went downstairs at half past six. My great-grandson was screaming his head off and keeping Katya and Tata up. I took him upstairs to give them a chance to doze a bit, and the moment we were alone together it was as if I had a band of brigands on my hands. My first defense was a box of matches: I lighted one after the other, but the effect soon wore off. Then I switched to the basket under the table, chasing it around the room with the keys to the chest of drawers in it. That staved off my downfall for two or three minutes, but the minutes passed and I resorted to a nose game, pressing a finger to my nose and mooing like an idiot each time. Boba enjoyed it: a great investigator of causes and effects, he was intrigued by the connection between finger and sound. He pressed his own dirty fingers to my poor nose some fifty times, thinking he had discovered a great law of nature. He was confirmed in his belief when I started tweaking his nose and making squeaky noises. But when the nose game too ran its course, Boba climbed up on the sofa and began pulling pictures off the wall, calling each one "pa-pa." (He was recently shown a picture of his father and told it was papa, so he logically concluded that all pictures are called papa.) After every one of the pictures was laid out on the floor, I gained a minute and a half of respite by burning some paper in the stove. Then I tried the matches, the nose, and the keys again, but in vain: he demanded new victims. I won him over with Klyuchevsky's *History*, letting him tear out four pages about the eccentricities of Ivan the Terrible. And when they had been duly destroyed and I could see no other source of deliverance, the keys came to the rescue after all: he pulled them out of the keyhole in the chest of drawers and then tried to put them back in. That investigation into the nature of things (*de rerum natura*) engaged him for approximately four minutes, after which his mouth suddenly turned down at the corners and he ran to the door screaming, "Mama!" Completely undone, I tried the earlier distractions yet again, but it wasn't until I found some beads of Katya's under my desk and wound them round a stick of Kolya's that he calmed down. It was the first morning in years when I felt free from my papers, my desk, my odious articles, and my literary impotence. < . . . >

Have been thinking a lot about Gorky. (His anniversary is coming up.) There were two years in my life when I saw him daily, and it was only natural that I wished to document for posterity everything he said. I would carry a small notebook with me and tried to record his every word. For a long time he failed to notice my perfidy, but one day he had a group of writers to his house, myself included, and I decided to try something new: I pinned a sheet of paper to Lunts's back and asked him to sit in front of me while Gorky spoke, as I would then be able to take notes easily. But Gorky unexpectedly placed us on the sofa and Lunts ended up next to me. Taking notes was anything but easy, but I did what I could. Noticing my outlandish posture, Gorky said, "What are you up to, *monsieur?*" I felt like a schoolboy caught cheating. He was furious. "I'm not so bad a writer myself," he said.

< . . . >

30 March.

The "nobility" gathered last night at Gorky's Nikitinskaya Street house < . . . >, including Zoshchenko, who was the reason I went. The dining room had three long tables and two short ones (at an angle) of well-dressed, well-fed, prize-winning members of the cream of Moscow society and their wives and daughters—and Zoshchenko with his burnt-out eyes, his martyred look, cut off from the world, crushed. There was nothing left of his former looks. He had once been a handsome melancholic, spoiled by fame and the ladies, generously endowed with lyrical Ukrainian humor, a man with a great fate ahead of him. I recall him with two other humorists, Zhenya Shvarts and Yury Tynyanov, and a group of young people in the House of the Arts, the walls resounding with laughter, when Zoshchenko was the unrivaled master of satire and humor and all eyes flashed smiles wherever he appeared.

Now he's a corpse in a coffin. It's even strange to hear him speak, and when he does it is dull and drawn out, in never-ending sentences. It's as if a talking device had been implanted in a cadaver. After a minute or so you can't stand it, you feel like running away or at least putting your hands over your ears. Witness the sad lines he wrote for *Chukokkala:*

> My genius, faded now like leaves in autumn,
> Is like my fantasy shorn of its former wings.

Because he used the old orthography, I said to him, "I remember you in the good old days."

"Yes those were the days. I was all jokes and pranks then. But what I write now is much nastier. Oh, the way I write now!"

And I could see in his eyes that he wasn't writing, that he couldn't write.

Yekaterina Pavlovna sat me to her right, in the place of honor, and I managed to have Zoshchenko seated to her left. He launched into a long explanation of Gorky's importance, citing a Chekhov letter ("and who was more honest than Chekhov"), but citing the same passage twice. < . . . > And on 3 April he is supposed to give a talk at the Gorky celebration.[285] What will he talk about? If he comes out with clichés like that, he'll only do himself harm and speed his demise. I asked him what he was planning to say. He said, "Oh, I don't know," and then, a little while later, "I'd best say nothing at all. I've been stigmatized, haven't I? I'm an outcast." < . . . >

Zoshchenko with gray, straggly hair, sunken temples, and those burnt-out eyes! An all too familiar Russian picture: talent smothered and killed. Polezhaev, Nikolai Polevoy, Ryleev, Mikhail Mikhailov, Yesenin, Mandelshtam, Stenich, Babel, Mirsky, Tsvetaeva, Mitya Bronshtein, Kvitko, Bruno Yasensky—crushed by the same boot one and all.[286]

31 March.

< . . . > Tomorrow, 1 April, the Village Soviet is at last taking over financial responsibility for the library. Or so I've been advised by phone. Which means that after handing it over to the District Soviet I kept it going at my own expense for six months.

---

285. The occasion was the ninetieth anniversary of Gorky's birth. (M.H.H.)
286. The first four suffered the wrath of the tsarist regime, the rest of the Soviet regime. (M.H.H.)

1 April.

I am seventy-six. **How stale and unprofitable.** I've never thought of myself as talented and despise everything I write, but looking back on it now I see a certain human element at work. Still, I've done nothing, nothing at all with my potential. < . . . >

Guests: Kaverin, Frida, Tess, Natasha Trenyova, Lida, Lyusha, Nika, Sergei Nikolaevich (the driver), Lyudmila Tolstaya, Nadezhda Peshkova, Lyovik, Hidas, Zoshchenko, and Margarita Aliger. Zoshchenko has really got me down. Clearly he must not give a talk at the Gorky celebration: he could ruin what little of his life remains to him. [. . .]

19 April.

< . . . > Pasternak is looking calmer. He brought up my "good deed" again. We talked about Henry James, Leonid Martynov, and Paustovsky. "Whenever I'm hospitalized," he said, "I think I can read only Chekhov. But this time I said to myself, 'Why not take Kuprin? With the Paustovsky foreword. And how weak, pretentious, and empty I found it.' " < . . . >

22 April.

Have been unable to write, read, or work for two days now. Had a visit from Tamara Ivanova yesterday. She has thrombophlebitis—she got it in Karlovy Vary and is just back—but nonetheless made it up the stairs to see me. Sholokhov was in Karlovy Vary too. She was disgusted with him: he is arrogant and stupid, he has no interest in culture, he's bored to death and won't even go to the pictures. He was there with his wife and family. He refused to bend his back at the spring, waiting for his wife to draw the water and hand it to him. [. . .]

I also had visits from the Pasternaks, Andronikov, and—later—Lida. Pasternak cuts a tragic figure: twisted lips, tieless. He told us he'd received a letter in German from Vilnius that said, "When you hear the hired assassins from the Voice of America praise your novel, you ought to burn with shame." (I haven't read *Doctor Zhivago*—all the way through, that is.) < . . . > But he also looks the genius: raw nerves, misfortune, fatality. He talked about Rabindranath Tagore. Someone has written from India asking what he thinks about him. Well, he can't stand him: he lacks the "solidity" Pasternak considers the essence of art. He borrowed Faulkner's *Light in August* from me. He went into town for the first time today since coming home. He bought gifts for the nurses and doctors.

29 April.

Am at the Kremlin's branch hospital outside Moscow. My room is luxurious, though not comfortable. I've made the acquaintance of Nikolai Nikolaevich Kún, the son of Béla Kún and brother of Ágnes. Fyodor Gladkov is in the room next door. He has tried several times to visit me, but I haven't been able to see him. I was horrified when I dropped in on him just now. The ravages of his disease have made him unrecognizable. I last saw him at the Second Congress of Writers, when he came out against Sholokhov. He claims it was then his illness began. He hadn't prepared to say anything at the Congress, he claims, but Suslov phoned him and said, "You must stand up to Sholokhov." So he did. And the next morning he received a call telling him: "We are satisfied with what you said and want you to run the closing meeting."

"And give a formal speech?"

"Yes, definitely."

That's what did him in, he claims. He received dozens of anonymous hate letters after coming out against Sholokhov. "If you are against Sholokhov, you are for the Yids and we will destroy you!"

He trembled all over as he spoke, the tears flowing down his cheeks. He lay there prostrate, even unto death.

"After the Congress I lost all desire (and ability) to write. To hell with it, I said. Look at the man in the street. People used to have principles, not the highest maybe, but still. Now all they do is drink, debauch, and steal. As for the authorities . . ." [. . .]

23 May.

I haven't slept for four nights now. I'm ashamed to show my face I look so sleepy and disheveled, so pitiful. I keep trying to write, but nothing comes of it. I've completely lost the habit. What can I do? I sometimes think it would be better to die. I can't conceive of life without writing. Looking back, I think how lucky I've been to have known inspiration so often, when your hand writes by itself, as if taking dictation, and all you do is rush to get the words down on paper. Even if the result is nothing more than "The Fly" or an article about Verbitskaya, those are the happiest times a person can experience.

Am reading the Blok-Bely correspondence. Bely is vain, fussy, hysterical, pretentious, and unruly; Blok is calm and radiant, though he too has his turbid moments, moments when he falters and goes limp. < . . . >

14 June.

< . . . > Dear Kassil has shown up out of the blue and told me Pasternak would be reading his poetry and autobiography tomorrow at the Writers House, which is inhabited not only by respected translators and literary critics but also by a good deal of riff-raff, "who will turn the reading into a riot—just what Surkov wants."

I rushed out to warn Pasternak, repeating to myself the lines from his hospital poem:

> All at once it was clear from the questions
> Of the nurse who kept shaking her head
> There was little hope left now: in essence
> He'd be leaving the hospital dead.

He was out for a walk, and he takes two-hour walks. I couldn't wait all that time. Zinaida Nikolaevna is against the reading too. She asked me to talk him out of it. We agreed that he would come and see me when he got back. It would be crazy for him to give a reading at this juncture. But how wonderful the poems are! How I relish "August," "Hospital," and "Snow."

Have just finished D. W. Winnicott's *The Child and the Outside World,* which came out in England in 1957. It's utter nonsense with a large dollop of psychoanalysis. *The Child and Sex* is an exercise in absurdistics. It has passages that read like Kuzma Prutkov. < . . . >

9 September.

My relationship with Pasternak is an awkward one: I love some of his poems, but do not care for certain translations or for his novel *Doctor Zhivago,* though I know only the first part and read it quite some time ago. He talks to me as if I had unreserved praise for everything he has written, and out of some sort of misguided courtesy I don't tell him where I stand. I adore his "Christmas Star," his "Hospital," "August," "To Women,"[287] and several more—they bring tears to my eyes—and I am very fond of him: he's a poet to the marrow of his bones—tempestuous, sincere, complex.

< . . . >

27 October.

The Pasternak affair is going to cost me three years of my life. I do so want to help him. I proposed that we go and see Furtseva together and that he tell her everything. Calmly, openly. He could say how upset he was by the articles being published about him by people with anti-Soviet views, but that he believed (and believe it he does) he was awarded the prize for his *entire* literary career. He could say he had been victimized by a group of political racketeers who published the novel against his will.

The following was written to be shown to the authorities.

[Added later in a different color ink.]

Here is what happened. My secretary, Klara Lozovskaya, arrived at eleven and, jumping for joy, informed me that Pasternak had been awarded the prize and been congratulated by Mikhailov, the Minister of Culture. Certain as I was that the Soviet government had nothing against the prize and unaware that *Doctor Zhivago* contained attacks on the Soviet system, I grabbed Lyusha and ran to congratulate him. He was happy, thrilled with his conquest, and told us that Vsevolod Ivanov had come to congratulate him the night before. I threw my arms around him and smothered him with kisses. It turned out to be his wife's birthday. I raised my glass to her. It was only then that I noticed the three photographers, two foreign and one Russian. The Russian was from the Ministry of Foreign Affairs and took a great many pictures. Also present was the wife of Titsian Tabidze, who had come from Tbilisi to enlist Boris Leonidovich's aid in bringing out a Russian edition of her husband's verse and had brought several bottles of marvelous Georgian wine. No one foresaw the imminent catastrophe. Zinaida Nikolaevna and Tabidze were talking over the kind of dress she would wear when accompanying "Borya" to Stockholm to receive the prize.

---

287. "Christmas Star" and "August" belong to the cycle "Poems of Doctor Zhivago." The exact titles of "Hospital" and "To Women" are, respectively, "In the Hospital" (1956) and "Women in Childhood" (1958).

I was very embarrassed at not having read *Doctor Zhivago* or, rather, Pasternak himself read me the draft of Part One on my balcony and I didn't particularly like it: it has some excellent passages, but taken as a whole it is insipid, egocentric, and on a much lower level than his verse. When Zinaida Nikolaevna asked me (a month or two ago) whether I'd read it, I said, "No, I don't read sensational books."

I forgot to say that no sooner had Lyusha and I arrived than Pasternak took us into a small room and told us that Fedin had called on him the day before (or was it that day?) and said, "I'm not going to congratulate you, because Polikarpov is at my place and he's demanding that you renounce the prize." To which Pasternak responded, "Under no circumstances."

We laughed. I thought it was a misunderstanding of some sort. After all, he was awarded the prize not only for *Zhivago* but also for his translations of Shakespeare, Schiller, Petőfi, and Goethe, for the prodigious labor of a lifetime, and every Soviet patriot should be grateful to him. < . . . >

Called on Fedin. He was down and out of sorts. "Pasternak will do us great harm with all this. They'll launch a fierce campaign against the intelligentsia now. He told me Polikarpov had gone off furious. "The last time he'd been to see me was when they slammed my Gorky book, *Gorky in Our Midst*." He said he felt sorry for Pasternak. "Polikarpov didn't come of his own accord, you know. They're waiting for Pasternak's answer 'at the top.' They'll make him run the gauntlet. And what can I do? I'm not just the nominal chairman; I really do run the Union. I'm obliged to come out against him. We'll publish the letter from the *Novyi mir* editorial board, the one we sent to Pasternak when we returned the manuscript to him." And so on.

Troubled by all this, I went back to Pasternak an hour or two later. < . . . > I told him there was a campaign being mounted against him and mentioned the *Novyi mir* letter. Most important, I told him about the notice I'd received from the Writers' Union inviting me to attend an emergency meeting tomorrow. Just then a courier arrived with the same notice for him. (I'd also seen the courier at Vsevolod Ivanov's.) His face grew dark; he clutched at his heart and could barely climb the stairs to his room.

There would be no mercy, that was clear. They were out to pillory him. They would trample him to death just as they had Zoshchenko, Mandelshtam, Zabolotsky, Mirsky, and Benedikt Livshits, and I had the crazy idea it was my job to rescue him from the gauntlet. There was only one way of doing so, and that was to go and see Furtseva first thing tomorrow morning and let her know that he himself was upset by the hullabaloo surrounding his name and that *Zhivago* had made its way abroad against his will. He should not steer clear of the Central Committee; he should show he opposed the bandits who were earning hundreds of thousands from his novel to say nothing of the political capital. < . . . > When Boris Leonidovich came downstairs, he rejected my proposal, but consented to write Furtseva a letter explaining his actions. He went back upstairs and ten minutes later (not more) came down with a letter, but one that seemed calculated to worsen the situation: "Higher powers command me to act as I do. I feel that the Nobel Prize recently granted me can only gladden the hearts of all Soviet writers." Having heard the letter, I lost hope. It was all wrong.[288] And suddenly I noticed I was ill: my nerves had got the better of me, and when I left I was nearly in tears. < . . . >

3 December.

For the entire month of November I was down with Pasternakitis. I was forced into writing a letter to explain how I had dared to congratulate a "criminal." Then there was Kolya's speech at the Union.[289] Not a single night did I sleep without a sedative. I wrote a lot of sclerotic nonsense: memoirs of the journal *Signal*. It took forever. I finished a new article about Oscar Wilde, but it too shows me doddering and senescent. The thirteenth edition of *From Two to Five*—shabby and replete with typos—is due out from Sovetskaia Rossiia any day now. I am proofreading *Nekrasov's Craft* and see to my disappointment what a poor book it is. The stamp of Stalinist terror is especially noticeable in the chapters on Pushkin and Gogol. Professor Asmus is staying at the Writers House here. He gave me best regards from Pasternak (whom I haven't seen since 25 October). Boris Leonidovich asked him to tell me he wasn't the least bit angry with Kolya.

4 December.

[. . .] "Pasternak is very generous," says Nilin. "Here in the writers' colony he rewards any favor richly. He gives the woman at the desk five rubles if

---

288. The letter was never sent.

289. The letter could not be located in Chukovsky's archive. "Kolya's speech at the Union" is a reference to Nikolai Chukovsky's public condemnation of Pasternak.

he uses the phone at the Writers House. An old man saw him at it and said, 'It's easy for him to throw his money around. He's sold out to the Americans. Have you read what the papers are saying? His money is all from America.'" < ... >

1959

->->->->->->->->->->

< ... >

7 January.

< ... > Pasternak came to see me today. He looks older, his cheeks are sunken, but no matter: he's full of life. I told him I hadn't slept for three months on account of his situation. "Well, I'm sleeping fine," he responded, and then came right to the point: "I've come to ask for a loan. Five thousand rubles. I have it, but I don't want to take it from Zina. And I don't want her to know."

The money was obviously for Olga Vsevolodovna.[290] I had taken five thousand out of my savings account just yesterday and was happy to give it to him. He started to talk.

"Goslit won't give Olga Vsevolodovna any translation work because of me. They even took back what work she had. I translated a play by Słowacki and handed it in. It was approved by the reviewers, but I've not been paid. I have an idea: supposing I gave Hemingway the power of attorney to collect my foreign royalties. I have no money coming in. But you should see the letters I've been receiving. Streams of greetings, expressions of sympathy . . ." < ... >

According to Tamara Vladimirovna, Pasternak doesn't read the papers. He hasn't read a single word about himself in the Soviet press. All his information comes from Olga Vsevolodovna. < ... >

---

290. Olga Vsevolodovna Ivinskaya was Pasternak's mistress and a prototype of Lara in *Doctor Zhivago*. (V.E.)

27 January.

Pasternak was here. He's worried they'll start up another campaign against him at the Twenty-First Party Congress and make him leave the country. He knows there's been a meeting of the ideological commission.

"Think of me what you will," I said to him, "but for heaven's sake don't put yourself in the position of being me, Pasternak, on one side, and you, the Soviet regime, on the other. Just write a long letter declaring your sympathy for what the Soviet regime is doing for the people and how you love the Seven-Year Plan, and so on."

"No, I can't. I'll tell them I'm only willing to be a translator, and refuse to write original verse."

"What do they care? They don't care two hoots about one or the other. What you need to do is write a detailed account of the circumstances under which you sent the novel abroad and why you now condemn what you did."

"Absolutely not. I'd rather be crucified." < . . . >

26 February.

< . . . > Have just read Agatha Christie's *Hickory Dickory Dock*. The action takes place in a London hostel for students from all over the world, though there are English students there too. As always in her novels they all seem perfectly innocent, simple, and nice at first, but then people start getting murdered and having all sorts of nasty tricks played on them, and for three quarters of the book the reader is forced over and over to look hard at each character and suspect each one of murder, theft, or other acts of villainy. [. . .] Only someone with a profound lack of faith in people could have written such a work. < . . . >

9 March.

< . . . > The nurses are told to act humanely. Many of them resist. They are flighty young things with the most philistine tastes. Kolya has just brought me a volume of Zabolotsky, Lyusha an album of Matisse. I can't for the likes of me imagine any one of my nurses appreciating the art in them. They come from a different planet. Radio, television, and the pictures have supplanted humanistic culture. Nurses are typical of the mass-

produced lower-echelon intelligentsia: they know the history of the Party but not the history of their country; they know Surkov but not Tyutchev. In other words, they're savages, barely human. A lot has been said about the younger generation. Well, I say it will be uncivilized, soulless, and ignorant. A male nurse has just been to see me. He is as deprived as the rest of them. It makes me feel I have no one to write for. < . . . >
< . . . >

23 April.

Have seen Pasternak three or four times in the past month. He is full of life; his eyes are bright; he's been to Tbilisi with Zina and come back looking younger and self-confident. He says he ran into Fedin near his house and shook his hand and why not? Once you start thinking, you can't shake anybody's hand!

"I've come for advice."

"You've never listened to me before. You don't need my advice."

He laughed and said, "True, true."

The reason he'd come was to find out whether I had a book about the peasant reforms of the sixties. He was interested in people like Milyutin, Kavelin, and Zarudny and in the committees they had served on.[291]

He also told me (and swore me to secrecy) that he'd been summoned by the public prosecutor and (he laughed) that proceedings had begun. "But the investigator told me, 'Don't worry. It's a load of rubbish. Things will turn out just fine.'

"And have you heard? I'm involved in another misunderstanding." And a terrible "misunderstanding" it is too. Two or three months ago he gave me a poem about himself as a "hunted beast." I hid it and showed it to nobody, thinking he'd written it on an impulse and it was more "mood piece" than "position piece." And now he's managed to get "The Beast" abroad, where it's been published![292] Only a madman would do such a thing, and I'm not sure there isn't a glint of madness in his eyes. [. . .]

291. In the last years of his life Pasternak worked on a play treating the aftermath of the emancipation of the serfs. Fragments of the work, *The Blind Beauty*, have been published, though it remained unfinished. (M.H.H.)

292. Reference to Pasternak's poem "The Nobel Prize," which appeared on 11 February in the *Daily Mail*. It began with "I'm as lost as a bear in a trap" and triggered further harassment of the poet. He was summoned by the Attorney General R. A. Rudenko, who threatened to open

27 April.

Saw Fedin in the woods on his way somewhere. He told me that since the volume *New Material on Mayakovsky* appeared, the Litnasledstvo series has been having a hard time.[293] Now that everything, including writers' biographies, has to be whitewashed, a book that makes public Mayakovsky's intimate (and, frankly, very bad) letters to Lili Brik and knocks him off his pedestal was bound to be received with animosity. The result was a decree declaring it harmful, a terrible blow to Zilbershtein. Here he masterminds a series of monumental books, devotes thirty years of his life to it, and people forget all about it, insult him, flay him, and trample him underfoot for one false step.

"The Academy of Sciences has set up a committee to look into the matter," said Fedin. "I'm the head of it."

"Wonderful! You can stand up for Zilbershtein."

"You must be a fool! What can I do but endorse the resolution?"

"You mean you'll sign?"

"I've no choice."

Whereupon he started confirming what I'd said about Zilbershtein: what a hard worker he was, a first-rate scholar, scrupulously honest, a fine organizer, and so on. < . . . > Poor Fedin. Yesterday they painted his fence green, and for that green fence,[294] for membership in the Academy, for honorary posts he has no need of he has to sign away his conscience. < . . . >

5 May.

Have been twice to see Fedin about the *Literaturnoe nasledstvo* affair, trying to get him to put in a good word for Zilbershtein. < . . . > What makes me sad is that the literary methodology I have used all my life—that of the

---

proceedings against him in connection with Article 69, which deals with treason against the state. In an interview with the United Press International correspondent in Moscow Pasternak claimed he had not authorized publication of "The Nobel Prize," and he denounced in no uncertain terms the reporter who had made it public.

293. *Litnasledstvo* stands for *Literaturnoe nasledstvo* (Literary Heritage), an important irregularly appearing series published by the Academy of Sciences. It contains documentary materials bearing on the major figures and movements in Russian literary history. (V.E.)

294. The houses of important personages in Peredelkino were protected by green fences. (M.H.H.)

unwhitewashed literary portrait—is now condemned, invalidated. Every-thing must be primer-shiny. The Central Committee resolution makes that amply clear. My *People and Books* has little chance of being reprinted now. The swine. Once more I'm out in the cold. They've kicked me out of children's literature, kicked me out of criticism, kicked me out of Nekrasov scholarship.

Tamara Vladimirovna tells me that Olga Vsevolodovna (Pasternak's friend, whom she wants nothing to do with) rang her recently and said, "Please, I beg of you, go to Pasternak and tell him to phone me, but don't let his wife know."

"Do you realize what you're asking of me? I'm a close friend of his wife's. I can't go behind her back."

"I beg of you! It's a matter of life and death."

What could she do? She went to see him. Zinaida Nikolaevna was playing cards downstairs with Selvinsky's wife (never mind that Selvinsky dragged him through the mud in the pages of *Ogonek*),[295] and she slipped into his office and did Olga Vsevolodovna's bidding.

Pasternak immediately rushed to the Writers House to use the phone.

It turned out that the Swedish ambassador had invited him to a recep-tion, and he had been informed by a certain official body that if he agreed to stay away from the reception and break off all relations with foreigners he would be paid for his Słowacki translation and a one-volume edition of his poetry would be published.

He agreed. < . . . >

6 May.

Saw Fedin in town yesterday. He came up to my car and said, "We managed to keep Zilbershtein on by the skin of our teeth. The battle lasted three hours. The Literaturnoe nasledstvo board has been puffed up to nine members. Vinogradov was of great help to Zilbershtein; he behaved very well."

Once more my tales are in trouble. It's RAPP all over again. I talked to Konstantin Fedotych at Detgiz yesterday, and he said (obviously repeat-

---

295. Reference to "Do Not Provoke Your Progeny, Good Fathers" in the November 1959 issue, which ends with the following stanza: "What use is your erstwhile poetic status, / The bounteous gifts of your soul's purest fire, / If now to cull the fame of a Herostrates / You stoop your native land to vilify?"

ing what he'd heard from the authorities), "We've had enough birdies and kitty cats. Our preschoolers need other things."

When I heard that from Mikhailov in December of last year, I thought it was a joke; now I see it's law. < . . . >

8 May.

< . . . > Yegolin is dead. Consummate scoundrel, lickspittle, and nonentity to boot. He used his elevated position in the Central Committee to wheedle editing jobs and made piles of money editing Chekhov, Ushinsky, and Nekrasov. For the (nominal) editing he did of Chekhov's works he earned more than Chekhov earned for writing them. < . . . >

10 June.

< . . . > Marshak and I had a conversation about the Symbolist poets. Nearly all their names begin with b: Bryusov, Balmont, Bely, Baltrušaitis, Blok.

"Right," said Marshak. "And Sologub ends with b. And Kuzmin was a b."[296] < . . . >

8 August.

Yesterday an Indian journalist turned up out of the blue (with Svetlana as a guide), the head of all Indian newspapers or some such thing and as far removed from me as the Brahmaputra. < . . . > After depriving me of two working hours, during which time he informed me he had been to America, talked to Eisenhower, made a tour of twenty or so countries, and was returning the following day to India < . . . >, my guest asked to visit Pasternak. I told him Pasternak was at work and had been done much harm by visiting foreigners, but he insisted on seeing him if only for a minute.

I hadn't seen Pasternak for two or three months. He is happy and healthy and still has that glint of madness in his eye. We met in the garden. His charming two-year-old grandson immediately came up to me and demanded I sit on a step with him and not budge. From a distance I could

---

296. Marshak is referring to the Russian word for "whore," *bliad'*. (M.H.H.)

hear Pasternak passing on his **greetings** to the whole Indian continent.
[. . .]

15 August.

Kataev has come back from America with a book about the beatniks called
The Holy Barbarians.[297] I finished it in one night; I couldn't put it down.
Capitalism had to produce its beatniks to revolt against the suffocating
American way of life, but how ugly and *tedious* a revolt it is.
< . . . >

"Why did you kill Jewish poets?" Kataev was asked at a press conference.

"And you answered, 'We didn't kill only Jewish poets, we killed Russian
poets too,' " I said.

"No, there was nothing to do but to lie. So I answered without blinking,
'We didn't kill any Jewish poets.' "

About Pasternak he had this to say: "You see him as a victim. Well,
save your sympathy: he has a splendid flat, a dacha, a car; he's rich, he
lives high off the hog—he earns a pretty penny from his books."

1960

→>-→>-→>-→>-→>-→>

10 April.

Have been in bed for nearly a month. First I had some heart problems,
then a sudden and virulent viral infection that has been dragging on for
some ten days. < . . . >

Pasternak came two or three days ago, but they wouldn't let him see
me. He came to return the five thousand rubles he'd borrowed last January
for a year. "Your father is so high-minded that he never even told you I
owed him five thousand rubles," he said, giving the money to Lida.

Unfortunately I wasn't high-minded at all: thinking I was about to die,
I had in fact told her about Pasternak's debt. < . . . >

297. Lawrence Lipton, *The Holy Barbarians* (New York, 1959).

21 April.

Fischer, Jr., whom I remember as a Pioneer, has come for a visit.[298] I remember his father well. He was an ardent supporter of the Soviet regime when he lived in Russia, singing the praises of Chicherin and Litvinov, then suddenly turned to Gandhi and became an orthodox Hindu.

The son is very much like the father. He says he wrote some anti-Soviet pieces for a while, but now that he's back in the country he's seen the light and will write an impartial book about the structure of Soviet society. Lida gave him Makarenko's *Road to Life.* [. . .]

23 May.

Pasternak's illness. Valentin Ferdinandovich Asmus came to see me yesterday. He visits Pasternak three times a day and talks to his doctors. He is convinced that it will be a miracle if Pasternak recovers: there is only a 10 percent chance he'll pull through. His hemoglobin is terrible, ditto his blood count. X-ray treatment is out of the question. < . . . >

31 May.

Lida brought me the dreaded news: "Pasternak is dead." He died at a quarter past one. Asmus apparently tried to reach me by phone.

He will be buried on Thursday the second. The weather has been unbelievably beautiful: hot and stable. The apple and cherry trees are in bloom. I've never seen so many butterflies, birds, bees, and flowers. I spend entire days out on the balcony. Every hour there's a miracle, every hour something new, while he, the singer of all these clouds, trees, and pathways (he portrays Peredelkino in "Christmas"), is now lying in state on a pitiful folding bed, deaf and blind, destitute, and we shall never again hear his impetuous, explosive bass or see his triumphant . . . (My head is aching. I can't write.) He was made for triumphs; he flourished amidst ecstatic cheers

298. "Fischer, Jr." is George Fischer, an American Sovietologist and author of *Soviet Opposition to Stalin* (1952), a study of the abortive attempt by Lieutenant General Andrei Vlasov, who was captured by the Nazis in 1942, to form a Russian liberation army and fight alongside the Germans while preserving a degree of political autonomy. (This book is presumably what Chukovsky means by his "anti-Soviet writings.") His father, Louis Fischer, a well-known journalist, was initially drawn to the Soviet Union, but grew increasingly critical of Stalin's regime. (V.E.)

from the audience; he was at his happiest on the podium; he needed to see the grateful, burning eyes of the young gazing up at him, to know they hung on his every word. Then he was kind, witty, cheerful, slightly co-quettish—in his element! And when they made him a monster, an outcast, a glowering criminal, he changed completely, began avoiding people. I remember how it irked him, the prime poet of the Soviet Union, to be unknown to *anyone* in the hospital ward where they put him.

> And you'll not wash away with all your blood pitch black
> The poet's equitable blood.[299]

(No, I can't go on writing. My head aches too much.)

6 June.

V. F. Asmus has just been to see me. Of all the professors and writers at Pasternak's grave he is the only one who made a speech. He is one of Pasternak's executors. His wife phoned from town to say that all kinds of books, gifts, and thank-you letters were pouring in.

Pasternak's sister has just arrived from England—too late for the fu-neral. Asmus met her while she was using the phone at the Writers House. She is staying with Zinaida Nikolaevna. The x-ray they took after he died showed he had lung cancer. The whole lung was affected, and he never felt a thing. Not until 6 May did he tell Asmus, "For some reason my upper back is aching."

Now the main problem is Olga Vsevolodovna. The last time I was at Pasternak's he showed me piles of letters he'd received from abroad, an entire dresser full. Where are they now? Asmus is afraid Olga Vsevolodovna has them—along with other materials.

8 June.

< . . . > Kornely Zelinsky, who instigated Koma Ivanov's dismissal from Moscow University on the basis of his close relations with Pasternak, has decided to try and rehabilitate himself after the fact and has made the following formal request to the rector of the university: "Please confirm that I made no written denunciation of V. V. Ivanov."

---

299. A quotation from Lermontov's poem on Pushkin's death.

The rector responded as follows: "K. A. Zelinsky made no *written* denunciation of V. V. Ivanov."

Zelinsky sent a copy of this correspondence to Vsevolod Ivanov. I have it from Tamara Vladimirovna Ivanova. She also told me that Asmus was summoned to the university on several occasions and interrogated about why he dared to call Pasternak a great writer.

"I am a writer," he told them, "a member of the Writers' Union. I assume I don't need anyone to tell me who is and who is not a great writer."

The last time Tamara Vladimirovna saw Pasternak was 8 May. He was full of jokes and had a lively conversation with her, and his doctor, Konchalovskaya, knowing full well he had had a heart attack, didn't tell him to lie there without moving. Indeed, she proved totally incompetent.

He gave Koma his play (the first three acts) to read. The final version. But the text is now obviously in Olga Vsevolodovna's hands, because Zinaida Nikolaevna has only the drafts. (It's about a serf actress who was blinded by her master.) Olga Vsevolodovna has Pasternak's entire archive, and no one knows what she plans to do with it.

Pasternak's brother and his son asked Koma whether he wished to see Olga Vsevolodovna. They told him she was next door. He said loudly and clearly that he had no desire to see her. < . . . >

16 June.

When they asked Shtein (Alexander) why he hadn't gone to Pasternak's funeral, he said, "I don't take part in anti-government demonstrations." < . . . >

13 August.

Back in Barvikha. < . . . >

14 August.

< . . . > Petrovykh, an amiable poetess, has been telling us about the problems the Goslit Akhmatova volume is having. The editorial board has thrown out the best poems and insists on including the "markedly Soviet" lines she wrote during the Stalinist years, when her son Lyova was in exile (or a labor camp). < . . . >

The fifteenth edition of *From Two to Five* is now in press. How I'd have liked to put a little more work into it. But I have to get going on Chekhov and redo *The Craft of Translation*. I happen to have run across Whitman again here at the sanatorium, and I'm as charmed by him as I was in my youth. I especially enjoyed "Crossing Brooklyn Ferry," where he talks to himself from the grave.

And I'm amazed at the horror and the ecstasy I felt reading J. D. Salinger's *Catcher in the Rye*. It's about a sixteen-year-old boy who despises vulgarity, yet is engulfed in it—his autobiography. "He rejects the things of this world" is how people would have put it fifty years ago. And what writing! The complexity of his soul, the contradictory desires rending it, tender and coarse together. < . . . >

< . . . >

11 September.

Yesterday I spent the entire evening with Dmitry Vasilyevich Pavlov, the Minister of Trade. He has written a book entitled *Leningrad Under Siege* and is now expanding it for the second edition. He read me excerpts from it and asked for my advice.

"One thing I deserve credit for," he said, "is to have been the first to name people who were executed. Popkov, for example."

He told me about how he managed to save several people close to Popkov. The head of a sweets factory was arrested for no other reason than that Popkov used to take showers at his factory. Pavlov got him out of jail, but he was still dismissed from his post and expelled from the Party. < . . . >

22 September.

Back in Peredelkino. < . . . >

It was 5 September, I think. The weather was beautiful, nice and dry. Two classes from School 589 came to see me. I had a headache and was lying in bed depressed when all of a sudden I was surrounded by all those wonderful, happy, boisterous children. I spent four hours with them and recovered completely. I didn't even feel tired. They gathered brushwood for a fire, raced with one another, and filled the woods with bedlam, laughter, and shouts. I had the feeling I'd never loved a woman as I loved those clear-throated children. All of them together. They're so much better than our Peredelkino (petit bourgeois) children. I recited a lot of my own works to them in the library; they listened attentively, then ran up and down the benches doing gymnastic stunts or climbed trees, girls as well as boys. [. . .]

12 October.

I don't know why, but I'm certain this will be the last book of my diary. I won't survive the winter; "I won't tread the new grass." I visited Marya Borisovna's grave today—*my* grave, actually: there's a place waiting for me by her side. So today while at my grave—with Lida—I said to myself: when all is said and done, I've lived a wonderful life. Even my grave is wonderful. [. . .]

28 October.

< . . . > I've fixed my death date: 21 February 1969. In any case, here is my will. I leave one quarter of my cash savings to Yevgeny Borisovich Chukovsky and three quarters to Lidia Korneevna Chukovskaya. The burial fees shall be paid by Nikolai Korneevich Chukovsky from his own funds. The furniture shall be equally divided amongst the heirs. *Chukokkala* shall go to Lidia Korneevna and Yelena Tsezarevna, as shall my diaries. They shall also receive my archives and enlist the aid of Klara Izrailevna Lozovskaya to examine and order them. They shall give Klara Izrailevna my desk as a keepsake. Tatyana Maximovna Litvinova shall be given such of my English books as she shall desire. The royalties for my books during the first year after my death shall be divided equally amongst my grandchildren; thenceforth they shall be given to my daughter Lidia Korneevna, who is very ill. Fair-minded and conscientious as I know her to be, I request that she distribute appropriate sums from the funds thus received to such of my grandchildren as may need them. < . . . >

29 October.

I am certain that Lida will continue to take part in the activities of the children's library. Marina and Klara and Lida and I have all put much love and time into the library, but Lida actually determined its current function and made it a reality. I hope to be able to add a third building to the complex, which, with Lida's active involvement, will make the operation that much more fruitful.

I'd like to see the late-June "Hail to Summer" bonfires become a tradition as long as Kolya, Lida, and Marina aren't forced off "our" land. But even if they are, they could carry on the tradition with the permission of the new tenants.

< . . . >

9 November.

What is literary creation? Linking unexpected words.

11 November.

< . . . >

[The following letter from Frida Vigdorova was pasted into the diary.]

> Dear Kornei Ivanovich: This information is confidential.
> The students of the Leningrad Institute of Precision Mechanics and Optics were undergoing training on a Coast Guard vessel (36190) in late August when they were sent ashore for a class. The class did not materialize, and the students decided to spend the time set aside for the class on shore. Such was their principal crime and one committed without malice: their behavior during their years at the institute and during their work in the virgin lands and on other training ships had shown them to be highly disciplined.
> When they returned to the ship, Captain Shadrin asked, "Who is the ringleader? Any of you with your own cars and papas in high places take a step forward!"
> "What about those whose fathers died fighting for their country?" asked a student by the name of Bernshtein.
> "I don't believe that the fathers of your kind died fighting for their country," he answered.
> Then he said to a student by the name of Viktor Kostyukov: "How could you, the son of a Russian proletarian, fall under the influence of ten Jews? I hope you haven't let the synagogue atmosphere rub off on you. When I was your age, I was flinging stones at Jews. Ten out of fifteen of the students sent to me are Jews. That's how it is in every institute. I'm going to do everything I can to save Russian science."
> Then he gave the students very bad evaluations, as a result of which

three of them—Funk, Kagan, and Dolgoi—were expelled from the institute.

The Political Board of the Baltic Fleet set up a committee to look into the matter and recommended that Captain Shadrin be asked to rewrite his evaluations. The new ones, which were every bit as biased, were also rejected by the Political Board, and Admiral Golovko had him punished and, if you remember, had some rather unflattering things to say about him in a conversation with you. Yet Comrade Vasilevsky of the Ministry of Higher Education continues to abide by those discredited evaluations.

Funk, one of the expelled students, is the son of a carpenter, Kagan the son of a metalworker, and Dolgoi, the third, the son of a tailor. The local Komsomol organization has intervened on their behalf with Kapustin, the head of the institute. Kapustin refused to reinstate them at first, but the day before yesterday he told institute and university officials that he would reinstate them if they return to Leningrad. They were supposed to leave today, but we have just learned by phone from Leningrad that a policeman has knocked on their door with a document ordering them to report immediately to the Military Enlistment Office. I understand that the army is a holy of holies, but justice must take precedence. Clearly the head of the institute promised to reinstate the students only because he was certain they would be conscripted, which would absolve him of the necessity of probing further.

All this has been going on for three months! And it is all so obvious, Kornei Ivanovich, and shameful . . .

It cannot, absolutely cannot be postponed another minute. It is essential for you to speak to the admiral in person and find out what he thinks firsthand. [. . .]

7 December.

The children's literature meeting opened today. It was enough to make one despair. Officials from all three boards were elected to the Presidium; real writers, like Barto, remained in the audience. The level is low and bureaucratic. Instead of saying outright, "Sing our praises, you hacks! Magnify and sanctify us!" the authorities make the standard speeches about Socialist Realism and the like. But everybody understands what's involved. [. . .]

19 December.

< . . . > At about four in the afternoon a Pobeda ambulance pulled up and asked how to get to Kozhevnikov's. He's had a heart attack. It's due

to Vasily Grossman's novel.[300] Grossman submitted the novel (a continuation of *Stalingrad Battles*) to *Znamia*, but it couldn't be published: it's an indictment of the commanding officers, it accuses the authorities of anti-Semitism, and so on. Kozhevnikov wanted to return it without making a fuss, but Polikarpov interfered: he'd read the novel and was furious. Kozhevnikov was so upset he upped and had a heart attack.

Kazakevich's novel about Lenin in Razliv has been removed from *Oktiabr'* because it shows Zinovyev with Lenin. < . . . >

27 December.

< . . . > Kolya says that Kazakevich sent Khrushchev the text of the novel that was removed from *Oktiabr'* and a three-hundred-word telegram. Three days later Kazakevich had a call from Khrushchev's secretary saying the novel was magnificent, just what was needed now, and he would let Nikita Sergeevich know how he felt.

Lida has lost a lot of weight. She looks sad and depressed.

1961

✦➤-✦➤-✦➤-✦➤-✦➤-✦➤-✦➤

4 January.

The year has begun terribly for literature. Kazakevich's novel has been removed from *Oktiabr'*, Vasily Grossman's novel from *Znamia*, and Ehrenburg's memoirs of Tsvetaeva, Pasternak, etc. from *Novyi mir*.

I have no desire to write about language. Language is not the point. A woman sent me a letter recently saying: "You keep writing about how poorly we speak. Why don't you write about how poorly we live?" < . . . >

13 January.

Look at the piece of idiotic nonsense Klara brought me yesterday:

300. See note 233.

385. Chukovsky, K. I. Word Culture. Molodaia gvardiia. 32 pgs. 50,000 copies. Price: 6 kopecks. (Autumn quarter)
Kornei Ivanovich Chukovsky is a close and loving observer of language. In this book, aimed at the younger generation, he writes of the richness of Russian, the culture of the living word, and the need to oppose the spread of dead bureaucratese in the written and spoken language.

I haven't the slightest intention of writing about the richness of Russian or of calling the book *Word Culture* or putting it out by the autumn. The whole thing is pure hogwash. The book will be ninety or a hundred pages long, and what I will say in it I don't know yet myself, though I'm hard at work on it every morning. The work proceeds as follows. I get up at five—or slightly later—and set to immediately. Sensing I won't last long, I write as much as possible—pushing forward, getting off the track, muddling things, putting quantity before quality—waiting for my heart to start bothering me. When I can't bear the pain any longer, I go and lie down—and read. I read whatever comes my way. A few days ago I finished a wonderful book, Nancy Mitford's *Voltaire in Love*. She's a fine writer. I envy her talent (and her cynicism). She manages to treat both Voltaire and Madame de Châtelet with the utmost delicacy, yet demonstrate on every page their self-interest, their careerism, and their readiness to stoop to the basest of deeds. < . . . >

I am currently reading Vladimir Nabokov's *Pnin*, a great work in praise of an upright Russian hurled into American university life. A poetic work, an intelligent work about the absentmindedness, immaturity, risibility, and spiritual grandeur of the half-baked Russian professor Timofei Pnin, a work shot through with sarcasm—and love. < . . . > In the course of the novel the author shares with the reader his memories of a Russian he met in Petrograd, Paris, and America. This man does not have a high opinion of his biographer. When the latter brings up a certain Lyudmila in his presence, Pnin cries out to the assembled company, "Don't believe a word he says . . . He makes up everything . . . He is a dreadful inventor" (p. 153). < . . . >

I was unfortunately able to confirm just that on the basis of my own experience. Quoting his father, Vladimir Dmitrievich Nabokov, the novelist writes in his memoirs that when I was at Buckingham Palace I asked King George V a question about Oscar Wilde. Rubbish! The King delivered a speech from a prepared text, as did Vladimir Dmitrievich. Talking to the

King was out of the question. It's just a story. He is trying to discredit his father.[301]

20 January.

Khrabrovitsky has given me Gippius's *Dmitry Merezhkovsky* published by the YMCA Press [in Paris]. It is a poor, hollow, sickly book all but devoid of images and color. It leaves you with no idea of who Merezhkovsky was. Instead of describing him, it describes the whirlwind of events surrounding him and gets dates and facts wrong to boot. (The description of their flight through Gomel is probably valid, but everything about the trip Alexei Tolstoy, Yegorov, and Nabokov take to London is taradiddle.) Besides, it is cold and heartless. < ... >

21 January.

A terrible anniversary: it is six years next month since Marya Borisovna died. I am reading over her letters to me.[302] < ... > All day I've felt in communication with her, close to her, and couldn't settle into anything, so I picked up one of my favorites, *The Gambler,* where Dostoevsky's genius comes across in all its purity: in the plot construction, the characters, the figure of the old woman, the dialogues, the nervous energy of the inspiration. < ... >

7 February.

< ... > Have just read the part of Ehrenburg's memoirs in *Novyi mir* where he goes into the deaths of Mandelshtam, Paolo Yashvili, Tsvetaeva,

301. Chukovsky has the following passage from Nabokov's *Speak, Memory* in mind: "In February 1916 Father visited England along with some other eminent journalists (among them Aleksei Tolstoy, Nemirovich-Danchenko, Chukovsky) at the invitation of the British government. There had been an official banquet, presided over by Sir Edward Gregg, and a funny interview with King George V whom Chukovsky, the *enfant terrible* of the group, insisted on asking if he liked the works of Oscar Wilde, 'dze uorks of Ouad.' The king, who was baffled by the interrogator's accent, and who, anyway, had never been a voracious reader, neatly countered by inquiring how the guests liked the London fog. Chukovsky used to cite this triumphantly as an example of British cant—tabooing a writer because of his morals" (*Speak, Memory* [New York, 1966], 254–55).

302. Marya Borisovna's letters have not yet been located in Chukovsky's archive.

and Mayakovsky. The emotional impact is less than it might be: too many people, too many names and places flicker past; you end up dizzy. Still, it's a heroic deed, an event. < . . . >

11 February.

A blissful day: I've been writing steadily from morn till night, not rereading what I put down. The only time I enjoy writing is when I feel I'm coming up with something new, something no one else has ever said. It's an illusion, of course, but I'm in heaven as long as it lasts.

1 April.

My birthday. I'm seventy-nine. Much to my surprise, I'm celebrating the first day of my last year free of trepidation. < . . . >

An old man has an interesting relationship to things: they are no longer his property. I shall never use up my pencils or wear out my shoes and socks. They no longer belong to me. The overcoat will go to Gulya, the English children's books to Andrei, the television set (I bought a new one yesterday) is more Lyusha's than mine. Zhenya recently gave me a fountain pen; it will soon go back to him. And they all know it. Yet they all make believe I'm the same as they are. < . . . >

1 May.

< . . . > Asmus is worried. Although he (along with Vilmont, Ehrenburg, and the Pasternak family) is Pasternak's executor, Goslit are publishing a volume of Pasternak's verse without his permission. Surkov has made the selection—and of a very small number of poems. It will be a slim volume. The executors have written a protest to the authorities, insisting that the choice of poems be made by them and the number of poems be increased. Zinaida Nikolaevna was against it. "I don't care how it looks," she said, "as long as they put it out quickly." So they wrote it in secret, and Lena will deliver it the day after tomorrow.

23 July.

I've had food poisoning and bronchitis and am more dead than alive. I haven't left the house for three weeks. I spend more and more time in bed.

I'm working on the language book. But today I have to get up: *The Nut-Tree Branch*, a play based on Romanian folk motifs, will be opening in our woods in half an hour. [. . .]

I'm looking out of the window. I've never seen such organization before. I put on my Indian headdress, go downstairs, and find a miracle: a magnificent set complete with tower, the children all dressed in silk, a great hustle and bustle backstage and perfect order onstage. A girl by the name of Marina Kostopravkina is playing the role of the heroine, who frees her brother from a witch's curse. The witch is played by Grunya Vasilyeva. Kotya Smirnov is a dragon, Zhenya—a giant chained to a rock. It's a little disappointing that the children's marvelous faces are covered: beneath those terrifying masks there are pink cheeks and shining eyes. No prompter is needed: they all know their parts. Fedin is in the audience: both his grandchildren are in the play. At five the cast is served a lavish tea. It's been a huge success. Dozens of children wish to sign up for the club.

I'm still racking my brains over the school slang article. It's painful to feel so devoid of talent.

30 July.

[. . .] The heat is terrible. I was at the cemetery. It's strange to think my grave will be next to Pasternak's. It's so immodest—impudent, even—on my part, but that's how it is. As long as the world goes round, Pasternak and I are fated to be neighbors. [. . .]

4 August.

Mitya had his first exam today: Russian literature. The topic he had to write on was "It is better to die on your feet than to live on your knees." He did a good job: he cited all kinds of heroic passages in works from "The Lay of the Host of Igor" to Bek's *Volokolamsk Road*. I was very nervous, from which I conclude that during the time he's been living here with me I've come to love him. < . . . >

Today, 6 August, two enormously important events are taking place. The first is the flight of the Vostok Two into space with German Stepanovich Titov on board. At this very moment, as I sit in my room writing these lines, German Stepanovich is flying in airless space around this tragic, absurd planet with its Shakespeares, Tolstoys, Chekhovs, Bloks, Schillers—

and Eichmanns. What is he feeling? I wonder what he has found out there in the void: immortality or death?

The second event is that I've finished (I can hardly believe it) my book *Alive as Life* after slaving away at it day and night for a whole year. I was afraid it would bear signs of my sclerosis, my insomnia, and my intimations of mortality, but it has turned out to be fresh and perhaps even useful . . .
< . . . >

23 August.

Literatura i zhizn' has published two articles questioning my reliability.[303] The newspaper is a kind of *Daily Hurrah*. It was angry with me for saying we have men-in-cases. There was a time when it was considered necessary to hide the existence of self-servers and do-nothings; now they practically call you an enemy of the people if you dare to say that some of our teachers are men-in-cases, though they are the ones producing them. < . . . >

Went to the *Litgazeta* and *Izvestiia* offices in town: I have to respond to *Literatura i zhizn'*. What a bore! [. . .]

28 August.

The bonfire was magnificent. Every one of the children showed unusual talent. There was an audience of about a thousand. It drizzled the whole time, but nobody seemed to mind. < . . . >

I'm in Barvikha.[304] It's damp. I'm slaving over my "scathing reply" to the *Literatura i zhizn'* attack. [. . .]

In the evening I went for a walk with Tvardovsky. He is hale and hearty, full of spirit, and amazingly open. We got onto the subject of Fedin's novel

303. On 12 August 1961 *Literaturnaia gazeta* published an article in which Chukovsky characterized "youth slang" as a protest against cliché-ridden bureaucratese and spoke sympathetically of Vasily Aksyonov's novella *A Ticket to the Stars* (1961) and its apt rendition of young people's speech patterns. Chukovsky was assailed in the newspaper *Literatura i zhizn'* for his statement that "school kids are sick and tired of the spic-and-span, saccharine, sanctimonious language that our men-in-cases still cultivate in the schools." ("The Man in a Case" is a Chekhov story about a hopelessly rigid schoolmaster.) A lively discussion ensued. On 9 September 1961 *Literaturnaia gazeta* published another Chukovsky article, this one entitled simply "Bureaucratese," its point being that the main trouble with Soviet language was the prevalence of the wooden turns of phrase characteristic of bureaucratic documents.

304. An elite sanitarium in the environs of Moscow. It later served as Yeltsin's residence.

The Bonfire. "It's pure calligraphy," he said, "devoid of content, but the form is good. He obviously doesn't know what a brigade-leader does as opposed to a kolkhoz chairman: he's never come in contact with that kind of thing. But he tries hard."

He called Paustovsky a philistine in love with beauty. "His autobiography is a lie: 'A wolf ran into the tent. I grabbed my rifle and shot it dead on the spot.'

"Talent is dying out in Peredelkino: Leonov no longer has it. Fedin no longer has it. Ditto Tikhonov and Vsevolod Ivanov. As for Sobolev, it must be awful for him to wake up in the middle of the night and remember that he's Sobolev." (He then told the story about Madame Soboleva and cancer.)

He had only bad things to say about Sergei Mikhalkov—"Already gray, and still a scoundrel"—but I'm glad he stood up for Dorosh and his village prose: "He hasn't had press reviews yet, but he has had a lot of letters."

On Leonov: "Have a look at book stalls when you're on the road and you'll see unbought copies of *The Russian Forest* all over Russia. And his Tolstoy speech—why, it's petty larceny! A patchwork of other peoples' thoughts. The authorities don't realize it's an empty shell: he got ten thousand rubles for it. It came out as a pamphlet too. It's unreadable, laughable." And so on and so forth.

We didn't say good night until twelve, and I didn't get to sleep until morning.

3 September.

Have been ill all week. A temperature of 37.4. Terribly depressed. After a hot shower came out into a drafty corridor.

Had several long talks with Tvardovsky. [. . .] "Look at Paustovsky's mannered style, and the philistines eat it up. And that Lev Nikulin—what a charlatan! Poor Kazakevich can't get a handle on soldier talk. It's all wrong the minute they open their mouths. His story has an idealized soldier presenting a gold watch to his commanding officer's widow. My Tyorkin would have sold it and spent the money on vodka. As for Marshak, he's a real character: he has his translations published with his own name at the top in large print, then the text, and down at the bottom in small print: Shakespeare."

He gave me *Distance Beyond Distance* with a kind dedication.

18 September.

Met our ambassador to Israel, who is just back from Jerusalem. He was invited to the villa of an American millionaire there, a man who had had business connections with the Soviet Union in his youth (which is why he was invited), and the first thing he saw was

Portrait of Kornei Chukovsky by Repin

So that's where it got to from America. Which makes its itinerary: Kuokkala, Rome, Moscow, New York, Jerusalem. I wonder where its next stop will be. And Repin made a formal gift of it to me. < . . . >

1962

➤-➤-➤-➤-➤-➤-➤-➤-➤

21 February.

< . . . > Yesterday I finished my work on Sasha Chorny (for the Small Series of the Biblioteka poeta) and sent it off to Leningrad. I've been reading through my *High Art* and see it for the chaotic and verbose book it is.

Today I received the official invitation from Oxford and a letter from S. A. Konovalov indicating the sorts of lectures they want me to give and so on. < . . . >

22 February.

< . . . > I've just recalled how my mother tried to preserve my innocence when I recited a ditty I'd picked up somewhere at the age of seven or so:

> Can there be a better life
> Than to be a soldier's wife?
> When off he marches to his base,
> Another comes to take his place.

"You've got it wrong," she told me. "The last line should read: 'She ups and follows him apace.' "

Vera Fyodorovna Panova has just been to see me. She's the best woman writer in the Soviet Union bar none and a simple soul with no pretenses whatever. [. . .] She is highly intelligent and extremely energetic. She is now on her way to Mosfilm, where they are shooting a screenplay of hers. She's written six in two years. < . . . >

24 February.

Olga Nikolaevna Vysotskaya has just been to see me. She brought me her memoirs of Meyerhold, with whom she lived in Terioki. Once a beauty— she is eighty now at least—she has retained the manners and mannerisms of a beauty. After Meyerhold she had a relationship with Gumilyov, by whom she had a son, Orest, who is currently . . . the head of a furniture factory. He is the half-brother of Akhmatova's son, Lev Gumilyov. [. . .]

1 March.

Elsberg has been expelled from the Writers' Union for doing in Babel and Levidov and trying to do in Makashin. But Lesyuchevsky, who did in Kornilov and Zabolotsky, is still at his post.[305] Kataev has told Kolya that someone has found a letter from Leonov to Stalin in which Leonov tries to get his play *The Invasion* staged by announcing that he is a pure-blooded Russian and our literature has too many cosmopolitan writers: Jews, southerners. < . . . >

5 March.

< . . . > Yesterday I had a fantastic letter from Oxford. The university wishes to bestow upon me the degree of "doctor of literature" for my literary achievements (!?). Am I truly worthy of such an honor? The only emotion I feel is amazement. But oh how I dread going into town—to the Writers' Union, to the Central Committee—and getting the ball rolling. < . . . >

---

305. At the time Nikolai Lesyuchevsky headed the Sovetskii pisatel' Publishing House and wielded inordinate power over the fate of writers and their works. He had clearly been implicated in the arrests of the poets Zabolotsky and Kornilov during the purges. The critic Yulian Oksman responded to his featured presence at the Bolshoi Theater Pushkin centenary celebration in 1936 by asking aloud, "What group is he representing? The murderers of poets?"

7 March.

Good heavens! How low can people stoop! Yugov, who also has a book about language coming out with Molodaia gvardiia, is apparently trying to get them to destroy the plates of my book and prevent it from appearing altogether.[306] < . . . > It was due out in early February, but was held back by Yugov and, in part, Syryshcheva, who had devised a cover consisting of a number of words discussed in the book done up in an ornamental script. The words were chosen at random, but the publishing house interpreted them as slander aimed at the Komsomol and banned the cover, which had already been printed in 175,000 copies. Syryshcheva received an official reprimand. < . . . >

But this Yugov character! During the war he feigned insanity here at Peredelkino, and how he toadied to me! For a long time I didn't know he was a simulator, and felt very sorry for him. < . . . >

17 March.

< . . . > My book *Contemporaries* has seven hundred pages. Klara, Marianna Shaskolskaya, and I have been proofreading it, and it suddenly seemed colorless, lopsided, full of hot air. I begged the publishing house to put off publication and give me a chance to fix it up, though in fact I feel it is beyond repair. True, the article on Chekhov's "Rothschild's Fiddle" is quite decent, but the censor will never pass it, because it goes against the idiotic theory that would have all literary characters either positive or negative. < . . . >

18 March.

< . . . > Lida tells me that when the initials BP (for Biblioteka puteshestvii [Travel Library]) were embossed on a book of hers, the censors ordered it removed for fear that it be mistaken for Boris Pasternak. < . . . >

30 March.

Yesterday I was "feted" at the Pioneer House and the House of the Children's Book. < . . . > Shklovsky made a wonderful comment: he said that

306. Alexei Yugov was a journalist and children's writer who lambasted Chukovsky's articles on the state of the Russian language.

before my tales children's literature was in the hands of El Cid and that my tales were the tales of Huckleberry Finn. < . . . >

All this hullabaloo and brouhaha, all these speeches and greetings and letters and telegrams (tons of them) serve only one purpose: to keep me from waking up and remembering that my life is over, that I've got one foot in the grave, and that I'm on the brink of seeing just how insignificant and powerless I am.

I have been awarded the Order of the Red Flag. At the same time as Yugov. < . . . >

Letter from Kazakevich.[307]

2 April.

I appeared at the Polytechnical Museum and on television. Once more I'm being taken for someone I'm not. What am I doing at the Polytechnical Museum? At least half of the crowd had to be turned away. The hall was packed—even the aisles were full—with every last person training lovesick gazes on me. Andronikov sang my praises for no less than a half hour. I felt an imposter. Heavens! The junk, the disgraceful rubbish I've written in my life! Like those awful articles for Ilya Vasilevsky in *Ponedel'nik*. It would take more than ninety years to make up for them. The clichés! Like "England on the Eve of War" or "The Silent Speak Out." Nor does the fact that I was sincere make it any better. What consolation is it to be a sincere idiot? I've received more than a thousand telegrams, from Akhmatova, Tvardovsky, Paustovsky, Isakovsky, etc. < . . . >

7 April.

Received the Order today at the Palace with that scoundrel of a nonentity Yugov at my side. I refused to shake his hand. Brezhnev spoke softly and was very glad that none of the laureates said a word. His favorite expressions are: "I am satisfied" and "it is with great satisfaction that I have learned . . . ," and so on. < .   >

---

307. Congratulating Chukovsky on his eightieth birthday, Kazakevich wrote: "You are among the few who have taught us to appreciate and understand our calling, our lofty craft. It is from you we have learned that the word written by the pen is more influential than commands and prisons, more enduring than granite or brass."

9 April.

Went to the pictures last night. It was disgusting. After five minutes I made a beeline for the door. Am reading Jane Austen's *Pride and Prejudice*. What marvelous, limpid, elegant prose. [. . .]

Tvardovsky has long since wanted to leave *Novyi mir*. "But if I go, all my dear friends there will drown." He uses his arm to show the wave that will come down over their heads. His eyes are bright, his voice confidential. "Nekrasov had an easier time publishing his *Sovremennik* than I have. He had a hostile government to contend with; I have my own."

He brought me a manuscript about the Stalinist camps by an unknown writer. It was given to him by Asya Berzer.[308]

He told me how he came to make his famous speech at the Twenty-Second Party Congress. He had something prepared, but there were too many writers as it was, so he left it in his coat. Suddenly they told him he was next. He talked about Kochetov, and people shouted, "Off with him!" which the papers described as "animation in the hall." When the audience mocked him, the papers wrote "laughter in the hall." < . . . > He talked about the Black Hundreds types and other such villains:[309] "They're not all that closely knit: they're perfectly happy to sell one another out. The one thing they share is that they're all nonentities." He radiates physical, moral, and creative strength. [. . .]

11 April.

< . . . > The day before yesterday Tvardovsky gave me a manuscript entitled *One Day in the Life of Ivan Danilovich* [*sic*], a splendid depiction of camp life under Stalin. I was thrilled and wrote a brief reader's report.[310] Tvardovsky told me the author was a mathematician, had written another story and some bad verse, and so on and so forth.

308. The manuscript in question, "Shch-854," was later published in *Novyi mir* under the title *One Day in the Life of Ivan Denisovich*.

309. See note 156.

310. Chukovsky's brief review, "A Literary Miracle," was the first assessment of Solzhenitsyn's novella. The statement "This story marks the appearance of a highly original and mature writer in our literature" coincides almost literally with what Tvardovsky had to say in his introduction to the work in *Novyi mir* (1962, no. 11).

12 April.

Just now, at three o'clock, Alexander Trifonovich Tvardovsky came straight from the Lenin Committee to inform me that I had been awarded a Lenin Prize. My reaction was one of joy and profound grief.

Wonderful Tvardovsky spent an hour or two with me. "What if it turned out you'd copied your whole book from Arkhipov?" he joked. He talked about Yermilov, who had come out against me, and N. N. Aseev and Kataev, who didn't make it. I'm the only one who got a prize for literary criticism. Vadim Kozhevnikov, who never greeted me before, has suddenly greeted me. A triviality, I know. The kind I'd rather not notice. < . . . >
< . . . >

18 April.

Had a visit from Sonya Petrovna Krasnova from Goslit. We came up with a plan for a six-volume set of my collected writings. Oh, the work I have to look forward to. < . . . >

22 April.

Did I ask for this? Surely I did not! The last thing I need is for them to show me, an old man plagued by insomnia, on television and for all sorts of insignificant people to write me letters addressed to "Kornei Chukovsky, Moscow or Leningrad," or to be pestered by reporters. The only way I was able to write my book was to get away, duck the crowds, forgotten by *Pravda* and *Izvestiia*. But my victory is important because it is a victory of the intelligentsia over the Kochetovs, Arkhipovs, Yugovs, Lidia Felixovna Kons, and other Black Hundreds types. It was the attacks of that idiot Arkhipov that got me the prize. The intelligentsia has won this round, but the Black Hundreds will certainly take their revenge. Yesterday's *Pravda* carried a very clever little article by Pogodin about my   I can hardly spit the word out—snobbery. < . . . >

For two weeks now workmen armed with pneumatic drills have been going at the Stalin statue opposite the main entrance here in Barvikha. The tr–tr–tr rings in my ears all day. It's like being at the dentist. < . . . >

30 April.

Yekaterina Pavlovna Peshkova has received a request from Maria Ignatyevna Benkendorf (Budberg), who lives in England, for an invitation. Yekaterina Pavlovna has acquiesced. "Of all Gorky's romantic interests," she told me today, "I had the least objections to Maria Ignatyevna. She is an interesting woman." But then she heard rumors to the effect that Maria Ignatyevna had sold the British press some diaries of Alexei Mikhailovich in which there is talk of Stalin. "He never kept a diary," she said, "but he may have jotted some remarks on loose sheets." And these remarks Maria Ignatyevna could sell. Yekaterina Pavlovna's face broke out in blotches, and she wrung her hands nervously. < . . . > "When Alexei Mikhailovich lay dying, she gave me a piece of paper in the hand of Kryuchkov but signed by Gorky. 'Alexei Mikhailovich asked me to have you give this to Stalin or, if that is impossible, to Molotov,' she said. I didn't even glance at it then; I just slipped it into my dressing-gown pocket. But when I did read it what did I find but his last will and testament! And not a word about me. Everything went to Kryuchkov!" (There were those blotches again.) Such are the memories torturing that poor soul.
< . . . >

19 May.

In 1903–4 I went to England a provincial, an ignoramus. That was sixty years ago: **Cadbury Cocoa** and **Beechamp's Pills,** *Review of Reviews.* I was so poor they drove me out of Russell Square to Titchfield Street, a street inhabited by the unemployed, by thieves and prostitutes, a veritable **slum**. It is now half past four. My plane takes off at half past eight. At eighty I feel nothing but fatigue.

21 May.

Had a very good flight. Marina and I had wonderful seats. [. . .] I learned I am a guest of the British Council. We went to the Embassy via Kensington Gardens—familiar places. I nearly wept with joy. The Englishman serving as my guide turns out to be the Norman I had met in Peredelkino! One day I saw a hatless young man walking along and guessed him to be an Englishman. I dragged him home, took out my book of Browning, and had him read to me "**Oh, Galuppi, Baldassaro, this is very sad to find!**" He turns out to work for the British Council. At the Hotel Rudolph in Oxford I was given two charming rooms, each with three mirrors, but with no desk. [. . .]

Went to the Bodleian Library. Marvelous! The letters of Swinburne, the complete works of Trollope, a splendid edition of Hazlitt, and the exquisite beauty of the place. The harmony of the architectural ensemble made a musical impression on me. I saw lovely drawings by Somov, Benois, Serov, Pasternak père and sketches of Lenin (done from life).

24 May.

A wonderful day. Cloudy, but no rain. A group of students came for me. They were with Pier Hotner, who says "Listen" before every sentence. We bought a razor and a bottle of ink. Then a car pulled up, and in it were Pier's wife and their eight-month-old boy, who has an intelligent face and large eyes, a charming little tyke. On the way we saw Alice's Shop, where Lewis Carroll bought sweets for children. In Carroll's honor we took a boat ride on the Isis, where precisely a hundred years ago he told the Liddell sisters the story of *Alice in Wonderland*. It's a lovely river with magnificent views and Magdalen Tower in the distance. A gray squirrel leaps through the grass like a kangaroo, swans glide along the water, and you have the feeling that both squirrel and swans have been here since 1320 or 1230. < . . . >

I forgot to mention that the ceremony that made of me a Doctor of Literature took place the day before yesterday. And a majestic operation it was. It took place at the Taylor Institution, because the building where such events usually take place is under reconstruction. They gave me a magnificent gown to don, placed robed and sceptered **bedels** (is "bedel" related to the Russian *pedel'* [bedel]?) on either side of me, and led me into a packed hall, where—stone-faced, yet amiable—the Vice Chancellor of Oxford University, A. L. P. Norrington, sat in front of me on a podium four steps off the ground. Worcester Professor A. N. Bryan (Brown) read a *laudatio* in which he mentioned *Crocodilius,* and when it was over I mounted the four steps and shook the Vice Chancellor's hand. The Vice Chancellor sat me next to him, and Professor Obolensky gave a brief sketch of my life. Then I delivered my Nekrasov lecture. I spoke with ease and aplomb—and a minimum of preparation—and to my amazement was extremely well received. I also recited some Swinburne and praised Soviet literary scholarship, naming Alexeev, Makashin, Mashinsky, Skaftymov, Vladimir Orlov, Oksman, Zilbershtein, and many others.[311] A reception followed on the premises. [. . .]

26 May.

Had two visits yesterday. Sir Maurice Bowra, the author of *Primitive Song,* fetched us and took us to his charming flat, the very flat where Christopher Wren lived in the sixteen hundreds. Never have I seen such musical proportions, such absolute harmony, such a combination of simplicity and opulence. It is an artistic experience to be in rooms like those, and he has many of them. And the books! All in perfect order: Italian, Greek, French, Russian, English. Upstairs there is a winter garden with cactuses. Sir Maurice is a bachelor and has a noiseless servant. **Chicken, chocolate pudding**. We talked about Robert Browning, Swinburne, and Watts-Dunton. Sir Maurice recited Fet, Homer, and Sappho. < . . . >

No sooner did I get home than the students were after me. They took me to St. Giles Street, where every day from half past two to half past three a twelve-student troupe put on a play about Robin Hood. [. . .] It's all great fun, unpretentious, and full of youthful spirit. At one point they tossed cabbage leaves out of the windows.

It began to drizzle, and I went back to the hotel and read Turgenev's "First Love" in Sir Isaiah's translation. It's a good translation. After a while Obolensky came for me in his tiny car and took me to see Sir Isaiah. Divine fields again and trees of supernatural beauty, an extraordinarily luxurious house—with a hint of bad taste—and delicious food, silent servants. Lady Berlin, the svelte, quiet, perfectly discreet granddaughter of a millionaire by the name of Ginzburg (who gave Antokolsky a house in Nice and was friends with Turgenev and Goncharov), took me to their son's room. It was huge, and half of it was taken up by an electric train (a toy) with tracks, stations, and the like. He has a collection of the most tasteless but harmless comic books. He was watching television (the wilds of Africa) and doing his Latin. I tested him on several conjugations; he got every one of them right. Obolensky drove us home and recited [A. K.

---

311. Chukovsky's Oxford lecture was not published in Russia until twenty-seven years later since it refers to scholars—Yury Oksman for one—who were taboo at the time. See Kornei Chukovsky, "Russkimi glazami," *Zvezda* 5 (1989): 189.

Tolstoy's] "Dream of State Councilor Popov" in his metallic voice. I forgot to mention that Shostakovich stayed with the Berlins when he received his honorary degree.

< . . . >

27 May.

< . . . > In the evening that nice Simmons (the librarian) drove Marina and me to his house for dinner. [. . .] I thought we were going to dine with Dr. Sparrow, warden of All Souls College and author of an article on the *Lady Chatterley's Lover* trial, with whom we talked about Rossetti, Swinburne, and Oscar Wilde. Sparrow showed me a magnificent edition of Wilde's correspondence that is coming out in June (he is writing a review of it). Everything was wonderful. I literally fell in love with Sparrow: he is energetic, intelligent, he has everything it takes. Then suddenly we were shown into the room next door, where about thirty scholars in morning coats and starched fronts stood waiting to sit down to table. The tables were laden with wines, fruit, and . . . sticks that looked like this

and that the gentlemen used to drag over the fruit bowl or wine of their choice. Sparrow kept up a continuous conversation with me, and for the first time I spoke English without noticing I was speaking a foreign language. < . . . >

2 June.

Made three public appearances yesterday. First, I recited "The Fly," "Wash 'Em Clean," and "The Wonder Tree" for the BBC's Russian Section. < . . . > At four we were taken to the University of London, a gigantic classical building, for a reception, then the lecture. Elizabeth Hill, professor at Cambridge, gave a long introduction, comparing me to old man Krylov, after which I went on for two hours, reciting my verse to thunderous applause, improvising a lecture on Nekrasov's style, and reminiscing about Mayakovsky. An unprecedented, unexpected **success**. Young and old flocked to hug me. The students were very excited, and the head of the university called the lecture **entertaining** and **instructive**. Then a ruddy, hefty chap by the name of Creighton took me to the England–USSR Club, where I performed again until I dropped. Damn my throat! It's sore again.

3 June.

I'm coughing. I performed at the Pushkin Club yesterday. < . . . > Before that I went to see Iona and Peter Opie.[312] They are truly wise: they have made a wise and happy life for themselves. They have written three basic books, written them together, and with what love and serenity. They've made their whole house a museum, a museum of children's books and toys. Since systematization and classification play a major role in their work, they keep their huge household in perfect order: thousands of folders, thousands of envelopes, thousands of pieces ready for museum exhibits. He has a youthful look and burning eyes; she has black eyes and is cordial and energetic. They have an ideal marriage, a life of conjugal cooperation. [. . .]

Today was a wonderful day. Marina and I took a stroll through London. [. . .] It was here we saw the Cenotaph, a monument to the Irish who fell in the war. And all of a sudden an orderly column of veterans of the Irish regiments in mufti, all gray or bald, came marching up, accompanied by trumpets blasting a funereal "God Save the Queen" and a priest in a white chasuble who later officiated at a service. Each of the old men had dozens of medals pinned to his breast, one was legless. Marina and I were terribly moved, so sorry for these old men on a festive sunny day that we started feeling sorry for ourselves and moved on to the beautiful immortal West-minster Abbey, passing monuments to Canning, Lincoln, and . . . George V. I was taken aback: in Moscow I am used to walking among monuments to my acquaintances: Repin, Mayakovsky, Gorky. But to find here in London an oversized, pompous monument to a man I had seen in the flesh, whose voice I'd heard—well, it was disconcerting. < . . . >

4 June.

[. . .] Mura Budberg came to see me with a deaf and blind woman by the name of Andronikova. "Akhmatova dedicated a poem called 'The Shadow' to me," she said.

---

312. Iona and Peter Opie were widely respected for *The Oxford Dictionary of Nursery Rhymes* (1951) and *The Lore and Language of Schoolchildren* (1959).

"Recite it, please," I said.
"I don't remember it." < . . . >

9 June.

Flying home. < . . . > There was a seven-year-old girl on the plane I got very close to. Her name was Tanya. She looked out at the fleecy clouds below us and said, "Soap country." The flight was uneventful. I might as well have been on a tram. It now seems perfectly natural that you see Denmark as it looks on the map, that passengers in first class keep to themselves while in tourist class they talk away, that the pilots are mere babes, and that jet flights are nothing special really. [. . .]

15 June.

< . . . > Called on Marshak yesterday. He is about to leave for the Crimea. He is in unusually good spirits. He recited some poems for me. The best was about Tsvetaeva.[313] He also read me his new William Blake translation. < . . . > He has written a review of the novella *One Day*, which Tvardovsky still means to publish in the August issue of *Novyi mir*. "After this work," he said, "writing bad literature will be impossible." < . . . >

Kennedy is coming here with Robert Frost, and Khrushchev is going to America with Tvardovsky—each with his poet.

16 June.

< . . . > A terrifying book has turned up on my desk: Ivanov-Razumnik's *Prisons and Exiles,* a chilling indictment of Stalin, Yezhov, and the campaign against the intelligentsia. They and all their henchmen wanted to wipe it out. They hated everyone who thought for himself, and failed to understand that the intelligentsia was stronger than any of them, because even if only one of the millions they tortured managed to slip out of their grasp, that one would damn them for now and forever and his verdict would be recognized by all mankind. < . . . >
< . . . >

---

313. Marshak's poem "To Marina Tsvetaeva" ends with the lines: "You managed to bring back to Russia / Yourself to the very last line."

28 June.

Am slaving over the second edition of *Alive as Life*. Mura has just come to mind. I can't calm down. < . . . >

Called on Zinaida Nikolaevna [Pasternak's wife] the day before yesterday. [. . .] She says that Pasternak told her on his death bed, "How glad I am to be leaving this vulgar world. It's vulgar there too (abroad)."

Just before his death the children had come to take their leave. Zinaida Nikolaevna asked whether he wanted to see Olga Vsevolodovna [his mistress], and he answered he did not. "Lida has the money," he told her. "She knows how to get it for you." But when Lida came from England, she turned out to have no money whatsoever.

"I'm a pauper!" said Zinaida Nikolaevna. "Whenever Borya's Shakespeare translations were staged, he would deposit all the royalties into my savings account. I had 120,000 rubles. But his illness was very costly: all those doctors' visits at five hundred rubles each. I've practically nothing left. The Litfond have just given me five hundred (five thousand of the old currency) and allowed me to stay on at the dacha rent free, but I have no pension and nothing to sell. When Olga was prosecuted for speculation, she said, 'Pasternak had about fifty suits and told me to sell them.' That's a shameless lie. Pasternak had one suit, which Surkov brought back from England from his late father, and his father's old boots, which Surkov brought as well. I buried him in his father's suit; I still have the boots. That is all. After Olga was arrested, two young *chekisty* [security officers] came to see me. They were very polite. I gave them the keys to the cupboards and said, 'Have a look for yourselves. None of his things are left.' Boris didn't care about clothes. He would work upstairs for days on end. Anyway, I'm a pauper. When I get down to my last kopeck, I'll go to Fedin and ask for a thousand rubles. I'll come to you too. I want to write to Khrushchev, but Lyonya [Pasternak's son] keeps discouraging me. The Litfond people are trying to get me a pension, but I don't know if they're making progress. Would you find out for me? And it would be very helpful if you, Tvardovsky, and Vsevolod Ivanov could ask the government to collect the royalties due Pasternak from abroad and give me a Soviet pension in exchange.

"Dr. Tager determined just before Pasternak's death that he'd had a year-old (that's how she put it) lung cancer. It began just when they started hounding him, and everybody knows that nerves affect the development of cancer. $<$ . . . $>$ I have no intention of leaving this estate; I'll do anything I must to save it. It can be made into a museum in due time. It's a pity I'm not well (she has had a heart attack) and can't go to his grave, but for me his grave is here." $<$ . . . $>$

29 June.

The Kopelevs—man and wife—have been to see Lida. It turns out he, Kopelev, is the one who got *Novyi mir* the *One Day* story Tvardovsky had me read.[314] [. . .]

1 July.

The most gloomy reports about the country's economic situation are rampant. After forty years of shouting that happiness—no, bliss—is around the corner, they've brought the country to the brink of starvation; after claiming they're competing with capitalist countries, they've failed so miserably—and in the very first round—that they've had to call it off completely . . . $<$ . . . $>$

3 July.

$<$ . . . $>$ Zhenya Pasternak has been here (three times) and told me (in his father's voice) that he and Zinaida Nikolaevna had been to see Ehrenburg, and Ehrenburg advised them to focus less on Pasternak's foreign royalties than on Zinaida Nikolaevna's pension. He's written a letter to Nikita Sergeevich [Khrushchev] that Tvardovsky, Shostakovich, Tikhonov, Fedin, and I are to sign. I've signed it, but getting the other signatures will be far from easy. Zhenya wants me to do it. I said I would. But Klara has saved me: she'll go to Maryamov and Fedin; she'll take care of it. $<$ . . . $>$

Have been reading Ehrenburg's memoirs in the June issue of *Novyi mir*. Everyone is in ecstasy. Well, my impression is, the man can't write. The only thing that saves him is the tragic theme of Russia caught in a trap. But why the rapid fire of undifferentiated names $<$ . . . $>$ with no

314. Solzhenitsyn writes about Kopelev's role in the fate of *One Day in the Life of Ivan Denisovich* in *The Oak and the Calf,* translated by Harry Willetts (New York, 1975), 16, 18, 19, 21, 25, as do Kopelev and his wife Raisa Orlova in *My zhili togda v Moskve* (Moscow, 1989), 76–81.

relief. It makes your head spin. And the bad verse he quotes (his own).
< ... >

6 July.

We had two Gorky widows to lunch: Mura Budberg and Yekaterina Peshkova. Mura is seventy-one, Yekaterina Pavlovna—eighty-two. Mura
brought a copy of the *New Statesman* with an incendiary article by Pritchett
on Gorky and the Russian people.[315] At lunch she drank vodka and cognac
and to my great dismay informed me she was negotiating with various
publishers about the translation of my memoirs. She's a colorless translator,
and I don't know how to get her away from my book. < ... >

7 July.

Vsevolod Ivanov came at five, and we drove to Barvikha in my car to see
Yekaterina Pavlovna in her new (post-fire) dacha. I grabbed my Zinaida
Nikolaevna folder on the way out.

The dacha is beautiful, a thousand times better than the old one, and
has two stories. In the kitchen we saw five or six old women cooking an
extravaganza of a meal, and in the sitting room—Tolstaya, Fedin, Leonov
and his wife, Academician P. L. Kapitsa, his wife, and Maria Ignatyevna
[Budberg], for whose sake we had gathered. I immediately opened the
folder. Kapitsa signed with gusto as did Vsevolod. Fedin frowned ("We're
doing everything we can for her as it is"), but signed. Leonov too gave his
signature. < ... >

Kapitsa—tired, but animated—told a disarmament joke:

The animal kingdom decided to disarm.

"I am for disarmament," said the lion. "Let us chop off all our horns."

"I am for disarmament," said the cow. "Let us chop off all our wings."

"I too am for disarmament," said the bear. "Long live peace! Come,
brothers, come into my arms!" < ... >

Kapitsa is a real wag. He says he is not only a Cambridge University
doctor of philosophy; he is a "donkey doctor" as well. Everyone is amazed.
It turns out he has also received a doctorate from the University of Oslo

---

315. Reprinted in V. S. Pritchett, "The Young Gorky," *Complete Collected Essays* (London,
1991), 179–83. (M.H.H.)

[*osel* is the Russian word for donkey]. He couldn't attend the ceremony: he was refused an exit visa. "They sent me a ring with the degree, but I've lost it." < . . . >

Kapitsa's wife also told a joke:

After Stalin's funeral a ghost carrying a wreath appeared in Red Square. The wreath bore the following inscription: "To the Posthumously Repressed Victim from the Posthumously Rehabilitated Victims."[316] < . . . >

Oh yes, and Kapitsa told us Vyshinsky has been posthumously repressed: his family banished from Moscow and forced to leave their dacha, which was in the village where the Kapitsas live. (And Vyshinsky was a member of the Academy!) < . . . >

I've always feared talking on the phone to the authorities, so I was nervous today when I phoned Comrade Lebedev, Khrushchev's secretary. And what did I hear but "How good to hear your voice. Congratulations on the Lenin Prize. You fully deserve it. I was so glad they gave it to you." And so on. I told him everything I had to say about Zinaida Nikolaevna < . . . > and read him virtually the entire letter. He approved the content, gave me the proper address, and promised to pass it on within the next few days. < . . . >

13 July.

Wonderful warm weather at last. Read my Zhitkov memoir over the radio; it was awful. Took a walk with Maryamov. He told me Shklovsky called Fedin the "commissar of his own security." < . . . >

19 July.

Arkady Belinkov is in a tragic state. He came to see me deathly pale and unable for a long time to get a word out. Then he wept and told me he had completely lost the ability to write. He had wanted to write a long article, "The Fate of Anna Akhmatova," and completed more than five hundred pages, but then something terrible happened to his brain and he was unable to turn the draft into a publishable text. "The thing is," he said, "I've had five books destroyed (manuscripts confiscated at the time

316. "Repressed" is a post-Stalin euphemism for "arrested or executed" during the Great Terror. In the same context "rehabilitation" means the restoration of civil rights to the "repressed." (V.E.)

of his arrest) and no rest for fifteen years. As soon as I returned from exile, I retook my exams at the Literary Institute so as to receive the diploma I was supposed to receive before my arrest (when he had already taken the exams)."

At this point he was so overcome by tears that again he was unable to speak. I was dumbfounded; I had no words of comfort. He gave me the first pages of his Akhmatova article. They are about how governments have oppressed and annihilated artists from time immemorial, and maybe that is so, but he goes on about it too long, so long that you begin to find it tiresome and want to argue with it. What about the *Odyssey*? And *War and Peace*. And *Romeo and Juliet*. And *The Brothers Karamazov*. [. . .]

30 July.

< . . . > Received a marvelously written article by a man named Medvedev about Lysenko and Prezent, the murderers of Academician Vavilov. I was beside myself.[317] < . . . >

16 August.

[. . .] Received a book from Yevtushenko. Had a visit yesterday morning at nine from Sergei Vladimirovich Obraztsov—with a kangaroo and baby elephant. The elephant had a funny way of wagging its trunk. Obraztsov was as magnetic as ever, bubbling over with talent and joie de vivre, up to his neck in work. He talked about the film he's making, recited a popular ditty, sang a song, and agreed to perform at our bonfire on the 19th if we provide him with a piano. Olga Vasilyevna has arranged for one with the military. [. . .]

Kornilov was here, and a fine man he is. He has a high forehead and closely cropped hair; he is very well-read, garrulous, poetic, and affectionate. He recited his "Anastasia," "To Anna Akhmatova," and excerpts from a new narrative poem. He rushes terribly and swallows the text, yet the result is irresistible! You feel the authenticity of every word. It's amazing. Even though most of his poems are couched in the harsh, caustic slang common to all thirty-year-olds run down by Soviet reality, the language he

317. A number of essays on the history of Soviet genetics by the dissident biologist Zhores Medvedev were widely disseminated in *samizdat*.

used in his conversation with me (for example) was still the *intelligentsia* language devoid of color or smell. < . . . >

28 August.

< . . . > Met Kataev today. He expounded his theory—which I found very close to the truth—that Tikhonov, Fedin, and Leonov had squandered their gifts in Peredelkino. He gave Yevtushenko as an example. "Here is what I told him," Kataev said. "Stop writing poems that please the intelligentsia, Zhenya. It's the road to ruin. Write what the upper echelons ask of you."

25 September.

< . . . > Kazakevich is dead. "I don't mind dying," he said on his death bed, "what I mind is not having finished my novel."

Anyone who says that has no concept of death. Though I'm just like him when you get down to it. My time has clearly come, but I'd mind terribly leaving unfinished the six-volume edition of my work. < . . . >
< . . . >

11 November.

< . . . > Have just had a visit from a group of gifted young linguists: Tanya Vinokur, Krysin, and Khanpira. Khanpira is a real bully when it comes to getting at the truth and bringing it out into the open; Tanya—who is very clever, has lived in Siam for two years, and has a fourteen-year-old son— read me a delightful article about clichés in which she points out new clichés like "conversation" and "forum" and so on. It is very elegant and witty. Krysin, the youngest of the three, is the thoughtful type. They have my *Alive as Life* under their wing. They told me that their institute has been commissioned to produce as many as three volumes to refute Stalin's linguistic doctrine, his "brochure," as the Central Committee puts it in its instructions. For five years the article was called the "brilliant work of the leader of Soviet science" and suddenly it was a "brochure." V. V. Vinogradov, who extolled the "brilliant work" more than anyone, is now in disfavor.[318]

318. See note 245.

When the Stalinist villain A. S. Shcherbakov died, they were going to erect a monument in his honor. They got as far as the pedestal and a plaque stating that the statue would follow. Now, Khanpira tells me, both pedestal and plaque have disappeared. Shcherbakov was on the cultural level of a janitor. When the artist for "We Shall Conquer Barmalei" denounced me for supposedly having said he was wrong to draw Stalin next to Lenin, I was summoned to the Kremlin, where Shcherbakov stamped his feet and covered me with profanity. I was shaken. I didn't know any regime would allow an illiterate scoundrel to scream at a graybeard writer. At the time both my sons were at the front, while his son (I knew for certain) had a cushy post in the rear. < . . . >

I stupidly agreed to talk about my memories of Mayakovsky to a Barvikha audience. When I finished, the wife of a district official (district officials, a sleepy crowd, now make up most of the population here) asked, "Why did Mayakovsky shoot himself?"

I wanted to ask how come she wasn't interested in why Yesenin hanged himself, why Tsvetaeva hanged herself, why Fadeev shot himself, why Dobychin threw himself into the Neva, why Mandelshtam died, why Gumilyev was executed, why Zoshchenko was persecuted, but fortunately I restrained myself.

19 November.

Had a visit from that nice Vadim Leonidovich Andreev and Olga Viktorovna, both of whom work for the UN. [. . .]

Apparently his brother Daniil was arrested for having hatched a plot to assassinate Stalin. The villains who brought him to trial knew perfectly well it was all nonsense, but they threw him in jail anyway. The basis for the accusation was a series of letters Vadim wrote from New York. Since they were all about his homesickness for Russia, nobody but a hangman could find anything criminal in them. [. . .]

They visited Anna Akhmatova. She was "in top form"—calm, healthy, vibrant—and spoke of the impending repeal of the Central Committee's resolution about her and Zoshchenko. < . . . >

23 November.

Had a visit from Lev Ozerov, the editor of the Pasternak volume. The trouble he's had with Pasternak. It's too much for him. Akhmatova says that when Pasternak visited her he would speak so indistinctly that the cleaning lady once said sympathetically, "We had a man like that in our village. You couldn't make out the half of what he said."

24 November.

Stalin's police thugs have come a cropper, and it's all Akhmatova's doing. The man in the street may think it a miracle: tens of thousands of *oprichniki* [Ivan the Terrible's henchmen] armed with every imaginable weapon, every imaginable torture, attacking a defenseless woman, and she proves stronger, she conquers them all. But *we* don't find it in the least surprising; *we* know that's how it always is. The poet's word is always stronger than the police's thugs. It can't be hidden, stamped out, or murdered. I know it from my own experience. In *From Two to Five* I make it look as though my tales were attacked only by individual pedagogues; in fact, they were the target of the state as a whole, backed by millions of officials, turnkeys, and soldiers, backed by a terrorized press. They trampled me underfoot, banned my works, ran smear campaigns against me—and came a cropper. And what brought them down? A runaway blanket and a miracle tree that grows boots.

Have just been out to pay my (enormous) rent and met Kataev. He is upset about *One Day*, which has been published in *Novyi mir*. "It's false," he said to my amazement. "It fails to show any protest."

"What protest?"

"Why, the protest of the peasants in the camp."

But that's the whole *truth* of the work. The butchers set things up in such a way that people lost all sense of justice. People can't think about conscience, honor, and humanity with the threat of death hanging over them. They agree to act as spies to keep from being beaten by the investigators. That's the whole point of the remarkable work. And Kataev says, "Why didn't Ivan Denisovich protest? If only under his blanket." How much did Kataev protest during the Stalin years? He wrote the same servile hymns as everybody.

Now I see how harmful Khrushchev's anti-Stalinist campaign is to the Black Hundreds types. Khrushchev read *One Day* and allowed it to be published, to the horror of the Polikarpovs of this world.

27 November.

Obraztsov came to see me the day before yesterday and told me publication of the journal *Literatura i zhizn'* was being halted for want of subscribers (there is no demand for Black Hundreds ideology). It will be replaced by *Literaturnaia Rossiia*. Leonid Sobolev, head of the Writers' Union Russian Republic branch, is in the process of selecting contributors to *Literaturnaia Rossiia* and is of course doing his best to keep as many as possible of the *Literatura i zhizn'* contingent so as to reproduce its anti-Semitic and overall Black Hundreds line. But to make it look reform-oriented, he has invited Shklovsky and Obraztsov on board. [. . .]

28 November.

At the American Embassy to meet the children's writer Munro Leaf. The guests included Kassil, his wife, Leaf, his wife, Leaf's interpreter, and the amiable director of the Children's Book House. The ambassador's wife turns out to be a translator. She has translated the Marquis de Custine's book about Russia, which is full of truths about Stalin (a hundred years before the fact—a miraculous prophecy).[319] Custine very well understood that the government was a façade, the epitome of violence and lies, but everything he wrote about the Russian people is poppycock and slander, because no other people revolted against its oppressors with such heroism and self-abnegation as Russians in the nineteenth century. < . . . >

1 December.

Fresh snow, plenty of it, unbelievably beautiful. Went out for a walk with Marina. Dropped in on Zinaida Nikoaevna Pasternak to let her know I'd talked to Chernoutsan about both Pasternak books, which are bogged down in the publishing houses—the prose volume at Goslit, the play translations at Iskusstvo. Chernoutsan promised to get things moving, and I thought I'd cheer Zinaida Nikolaevna up by telling her, but she was not particularly interested.

"What about my pension?" she asked.

319. Phyllis Penn Kohler's translation of the Marquis de Custine's *La Russie en 1839* first appeared under the title *Journey for Our Time* (New York, 1951) and was reprinted as *Custine's Eternal Russia* (Miami, 1976). (M.H.H.)

So they still haven't given her one. < . . . >

Khrushchev went to the Manège exhibition and shouted obscenities at Neizvestny the sculptor and a group of the other young artists showing there. He also came down hard on Falk.[320]

Tamara Ivanova came to see me with Misha (who showed his landscapes at the Manège). They brought a protest, formulated and signed by Vsevolov Ivanov, against Khrushchev's remarks. I signed it. [. . .]

10 December.

< . . . > "The main thing," says Akhmatova, "is not to lose your despair." She has recorded her *Requiem*.

16 December.

Sibirskie ogni has accepted Lida's novella *Sofia Petrovna* for publication, but with the stupidity peculiar to editors they insist on the title *One in a Thousand*. Lida, who is a fanatic when it comes to noninterference on the part of editors, has rejected all their emendations. On the other hand, six months ago it would have been impossible to dream of bringing that kind of work into the open. For years the manuscript had to be hidden like a dangerous crime you could be executed for. Now she's gone to *Novyi mir*, *Znamia*, Sovetskii pisatel', and *Moskva*, and although they all read and rejected it *Sibirskie ogni* has decided to publish it in February. Still, everything depends on tomorrow's meeting with Khrushchev. It's not out of the question that tomorrow will spell an end to liberalism in general, and that will be the end of *Sofia Petrovna*.[321] [. . .]

1962 is ending on a sad note. I signed a letter protesting against Khrushchev's attacks on the young artists, and at yesterday's meeting I got raked over the coals by Khrushchev himself. Even though my tastes were formed by Repin's paintings and Nekrasov's verse, I cannot reconcile myself to

320. Khrushchev's outburst against abstract painting while visiting a mildly unorthodox exhibition led to a crackdown on the liberal tendencies in the arts associated with the thaw. (M.H.H.)

321. A short novel about an ordinary woman whose timid conformism is sorely tested by the arrest of her son during the purges. It did not in fact appear in *Sibirskie ogni* and could not be published in the Soviet Union until the glasnost years. It appeared in English first as *The Deserted House*, translated by Aline Werth (London, 1967), then as *Sofia Petrovna*, translated by Aline Werth and emended by Eliza Kellogg Klose (Evanston, Ill., 1994). (V.E.)

our Serovs, Alexander Gerasimovs, and Loktionovs, who consider themselves Repin's successors. I hate despotism in art.

I don't cherish tender feelings for Neizvestny, but the way they have treated him fills me with intense indignation.

Things were simple in Stalin's time: you walloped the intellectuals, did away with anybody who thought for himself. Now it's much harder. You've got a large, new *technical* intelligentsia the government is dependent on, and this large new group has taken on the function of the humanistic intelligentsia and constitutes a kind of public opinion.

1963

+>-+>-+>-+>-+>-+>-+>

Morituri te salutant!

8 January.

I have always written my diaries for myself, thinking, "I'll sit down and read it in a year, two years, ten, twenty years." Now that I have almost no future, I've lost all desire to keep a diary: I don't wish to write about my life for outsiders, nor have I the time to do so. < . . . >

17 January.

Thirty degrees below zero. [. . .] Gennady Matveevich is supposed to be bringing me the new edition of my poor *Nekrasov's Craft*. It's the fourth edition and has received a Lenin Prize. It leaves me completely cold: it's the worst of my books. It was written during the damned personality cult, when I was trying to write unobtrusive things, because being obtrusive was extremely dangerous. Trying to remain in the shade, I wrote a little article called "Pushkin and Nekrasov" for the Pushkin anniversary and a little article called "Gogol and Nekrasov" for the Gogol anniversary, and so on. Before that (or at that time) I spent several years writing commentaries to Nekrasov's verse—that too to keep in the literary background away from Stalin's police thugs. I am loud, I stand out, so I chose a quiet backwater

and wrote *sotto voce*. When I think of how excited I was while working on
"The Poet and the Hangman," "The Life and Fate of Nikolai Uspensky,"
and "Nat Pinkerton," how can I call *Nekrasov's Craft* anything more than
handicraft? < ... >

15 February.

Paustovsky is currently taking a rest at the Writers House. Yesterday Lida
said he wanted to see me. [...]

What he wanted to see me about is the following: the idiots in charge
of Karelia have decided to destroy all its wooden country churches. He has
pictures of them on his desk. They are magnificent—intricately orna-
mented, but falling apart. They cry out for restoration. Only a monster, a
benighted ignoramus of a monster could think of destroying them. < ... >
We talked of sending a telegram to the authorities calling for an end to
such barbarity. [...]

The second issue of *Novyi mir* has been held up. It was supposed to
contain Ehrenburg's memoirs of Soviet anti-Semites and their victims.

Paustovsky says that *Pravda* and *Izvestiia* are going to run articles
blasting Solzhenitsyn's two new stories. "There's one thing that frightens
me about Solzhenitsyn," he said. "He's an enemy of the intelligentsia. You
can feel it in everything he writes. That's why he so likes Tvardovsky, who
every time he sees me gives me a reproachful look and says, 'You know,
your *Golden Rose* smacks of the intelligentsia.' But fate has had the last
laugh on Tvardovsky: the journal he edits is the most representative of the
Soviet intelligentsia."

17 February.

Paustovsky came again yesterday. Even before he got to the top of the stairs
(panting), he said, "Have you read *Izvestiia* on Yermishka?"

Izvestiia is apparently running an entire page of letters from benighted
readers backing Yermilov and reviling Ehrenburg the Jew, intellectual, and
Westernizer.[322]

322. Reference to a rash of letters triggered by the exchange between Vladimir Yermilov and
Ilya Ehrenburg over the latter's *People, Years, Life*. In an article entitled "Why We Must Argue"
(*Izvestiia*, 29 January 1963) Yermilov accused Ehrenburg of "exaggerating the importance of
modernist art and ignoring the self-quest of the art of the Revolution." He is still more annoyed
by the passages prescribing the "art of silence" as a means of coping with the iniquities of the

Paustovsky brought the draft of his letter to Nikita Sergeevich [Khrushchev] about the destruction of the wooden churches. The suppressed anger is wonderful. After we'd gone over it, Tanya made a clean copy, incorporating the minor changes I'd made, which Paustovsky fully accepted. [. . .]

On Babel: "He would lie to everyone about everything. Even trivialities. He would surround himself with mystery. If he was going to Petersburg, he'd say (even to a neighbor's ten-year-old daughter), 'I'm off to Kaluga.' When some Party types came to search his father's agricultural equipment warehouse (McCormick) in Odessa, Babel's mother locked her husband in a room to keep him from blabbering. The search went fine—they didn't find anything—but Babel's mother unlocked the room too soon, and her husband jumped out, made a rude gesture at them, and shouted, 'Thought you'd find something, eh? Well, out you go, empty-handed!' So back they came, discovered a cellar, and found a bundle of dollars, some gold, etc." [. . .]

21 February.

Eight years have passed since my dear Marya Borisovna died. I am visiting her grave today, as always, without a single feeling, my only justification being that soon, very soon I shall lie at her side forever and atone for all the wrongs I did her, voluntary and involuntary.

Am working on *The Art of Translation*, stupid me, when I should be compiling the sixth, pre-1917 volume of my collected works. Reading those early pieces now, I can see they show a certain talent, something I never noticed while writing them.

Went to the cemetery with Lida. A February blizzard, fog. I stood and thought. There was snow on my grave. I have a clear picture of Peredelkino without me. People will say, "That happened back when old man Chukovsky was alive." The furniture and books will be divided up among the children and grandchildren, and no matter how hard I think I cannot fathom what posthumous fame is, what good it does, what pleasure it is meant to give the dead. < . . . >

---

era, and mockingly attributes to Ehrenburg the slogan "I Can Keep Silent" (an allusion to Tolstoy's famed outcry "I Cannot Keep Silent," a denunciation of the political repression that followed the 1905 Revolution). The fact that editors of *Izvestiia* sided with Yermilov indicated an ominous chill in the cultural climate.

1 March.

< . . . > Called on Paustovsky. He repeated the following aphorism (he
got it from Babel, I think): "All you need to be well-educated is to read
seven or eight books. Yes, but first you need to read twenty thousand or
so."

3 March.

1) Yevgenia Borisovna Zbarskaya has received a very small pension since
her husband died. I sent a note to Sholokhov (who was a close acquaintance
of them both), and he wrote the necessary letter. She is coming today to
have me sign it together with him.

2) Professor Weil and his guitar. A very nice young man. A Gorky
enthusiast. Wants to write a book about him. < . . . >

Received a letter from Solzhenitsyn!

5 March.

Received an awful translation of my *Contemporaries* (Chekhov and Andreev)
from M. I. Benkendorf [Budberg]. Am sending her a letter and the following telegram: STOP TRANSLATING TILL YOU GET MY LETTER.

Literature, art, and the cinema are in for a frontal attack at the Central
Committee the day after tomorrow, 7 March. I saw Paustovsky and Yashin
at the Writers House. Yashin was in a panic. He told the Armenian joke
about Karapet[323] who escapes from a lion by lowering himself on a rope
into a well, but looks down to see a crocodile at the bottom of the well—
"But Karapet does not despair"—and looks up to see a mouse nibbling
away at the rope—"But Karapet does not despair."

Well, Yashin does. The peasants from the kolkhoz he describes in his
Vologda Wedding have sent him a letter telling him he got them absolutely
right. He carries the letter around with him, all atremble: "I've got six
children. What will become of them if I stop getting published?"

Paustovsky is gloomy: "They've got it all worked out beforehand, like
a mass. And there's no place for me in their liturgy. I tried to speak at all

323. Karapet is an imaginary character who serves as the protagonist for a special brand of
ethnic humor in Russia, the "Armenian joke." (V.E.)

three congresses, and all three times they refused to give me the floor." We have both had phone calls from the Central Committee telling us to be sure to attend the meeting. < . . . >

7 March.

It's a pity I'm ill and can't make it to today's meeting in the Kremlin.[324] I don't know what will happen there, but if I weren't eighty-one, I'd take a "most active part." There are lots of rumors, though. They say Sholokhov has prepared a speech that will be the end of *Novyi mir*, Tvardovsky, and Solzhenitsyn, a speech that will extol Yermilov and decimate the intelligentsia, and so on. < . . . >
< . . . >

20 March.

Paustovsky has just left. He had a reading at the Electro-something-or-other Institute, and at the end the students gave him a bouquet—for Ehrenburg. "And I just happened to be going to see him," said Konstantin Georgievich. "He's doing very poorly. He doesn't get out of his chair. The phone keeps ringing with expressions of sympathy, and he just sits there, numb. As for his wife—she's a terrible sight." [. . .]

26 March.

Twenty days ago Natasha Roskina phoned me for an interview in connection with "Children's Week." I told her a lot of boring stuff, and suddenly the day before yesterday she rang to say in an innocent voice that she'd

---

324. Solzhenitsyn described this encounter of the government with the intelligentsia as follows: "The second Kremlin meeting on 7–8 March 1963 was one of the most painful pages in the history of Khrushchev's rule. It was rigged so that the Stalinists had a preponderance of 5 to 1 . . . , and the air was filled with harsh invectives and destructive hostility toward anything that gave the faintest whiff of freedom. . . . It took only a short time . . . to recreate the atmosphere of intolerance we had known in the thirties" (*The Oak and the Calf,* 62). Kaverin recalled that Ehrenburg was "the main target of the attack, that Khrushchev called his *People, Years, Life* "a look from a Paris attic at the history of the Soviet state." Ehrenburg tried to remonstrate, "but was promptly forced into silence. He was roundly insulted. Instantly a vacuum formed around him" (*Epilog,* 381).

added a few lines about my response to Khrushchev's literature speech. Since that's all *Litgazeta* is interested in these days, she decided to insert a paragraph or two saying I don't see any difference between the (Stalinist) fathers and sons. It was like a punch in the nose. I was horrified. I asked her to come and see me, and when she came I demanded that her shameless fabrications be removed from the interview. Then I realized that in these sad times any statement with the slightest hint of ooh-la-la was reprehensible, so I demanded that the entire interview be withdrawn. She didn't guarantee success, but said she would see what she could do. That was on Saturday. On Monday (yesterday) after two sleepless nights I went to *Litgazeta,* straight to the editor, and said, "I'm sure you understand that I, as an intellectual of the old school, can have little sympathy for what is going on in literature today. I'm delighted the 'sons' hate their 'fathers,' and if you print words I never said I'll make my convictions public—not that I've ever hidden them."

And many more wild words. He promised. But I didn't sleep that night either (or, rather, I did sleep, but fitfully, knowing the gangster-like tactics of the press nowadays) and kept thinking that promise or no promise the article might still appear and with heaven only knows what ascribed to me. I had heard just such a story from Ilya Zverev (Izold). He once submitted a very liberal article to *Litgazeta* and went off to Poland. While he was gone, they altered the orientation of the article and added their own ending, consisting of a string of quotes from a Khrushchev speech; they made it the exact opposite of what Zverev had meant to say.

But I was luckier, thank God. < . . . >

12 April.

It's depressing—slaving away at the translation book. Dull, stupid drudgery. Spending as much as three hours to squeeze out two lines . . .

The talk about what's going on in literature is all terrible. Yesterday I heard a rumor that Yevtushenko had shot himself. Well, why shouldn't he? The system that murdered Mandelshtam, Gumilyov, Korolenko, Dobychin, Mayakovsky, Mirsky, Marina Tsvetaeva, Benedikt Livshits, and tortured Belinkov and so on and so forth could easily drive Yevtushenko to suicide.

People also say that some reporters asked Solzhenitsyn what he thought of the current bestialization of literature and responded, "You're keeping me from my work. If *you* don't leave immediately, *I* will." < . . . >

6 June.

Solzhenitsyn came to call today. He bounded up the stairs like a young man. He was wearing a light summer suit; his cheeks were rosy, his eyes youthful and smiling. So he's not so badly off as they said. "The tumor was the size of two fists, but it's gone down now thanks to the Tashkent doctors who took care of me and were very good." He talked a lot about his years in prison. "I could have made money by teaching the old women in the prison reception room what could be passed on to prisoners and what could not." [. . .] He looked through *Chukokkala* and showed interest in the pre-Revolutionary entries. "I'm writing a Petersburg tale; I've been wanting to write one for ages. I've just written a story about a group of young people building a new technical college, and just as they finish building it they are expelled. We have three technical colleges in Ryazan, and two were built like that."

"Seventy-five percent," I said.

"Sixty-six," he said. I'd forgotten he taught mathematics.

He was thrilled with Tallin: "It's the only city in Estonia that still has medieval monuments. And what monuments!" (He enumerated them.) "There are also things to see in the northwestern tip of Estonia." (He named the place.) "I'm planning a bike trip there with a friend."

We drove to the cemetery and looked at Pasternak's grave. It is covered with white dogrose. There are lots of flowers inside as well. Then we went to see Marya Borisovna's grave (and mine). There too the vegetation is rich: cherry trees, rowan trees, acacias. We stood there for a long time, and as always I left in peace.

I've been neglecting my diary, and in the meantime Akhmatova has been to see me (two Wednesdays in a row). Slow and majestic, but wild-eyed. She can't get over Makovsky's having written something unacceptable about her relationship with Gumilyov. "He didn't know us when we were first married."

< . . . >

14 September.

Zinaida Nikolaevna Pasternak says, "I was so distraught I wrote furious letters to Fedin and Tikhonov saying I was living in poverty, I hadn't yet

been granted a pension, the publishing house had cut Borya's minuscule volume of poetry in half, I hadn't received a kopeck from abroad. < . . . > Fedin said the dacha would be paid for, I would be given a lump sum instead of a pension, the Biblioteka poeta Pasternak volume would run to three hundred or three hundred and twenty pages (not a hundred and seventy-five pages, as the contract said), and so on. When I mentioned *Doctor Zhivago*, he looked embarrassed and said, 'It will have to wait. This is not the time for it.' But the following day Khesin phoned from the Office of Authors' Rights and asked for *immediate* information about the heirs." (They obviously want to transfer the foreign royalties here.)
< . . . >

2 October.

The pond has a golden ripple on it, and the surrounding trees seem under a spell. A. A. Soldatov and I have been basking in the sun for three hours, talking lazily.

"Just think," Soldatov said when we turned to the Stalin years, "At Arkos alone five managers were relieved of their functions and shot. They've all been rehabilitated now, right? (He likes to add "right?" to whatever he says.) Five managers! You can be sure that the third, fourth, and fifth thought of saving their necks rather than running the plant." Then he paused and said, "Party members were hit particularly hard."

Which is wrong, of course. The *intelligentsia* was hit particularly hard. Writers like Benedikt Livshits, Osip Mandelshtam, Marina Tsvetaeva, Gumilyov, Mirsky, Kopelev, Solzhenitsyn, Dobychin, Zoshchenko, Akhmatova, Eikhler, Zabolotsky, Babel, Mikhail Koltsov, Alexander Vedensky, Kharms, Vasilyeva, Bruno Yasensky, Pilnyak, Yelena Tager.
< . . . >

12 October.

< . . . > Went out for a walk and saw Marshal Sokolovsky coming toward me. We fell into conversation, and before long he was attacking Solzhenitsyn. "*Ivan Denisovich* is a sermon in camp talk. Who needs (!) camp talk? And if you want to reveal what happened under Stalin, then be clear about

it. He drops a word or two about Stalin and makes a run for it!" And so on.

"Then there's 'Matryona's House.' Some ideal he picks: a smelly old peasant woman complete with icons! And not a single positive Soviet character by way of contrast!"

I objected with a yelp, but he would have none of it: "A sermon in camp talk."

He was slightly better disposed toward "An Incident at Krechetovka Station," but there was hatred in his eyes the whole time we argued. < . . . > He has a guttural, Ukrainian *g* and curses like a trooper, but he's afraid of camp talk. [. . .]

27 October.

< . . . > The local bureaucratic Olympus behave like pigs. First of all, they don't think: all their thinking is done for them by Marx-Engels-Lenin; they have no curiosity, no doubts, no spiritual needs. All that's left is living high at public expense, taking meals at the Kremlin dining room, and spending time at Barvikha listening to the official radio, playing dominoes, and watching football on television. They love undergoing medical treatment and have ten or twenty treatments at a time. Their conversations run along the following lines:

"I don't seem too thirsty for some reason."

"Well, have something salty to eat. Salt makes you thirsty."

"Right, right." [. . .]

The day before yesterday a visiting bigwig came up to me and said, "I'm the one in the Chamber of Deputies who represents the area Matryona comes from. Your Solzhenitsyn made it all up. She's not like that at all."

No matter how I tried to convince him that a writer has the right to transfigure reality, he kept repeating, "He turned everything around, he got it all wrong. A writer should tell the truth." < . . . >

1964

< . . . >

10 January.

Took a walk with Andrei Andreevich Gromyko, a man of great experience, and his wife. Told them about Pasternak and all the money that's going to waste in the States in royalties for the foreign editions of *Doctor Zhivago.* Wouldn't it make sense, I said, to collect the hard currency and pay it to Pasternak's wife in Soviet currency?

Arrived home to find Boris Pasternak, *Fifty Poems,* chosen and translated by Lydia Pasternak Slater (Unwin Books) on my desk. The introduction is fine—biographies of his mother and father and excerpts from his poems—but the translations, well, prose would have been better. Most of the poems are rendered in a Yakub Kolas rhythm, and only the even lines rhyme. I can just imagine how much Pasternak would have suffered had he seen them. No editorial board here would have let a translation like that into print. So I was wrong to pitch into poor Miriam Morton and Maria Ignatyevna [Budberg] for their translations of my work. < . . . >

11 January.

Have been thinking about Mama. She once gave me a paper ruble and sent me off to Dzenkevich's pharmacy for a bottle of Botkin drops. I stuck the ruble in my glove, but the glove had a whole in it and by the time I got to the pharmacy the ruble was gone. I ran home in tears with no ruble and no drops, and Mama said, "But think of the person who found the ruble, a poor woman who . . ." And so on. < . . . >

24 January.

It was as if a drunkard had belched in my face. No, worse. I've just had a visit from a certain Sergei Sergeevich Tsitovich, who announced with a wink that Pervukhin and Voroshilov have Jewish wives, that Marshak has no feeling for Russia (because he's Jewish) and was a Zionist in his youth, that Engels's will says socialism is doomed if you let Jews get involved, that Averchenko's real name is Livshits and Koni (Anatoly Fyodorovich) is really Kohn, and so on. I just sat there, numb with horror. He gave me the feeling he had influential support, concrete political forces behind him. < . . . >

< . . . >

2 February.

Marshak arrived at Barvikha yesterday and has taken up residence in "semi-deluxe" room twenty-three on the ground floor. Tears came to my eyes at the sight of him: he is tiny, wizened, sapped by his illness, yet bubbling with energy. Even before I sat down, he was going on about himself, his strong sense of self-involvement completely justified by the fact that he is phenomenally inspired and fairly radiates creativity. He spoke about Blake and how Gorky said and even wrote to him: "Translating that Blake is a waste of your time." He spoke of Solzhenitsyn, who had paid him a visit the day before yesterday to thank him for the *Pravda* article he'd written. It was originally meant to be broadcast over the radio. He has very positive things to say about Solzhenitsyn: "He's a fine person: he likes my translations of Shakespeare's sonnets." [. . .]

He talked to me about a conversation he'd had with Kosolapov, the head of Goslit, about the contract Kosolapov had broken with the poet Brodsky: " 'You were a coward,' I told him. 'You must have him sign another contract with you.' " And so on.

He talked down to me—he didn't merely talk, he "bestowed his wisdom upon me" and "gave generously of his riches"—yet I was moved by the great victory of the spirit over the flesh, of life over a death besieging him on all sides, and I left with a pang of compassion *for the two of us.*

By the way, my heart is still giving me trouble. It was better yesterday, but today . . .

3 February.

The pain is back. < . . . >

Ilyichev's deputy told me during a walk we took together yesterday that many of Lenin's manuscripts do not figure in his collected works. One of them is about how Voroshilov destroyed the army. "We don't publish them out of pity for the old boy." $<\ldots>$

7 February.

There was a screening of Chaplin's *Modern Times* last night, and Marshak was there. He can see everything, even the small captions, but his hearing has deteriorated. His self-infatuation is as all-encompassing as ever. I saw him back to his room and noticed he had the latest issue of *Novyi mir* on his desk. I picked it up eagerly. "It's got my literary epigrams. Read them." I read to him the poems he had read to me yesterday and the day before. When I started leafing through the issue, he took it from me. He told me for the second time the story of how he had responded to his son's boss when the man said, "I'll break up this synagogue" even though only three percent of the people in the office are Jewish. I had thought of going and reading to him daily, but now I see it's impossible: if you don't read to him about himself, he launches into a monologue.

Chaplin is an unparalleled genius, of course: he made circus clowning lyrical.

17 February.

$<\ldots>$ I see Marshak every day. He goes on about himself or turns what he's saying into a series of unconnected aphorisms and tries to make it seem he's come up with them on the spot. Some of the aphorisms are good—for instance the one about Lugovsky's verse being like the water a painter washes his brushes in: it may be full of color, but it's still only water. Or the one about how our critics have hands but no fingers. And so on. Now he's reworking his Shakespeare sonnet translations: he did them originally as if they were addressed to a woman, when they were obviously addressed to a man. $<\ldots>$

Frida Vigdorova and Lida are doing everything they can for the Leningrad poet Iosif Brodsky, who is being hounded by a group of bad Leningrad poets calling themselves "Russists." He is going on trial tomorrow for moral turpitude. Frida and Lida have worked out a slew of things that we, Marshak and Chukovsky, can do to hold up the trial. Marshak is more than willing to champion the poor poet: he's making all sorts of phone calls, doing everything he can.

< . . . > During breaks between the calls Mitya [Dmitry Chukovsky, his great-grandson] talked about Solzhenitsyn's visit to the Studio of the Moscow Art Theater to see its production of *An Incident at Krechetovka Station*. A large crowd had gathered to catch a glimpse of him and kept waiting and waiting, wondering what was making him so late, until he was discovered sitting in the third row, unrecognized. When they realized who he was, he asked to speak to the actors in private. He wanted nothing to do with the public and was especially disturbed to learn there were journalists present. "Everything I have to say to readers I say in my works. I need no mediators." He said such unpleasant things about journalists that one of them went off in a huff.

Marshak listened carefully and suddenly said in a perfectly plain voice, "I don't feel well" and fainted. Mitya practically had to carry him to his room (number twenty-three). We called a doctor, opened the window, and in a few minutes he came to. "I thought I was dying," he said in the same plain voice.

Mitya was highly impressed. No sooner was Marshak in possession of his faculties than he said, "Phone Lida about Iosif Brodsky."

There is a certain majesty to his character.

18 February.

[. . .] I don't know what's been happening with Brodsky. I wonder why Marshak had me pay for the telegrams as well as formulate the texts.[325]
< . . . >

19 February.

Damn the Benkendorfs and Dubelts of this world, whatever regime they defend! The violence they do to literature! Poor, miserable Poskrebyshev [Stalin's henchman]—his infamy shall echo through the ages. Zhdanov never dreamed how he branded himself and his descendants with his illiterate and boorish attack on Akhmatova and Zoshchenko. That is what

325. Chukovsky and Marshak sent the following telegram to the Leningrad People's Court: "Iosif Brodsky is a gifted poet and a skillful and hardworking translator. We ask the court to take our opinion of the young man's unquestionable literary talent into consideration." The court refused to include the telegram in the proceedings because it had not been notarized.

I want to write in the copy of *From Two to Five* that Lebedev has brought for my autograph. [...]

20 March.

Getting close to eighty-two. The doctor who came to see me yesterday is clearly the one who will lay me in my grave. She told me there's a note in my medical history saying, "Considers himself healthy."

No, I consider myself ill, but I so hated undergoing treatment and having my doctor at the time pester me with her daily visits (she was very stupid) that I told her day after day, "I feel wonderful."

< ... >

25 June.

The head of the Supreme Court, L. N. Smirnov, came to see me yesterday. < ... > He is stout and has a high forehead and tired features. He perked up when I mentioned Iosif Brodsky. "You know, I've received two letters about him. Both from Leningrad. One in English. Written by a student. He'd torn a sheet of paper out of a notebook. A funny letter."

"You may find it funny, but Brodsky is suffering. He's a sick man hauling manure at the beck and call of some brutes." And so on.

"A very funny letter."

I told him about the malicious Prokofyev, who for his own obscure reasons had it in for Brodsky, and the ignoramus of a judge. < ... > He said he was feeling tired and had to get back to Moscow: he had a lot of cases to read through—murders, rapes, and more murders. He would be sentencing a few people to be shot.

He's got a nice face. He's an *intelligent*. His last words were: "How good that you love children."

< ... >

28 June.

Much to my horror I see that my "Zoshchenko" is worthless. I've been working on it since 1 March. All I wanted was ten pages, but I couldn't even come up with that. < ... >

5 July.

Three days ago Lida went out of our gate to go to the Writers House and saw a car coming. She ran off to the side of the road, but failed to see the bicycle behind it. The bicycle knocked her off her feet and she fell on her left side, which was badly bruised.

While proofreading *From Two to Five,* I needed a footnote from Marshak's *Education Through the Word.* I picked up the book, found the page I needed, and was inserting the reference into the proof when the phone rang and Volodya Glotser said three very ordinary words: "Marshak is dead." It was like an electric shock. My hands began to tremble. I couldn't think. And then I did have an awful thought: What if Lida finds out? Bedridden and in the state she's in, she can't possibly go to the funeral or write about him.

7 July.

< . . . > Sofya Krasnova, the nonentity of an editor of my collected works, came to see me yesterday. The galleys of Volume One are abominable— the choice of illustrations arbitrary, the layout of the poems ridiculous— but the cost sheet is complete and no changes are possible. I thought there would be a mock-up, but nobody showed me one. It really made me angry. Fifty years ago, when I was editing Repin's memoirs, it took three days to get the illustrations and the general layout right, and nobody batted an eyelid; now with our planned economy it takes practically a decree from the Council of Ministers to move a few pages: the cost sheet is complete. < . . . >

8 July.

The more I think about Marshak the more terrified I am. There he was in the claws of death—he had a table strewn with medicines next to his bed— hanging on to life by the force of his spirit and the thought of his work. He couldn't walk, he'd grown deaf and blind, he'd shriveled up like a balloon with the air let out, but he had a pile of papers on his desk, and as long as he could command those papers, as long as he could go on creating the drafts that with endless and unstinting labor he turned into poetry, songs, epigrams, the Russian Burns, and the Russian Blake, he held his own on planet Earth. This "planet Earth" has been around for millions of years, and all at once, after millions of years of nonbeing, a man comes into being for a split second, and once that split second is over he vanishes back into nonbeing. [. . .]

24 August.

The past month and a half have made it clear I'm moving into the "pre-death" phase. I have heart spasms and feel phenomenally weak. I've been in bed for forty days, done almost no work, and am constantly having medicine jabbed into me. Today I will start recording The Official Account of My Death.

< . . . >

10 September.

Camphor.

It's all nonsense. Dying is not so awful as people make it out to be. Having spent my whole life studying writers' biographies, I know how a good many men died, men like Nekrasov, Turgenev, Saltykov-Shchedrin, Vasily Botkin, Leonid Andreev, Fonvizin, Zoshchenko, Walt Whitman, Oscar Wilde, Sologub, Heine, Mickiewicz, Goethe, Byron, and a number of others, including Kuprin, Bunin, Koni, and Lev Tolstoy. I've studied their methodology of dying; I know what the dying do and say and what happens after their funerals. In 1970 Lyusha will say, "This was here when Grandfather was alive." [. . .] Or "That's the balcony where Marshak used to sit," somebody will say, walking past the dacha, to which his friend will say, "Marshak? You mean Chukovsky!" There will be obituaries in *Litgazeta* and *Nedelia*, but in 1975 I'll be revealed as an uninspired, highly overrated writer (which is in fact the case) and put out to pasture.

Solzhenitsyn came at half past ten looking younger than ever. He refused coffee and asked for tea. We embraced. He told me about his new novel [*The First Circle*] in confidence. Tvardovsky is wild about it, ecstatic. < . . . > It is five hundred and fifty pages long. Three days (two and a half, actually) in 1949. Prison and interrogations. Even Stalin puts in an appearance. Tomorrow he will tell Tvardovsky to let me read it.

When I told him I was writing about Zoshchenko, he said, "I've read a lot of him, but don't like him. I find his humor coarse." < . . . >

Later: Tvardovsky didn't give me the novel. He's taken a sudden violent disliking to me.

23 October.

Cheever paid me a visit yesterday. He's the spitting image of Wells: he's got the same hair color, the same smile, the same build, the same rosy complexion. He stayed a long time, four hours, preferring to miss the first two acts of the Bolshoi performance he had tickets for. I was down with flu and it was hard for me to sit—I wanted to go to bed—but I so like him and enjoy his presence. He hugged me when he left. If he knew what a bad little article I'd written about him.

It was Tanya who kept the conversation going for the most part. She positively shone in his presence. Her translation of his "Swimmer" is wonderful. < . . . >

Since I last made an entry, Khrushchev has been removed from office, three cosmonauts have been launched into space, and the Labour Party has won the British elections, but I'll leave it to others to write about such matters. I will only note that Updike arrived in Moscow yesterday.

Cheever is like a member of the family.

21 November.

< . . . > Now that Khrushchev has been dethroned, the government is keeping mum, and the man in the street doesn't know under whose auspices he will be led along the "Leninist path," there are a number of epigrams, songs, jokes, and ditties being written.
< . . . >

26 November.

Once, when he was about six, Kolya looked through my books and said, "When Papa dies, I'll have these books bound and throw those books out."

Now that the time is drawing near, I can see Kolya doing just that. They'll have a hard time with the books. Lately English books have occupied a particularly large place in my library. None of my heirs has any interest in reading English books.

Gave a reading of my Andreev memoirs on the radio. The new head of radio and TV perceived something felonious in a recent TV program called *The Circus* and dismissed three people. The feebleminded swine of a nonentity. They haven't learned a thing, these thugs. All they believe in is flogging and bugging. [. . .]

7 December.

Have just had a call from Laskina at *Moskva*. She liked my Zoshchenko article: "You have taught us to read Zoshchenko," she said.

"So you think I'm more critic than memoirist."

"Right. You'll want to trim the memoir part." [. . .]

Pasternak's son, Yevgeny Borisovich, has just phoned to ask me for an introduction to a book of his poems being put out by Goslitizdat. Oh ho ho!

I'm a swine for not writing about Chekhov.

Tanya tells me she saw a film in the flat of someone who works for the American Embassy. He had sent an invitation to the Foreign Committee of the Writers' Union. There were four of them altogether—Tanya, Volzhina, and two young translators—and they assigned four informers. When they were in the lift, one of them asked one of the translators to open his briefcase and show him the books the man from the Embassy had given him. < . . . >

Akhmatova is in Italy. Who would have believed it! She has

> Not a bone unbroken
> Not a vein unstretched

and suddenly there she is in Italy for her own coronation.[326] < . . . >

8 December.

Lida arrived from Komarov yesterday with the following story. The Lerner who played such a despicable role in the Brodsky affair was now, as a member of the Voluntary People's Militia, on the trail of a certain physicist. It seems a woman had taken to visiting his hotel room, and Lerner, striking a moral pose, frightened the man at the desk into letting him into the room. But since the physicist was an atomic physicist, he had two bodyguards, and they beat him up and took him to the head of the hotel, who confiscated his documents. < . . . >

---

326. Akhmatova had gone to Italy to receive the prestigious Aetna-Taormina award. The lines are from Nekrasov's *Who Lives Well in Russia* (chapter 7, "The Governess").

10 December.

< . . . > Olenka Andreeva, Leonid Nikolaevich's granddaughter, was here on a visit. She is translating *The Idiot* with her husband in New York and setting up an exhibition of her drawings in Paris. She also spends time with her parents in Geneva.

In the evening I had a meeting with three Party members: Yelizar Maltsev, Pavel Nilin, and . . . enko [full name missing]. They stand quite a bit to the left of non-Party members and wax ironic when it comes to the current reforms. < . . . >

11 December.

"You can't turn a toilet into the Mona Lisa," said Simon Dreiden when he heard that *Litgazeta* had rejected my Zoshchenko article.

Had a phone conversation with a Zalman Akhraimovich, the head of one or another department there. He said my article wasn't newspaper material. "I have been writing newspaper articles for sixty years. I should very much like to write something that is not newspaper material and am unable to do so. My article is perfectly good newspaper material. The problem is that you are a coward. Here I give you a chance to show your readers at subscription time how honest you are—and you are well aware that the article would bring you hundreds of subscribers—yet you prefer to take sides with the forces that trampled Zoshchenko underfoot."

15 December.

[. . .] Had a visit yesterday from Yelizar Maltsev. A very fine man. He talked an hour and a half about a meeting at the Party Municipal Committee. He was terribly uneasy and upset and kept jumping up and down, laughing nervously, and raising his voice as he spoke. < . . . > What has all this to do with literature? I thought to myself. The only way to be a writer is to ignore the functionaries he was talking about, forget they ever existed. Only then can writers be true heirs of Belinsky, Tyutchev, Herzen, and Chekhov. Why should a frightened yet brazen-faced functionary stand between Chekhov and me? I may be an unworthy microscopic heir of writers like Chekhov, Turgenev, Kuprin, and Bunin, but I *am* their heir, and they—my legitimate ancestors—are the people I think about day in and day out, not those idiot functionaries. [. . .]

17 December.

< . . . > Kolya has just returned from Italy; he was there with Marina. Marina saw the Akhmatova celebration on television. She says Tvardovsky gave a ridiculous speech about how Akhmatova "also enjoys recognition and respect in the land of her birth."

Mendeleev, an editor at *Nedelia,* came to see me with my Akhmatova article. It will appear in the coming issue. He was reeking of vodka—no paragon of virtue he—but hurray! The conspiracy of silence surrounding Akhmatova is over!

Though for some reason I'm still worried about her. [. . .]

21 December.

A Marya Borisovna day. Took a walk with Zalygin, who lives in Novosibirsk. The citizens of Novosibirsk won't venture outside after dark these days, because a group of perfectly Soviet youths recently murdered twelve people there for no apparent reason. The merry band had gone out for a stroll of an evening, swinging a weight on a rope. They ran into a group of people on their way home from the theater and said, "This man here and that woman." Up went the weight and down went two bodies, whereupon these products of Soviet reality moved on to their next set of murders. When a local reporter wrote a sketchy, highly censored article about the incident, she was summoned by the Municipal Committee. "How dare you defame our city?" they said. "That kind of thing goes on everywhere."

On our walk < . . . > we met Vadim Kozhevnikov, who used to pass me without a greeting, but suddenly acknowledged me and made a whole round with us, showing off his liberal views—this the man who brought Vasily Grossman's novel to the attention of the Central Committee, as a result of which the novel was placed under arrest and Grossman perished.[327] Now he calls *Oktiabr'* a Black Hundreds journal and the author of *Rot* a Black Hundreds writer. < . . . >

327. See note 233.

25 December.

Took a walk with Sima Dreiden. He told me a shocking story with a deep meaning to it. An *intelligent* took up residence (against his will) in a railway trackman's hut. The trackman was illiterate. The *intelligent* went to great lengths to teach him to read. The man was slow, but eventually mastered the basics of grammar. He very much wanted to become a train guard, but to do so he needed to memorize dozens of rules and take an exam, and the *intelligent* helped him there as well. As a guard he would buy large quantities of oranges and other fruit in the south and sell it at a profit in the north. He grew rich. Meanwhile the *intelligent* was arrested. After serving out his time in the camps, he returned home and was rehabilitated. From his file he learned that no sooner had the noble railwayman become literate than he wrote a denunciation stating that "XY has ties with people abroad." < . . . >

1965

✦➤-➤-➤-➤-➤-➤-➤-➤-➤➤

14 January.

[. . .] Went to town to see about having my "Zoshchenko" moved from the May to the April issue of *Moskva*. It turns out to have moved by itself—to June: April is a Lenin issue, May is devoted to the victory over fascism.

From *Moskva* to *Pravda*, where the bald, gray-faced Nikolai Alexandrovich Abalkin read the Vasentsov article aloud in my presence and said, "A fine article, excellent, and, most important, a necessary article: we need to educate (!) our youth (!) in the spirit of national and even nationalistic ideals. Where is our youth headed? It has lost all restraint, nothing is sacred, and so on. The last thing I intended was for my article to restrain our youth! He promised to publish it. *Pravda* makes a dark, dungeon-like impression. < . . . >

Despite insomnia, stomach and heart pains, and friends' entreaties, I went to the Writers' Union the day before yesterday to give a talk at a Zoshchenko evening, the first in twenty years. Although there was a large audience, we were forced to use the Small Auditorium. There was not a single poster anywhere, not even in the Writers House. The program was to include Kataev, Shklovsky, Chukovsky, Kaverin, and Ilyinsky, but Kataev and Shklovsky were afraid to show their faces. Shame on them. They both did their share of whooping during the official campaign against Zoshchenko.

It was freezing cold. I had to wear boots. My talk was well received: people clapped a lot and cried out, "Thank you!"

Lev Slavin served as moderator. He gave a marvelous introduction. He said there is a whole contingent of splendid writers whose names don't even come up in histories of Soviet literature: Babel, Platonov, Khatsrevin, Lapin, and—of course—Zoshchenko. We will stand up for them, and so on.

Kaverin's talk was brilliant and courageous, dripping with indignation against the butchers who were Zoshchenko's downfall. [. . .]

16 January.

[. . .] Two weeks ago Yevtushenko gave a radio recitation of a poem about a ship tossed hither and yon (that is, Lenin's Party). The authorities were furious and fired two people connected with the program. < . . . >

It is the authorities' design that the Writers' Union and all journals be headed by swine. Elections for leading Writers' Union positions are coming up, and Lida is terribly worried. If the elections weren't bogus, the swine would be out on their ears, but the authorities will certainly find a way to foist their swine on the Union, so what's the point in worrying? The outcome is determined in advance. If Lida rushes into the fray, it is because she wants the younger generation to see that there is such a thing as a struggle for justice(?!). [. . .]

18 January.

The writers are jubilant: the Leningrad Writers' Union held reelections, and not only was Prokofyev, who put together the "Brodsky affair," trounced but the Brodskyites—Grudinina, Dolinina, Etkind, etc.—got on the board. The entire literary world is thrilled at even so minor and fragile a victory. < . . . >

21 January.

A Marya Borisovna day. In a month she will have been in the grave for ten years, waiting for me to join her.

Raisa Orlova came for a visit and told me all about the elections to the Writers' Union board. Thousands of writers spent the whole day in that stultifying atmosphere, fantasizing that literature would change if B or C got elected instead of A even though one condition has not changed: all power over the writers remains in the hands of the people who did in Babel, Zoshchenko, Mayakovsky, Mandelshtam, Gumilyov, Livshits, Tager, Tsvetaeva, Yasensky, Pasternak, and hundreds of others.

12 February.

< . . . > I've just finished a piece on the Bible. Writing the word Bible with a capital letter is apparently unacceptable, and it's better not to mention that it's a Jewish book. [. . .]

29 March.

Akhmatova promised to visit on Wednesday (the 24th), but I wanted to take part in the Children's Book Festival in the Hall of Columns first. < . . . > Sitting on the podium and looking out into the fine hall, I remembered that this was where we paid tribute to Gorky and Kirov and this is where Lermontov had a reading at the age of fourteen. Little girls wearing wreaths filed into the front rows, the television people got set up, Kassil said something about cosmonauts, and all of a sudden things started swimming before my eyes and I barely made it to a sofa in the lobby. < . . . > They called an ambulance, and after an intravenous vasodilator I got back to Peredelkino, though more dead than alive.

Akhmatova is in Peredelkino (with Frida), but I'm in no shape to see her, so she will leave and I'm condemned to lying here immobile and gulping down all sorts of poisonous medications. I should be proofreading "Whitman" for my third volume, and instead here I am lying "like a fool, as yet unborn or newly dead," and dear, sweet Marina is reading me Goncharov's *Frigate Pallada*, specially written for people like me who are forbidden to use their brains. It's wonderfully written, but vapid. < . . . >

4 April.

From today on I am in cubicle ninety-three of the Kremlin's Suburban Hospital, in other words, in heaven. < . . . > Today I will see Yasinovskaya, the very practical and judicious editor of my Bible book. I'm sorry I agreed to write it. It will earn me the attacks of believers and non-believers, believers, because I speak of the Holy Scriptures as a sequence of interesting myths, and non-believers, because I am promoting the Bible. [. . .]

12 April.

< . . . > Have got to proofread *Contemporaries* even though I very much dislike Korolenko, Lunacharsky, and Repin now. I've always thought Lunacharsky was a gifted yahoo, but a yahoo all the same, and the only reason I decided to write about him was that unlike the current minister of culture he was an educated man. The article about Repin dates from shortly after his death, when praising him was forbidden. Now his name is synonymous with things reactionary, and fashion would dictate withholding praise, but what do I care for fashion—though I do agree with Vladimir Nabokov when he calls *Pushkin Taking an Examination* and *Onegin's Duel with Lensky* silly little daubs.[328]
< . . . >

9 May.

The first cuckoo. Plaintive and importunate, never-ending. As if next door. And—am I really hearing it once more?—the polyphonic chorus of birds coming from the woods, wave upon wave, surging, desisting, and surging again. < . . . >
   Conversation with an African from Kenya:

HE. You speak excellent English.
I. Oh, no! I can only read.

328. Vladimir Nabokov had this to say about Repin in his autobiographical *Other Shores:* "I even pictured—God forgive me—that most mediocre painting of that mediocrity Repin depicting a forty-year-old Onegin aiming at a curly-headed Sobinov" (*Drugie berega* in *Sobranie sochinenii v 4-kh tomakh* [Moscow, 1990] 245). Nabokov did not include this sentence in the final English-language version of the work, *Speak, Memory.*

HE (*puzzled*). You read English books?
I. Yes, I love them.
HE. You do? We hate the English.
I. Shakespeare. Ben Jonson. Thackeray, Samuel Johnson, Dickens.
HE. We hate them all. We hate colonialism.
I. But what about Byron, Bernard Shaw, William Morris?

His forehead wrinkled as if he had bit into something sour. And there are millions like him. All of a piece.

It's so chillingly simplistic. People with true culture will soon be as isolated as, say, Herzen or Tyutchev, and everything they represent will be smothered by mass semi-culture. It will be like the eighteen-sixties, but worse, more satanic.[329] For the likes of him even **pop literature** is too high a goal: two or three ready-made thoughts will hold him for a lifetime. Yet he's a perfectly nice person, full of animation, with a high forehead and sparkling young eyes.

A recently published collection of articles from the *Times Literary Supplement* includes a review of my *Alive as Life,* which received not a single review in Russia.[330] While leafing through this **highbrow** publication, I was brought a copy of *Iunost'* with Yevtushenko's long poem "The Bratsk Hydraulic-Electric Station," and what had been a clever book turned into a handful of dust. What is remarkable about the poem is that it treats a subject that is our very lifeblood. [. . .]

17 May.

I gave Doctor XY a hundred rubles (in other words, a thousand old rubles) and talked to her about the hospital where I was. The hospital is a scandal: Central Committee members and other bigwigs have created a paradise for themselves and couldn't care less about the commoners. The latter are subjected to dirty beds, starvation rations, a lack of essential medicine, and coarse, loudmouthed nurses, while the former and their wives receive victuals galore, medicine galore, courtesy galore—everything their hearts desire. [. . .]

329. Reference to the resurgence of the anti-aesthetic and crudely utilitarian ethos of the Russian radical intelligentsia in the 1860s. (V.E.)
330. "Brush Up Your Russian," *Times Literary Supplement,* 16 January 1964.

27 May.

Akhmatova rang yesterday. I gave her a number of foolish pointers for her upcoming coronation,[331] mentioning in passing what a fine person Sir Isaiah Berlin is, how warm and kindhearted, etc. And now Lida tells me that A.A. knows Berlin better than I do because she had an affair with him in the forties in Leningrad (or Moscow), that she has dedicated many poems to him (the poem about the "mysterious meeting manqué"), that he in fact initiated the coronation. He is highly influential and will certainly assure her a welcome with all due pomp.

What a long Don Juan list she has.[332] Plenty to mull over at night. [. . .]

31 May.

[. . .] They told Akhmatova she'd be going on Friday, then on Tuesday, but they gave her the visa on Monday. *Litgazeta* did an interview with her and published some translations she did from the Egyptian.

Natasha Belinkova brought me my Zoshchenko article all mangled by the censor. The Serapion Brothers are completely out of bounds. The article is due to appéar in the June issue of *Moskva.* < . . . >

8 June.

Not a peep about Akhmatova in the papers.

[. . .] Our idiots, by persecuting Pasternak and putting Brodsky on public trial, made them famous on five continents. [. . .]

14 June.

The Vinogradovs came to see me yesterday. [. . .] Somebody sent Viktor Vladimirovich and his wife a deluxe edition of Camus and two other books.

331. By "coronation" Chukovsky means the ceremony at which Akhmatova was awarded a doctorate in literature *honoris causa* by Oxford. (V.E.)

332. *Pushkin's Don Juan List* is a monograph detailing the poet's numerous conquests. Even though Akhmatova's encounter with Isaiah Berlin was a memorable experience for both parties, as witnessed by the moving pages Berlin devoted to it in *Personal Impressions,* it was scarcely another "conquest." (V.E.)

The censor informed him that they had retained the books and that he could come and read them on their premises should he so desire. < . . . >

17 June.

S. A. Konovalov came with news of Akhmatova. She is staying with Berlin; she had breakfast with the Vice Chancellor; she had an interview in the *Times* and a picture. He brought an excerpt from the interview in which she says that the younger generation is fearless, that the best poets (such as Maria Petrovykh) are not published, that she went hungry in her day, that it was impossible to tell on what basis Stalin chose his victims, and so on. I was mortified by the interview; Lida found it to her liking: "Akhmatova was always heroic." [. . .]

27 June.

Sunday. Clear weather.

~~Yesterday I had a minor cerebral crisis.~~

Early this morning Zhenya Pasternak brought over an advance copy of a Biblioteka poeta volume with BORIS PASTERNAK written in bold letters on the cover! He is taking it to the hospital for Zinaida Nikolaevna. A red-letter day! < . . . >

1 July.

Received a copy of *Moskva* with my Zoshchenko article. They've made the most God-awful mess of it. Instead of the caricature I sent them they published a dour portrait: *Zoshchenko at His Desk.* The violence they do to authors goes so far as to be humorous. I once sent a letter to *Komsomol'skaia Pravda* expressing my gratitude to the Bonfire participants, and the editorial board turned it into an article entitled "Burn, Brightly Burn" and *corrected my style!* Without my permission.

2 July.

Mikhail Alexandrovich Lifshits, who is staying at Paustovsky's dacha, has just told us about a neat and courteous little old man he often sees in the courtyard of his Moscow house, a pensioner who loves children. The man's job was to carry out sentences. To put it plainly, he was a hangman. "He gets a *very* good pension. You should see the way he dresses. And there's a perpetual smile on his face." < . . . >

Koma came to give me a copy of Vygotsky's book, which he has annotated.[333] He asked me to sign a telegram to Mikoyan about concern for Brodsky. I was only too happy to sign and gave Koma ten rubles towards the cost of the telegram. The telegram calls Brodsky a remarkable poet. I don't think so. He is too free-and-easy. [. . .]

15 August.

< . . . > Listening to the radio today, I realized for the first time in my life that radio is the opium of the people. In a country whose economy is in desperate straits and whose political system is based on absolute slavery it presents tiny isolated bright spots, rarities, as general phenomena and labels all regimes but ours as slave-based. < . . . >

By the same token one can say that newspapers are the opium of the people, soccer is the opium of the people. And upbeat songs meant to mask the general despondency. And upbeat people: "Do tell us, Ivan Pafnytyich, how your kolkhoz has managed to achieve such amazing results."

The sky is a leaden gray. There hasn't been a scrap of blue for a whole week. And the wind is wild. We've had rainy summers before, but nothing like this. I can see a rick of hay from my window. It is rotting before my very eyes. The entire harvest is headed in the same direction.

18 August.

Received a letter from Isaiah Berlin. He reports from Italy that the local papers are writing about my introduction to Pasternak's verse.[334] Simmons

333. Lev Vygotsky, *Psikhologiia iskusstva* (Moscow, 1965). Koma is the nickname of Vyacheslav Ivanov, who wrote the following dedication to Chukovsky: "Read this book extraordinary. / Don't forget the Koma-ntery."

334. Chukovsky had great difficulty publishing his introduction to the first collection of Pasternak's verse since the *Doctor Zhivago* affair. He wrote it at the request of the poet's son. The editor insisted that Pasternak's literary past be characterized as "complex and contradictory," and Chukovsky refused to comply. The edition was accordingly provided with an afterword by Nikolai Bannikov, who lectured his readers as follows: "Not being a social thinker, Pasternak was naturally unable to solve the problems raised in the novel. . . . His deplorable errors, especially those committed during the last years of his life, are well-known. . . . He was undercut and hobbled by his ideological stance and his social alienation and isolation."

has sent an idiotic *Times* article from Oxford about same. A Canadian doctor has sent a similar article from the Canadian press: "Pasternak Poems." I'll have to tell Yevgeny Borisovich. [. . .]

Lyusha has brought terrible news: a group of Black Hundreds bigots has let loose at a plenary session and launched a new campaign against literature, *Novyi mir*, Brodsky, and anyone who dares have an opinion of his own.[335] < . . . >

Heard a divine Rachmaninoff performance (Third Concerto). Marvelous emotional energy: a tumultuous and defiant background to a crystalline lyrical voice, an ecstatic lament, several passages of pure gold. And suddenly a pause—followed by thoughtful, slow, naive sounds ready to die, bordering on silence, near silence—nocturnal, isolated, whispered, conversing among themselves—and then day breaking, the heat of the sun and the passions, the deceptive allurements and values of life, the wild pounding of the blood, youth, yea-saying, health . . .

For how long? How long does anything last on earth? Then came a trill and suddenly—fitful, explosive streams turning into a dance, festive (magnificent, dauntless, artless) sounds, and whispers again, though by then I was exhausted and had stopped listening. Even so, the crystal and gold stayed with me all day. < . . . >

Radio is a terrible thing. The youth programs are pure treacle. "All roads are open to you," Gagarin intones, priest-like. But if Lyusha wants to go to Holland or I want to write that Leonov's *Russian Forest* is a bad book, the road is closed. < . . . >

24 August.

Went to the park. Spent a blissful day by the lake. Met Lebedev and Tseitlin (from *Izvestiia*). Their style, as before, was mocking, ironic, yet at

---

335. Echoes of this meeting occur on the pages of Solzhenitsyn's sketches of literary life: "We can say with near certainty that what was planned was an abrupt return to Stalinism, . . . that in August an important ideological conference took place at which it was explained that the struggle for peace went on, the Soviet people *must not be disarmed*. . . . It was time to *resurrect the useful concept* 'enemy of the people'. . . . The spirit of Zhdanov's decrees on literature was sound—*Novyi mir* must be looked at *more closely* to see why the bourgeoisie praises it so much. (There was something about me, too: I had distorted the picture of the camp-world, where only communists suffer and our enemies were imprisoned with good reason)" (*The Oak and the Calf*, 98–99).

the same time gentle. Lebedev said that the Russian intelligentsia felt very hurt that Sholokhov hadn't been made a Hero of Labor! "Intellectuals don't care about decorations," I cried, "about pieces of tin pinned to the chest! And if ours do, what kind of intellectuals are they!" And so on. < ... >

15 September.

Beautiful weather. Feeling better. A major event: Bulgakov's *A Novel of the Theater*.[336] A miracle. It came out in the August issue of *Novyi mir*. A dazzling achievement. There are pages worthy of Gogol.

My little Pasternak article in *Iunost'* has been the object of much unexpected praise. [...]

21 September.

Solzhenitsyn has just left. His beard is long, his cheeks rosy; he looks taller than before. But he's terribly upset. The thing is, he was foolish enough to pick up the three copies of the unfinished novel he'd left at *Novyi mir* and take them to an anthroposophist friend in a suitcase. That night his friend was visited by some "archangels" supposedly after his theosophical books, and suddenly they asked, "What have you got in that suitcase? Underwear?" And that was the end of the novel.[337]

His enemies have been slandering him, spreading rumors to the effect that he was a *vlasovets*,[338] betrayed his country, didn't fight at all, or surrendered to the enemy. His dream is to move to the town of Obninsk, where there's an atomic research center. His wife had a job in Ryazan, but she was recently fired, and he's homeless, lost, anticipating some awful event, a summons, prison even. [...]

---

336. Bulgakov's *A Novel of the Theater* (published in English as *White Snow*, translated by Michael Glenny [London, 1967]) is a satirical roman à clef that closely reflects Bulgakov's disagreeable experiences with the Moscow Art Theater. (V.F.)

337. On 11 September a KGB search at the apartment of a friend of Solzhenitsyn's produced a manuscript of *The First Circle*. More information on the search may be found in *The Oak and the Calf*, 102.

338. A soldier who went over to Andrei Vlasov, a Soviet general who turned coat in 1942. (M.H.H.)

28 September.

< . . . > Solzhenitsyn arrived at one o'clock with wife and chattels in tow. Tomorrow morning he is moving into Kolya's room.

29 September.

Solzhenitsyn has moved in. From our conversation it is clear he is completely absorbed by his own work and not particularly interested in, say, Pushkin, Leonid Andreev, or Kvitko. I recited my favorite poems to him. He didn't care for them. But he can go on endlessly about the camps. [. . .]

30 September.

Alexander Isaevich recited a powerful poem about the Russian attack on Germany—and gave a powerful recitation. I felt part of that stream of frenzied people. It went on for fifty minutes. There was something elemental about it. It was extremely strong. He wrote it fifteen years ago. It opens with a rushing cataract of words, a frantic energy, and ends in tranquility with the rape of a German girl.

Boris Zakhoder came to see me. He brought his translation of *Winnie the Pooh*. The September issue of *Iunost'* has a marvelous cycle of his poems, but he can't find a publisher. He's thinking of translating *Alice in Wonderland*.

2 October.

That nice Natalya Stolyarova, Ehrenburg's secretary, came to see me bearing gifts from Vadim Andreev in Paris. [. . .] Stolyarova told us that Sinyavsky had confessed to being one of the "Abram Tertzes."[339] She saw some of the old émigrés in Paris, a dying clan. Thirty invalids from the poor house including Adamovich and Odoevtseva.

339. Two dissident writers, Andrei Sinyavsky and Yuly Daniel, were arrested and tried for having published anti-Soviet works abroad under the pseudonyms of Abram Tertz and Nikolai Arzhak. Their trial was a turning point in the Russian dissident movement: both refused to repent, and their imprisonment triggered public protest within the Soviet Union as well as in the West. (V.E.)

3 October.

[. . .] Solzhenitsyn went to Moscow yesterday. He may come back today or not until Thursday. Now that I know him better, I see he's basically interested in one thing only, which he treats in "An Incident at Krechetovka Station" and *Ivan Denisovich*. Everything else is hazy. He doesn't care about literature as such; he sees it only as a means of protesting against his enemies. He has a clear idea of where he is going and proceeds accordingly.
< . . . >
< . . . >

5 October.

Terrible insomnia. Mustard poultices. Three doses of dimedrol.

   Went down to the lake with that nice man Soldatov and suddenly felt dizzy. We came back, and Soldatov and his wife gave me some shocking news: Maria Ignatyevna Budberg had gone into a shop, put several dozen pounds worth of merchandise into her bag, and paid for only a small part of it. "She must have been drunk," said Rufina Borisovna. Her conduct in court was quite nonchalant: "I stole a few more things in another shop that day," she said. The newspapers pointed out that she was a native of Russia. How surprised Gorky and Wells, her famous **lovers,** would have been.

8 October.

< . . . > The Soldatovs say Akhmatova told them that she didn't like Chekhov because he was an anti-Semite and that she put Dostoevsky at the top of her list. < . . . >

28 October.

< . . . > Khrapchenko told us about instances of people with no knowledge of foreign languages appropriating solid works of scholarship written by their underlings (Shcherbina). The late Alexandrov, a member of the Academy of Sciences, went about it as follows: he summoned a gifted young scholar and said the GPU had been inquiring about him and he was heading for a disaster; the only way out was to write a book praising Stalin's articles on linguistics. The young man was panicked into doing so, and Alexandrov

kept up the scare tactics until he had three hundred or so pages to put his name on. < ... >

5 November.

Klara came to see me with Mitya and Lyusha. I was thrilled. Klara hugged me from behind and, while I was babbling on about something, said, "Nikolai Korneevich died yesterday afternoon."

The words were so unbelievable they seemed to be in a foreign language. It turns out that Kolya—who had been here three days ago, perfectly calm and collected, and taken a walk along the lake with me—fell asleep after lunch and never woke up. He died quietly, with no pain. Marina went into the room, saw Kolya lying there dead, and went out into the kitchen in a trance to finish washing up.

Then Oblonskaya came—she is editing Whitman with me—and that saved me. We spent the whole day working on *Leaves of Grass*. She's a clever girl and a hard worker, and I kept a grip on myself. < ... >

I was distraught and unable to show this most awful PAIN. Kolenka! From the moment in 1905 when Marya Borisovna showed me the little big-head in Odessa under the oleanders, I accepted the idea that the future was his, not mine. < ... > Forgive me, Kolya. I never meant to outlive you. I never dreamed I would see clouds, trees, flowers, or books when they were all dust to you.

8 November.

I can't stop thinking about Kolya. He wrote a story that can't be published now. He left approximately seven hundred pages of memoirs. < ... >

15 November.

My heart is so out of joint that they had to bring me to Kuntsevskaya Hospital. < ... > Ward 515 is very noisy. I've given an ultimatum: if they don't move me to 500, which is quiet, I'm going home. < ... >

28 November.

< . . . > Have read another Solzhenitsyn story. He is a true master. It's called "The Right Hand."[340] Another work about man's inhumanity to man. [. . .]

Wrote a long letter for Solzhenitsyn yesterday. We are collecting signatures. Sergei Smirnov, Kapitsa, Shostakovich, and Paustovsky have signed so far. I wonder if Tvardovsky will.[341]
< . . . >

6 December.

< . . . > Got up with a clear head and tried to come up with ways to mangle my "Poet and Hangman" for the censor. [. . .]

27 December.

< . . . > Everyone is talking about the Sinyavsky affair. All literary institutions are issuing public statements censuring him at the bidding of the authorities, but nobody has seen the incriminating works.
< . . . >

29 December.

I've finally broken loose from this awful prison. My temperature is thirty-seven, and what a joy to make my wobbly way to the car and head for the deep snows of Peredelkino.

340. Like *The Cancer Ward,* "The Right Hand," written in 1960, is based on Solzhenitsyn's experiences in a Tashkent hospital. (M.H.H.)

341. The letter—addressed to Pyotr Demichev, Secretary of the Central Committee, and signed by Paustovsky, Shostakovich, Chukovsky, Kapitsa, and Smirnov—urged that a Moscow apartment be placed at Solzhenitsyn's disposal. Two weeks later Solzhenitsyn was offered an apartment in Ryazan (the town in central Russia where he had resided since 1957), which, as the text of the petition clearly indicates, no one had requested. Tvardovsky's name does not appear.

1966

++>-+>-+>-+>-+>-+>-+>

6 January.

Iosif Brodsky came to call. He impressed me as a very self-assured, even self-satisfied young man. His verse is muddled, but not worthless. He did not thank me for the effort I put in on his behalf. His love of English poetry is bogus: he scarcely knows the language. Yet he is pleasant enough. He speaks of Akhmatova with great respect. < . . . >

18 January.

< . . . > *Anna Akhmatova died yesterday.*

5 March.

She died in Domodedov of her fifth heart attack. We kept it from Lida: she had just had an attack of arrhythmia, a severe one, and I was afraid she'd have rushed off to Leningrad for the funeral.

I had known Akhmatova since 1912. I see before me a slim, coquettish girl with a hooked nose and believe in her more than I do in the old woman with the bloated, flaccid face. The imbeciles in charge arranged for the secret removal of her body. There wasn't a word about the funeral in any paper. As a result, only a small chance group gathered at the Writers' Union: Yevtushenko, Voznesensky, Ardov, Marina, Tanya, Tarkovsky, and a few others. Tarkovsky said, "Life for her has ended; now comes immortality."

9 March.

< . . . > Sent the following telegram to the Writers' Union: "What is surprising is not that she has died but that she was able to live so long after what she went through—and to be so good, so majestic, so proud. We must start compiling her monumental biography immediately. It will be an instructive book."

I have learned there was a meeting of writers at the Union on the ninth, a heated protest against the vile silence surrounding the funeral. It was done on the Central Committee's orders. Not so much as a notice was posted anywhere. They thought they could keep it under wraps. But at the meeting even the most demure shouted, Shame! Mikhalkov—who made the famous pronouncement "Thank God we have the GPU!"—was censured unanimously. Tamara Ivanova was especially admirable.

25 March.

Have been in the hospital's Infection Wing, room ninety-three, for ten days now. When I came, my temperature was normal; now it's 37.5. In the process of proofreading the third volume of my collected works I reread the article on Beecher Stowe. It's a disgrace—banal, contrived baby talk. If, when I was young and on the warpath for new forms of criticism, I had been shown that article, written in the days of Stalin for Detgiz (and rejected by Detgiz, since the Chukovitis campaign was in full swing at the time)—if I had been shown that bloodless, insipid little article, I'd have burst into tears. I've devoted my whole life to putting an end to facile, sanctimonious articles like that, and suddenly I offer one up to my readers as a model, a musty old thing without a spark of the Chukovsky in it.

Klara has brought thirty copies of the Pasternak volume with my watered-down introduction. Somebody had tampered with it, going so far as to introduce words I find odious. Since I refused in my text to take Pasternak to task for the supposed errors of his ways, the drunkard Bannikov did so in his, even though he worships Pasternak much more than I do. True, he wrote several decent pages, but then he turned on *Doctor Zhivago* and delved into Pasternak's fallacious ideological positions and his "state of detachment and isolation." If detachment were a vice, we'd not celebrate Thoreau. And the moment Bannikov starts lying, his style changes. He writes: "Pasternak's errors and delusions" (359, as if errors and delusions were not synonyms); "in minds and (?) souls" (338), "morally ethical" (357).

I must add the following to my letter to Kosolapov: "May I take this opportunity to inform you how painful it is to feel the weight of the censorship on my collected works. You have cut several lines about Yulian Grigoryevich Oksman from my Tynyanov article, even though his name now appears widely. And why did you exclude my lively Jack London article? Has London joined Oksman on the black list? I should have thought that when you undertook to publish the works of Chukovsky you knew what Chukovsky means."

< . . . >

1 April.

< . . . > Sholokhov's despicable speech in response to our attempts to defend Sinyavsky so upset me that I was up all night even after a triple dose of sleeping pills.[342] Why did Lyusha read me the speech? The Black Hundreds are closing ranks; they have drafted a program to massacre and stifle the intelligentsia. I suspect the speech will make Sinyavsky's life at the labor camp even more arduous.

3 April.

< . . . > Worked all day with Lyusha on Chukokkala. She is such a pleasure to work with—so well organized, so adept at distinguishing good material from bad, so literary—that if I weren't ill I'd enjoy the project immensely. < . . . >

12 April.

< . . . > Am trying to write about Sologub for Chukokkala. It's not easy. Just about anything connected with Chukokkala is illegal these days. Chukokkala aims at resurrecting Yevreinov, Sologub, Gumilyov, Annenkov, Vyacheslav Ivanov, and suchlike remarkable figures; the authorities prefer to hush them up. There's nothing I can do.

18 April.

There is a funeral service for Kolya at the Writers House, and I am here. I've been terribly restless all day. I can't get anything done. I had a visit from a rather thick-skulled individual this evening, and I was so on edge, hysterical even, that I'm ashamed to think of it. [. . .] But all I can see is

342. In his speech at the Twenty-Third Party Congress, Sholokhov said, inter alia, "I feel ashamed for those who offer their services and ask to be allowed to vouch for the convicted outcasts. (Stormy applause.)"

a round-headed seven-year-old running from rock to rock at the Bartner dacha on the Kuokkala seashore, telling himself fantastic stories or running into the water and shouting, "Papa, let's get a bunny—gosh, this water is cold!—rabbit."

I can't believe he is lying in a coffin and spring streams are flowing, seeping up to his skull. And today is the first day the nightingales are calling. What a curse.

< ... >

19 July.

Solzhenitsyn and his wife came to see me yesterday. I had just finished his *Cancer Ward*. He is afraid that the "powers that be," having got hold of his worst pieces, have published them for internal distribution so that members of the government can pronounce their sentence upon him. He praised my *From Chekhov to Our Times*, but hasn't read Kataev yet. There is hope that *Novyi mir* will publish *The Cancer Ward*. Tvardovsky gave his approval, but then went on a bender, his third this summer. He is proposing a new title: *From Thursday to Wednesday*. < ... >

I asked his wife whether they have any money. She said they had, even some hard currency. She earns three hundred rubles a month as a chemist. Besides, Alexander Isaevich says that wealth comes from spending little rather than from earning a lot. When I told him he needed new shoes, he said, "I bought these only ten years ago."

I'm working on the introduction to a Leningrad collection of Akhmatova's verse. < ... >

20 July.

Now that she has grown a little wiser, sweet little Marina has stopped propagating nonresistance to evil. It used to be that when you took a toy away from her, she would be perfectly willing, even glad to pick up another. She was happy no matter what. Phlegm personified. But now the moment something rubs her the wrong way she starts screaming at the top of her lungs. She eats *kisel'* [a cold pudding] and soup in enormous quantities and is as sweet as can be. I try to spend every free moment at her cradle. Her greatest current aspiration is to sit up: she's tired of lying. If I put a stick across her pram, she'll grab it and pull herself up, which is fine, but then she tries to cling to it with her lips and I have to put her on her back again. Given her stalwart character, she doesn't hold it against me or cry; she just reaches out for the stick again.

Solzhenitsyn has had another setback: Tvardovsky, who accepted *The Cancer Ward* for *Novyi mir* before his bender, has now, after the bender, rejected it in no uncertain terms. < . . . >

1967

➤-➤-➤-➤-➤-➤-➤-➤-➤

14 January.

< . . . > Am reading over an old report of the Writers' Union meeting about Pasternak.[343] The speeches by Pertsov and Kornely Zelinsky were particularly vile. Lida came for a half hour yesterday and told me all about how the Punins[344] have squandered Akhmatova's legacy.

8 February.

Hard at work on the fifth volume of my collected works. Very boring articles with none of me in them. They all bear the seal of the tedium imposed on us by the personality cult. I remember how grim I felt writing them. I never smiled. [. . .]

3 March.

< . . . > The *Times Literary Supplement* calls Lida's novel **"a classic of the purges"** and compares it to *Ivan Denisovich* and *Requiem*.[345] < . . . >

343. Reference to the 21 October 1958 meeting of the Moscow branch of the Writers' Union, which voted to expel Pasternak. The proceedings were first published in the New York–based Russian émigré journal *Novyi zhurnal* 83 (1966): 185–227. The same issue featured the first installment of Lidia Chukovskaya's novella *Sofia Petrovna* (5–45, see note 321), which may account for the fact that Chukovsky was able to get hold of a journal that was otherwise banned.

344. The family of Akhmatova's third husband. (V.E.)

345. "Lida's novel" is Lidia Chukovskaya's *Sofia Petrovna*. *Requiem* is Akhmatova's lyrical cycle about the Great Terror and, more specifically, the plight of a mother with a son in the gulag. (V.E.)

14 March.

Tanya has a kind of faded look, as if she'd been sprinkled with ashes. I showed her "The Poet and the Hangman," which I am reworking, and she helped me with the structure. We composed a letter to an American who has offered to translate my tales. **They are untranslatable,** we wrote. She read me the transcript of a trial in which a young man who had made a frank declaration of his beliefs was sentenced to three years' hard labor even after his lawyer had proved him innocent in a brilliant peroration. I believe the youth's name was Khaustov.

Am hard at work on the Nekrasov commentary for the Biblioteka poeta edition of Nekrasov. To my amazement I see that the commentary I wrote to the satirical narrative poem "Contemporaries" was copied pretty much in its entirety by Teplinsky, who then published it as his own. < . . . >
< . . . >

24 March.

< . . . > Today is Lida's birthday. Sixty years ago I went to the Palais Royal, which had a telephone booth downstairs, to ring Dr. Gerzon's maternity hospital, and found out it was a girl. Bunin was standing in back of me (there was a short queue), and when he heard I'd had a girl he congratulated me in a dry, ironic voice. [. . .]

31 March.

Raging, never-ending snow. < . . . > And as is only fitting for an eighty-five-year-old I am stretched out with a crisis of the brain, because I took it into my head to work on the fifth volume with Simon Dreiden. Telegrams and letters from well-wishers have been pouring in, the most touching from Solzhenitsyn in Ryazan. [. . .]

20 May.

In bed. I can't shake this pneumonia. A happy, bearded, and rosy-faced Solzhenitsyn came to see me today. He's finished the second part of his *Cancer Ward*. On Tvardovsky's duplicity he quotes the man himself: "You hold on to grudges for too long. We must learn to forget. You forget nothing." To which he responds (majestically), "It is the writer's duty to forget nothing."

He is bright-eyed and looks like a lay brother, but his eyes are sharp and penetrating, the eyes of an artist. Of the three people involved in the conversation he was the only one who noticed I was exhausted. I was in fact fagged out, and when he saw that he stopped talking or, rather, cut his story short.

I had never seen him so "collected," so energetic and "steeled." He told me he's written a letter to the Writers Congress that opens on 22 May, a letter making insane demands including full freedom of the press (the abolishment of censorship). He describes how agents of the State Security confiscated his novel. The style is highly emotional. Why haven't the stories published separately in *Novyi mir* come out in book form? he protests.

I am deeply sympathetic—his heroism is remarkable, his talent evident in every word—but a state may well not survive its writers' telling its people the truth. Had the subjects of Nicholas I suddenly demanded that he publish "Belinsky's Letter to Gogol," he would have refused in the interest of state security.[346] You have to put yourself in Semichev's [De-michev's] shoes: if he grants writers their freedom, he'll have hundreds of Saltykov-Shchedrins on his hands raising a great hue and cry over the Injustice that reigns in our land and appealing to all mankind under the banner of TRUTH AND JUSTICE. And what will happen to the army of prop-agandists, what will happen to the thousands of provincial newspapers for which the word of the Center is law? There is no doubt that Solzhenitsyn will go down in literature and history as one of the most noble-minded champions of freedom, yet there is an element of nontruth in his truth: think of all the fine, bright, selfless people among the Communists, people who created—or tried to create—the basis for universal happiness. It is wrong to erase them from history just as it is wrong to forget that freedom of speech is essential to only a very limited circle; most people (even most intellectuals)—doctors, geologists, officers, pilots, architects, carpenters, masons, chauffeurs—do their jobs without it.

See what nonsense I can write? And all because of my poor diseased brain. [. . .]

---

346. The letter Belinsky wrote to Gogol after reading his *Selected Passages from Correspondence with Friends*, a tract he found conformist and retrograde, is an impassioned indictment of the Russia of Nicholas I. (V.E.)

30 May.

Room thirty. Have read a book about Tynyanov and the second issue of *Prometei.* Tynyanov's autobiography is a marvel—all concrete imagery and artistic detail. One would think it had been written by a great novelist rather than a scholar. And what a memory for the picturesque images surrounding him as a child.

There is no indication in the book that he was a Jew, but the meticulous mind evident in his *Vazir Mukhtara* is as often as not characteristic of the Jewish mind. Compare Alexei Tolstoy's novels with Tynyanov's. In Tynyanov the characters have ideas, the ideas collide and fight, and ideology is always in the foreground, ideology underpinned by art; in Alexei Tolstoy the carnal reigns.

The doctors have made their rounds. They all hate Svetlana Allilueva-Stalina.[347] It's unanimous. The authorities really put their foot in it, and now they're busy sullying her name in the papers, but unanimity reigns throughout the country and even honest people have fallen into the trap.

> The whole of Russia twists and turns
> And will not stop till she is cured.
>
> Barbiturates—
> They enervate us,
> Make us such degenerates.

Nurse Dusya has just exhorted me to stop working. "You need your rest. How many years have you got left anyway? One or two at most."

She was only trying to be nice.

Spent two days reading Erle Stanley Gardner's *The Case of the Beautiful Beggar.* A piece of trash, but I couldn't put it down. < . . . > Am now reading Golding's *Lord of the Flies.* It's terrific.

The *New Yorker* is running Edmund Wilson's notebooks. What complacency and poverty of thought!

Have read the first part of Bertrand Russell's autobiography. For all his democratic ideals he remains a British aristocrat. He writes a beautiful, classically limpid English. He is funny, marvelously independent in his

347. The news that Stalin's daughter, Svetlana Allilueva, who was visiting India at the time, chose not to return to Russia triggered a vitriolic campaign against her in the Soviet media. (V.E.)

opinions, and frank about his sexual vagaries. Neither mathematics nor philosophy has killed the man in him.

Have read *Papa Hemingway*, an overly familiar, vulgar book with a terrible ending—about the madness of a great writer. < . . . >

6 August.

[. . .] Had breakfast with Solzhenitsyn today. He is radiant: he looks younger and has filled out. He told the wonderful story of the deferential and dismayed reception that Voronkov, Markov, and Sobolev gave him in Fedin's office. Markov was frightened when he put a sheaf of papers on the table: could it be yet another exposé aimed at world public opinion? They gave him a friendly scolding: why didn't he send his letter to the Presidium instead of distributing it to each member of the Congress?

"I've been sending these letters to various individuals for two years now," he said, indicating the papers he'd put on the table, "and not once have I received a response. Here is a copy of a letter to Brezhnev. Brezhnev failed to answer it. Here is a copy of a letter I wrote to *Pravda*. No response. Here is a letter to you at the Writers' Union. You didn't answer either."

Markov, Voronkov, and Sobolev looked amazed: clearly Leonid Ilyich [Brezhnev] never received your letter. In a word, they all fawned on him. "Shall we close the window? Is there too much of a draft?" And when he asked for some water, trays with glasses of tea and all manner of refreshments suddenly made their appearance.

Tvardovsky, who had brought Solzhenitsyn, asked, "Do you think your *Cancer Ward* will be published abroad?"

Solzhenitsyn: "It's highly probable. At last count there were no less than five hundred typescripts in circulation. It is pointless to hope that not one of them has made its way abroad."

"Then what shall we do?" the judges asked the defendant in desperation.

"There's only one way out," said Tvardovsky. "Publish *The Cancer Ward* in *Novyi mir*."

They talked about the slanderous accusations being made against Solzhenitsyn—that he had been a deserter and even a kapo in a German POW camp, and so on—and magnanimously promised to defend his good name.

He felt he had come out on top and claims that the government will pull in its horns in the near future. "For the next three months at least I can be certain they won't stab me in the back." He carries himself with equanimity and exudes joy. < . . . >

15 August.

[. . .] What turbid, pretentious rubbish Nabokov's *Invitation to a Beheading* is. I put it down after forty pages. [. . .]

12 September.

Lida was here yesterday looking very thin. < . . . > She is excited about the commentary she is doing for Akhmatova's verse. I am sure it is excellent. She's read the new edition of my *Contemporaries* and approves of "Zhitkov," "Chekhov," "Leonid Andreev," and "Kuprin." She rates the Akhmatova chapter lower than the others and finds the memoir section especially weak. I feel it too. < . . . >

17 September.

[. . .] Had a letter telling me that Yelena Kiselyova is alive. The daughter of a mathematician who wrote algebra and geometry textbooks, she studied with Repin and we had a tumultuous (if short-lived) affair in 1915. I remember how exciting I found the red parasol she took to the beach. She's close to ninety by now, but what I wouldn't give to see her with it on the beach!

My memory is weaker by the day. Yesterday I couldn't remember where these lines by Pushkin come from:

> Why does the bright-eyed Desdemona
> Love the jealous Moor of Venice? [. . .]

23 September.

Solzhenitsyn was here. He underwent a five-hour hearing at the Secretariat of the Writers' Union yesterday, a grueling cross-examination at the hands of Fedin, Surkov, Voronkov, and others. < . . . >

6 October.

[. . .] Semyon Lipkin was here with some very intelligent things to say about Akhmatova. Late one evening she phoned to summon him immediately about "a very important matter." Concerned, he rushed to her flat. "Look at this," she said, holding out an article in a French newspaper. Lipkin read the article. It was a rave review. But Akhmatova was outraged: "How despicable!" The article turned out to have said that Gumilyov left her. "No, *I* left *him*. And that vile article . . ."

8 October.

The titmice have arrived. They're pecking at the window. [. . .]

16 October.

My wonderful Mitya was here and told the following story. One day Olesha came out of the Astoria Hotel drunk and called out to a man with gold braid on his coat, "Porter! Get me a cab!"

   "I'm not a porter," said the man. "I'm an admiral."
   "Then get me a ship!"

22 October.

[. . .] Sent a review of the Yesenin-Erdman *Pugachov* to the Taganka Theater. The Theater's director, Yury Petrovich Lyubimov, had asked me to write it because the Theater was under attack by the authorities, which rightly saw the play as a lampoon of current conditions.

   Am completely done in by proofreading the fifth volume of my collected works. The Sleptsov chapters are particularly contemptible: my assumption at the time I wrote them was that revolution is good and peaceful progress bad, a formulation now abhorrent to me: the past forty years have convinced me irrevocably that our revolutionary ideas were disastrous and led to [unfinished]

26 October.

After perusing my old diaries (1921–24), Tanya said, "My, how unhappy you were. It pains me to read them." I didn't know I was unhappy. I keep feeling outbursts—wild outbursts—of happiness.

30 October.

< . . . > The school in Choboty has a new teacher of Russian language and literature who tells the children that under the autocratic regime all poets perished in duels. None died a natural death. When one little girl asked innocently, "But why did Mayakovsky and Yesenin commit suicide under the Soviet regime?" she was pronounced a dangerous troublemaker and there were attempts to expel her from the school. She was fortunate to escape with a stern reprimand and a bout of humiliation in the presence of her fellow pupils. < . . . >

Finished the second run-through of the fifth volume. I'm terribly depressed at the idea of including "Lenin and Nekrasov," which represents old ideas, ideas I no longer agree with. < . . . >

I know full well that this autumn is my last, and the odd thing is it doesn't sadden me in the least. My false teeth are the only stable part of my organism; the rest is all rags, bits and pieces—only the teeth are immortal. I am sentenced to death—not as a mortal but as the victim of capital punishment—and I know my sentence cannot be commuted to hard labor for life:

> In vain I appeal, "Tarry! Wait!"[348]
> And still I exult and rejoice. An unexpected feeling. [. . .]

2 December.

[. . .] It goes without saying that every soldier in the War was issued a copy of Stalin's *Foundations of Leninism* along with his gun and greatcoat. We had some soldiers stationed on my Peredelkino estate, and when they left for the front each of them tossed the book into a corner of my room. There were about sixty copies. I asked the office of the writers' colony to take the books, and they promised they would, but they didn't mean it. So one night, knowing I was committing a political crime, I tossed them into a small ditch in the woods and covered them with dirt, and there those awful holy scriptures of our Mao have been peacefully rotting these twenty-four years.

< . . . >

---

348. The line is from "Prelude to Songs of Farewell" by the nineteenth-century poet Alexei Zhemchuzhnikov.

8 December.

< . . . > Yasinovskaya was here with glad tidings: the Bible we edited is going to press any day now! But with one absolute proviso: the word "Jerusalem" must be completely excised. When I started work on the project in 1962, I was told to excise the words "Jews" and "God" (I violated both prohibitions), but it never entered my mind that the censor would make the word "Jerusalem" taboo.

10 December.

< . . . > Am reworking an old article on Sologub for volume six, when what I want to be writing about is Nabokov's Pushkin.

25 December.

Kaverin has just left. He was in a good mood. "*The Cancer Ward* has been set in pages for the December issue of *Novyi mir*," he said, "and a book of Solzhenitsyn's stories has been approved for publication. Apparently the Italian and English Communist Parties insisted upon it."

Solzhenitsyn told Kaverin, "I'm convinced the Soviet Union is going to start taking a Western tack. It has no other tack to take." [. . .]

26 December.

Met Zalygin, who said *The Cancer Ward* wouldn't be in the December issue. It's been moved to the January issue.

27 December.

Have renewed my acquaintance with Shaginyan. < . . . > She tells me she has discovered that Lenin's mother was the daughter of a converted Jew by the name of Blank, the moneybags of his shtetl. His real name was Izrael, and he received the name of Alexander at his baptism. When Shaginyan went to Pospelov with her discovery, Pospelov was horrified—"I don't dare report it to the Central Committee"—and she was forbidden to publish a word about it.[349] < . . . >

349. Marietta Shaginyan's *The Ulyanov Family: A Chronicle Novel* (1958) contains a chapter entitled "Lenin and His Paternal Ancestors." Documents which came to light in the mid-sixties

29 December.

< . . . > The BBC has broadcast a protest written by Pavel Litvinov against an article in *Vecherniaia gazeta* calling Bukovsky a hooligan.[350] The protest seems to have been sent abroad by Pavel himself. < . . . > Tanya tells me that the moment the BBC broadcast the item about Pavel Litvinov our Soviet geniuses decided to vent their spleen on the late Maxim Litvinov. It just so happens there was a ceremony the other day commemorating some event in Soviet diplomacy and the newspapers failed to mention him. Not even *Moscow News* [an English-language newspaper published in Moscow] mentioned him. So Tanya made some inquiries, and yes, there had been an order to pass over Litvinov's name in silence, thereby making him responsible for the sins of his grandson twenty-five years after his death. < . . . >

1968

-+->->->->->->->->-

11 January.

< . . . > Tanya is back. She has written a scathing letter to *Izvestiia* about the trial of the four and made another attempt to force her way into the courtroom with her nephew Pavel.[351] I see it as a pre-Decembrist move-

---

indicate that Lenin's maternal grandfather was a converted Jew and that there were some Kalmyks on his father's side. A detailed genealogical survey of the Ulyanov family—G. M. Deich, *Evreiskie predki Lenina: Neizvestnye arkhivnye dokumenty o Blankakh* (New York, 1991)—includes Shaginyan's letter about her findings and the prohibitions by which her *Ulyanov Family* was shackled. Deich chronicles the dismissals of the archivists who gave researchers access to materials pertaining to the Ulyanov family. He concludes his narrative as follows: "What was then V. I. Lenin's nationality? I answer confidently: Russian. He is Russian in his culture, language, and upbringing; a hereditary Russian nobleman."

350. The article, which appeared on 4 September 1967, reported that Vladimir Bukovsky, a young human-rights activist, had been sentenced to three years' imprisonment for "anti-social activity." In fact, he was charged with having organized a Pushkin Square demonstration the previous January in defense of a group of dissidents detained at the time.

351. Four dissidents—Y. T. Galanskov, A. I. Ginzburg, V. I. Lashkova, and A. A. Dobrovolsky—stood trial in January 1968. Pavel Litvinov and Larisa Bogoraz (the wife of Andrei Sinyavsky's co-defendant, Yuly Daniel) circulated a statement stigmatizing the trial as "a stain on our country and a throwback to the infamous trials of the thirties."

ment, the first in a series of heroic deeds and sacrifices on the part of the Russian intelligentsia that will turn Russian history into an ever widening torrent of blood. This is only the beginning, only a trickle. General Grigorenko is a particularly interesting figure, a typical throwback to the generation of the 1860s, which had its generals too. I wonder whether the army of protesters is increasing or whether there are twelve all told: Tanya, Pavlik, Grigorenko, Koma Ivanov, and precious few more.

Pavlik delivered his statement openly to foreign correspondents. It calls for judging the judges who staged the trial of the four, brands Dobrovolsky a traitor, and charges that the sentences had all been decided beforehand and the courtroom stacked with GPU agents. The statement is co-signed by Daniel's wife.

The English Communist Party announced in the *Morning Star* that our embassy in London had misled English Communists by assuring them the trial would be open to the public. < . . . >

17 January.

< . . . > Heard a BBC broadcast calling me a leading light and praising me for "working" side by side with my daughter. Learned of Lida's letter to Sholokhov from the American press.[352] < . . . >

Am reading the Syomin novel again.[353] It's very good.

20 January.

< . . . > Tanya tells me that Ivy,[354] an old woman by now, has upped and given an interview to a *Morning Star* reporter, sanctioning the actions of Pavel, her mad grandson, who by the way was called up yesterday by the Military Registration and Enlistment Office. < . . . >
< . . . >

---

352. Lidia Chukovskaya's open letter to Sholokhov in defense of Sinyavsky and Daniel was widely circulated in *samizdat,* broadcast by the Russian émigré radio stations, and published in foreign newspapers. For her father's peace of mind she did not tell him of her bold act, which could have had serious consequences. The letter was first published in *Gorizont* 3 (1989).

353. Vitaly Syomin's *Seven in One House,* which was published in *Novyi mir* 5 (1965).

354. Ivy Litvinova (see note 366).

29 January.

Had a visit from a genius: Kostya Raikin. < . . . > He is a phenomenally well-built, elegant young man with an exceptionally thoughtful, expressive face. He is studying mime and does etudes with his body: "A Wind, an Umbrella, and I," "The Indian and the Jaguar," "Along the Arbat," "On the Bus." His powers of observation are amazing, and he subordinates every inch of that supple, graceful, powerful body to his designs. A pity there was no music. I was entranced, overwhelmed by the proximity of such a gem. His very presence excludes vulgarity; he heightens the spiritual atmosphere around him. Watching his gestures, I realized for the first time (and high time it is, too) how much more beautiful, more harmonious, and more intelligent a young man's body is than a young woman's. A. N. Tolstoy was right when he wrote:

> A naked girl's a hag,
> A life-producing bag.

< . . . >

21 February.

Thirteen years to the day since Marya Borisovna's death, and I carry on with my haphazard, meaningless, fatuously industrious existence.

< . . . > Have written a brief article in defense of Grekova, who is being persecuted by a frenzied military for her story "The Entrance Examination." [. . .] It was read during the discussion of the story by the Party's Prose Section (on 16 February). [. . .]

I rang Grekova and said by way of consolation, "Things will iron themselves out."

"I don't want things to iron themselves out," she replied. "I want to show up those scoundrels for what they are." < . . . >

12 March.

Arrived here [Room 93, Ward for Infectious Diseases] healthy, but have caught a cold (my temperature is 37.3). [. . .]

6 April.

Am reading Bunin's *Liberation of Tolstoy*. One malicious man, who realizes that kindness is the highest good, writes here about another malicious man, who craves madly to squeeze the last drops of kindness out of himself. Tolstoy was staggeringly irascible, ambitious, self-centered, and overbearing, Bunin—envious, easily offended, and rancorous.

LAST WILL AND TESTAMENT

The royalties for all my children's books—*The Silver Escutcheon, Jack the Giant Killer, Wash 'Em Clean, Bibigon,* and the miscellany *Chukokkala*—I leave to my granddaughter Yelena Tsezarevna Chukovskaya.

The royalties for all my adult books—*Contemporaries, From Two to Five, Nekrasov's Craft, A Book About Alexander Blok, Alive as Life, A High Art, Walt Whitman, People and Books,* etc.—I leave to my daughter Lidia Korneevna Chukovskaya.

All the Russian books in my personal library I leave to the library of the Writers House; all the foreign books—to the Library of Foreign Literature.

I leave Lida all my money—except for the sums set aside for Tatyana Maximovna Litvinova, Klara, and Marianna Shaskolskaya—and all the furniture she wishes to keep or distribute to the family except for the secretary, which I leave to Marina.

From the money I leave to her I ask Lida to give Yevgeny Borisovich Chukovsky a monthly stipend and, as far as possible, to provide financial support for the library I have built.

I ask that the trees at the grave site be cleared and that my grave be marked with a tombstone matching Marya Borisovna's.

All the books dealing with Nekrasov I leave to the Nekrasov Museum in Leningrad.

10 May.

Have been writing all this in the Kremlin Suburban Hospital, where I arrived pretty much healthy and have now had three bouts of disease.[355] I have had a high temperature the whole time, my erythrocyte sedimentation

---

355. "All this" refers to the short book of memoirs, *What I Remember,* that Chukovsky wrote while hospitalized. For excerpts see the Appendix.

rate is astronomical, and as I couldn't write anything decent I wrote pop-pycock. < ... >

23 May.

< ... > My book *A High Art* is in galleys at Sovetskii pisatel'. It was about to come out when the publishing house suddenly noticed the name Solzhenitsyn in the text and withheld publication. That makes the third book of mine withheld from the 1968 lists: *Chukokkala, The Tower of Babel,* and *A High Art.*[356] A bit much for one person, I'd say.

24 May.

Terrible news: that traitor Blinov apparently "forgot" to include *My Whitman* in the 1968 list. All that work and the book's in a state of limbo. Book number four down the drain this year. < ... >

25 May.

[...] Had a visit at five from Yury Petrovich Lyubimov, head of the Taganka Theater and the victim of a *hongweibing*[357] attack on his work there. Ella Petrovna is his literary manager. They want to put my *Chukokkala* on stage. He told a very funny story about Khrushchev's visit to the Sovremennik Theater complete with Khrushchev imitation. < ... >

27 May.

A very tired Tanya came to see me. She's not through with Meredith yet, but the end is in sight. Her brilliant translation of Cheever's "Geometry of Love" is out in the latest issue of *Inostrannaia literatura.*

356. *Chukokkala* was not published until 1979. During the last years of his life Chukovsky was engaged in editing a volume of Bible stories for children, but publication was thwarted by the censors. It finally appeared, under the title *The Tower of Babel,* twenty years after Chukovsky's death. *A High Art,* Chukovsky's treatise on the art of literary translation, was held up because it contained passages dealing with the English translations of Solzhenitsyn's *One Day in the Life of Ivan Denisovich.*

357. The Chinese term for the notorious Red Guards, *hongweibing,* gained currency in the Soviet Union during the Chinese Cultural Revolution. Chukovsky uses it figuratively as the epitome of wanton brutality and lawlessness.

Have just recalled what Lyubimov told me about a heroic deed on the part of Paustovsky. Paustovsky was very ill, but agreed to phone Kosygin. "This is the writer Paustovsky," he said to him. "Before I die, I want to appeal to you to keep the cultural values of our country alive. If you remove Lyubimov from his post, his theater will collapse and a great cause will be lost" and so on.

Kosygin promised to look into it, and as a result Lyubimov kept his theater, though he did get a stiff "warning" from on high. [. . .]

3 June.

< . . . > Have been in a dither since morning after reading the libelous attack by those *Ogonek* bandits in the Mayakovsky article.[358] Not that I was particularly disturbed by it. But I'm afraid it's the start of an all-out campaign against me, a way of taking revenge for my friendship with Solzhenitsyn, for signing petitions and letters of protest, for [entry breaks off here] . . .

10 June.

[. . .] I must write something about N. F. Belchikov's vile project to put out Chekhov's early works "in chronological order." Why does Chekhov always end up being edited by miscreants? The first Complete Works was edited by the Stalinist lout Yegolin. It's the oyster train all over again![359]

I've got a new idea for a Chekhov chapter: he would start a story or play with a minus and end it with a plus. I can't quite put it into words, but here is an example: "The Bear" begins with hatred and the threat of a duel and ends with a kiss and a wedding. Gradually turning a minus into

358. A. Koloskov, "Tragediia poeta," *Ogonek* 23 (1968). Mayakovsky's tragedy, according to Koloskov, was that his critics misunderstood and harassed him. "In a book that appeared in 1922 Kornei Chukovsky characterized Mayakovsky as 'a poet of catastrophes and convulsions' and maintained that he 'lacked a feeling for his homeland,' 'every shout of his is cerebral, manufactured,' 'his fire is artificial,' 'he is a Vesuvius spouting cotton,' 'everything smacks of invention, contrivance.' " In fact, the snippets quoted have little in common with Chukovsky's piece, which appeared not in a book in 1922 but in the journal *Dom iskusstva* in 1921. The article, "Akhmatova i Maiakovskii," has been reprinted in *Voprosy literatury* 1 (1988).

359. Chekhov died in Germany. His body arrived in Russia on a train with FOR OYSTERS written on it. Chukovsky is bemoaning the shoddy treatment to which Chekhov has been subjected. (M.H.H.)

a plus calls for great virtuosity of dialogue. Take "An Expensive Dog," for instance. A man sells his dog and is then willing to pay for it to be carted away. < . . . >

28 June.

A hard day for Lida: Lengiz have informed her that four poems and several lines from *A Poem Without a Hero* will be removed from her one-volume Akhmatova. She wrote letters to Lengiz, Zhirmunsky, Surkov, and somewhere else protesting against the cuts. Unfortunately, the lines eliminated from *A Poem Without a Hero* tell about how Akhmatova spent several years with a pistol at her head, and it is perfectly understandable that given the way the winds are blowing nowadays making lines like that public is out of the question. But Lida is adamant; she won't bend. She told Lengiz that if they eliminate the pistol she will take her name off the book, because she must answer to the world for the text of the poem. Nekrasov had a different view of such things: he understood that the censor's fanaticism does not last forever.

29 June.

Kruchonykh is dead, and with him the pleiad of poets surrounding Mayakovsky has come to an end. [. . .]

Litgazeta is running a despicable article about Solzhenitsyn with an attack on Kaverin as well.[360]

< . . . >

7 July.

< . . . > There's a speech by Brezhnev in the papers. He mentions me. I wonder if I shouldn't write him a letter about the books of mine that have been withheld from publication.

360. The editorial in *Literaturnaia gazeta* (6 June 1968), "The Ideological Struggle and the Responsibility of the Writer," was directed primarily against Solzhenitsyn in connection with the publication of his *Cancer Ward* in the West. Another target was Kaverin: "Fanning the provocative flames over *The Cancer Ward*, the radio stations hostile to us have seized upon another 'document' and call it 'Kaverin's open letter.' . . . There is no point in dwelling on this letter in detail. Suffice it to say that even though he has been listening daily to its rendition by various émigré 'voices,' Kaverin has not deemed it necessary to repudiate the hostile chorus."

Rumor has it that one of the most ardent anti-Semites has been thrown out of the government and that *Ogonek* is in hot water because of its Mayakovsky articles.[361]

8 July.

Rumor has it that *Litgazeta* will run some articles challenging the *Ogonek* "Mayakovsky." The articles are supposedly commissioned by the Central Committee.

11 July.

[. . .] Solzhenitsyn has decided to refrain from responding to the *Litgazeta* attack. Rumor has it that Tvardovsky will be requesting an audience with Brezhnev to propose either that *Novyi mir* be abolished or censorship be toned down. Now you have to collect material for three issues to put out one. < . . . >

24 July.

Sofya Krasnova came to inform me that my "Surveys," which were supposed to be included in Volume Six, have now been removed as well. I thought I was having a heart attack. I ran out into the woods, my arms and legs trembling. I felt like an old man being trampled to death.

Poor Russian literature! All it is allowed to do is praise the authorities. < . . . >

2 August.

Vladimir Glotser and I have prepared Volume Six for publication. Bonetsky and Sofa, whom we were expecting, came at four sharp. No sooner had I set out all the articles of the mangled volume on my desk than Bonetsky launched into an incredible monologue: I was obliged to write a foreword

361. See note 359 above and another *Ogonek* article about Mayakovsky by Koloskov, "Liubov' poeta" (*Ogonek* 16 [1968]). The tenor of the latter was unmistakably anti-Semitic, its author pitting the "truly Russian" young émigré Tatyana Yakovleva, with whom Mayakovsky had fallen in love while in Paris, against his allegedly manipulative Jewish intimates, Lili and Osip Brik. (V.E.)

about the long, circuitous path to Marxism-Leninism—a path "with great complications and contradictions"—I had taken during my career as a writer and to announce that I had finally arrived at the truth, as was evident from books like *Nekrasov's Craft* and so on. But some of the articles in this volume contain mistakes that can be explained by the fact that I wrote them before Marxism-Leninism had shed its grace upon me.

I was so upset by this balderdash that my heart started pounding something awful and I made a number of stupid remarks. But then I read out loud the foreword I had taken such pains to write with the assistance of Marianna Petrovna and Glotser, and to my amazement the disciple of Marx and Engels was perfectly happy with it and said, "Just what we need!"

My "Surveys" are now reinstated. All I have to do is remove the reference to Gorky's *Mother* or *Maman*, as Bonetsky called it playfully. < . . . >

7 August.

Watched Marinochka for a long time from my window. She was picking up sand from a pile some distance from the house and bringing it closer. There was no one around. "What are you doing?" I called out. She looked uneasy and wanted to go on playing by herself, so she said (oh how shrewd a child can be!), "Move away from the window or you'll catch cold!" < . . . >

17 September.

Having a hard time with my books. They won't release the Bible, though they've printed fifty thousand copies. They're withholding *Chukokkala*. They've torn the sixth volume apart and thrown out the best articles and the best parts of the rest of them. *A High Art* has been sitting there since May: they demand I excise Solzhenitsyn.

I am on an even keel, though now that I'm so old I find it painful to see the dreams of so many—our Belinskys, Herzens, Chernyshevskys, Nekrasovs, and countless members of the People's Will and Social Democrat Parties—to see their dreams crushed and the paradise on earth for which they were willing to give up their lives nothing but a debauch of lawlessness and police brutality. < . . . >

25 September.

Yelena Sergeevna Bulgakova came to call today looking very young. She has many interesting memories of Bulgakov. We have the same opinion of Nemirovich-Danchenko and the Moscow Art Theater in general. Bulgakov couldn't stand the Theater, she said. When he was mortally ill, he would wake her and tell her how much he hated it, and making fun of Nemirovich-Danchenko would help him to forget his pain. He was gearing up to make fun of him in the second part of *A Novel of the Theater*.[362] [. . .]

1 October.

< . . . > Daniel's wife must be crazy![363] She's abandoned her son, turned her back on her jailed husband, and is begging to be put in jail. The lawyers defending her and Pavel in court are true heroines, putting their careers on the line as they are. The Constitution requires lawyers in political cases to admit their clients' guilt and plead only for clemency. The defendants of Pavel and Larisa rejected that procedure from the outset. [. . .]

7 October.

I committed a vile act today, alas: I crossed out the references to Solzhenitsyn in *High Art*. There weren't many. I had to mangle only four pages. But I'd held out for seven months: for seven months I'd refused to let them publish my book, for seven months I'd suffered at the thought of its being hidden away somewhere, already typeset, nearly ready to go to the bookshops. And now that they tell me they will break up the type if I leave that odious name, I see I'm not a hero at all, just a writer willing to let his book undergo any kind of mutilation because a book is after all the fruit of many years' work, arduous work if not always successful. People predicted that bending to the censor's terror would cause me great torment, but in fact all I feel is grief. I'm callous by now. [. . .]

362. See note 336.

363. Reference to Larissa Bogoraz who, with Pavel Litvinov and several fellow dissidents, took part in a demonstration in Red Square on 25 August 1968 protesting the Soviet invasion of Czechoslovakia. Also see note 352. (V.E.)

9 October.

My room is full of floodlights and cameras: I'm being filmed for *Chukok-kala.*[364] Since I don't find such things annoying and the crew is perfectly nice, talking in front of the camera didn't tire me in the least. It's much easier than writing. I remarked to the director, Marianna Tavrog, that the film would be lopsided without Mandelshtam, Gumilyov, or Zamyatin. It was as if the camera were shackled. [. . .] Ivy's story in the *New Yorker* is very good.[365]

10 October.

Shooting for *Chukokkala* went on today. It's a terrible thing that so light-hearted and playful a book has been made sanctimonious and official by the censor. < . . . >

12 October.

Yasinovskaya came to see me about *The Tower of Babel*. People at the Central Committee are up in arms against the book because of Moses and Daniel. "Moses is no mythical character; he is a figure in Jewish history. As for Daniel, he is grist for the Zionists' mill." In other words, they will never stop quibbling. [. . .]

13 October.

Tanya came this evening, with fiery eyes, grief-stricken, possessed. All she can talk about is the trial against Pavlik, Delone, Bogoraz, and the rest of them.[366] She can't get over how brave they were, and gave a detailed report of the proceedings, which were far from legal. There was despair in her every word, her every gesture.

364. A documentary, *Chukokkala*, premiered two months after Chukovsky's death.

365. Ivy Litvinov, "She Knew She Was Right," *New Yorker* 44 (1968): 42–49. A number of Ivy Litvinova's stories came out in the *New Yorker* at this time, and a collection of them appeared as Ivy Litvinov, *She Knew She Was Right* (New York, 1971). (M.H.H.).

366. Reference to the court proceedings of 9–11 October against participants in the Red Square demonstration protesting the Soviet invasion of Czechoslovakia. Pavel, Tanya, Flora, and Misha are members of the Litvinov family.

Now that the *hongweibing* are ganging up against intellectuals and the very word "intellectual" has become a term of abuse, it is important to remain in the ranks of the intelligentsia and not abandon them—for jail. We need our intelligentsia to carry on our day-to-day intellectual existence. Would it have served any purpose for Chekhov or Constance Garnett to serve time?

18 October.

Solzhenitsyn came yesterday evening. I was hoping he was here for a fortnight, but he stayed only twenty-four hours. We always kiss when he visits, and his lips are cool and fresh, his eyes clear, but his young face has begun to wrinkle. His wife Natasha, who works at a research institute in Ryazan, has been given signals indicating she will be dismissed before long. A newly arrived goody-goody of a "scientist" is clearly up for her position. [. . .]

25 October.

Our own *hongweibing* are performing new feats: they've routed Biblioteka poeta. After all, Orlov was geared up to publish Akhmatova, Gumilyov, Mandelshtam—"intellectual" poets—to the detriment of balalaika poets < . . . > and a few others have been dismissed because Etkind's book on translators says that Akhmatova, Zabolotsky, and many more were deprived of the possibility of publishing their verse and were therefore constrained to devote all their energy to translating.

Had a funny talk with that nice poet Chukhontsev. I'd given him an anthology of English verse and asked when I ran into him what he'd thought of it.

"It's very good," he said. "I especially like the poet Anon. Who is he? When did he live?"

I was a bit thrown at first, but then it came to me: he was asking about **Anonymous!** < . . . >

31 October.

Marinochka said to me today, "Volodichka has no great-grandfather. Most boys and girls don't have great-grandparents. They die too soon. When are you going to die?"
< . . . >

2 November.

< . . . > Yevtushenko was here from six to eleven p.m. A great event for me. We talked about an anthology that an American publisher has commissioned him to put together. He displayed a vast knowledge of early literature. He rejects Vyacheslav Ivanov and Bryusov. He made an excellent choice of Mayakovsky's verse. He is guided by the highest standards and deep understanding. He says that since our invasion of Czechoslovakia he's had what might be called a breakthrough: he's come out with a torrent of verse. He recited five wonderful poems. One is about three rotting peasant houses inhabited by two old women and an ill man and juxtaposed to a Moscow rotten to the core and the false and sordid life that goes on there. Then there is one about an old woman who finds herself in a shop that sells goods for Western currency and, imagining she can buy the most luxurious things, thinks she has entered the realm of Communism—only to be shown the door when she can proffer only Soviet currency. And another one about the troops that invaded Czechoslovakia. The poems are remarkable, as is he.[367] He's a major figure with a great destiny. As I've always said, he is the needle that touches the sorest nerve in the tooth; he experiences the life of the country as if it were his toothache.

"I'm a lyrical poet," he said, "really I am, but I somehow can't stop writing about political matters, damn them." < . . . >

13 November.

> Pushkin! Songs of secret freedom
> We have learned to sing from you.
> Give us strength in times of evil

---

367. The poems in question are "A Hundred Versts from the Capital of All Hopes," "A Russian Miracle," and "Tanks in the Streets of Prague."

Help us in our struggle mute.
Blok[368]

22 November.

Yevtushenko this evening. Our dominant figure. He's on tenterhooks: today is the day Oxford will either accept or reject him (he is up for a professorship there). "That damned Amis" has publicly declared him an "official" poet, "and Amis is a Fascist, he's for the war in Vietnam, the bastard! They know nothing of what goes on here. They don't understand a thing!"[369] Other statements: "I'd give ten years of my life to see *The First Circle* published in Russia. There is no solidarity among writers here, and that is our undoing." And he laid out a fantastic plan to seize power at the Moscow Division of the Writers' Union! Then he recited some poems, the best of which was about "creeping birches," that is about himself and his fate as a poet. In the end, that's what all his poems are about. We went for a walk.
< . . . >

23 November.

Today the second most central literary figure, Alexander Isaevich, came to see me, his beard longer, his face gaunter. He arrived in Moscow yesterday and was so worn out from his day there that he came here for a good sleep. He's in good spirits, though. He told me about some cheeky letters he'd written to the Ryazan Division of the Writers' Union. The secretary of the Ryazan District Committee had expressed a desire for a talk with him and asked him to come to his office. He had responded (through the Writers' Union) that as he was not a Party member he did not feel obliged to go and see him but that if he was willing to go to the Writers' Union he,

368. The key stanza in Blok's poem "To the Pushkin House," written six months before his death. Blok drew the phrase "secret freedom" from a poem by Pushkin, "To N. Y. Plyuskovaya" (1818), in which the persona calls his "incorruptible voice" "an echo of the Russian people." (V.E.)

369. Yevtushenko's version of the Oxford episode, as recorded by Chukovsky, is not entirely accurate. For one thing, he was considered for an honorary fellowship rather than a professorship; for another, Kingsley Amis was not the only person to query Yevtushenko's candidacy; and, needless to say, neither Amis's pronounced conservative leanings nor his alleged support for the American involvement in Vietnam provides sufficient basis for labeling him a Fascist. (V.E.)

Solzhenitsyn, would be willing to talk to him, though not in private, of course (since we have no secrets). [. . .]

3 December.

Saw an article in the *Times* about Oxford's rejection of Yevtushenko and decided to take it to him. A motorcycle policeman happened to be passing and gave me a lift. "Yevtushenko is ill," the nanny told me. It turned out he'd been in Moscow for three days doing nothing but drinking. "I financed the binge with the money we'd saved for a tape recorder." He was ashamed to look his wife in the eye. He read me a poem about a blue fox and a poem about whales. "I'm surprised they printed the poem about the fox," he said. "They must have thought I was really writing about foxes. It was the caption 'Alaska' that fooled them." < . . . >

1969

➤➤➤➤➤➤➤➤

6 March.

Went to Kassirsky Hospital yesterday. The staff is excellent, the doctors first-class, but I'm in a bad way: my medicines are poisoning me.
< . . . >

7 March.

< . . . > It's awful, a disgrace: I have a TV addict for a neighbor. There's a continuous bark coming through the wall. It doesn't stop till midnight. Had I had the slightest inkling I'd be neighbors with a savage, I'd have rather died at home in bed. < . . . >
< . . . >

31 March.

< . . . > The most interesting person here is Valentina Georgievna Antipova, an auditor for railway construction plants in the Urals, Siberia, and

the Far East. She puts her heart and soul into bringing up her sixteen-year-old son, and a fine lad he is. She has seen an enormous amount of life. She knows all the cities of Siberia the way I know Peredelkino. She is open-minded and independent. She left her husband long ago and has had to develop certain masculine traits willy-nilly. She is critical of contemporary life and refused to join the Party after the Komsomol even though her father is a longtime member. It's a pleasure to talk to her: she has a lively, active, skeptical mind.

But . . . she has absolutely no idea that Russia has writers and artists the likes of Mandelshtam, Zabolotsky, Gumilyov, Zamyatin, Somov, Boris Grigoryev; Pasternak's "Christmas" was not an event in her life; she fails to realize that *The Master and Margarita* and *A Novel of the Theater* are our pride and joy as a nation; "Matryona's Home" and *The First Circle* mean nothing to her, she can perfectly well do without them.

Since I have long since suspected such people exist, I decided to observe her closely, and I now see that it comes from being exposed exclusively to newspapers, the radio, magazines like *Nedelia* and *Ogonek*, which not only impose bad art on their audiences but conceal good art from them. By pushing such bald-faced hacks as Serafimovich, Gladkov, and Nikolai Ostrovsky to the fore, the government doggedly hides the verse of Akhmatova, Mandelshtam, and Gumilyov and the novels of Solzhenitsyn from the population. It surrounds the names of Sologub, Merezhkovsky, Bely, and Gippius in mystery, forcing people to like Mayakovsky's worst verse, Gogol's worst stories. Radio and television are run by Cerberuses who let not a single subversive name past. In other words, I see her as a great soul deprived of its birthright.

The man next door in Room 202 is an optician, Professor R. Like every self-satisfied specialist he can speak only about his specialty. No sooner had we met than he set forth his "system," which he has applied to art. [. . .] His views are based on the presupposition that good art is created by healthy people. An artist with bad eyesight is a bad artist. He speaks of the color blind as if they were criminals. He believes that if he can prove that Van Gogh was color blind he will have compromised him. (What about Turner?)

"Does that mean that if Dostoevsky hadn't been an epileptic he'd have been a better writer?" clever Inna Borisovna asked him.

"Definitely," he replied, the ass.

"And if Goya had been healthy, his marvelous 'Caprichos' would have been even better?"

"Of course."

According to the idiot professor, Vrubel's scale of blues is the result of his color blindness, and the fact that it was a turning point in his art and a contribution to art in general (since he used it to shame and overthrow the pallid Itinerant artists)—that never occurred to him. The very concept of "healthy art" is rotten to the core. It owes its existence to Soviet gendarmes and caused the Impressionist masterpieces acquired by Shchukin and left by him to the people to be hidden away in basements. Because all artists were required to be "Realists," what you got were those awful Laktionovs and Gerasimovs, more photographers than painters. But even Soviet ideologues have had to pull in their horns: there has been a Matisse exhibition, the artists connected with the World of Art are being resurrected, names like Seurat, Sisley, Manet, and Monet are no longer used as invective, and so on. [. . .]

29 April.

< . . . > Have greatly enjoyed the company of I.A.K. from Room 209 lately. His coarse features notwithstanding, he is refined, decent, generous, and considerate. Quite talented too. His witty retorts at the dinner table have us in stitches. He is hardworking, persistent, and selfless. Yet he is incredibly removed from general culture. He is a singer and a good one, too, I believe. But there was a reason why starting as a young man Chaliapin hobnobbed with Tolstoy, Chekhov, Gorky, Andreev, Balmont, Golovin, Kustodiev, and Sudeikin; there is a reason why Sobinov was one of the best-read people of his day and Lyadov quoted Saltykov-Shchedrin and Dostoevsky in his conversations. All Igor Al. can quote—not having had a general, humanistic education—are the disgusting banalities of contemporary Party-line poetasters. I find it odd to see a young person who knows no Zabolotsky, no Mandelshtam, no Akhmatova, Solzhenitsyn, Derzhavin, or Baratynsky. He is trying to write, and the richness of his character does come out in his writings, but then so do the hackneyed devices, the banal epithets, the lack of taste and literary finesse.

And he is one of our corridor's most noteworthy residents. The rest have been idiotized and homogenized by newspapers, radio, and TV: you can tell in advance how they will react to anything. They're not people; they're furniture—a set of chairs or the like. Saltykov-Shchedrin and Kuzma Prutkov once pooh-poohed the prospect of unanimity of thought being imposed upon Russia. Well, now the prospect has become reality. Everyone shares the official way of thinking; clear-cut individualists are few and far between. [...]

Made the acquaintance of Bagritsky's wife yesterday. She's entirely gray and has had a hard life: she was arrested and spent eighteen years in a camp.

At mealtimes the women go on about petty female concerns: whether kefir is good for you, what the best way to fry carp is, whether blue is more becoming to someone than green. There's not a single thought, not a single human word. They read the newspapers daily, but mostly for the weather and the TV and radio programs. < ... >

DEATHBED NOTES

16 June.

Had a sudden visit from Solzhenitsyn and his wife yesterday. We embraced, then lunched on the balcony. The weather is heavenly: our lilacs have been particularly luxuriant, the cuckoo's call is more cheerful than usual, the trees incredibly green. Alexander Isaevich is working on a novel dealing with the first German war (1914–17) and is completely wrapped up in it. "But I've been having trouble lately. I find it very easy to write about what I've experienced. I can't seem to make things up."

His wife nods. "And when he gets stuck," she says, "he's gloomy and irritable." His wife, Natasha, keeps his archive of nineteen folders, one of which is for honorary titles. He's an academician, after all: he's been made a member of a literary academy in Paris and an honorary member of an American academy. [...]

25 July.

< ... > The current spiritual atmosphere in the USA is very bad. Yelizar Maltsev has just returned. His father, an illiterate peasant who worked there as a forest ranger, was thrown into the water by some poachers and drowned. Yelizar still has two sisters there. One is a waitress in a café, the other a musician. He spent a month gathering material for a story about

his father (though Korolenko told a similar tale in "Without a Language"). Yelizar was "without a language" himself: he met only Russians. He says people behave like crooks and the Negroes are troublemakers, and so on. We heard it all from Yelizar's wife, Alexandra Ivanovna, a nice woman who after reading *Anti-Dühring* became an Orthodox Christian (she had been a member of the Komsomol).[370] It's a mass phenomenon: good people are retreating to religion in protest against the blood-stained lies permeating our society.

< . . . >

I'm completely absorbed in the Americans' flight to the moon. Our internationalists, who go on and on about space travel as a world-scale phenomenon, are full of envy and hatred for the American heroes and have made the public feel likewise. While "tender feelings fairly rend my breast," tender feelings for the Americans, Lida's cleaning lady Marusya says, "I hope they croak on the way." Schoolchildren are told that the reason Americans are sending humans to the moon is that they are inhuman, callous. We send equipment, instruments, and those dreadful Americans send live people! In other words, our poor fanatics refuse to feel part of humanity. What's more, they forget they once boasted that *they* would be the first people on the moon. "Only Communism will make manned space flights possible," our propagandists once proclaimed like a broken record. Thanks to the ability of the Russian people to forget its immediate past, today's propagandists can state with impunity: "Only heartless capitalism would send manned flights to the moon." The lying crooks! < . . . >

Tanya has just phoned to say the astronauts have returned safely to earth! An earth capable of producing both villains and heroes, prodigious wise men and prodigious ignoramuses—and then serves as grave for them both. An enormously round bipolar cemetery that from afar (the moon) seems but a pretty star. < . . . >

2 August.

Had a visit from Yevtushenko and an artist whose name I can't remember. He recited some inspired verse and did so with such artistry that I regretted there weren't ten thousand people there to listen blissfully with me. He

---

370. Friedrich Engels's *Anti-Dühring* (1878) is a fundamental work of Marxist theory and one that greatly influenced Lenin.

recited one poem about how no matter how we hurt and suffer we should thank fate for the very fact of our existence. His poems are so inspiring they should be printed on leaflets for distribution to prisons, hospitals, and other institutions where people are tortured and oppressed. Then he recited a poem he'd brought back from Siberia, where a boat he was rowing on a river was grounded on a rock. Very Russian, very folk-like. He spent some time in Kazan—he is writing about Lenin in the eighties—and the secretary of the District Committee gave him an amusing document. Nobody is publishing his poetry. One poem was rejected by twelve editorial boards. Another, in which he writes about the charms of early morning Moscow and how wonderful Moscow is at night, was banned: "So you like it better when the authorities are asleep, do you?"

He was going to play Cyrano de Bergerac in a film, but the Central Committee put its foot down. You can have anyone you like, the director was told, but not Yevtushenko.

The director dropped the project.

He brought me a poem about America.[371]

4 September.

September already! And what an eventful few weeks. The police raided my dacha to remove the Reeves, who had come for a visit with their three children.[372] < . . . > I started writing about detective stories and gave it up. I started writing about Sir Max Beerbohm and gave it up. Now I'm writing about how my tales came about, but my memory is failing and I'm afraid I'll get things wrong. [. . .]

Doctor Khomenko came at about six and discovered I had jaundice. She drove me to the Ward for Infectious Diseases of the Kremlin Suburban Hospital, < . . . > where Room 93, my favorite, had just been vacated. And who should I find there but Alexandra Georgievna, my favorite nurse. < . . . >
< . . . >

371. Probably "Under the Skies of the Statue of Liberty" (1968) (V.E.)

372. Professor Franklin D. Reeve—an American scholar, translator, and poet, the author of *Robert Frost in Russia* and *The Russian Novel*—paid Chukovsky a visit at Peredelkino with his wife and three young children. His wife, Helen, was writing a dissertation on Nekrasov and hoped to discuss it with Chukovsky. The conversation had barely begun when the police appeared and forced the Reeves to leave. Peredelkino is far enough outside Moscow to have been off-limits to Westerners.

7 October.

"Gallstones is no joke," said Nurse Sima as she gave me an injection.

So that's it! I've got gallstones. Due to the sleeping pills I've been taking since I was twenty or so, Maria Nikolaevna told me yesterday.

I keep trying to write, but it doesn't work.

After lengthy palpation Maria Nikolaevna decided my liver was diseased and put me on intravenous feeding. I am even more yellow than before. I'd better hurry, because I know my head will be weaker tomorrow than it is today. There's a sign over my door that says "Possibly Botkin's Disease."

< . . . >

16 October.

The following is a list of the books I've written:

1. *Nekrasov* (1930, Federatsia)
2. *A Book About Alexander Blok* (1924)
3. *Contemporaries*
4. *Alive as Life*
5. *A High Art*
6. *From Two to Five*
7. *Chekhov*
8. *People and Books of the Sixties* and other essays ("Tolstoy and Druzhinin," "Sleptsov's Cryptogram of *Hard Times*," etc.)
9. *Nekrasov's Craft*
10. Articles included in the sixth volume of my *Collected Works*
11. Articles (to be) included in the seventh volume
12. *Repin*
13. *My Whitman*
14. *The Silver Escutcheon*[373]
15. *Sunny*

I hereby bequeath the copyright to all these books to my daughter Lidia Korneevna and my granddaughter Yelena Tsezarevna. I also leave the future of my archive, my diaries, and *Chukokkala* to Yelena Tsezarevna Chukovskaya.

---

373. A slightly fictionalized version of Chukovsky's Odessa school years. (V.E.)

The first day without vomiting. Felt something close to an appetite.

< . . . >

[Letter pasted into the diary]

Dear Lida,

Not only can I not get to my feet; I simply cease to exist the moment I make an attempt to raise my body. My stomach is poisoned, my kidneys too, and my liver. A fortnight ago I suddenly lost the ability to write, the following day to read, then to eat. The very word "food" makes me nauseous.

I scarcely need say that I leave you and Lyusha all the rights to my archives, my books *Alive as Life, Chekhov, A High Art, My Whitman, Contemporaries, From Two to Five, Repin, Nekrasov's Craft, Chukokkala, People and Books, Nekrasov* (1930), *A Book About Alexander Blok*. You will also receive the royalties for "Chatterbox [The letter breaks off here.]

20 *October.*

The books I adapted: *The Baron Münchhausen, Robinson Crusoe, The Little Ragamuffin, Doctor Ouch-It-Hurts*

The books I translated: Wycherley, *The Plain Dealer;* Mark Twain, *Tom Sawyer,* the first part of *The Prince and the Pauper;* Kipling's "Rikki-Tikki-Tavi," English nursery rhymes

My tales: "Bruin and the Fox," "Bruin and the Moon," "Praise Be to Ouch-It-Hurts," "Ouch-It-Hurts," "The Telephone," "The Giant Cockroach," "Wash 'Em Clean," "Chatterbox Fly," "The Crocodile," "The Wonder Tree," "The Stolen Sun," "Bibigon"

And an appendix of all my riddles and ditties—

I leave them all to my daughter Lidia Korneevna and my granddaughter Yelena Tsezarevna Chukovskaya to do with them as they see fit.

How to legalize this I don't know.

21 *October.*

A Marya Borisovna day.

Yesterday the sixth volume of my collected works arrived. It was sent by Sofya Krasnova with a very nice cover letter, but I have neither the strength nor the desire to look at this long-awaited progeny of the censor's arbitrary will. < . . . >

24 October.

A terrible night.

APPENDIX

Excerpts from
"What I Remember; or,
Fiddle-Faddle"

(Written in Hospital with a High Temperature) 1968 [. . .]

Rozanov read very little. "Writing *On Understanding* is enough. It's a big book," he boasted in his childlike manner. "It costs five rubles."

He had a bas-relief of Nikolai Nikolaevich Strakhov hanging in his office and a portrait of Nikolai Yakovlevich Danilevsky on his desk. "Danilevsky was right to argue that Darwinism is rubbish. Let's say I cut my finger. A most sagacious power stops the bleeding, places a scab over the incision, and does its delicate work beneath the scab, and when the scab falls away there is not a trace of the incision, the skin is as smooth as if it had never been cut. Nature has carried out a number of clear-cut operations contributing to the well-being of the individual, but what has that to do with the struggle for existence? Believing in God is easier than believing in the struggle for existence."

He very much wanted Repin to paint his portrait. Repin refused point-blank. "He has a red face. He looks just like . . ."

After learning that Repin would not paint his portrait, Rozanov started attacking him and Natalya Borisovna in *Novoe vremia* and *Opavshie list'ia*. He also came down on my portrait of Repin's work. But it was all perfectly innocent: the first time we met he said, "That was a dirty trick I played on you."

* * *

I remember how Konstantin Nabokov took a fancy to me after my first Whitman translations. Emaciated, his face gaunt and haggard, and wearing a fine Paris-tailored suit, he came to visit me in Kuokkala on his way back from a trip abroad even before he'd gone to see his mother in her Siverskaya Street flat (the Nabokovs owned all Siverskaya Street). I had no money. A big family. All we had for dinner was pea soup. I happened to be going on a lecture tour—I was lecturing about Oscar Wilde, I believe, and he came with me to Moscow, Vilnius, and Vitebsk, attending the same lecture over and over. And because he stayed at expensive hotels and took me to expensive restaurants, my earnings diminished considerably. Back in Moscow I deduced from several things he did that he was a homosexual and that his love for me was the love of an urning. But he was very civil and loved art and poetry. Later we met in London, where he was first secretary at the Embassy, and our friendship ran its course, but we were good friends in Petersburg.

*   *   *

The scorn Akhmatova had for Shklovsky! She inherited it from Blok, who treated him squeamishly, as if he were a leper. "Shklovsky," he said, "belongs to that manifold category of critics who, understanding nothing about art and unable to distinguish good art from bad, prefer to create theories of art, schemes. They evaluate a work not on the basis of its artistic qualities but on the basis of whether it supports (or fails to support) the scheme they have devised before the fact."

*   *   *

I am reading the fifth edition of the *Anthology of Children's Literature*. The choice is terribly forced. The progenitor of children's literature, for instance, is—by order of the authorities—none other than Mayakovsky. I read his poem *What I Want to be When I Grow Up*. He clearly wrote it with his left hand, and a very active left hand he had too. What a profound lack of respect for children! How could he be so sloppy? The following is about a plane:

> Fly up, motor, to the skies,
> Hear the birdies sing
> Instead of the lowlands.

Why do the birds sing *instead of* the lowlands? Do lowlands sing at all? Do planes fly up to the skies to hear birds sing? And even if you could find a pilot willing to listen to birds, wouldn't the propeller drown out their song? Besides, where do you find most songbirds if not in the lowlands? And the diction is so illiterate, so out-of-date: the fulsome praise of the workers, the story about the construction of a multistoried building using *scaffolding*. It is only because I so love Mayakovsky that it pains me that the authorities are forcing the worst things he wrote on children. The Prosveshchenie [Enlightenment] Publishing House should change its name to Zatemnenie [Eclipse]. The anthology has a great deal of Baruzdin but no Maikov, no Polonsky, no Kharms, no Voznesensky, no Panteleev.

* * *

< . . . > I once gave Pozdnyaev some material [for *Literaturnaia Rossiia*] including a note Gorky had written condemning the anti-Semitic content of a Bobrov engraving and defending the Jews. Pozdnyaev took it but did not publish it. "The engraving does not reproduce well," he said, looking me shamelessly in the eye.

* * *

[. . .] Several memories from the distant past.

A gigantic hall crammed with people. Seven hundred people if not more. Students with blazing eyes and a number of highly galvanized ladies. More than a thousand hands ready to applaud, passionately anticipating the appearance of their hero.

Their hero was Semyon Yushkevich, a popular writer, the author of the heartrending *Leon Drei* and suchlike overwrought creations which, though not particularly accomplished, abounded in "hot" topics. He had become famous ever since his novels, stories, and sketches began to appear in Gorky's *Znanie* miscellanies side by side with Gorky, Kuprin, and Leonid Andreev. And now this resident of Odessa was making an appearance before his Kiev admirers to give a reading of his latest story.

But what was holding him up? Ten minutes after the appointed hour the stage—with its crimson armchair, table, and pitcher of water—was still bare. Fifteen minutes—and still no Yushkevich.

Suddenly a foppishly dressed but dismayed and trembling young man came out on stage and informed the audience, nearly sobbing, of a terrible catastrophe: their beloved Yushkevich had just sent a telegram saying that he would be unable to oblige Kiev with his precious person as that person had come down with a sudden cold.

A general groan emerged from the audience. Then sighs of disappointment and grief. As they started dying down, the young man hastened to reassure the audience by saying, "However we do have another writer with us this evening, a writer also known for his participation in *Znanie*. His name is Ivan Alexeevich Bunin, and he has graciously consented to give us a reading of some of his works."

The audience simply sat there, morose as ever, whereupon the young man added in an unexpectedly animated bass: "Anyone so wishing may receive his money back."

Anyone turned out to be most everyone. Young and old, pushing and shoving, they elbowed their way to the doors as if the hall were on fire. They all could think of nothing else than retrieving their rubles and kopecks before the box office closed.

In the midst of all this Bunin made his appearance with a proud, resentful, immobile face. Instead of going up to the table, he stopped at the left-hand side of the stage and waited for the flight of the crazed multitude to run its course. Meanwhile, the few diehards, about fifty in number, clambered noisily up to the front rows. Bunin remained in the same fixed pose, pale, thin, and haughty.

He opened with his poem "The Scarecrow." It is his only poem with a civic theme: it depicts fetid Russian autocracy as a pitiful kitchen-garden scarecrow:

> Out back behind the threshing barns
> Of peasants well-to-do
> *He* stands—eleven centuries,
> A truly Russian brute.

But no one grasped the allegory. The fact that "eleven centuries" refers to the precise date of the origin of autocracy in Russia went unnoticed. Now most of the people who had decided to stay jumped up and made a dash to the exit.

"All trees and bees," was the judgment of a pursy, jowly man rushing out with two sour-faced maidens in tow. Of deserters there was no end. Soon only a handful of people were left. We squeezed together down near the footlights, practically on top of the mortified speaker, clapping wildly to offset the humiliation he was going through. But he peered down at us with icy eyes and recited his verse in a dry, hostile, alienated voice, lest we should think he valued our demonstrative show of love in the slightest. At one point a fledgling of a student, showing off his familiarity with Bunin's poetry, called upon him to recite "Stonemason, Stonemason, in Your White Apron"—unaware that it was by Bryusov. That was the last straw for Bunin.

Without so much as a glance at the offender he turned on his heel and made a proud exit.

The incident took place, as far as I can remember, at the Commercial Club. I met Bunin at the entrance and the two of us set off on a ramble through the streets of Kiev. We said not a word about what had just gone on, but it clearly colored his mood. The first words out of his mouth were abuse for his literary colleagues: Leonid Andreev and Fyodor Sologub and Merezhkovsky and Balmont and Blok and Bryusov and last but not least the ill-starred Semyon Yushkevich, who had made things so unpleasant for him. He was quite even-tempered about it and spoke in a steady, even monotonous voice, but it was obvious that he regards the ideas he was setting forth as conventional, old hat, points he had made a thousand times before.

I liked his works and felt he had the right to consider himself misunderstood and underrated, but I found his unkind remarks profoundly misguided. He talked about writers as if every one of them pandered to the crowd to further their careers. Leonid Andreev, who was the leading literary light at the time, he likened to a booming barrel and accused him of a total ignorance of Russian life and a penchant for cheap rhetoric; Balmont he called a vulgar chatterbox, Bryusov a complete nonentity duping simpletons with his supposed erudition. And so on and so forth. In his eyes they were all usurpers of his own glory.

Listening to his monologue that night, I realized what a hard time he had living in literature, where he saw himself as the only righteous man among a flock of sinners making their way in the world. The only thing he could do, given his feeling of superiority, was to treat them with fastidious arrogance. I was especially struck by his caustic remarks about Gorky. "It is morning at Kuokkala," he said. "The samovar on the dacha terrace is boiling away. Gorky comes downstairs before anyone and unrolls the day's newspapers with impatient fingers. Every paper has stories about him. He smirks. A half hour passes. He lays the papers aside. The ladies come down for tea, and they too make first for the papers.

" 'Look, Alexei Maximovich! They mention you here, and here's a whole column devoted to your book.'

" 'I can't be bothered,' he replies, feigning indifference."

I swallowed it all hook, line, and sinker, never thinking to ask how Bunin found out what went on in the privacy of Gorky's terrace.

Bunin maintained friendly relations with Gorky and Leonid Andreev.

He could not have been said to go unrecognized. The true connoisseurs of literature, its supreme arbiters, Chekhov and Gorky, appreciated his gift immediately upon reading his early poems and stories. The Academy of Sciences bestowed the title of academician on him. But the reading public long remained apathetic. [. . .]

Another memory, from a later date. The Finland Station in Petersburg. Summer. Sweltering, stuffy heat. Leonid Andreev and Bunin get off the train. A crowd of onlookers is jumping for joy: "Andreev! Andreev! Andreev!" Pushing and shoving, flushed and sweaty, they surge forward to catch a closer glimpse of the super-famous author of "The Abyss."

"Who's that next to him? The skinny fellow."

"Bunin!" I say in as spirited a voice as I can muster.

But all I hear around me is the same incantatory "Andreev! Andreev! Andreev!"

Bunin, who considered himself head and shoulders above Andreev, can scarcely have been pleased.

[. . .] I repeat, Bunin did enjoy a certain success, he was not belittled, the press ran positive reviews of his work, but compared with the mountains of articles each new work of Gorky—and later Leonid Andreev—called forth the number of reviews devoted to Bunin's works seems microscopically small. Although he eventually came out against the Symbolists with jeering contumely, there was a time when he grudgingly attempted to join ranks with them, and he subsequently published in the *Znanie* collections, though according to his later statements he felt the odd man out there as well. He was never one for slogans or calls to action or sermons. He had a pure, poetic view of life, he was an exquisite craftsman and had an elegant style all his own, but those were not the qualities valued by the general reading audience at the time.

*   *   *

The history of my Repin portrait. Repin always painted several pictures at once. I posed for two: *The Black Sea Freemen* and *The Duel*. I would strip to the waist and lie on the carpet as a wounded duelist. In 1910 he asked me if I wanted him to paint my portrait. It was a success. He made me a gift of it. But in 1912 he had a show in Rome and asked me for permission to exhibit it there. It was sent to Rome. A month later he came and told me rather sheepishly that it had been sold to a couple named Tseitlin.

"It was all a mistake," he explained. "I insured it for a very small sum, and the people running the exhibit thought it was the *price* of the portrait and sold it for a song."

I was upset, and to console me Repin promised to do another portrait.

In 1916, when I was in Paris with Alexei Tolstoy, Vladimir Nabokov, and Vasily Nemirovich-Danchenko, a smooth-spoken Mr. Tseitlin came to our hotel and invited us to dine in the name of his wife. We accepted. The Tseitlins proved enlightened and hospitable people, at home in the ways of the world.

After desert Madame grabbed me by the hand and took me to a far-off room, where I saw a portrait of her children done by Bakst and my portrait done by Repin. I told her that the portrait had been given me by the artist, that they had bought it for the insurance fee, and that I was ready to pay her that sum on the spot. The impulsive Madame Tseitlin was ready to have a ladder brought and the painting taken down, but her husband, who happened to come into the room, objected. "Look where you're taking the portrait. There's a war on. You have to go to Petersburg by sea, through Scandinavia. The portrait could end up in the water or in German hands. As soon as the war ends, we'll take it to you."

The war ended with the Bolsheviks and Lenin's decrees, and even so the Tseitlins returned to Moscow. Krandievskaya (Alexei Tolstoy's wife) writes in her notes about how the Tseitlins, all of whose property had been confiscated, made their way to Odessa with the Tolstoys. My portrait, confiscated with the rest of their property, ended up at the Tretyakov Gallery. It was put in the room where Nesterov's portrait of Pavlov was hanging, but remained there less than a month. Some official came along and exclaimed, "What's Chukovsky doing here?" and the portrait was removed to the basement.

The next time I was in Moscow I saw it in the Torgsin window.

"We'll be only too glad to sell it to you, but only for hard currency or gold."

So off I went, and a month later I learned that the portrait had been sent to America. That must have been in 1933. A year later I returned to Moscow and stayed at the National. One evening when I went into the lobby, the porter called out my name and handed me a letter. **"Are you really Mr. Chukovsky?"** the woman standing next to him asked in a singsong voice.

We fell into conversation. She told me that the Repin portrait had been bought by her husband and was (I believe) in Illinois. I explained that it was family property and asked her to sell it to me for Soviet currency. She promised to talk it over with her husband. Her husband worked for the Association for Trade with America, so Soviet currency was something he could use. We agreed that he would bring the portrait from Illinois and I would pay for it in rubles. Since she (her name was Mrs. Edwards or something along those lines) was also staying at the National, we would have coffee every morning together and we became close friends. Then she left to join her husband and did not return for quite some time.

Meanwhile the year of Stalin's terror, 1937, was upon us. Our home-grown Red Guards were on the warpath, bent on the mass destruction of the intelligentsia. Many of those nearest and dearest to me—writers, translators, physicists, artists, actors—were arrested for no reason at all. Every night I awaited my turn.

And in the midst of all that I had a visit from a messenger with Astoria written on his cap (he came from the Hotel Astoria). He handed me a parcel and a letter. When I opened the parcel, I found volumes of Walt Whitman and O. Henry along with some socks, some pencils, and a few other things. I never even looked at the envelope or tried to learn who the parcel was from; I simply wrapped everything up again in the parcel they had come in and handed it and the unopened letter back to the messenger. "Here, take it. Here," I mumbled in desperation. "I didn't read a thing. I didn't look at a thing. Take it back. Take it all back," because contact of *any* citizen with a foreigner automatically turned that citizen into a spy in the eyes of the Red Guards. The Red Guards could not conceive of an intellectual not being a spy. As I thought the letter and parcel had come from the Edwardses and that the letter contained the news that my portrait had made its way to Leningrad, I was convinced the portrait had disappeared from sight—my sight, at least—forever.

But no! In the fifties at Barvikha I met our ambassador to Israel, and he told me he had spent a lot of time in Jerusalem at the home of a wealthy man by the name of Sherover, where he had had occasion to admire my portrait. I immediately forgot the rich man's name of course, but later in the course of my correspondence with a very fine woman by the name of Rakhil Margolina I mentioned my portrait. She found out that the portrait was in the possession of Mr. Sherover, a great friend of the USSR. I entered into correspondence with Sherover and learned that upon his death the portrait would go to the Tretyakov Gallery. He was kind enough to send me a photograph of the portrait. < . . . > He paid me a visit in 1968—a typical American businessman.

* * *

[. . .] Anastasia Chebotarevskaya was a small woman with enormous drive. After she and Sologub became a couple, she kept telling him what a brilliant poet he was: Gorky couldn't hold a candle to him. He came to think of Gorky as his rival, and she started a (tiny) journal for the specific purpose of exalting Sologub and disgracing Gorky. The newlyweds moved from Vasilyevsky Island to Razyezhaya, where she decorated the rooms with pretentious splendor—I recall some ridiculous embroideries hanging on the walls—and created a salon. To support this life of luxury, Sologub turned into a hack, a graphomaniac: he increased his literary output tenfold and inundated newspapers and journals with instant stories and verse. Occasionally he went so far as to plagiarize. His gift made itself felt more and more rarely.

And all of a sudden something terrible happened: Anastasia Nikolaevna fell in love with XY and lost all interest in Sologub. Their life was hell. Anastasia Nikolaevna's love was unrequited, and the poor woman sought to console herself by visiting friends and telling them of her hopeless passion. Finally she could stand it no longer. She ran out of the house, threw herself into the river, and drowned. I have the article Sologub wrote about her suicide for the paper:

Miscellaneous

Will anyone who witnessed the accident that occurred on the evening of 28 September on Tuchkovy Bridge, when a woman was removed from the water and taken to Bolshoi Prospect, please report all pertinent information to Fyodor Sologub (Zhdanovskaya Embankment 3, flat 26). The same request holds for anyone who knows of what happened subsequently to the ill woman, who left home in a gray coat, a red suit with black trimming, and gray boots. Distinguishing features: early forties, dark, thin, black hair, large eyes, wedding ring.

As I say, at one point Sologub took to plagiarism. *Russkoe bogatstvo* published an article revealing his literary embezzlements. Apparently he had borrowed almost an entire chapter from a French novel. I happened to meet him at the Zamyatins' shortly after the article appeared, and he asked me, playfully dangling his foot as usual, "See how your *Russkoe bogatstvo* friends disgraced themselves?"

"They disgraced themselves?"

"And how! They caught me stealing four pages from a third-rate French writer and failed to notice I'd copied the next four from Charlotte Brontë. Shame on them! The work of a vulgar hack they know inside out, while they haven't a clue about a classic."

* * *

He never reminisced about Chebotarevskaya.

* * *

The first time I saw Kropotkin was in the Reading Room of the British Museum. He was rather short and his eyes were calm, but he was broad-chested and had a military bearing. Everyone called him Prince Kropotkin. At the time the Reading Room had boards on legs, a high table of sorts, for tired readers to relax at. < . . . > He would strike a somewhat statu-esque pose and stand there like a monument, the better to let mankind admire him. < . . . > Impressive and dignified as he was, he had an irra-tional fear of spies. He refused to talk to V. F. Lazursky, a mild-mannered university lecturer and former tutor to Tolstoy's children, who had been sent to London to write a dissertation on Steele and Addison: "An agent of Petersburg. No doubt about it."

I made the acquaintance of his daughter Sasha at Repin's. She was a healthy, round-cheeked girl, not in the slightest devoted to her father's doctrines. She spoke with an English accent. Blok later called her a "true daughter of Ryurik" [the semi-legendary founder of the Russian medieval dynasty], obviously unaware of the fact that her mother was a Jewess.

Kropotkin returned to Russia in 1917 (I believe) at Kerensky's invi-tation and took up residence on Kamenny Island in the house of the for-mer Dutch ambassador, who had gone back to Holland. The house suited the Kropotkin style to a T: it had the same impressive and dignified quality.

"Papa would very much like to meet you," Sasha told me one day when I saw her walking along Nevsky Prospect. "He's read your articles on Nekrasov and some article you wrote for *Russkoe slovo* (probably the Jack London article). He receives on Sundays."

Early the next Sunday morning I hastened to Kamenny Island and the Dutchman's cozy yet ministerial house. The reception hall was small, but imposing and even a bit intimidating. There were already a few people waiting silently for Pyotr Alexeevich by the time I got there. He was at the Winter Palace "at Kerensky's request."

At last he was announced—"He has arrived!"—and a few minutes later he appeared at the door—short and broad-chested, his beard neatly trimmed, ready to please. We all stood, then took our seats, and he began going from one to the next, hearing out each of us patiently. It would have been perfectly natural if we had had petitions in our hands.

One group of silent "petitioners" turned out to be American business-men. Knowing that we were behind in matters of transport, they were out to sell our Russian and Siberian railways American **switches** and showed Kropotkin samples on the spot. All they wanted of him was that he should show their wares to Kerensky and help them to secure a contract.

"Fine," said Kropotkin, "I'll tell him."

Taking their leave, the Americans pulled out their favorite phrase: "Why don't you come and visit us in the States?"

"I'd be only too glad to, but I can't," he replied. "I am forbidden to enter the country."

"Why?"

"Because I'm an anarchist."

"**Are you really an anarchist?**" they asked in amazement.

It was in fact hard to imagine that this portly, well-fed, and important elderly gentleman had any connection to the gangs of bomb throwers who had terrorized the residents of Chicago several years previous.

Once he had seen the Americans out, Kropotkin came up to me. He started our acquaintance in a very strange way: after the formalities he struck a pose and declaimed the long Nekrasov poem that begins:

> I was a mere lad of four
> When my father said . . .

Not daring to interrupt him, I listened to it all the way through. When he had finished, he said, "Completely unknown and never published."

I knew the poem. I must have found it in some old publication. I told him so in a quiet, even guilty voice, but he must not have heard me too well, because every time we met after that he declaimed that poem.

Several days later I had an unexpected guest: Ivan Dmitrievich Sytin accompanied by his factotum Rumanov. It was the first time I'd seen him so dismayed, though he did tend to be gloomy: in 1914 he published my

Walt Whitman, which was confiscated by the police, and for two whole months he pouted at me. < . . . >

"What can we do?" his alter ego Arkady Veniaminovich Rumanov asked me. "What can we do, dear Kornei Ivanovich? We've been meaning to publish the works of Merezhkovsky at *Russkoe slovo,* but Merezhkovsky is so sanctimonious—'Redeem, O Lord, Thy people'—not the sort of thing to tempt today's reader. What we need is something militant, revolutionary. We've been thinking of Hauptmann's *Weavers . . .*"

I had a sudden bright idea.

"What about Kropotkin? His *Memoirs of a Revolutionist, The Conquest of Bread, Mutual Aid in the Animal Kingdom,* and so on."

Sytin gave Rumanov an inquisitive look, a flash of hope illuminating his bat-like face. Prancing around my tiny room and moving back and forth between the formal and informal *you,* he asked me to make a list of Kropotkin's works. I took out a narrow slip of paper and did so at once. Within the hour we were at the Dutchman's house on Kamenny Island. Kropotkin gave us a warm reception and immediately paid Sytin all kinds of compliments: "The things you have done for the advancement of learning . . . The ways you have served culture . . ."

Though accustomed to such praise, Sytin always reacted as if hearing it for the first time. He bowed and scraped and pressed the Prince's hand between his own. "We've come to make you a proposition," he said. "We're ready to draw up a contract on the spot."

Rumanov explained to Kropotkin what they had in mind. Kropotkin took my slip of paper and examined it carefully through his gold-rimmed spectacles. Then he added a title to the list—*A History of Russian Literature,* I believe, a work I had excluded from the list because I thought it crude and naive.

"But God be my witness," said Sytin (who liked to play the old-fashioned merchant and was quite good at it), "God be my witness, given the current circumstances we can't give you more than ten thousand. Ten thousand now, when you sign, and ten thousand when we see what the response is like. We have no choice. We used to go as high as sixty thousand, but nowadays, God be my witness . . ." And so on.

Kropotkin waited calmly for him to finish and said, "You know, we anarchists consider it immoral to accept money for our mental labors. I shall be gratified if my works finally reach a Russian audience, and that gratification is all I need. I grant you the rights free of cost."

Sytin's expression changed completely. He bade a hasty farewell and strode rapidly to the small car we had come in (by some miracle Rumanov had managed to save the *Russkoe slovo* car). Sytin held his peace as the car bumped and wobbled its way through the potholes, but once we came out into Kamenny Island Prospect he said in a sullen, reproachful voice, "The fool! Doesn't take money for his books. Books are obviously worth dogshit."

* * *

[. . .] Gorky had a weak character and was easily influenced; Chekhov had an unusually strong character, an iron will. Perhaps that is why Gorky glorified the strong, the willful, the all-powerful and Chekhov—the weak-willed and defenseless.

* * *

I once saw Mikhail Kuzmin dining at the *Vienna* with a small group of people I didn't know. They asked me to their table. Indicating the stout woman sitting next to him, Kuzmin said, "For all you've written about Nekrasov, I bet you don't know that this bacchante is the daughter of Avdotya Yakovlevna Panaeva."

"How dare you!" the bacchante shouted, furious. "I never tell any-body—anyone at all—that I'm her daughter!"

The bacchante turned out to be Nagrodskaya, the author of the sensational novel *The Wrath of Dionysus*. Out of the blue she let drop that she owned a notebook in the hand of Nekrasov.

I had to get it from her.

She lived in Pavlovsk. Not trusting to my own ability, I took two friends along: Emil Krotky and Isaak Babel. Krotky and I went into the house together; Babel remained in the garden. Krotky immediately spoiled everything. He began telling her what a treasure she had and how precious every line of Nekrasov's was to posterity and so on and so forth.

To neutralize so unfortunate an ally, I called upon Babel. Babel listened morosely to our conversation the way a great artist listens to rank dilettantes, then signaled us to hold our tongues.

"May I have a word with you, Yelena (or Yelizaveta?) Apollonovna?" he asked. "In private."

He went into the next room with her. She clearly felt more comfortable with him than with us. His dimpled, pseudo-naive face had obviously made an impression on her.

We waited a long time, and when he finally emerged, his face was red and his high forehead covered with beads of sweat. He was holding the (now famous) black notebook, which he handed to me with his usual ironic semi-bow. My hands shook as I gave Nagrodskaya a receipt for it.

After we'd left the house, I asked Babel the magic word he'd used to get her to agree to part with her treasure.

"I didn't say a word about Nekrasov; I talked about *The Wrath of Dionysus*. I praised it to the skies. I told her it meant more to me than Flaubert and Huysmans; I told her I was under her influence. And when she invited me back next Friday to read the opening of her new novel, I said, 'What does a yellowed archival document mean to you with your firm grip on the present and future? You don't realize how talented you are.' "

"But *The Wrath of Dionysus* is a terrible novel!" I said.

"I wouldn't know," he replied. "I haven't read it."

* * *

When Marshak came back from the Caucasus in 1920 or 1921, Gorky refused to see him for a long time. "Of course I remember him," he would say to me, "but I'm busy now. I can't."

< . . . > He had brought back a ballad in the Scottish vein, and I said, "Why ballads? They're all wrong for young children. Children need a trochaic line with a variable number of feet; it's the most natural rhythm for them. And children's verse must be structured in such a way that each stanza calls for its own drawing, which means that each stanza must have its own imagery."

Two or three days later he returned with "The Fire," a narrative poem based on the "Wash 'Em Clean" model, and he began calling me his teacher. I was delighted at how quick he was to adapt, and did everything I could to promote his work. Fedin recently reminded me of how I would take Marshak to see him, trying to increase the literary circle of the then-neophyte children's writer.

I had a secretary by the name of Pambe (Ryzhkina) who came up with an English book about the young of various animals in a zoo. The drawings had been done by a well-known English animal artist (I forget his name). Pambe translated it and showed it to Klyachko at Raduga. Klyachko agreed to publish it (mostly for the illustrations). Then Marshak saw Pambe's book. He took a liking to the illustrations and composed a text of his own to go with them. That was how *Coming of Age in a Cage* came about, its first edition featuring the illustrations from the English book Pambe had taken to the publisher in the belief that they would appear with her text.

Then and later Marshak's predatory, pirate-like tendencies were very much in evidence. For all that, I had to admit that Marshak was a superb writer who created some immortal works, who was capable of producing translations (of the English **nursery rhymes,** for instance) that are nothing short of miracles, who worked tirelessly and had a right to be predatory.

When I was translating Kipling's *Just So Stories,* I intended to translate the verse accompanying each story. I managed to do only four lines. I gave them to Marshak, who put them into circulation over his own name, but also translated all the rest of the verse himself and with a mastery I would never have been able to muster. He took Kharms's "They Lived in Flat 44" and turned it into a masterpiece of a poem. By the forties and fifties my attitude toward Marshak had changed radically. He softened as he approached old age, and his tragic disease made me take pity on him. < . . . >

Marshak had a unique mind. He read almost nothing (his wife supplied him with the necessary quotations from Belinsky and others); he was completely ignorant of literary history (with all its Mikhailovskys, Merezhkovskys, Dostoevskys), but he knew hundreds of folk songs—Scottish, Jewish, Russian, Ukrainian, Bulgarian, and so on. He knew practically the whole of Pushkin by heart, and he loved the poets he translated—Shakespeare, Keats, Shelley—with a passion. He knew Burns. When he died, I mourned him as if he had been one of the family.

* * *

I want to write about an act of cowardice I committed.

When during the anti-Chukovsky campaign in the thirties my tales were banned, my name made a term of abuse, when I was driven to the brink of ruin and despair, I was visited by a tempter (a man by the name of Khanin, I believe) who tried to persuade me to make a public repentance, to renounce in writing the error of my ways and announce that I would henceforth write only orthodox books. He even gave me a title for them: *Merry Kolkhozia.* There was illness in the family, I was ruined, isolated, desperate, and I signed the statement that scoundrel had prepared. It said that I censured my former works—"The Crocodile," "Wash 'Em Clean," "Fyodor's Grief," "Doctor Ouch-It-Hurts"—and regretted they had caused so much harm; it said that I promised henceforth to write in the spirit of Socialist Realism and specifically to create a *Merry Kolkhozia.* That Party flunky Khanin, exulting at his victory over an ill and tormented writer, published my renunciation in the papers, and my tormentors besieged me with demands for "full-fledged, *progressive* works."

My head was bursting with ideas for wonderful new tales, but those monsters had convinced me that nobody needed my kind of tale and I wrote not a line. To make matters worse, my former supporters drifted away and I saw myself as a reprobate.

Retribution was not long in coming: Murochka fell mortally ill. I made a few insignificant stylistic changes in the renunciation Khanin had written, and signed it with my name.

Khanin took it to Moscow. When I heard he was planning to make the shameful document public, I authorized Vanya Khalturin to try and get it back, but it was too late, and I was ashamed to look my nearest and dearest in the eye.

Two or three months passed, and I realized I had made a terrible mistake: people I respected turned their heads when I passed, and I gained no advantage whatever. From then on I made it a rule never to give in to the exhortations of our despicable, brazen, benighted bandit Khanins doing their bosses' bidding.

Periodicals, Publishing Houses, Abbreviations, and Acronyms

The source for the abbreviations and acronyms is D. I. Alekseev, *Slovar' sokrashchenii russkogo iazyka* (Moscow: Russkii iazyk, 1983).

Academia. A publishing house specializing in scholarly editions.

Adskaia pochta [Hell's Post]. A prerevolutionary literary journal.

Biblioteka poeta [Poet's Library]. A prestigious series of annotated one-volume editions of major Russian poets.

Begemot [The Hippopotamus].

Cheka = Chrezvychainaia komissiia po bor'be s kontrrevoliutsiei, sabotazhem i spekuliatsiei [Extraordinary Commission for Combating Counter-Revolution, Sabotage, and Speculation]. The official name of the secret police from 1918 to 1922.

Den' [The Day].

Derevenskaia gazeta [Village Gazette]. A publishing house.

Detgiz = Gosudarstvennoe izdatel'stvo detskoi literatury [State Publishing House of Children's Literature].

Detizdat = Izdatel'stvo detskoi literatury [Publishing House of Children's Literature].

Dom detskoi knigi [Children's Book House].

Dom iskusstv [House of the Arts].

Dom literatorov [Writers' House].

Dom tvorchestva [House of Creation].

Epokha [The Epoch]. A publishing house.

Epokha [The Epoch]. A nineteenth-century journal.

GIKhL = Gosudarstvennoe izdatel'stvo khudozhestvennoi literatury [State Publishing House of Literature]

GIZ = Gosudarstvennoe izdatel'stvo [State Publishing House].

Glavlit = Glavnoe upravlenie po delam literatury i izdatel'stv [Central Board of Literature and Publishing Houses]. The board of censors.

Glavprosvet = Glavnoe upravlenie po delam prosveshcheniia [Central Board of Education].

Gorkom = Gorodskoi komitet [Municipal Committee].

Gosizdat = Gosudarstvennoe izdatel'stvo [State Publishing House].

Goslit, Goslitizdat = Gosudarstvennoe izdatel'stvo khudozhestvennoi literatury [State Publishing House of Literature].

GPU = Gosudarstvennoe politicheskoe upravlenie [State Political Board]. Secret police.

Gublit = Gubernskii otdel literatury i izdatel'stv [Regional Department of Literature and Publishing Houses].

GUS = Gosudarstvennyi uchenyi sovet [State Learned Council]. A branch of the People's Commissariat of Education.

Informburo = Informatsionnoe biuro kommunisticheskikh i rabochikh partii [Information Bureau of Communist and Workers Parties].

Inostrannaia literatura [Foreign Literature]. A monthly devoted to translations of contemporary world poetry and fiction.

Intourist = Innostrannyi turist [Foreign Tourist]. The state tourist agency.

Iskusstvo [Art]. A publishing house.

Iskusstvo v shkole [Art in the School].

Istoriia zavodov [The History of Factories].

Iunost' [Youth]. A literary monthly founded in 1955 and often associated with the thaw.

Izdatel'stvo pisatelei [Writers' Publishing House].

Izvestiia [Information]. The Soviet government daily.

Kommunist [The Communist].

Komsomol = Kommunisticheskii soiuz molodezhi [Communist Youth League].

Komsomolka = *Komsomol'skaia Pravda* [Komsomol Truth].

Komsoml'skaia Pravda [Komsomol Truth]. The Komsomol daily.

Krasnaia gazeta [Red Gazette].

Krasnaia nov' [Red Virgin Soil]. A major literary journal appearing between 1921 and 1942 and associated with the writers known as Fellow Travelers.

Krasnaia Pravda [Red Truth].

Krasnaia zvezda [Red Star].

Krokodil [Crocodile]. Soviet humor magazine.

Krug [Circle]. A publishing house.

KSU = Komitet sovetskikh uchenykh [Committee of Soviet Scholars].

Kubuch = Komissia po uluchsheniiu byta uchenykh [Commission for the Improvement of Scholars' Living Conditions].

LEF = Levyi front iskusstva [Left Front of Art]. A literary group of the twenties in which leading representatives of Futurism and Formalism joined forces.

Lengiz = Leningradskoe otdelenie Gosudarstvennogo izdatel'stva [Leningrad Department of the State Publishing House].

Letopis' [Chronicle]. Liberal literary and political journal founded by Gorky in 1915.

Letopis' Doma literaterov [Chronicle of the Writers' House].

Literatura i zhizn' [Literature and Life].

Literaturka. See *Literaturnaia gazeta*.

Literaturnaia gazeta [Literary Gazette]. A literary weekly and organ of the Writers' Union since 1934.

Literaturnaia Moskva [Literary Moscow].

Literaturnaia mysl' [Literary Thought].

Literaturnaia ucheba [Literary Studies]. A literary journal founded by Gorky in 1930 to raise the level of Soviet literature and literary criticism.

Literaturnoe nasledstvo [Literary Heritage]. A series of miscellanies published by the Academy of Sciences since 1931 and containing archival, biographical, bibliographical, iconographical materials relevant to major Russian authors.

Literaturnyi sovremennik [Literary Contemporary]. A Leningrad-based literary journal during the thirties.

Litfond = Literaturnyi fund [Literary Fund]. The organization in charge of the social welfare of Writers' Union members.

Litgazeta. See *Literaturnaia gazeta*.

Litsovremennik. See *Literaturnyi sovremennik*.

MGU = Moskovskii gosudarstvennyi universitet [Moscow State University].

Molodaia gvardiia [Young Guard]. A publishing house.

Molodaia gvardiia [Young Guard]. A literary journal founded in 1922 and specializing in works for young adults.

MONO = Moskovskii otdel narodnogo obrazovaniia [Moscow Department of the People's Education].

MOPR = Mezhdunarodnaia organizatsiia pomoshchi bortsam revoliutsii [International Organization for Aid to Revolutionaries].

Mosfilm [Moscow Film Studios].

Moskovskaia pravda [Moscow Truth].

Moskovskii rabochii [Moscow Worker]. A publishing house.

Moskva [Moscow]. A literary journal founded in 1957 known for publishing major Soviet and Western writers.

Moskvitianin [The Muscovite]. An important nineteenth-century "thick" journal with a conservative, nationalist bent.

Murzilka [Murzilka]. A children's magazine.

Muzgiz = Gosudartvennoe muzykal'noe izdatel'stvo [State Publishing House of Music].

Mysl' [Thought]. A publishing house.

Nachala [Beginnings].

Nakanune [On the Eve]. The Berlin-based organ of the Change of Landmarks group in the 1920s.

Na literaturnom postu [On Literary Guard]. The journal that provided the theoretical basis for proletarian literature (1926-32).

Narkomindel = Narodnyi komissariat inostrannykh del [People's Commissariat of Foreign Affairs].

Narkomprod = Narodnyi komissariat prodovol'stviia [People's Commissariat of Food].

Narkompros = Narodnyi komissariat prosveshcheniia [People's Commissariat of Education].

Narkomzdrav = Narodnyi komissariat zdravookhraneniia [People's Commissariat of Health].

Nashi dostizheniia [Our Achievements].

Nauka i religiia [Science and Religion].

Nedelia [The Week].

Nemetskaia gazeta [The German Gazette]. Saint Petersburg newspaper.

Niva [The Field]. A prerevolutionary literary journal.

Novaia Rossiia [New Russia].

Novaia russkaia kniga [The New Russian Book]. A literary journal coming out in Berlin in the twenties.

Novaia zhizn' [New Life]. A Socialist newspaper critical of the Bolsheviks edited by Gorky in 1917–18.

Novoe vremia [New Times].

Novosti [News].

Novyi mir [New World]. A literary monthly founded in 1925 and known for its liberal stance.

Novyi zritel' [New Spectator].

NKVD = Narodnyi komissariat vnutrennikh del [People's Commissariat of Internal Affairs].

Ogiz = Ob"edinenie gosudarstvennykh izdatel'stv [Association of State Publishing Houses].

Ogonek [Small Fire]. A popular illustrated monthly.

Oktiabr' [October]. A literary monthly founded in 1924 to feature proletarian writers and promoting a conservative line throughout the Soviet period.

Orgkomitet = Organizatsionnyi komitet [organizational committee].

Otechestvennye zapiski [Notes of the Fatherland]. A "thick" journal published from 1839 to 1884, home first to the Westernizers and later to the Populists.

Otkomkhoz = Otdel kommunal'nogo khoziaistva [Communal Housing Department].

Pechat' i revoliutsiia [Press and Revolution]. A bibliographical monthly published from 1921 to 1930.

Petrokomnetr [Petrograd Commission for Non-Workers].

Pionerskaia Pravda [Pioneer Truth]. The organ of the Pioneer movement.

Pisatel' i chitatel' [Writer and Reader].

Ponedel'nik [Monday]. A prerevolutionary newsweekly.

Poslednie novosti [The Latest News].

Pravda [Truth]. The Communist Party daily.

Priboi [Surf]. A publishing house.

Proletarii [The Proletarian]. A publishing house.

Proletcult = Proletarskaia kul'tura [Proletarian Culture]. A cultural organization under the aegis of the People's Commissariat of Education (1917–32) and designed to promote proletarian values.

Prozhektor [Floodlight].

Pushkinskii Dom [Pushkin House]. A Leningrad institute for the study of Russian literature.

Raduga [Rainbow]. A publishing house.

Raisovet = Raionnyi sovet [District Soviet].

RAPP = Rossiiskaia assotsiatsiia proletarskikh pisatelei [Russian Association of Proletarian Writers]. The literary organization that put an end to experimentation in the twenties and laid the foundation for Socialist Realism.

Rech' [Speech]. A liberal Saint Petersburg newspaper founded in 1906 as the central organ of the Constitutional Democratic Party and banned after the October Revolution.

Russkaia mysl' [Russian Thought].

Russkaia starina [Russian Antiquity]. A nineteenth-century journal.

Russkaia volia [Russian Will].

Russkii sovremennik [The Russian Contemporary].

Russkoe bogatstvo [Russian Wealth]. A prerevolutionary literary monthly founded in 1876 and specializing in Realist writers.

Russkoe slovo [The Russian Word]. A prerevolutionary journal.

Sibirskie ogni [Siberian Fires]. A Siberian literary journal.

Slovo [The Word]. A prerevolutionary literary journal.

Smekhach [The Wag].

Soiuzpechat' [All-Union Press]. The centralized book distribution agency.

Soiuz prosveshcheniia [Board of Education].

Sotsvos = Podotdel sotsial'nogo vospitaniia otdela narodnogo obrazovaniia [Subdivision of Social Education of the Department of the People's Education].

Sovnarkhoz = Sovet narodnogo khoziaistva [Council of the Economy].

Sovnarkom = Sovet narodnykh komissarov [Council of the People's Commissars].

Sovremennik [The Contemporary]. The major literary journal in the nineteenth century. *Sovremennik* is also sometimes used by Chukovsky in the diary as an abbreviation for *Russkii sovremennik* (see above).

Sovremennik [The Contemporary]. Liberal Moscow theater.

Sovremennoe slovo [The Contemporary Word].

Sovremennyi Zapad [The West Today]. A journal founded by Chukovsky in 1922, it proved too liberal for the regime.

Teatr [Theater]. The leading Soviet theater journal.

Teatr i iskusstvo [Theater and Art].

Torgsin = Vsesoiuznoe ob"edinenie po torgovle s inostrantsami [All-Union Association for Trade with Foreigners].

TsDRI = Tsentral'nyi dom rabotnikov iskusstva [Central House of Art Workers].

Tsentral'nyi komitet po uluchsheniiu byta uchennykh [Central Committee for the Improvement of Scholars' Living Conditions].

TsK = Tsental'nyi komitet [Central Committee of the Communist Party].

VAPP = Vserossiiskaia assotsiatsiia proletarskikh pisatelei [All-Russian Association of Proletarian Writers]. The predecessor to RAPP.

Vecherniaia Moskva [Evening Moscow]. An evening daily.

Vestnik [The Herald]. A journal Blok published in his childhood.

Vestnik znaniia [Herald of Knowledge].

Vesy [Scales]. The leading journal of the Russian symbolist movement, published in Moscow from 1904 to 1909.

VKP(b) = Vsesoiuznaia kommunistichskaia partiia (bol'shevikov) [All-Union Communist Party (Bolsheviks)].

VLKSM = Vsesoiuznyi leninskii kommunisticheskii soiuz molodezhi [All-Union Leninist Young Communist League].

Voprosy istorii [Issues of History]. The most prestigious history journal in the Soviet era.

Vremia [Time]. A publishing house.

Vremia [Time]. A nineteenth-century journal.

Vserosskomdram = Vserossiiskoe obshchestvo kompozitorov i dramaturgov [All-Russian Society of Composers and Playwrights].

Yezh [The Hedgehog].

Zapiski mechtatelei [Dreamers' Notes].

Zaria Vostoka [Dawn of the East]. A newspaper.

Zateinik [The Joker].

Zavtra [Tomorrow]. The title of an independent cultural journal Chukovsky tried to start in 1919.

Zemlia i fabrika [Land and Factory]. A publishing house.

Zhizn' iskusstva [The Life of Art]. An important journal of the avant-garde, published in the twenties.

ZIF = Zemlia i fabrika.

Znamia [The Flag]. A monthly literary journal founded in 1930 to give voice to a conservative stance.

Biographical References

Abalkin, Nikolai Alexandrovich (1906–1986). Literary critic. Appointed deputy editor of *Pravda* in 1949.

Adamovich, Georgy Viktorovich (1892–1972). Minor Acmeist poet, leading literary critic of the interwar emigration.

Addison, Joseph (1672–1719). English satirist.

Afinogenov, Alexander Nikolaevich (1904–1941). Playwright.

Agranovsky, Abram Davydovich (1895–1951). Journalist.

Akhmatova, Anna Andreevna (pseudonym of Anna Andreevna Gorenko, 1889–1966). Major lyric poet. Along with Nikolai Gumilyov and Osip Mandelshtam she was a leading figure in the Acmeist movement, a post-Symbolist school of poetry stressing lucidity, precision, and restraint. She won immediate acclaim for her two first collections of verse, *Evening* (1912) and *The Rosary* (1914). Although she is commonly characterized as a poet of love and intimacy, a note of public concern and apprehension entered her third volume, *White Flock* (1917), and remained one of her trademarks. She was virtually silenced during the Stalinist period, and in 1946 she and Mikhail Zoshchenko became the targets of a scurrilous attack by Stalin's cultural henchman Andrei Zhdanov, who called her "half-harlot, half nun." In the post-Stalin period Akhmatova received a modicum of official recognition at home and several prestigious awards abroad. In her last years she served as a model to a group of gifted young Leningrad poets including Joseph Brodsky. Neither her poetic cycle *Requiem*, a dirge for the victims of the Great Terror, nor the full text of her *A Poem Without a Hero*, a remarkable attempt to capture the feverish atmosphere of prewar literary Petersburg, could be published until glasnost.

Alexandrov, Georgy Fyodorovich (1908–1961). Director of the Institute of Philosophy from 1947, member of the Academy of Sciences, Minister of Culture in 1954–55.

Alexeev, Vasily Mikhailovich (1881–1951). Sinologist.

Alexinsky, Mikhail Andreevich (1889–1938). Member of the People's Commissariat of Education. Victim of the Great Terror.

Aliger, Margarita Iosifovna (1915–1992). Poet.

Allilueva, Svetlana Iosifovna (1926–). Stalin's daughter. She defected to the United States in 1967 and has written several volumes of memoirs.

Amfiteatrov, Alexander Valentinovich (1862–1938). Poet, journalist, critic, and publisher.

Andersen, Nexø Martin (1869–1954). Danish proletarian novelist.

Andreev, Andrei Andreevich (1895–1971). Secretary of the Central Committee, member of the Politburo.

Andreev, Daniil Leonidovich (1906–1959). Writer, son of Leonid Andreev.

Andreev, Leonid Nikolaevich (1876–1919). Prominent turn-of-the century short-story writer and playwright. Stories like "Red Laughter" (1904) and "The Seven Who Were Hanged" (1908) created a stir because of their daring subject matter. His plays, the most famous of which are *The Life of Man* (1908) and *He Who Gets Slapped* (1915), are more in the Symbolist or allegorical vein.

Andreev, Vadim Leonidovich (1902–1976). Poet, member of the French Resistance, son of Leonid Andreev.

Andronikov (Andronikashvili), Irakly Luarsabovich (1908–1990). Soviet writer, literary critic.

Angert, David Nikolaevich (1893–1977). Head of the Lenotgiz editorial board.

Annenkov, Yuri Pavlovich (1889–1974). Modernist painter and sculptor known for portraits of both literary contemporaries and high-ranking Bolsheviks.

Annensky, Nikolai Fyodorovich (1843–1912). Journalist, statistician.

Antokolsky, Mark Matveevich (1843–1902). Sculptor.

Antokolsky, Pavel Grigoryevich (1896–1978). Poet.

Ardov, Viktor Yefimovich (1900–1976). Satirist, playwright.

Arkhipov, Vladimir Alexandrovich (1913–1977). Literary scholar.

Arnshtam, Lev Oskarovich (1905–1979). Film director, screenwriter.

Aronson, Naum Lvovich (1872–1943). Sculptor.

Arosev, Alexander Yakovlevich (1890–1938). Writer, publisher. Victim of the Great Terror.

Artsybashev, Mikhail Petrovich (1878–1927). Writer known for his lurid subject matter.

Aseev, Nikolai Nikolaevich (1889–1963). Neo-Futurist poet. Close associate of Mayakovsky, member of LEF.

Asmus, Valentin Fernandovich (1894–1975). Philosopher, literary scholar.

Atsarkin, Alexander Nikolaevich (1904–1988). Editor.

Averbakh, Leopold Leopoldovich (1903–1937). Literary critic. A leading spokesman for RAPP. Victim of the Great Terror.

Averchenko, Arkady Timofeevich (1881–1925). Humorist.

Azadovsky, Mark Konstantinovich (1888–1954). Literary scholar, folklorist.

Babel, Isaak Emmanuilovich (1899–1940). Major early Soviet short-story writer and playwright. He is best known for the brilliant language and imagery of his story cycles *Red Cavalry* (1926), about the 1920 Polish campaign, and *Odessa Tales* (1927), about a flamboyant Jewish gangster. By the time of the First All-Union Congress of Writers in 1934, however, he could speak of himself as a "past master at the art of silence," and he was arrested in 1939 and shot in 1940.

Bagritsky (pseudonym of Dzyubin), Eduard Georgievich, (1895–1934). Poet best known for his Civil War saga in the vein of revolutionary romanticism.

Bakst, Lev Samoilovich (1886–1924). Modernist painter and stage designer.

Bakunin, Mikhail Alexandrovich (1814–1876). Political writer and thinker, a major theorist of anarchism.

Balmont, Konstantin Dmitrievich (1867–1942). Early Symbolist poet whose lush sound painting and exuberant celebration of the self in works like "Let Us Be Like the Sun" (1903) introduced Russian readers to the Modernist sensibility.

Baltrušaitis, Jurgis (1873–1944). Lithuanian Symbolist poet writing primarily in Russian.

Balukhaty, Sergei Dmitrievich (1882–1945). Literary scholar.

Baranov, Nikolai Mikhailovich (1834–1901). Governor of the Nizhny Novgorod province.

Baratynsky, Yevgeny Abramovich (1800–1844). Major Romantic poet.

Barto, Agnia Lvovna (1906–1981). Well-known Soviet children's poet.

Baruzdin, Sergei Alexeevich (1926–1991). Children's writer known for his Party-line verse and stories.

Bedny, Demyan (pseudonym of Yefim Alexeevich Pridvorov) (1883–1945). Soviet poet and fabulist.

Beilis, Mendel (1873–1934). Jewish defendant in the infamous 1913 ritual murder trial.

Belchikov, Nikolai Fyodorovich (1890–1979). Literary scholar.

Belinkov, Arkady Viktorovich (1921–1970). Dissident literary critic. He attempted a trilogy about the fate of the Russian intellectual under an authoritarian regime.

Belinsky, Vissarion Grigoryevich (1811–1848). Pioneer of Russian literary criticism who determined its predominantly social orientation during the nineteenth century and is often called the father of the Russian intelligentsia.

Belitsky, Yefim Yakovlevich (1895–1940). Publisher.

Bely, Andrei (pseudonym of Boris Nikolaevich Bugaev, 1880–1934). Leading

Symbolist poet, novelist, literary critic, and memoirist. His *Petersburg* (1913–22) represents the climax of Symbolist prose. In addition to fiction and lyric verse Bely produced a significant body of literary criticism, and his four volumes of memoirs are a compelling if often unreliable re-creation of the Symbolist era.

Benkendorf, Alexander Khristorovich (1785–1844). Head of the secret police under Nicholas I.

Benkendorf, Maria Ignatyevna. *See* Budberg, Maria Ignatyevna.

Bennett, (Enoch) Arnold (1867–1931). English journalist, novelist, and playwright.

Berdyaev, Nikolai Alexandrovich (1874–1948). Russian philosopher and publicist.

Beria, Lavrenty Pavlovich (1899–1953). Head of the Soviet secret police from 1938. Played a major role in Stalinist purges. Arrested and executed soon after Stalin's death.

Berkovsky, Naum Yakovlevich (1901–1972). Literary critic.

Berzer, Anna Samoilovna (1917–1994). Editor of *Literaturnaia gazeta*, then head of fiction at *Novyi mir*.

Bestuzhev, Nikolai Alexandrovich (1791–1855). Writer, painter, one of the leaders of the 1825 Decembrist insurrection.

Blok, Alexander Alexandrovich (1880–1921). Leading Symbolist poet. In his lyrical verse the romantic quest for an elusive love object gives way to self-mockery and a guilt-ridden involvement with Russia's national destiny culminating in "The Twelve" (1918), the most significant poetic response to the October Revolution. Yet Blok's intoxication with what he called the music of the revolution was short-lived. In a remarkable speech given just before his death he warned against the creeping regimentation of literature.

Bobrov, Sergei Pavlovich (1889–1971). Poet, translator, essayist.

Bondi, Sergei Mikhailovich (1891–1983). Eminent Pushkin scholar.

Bonetsky, Konstantin Iosifovich (1914–). Editor at Khudozhestvennaia literatura Publishing House.

Boronina, Yekaterina Alexeevna (1908–1955). Children's writer. Lidia Chukovskaya's classmate.

Botkin, Vasily Petrovich (1811–1869). Liberal literary critic.

Brezhnev, Leonid Ilyich (1906–1982). Soviet leader.

Brik, Lilia Yuryevna, "Lili" (1891–1978). Addressee of Mayakovsky's most effective love poems. Wife of Osip Brik.

Brik, Osip Maximovich (1888–1945). A Formalist critic and leading member of LEF.

Brodsky, Joseph (1940–1996). Major poet and essayist. A protégé of Anna Akhmatova, he began writing poetry with a pronounced metaphysical bent as an adolescent. In 1964 he was tried and sentenced as a "social parasite" to five years' exile at hard labor in the Arkhangelsk region. As a result of a worldwide outcry, he was allowed to return to Leningrad after twenty months, but was subsequently forced into exile. In 1972 he settled in the United States, where his poetic talent matured and its range expanded. He shows deep affinities not only with Akhmatova but also with Mandelshtam, the English metaphysical poets, T. S. Eliot, and his friend W. H. Auden. He was awarded the Nobel Prize for Literature in 1985 and served as Poet Laureate of the United States.

Broshniovskaya, Olga Nikolaevna. Translator.

Brovman, Grigory Abramovich (1907–1984). Literary critic.

Brushtein, Alexandra Yakovlevna (1884–1968). Author of plays and stories for children.

Bryusov, Valery Yakovlevich (1873–1924). Major Symbolist poet, novelist, and literary critic.

Bubnov, Andrei Sergeevich (1883–1938). People's Commissar of Education from 1929. Victim of the Great Terror.

Buchanan, George William (1854–1924). British diplomat.

Buckle, Henry Thomas (1821–1862). British historian.

Budberg, Maria Ignatyevna (née Zakrevskaya, first marriage to Benkendorf, 1892–1974). Translator, secretary of Maxim Gorky.

Budyonny, Semyon Mikhailovich (1883–1973). Military leader, commander of the First Cavalry during the 1920 campaign against Poland.

Bukharin, Nikolai Ivanovich (1888–1938). Bolshevik leader and Marxist theoretician. Accused of counterrevolutionary activities and espionage, he was arrested, put on public trial in 1938, and subsequently executed.

Bulgakov, Mikhail Afanasyevich (1891–1940). Prominent novelist and playwright. A master at combining the fantastic and the everyday to produce biting and hilarious satire, he is most remembered for his long-suppressed novel *The Master and Margarita* (1929–40).

Bulganin, Nikolai Alexandrovich (1895–1975). Communist dignitary. Chairman of the Council of Ministers between 1955 and 1958.

Bunin, Ivan Alexeevich (1870–1953). Prominent novelist, short-story writer, and poet. He depicts the disintegration of traditional rural life in rich, flowing prose. An arch foe of Bolshevism, he left Russia shortly after the Revolution and in 1933 became the first Russian to win the Nobel Prize for Literature.

Burlyuk, David Davidovich (1882–1967). Modernist painter and poet, spokesman for the Cubo-Futurist faction of the Russian avant-garde.

Butkov, Yakov Petrovich (1821–1857). Short-story writer focusing on the hapless denizens of Saint Petersburg.

Butler, Samuel (1835–1902). English novelist known for *The Way of All Flesh* (1903).

Bystryansky, Vadim Alexandrovich (1886–1940). Journalist, member of the Gosizdat editorial board.

Caine, Thomas Henry Hall (1853–1931). English novelist.

Canning, George (1770–1827). British statesman.

Čapek, Karel (1890–1938). Czech playwright, novelist, journalist, and translator. A leading cultural figure during the first Czechoslovak Republic, he is best known outside the country for his play *R.U.R.* (1921), which introduced the word *robot* into European languages.

Carlisle-Andreeva, Olga Vadimovna (1930–). Painter, writer, translator. Granddaughter of Leonid Andreev.

Carpenter, Edward (1844–1929). British social reformer and writer. Acquaintance of Walt Whitman's.

Chaadaev, Pyotr Yakovlevich (1794–1856). Author of *Lettres philosophiques* (1829–31), which condemned Russian cultural backwardness and called for integration into the European tradition. After publishing the first letter, Chaadaev was officially declared insane and placed under house arrest.

Chagin, Pyotr Ivanovich (1898–1967). Editor of *Krasnaia gazeta.*

Chaliapin, Fyodor Ivanovich (1873–1938). Internationally known opera singer.

Chamberlain, Joseph (1836–1914). British statesman and father of Neville Chamberlain.

Chapygin, Alexei Pavlovich (1870–1937). Writer.

Charskaya, Lidia Alexeevna (1875–1937). Popular writer of novels for and about young women.

Chatterton, Thomas (1752–1770). English poet.

Chebotarevskaya, Anastasia Nikolaevna (1876–1921). Translator, literary critic.

Chekhonin, Sergei Vasilyevich (1878–1934). Painter, stage designer.

Chekhov, Anton Pavlovich (1860–1904). Playwright and short-story writer.

Chernov, Viktor Mikhailovich (1876–1952). Leader of the Socialist Revolutionary Party, Minister of Agriculture in the Provisional Government. Chairman of the short-lived Constituent Assembly (1918).

Chernyshevsky, Nikolai Gavrilovich (1828–1889). Writer, critic, political activist. His master's thesis, "On the Esthetic Relation of Art to Reality" (1855), posits the superiority of reality over art, and his enormously influential novel-tract *What Is to Be Done?* (1862–64) sets forth the materialistic idea of "enlightened self-interest."

Chertkov, Vladimir Grigoryevich (1854–1936). Journalist. Tolstoy's amanuensis during his later years and a bitter antagonist of Tolstoy's wife.

Chicherin, Georgy Vasilyevich (1872–1936). Commissar of Foreign Affairs from 1918 to 1930.

Chikobava, Arnold Stepanovich (1898–1985). Linguist.

Chorny, Sasha (pseudonym of Alexander Mikhailovich Glikberg) (1880–1932). Popular satirist and parodist.

Chudovsky, Valerian Adolfovich (1882–1938). Literary critic. Victim of the Great Terror.

Chulkov, Georgy Ivanovich (1879–1939). Minor Symbolist poet and essayist.

Churlionis, Mikalojus Konstantinas (1875–1911). Lithuanian Symbolist, painter, composer.

Cournos, John (1881–1966). English writer and translator.

Custine, Adolphe de (1790–1857). French diplomat known for *La Russie en 1839*, an anecdotal but insightful account of Russian absolutism.

Dal, Vladimir Ivanovich (1801–1872). Writer, lexicographer, linguist. He compiled the monumental and in some ways still unsurpassed *Explanatory Dictionary of the Living Russian Language* (1863–66).

Dan, Fyodor Ilyich (1871–1947). Leading Menshevik.

Daniel, Yuly Markovich (1925–1988). Writer and translator. In 1965 he was tried for publishing a cycle of stories in the West under the pseudonym Nikolai Arzhak and was sentenced to five years' hard labor.

Danilevsky, Nikolai Yakovlevich (1822–1885). Political writer with a strong Slavophile orientation. Author of the influential tract *Russia and Europe* (1869).

Davydov, Denis Vasilyevich (1784–1839). Member of the Pushkin pleiad known as the "hussar poet."

Delvig, Anton Antonovich (1798–1831). Member of the Pushkin pleiad known for his idylls and romances.

Dementyev, Alexander Grigoryevich (1904–1984). Deputy editor of *Novyi mir*.

Demichev, Pyotr Nilovich (1918–). Secretary of the Central Committee.

Denikin, Anton Ivanovich (1872–1947). General, a leader of the abortive White Resistance to the Bolsheviks.

Denisevich, Tolya. Leonid Andreev's sister-in-law.

Derzhavin, Gavrila Romanovich (1743–1816). Premier lyric poet of the age of Catherine the Great known especially for his sonorous odes.

Deutsch, Babette (1895–1962). American translator.

Diky, Alexei Denisovich (1889–1955). Actor, stage director.

Dobrolyubov, Nikolai Alexandrovich (1836–1861). Russian radical critic who treated fiction as a springboard for sociopolitical diagnoses.

Dobuzhinsky, Mstislav Valerianovich (1875–1957). Painter, graphic artist, stage designer with Modernist tendencies.

Dovzhenko, Alexander Petrovich (1894–1956). Leading Soviet film director especially acclaimed for *Earth* (1930), a film about collectivization.

Dreiden, Simon Davydovich (1906–1991). Drama critic.

Druzhinin, Vasily Grigoryevich (1859–1937). Historian of religion, bibliographer.

Druzin, Valery Pavlovich (1903–1980). Literary critic.

Dubelt, Leonty Vasilyevich (1792–1862). Police chief under Nicholas I.

Dubrovina, Lyudmila Viktorovna (d. 1977). Member of the staff of the Central Committee. Head of Detgiz.

Dudintsev, Vladimir Dmitrievich (1918–1998). Writer. He created a stir with *Not by Bread Alone* (1956), a novel openly critical of the Party.

Duncan, Isadora (1878–1927). Innovative American dancer. Married to Sergei Yesenin.

Dymov, Osip (pseudonym of Iosif Isidorovich Perlman, 1878–1959). Journalist, humorist.

Dzerzhinsky, Felix Edmundovich (1877–1926). Bolshevik leader, founder of the first Soviet secret police organization.

Dzhugashvili. *See* Stalin.

Efros, Abram Markovich (1888–1954). Art critic and translator.

Ehrenburg, Ilya Grigoryevich (1891–1967). Prolific writer and journalist. His first novel, *The Extraordinary Adventures of Julio Jurenito* (1922), marked him as a freewheeling muckraker. Toward the end of his life he played a significant role in the post-Stalin cultural ferment as author of the novel *The Thaw* (1954–1956) and of the wide-ranging and relatively candid memoirs *People, Years, Life* (1961–65).

Eikhenbaum, Boris Mikhailovich (1886–1959). Literary historian and theorist. A key figure in the Formalist school of literary scholarship, he became a target of official abuse during the postwar cultural purge, but resumed full-scale scholarly activities during the late fifties.

Eikhler, Genrikh Leopoldovich (1901–1953). Detgiz staff member.

Eikhvald, E. E. A doctor.

Eikhvald, Yekaterina Nikitichna. Widow of Dr. E. E. Eikhvald.

Eizen, Ilya Moiseevich. Journalist.

Elsberg, Yakov Yefimovich (1901–1972). Critic.

Epshtein, Iosif Moiseevich (1895–1980). Urologist.

Epshtein, Moisei Solomovich (1890–1938). Head of the Social Education Subdivision of the Department of People's Education. Victim of the Great Terror.

Etkind, Yefim Grigoryevich (1918–1999). Eminent literary scholar, comparatist, translator, and theoretician of translation. He was forced into emigration after appearing as a defense witness in Brodsky's trial and taught Russian literature in Paris for a number of years.

Fabritsius, Yan Frantsevich (1877–1929). Military commander. Civil War hero.

Fadeev, Alexander Alexandrovich (1901–1956). Prominent Soviet novelist and

Party activist. He was a leader of RAPP and headed the Soviet Writers Union between 1946 and 1954. He shot himself shortly after Khrushchev's Secret Speech in 1956.

Falk, Robert Rafailovich (1886–1958). Painter. Member of the World of Art group.

Fausek (née Andrusova), Yulia Ivanovna (1863–1943). Pedagogue, psychologist. Author of studies on the Montessori system and of children's books.

Favorsky, Vladimir Andreevich (1886–1964). Illustrator of Soviet editions of the Russian classics.

Fedin, Konstantin Alexandrovich (1892–1977). Prominent Soviet writer and literary dignitary. In the twenties he was a member of the freewheeling Serapion Brotherhood, but eventually adjusted to the demands of Socialist Realism. As a pillar of the literary establishment Fedin explained to Pasternak in temperate but orthodox prose why *Doctor Zhivago* was unfit for publication in the Soviet Union.

Fet (Shenshin), Afanasy Afanasyevich (1820–1892). A master of nineteenth-century Russian lyric poetry.

Filosofov, Dmitry Vladimirovich (1872–1940). Journalist and critic.

Fonvizin, Denis Ivanovich (1744–1792). Leading Russian comic playwright of the eighteenth century.

Forsh, Olga Dmitrievna (1873–1961). Writer. Her *Ship of Fools* (1931) gives a vivid portrayal of the Petrograd House of the Arts in the early twenties.

Fourier, Charles (1772–1837). French social philosopher who proposed a utopia based on communal living in what he called phalansteries.

Furtseva, Yekaterina Alexeevna (1910–1974). Minister of Culture under Khrushchev.

Fyodorov, Alexander Mitrofanovich (1868–1949). Poet, translator.

Gabrichevsky, Alexander Georgievich (1891–1968). Literary scholar, translator.

Galkin, Samuil Zalmanovich (1897–1960). Poet, playwright.

Ganetsky, Yakov Stanislavovich (1879–1937). Journalist, Party activist.

Gardner, Erle Stanley (1889–1970). American detective-story writer.

Garnett, Constance (1862–1946). English translator of the Russian nineteenth-century classics.

Garshin, Vsevolod Mikhailovich (1855–1888). Important short-story writer.

Gerasimov, Alexander Mikhailovich (1881–1963). Official painter. Head of the Academy of Fine Arts between 1947 and 1957.

Gernet, Nina Vladimirovna (1904–1982). Children's writer.

Gessen, Iosif Vladimirovich (1886–1943). Prominent figure in the Constitutional-Democratic (Kadet) Party. In emigration he edited the multivolume *Archive of the Russian Revolution*.

Ginzburg, Lidia Yakovlevna (1902–1990). Eminent literary scholar known for her penetrating studies of the Russian classics.

Gippius, Tatyana Nikolaevna (1877–1957). Painter, sister of Zinaida Gippius.

Gippius, Vasily Vasilyevich (1890–1942). Leading Gogol scholar.

Gippius, Zinaida Nikolaevna (1869–1945). Poet and critic. Together with her husband, Dmitry Merezhkovsky, she played a leading role in the turn-of-the-century spiritual ferment. Although the faith for which Gippius' persona gropes remains unattainable, the masterfully orchestrated quest makes her one of the most significant religious poets in the language. Writing under a male pseudonym, she also produced incisive if astringent and partisan literary criticism.

Glazunov, Alexander Konstantinovich (1865–1936). Composer.

Glotser, Vladimir Iosifovich (1931–). Pedagogue, literary critic.

Gollerbakh, Erikh Fyodorovich (1895–1945). Art historian, literary scholar.

Golovin, Alexander Yakovlevich (1863–1930). Stage designer.

Gorchakov, Alexander Mikhailovich (1799–1883). Diplomat, Pushkin's classmate.

Gorky, Maxim (pseudonym of Alexei Maximovich Peshkov, 1868–1936). Major fiction writer, playwright, public figure. His early stories idealized picturesque outcasts in the vein of romantic naturalism. His unabashedly didactic first novel, *Mother* (1906), reflects his involvement with Russian Marxism and was later acclaimed as a classic of proletarian literature. While he repeatedly tried his hand at drama, his only unquestionable success was the flawed but powerful *Lower Depths* (1901). His most enduring literary contributions are his autobiographical trilogy—*Childhood* (1913), *In the World* (1916), *My Universities* (1922)—and his perceptive reminiscences of Lev Tolstoy. During the early years of the Revolution Gorky maintained an ambivalent attitude toward the Bolshevik regime, rescuing uprooted writers and artists from near-starvation and masterminding a series of popular editions of world classics. Although he left the Soviet Union and lived in Sorrento for ten years, ostensibly for reasons of health, he gradually assumed the role of patron of Soviet culture.

Gorodetsky, Sergei Mitrofanovich (1884–1967). Minor modernist poet and essayist.

Grabar, Igor Emmanuilovich (1871–1960). Painter, art historian.

Granovsky, Timofei Nikolaevich (1813–1855). Liberal historian and public figure.

Grebenshchikov, Yakov Petrovich (1888–1935). Book collector and librarian.

Grekova, I. (pseudonym of Yelena Sergeevna Ventsel, 1907–2002). Writer.

Griboedov, Alexander Sergeevich (1795–1829). Playwright, diplomat. He is remembered primarily as the author of a brilliant comedy of manners, *Wit*

Works Woe (1824), marked by satirical bite and a deft use of conversational verse.

Grigorenko, Pyotr Grigoryevich (1907–1965). General, human rights activist.

Grigoryev, Apollon Alexandrovich (1822–1864). Poet and an influential Romantic literary critic.

Grigoryev, Boris Dmitrievich (1886–1939). Painter.

Grishashvili (pseudonym of Manuslaishvili), Iosif Grigoryevich (1889–1965). Georgian poet.

Gromyko, Andrei Andreevich (1909–1989). Soviet diplomat and statesman. He became Soviet Ambassador to the United States in 1943 and Minister of Foreign Affairs in 1957.

Grossman, Leonid Petrovich (1888–1965). Eminent Dostoevsky scholar.

Grossman, Vasily Semyonovich (1905–1964). Novelist. His early works reflected standard Soviet concerns and techniques, but with time he developed into a critic of the regime, and his final works—the essayistic *Everything Flows* (1953–1963) and epic *Life and Fate* (1980)—circulated in samizdat but were not published until glasnost.

Grot, Nikolai Yakovlevich (1852–1899). Eminent philosopher and psychologist, professor at Moscow University.

Gruzdev, Ilya Alexandrovich (1892–1960). Literary critic.

Grzhebin, Zinovy Isaevich (1869–1929). Painter, publisher.

Guber, Pyotr Konstantinovich (1886–1938). Literary critic, author of *Pushkin's Don Juan List* (1932). Victim of the Great Terror.

Gudzy, Nikolai Kalinnikovich (1887–1965). Eminent literary historian.

Gukovsky, Grigory Alexandrovich (1902–1950). Eminent literary historian.

Gumilyov, Nikolai Stepanovich (1886–1921). Major poet and literary critic. Akhmatova's first husband and one of the founders of the Acmeist movement. He is best known for his poems of male bravado and exotic climes (he made two long journeys to Africa). In August 1921, just as the more inward-looking and complex volume *The Pillar of Fire* was about to appear, he was arrested by the Cheka, accused of complicity in an anti-regime conspiracy, and executed.

Haggard, H. Rider (1856–1925). English author of popular romances.

Hauptmann, Gerhart (1862–1946). German playwright.

Hervegh, Georg (1817–1875). German poet.

Herzen, Alexander Ivanovich (1812–1870). Distinguished political writer and memoirist, a seminal figure in the Russian radical tradition. His major achievements were the essays collected in *From the Other Shore* (1847–50) and his masterful memoirs, *My Past and Thoughts* (1852–55). The periodicals he edited while a political émigré in London had a significant impact on emerging public opinion in Russia.

Hidas, Antal (1899–1980). Hungarian writer.

Hill, Dame Elizabeth (1900–1996). English Slavist, professor at Cambridge University.

Huysmans, Joris-Karl (1848–1907). French novelist whose *Against Nature* (1884) provided the prototype for literary decadence.

Igelström, Andreas (1860–1927). Finnish professor of Russian literature.

Ilyichev, Leonid Fyodorovich (1906–1990). Head of propaganda for the Central Committee from 1958 to 1965.

Inber, Vera Mikhailovna (1890–1972). Poet. She is remembered chiefly for her depiction of the Leningrad blockade during World War II.

Ionov (pseudonym of Bernshtein), Ilya Ionovich (1887–1942). Head of the Petrograd branch of the Gosizdat.

Isakovsky, Mikhail Vasilyevich (1900–1973). Poet. Many of his patriotic poems were set to music and became popular songs.

Ivanov, Georgy Vladimirovich (1894–1958). Acmeist poet. He is considered one of the most gifted poets in exile. His *Petersburg Winters* (1928) is a vivid if unreliable memoir of the Petersburg literary scene between 1913 and 1920.

Ivanov, Vsevolod Vyacheslavovich "Koma" (1895–1963). Prominent Soviet fiction writer, member of the Serapion Brotherhood. A master of ornamental prose, he earned early acclaim for his stark, hard-hitting depiction of the horrors of the Civil War in Central Asia as in *Armored Train 14–19* (1922).

Ivanov, Vyacheslav Ivanovich (1866–1949). Leading Symbolist poet and theorist, classical scholar. He was a master of learned and richly orchestrated verse.

Ivanov, Vyacheslav Vsevolodovich (1929–). Distinguished linguist, literary scholar, cultural historian, and public figure. Son of Tamara and Vsevolod Ivanov. The regime long hindered his duties at Moscow University, and he now teaches at the University of California, Los Angeles.

Ivanova, Tamara Vladimirovna (1900–1996). Actress, translator, memoirist. Wife of Vsevolod Ivanov.

Ivanov-Razumnik (pseudonym of Ivanov), Razumnik Vasilyevich (1878–1946). Leftist literary critic. He was active in the fellow-traveler Scythian movement, which affirmed Russia's semi-Asiatic identity.

Ivinskaya, Olga Vsevolodovna (1912–1995). Translator. Pasternak's mistress of many years and prototype of Lara in *Doctor Zhivago*. The liaison earned her a number of years in the Gulag.

Izgoev (pseudonym of Alexander Solomonovich Lande, 1872–1935). Journalist.

Jakobson, Roman (1896–1982). Distinguished linguist and literary theorist. Closely affiliated with the Russian poetic avant-garde, he was one of the architects of the Formalist School in literary scholarship and subsequently of Prague Structuralism. Continuing his scholarly activity in the United States, he trained two generations of American Slavists at Columbia and Harvard.

Kachalov, Vasily Ivanovich (1875–1948). One of the leading actors at the Moscow Art Theater.

Kaganovich, Lazar Moiseevich (1893–1991). Bolshevik leader.

Kalinin, Mikhail Ivanovich (1875–1946). Prominent early Bolshevik. Titular head of the Soviet state for many years.

Kamenev (pseudonym of Rozenfeld), Lev Borisovich (1883–1936). Prominent early Bolshevik. Together with Stalin and Zinovyev he formed the ruling Party triumvirate after Lenin's death. He also headed the Academia Publishing House. Victim of the Great Terror.

Kameneva, Olga Davidovna (1883–1941). Head of the Theater Division of the People's Commissariat of Education. Trotsky's sister, Kamenev's first wife. Victim of the Great Terror.

Kameneva, Tatyana Ivanovna (1895–1937). Worked for Academia Publishing House. Kamenev's second wife. Victim of the Great Terror.

Kamensky, Anatoly Pavlovich (1876–1941). Writer.

Kamensky, Vasily Vasilyevich (1884–1961). Futurist poet and playwright.

Kamo (Party pseudonym of Simon Arshakovich Ter-Petrosian, 1881–1922). Political activist involved in acts of armed robbery. Protégé of Stalin.

Kapitsa, Olga Yeronimovna (1866–1937). Children's writer. Mother of Pyotr Kapitsa.

Kapitsa, Pyotr Leonidovich (1894–1984). Physicist. Co-recipient of the Nobel Prize for Physics in 1978.

Karakhan, Lev Mikhailovich (1889–1937). Soviet diplomat. Victim of the Great Terror.

Karamzin, Nikolai Mikhailovich (1766–1826). Writer, historian, one of Russia's first men of letters. He was the main exponent of Sentimentalism in Russian literature and author of a monumental *History of the Russian State* (1818–24).

Kassil, Lev Abramovich (1905–1970). Children's writer.

Kataev, Valentin Petrovich (1897–1986). Soviet novelist and playwright.

Kavelin, Konstantin Dmitrievich (1818–1885). Liberal historian, journalist, public figure.

Kaverin (pseudonym of Zilber), Venyamin Alexandrovich (1902–1989). Writer, literary scholar, memoirist. He was a prominent member of the Serapion Brotherhood and held out for experimental prose as long as the political situation allowed it. He played a major role in the revival of literature after Stalin's death. In his later years he turned to autobiography, most notably the remarkably candid memoir *Epilogue,* which was published posthumously at the peak of glasnost.

Kayden, Eugene Mark (1886–1984). American translator of Russian poetry.

Kazakevich, Emmanuil Genrikhovich (1913–1962). Writer. He participated in the post-Stalin literary ferment as an editor of the miscellany *Literary Moscow.*

Kerzhentsev (pseudonym of Lebedev), Platon Mikhailovich (1881–1940). Journalist, diplomat.

Khalatov, Artemy Bagratovich (1896–1937). Chairman of the board of Glavlit. Victim of the Great Terror.

Khalturin, Ivan Ignatievich (1902–1969). Authority on children's literature.

Khardzhiev, Nikolai Ivanovich (1903–1996). Literary and art historian, authority on the Russian avant-garde.

Kharms (pseudonym of Yunachev), Daniil Ivanovich (1905–1942). Writer. Though now remembered as the author of brilliantly absurdist stories and plays and one of the founders of the radically experimental OBERIU (acronym for "Association for Real Art"), he earned his living by writing for children. He died in prison.

Khatsrevin, Zakhar Lvovich (1903–1941). Writer and journalist.

Khlebnikov, Velimir (pseudonym of Viktor Vladimirovich, 1895–1922). Leading Futurist poet. His bold and brilliantly idiosyncratic verbal experimentation made him a seminal figure in the Russian avant-garde.

Khodasevich, Vladislav Felitsianovich (1886–1939). Major poet, essayist, memoirist. He is known for his classically pure language and timeless subject matter. He emigrated in 1922.

Khomyakov, Alexei Stepanovich (1804–1860). Poet, playwright, essayist. Leading spokesman for the Slavophile trend within the budding Russian intelligentsia.

Khrapchenko, Mikhail Borisovich (1904–1986). Secretary of the Language and Literature Section of the Academy of Sciences.

Khrushchev, Nikita Sergeevich (1894–1971). Soviet leader.

Kirov, Sergei Mironovich (1886–1934). Party leader. His assassination in December 1934, possibly with Stalin's complicity, helped to trigger the Great Terror.

Kiselyova, Yelena Andreevna (1873–1974). Painter.

Kleist, Heinrich von (1777–1811). German writer.

Kloots, Anacharsis (pseudonym of Jean-Baptist, 1755–1794). French Enlightenment philosopher.

Klyachko-Lvov, Lev Moiseevich (1873–1934). Journalist. Owner of the Raduga Publishing House.

Klyuchevsky, Vasily Osipovich (1841–1911). Leading Russian historian. Author of the magisterial *History of Russia* (1906–1910).

Knipovich, Yevgenia Fyodorovna (1898–1988). Literary scholar.

Kobetsky, Mikhail Veniaminovich (1881–1937). Soviet Ambassador to Denmark from 1924 to 1933. An Odessa schoolmate of Chukovsky's. Victim of the Great Terror.

Kochetov, Vsevolod Anisimovich (1912–1973). Writer known for his crude lampoons of the liberal intelligentsia.

Kogan, Pyotr Semyonovich (1872–1932). Marxist literary critic, author of a polemical tract on early Soviet literature.

Kolas, Yakub (1882–1956). Belorussian poet.

Koltsov, Alexei Vasilyevich (1809–1842). Peasant poet whose verse was permeated with the imagery and phraseology of the Russian folk song.

Koltsov, Mikhail Yefremovich (1898–1940). Writer, one of the most gifted *Pravda* journalists. Victim of the Great Terror.

Koltsova, Yelizaveta Nikolaevna. Wife of Mikhail Koltsov.

Komarov, Nikolai Pavlovich (1886–1937). Deputy chairman of the Leningrad Regional Executive Committee.

Komarovskaya, Nadezhda Ivanovna (1885–1967). Actress.

Komissarzhevskaya, Vera Fyodorovna (1864–1910). Internationally known turn-of-the century actress and stage director.

Kon, Lidia Felixovna (1895–1968). Literary scholar, translator.

Konashevich, Vladimir Mikhailovich (1888–1963). Painter.

Koni, Anatoly Fyodorovich (1844–1927). Prominent legal expert, memoirist, public figure.

Konovalov, Sergei Alexandrovich (1899–1982). British Slavist. Professor of Russian literature at Oxford.

Konyukhova, Yelena Nikolaevna (d. 1982). Editor at Sovetskii pisatel' Publishing House.

Kopelev, Lev Zinovyevich (1912–1997). Literary scholar specializing in German literature, human rights activist. He is particularly known for his forthright memoirs, *To Be Preserved Forever* (1977) and *Education of a True Believer* (1985), which could not be published until glasnost.

Kornilov, Boris Petrovich (1907–1938). Poet, follower of Yesenin. Victim of the Great Terror.

Korolenko, Sofia Vladimirovna (1886–1957). Literary scholar, daughter of Vladimir Korolenko.

Korolenko, Vladimir Galaktionovich (1853–1921). Prolific writer. His well-known "Makar's Dream," like most of his stories and journalistic sketches, is marked by a profound compassion for the underdog.

Kosarev, Alexander Vasilyevich (1903–1939). Party activist.

Kostylyov, Valentin Ivanovich (1884–1950). Writer. Victim of the Great Terror.

Kosygin, Alexei Nikolaevich (1904–1980). Communist dignitary, appointed chairman of the Council of Ministers in 1964.

Kotlyarevsky, Nestor Alexandrovich (1863–1925). Literary scholar.

Krasin, Leonid Borisovich (1870–1926). Commissar of Foreign Trade in the twenties.

Krasnova, Sofya Petrovna (1919–). Editor at Goslitizdat.

Kristi, Mikhail Petrovich (1875–1956). Plenipotentiary of the People's Commissariat of Education in Petrograd.

Krivitsky, Alexander Yulyevich (1910–1986). Deputy editor-in-chief of *Novyi mir*.

Kron, Alexander Alexandrovich (1909–1983). Writer, playwright.

Kropotkin, Pytor Alexeevich (1842–1921). Internationally known anarchist theoretician from a princely family.

Krotky, Emil (1892–1963). Poet-satirist.

Kruchonykh, Alexei Yeliseevich (1886–1968). Futurist poet. He was noted for extreme verbal experimentation including play with nonsense syllables.

Krylov, Ivan Andreevich (1769–1844). Russia's leading fable writer.

Kryuchkov, Pyotr Petrovich (1889–1938). Secretary of Gorky's wife, M. F. Andreeva, then of Gorky himself.

Kuibyshev, Valerian Vladimirovich (1888–1935). Prominent early Bolshevik.

Kukolnik, Nestor Vasilyevich (1809–1868). Writer.

Kupala, Yanka (pseudonym of Ivan Dominikovich Lutsevich, 1882–1942). Belorussian poet.

Kuprin, Alexander Ivanovich (1870–1938). Novelist and short-story writer with an eye for society's ills.

Kustodiev Boris Mikhailovich (1878–1927). Painter strongly drawn to folkloric stylization.

Kuzmin, Mikhail Alexeevich (1872–1936). A fine modernist lyric poet. His masterful *Alexandrian Sonnets* (1905–8) express a homoerotic sensibility.

Kuznetsov, Yevgeny Mikhailovich (1900–1958). Theater critic.

Kvitko, Lev (Leib) Moiseevich (1890–1952). Yiddish poet whom Chukovsky held in high regard. He was executed in 1952 with a number of other Jewish literary figures.

Lagansky, Yeremei Mironovich (1887–1942). Journalist.

Laktionov, Alexander Ivanovich (1910–1972). Artist.

Laplace, Pierre Simon (1749–1827). French astronomer and mathematician.

Leaf, Munro (1905–1976). American children's writer.

Lebedenko, Alexander Gervasovich (1892–1975). Writer of historical fiction.

Lebedev, Boris Fyodorovich (1877–1948). Journalist. Son-in-law of Pyotr Kropotkin.

Lebedev, Vladimir Semyonovich (1915–1966). Khrushchev's secretary.

Lebedev, Vladimir Vasilyevich (1891–1967). Artist.

Lebedev-Polyansky, Pavel Ivanovich (1881–1948). Critic. Head of Glavlit in the twenties.

Leonov, Leonid Maximovich (1899–1994). Prominent Soviet writer. He began his literary career as a fellow traveler. His ambitious and complex *Thief* (1927) viewed the NEP realities through an unmistakably Dostoevskian prism, but in the thirties he became a leading exponent of Socialist Realism.

Lepeshinsky, Panteleimon Nikolaevich (1868–1944). Prominent early Bolshevik; journalist, editor, memoirist.

Lermontov, Mikhail Yuryevich (1814–1841). Russian's prime Romantic poet. Adept at both lyrical and narrative verse, he is equally revered for having created one of the first major Russian novels, *A Hero of Our Times* (1840), a cluster of stories linked by a common protagonist. He responded to Pushkin's duel with the lyrical invective "The Death of the Poet."

Leskov, Nikolai Semyonovich (1831–1895). Major fiction writer and journalist. He established the narrative technique known as *skaz*, which aims to give the illusion of lively, semi-literate speech.

Levidov, Mikhail Yulyevich (1891–1942). Literary critic, journalist, playwright.

Libedinsky, Yury Nikolaevich (1858–1959). Writer.

Lidin (pseudonym of Gomberg), Vladimir Germanovich (1894–1979). Writer, critic.

Lifshits, Mikhail Alexandrovich (1905–1983). Literary scholar, authority on Marxist aesthetics.

Lipkin, Semyon Izrailevich (1911). Poet, translator.

Litvinov, Maxim Maximovich (1876–1951). Prominent Soviet diplomat. He was Commissar for Foreign Affairs between 1930 and 1939 and Ambassador to the United States between 1941 and 1943.

Litvinov, Pavel Mikhailovich (1940–). Human rights activist.

Litvinova, Ivy (1889–1977). Writer, translator. British-born wife of M. M. Litvinov.

Litvinova, Tatyana Maximovna (1918–). Translator, human rights activist. Daughter of Ivy and Maxim Litvinov.

Livshits, Benedikt Konstantinovich (1886–1938). Futurist poet; author of an important memoir, *The One-and-a-Half-Eyed Archer* (1933).

Lofting, Hugh (1886–1947). American writer.

Lomonosova, Raisa Nikolaevna (1888–1973). Correspondent of Chukovsky, Pasternak, and Tsvetaeva.

Lozinsky, Mikhail Leonidovich (1886–1955). Poet, translator, friend of Akhmatova.

Lugovsky, Vladimir Alexandrovich (1901–1957). Poet.

Lunacharsky, Anatoly Vasilyevich (1875–1933). Bolshevik dignitary, critic, playwright. As Commissar of Education from the beginning of the regime until 1929, he masterminded the initial stage of Soviet culture.

Lundberg, Yevgeny Germanovich (1887–1965). Writer, literary critic.

Lunts, Lev Natanovich (1901–1924). Playwright, short-story writer, essayist. The principal spokesman for the Serapion Brotherhood, he composed its manifesto "Why We Are Serapion Brothers" in 1922.

Lurie, Artur Sergeevich (1891–1966). Composer, close friend of Akhmatova.

Lyadov, Anatoly Konstantinovich (1855–1914). Composer and music teacher.

Lysenko, Trofim Denisovich (1898–1976). Agronomist. His crackpot but ideologically desirable theory of the inheritance of acquired characteristics enjoyed Stalin's support and set back Soviet genetics for years.

Lyubimov, Alexander Mikhailovich (1879–1955). Painter.

Lyubimov, Yury Petrovich (1917–). Internationally known theater director.

McKay, Claude (1890–1948). Prominent African-American poet.

Maeterlink, Maurice (1862–1949). Belgian Symbolist playwright.

Maikov, Apollon Nikolaevich (1821–1897). Eclectic poet, friend and confidant of Dostoevsky.

Maisky, Ivan Mikhailovich (1884–1975). Historian, diplomat.

Makarenko, Anton Semyonovich (1888–1939). Writer, pedagogue. In the widely read *Pedagogical Poem* (also known in English as *The Road to Life*, 1933–35), he describes his experiences as a principal of a school for juvenile delinquents.

Makashin, Sergei Alexandrovich (1906–1989). Literary scholar.

Makovsky, Konstantin Yegorovich (1839–1915). Painter, member of the Itinerants group.

Maltsev, Yelizar Yuryevich (1916–). Writer.

Malyavin, Filipp Andreevich (1869–1940). Artist.

Mandelshtam, Iosif Yemelyanovich (1846–1911). Literary historian.

Mandelshtam, Osip Emilyevich (1891–1938). Major poet and essayist. A member of the Poets' Guild and leading Acmeist, he cultivated an elliptical, highly metaphorical style. He sang the ideals of classical antiquity and Western civilization, the fatidic, hieratical function of poetry. A line in a 1917 poem—"the wolfhound age leaps at my throat"—proved prophetic: in 1934 he was arrested for a pungent epigram on Stalin and exiled to Voronezh, where he managed to write some of his most stunning poetry. He was arrested again in 1938 and died, probably of starvation, in a transit camp. His work has been highly influential among both Russian and non-Russian poets.

Margolina, Rakhil Pavlovna (d. 1973). Correspondent of Chukovsky.

Markov, Georgy Mokeevich (1911–1991). First Secretary of the Soviet Writers' Union.

Marr, Nikolai Yakovlevich (1864/65–1934). Prominent linguist. His highly idiosyncratic views on the origin of language were debunked by none other than Stalin in the pages of *Pravda*.

Marshak, Samuil Yakovlevich (1887–1964). Poet, translator, children's writer. He was steeped in both Russian and English folklore. His translations of Shakespeare's sonnets as well as of Burns, Blake, and Edward Lear are highly prized.

Martynov, Leonid Nikolaevich (1905–1980). Poet, translator.

Mashinsky, Semyon Iosifovich (1914–1978). Literary scholar.

Maspero, Gaston (1846–1916). French Egyptologist.

Matveeva, Novella Nikolaevna (1934–). Poet.

Matyushkin, Fyodor Fyodorovich (1799–1872). Admiral. Pushkin's classmate.

Mayakovsky, Vladimir Vladimirovich (1893–1930). Leading Futurist poet. His early verse—such as "Cloud in Trousers" (1914–15) and "The Backbone Flute" (1915)—shows dazzling verbal inventiveness, blending vehement social protest with personal anguish. In 1917 he was ready to place his talent at the service of the Revolution. He sought to further the cause in his satiric morality play *Mystery Bouffe* (1918), his burly Communist epic *One Hundred and Fifty Million* (1920), celebratory poems like "Vladimir Ilyich Lenin" (1924), and even propaganda ditties. Increasingly disillusioned in both his public and private life, he committed suicide in 1930. Five years later Stalin anointed him as "the best and the most talented poet of the Soviet era."

Mei, Lev Alexandrovich (1822–1862). Poet whose Romantic verse was often set to music.

Mekhlis, Lev Zakharovich (1889–1953). Journalist, editor of *Pravda* in the thirties.

Menzhinskaya, Lyudmila Rudolfovna (1876–1933). Pro-Rector of the Krupskaya Institute for Communist Education.

Merezhkovsky, Dmitry Sergeevich (1866–1941). Novelist, poet, critic, essayist, religious thinker. One of the most influential figures of the Symbolist era, he explored the dichotomy between Hellenic paganism and Christian spirituality in both his historical fiction (for example, the trilogy *Christ and Antichrist* [1896–1905]) and literary criticism (*Tolstoy and Dostoevsky* [1901–?]). He and his wife, Zinaida Gippius, were vociferous foes of Bolshevism, and the two became prominent figures in the Russian émigré community in Paris.

Meshcheryakov, Nikolai Leonidovich (1865–1942). Head of Gosizdat.

Messing, Stanislav Adamovich (1890–1937). Head of the Leningrad GPU. Victim of the Great Terror.

Meyerhold, Vsevolod Emilyevich (1874–1940). Internationally acclaimed avant-garde stage and film director. Perished during the Great Terror.

Mickiewicz, Adam (1798–1855). Polish national poet. He is known for the Faustian drama *Forefathers' Eve* (1832) and the epic poem *Pan Tadeusz* (1834). During his enforced stay in Russia between 1826 and 1829 he found a soulmate in Pushkin.

Miezelaitis, Eduardas (1919–1997). Lithuanian poet.

Mihajlov, Mihajlo (1934–). Yugoslav journalist.

Mikhailov, Mikhail Larionovich (1829–1865). Poet, journalist.

Mikhailovsky, Nikolai Konstantinovich (1842–1904). Sociologist, essayist. A major spokesman for Russian populism.

Mikhalkov, Sergei Vladimirovich (1913–). Writer. Secretary of the Soviet Writers' Union. Author of the words for the Soviet national anthem.

Mikhalkov-Konchalovsky, Andron Sergeevich (1937–). Filmmaker. Son of Sergei Mikhalkov.

Mikoyan, Anastas Ivanovich (1895–1978). Communist leader. An influential figure during Khrushchev's ascendancy.

Milyukov, Pavel Nikolaevich (1859–1943). Public figure and historian. He was leader of the Constitutional-Democratic (Kadet) Party and Minister of Foreign Affairs in the Provisional Government and editor of the Paris-based liberal émigré newspaper *Poslednie novosti.*

Milyutin, Nikolai Alexeevich (1818–1872). Deputy Minister of Internal Affairs under Alexander II. He was a key figure in implementing the emancipation of the serfs decreed in 1861.

Minsky (pseudonym of Vilenkin), Nikolai Maximovich (1855–1937). Poet and essayist. Although his poetry, couched in the vein of social protest, is traditional in form, his essays were harbingers of Russian modernism.

Mirolyubov (pseudonym of Mirov), Viktor Sergeevich (1860–1939). Singer, editor-publisher.

Mirsky (Svyatopolk-Mirsky), Dmitry Petrovich (1890–1939). Distinguished literary critic of aristocratic birth. While an émigré in London, he wrote the masterful *History of Russian Literature* (1926) in English. He returned to the Soviet Union in the mid-thirties. Victim of the Great Terror.

Molotov (Skryabin), Vyacheslav Mikhailovich (1890–1986). Prominent Bolshevik leader. He was head of government in 1930–41, and foreign minister between 1939 and 1949.

Muizhel, Viktor Vasilyevich (1880–1924). Short-story writer and playwright.

Muromtsev, Dmitry Nikolaevich. Ivan Bunin's brother-in-law.

Musorgsky, Modest Petrovich (1839–1881). Major Russian composer.

Nabokov, Vladimir Dmitrievich (1869–1922). Politician. Father of the novelist Vladimir Nabokov. A prominent figure in the Constitutional-Democratic (Kadet) Party, he was assassinated by a right-wing fanatic.

Nabokov, Vladimir Vladimirovich (1899–1977). Major Russian and later American novelist, poet, memoirist, and literary critic. He published his Russian works, culminating in the masterful novels *The Gift* (1937–38) and *Invitation to a Beheading* (1938), under the pseudonym Sirin. Among the highlights of his post-1940 American period are *Lolita* (1955), a masterful treatment of a risqué subject; *Pnin* (1957), a comic novel about a Russian displaced on an American campus; and a brilliant pastiche, *Pale Fire* (1962). He also published a compelling study of Nikolai Gogol (1944) and a four-volume annotated English translation of Pushkin's *Eugene Onegin* (1964).

Nechaev, Sergei Gennadievich (1847–1882). Russian revolutionary and nihilist who served as a model for the character of Pyotr Verkhovensky in Dostoevsky's *Demons*.

Neizvestny, Ernst Iosifovich (1925–). Nonconformist sculptor who eventually emigrated.

Nekrasov, Nikolai Alexeevich (1821–1877). Major poet, public figure, publisher of the important radical journal *Sovremennik*. His most ambitions poem, *Who Is Happy in Russia?* (1866–1876), is a kind of populist epic. A man of compassion and moral outrage, Nekrasov enjoyed great popularity in his day. It fell to Chukovsky to demonstrate that the champion of the dispossessed was also a resourceful craftsman.

Nekrasov, Viktor Platonovich (1911–1987). Writer. His *In the Trenches of Stalingrad* (1946) won a Stalin Prize despite its honest, unflinching portrayal of the battle, and his novella "Kira Georgievna" (1962) placed him in the forefront of "thaw" literature. He was forced to emigrate in 1974.

Nemirovich-Danchenko, Vasily Ivanovich (1844–1936). Journalist, war correspondent, writer.

Nemirovich-Danchenko, Vladimir Ivanovich (1858–1943). Stage director and playwright. The founder, with Stanislavsky, of the Moscow Art Theater.

Neradovsky, Pyotr Ivanovich (1875–1962). Painter. Curator of the Russian Museum in Leningrad.

Nesterov, Mikhail Vasilyevich (1862–1942). Painter.

Nikitin, Ivan Savvich (1824–1861). Minor poet in the folk vein.

Nikitin, Nikolai Nikolaevich (1895–1963). Writer. Member of the Serapion Brotherhood.

Nikitina, Yevdoxia Fyodorovna (1895–1973). Head of Nikitinskie subbotniki, a cooperative publishing house.

Nikulin, Lev Veniaminovich (1891–1967). Author of adventure and historical novels.

Nilin, Pavel Filippovich (1908–1981). Journalist and writer.

Oblonskaya, Raisa Yefimovna (1924). Translator.

Obolenskaya, Yekaterina Mikhailovna (1889–1964). Editor at Detgiz.

Obolensky, Dmitry Dmitrievich (1918–). Professor of History at Oxford University. His major work is *Byzantium and the Slavs* (1971). He edited *The Penguin Book of Russian Verse* (1962).

Obraztsov, Sergei Vladimirovich (1901–1992). World-renowned puppeteer.

Odoevtseva, Irina Vladimirovna (pseudonym of Iraida Gustavovna Geinike, 1895–1990). A late Acmeist poet. Wife of Georgy Ivanov.

Ogaryov, Nikolai Platonovich (1813–1877). Romantic poet and co-editor with Herzen of the influential London-based newspaper *Kolokol*.

Oksman, Yulian Grigoryevich (1894–1970). Eminent scholar of nineteenth-century Russian literature.

Oldenburg, Sergei Fyodorovich (1863–1934). Scholar; authority on the Far East, especially India.

Olesha, Yury Karlovich (1899–1960). Prominent writer. His major literary success was *Envy* (1927), a brilliantly crafted novel that provoked a lively controversy because of its ambiguous treatment of the conflict between a bumptious Soviet entrepreneur and an "envious" but sensitive misfit. After 1932 Olesha's production slowed to a trickle.

Opie, Iona (1923–) and Peter (1918–1982). British scholars and collectors of children's folklore.

Ordzhonikidze, Grigory Konstantinovich (known as Sergo, 1886–1937). High-ranking Georgian Communist. He committed suicide in 1937.

Orlov, Alexander Sergeevich (1871–1947). Literary historian. Member of the Academy of Sciences.

Orlov, Vladimir Nikolaevich (1908–1985). Literary scholar. Author of the standard biography of Alexander Blok.

Orlova, Raisa Davidovna (1918–1989). Scholar of American literature, memoirist. Wife of Lev Kopelev.

Ostrovsky, Nikolai Alexeevich (1904–1936). Writer known as the author of the classic Soviet novel *How the Steel Is Tempered* (1932–34). Its hero, Pavel Korchagin, was widely hailed as a model for Soviet youth.

Otsup, Nikolai Ardievich (1894–1958). Minor Acmeist poet.

Owen, Robert (1771–1858). British social reformer.

Ozerov, Lev Adolfovich (1914–1996). Literary historian.

Panaeva, Avdotya Yakovlevna (1819–1893). Writer, memoirist.

Panfyorov, Fyodor Ivanovich (1896–1960). Socialist-Realist novelist.

Panova, Vera Fyodorovna (1905–1973). Writer known for her sensitive portrayal of individuals.

Panteleev, L. (pseudonym of Alexei Ivanovich Yeremeev, 1908–1987). Writer known for his aversion to ideological clichés.

Parny, Évariste (1753–1814). French poet.

Pasternak, Boris Leonidovich (1890–1960). Major poet and prose writer. He began his poetic career before the Revolution, but found his distinctive and singularly effective brand of Modernism in the collections *My Sister Life* (1922) and *Themes and Variations* (1923), which won acclaim from critics and fellow poets alike. As the intellectual climate of the thirties grew increasingly inhospitable to poetic self-expression, he devoted much of his creative energy to translating Western classics, notably Shakespeare, Goethe, Schiller, and Keats. He completed his first full-length novel, *Doctor Zhivago*, at the end of 1955, but even in the fairly permissive cultural atmosphere of the time the relatively liberal journal *Novyi mir* turned it down, judging it a repudiation of the October Revolution. In the meantime, translations of the novel had brought him to the attention of the Western reading public, and in 1958 he was awarded the Nobel Prize for Literature. Compelled by the regime to reject it, he died a broken man.

Pasternak, Leonid Osipovich (1862–1945). Painter, especially known for his portrait of Lev Tolstoy. Father of Boris Pasternak.

Paustovsky, Konstantin Georgievich (1892–1968). Writer, essayist. He was at his best in his gracefully meandering autobiography, *The Story of My Life* (1945–63), and his largely descriptive stories and sketches. He took active part in the post-Stalin literary ferment and served as a mentor for a new breed of Soviet writers.

Pavlenko, Pyotr Andreevich (1899–1951). Journalist, writer.

Pavlov, Ivan Pavlovich (1849–1936). Distinguished physiologist. He developed the influential concept of the conditioned reflex.

Petőfi, Sándor (1823–1849). Hungarian national poet.

Petrov, Nikolai Nikolaevich (1876–1964). Surgeon.

Petrov, P. D. Inspector at the Leningrad Gublit.

Petrov, Sergei Mitrofanovich (1905–1988). Director of the Literary Institute during the fifties.

Petrov, Yevgeny Petrovich (pseudonym of Yevgeny Kataev, 1903–1942). Major satirist. He was co-author, with Ilya Ilf (Ilya Arnoldovich Fainzilberg), of the popular comic novels *Twelve Chairs* (1928) and *The Golden Calf* (1931) and an entertaining travelogue, *One-Story America* (1936).

Petrovykh, Maria Sergeevna (1908–1979). Poet, translator.

Pilnyak (pseudonym of Vogau), Boris Andreevich (1894–1938). Prominent writer. In 1922 he published one of the first major Soviet novels, *The Naked Year*, but by 1929 he was attacked for publishing abroad a mildly heterodox novella, *Mahogany*, and tried to make amends in a celebratory Socialist-construction novel, *The Volga Flows to the Caspian Sea* (1930). Victim of the Great Terror.

Pisarev, Dmitry Ivanovich (1840–1868). Literary critic. He was the most combative and most gifted spokesman for radical intelligentsia of the 1860s and the epitome of the utilitarian approach to literature.

Piskunov, Konstantin Fyodorovich (1905–1981). Head of the Moscow branch of Detgiz.

Platonov, Andrei Platonovich (pseudonym of Platon Klimentov, 1899–1951). Major writer. A dedicated Communist, he began his literary career with "cosmic" revolutionary poetry and science fiction animated by a dream of the imminent physical transformation of the world, but a growing concern over the fate of the revolutionary project pervades his two full-length novels, *Chevengur* (1926–1929) and *The Foundation Pit* (1929–1930), both of which had to await glasnost for publication in his country.

Podarsky (pseudonym of Nikolai Sergeevich Rusanov, 1859–1939). Journalist.

Pokrovsky, Mikhail Nikolaevich (1868–1932). Historian. Deputy Commissar of Narkompros, Chairman of GUS.

Polevoy, Nikolai Alexeevich (1796–1846). Literary critic, journalist, historian. Editor of the influential journal *Moskovskii telegraf* (1825–34).

Polevoy, Xenofont Alexeevich (1801–1867). Critic and journalist.

Polezhaev, Alexander Ivanovich (1805–1838). Romantic poet.

Polikarpov, Dmitry Alexeevich (1905–1965). Communist dignitary; head of the cultural department of the Central Committee (1955–65). Secretary of the board of the Soviet Writers' Union.

Polonsky, Yakov Petrovich (1819–1898). Prolific man of letters.

Polyakov, Fyodor Petrovich (1860–1925). Physician, professor.

Popov, Vasily Stepanovich. General.

Poskrebyshev, Alexander Nikolaevich (1891–1965). Stalin's secretary.

Pospelov, Pyotr Nikolaevich (1898–1979). Editor-in-chief of *Pravda* (1940–49). Head of the Institute for Marxism-Leninism (1953–1960). Academician.

Postupalsky, Igor Stefanovich (1907–1990). Literary scholar, poet, and translator.

Pozdnyaev, Konstantin Ivanovich (1911–). Editor-in-chief of *Literaturnaia Rossiia*.

Prezent, Isaak Izraelevich (1902–1969). Official philosopher. Close ally of Lysenko.

Prokofyev, Alexander Andreevich (1900–1971). Poet. A key figure in the Leningrad Writers Union (1945–48).

Proshian, Prosh Perchevich (1883–1918). Prominent Bolshevik.

Prutkov, Kozma. The collective pseudonym of Alexei (1821–1908) and Vladimir (1830–1884) Zhemchuzhnikov and Alexei Konstantinovich Tolstoy (1817–1875). A remarkable team of satirists and parodists.

Przybyszewski, Stanisław (1868–1927). Polish Symbolist playwright, prose writer, essayist.

Pumpyansky, Lev Vasilyevich (1894–1940). Literary scholar, close associate of Mikhail Bakhtin.

Punin, Nikolai Nikolaevich (1888–1953). Avant-garde art critic and influential member of Fine Art Section of the Commissariat of Education in the twenties.

Rachmaninoff, Sergei Vasilyevich (1873–1943). Major Russian composer.

Radishchev, Alexander Nikolaevich (1749–1802). Writer. He is now read primarily as the author of *A Journey from Petersburg to Moscow* (1790), a strong indictment of serfdom.

Radishchev, Leonid Nikolaevich (1905–1973). Children's writer, author of tales about Lenin.

Radlova, Anna Dmitrievna (1891–1949). Poet and translator.

Raikin, Konstantin Arkadievich (1950–). Actor.

Rassadin, Stanislav Borisovich (1935). Literary critic.

Redko, Alexander Mefodievich (1866–1933). Literary scholar, ethnographer.

Redko, Yevgenia Isaakovna (1869–1955). Actress.

Remizov, Alexei Mikhailovich (1877–1957). Major writer. His novels, folkloric vignettes, short stories, parables, and apocrypha epitomize the ornamental style in Russian modernist prose. After emigrating to Paris, he continued to work in a number of genres, the suggestive essays on dreams in Russian literature, *The Fire of Things* (1954), being especially memorable.

Remizova, Serafima Perlovna (1876–1941). Wife of Alexei Remizov.

Repin, Ilya Yefimovich (1844–1930). Major Realist artist especially known for his historical and genre paintings. For years he was Chukovsky's friend and neighbor in the Finnish town of Kuokkala. Although many of his canvases— the famous *Volga Boatmen*, for example—imply social criticism, he was unremittingly hostile to the Soviet regime and remained on the Finnish side of the border after the Revolution.

Repin, Yury Ilyich (1875–1954). Minor painter. Son of Ilya Repin.

Rerikh, Nikolai Konstantinovich (1874–1947). Important painter. Member of the World of Art group. His work typically combines modernist techniques with traditional Russian themes.

Rodchenko, Alexander Mikhailovich (1891–1956). Avant-garde painter, sculptor, and photographer. Member of LEF.

Rolland, Romain (1866–1944). French novelist with Communist sympathies.

Roskina, Natalya Alexandrovna (1928–1989). Memoirist, literary scholar.

Rothstein, Andrew (1898–?). English historian, journalist. Member of the Communist Party of Great Britain.

Rotov, Konstantin Pavlovich (1902–1959). Graphic artist.

Rozanov, Vasily Vasilyevich (1856–1919). Controversial turn-of-the-century thinker and essayist. His religious and philosophical meditations often challenge traditional Christianity in favor of a naturalistic cult of sex and procreation.

Rozenel, Natalia Alexandrovna (1902–1962). Actress. Wife of Anatoly Luna-
    charsky.

Rozenko, A. Head of Molodaia gvardiia Publishing House.

Rumanov, Arkady Veniaminovich (1876–1942). Journalist, head of the publish-
    ing house of A. F. Marks.

Rustaveli, Shota. Twelfth-century Georgian poet.

Rybakov, Anatoly Naumovich (1911–1998). Writer. He was known in his day
    for *Heavy Sand* (1979), the first Soviet novel to touch on the Holocaust,
    and the mildly unorthodox *Children of the Arbat* (1987).

Rykov, Alexei Ivanovich (1881–1938). Prominent early Bolshevik, member of
    the Central Committee from 1920 to 1934. One of the principal defendants
    in the show trials, he perished in the Great Terror.

Sadofyev, Ilya Ivanovich (1889–1965). Poet.

Sadovsky, Boris Alexandrovich (1881–1952). Minor Symbolist poet.

Safonova, Yelena Vasilyevna (1902–1980). Artist.

Saltykov-Shchedrin, Mikhail Yevgrafovich (1826–1889). Major satirical writer.
    His best-known works include the caustic *History of a Town Glupovo* (1869)
    and the somber family chronicle *The Golovlyovs* (1875–80).

Samarin, Yury Fyodorovich (1819–1876). Political figure, historian.

Sazonov, Pyotr Vladimirovich. Administrator at the Petrograd House of the
    Arts.

Schulz, F. von. Professor of Russian literature at Helsinki University.

Seifullina, Lidia Nikolaevna (1889–1954). Popular fiction writer of the twen-
    ties. Her novel *Virineia* (1924) depicts a peasant woman's struggle for eman-
    cipation.

Severyanin, Igor (pseudonym of Igor Vasilyevich Lotarev, 1887–1941). Poet.
    He was a leader of the Ego-Futurist faction of the Russian avant-garde.

Shabad, Yelizaveta Yulyevna (1878–1943). Pedagogue.

Shaginyan, Marietta Sergeevna (1888–1982). Novelist. In her successful *Mess
    Mend* (1923–25) she pioneered a distinctively Soviet detective novel. *Hy-
    drocentral* (1931) is a carefully researched production novel.

Shakhmatov, Alexei Alexandrovich (1864–1920). Distinguished Russian lin-
    guist.

Shaskolskaya, Marianna Petrovna (1913–1985). Physicist.

Shchedrin, Mikhail Yevgrafovich. See Saltykov-Shchedrin, Mikhail Yevgra-
    fovich.

Shchepkina-Kupernik, Tatyana Lvovna (1874–1952). Writer, translator.

Shcherbina, Vladimir Rodionovich (1908–1989). Literary critic.

Shchogolev, Pavel Yeliseevich (1877–1931). Pushkin scholar.

Shchukin, Sergei Ivanovich (1854–1937). Moscow merchant and art collector
    known for his collection of French Impressionists.

Shenrok, Vladimir Ivanovich (1853–1910). Literary historian.

Shevchenko, Taras Grigoryevich (1814–1861). Ukrainian national poet.

Shileiko, Vladimir Kazimirovich (1891–1930). Assyrologist. Akhmatova's second husband.

Shklovsky, Isaak Vladimirovich (pseudonym Dioneo) (1865–1935). Journalist, literary critic, ethnographer.

Shklovsky, Viktor Borisovich (1893–1984). Literary critic, writer. One of the founders of the Society for the Study of Poetic Language (OPOYAZ), the center of the Formalist school of literary scholarship, he became its leading spokesman. His programmatic essay "Art as Device" launched the influential concept of "defamiliarization" or "making it strange" (*ostranenie*) as a central literary strategy. He cultivated half-documentary, half-fictional literary modes in such works as *Sentimental Journey: A Memoir* (1913–22) and "Zoo or Letters Not About Love" (1923). In the thirties, when Formalism was declared off-limits, he turned to film criticism and script writing.

Sholokhov, Mikhail Alexandrovich (1905–1984). Major Soviet writer. His reputation rests mainly on the epic novel *And Quiet Flows the Don* (1928–40), a vivid and richly textured portrayal of life in the Cossack village in the years 1912–1920 (though his authorship of the work has been periodically questioned). The equally epic, though less impressive *Virgin Soil Upturned* (1932–60) belongs to the genre of the collectivization novel. He received the Nobel Prize for Literature in 1965, but wrote little thereafter, distinguishing himself rather by intemperate attacks on dissident writers.

Shostakovich, Dmitry Dmitrievich (1906–1975). Major Russian composer.

Shtein, Alexander Petrovich (1906–1993). Playwright.

Shvarts, Yevgeny Lvovich (1896–1958). Playwright. His strongest plays—*The Naked King* (1934), *The Shadow* (1940), and *The Dragon* (1943–44)—turn fairy-tale motifs into covert but telling satire.

Shveitser, Vladimir Zakharovich (1889–1971). Journalist.

Simmons, Ernest (1903–1972). American Slavist. Professor of Russian literature at Columbia. Dostoevsky scholar and biographer of Tolstoy and Chekhov.

Simmons, John Simon Gabriel (1915–). English Slavist. Professor of Russian literature at Oxford. Eminent bibliographer.

Simonov, Konstantin Mikhailovich (1915–1974). Prolific novelist, poet, playwright. Everything he wrote was officially sanctioned, and he was a key figure in the Writers' Union.

Sinyavsky, Andrei Donatovich (1925–1997). Literary critic and fiction writer. Arrested in 1965 for publishing a heterodox novella, "The Trial Begins," abroad under the pseudonym Abram Tertz, he was condemned to seven years' hard labor. In 1973 he emigrated to France and taught Russian literature at the Sorbonne. Among his important works are the seminal essay "On Socialist Realism" (1956), an essay on Pasternak, a study of Gogol, and a whimsical causerie devoted to Pushkin.

Skaftymov, Alexander Pavlovich (1890–1968). Literary scholar, author of a Formalist study of the Russian heroic ballads.

Slater, Lydia Pasternak (1903–1989). Boris Pasternak's sister. She emigrated to England, where she worked as a translator.

Slavin, Lev Isaevich (1896–1984). Novelist, playwright, war correspondent.

Sleptsov, Vasily Alexeevich (1836–1878). Radical writer, journalist, social activist. His short novel *Hard Times* (1865) tackles the contradictions of the recent emancipation of serfs with skill and tough-minded cogency.

Slezkin, Yury Lvovich (1885–1947). Writer.

Slonimsky, Mikhail Leonidovich (1897–1972). Writer, member of the Serapion Brotherhood. His first novel, *The Lavrovs* (1926), depicts the disintegration of an intelligentsia family.

Słowacki, Juliusz (1809–1849). Great Polish Romantic poet and dramatist.

Sluchevsky, Konstantin Konstantinovich (1837–1904). Lyric poet whose late verse foreshadows Russian Symbolism.

Smirnov, Ivan Ivanovich (1909–1965). Historian.

Smirnov, Lev Nikolaevich (1911–1986). Chairman of the Supreme Court of the Russian Federation from 1962 to 1972.

Smirnov, Nikolai Ivanovich (1893–1937). Party activist, head of Ogiz. Victim of the Great Terror.

Smirnov, Sergei Sergeevich (1915–1976). Writer. Editor-in-chief of *Literaturnaia gazeta* (1959–60).

Smirnov, Vasily Alexandrovich (1904–1979). Secretary of the board of the Writers' Union from 1954 to 1959.

Sobinov, Leonid Vitalyevich (1872–1934). Singer.

Sobolev, Leonid Sergeevich (1898–1971). Writer. A key figure in the Writers' Union.

Soboleva, Olga Ioannovna. Wife of L. S. Sobolev.

Soldatov, Alexander Alexeevich (1915). Soviet Ambassador to Great Britain between 1960 and 1966.

Sologub (pseudonym of Teternikov), Fyodor Kuzmich (1863–1927). Symbolist poet and novelist. His lyric verse orchestrates the turn-of-the century mood of vague yearning with skill and grace. His major achievement as a novelist is the unsettling *Petty Demon* (1907).

Solovyov, Vladimir Sergeevich (1853–1900). Lay theologian, philosopher, poet. In his early works he championed a rapprochement between the Catholic and Orthodox churches. His identification of Sophia, divine wisdom, with the Eternal Feminine deeply affected Alexander Blok and other younger Symbolists.

Solts, Aron Alexandrovich (1872–1945). Party activist, member of the Supreme Court of the USSR.

Solzhenitsyn, Alexander Isaevich (1918–). Major writer. His literary debut, *One Day in the Life of Ivan Denisovich* (1962), made history as the first portrayal of a Soviet labor camp. His next two novels, *The First Circle* and *The Cancer Ward,* were briefly considered for publication but ultimately blocked by the literary establishment. In 1973 the KGB seized the manuscript of his *Gulag Archipelago,* a massively documented indictment of the Soviet forced labor system, and he was deported to the West. Settling in Vermont, he worked on a panoramic series of historical novels designed to identify the roots of the disaster that befell Russia in 1917. With the fall of the Soviet Union he returned to his native country, where he continues to serve as a gadfly.

Somov, Konstantin Andreevich (1869–1939). Painter and graphic artist. Founding member of the modernist World of the Art group.

Spasovich, Vladimir Danilovich (1829–1906). Jurist.

Speranskaya, Yelizaveta Petrovna (1878–?). Wife of G. N. Speransky.

Speransky, Georgy Nesterovich (1873–1969). Prominent pediatrician.

Ståhlberg, Kaarlo Juho (1865–1952). President of Finland from 1919 to 1925.

Stalin (pseudonym of Dzhugashvili), Iosif Vissarionovich (1879–1953). Soviet leader.

Stanislavsky, Konstantin Sergeevich (1863–1938). Prominent actor and stage director. The founder, with Nemirovich-Danchenko, of the Moscow Art Theater, he developed the school of acting known as the Method in the West.

Stasov, Vladimir Vasilyevich (1824–1906). Art and music critic, art historian.

Stead, Estelle. Daughter and biographer of W. T. Stead.

Stead, William Thomas (1849–1912). English journalist.

Stenich (pseudonym of Smetanich) Valentin Iosifovich (1898–1938). Translator. Victim of the Great Terror.

Stepanov, Nikolai Leonidovich (1902–1972). Pushkin scholar and authority on twentieth-century Russian poetry.

Stephen, Leslie (1832–1904). English writer and critic.

Stolyarova, Natalia Ivanovna (1912–1984). Ilya Ehrenburg's secretary. Human rights activist.

Strakhov, Nikolai Nikolaevich (1828–1896). Influential literary critic of a mildly conservative, nationalist persuasion.

Struve, Alexander Filipovich (1874–?). Head of literature for the Moscow Proletcult.

Stupniker, Alexander Maximovich (1902–?). Journalist.

Sudeikin, Sergei Yuryevich (1882–1946). Stage designer.

Sudeikina, Olga Afanasyevna (1885–1945). Actress. A friend of Akhmatova, she appears in her "Poem Without a Hero."

Sully, James (1842–1923). British child psychologist.

Surkov, Alexei Alexandrovich (1899–1983). Poet known for his wartime lyric verse. Conservative head of the Writers' Union between 1953 and 1959.

Svyatopolk-Mirsky, Dmitry Petrovich. See Mirsky, Dmitry Petrovich.

Syomin, Vitaly Nikolaevich (1927–1978). Novelist of the post-Stalin period.

Sytin, Ivan Dmitrievich (1852–1934). Publisher and bookseller.

Tabidze, Titsian (1895–1937). Distinguished Georgian poet. A friend of Pasternak. Victim of the Great Terror.

Tager, Yelena Mikhailovna (1895–1964). Writer, translator.

Tan (pseudonym of Bogoraz), Vladimir Germanovich (1865–1936). Writer, ethnographer. His science fiction shows the influence of H. G. Wells.

Tarkovsky, Arseny Alexandrovich (1907–1989). Poet, translator. His first collection of verse, *Before the Snow* (1962), brought him immediate recognition.

Tatlin, Vladimir Yevgrafovich (1885–1953). Eminent Constructivist painter and sculptor.

Teplinsky, Mark Veniaminovich. Nekrasov scholar.

Tess (pseudonym of Sosyura), Tatyana Nikolaevna (1906–1984). Journalist.

Tikhonov, Alexander Nikolaevich (1880–1956). Writer, publisher.

Titov, German Stepanovich (1935–2000). Soviet cosmonaut.

Toller, Ernst (1893–1939). German Expressionist playwright.

Tolstaya, Lyudmila Ilyinichna (1906–1982). Wife of A. N. Tolstoy.

Tolstoy, Alexei Konstantinovich (1817–1875). Poet, novelist, and playwright. Known for his ballads and historical dramas.

Tolstoy, Alexei Nikolaevich (1882–1945). Classic Soviet novelist. After the October Revolution he went into voluntary exile, but returned in 1923. He is known chiefly for panoramic historical novels (*Road to Calvary* [1921–40] and *Peter the First* [1929–43]) and science fiction (*Aelita* [1922]).

Tomashevsky, Boris Viktorovich (1890–1957). Formalist literary historian and theorist. He is known mainly as a Pushkin scholar and an authority on prosody.

Trenyova, Natalia Konstantinovna (1904–1980). Translator.

Tretyakov, Sergei Mikhailovich (1892–1937). Writer. Spokesman for LEF. Victim of the Great Terror.

Tsvetaeva, Marina Ivanovna (1892–1941). Major poet. Spurning Symbolists, Acmeists, and Futurists alike, she developed into one of the most boldly innovate Russian Modernists. In 1922 Tsvetaeva left Russia and after a brief stay in Berlin and a more extended one in Prague landed in Paris, where her verse matured and blossomed, a verse both intimate and powerful with roots in Russian folklore and Russian and classical poetry, a dramatic verse incorporating a multitude of voices, a verse in which sound, rhythm, and meaning vie for primacy. Turning to prose in the thirties, she wrote a number of vivid literary memoirs and illuminating critical essays. In 1939 she chose to return to the Soviet Union. Personal tragedy and ostracism on the part of the literary community drove her to suicide in 1941.

Tsypin, Grigory Yevgenievich (1899–1938). Journalist, head of Detgiz. Victim of the Great Terror.

Tynyanov, Yury Nikolaevich (1894–1943). Major literary scholar and writer. A member of the Petrograd Society for the Study of Poetic Language (OPOYAZ) and one of the most influential and articulate exponents of the Formalist approach to literature, he wrote a number of brilliant essays—for example, "The Literary Fact" (1924) and "Literary Evolution" (1927)—probing the boundary between literature and life and the phenomenon of literary history. He also wrote magisterial studies of Pushkin—most notably, *Archaists and Innovators* (1926)—and drew on his prodigious knowledge of the Pushkin era for his historical fiction: *Kyukhlya* (1925), *The Death of Vizier Mukhtar* (1927), "Lieutenant Kizhe" (1928), and the unfinished *Pushkin* (1935–43).

Tyutchev, Fyodor Ivanovich (1803–1873). Major Russian lyric poet. His masterful nature poems and meditative poetry are informed by the spirit of German Romantic philosophy.

Uspensky, Nikolai Vasilyevich (1837–1889). Writer. His stories, which deal with the life of the underprivileged, are marked by relentless Realism.

Utyosov, Leonid Osipovich (1895–1982). Famous music-hall artist.

Vaginov (pseudonym of Vagenshtein), Konstantin Konstantinovich (1899–1934). Writer. After starting out as an Acmeist poet, he joined the OBERIU group and switched to experimental prose.

Vasilyev, Pyotr Vasilyevich (1899–1975). Painter.

Vatson, Maria Valentinovna (1848–1932). Poet, translator.

Vavilov, Nikolai Ivanovich (1887–1943). Eminent geneticist. For opposing Lysenko's crackpot notions he was deposed as the head of the Academy of Sciences and arrested in 1940. He died in the Saratov prison.

Veltman, Alexander Fomich (1800–1870). Prolific prose writer and poet. He was popular for various modes of Romantic fiction—historical, Gothic, fantastic, and folkloristic.

Vengerov, Semyon Afanasyevich (1855–1920). Prominent literary historian. Professor of Russian Literature at Saint Petersburg University on the eve of World War I.

Vengerova, Zinaida Afanasyevna (1867–1941). Historian of West European literature.

Vengrov, Natan (1894–1962). Children's writer. Head of children's literature for the Moscow Gosizdat.

Verbitskaya, Anastasia Alexeevna (1861–1928). Prolific writer, journalist, playwright. She owed her popularity to a focus on the love life of the educated Russian woman.

Vigdorova, Frida Abramovna (1915–1965). Writer, human rights activist.

Vilmont, Nikolai Nikolaevich (1901–1986). Literary scholar, translator.

Vinogradov, Viktor Vladimirovich (1895–1969). Prominent philologist and literary scholar. His works include an early monograph on Anna Akhmatova, acute essays on Gogol, and full-length studies of Pushkin's language.

Virta, Nikolai Yevgenievich (1906–1976). Novelist, playwright, journalist.

Vladimirtsev, Boris Yakovlevich (1884–1931). Orientalist.

Vlasov, Andrei Andreevich (1900–1945). Soviet general who went over to the Germans in 1942. Executed in 1945.

Vlasov, Mikhail Fyodorovich (d. 1965). Economist.

Voitolovsky, Lev Naumovich (1877–1941). Literary scholar.

Volin, B. (pseudonym of Boris Mikhailovich Fradkin, 1886–1957). Head of Glavlit from 1931 to 1935.

Voloshin, Maximilian Alexandrovich (1877–1932). Major poet, literary critic, painter. He began as a Symbolist, then wrote poignant and eloquent responses to the atrocities of the Revolution and the Civil War. His house on the Crimean coast became a refuge for poets and artists.

Volynsky, A. (pseudonym of Akim Lvovich Flekser, 1863–1926). Modernist literary and art critic.

Voroshilov, Kliment Yefremovich (1881–1969). Party and military dignitary.

Vostokov, Alexander Khristoforovich (1781–1864). Poet. Pioneering Slavic philologist, grammarian, and lexicographer.

Vovsi, Miron Semyonovich (1897–1960). Prominent Soviet physician, cardiologist. A specialist in the physiology and pathology of internal organs.

Voznesensky, Andrei Andreevich (1933). Poet. Together with Yevtushenko he made his initial impact in the mass poetry readings of the Khrushchev era. His spirited verse is marked by a proclivity for verbal play and other trappings of modernism.

Vrubel, Mikhail Alexandrovich (1856–1910). Leading Russian Symbolist painter.

Vvedensky, Alexander Ivanovich (1904–1941). Avant-garde poet and leading member of the OBERIU. He found refuge at Detgiz, which published his poetry and prose for children.

Vyazemsky, Pyotr Andreevich (1792–1878). Poet, literary critic. He was an articulate champion of Romanticism in Russia.

Vyrubova, Anna Alexandrovna (1884–1964). Lady-in-waiting to the Empress Alexandra Fyodorovna.

Vyshinsky, Andrei Yanuaryevich (1883–1954). Public prosecutor in the show trials of the thirties.

Wasilewska, Wanda (1905–1964). Left-wing Polish novelist. She helped to found the Soviet-sponsored "Union of Polish Patriots," which provided the nucleus for the first postwar Polish government.

Watts, George Frederick (1817–1904). English painter.

Winnicott, D. W. (1896–1973). English child psychologist.

Winter, Ella (1898–1971). American journalist. Wife of the journalist John Reed, author of *Ten Days That Shook the World*.

Yagoda, Genrikh Grigorievich (1891–1938). Head of the Soviet secret police between 1934 and 1936.

Yakir, Iona Emmanuilovich (1896–1937). Army commander. Victim of the Great Terror.

Yakir, Pyotr Ionovich (1827–1982). Human rights activist. Son of I. E. Yakir.

Yakovleva, Varvara Nikolaevna (1884–1941). Deputy Commissar of Narkompros. Victim of the Great Terror.

Yampolsky, Isaak Grigoryevich (1903–1991). Literary scholar. Specialist in nineteenth-century Russian radical writers.

Yarmolinsky, Avrahm (1890–1975). Librarian, literary scholar. Head of the Slavonic Division of the New York Public Library and editor of *A Treasury of Russian Verse* (1949).

Yasensky, Bruno (Bruno Gasienski, 1901–1938). Left-wing Polish Futurist poet and Soviet writer. Victim of the Great Terror.

Yashin (Popov) Alexander Yakovlevich (1913–1968). Writer.

Yashvili, Paolo (Pavel) Dzhibrazlovich (1895–1937). Georgian poet. Friend of Pasternak. Victim of the Great Terror.

Yasinovskaya, Anna Viktorovna. Editor at Detgiz.

Yegolin, Alexander Mikhailovich (1896–1959). Literary scholar. He worked on Nekrasov and Herzen and headed the Gorky Institute of World Literature from 1949 to 1951.

Yermilov, Vladimir Vladimirovich (1904–1965). Influential literary critic. He often served as an official hatchet man.

Yershov, Pyotr Pavlovich (1815–1869). Poet.

Yesenin, Sergei Alexandrovich (1895–1925). Major poet. His verse is characterized by rich imagery and colorful diction. Stylizing himself as the "last village poet" trapped in the age of urbanization, he began with melancholic evocations of the countryside, but the bohemian—not to say debauched—existence he came to live in the city gradually invaded his verse. He took his own life, writing a versed suicide note in his own blood.

Yevdokimov, Ivan Vasilyevich (1887–1941). Author of biographical novels about Russian painters.

Yevgenyev-Maximov, Vladislav Yevgenyevich (1883–1955). Literary scholar.

Yevreinov, Nikolai Nikolaevich (1879–1953). Prominent stage director, theorist of the theater, playwright.

Yevtushenko, Yevgeny Alexandrovich (1933–). Poet. Blending a facile lyricism with liberal commitment, he best represents the post-Stalin "thaw" sensibility in poetry. An effective performer, he dominated the mass poetry readings of the Khrushchev era and made a discernible political impact with hortatory poems decrying the legacy of Stalinism ("Stalin's Heirs") and Soviet anti-Semitism ("Babi Yar"). He continued in a similar vein until the fall of the regime. Since then he has lived largely in the West.

Yezhov, Nikolai Ivanovich (1895–1940). Bolshevik leader, head of the secret police in 1936–38. A central figure in the purge trials.

Yugov, Alexei Kuzmich (1902–1979). Writer.

Yuryev, Yury Mikhailovich (1872–1948). Actor.

Yushkevich, Semyon Solomonovich (1868–1927). Writer.

Zabolotsky, Nikolai Alexeevich (1903–1958). Major poet. His first collection of verse, "Columns" (1929), treats Leningrad life in the twenties as a phantasmagoria. It was received by the Party critics with hostility, which was exacerbated by his remarkable, highly idiosyncratic narrative poem about collectivization, *Triumph of Agriculture* (1933). He was arrested in 1938 and spent eight years in the gulag. His late poetry, though more traditional, exhibits great formal mastery.

Zaitsev, Boris Konstantinovich (1881–1972). Émigré fiction writer, biographer.

Zakhoder, Boris Vladimirovich (1918–2000). Children's writer, translator.

Zalygin, Sergei Pavlovich (1913–2000). Fiction writer and essayist. He edited *Novyi mir* after the fall of the Soviet Union.

Zamirailo, Viktor Dmitrievich (1868–1939). Artist.

Zamoshkin, Nikolai Ivanovich (1896–1960). Literary critic.

Zamyatin, Yevgeny Ivanovich (1884–1937). Major modernist writer and essayist. A mentor to the Serapion Brotherhood, he provided distinctive and heterodox perspectives on post-October realities in his early stories. His anti-utopian novel *We*, which had great influence in the West, dates from 1920, but was banned in the Soviet Union until the advent of glasnost. Its publication abroad triggered a vicious campaign against him, but as a result of Gorky's intercession he was allowed to emigrate to Paris.

Zarudny, Mitrofan Ivanovich (1836–1883). Lawyer.

Zbarsky, Boris Ilyich (1885–1954). Biochemist involved in the embalming of Lenin's corpse.

Zelinsky, Kornely Lutsianovich (1896–1970). Literary critic and theorist associated with the Constructivists.

Zhabotinsky, Vladimir Yevgenievich (1880–1940). Journalist. Internationally known Jewish public figure. Before the Revolution he wrote political commentary under the pseudonym of Altalena and translated the great Hebrew poet Chaim Nachman Bialik. He later he became a right-wing Zionist leader.

Zhirmunsky, Viktor Maximovich (1891–1971). Eminent literary scholar and comparatist. His methodological position was close to that of the Formalists.

Zhitkov, Boris Stepanovich (1882–1938). Children's writer, Chukovsky's schoolmate.

Zhukovsky, Stanislav Yulianovich (1873–1944). Artist.

Zhukovsky, Vasily Andreevich (1783–1852). Major poet. A key figure in Russian pre-Romanticism, he was especially noted as a translator of German and English romantic ballads.

Zilbershtein, Ilya Samoilovich (1905–1988). Literary scholar known for his textological expertise. A founder of *Literaturnoe nasledstvo.*

Zinovyev (Radomyslsky), Grigory Yevseevich (1883–1936). Party leader. He was chairman of the Petrograd Soviet after the October Revolution and head of the Communist International from 1919 to 1926. He led the left opposition in the Central Committee in 1925. Victim of the Great Terror.

Zinovyeva-Annibal, Lidia Dmitrievna (1866–1907). Writer.

Zorgenfrei, Vilgelm Alexandrovich (1882–1938). Minor Symbolist poet, translator. Victim of the Great Terror.

Zoshchenko, Mikhail Mikhailovich (1895–1958). Premier Soviet humorist. His hilarious sketches of Soviet everyday life, cast in the form of monologues of half-literate city bumpkins, made him one of the most popular writers of his day. The quasi-autobiographical *Before Sunrise* (1943), in which he sought to get to the root of his chronic depression, lay him open to charges of subjectivism and "psychologism." In 1946 he and Anna Akhmatova were targeted in a cultural purge and expelled from the Writers' Union.

Zverev, Ilya (pseudonym of Izold Yudovich Zondberg, 1926–1966). Writer.

Index

Abalkin, Nikolai Alexandrovich, 500
Academia Press, 204, 268, 274, 278, 280, 282, 291, 293, 307, 310, 311, 314
Academy Capella, 276, 278
Acmeists, 61–62
Adrianov, Sergei Alexandrovich, 107
Afinogenov, Alexander Nikolaevich, 283, 341, 342
Aikhenwald, Yuly Isaevich, 104–105, 117
Akhmatova, Anna Andreevna, xi–xii, 155, 389; Chukovsky's visits with, 66, 67, 97–98, 99–100, 106–108, 116–117, 125, 126, 128, 131–132, 141–143, 148–149, 317, 337–338, 399–400, 407; Chukovsky's work on, 67, 111, 523; concerned about her reputation, xi, 97, 100, 107–108, 117, 139, 486, 524; death of, 514–515; denunciations and censorship of, xi, 357n, 358, 360, 384, 474, 476, 477, 487, 492, 499, 533; discussions on writers, 81, 97–98, 99–100, 113, 125, 126, 128, 133, 476–477, 511, 551; financial concerns of, 97–98, 108, 112, 116, 131, 133, 134, 137–138, 142, 148; health problems of, 97, 126, 129, 132, 133, 143; honors to, 337n, 497, 499, 505–506; other writers on, 473, 474, 514, 538; personal traits of, xii, 81, 112, 116–117, 138, 383–384, 399–400; poetry by, 67, 69–70, 87, 97, 99, 100, 103, 108, 116, 128, 317, 379, 400, 407, 446, 468, 479, 505, 517, 518n, 523, 533; translations by, 384
Akhraimovich, Zalman, 498
Alexander II, Tsar, 19n
Alexandrov, Georgy Fyodorovich, 349, 375, 393–395, 399, 511–512

Alexinsky, Mikhail Andreevich, 237
Aliger, Margarita Iosifovna, 405, 412, 413, 417, 423, 431
Allilueva-Stalina, Svetlana Iosifovna, 442, 521
All-Russian Writers' Union. See Writers' Union
Alyansky, Sammil Mironovich, 88, 136, 293, 323, 355, 422
American Relief Administration, 121–122, 127
Amfiteatrov, Alexander Valentinovich, 67
Amis, Kingsley, 540
Andreev, Leonid Nikolaevich, 15, 18, 22, 58, 115, 241, 333, 554, 555; Chukovsky's writing on, 56–57, 103, 124, 483, 496, 523; death of, 495; personal traits of, 39, 55, 56, 57, 103, 339
Andreev, Vadim Leonidovich, 476, 510
Andreeva, Marya Fyodorovna, 50, 84, 353
Andreeva, Olga Vadimovna (Olga Carlisle), 498
Andronikov, Irakly Luarsabovich, 373, 376–377, 381, 399, 431, 461
Angert, David Nikolaevich, 277–278
Angert, Raisa Grigoryevna, 277
Annenkov, Yuri Pavlovich, 6, 80, 100, 114, 115, 117, 124, 133, 155, 201, 516
Antipova, Valentina Georgievna, 541–542
Anti-Semitism, 16, 22, 236, 386n, 432, 443, 449–450, 451, 459, 478, 481, 489, 490, 491, 502, 534, 552
Antokolsky, Mark Matveevich, 19, 402, 466
Ardov, Viktor Yefimovich, 514
Arkhipov, Vladimir Alexandrovich, 463
Arosev, Alexander Yakovlevich, 318

Aseev, Nikolai Nikolaevich, 463
Asmus, Valentin Fernandovich, 444, 445, 446, 454
Austen, Jane, 462
Averbakh, Leopold Leopoldovich, 256, 257
Averchenko, Arkady Timofeevich, 314, 490
Azov, Vladimir Alexandrovich (head of House Committee), 53

Babel, Isaak Emmanuilovich, 167–168, 185, 233, 374, 430, 459, 482, 483, 487, 501, 502, 562–563
Bagritsky, Eduard Georgievich, 261*n*, 298
Bakst, Lev Samoilovich, 15, 266
Bakunin, Mikhail Alexandrovich, 423
Balmont, Konstantin Dmitrievich, 49, 554
Balzac, Honoré de, 295, 318
Bannikov, Nikolai, 507*n*, 515
Battleship Potemkin (film), 12*n*
Batyushkov, Fyodor Dmitrievich, 47
Baumvol, Rakhil Lvovna, 388
Bazov, Herzl, 285
Bedny, Demyan, 142, 215, 324–325
Beerbohm, Max, 546
Beketova, Marya Andreevna, 127
Belchikov, Nikolai Fyodorovich, 532
Belinkov, Arkady Viktorovich, 473–474, 485
Belinsky, Vissarion Grigoryevich, xvi, 6, 195, 313, 358, 362, 409, 498, 520
Belitsky, Yefim Yakovlevich, 77, 132, 186
Belskoye Ustye colony, 92, 94–95
Beluga, Khanka, 145
Bely, Andrei, 15, 29, 45*n*, 80, 97, 108, 298, 312, 371, 433
Benkendorf, Alexander Khristorovich, 82, 209, 492
Benkendorf, Maria. *See* Budberg, Maria Ignatyevna
Bennett, Arnold, 120
Berdyaev, Nikolai Alexandrovich, 17
Beria, Lavrenty Pavlovich, 377, 382, 388, 394, 396–397
Beria, Sergo Lavrentyevich, 377, 387
Berlin, Isaiah, 466–467, 505, 506, 507
Berzer, Anna Samoilovna, 462
Bestuzhev Courses, 133

Bible, 26, 108, 502, 503, 526, 535
Biblioteka poeta (Poets' Library), 262, 304, 305, 506, 519, 538
Blake, William, 236, 237, 469, 490
Blok, Alexander Alexandrovich, 38–39, 44, 65, 131, 191, 333, 551, 554; books about, 97, 204, 240, 402–403; Chukovsky's readings on, 85–86, 132, 402; Chukovsky's writings on, 112, 132, 178, 352, 402, 411; death of, 95–96, 99, 127; on humanism, 45–46; letters of, 204, 433; in Moscow, 87–88; personal traits of, xi, 52, 53, 58, 60, 70, 84, 96, 164, 433; poetry by, 63, 73, 77, 80, 87, 96, 128, 135, 216, 286, 539–540; political attacks on, 53, 84, 89–90, 97, 98; on Pushkin, 81–82; readings by, 50–51, 59, 88, 90; *Snow Mask,* 98; *The Twelve,* 52, 63, 80, 82, 96, 103, 112, 151*n;* and World Literature project, xi, 18, 41, 45, 59, 60, 61–62, 68–69, 73–74, 77, 96
Blok, Lyubov Dmitrievna, 88*n*, 96, 127, 165, 185–186
Bogdanovich, Tatyana Alexandrovna, 372
Bogoraz, Larissa Iosifovna, 536, 537
Boldyrev, Ivan Sergeevich, 419
Bolsheviks: arrests made by, 48, 132; artists denounced and attacked by, xi, 99, 410*n;* Chukovsky's official dealings with, 38, 52; complaints about, 38, 45, 74, 84, 113*n*, 159; and Gorky, x–xi, 43, 45, 48, 51, 55, 57, 71, 79–80, 84, 276; and Mensheviks, 157; power seized by, 32*n;* publications of, 107; public demonstrations by, xii, 31
Bolshoi Dramatic Theater, 86, 135, 181, 182
Bondi, Sergei Mikhailovich, 59, 378
Bonetsky, Konstantin Iosifovich, 534–535
Bonnier, Sofya Pavlovna, 353
Borisovna, Marya. *See* Chukovskaya, Marya Borisovna
Boronina, Yekaterina Alexeevna, 388
Boswell, James, *Life of Johnson,* 392
Botkin, Vasily Petrovich, 495
Bowra, C. M. (Maurice), 466
Brezhnev, Leonid Ilyich, 461, 522, 533, 534

Brik, Lilia Yuryevna, 74, 75, 76–77, 124, 233, 235, 241, 321, 440, 534*n*

Brik, Osip Maximovich, 75, 534*n*

Brodsky, Iosif Alexandrovich (Joseph Brodsky), xvii, 412*n*, 490, 491–492, 493, 497, 501, 505, 507, 508, 514

Bronshtein, Matvei Petrovich, xiv, 334*n*, 336, 337, 430

Browning, Robert, 10, 464

Bryusov, Valery Yakovlevich, ix, 15, 18, 29, 63, 135, 164, 233, 268, 424, 539, 553, 554

Bryusova, Zhanna Matveevna, 268

Bubnov, Andrei Sergeevich, 308, 324, 325

Budberg, Maria Ignatyevna (Benkendorf), 53, 66–67, 464, 468, 472, 483, 489, 492, 511

Budnikov, Fyodor Ilyich, 255

Budyonny, Semyon Mikhailovich, 287, 374

Bukharin, Nikolai Ivanovich, 183, 300

Bukhnikhashvili, Grigory, 285

Bulgakov, Mikhail Afanasyevich, 410, 509, 536

Bulgakova, Yelena Sergeevna, 536

Bunin, Ivan Alexeevich, 24, 136–137, 236, 356, 402, 495, 498, 519, 530, 553–555

Butkov, Yakov Petrovich, 196

Butler, Samuel, 39, 410

Byron, George Gordon (Lord), 11, 15, 128, 155, 495

Byronism, 59*n*

Bystrova, Lyudmila Modestovna, 136, 149, 153, 171, 182, 187

Bystryansky, Vadim Alexandrovich, 104

Caine, Thomas Henry Hall, 386

Čapek, Karel, 144

Carlyle, Thomas, 39, 347

Carpenter, Edward, 35

Carroll, Lewis, xvi, 465

Cellini, Benvenuto, 122

Chaadaev, Pyotr Yakovlevich, 5

Chagin, Pyotr Ivanovich, 206

Chaliapin, Fyodor Ivanovich, 24, 39, 44, 50, 51, 53, 65, 87, 142, 231

Chaliapina, Marya Valentinovna, 66

Chaplin, Charlie, 491

Chapygin, Alexei Pavlovich, 276–277

Charskaya, Lidia Alexeevna, 113–114

Chatterton, Thomas, 14

Chebotarevskaya, Anastasia Nikolaevna, 558, 559

Cheka, 55, 80, 94, 114, 236, 289, 306, 470

Chekhonin, Sergei Vasilyevich, 303

Chekhov, Anton Pavlovich, 7, 69, 160, 249, 371, 498, 532–533; anecdotes about, 19, 24, 50, 83, 109, 152, 328, 353, 381, 387, 431; censorship of, 235, 460, 538; Chukovsky's work on, 14–15, 24, 348, 352, 353, 354, 402, 408, 413, 423, 424, 427–428, 447, 460, 483, 523; death of, 386–387, 532*n*; personal traits of, 15, 164, 214, 430, 562

Chekhov, Mikhail Alexandrovich, 184, 249

Chekhova, Marya Pavlovna, 387

Chernov, Viktor Mikhailovich, 114

Chernyshevsky, Nikolai Gavrilovich, xvi, 8, 22, 33, 195, 207*n*, 213, 244, 271, 282, 311, 313*n*, 336, 388

Chesterton, G. K., 72, 85, 106, 108, 109, 138

Chicherin, Georgy Vasilyevich, 215

Chikobava, Arnold Stepanovich, 369

Chorny, Sasha, 458

Christie, Agatha, 438

Chudovsky, Valerian Adolfovich, 59, 97–98

Chukovskaya, Lidia Korneevna (daughter), 168, 350, 384; birth of, 18*n*, 519; childhood of, 18, 23, 24, 28, 30, 36, 46, 141; and children's library, 448–449, 530; editorial work of, 111, 363, 390; health problems of, 254, 363, 448, 451, 494, 514; and her father, 47, 170, 186, 336, 342, 372, 431, 448, 530, 547–548; husband's arrest and execution, xiv, 334, 337; and official censorship, xvii, 414, 491, 501, 533; personal traits of, 145–146, 148, 170, 178, 448; speeches of, 415; student years of, 76, 105–106, 111, 148; translations by, 155; writings of, 213, 323, 336, 337, 346, 381, 408, 414, 460, 479, 518*n*, 523, 528; and Zoshchenko, 400, 401

Chukovskaya, Marina (great-granddaughter), 517–518, 535, 539

Chukovskaya, Marina Korneevna "Mura"/
"Murka" (daughter): childhood of, 100–
101, 106, 119, 120, 128, 130–131, 137,
146, 158–159, 163, 164, 165–166, 168–
169, 174, 185, 189, 193, 195, 213, 263;
death of, 254–255, 259, 265, 273; illnesses of, 196–198, 240, 243, 245–246,
247–248, 249–250, 252–255; infancy of,
73, 79, 81; and *Murka's Book*, 130–131,
135–136; Chukovsky's visits to grave and
memories of, 273, 284, 330, 470
Chukovskaya, Marina Nikolaevna (Kolya's
wife), 139–140, 141, 336, 342, 348, 359,
448, 464, 468, 502, 512, 514, 530
Chukovskaya, Marya Borisovna (wife), 3, 8–
9, 31, 158, 163, 285, 363; death of, 391–
393; health problems of, 67, 68, 366,
370, 372; and husband's birthdays, 47–
48; and Kolya's birth, 10, 512; and
Mura, 81, 164, 185, 198, 243, 246, 248,
255, 263; and shortages, 82–83, 122, 265;
socializing, 19, 22, 294, 320; traveling,
341–342, 345, 347; Chukovsky's visits to
grave and memories of, 395, 397, 401,
414, 423, 448, 453, 482, 486, 499, 502,
529, 530
Chukovskaya, Natalya Nikolaevna "Tata"
(granddaughter) 348, 350n, 409
Chukovskaya, Yelena (Elena) Tsezarevna
"Lyusha" (granddaughter), xiv, 350n,
367, 372, 384, 434, 448, 495, 516, 530,
547
Chukovsky, Boris Korneevich "Boba"
(son), 170, 175, 207, 342, 344, 346; birth
of, 23n; childhood of, 28, 46, 47, 66, 81,
111, 114; personal traits of, 145, 147,
178
Chukovsky, Boris Yevgenyevich "Boba"
(great-grandson), 428–429
Chukovsky, Dmitry Nikolaevich "Mitya"
(great-grandson), 492, 524
Chukovsky, Kornei: on aging, 109–110,
166, 170, 177, 316, 328, 354, 363, 368,
431, 454, 461, 482, 493, 495, 525; birth
and early years of, ix, 161–162, 328–329;
boredom and depression of, 8, 73, 118–
119, 124–125, 129, 143, 176, 182, 210,
271–272, 335, 355, 358, 363, 366–367,

372, 387, 403, 432–433, 457; on censorship, xv, xvii, 20, 24, 136, 142, 149, 150,
151, 153–158, 165, 171–173, 174, 176,
177–178, 179, 182, 183, 184, 187, 188,
195–196, 201, 205–206, 207–208, 214–
216, 240, 271, 279, 290, 295–296, 307–
311, 323–324, 348–350, 352, 353, 354,
365–366, 403, 460, 477, 505, 506, 515–
516, 524, 526, 531, 532, 533, 534–535,
536; with children, 326, 327, 330–331,
333–334, 344, 350, 371, 418, 447–448;
children's letters to, 210, 245; children's
library of, 418–421, 427, 430, 448–449,
455; on children's theater, 60, 114–115;
on cultural continuity, xviii, 542–544,
545; disillusionment of, xvi, 174–175,
176, 181, 363, 364, 365, 367, 368, 372,
380, 394, 413, 536; estate of, 448, 496,
530, 547–548; on fatherhood, 30, 81, 119;
finances of, 42, 60, 63, 64, 65, 74, 81,
85, 106, 111, 117–118, 130, 132, 136,
137, 146, 155, 174–175, 180–181, 182,
186–187, 190, 205, 206, 213, 258, 264–
265, 273, 274, 278, 364, 368; in Finland,
21, 158, 159–160, 162, on food shortages, 64, 81, 82–83, 85–87, 111; as
grandfather, 170, 367, 372, 409, 428–
429, 455, 517–518; happiness of, 9–10,
524; health problems of, 64, 174–175,
177, 239, 254, 261, 265, 269, 278–279,
282, 296–299, 323, 331, 345, 363, 411,
427, 438–439, 443, 447, 454, 457, 484,
495, 502–504, 506, 512–513, 515, 519,
529, 530–531, 541, 546–548; on his
birthday, 47–48, 85, 166, 189, 316, 331,
341, 346, 355, 368, 372–373, 397, 416,
431, 454; on his mother, 151, 161, 166,
489; honors to, xvi, 382, 416–417, 460–
461, 463, 473, 480; imprisonment of,
397n; insomnia of, 15, 28, 29, 31, 48, 50,
56, 60, 63, 64, 74, 82, 85, 101, 106, 143,
155, 160, 190, 207, 234, 269, 302, 304,
320, 338, 354, 360, 427, 436, 511, 516;
on language, 18, 63, 451–452, 455, 456n,
460; library destroyed, 350; in London,
ix, 9–10, 464–469; and Masha (*see* Chukovskaya, Marya Borisovna); in Moscow,
87–88, 123, 270, 274, 280–282, 290, 294–

295, 302; near-drowning of, 31; Oxford doctorate to, xvi, 458, 459, 464–469; papers of, 160–162, 448, 547–548; on photography, 11; political attacks on, xiii–xiv, xvii, 83–84, 85, 111, 125, 151–152, 153, 194, 309, 317, 323, 336, 340, 351, 352, 355–356, 357, 361, 441, 456, 463, 477, 515, 564–565; portraits of, 15, 19–20, 265–266, 315, 458, 555–558; readings and talks by, 50–51, 52, 69, 88, 122–124, 154, 183, 189, 204, 216, 279, 287, 292, 302, 312–313, 316–317, 336, 341, 345, 348, 353, 370, 394, 402, 422, 423, 465–468, 473, 476, 496, 500–501; on the Revolution, 11–13, 289, 301, 478; self-criticism of, 8–9, 16, 17, 524; translations by (*see* Chukovsky, Kornei, translations by); trip to Tashkent, 341–347; unemployment of, 190; writings of (*see* Chukovsky, Kornei, writings)

Chukovsky, Kornei, translations by, x, xi; *Apostles*, 180, 181, 182; *Art of Translation*/"Rules for Translators," 40, 304, 308, 310, 335, 447, 482, 485; Byron, 11; Fielding, 380; Kipling, 16, 564; O. Henry, 113, 119, 176, 189, 212, 385; *Playboy of the Western World* (Synge), xiii, 115–116, 119; "Rain" (Maugham), 176, 178, 179, 180, 181, 184, 190; *Robinson Crusoe* (Defoe), 341, 380; D. G. Rossetti, 14; *Sadie*, 180, 181, 184, 190; Twain, 409–410, 423; for World Literature project, 39–42

Chukovsky, Kornei, writings: on Akhmatova, 67, 111, 523; *Alive as Life*, 456, 470, 475, 504; on Andreev, 56–57, 103, 124, 483, 496, 523; anthologies, 324, 340*n;* "Barmalei," 149, 207–208, 302, 346*n*, 348, 350, 351*n*, 352, 379, 476; "The Barrel Organ," 205; "Bibigon," 354, 355–356, 357, 361, 362, 379, 380, 397; on Blok, 112, 132, 178, 352, 402, 411; "Blue Grandpa," 147; *Books and People*, 423, 441; *Borodulia*, 175, 177, 180, 210; "The Chatterbox Fly," 130, 171, 173, 302, 364, 433, 467; on Chekhov, 14–15, 24, 348, 352, 353, 354, 402, 408, 413, 423, 424, 427–428, 447, 460, 483,

523; on Chesterton, 85; children's books, xiii, xvi, 132*n*, 165, 282, 290–292, 308, 322, 335, 341, 530, 547; *Chukokkala*, 268, 277, 283, 430, 448, 486, 516, 531, 535, 537; collections of, 463, 475, 482, 494, 515, 524, 525, 526, 534–535, 548; *Contemporaries*, 460, 483, 503, 519, 523; *A Contemporary Eugene Onegin*, 10–11; "The Crocodile," xiii, xv, 7, 28–29, 76, 102, 136, 147, 171, 174, 179, 180, 181, 183, 186, 187, 188, 209, 214–216, 254, 266, 275, 307–311, 312, 315, 325, 379, 402, 405, 465; "Desdemona's Asthma," 335–336; diary (notes on), vii, ix, xii, xiv, 3, 397, 407, 416, 480, 524; *Doctor Ouch-It-Hurts*, 155, 205, 324, 380, 402; "Fedora's Misfortune," 166, 167; "Fifty Piglets," 154–155, 221; "The Fly's Wedding," 171–172; *From Chekhov to Our Times*, 286, 517; "From Dilettantism to Science," 381–382; *From Two to Five*, xvii, 293, 299, 315, 317, 323, 380, 397, 401, 402, 403, 408, 436, 447, 477, 493; on Futurism, 111, 119; "The Giant Cockroach," xiii, 116, 117–118, 146, 147, 171, 405; on Gorky, xiii, 130, 136, 175, 348, 416, 429; *A High Art*, 531, 535, 536; *KKK*, 174; literary criticism, xiii, 463; on Mayakovsky, 51, 76, 104, 352, 375, 532; *Men of the Sixties*, 8, 274, 293; *Murka's Book*, 130–131, 132, 135–136; on Nekrasov (*see* Nekrasov, Nikolai Alexeevich); on Panaeva, 212, 213, 365; on Pasternak, 507*n*, 508, 509, 515; "A Perennial Issue," 7; play about Tsar Puzan, 31; *The Poet and the Hangman*, 97*n*, 513, 519; *The Poet's Wife*, 97*n*; *Porcupines Laughing*, 192; on Pushkin, 366, 436, 480; on Radlova, 335, 336; on Repin, 85, 308, 311, 312–313, 319, 324, 335, 352, 353, 380, 494, 503, 550; "Robin Bobin Barabek," 323; "The Samovar Revolt," 165; "Sensical Nonsense," 216–217; *Small Children*, 279, 282; songs, 292; "Sunny Girl," 254, 274; "The Telephone," 333; *The Tower of Babel*, 531; on Tynyanov, 380, 515; "Wash 'Em Clean," xiii, 116, 118, 123,

Chukovsky, Kornei, writings (continued)
136, 146, 165, 171, 215, 270, 364, 467,
563; *What I Remember*, 530*n*, 550–565;
"White Mouse," 178; on Whitman, 119,
270, 274, 373, 379, 380, 395, 502, 512,
531, 550, 561; *Who Lives Well in Russia*,
275, 368; on Wilde, 119, 436; "The
Wonder Tree," 130, 341, 467; on Zhitkov, 380; on Zoshchenko, 493, 495, 496,
497, 498, 500–501, 505, 506

Chukovsky, Nikolai Dmitry "Kolya" (son)
98, 166, 175, 348, 359; birth of, 9*n*, 10;
childhood of, 16, 18, 20, 23, 28, 30, 31,
36, 46, 140–141, 151, 402; death of, 512,
516–517; diaries of, 40; and food shortages, 82, 86; and his father, 86, 372, 448;
marriage of, 139–140, 141; in the navy,
336, 342, 346; novels of, 147–148, 149,
151, 155, 260–261, 357, 414; and Pasternak, 436*n;* personal traits of, 40, 141,
372; poetry of, 40, 41, 83, 147; political
attacks on, 357–358; stories of, 408, 412;
translations by, 141, 148, 180, 213, 319

Chukovsky, Yevgeny Borisovich "Zhenya"
(grandson), 448, 530

Chulkov, Georgy Ivanovich, 16, 411

Classicism, 59*n*

Club of Children's Writers, 300

Coleridge, Samuel Taylor, 66

Communist Party, 79–80, 162, 200, 275,
301, 309, 314*n*, 357*n*, 528

Constructivists, 261

Czechoslovakia, Soviet invasion of, xvii,
536*n*, 537*n*

D'Angelo, Sergio, 407*n*

Daniel, Yuly Markovich, 510*n*, 527*n,* 536

Dante Alighieri, 291, 414

Darwin, Charles, 13, 16, 141

Davydov, Denis Vasilyevich, 60

Defoe, Daniel, *Robinson Crusoe*, 341, 380

Delvig, Anton Antonovich, 61

Deniken, Anton Ivanovich, 70

Derevenskaia gazeta, 258

Deutsch, Babette, 137, 266

Diaghilev, Sergei Pavlovich, 98

Dickens, Charles, 42, 51, 72, 74, 372

Dobrolyubov, Nikolai Alexandrovich, 8,
125, 128, 195, 313*n*

Dobrovolsky, Alexei Alexandrovich, 527*n*,
528

Dobuzhinsky, Mstislav Valerianovich, 79,
83, 92*n*, 95, 149, 208

Dobychin, Leonid Ivanovich, xvi, 485, 487

Dorofeev, Viktor Petrovich, 365–366

Dostoevsky, Fyodor Mikhailovich, 34, 79,
101, 177, 205, 207*n*, 240, 314*n*, 352; *The
Brothers Karamazov*, 94; *Demons*, 313*n;*
The Diary of a Writer, 62; *The Gambler*,
453; *The Idiot*, 18; influence of, 13, 60,
112, 129, 142; personal traits of, 214

Doyle, Arthur Conan, 72, 412

Drabkina, Lizabeta Yakovlevna, 289

Dreiden, Simon Davydovich, 393, 498,
500, 519

Dubrovina, Lyudmila Viktorovna, 360–361

Dudintsev, Vladimir Dmitrievich, 411

Duduchava, Alexander Iosifovich, 285

Dumas, Alexandre, 295, 352

Duncan, Isadora, 100, 140, 360

Dzerzhinsky, Felix Edmundovich, 55*n*, 238

Easter kiss, 50

Efros, Abram Markovich, 139, 142, 275

Ehrenburg, Ilya Grigoryevich, 348, 379,
380, 386, 389, 422, 451, 453, 454, 471,
481–482, 484

Eikhenbaum, Boris Mikhailovich, 59, 117,
125, 152, 154, 155, 160, 163, 211, 262,
276, 303

Eikhler, Genrikh Leopoldovich, 487

Eikhvald, Yekaterina Nikitichna, 38

Eisenstein, Sergei, 12*n*

Eizen, Ilya Moiseevich, 43

Eliot, George, 112

Elsberg, Yakov Yefimovich, 459

Epshtein, Moisei Solomovich, 308

Etkind, Yefim Grigoryevich, 501, 538

Fadeev, Alexander Alexandrovich, 257,
283, 301, 377, 414–415; and Akhmatova,
337, 338; and Chukovsky's writings, 336,
355, 360, 361, 383; as Party activist, 339,
348, 357, 374, 385, 390, 406; suicide of,

Index

617

xvi, 405–406; as writer, 313*n*, 314*n*, 406; and Writers' Union, 348, 362, 380, 383
Faulkner, William, 415, 432
Fausek, Yulia Ivanovna, 181
February Revolution (1917). *See* Revolutions
Fedin, Konstantin Alexandrovich, 143, 203, 280, 349, 357, 376, 384, 455, 472, 473; in Academy of Sciences, 174, 440; at Blok memorial, 402; home destroyed, 364; letters of, 425; and *Literaturnoe nasledstvo*, 440, 441; and Pasternak, 359, 407, 408, 435, 439, 470, 471, 486–487; on Russian literature, 379, 416, 418, 440, 563; and Serapion Brotherhood, 93; and Solzhenitsyn, 522, 523; on his wife's death, 373; as writer, 156, 179, 199, 389, 435, 456–457, 475; and Writers' House, 98, 99; at writers' meeting, 411–412; and Writers' Union, 348, 380, 383, 386, 417, 424, 426, 523; and Zoshchenko, 299; and *Zvezda*, 157
Fedina, Dora Sergeevna, 337, 364, 373
Fedina, Ninochka, 337
Fedotych, Konstantin, 441–442
Feltrinelli, Giorgio, 407*n*
Fet, Afanasy Afanasyevich, 49, 204, 398
Fielding, Henry, 366, 379, 380, 388, 392
Filatov, Alexander Konstantinovich, 418, 419
Filosofov, Dmitry Vladimirovich, 28
Fischer, George, 444
Flaubert, Gustave, 6, 101
Fonvizin, Denis Ivanovich, 495
Formalism, 59*n*, 160, 173, 275–276, 303
Forsh, Olga Dmitrievna, 127, 262–263
Fourier, Charles, 34, 129
Freud, Sigmund, 145
Frost, Robert, 469
Frunze, Mikhail Vasilyevich, 404*n*
Furtseva, Yekaterina Alexeevna, 411–412, 424, 434, 436
Futurism, 111, 119, 235*n*

Gabrichevsky, Alexander Georgievich, 269
Gagarina, Princess, 83
Galenskov, Y. T., 527*n*

Ganetsky, Yakov Stanislavovich, 288
Gardner, Erle Stanley, 521
Garnett, Constance, 538
Gegenada, S. S., 285
Gerasimov, Alexander Mikhailovich, 480
Gerasimova, Valeria Anatolyevna, 405
Gershenzon, Mikhail Osipovich, 215
Gessen, Iosif Vladimirovich, 114, 205
Gide, André, 379
Ginzburg, Alexander, 527*n*
Gippius, Zinaida Nikolaevna, 28, 38–39, 52, 453
Gladkov, Fyodor, 432
Glotser, Vladimir Iosifovich, 494, 534, 535
Goethe, Johan Wolfgang von, 266–267, 435, 495
Gogoberidze, Lina, 285
Gogol, Nikolai Vasilyevich, 60, 79, 160, 203, 213, 242, 436, 520; *Dead Souls*, 62*n*; influence of, 15, 371, 388, 509; *The Inspector General*, 13*n*, 206, 251, 394*n*; *The Robbers*, 62
Golding, William, 521
Gollerbakh, Erikh Fyodorovich, 107
Golovenchenko, Fyodor Mikhailovich, 360
Gorbachov, Georgy Yefimovich, 157
Gorky, Maxim, 26–28, 48–50, 54, 82*n*, 96, 102, 109, 156, 178, 260, 274, 303–304, 311, 464, 554–555; and arrests, 53, 66–67, 92–93; and Bolsheviks, x–xi, 43, 45, 48, 51, 55, 57, 71, 79–80, 84, 276; celebrations and honors for, 46–47, 48, 276–277, 377, 429–430; and censorship, 51, 142, 152, 158, 235, 290, 293, 310; and children's book commission, 295; Chukovsky's writing on, xiii, 48, 130, 136, 142, 175, 348, 416, 429, 535; comparisons of others with, 56, 276, 558; death of, 326; on food shortages, 86–87; health problems of, 282, 297; in others' writings, xiii, 55, 130, 136, 280, 387, 425, 435, 472; and Pasternak, 371; on peasant as enemy, 45, 46, 86, 91; personal traits of, x, xi, 26, 44, 50, 55, 56, 57, 58–59, 61, 74, 80, 90, 143, 164, 262, 335, 371, 562; political attacks on, 73, 286, 314; readings by, 50–51; reputation of, 57, 86;

Gorky, Maxim (continued)
   and Serapion Brotherhood, 93–94; and
      Stalin, 296, 297; stories of, 27, 41, 44, 53–
      54, 61, 65–66, 230, 233, 277, 287–289,
      318, 320, 333, 374–375, 383, 490, 563–
      564; and Tolstoy (Alexei), 136, 300; and
      Tolstoy (Lev), x, 48–49, 61, 159; and
      World Literature project, x, 39–42, 45–
      47, 55, 57–58, 61, 62, 63, 67, 68–69, 72–
      73, 77, 79–80; writings of, 51, 233, 276,
      291, 313–314, 378
Gorlin, A. N., 157
Gorodetsky, Sergei Mitrofanovich, 61, 237,
      240, 402
Gorokhov, L. B., 200, 205
Gosizdat Editorial Division, 126, 132; and
      arrests, 162; bankruptcy of, 130; breakup
      and reorganization of, 156–157, 163; and
      censorship, 178, 180, 181, 205, 321; and
      Chukovsky's work, 123, 130, 151, 183,
      195, 265, 380; and GUS, 200n; and pa-
      per factory, 144; readings at, 130, 211;
      and Repin, 159; and Revolution, 210;
      and Tolstoy, 212; and Trotsky, 151, 153;
      and World Literature, 122, 157; and
      writers' letter, 152
Goslitizdat, 365–366, 370, 380, 413, 454
Government House, 258, 290
Grabar, Igor Emmanuilovich, 302–303, 315
Granovskaya Yelena Mavrikievna, 180, 190
Grekova, I., 529
Griboedov, Alexander Sergeevich, 76, 194,
      209
Grigorenko, Pyotr Grigoryevich, 528
Grigoryev, Apollon Alexandrovich, 45
Grishashvili, Iosif Grigoryevich, 314–315
Gromova, Vera Alexeevna, 335
Gromyko, Andrei Andreevich, 489
Grossman, Leonid Petrovich, 231, 398, 499
Grossman, Vasily Semyonovich, 347, 358,
      383, 451, 499
Gruzdev, Ilya Alexandrovich, 93, 251
Grzhebin, Zinovy Isaevich, 26, 44, 51n, 53,
      55, 56, 59, 60, 61, 68, 69, 73, 93, 104,
      125
Guber, Pyotr Konstantinovich, 82, 129
Gudzy, Nikolai Kalinnikovich, 376
Gumilyov, Lev Nikolaevich, 459

Gumilyov, Nikolai Stepanovich, 43, 59, 82,
      191, 240, 243, 516; and Akhmatova, xii,
      125, 131, 132, 384, 459, 486; and Blok,
      45, 52; execution of, xvi, 99, 100, 476,
      485, 487, 502; family of, 90–91, 100, 459;
      personal traits of, 60, 80, 102, 164; read-
      ings by, 50–51, 70; rules for translators
      from, 40, 42; translations by, 66, 128;
      and World Literature project, 45, 60, 61–
      62, 68
Gumilyova, Anna Nikolaevna Engelhardt,
      90–91
GUS (State Learned Council), 200, 205,
      209, 214–215, 217, 237
Gusev, N. N., 16n

Haggard, H. Rider, 42
Hardy, Thomas, *Far from the Madding
      Crowd*, 85, 102, 105, 108–109, 110, 111,
      353
Heine, Heinrich, 45, 46, 163, 173, 194,
      209, 300, 319, 495
Henry, O., 39, 88, 113, 189, 194, 212, 385;
      Cabbages and Kings, 119, 176
Hermitage: Chukovsky's visit to, 127–128;
      paintings sold by, 302–303
Herzen, Alexander Ivanovich, xvi, 311,
      409, 498
Hidas, Antal, 431
Hikmet, Nazim, 423
Holitscher, Arthur, 73–74
House of Scholars, 73, 81, 108, 252, 299,
      353
House of the Arts, 60, 65, 69, 71–72, 73,
      74–75, 83, 84, 86, 96, 102n, 109, 243,
      264, 429
House of the Children's Book, 460, 478
House of the Press, 89–90, 122, 210
House of Writers, 54–55, 81, 84, 98–99,
      113, 433, 436–437, 441, 483, 501
Hugo, Victor, 39–40, 253
Humanism, 45–46

Ibsen, Henrik, 17
Ilf, Ilya Arnoldovich, 283, 284
Ilyin (= Ilya Yakovlevich Marshak), 280,
      321
Imperial Academy of Fine Arts, 16n

Inber, Vera Mikhailovna, 283, 360
Ionov, Ilya Ionovich, 56, 81, 156–157, 158, 162, 174, 258, 282
Irving, Washington, 113, 407
Isaakyan, Avetik, 234
Isakovsky, Mikhail Vasilyevich, 383
Italian Society, 89–90
Iunost', 389, 504, 509, 510
Ivanov, Vsevolod Vyacheslavovich, 90, 115, 200, 211, 383, 404, 416, 457, 472, 479; and Pasternak, 434, 435; and Writers' Union, 348, 380, 398; writings of, 257, 283, 374
Ivanov, Vyacheslav Ivanovich, 15, 96, 507, 516, 539
Ivanov, Vyacheslav Vsevolodovich "Koma," 445–446, 528
Ivanova, Tamara Vladimirovna, 377, 379, 398, 425–427, 431, 441, 479, 515
Ivanov-Razumnik, Razumnik Vasilyevich, xv–xvi, 45*n*, 60, 61, 132, 195, 469
Ivinskaya, Olga Vsevolodovna, 437, 441, 445, 446, 470
Izvestiia, 300, 362, 463, 481

James, Henry, 101–102, 352–353, 425, 431
Jerome, Jerome K., 197
Joyce, James, 275

Kachalov, Vasily Ivanovich, 135, 231, 232
Kalinin, Mikhail Ivanovich, 91, 303, 341
Kalitskaya, Vera Pavlovna, 184
Kamenev, Lev Borisovich, 153, 168, 215, 251, 274, 282, 298, 303–306, 310, 311–312
Kameneva, Tatyana Ivanovna, 305, 312
Kamensky, Anatoly Pavlovich, 6
Kamensky, Vasily Vasilyevich, 15
Kant, Immanuel, 62
Kapitsa, Olga Yeronimovna, 184, 472–473
Kapitsa, Pyotr Leonidovich, 472–473, 513
Kaplun, Boris Gitmanovich, 68, 69, 78–79
Karakhan, Lev Mikhailovich, 269–270
Kashtelyan, Sammil Borisovich, 156, 205
Kataev, Valentin Petrovich, 374, 378, 382, 389, 443, 459, 463, 475, 477, 501
Kaverin, Venyamin Alexandrovich, 369, 400, 410, 416*n*, 418, 431, 484*n*; on cen-

sorship, xiv–xv, 355–356; and Chukovsky's work, 355–356; and Solzhenitsyn, 526, 533; and Tolstoy, 212; and Tynyanov, 319–320, 380; and Zoshchenko, 377, 501
Kaverina, Lidia Nikolaevna, 425
Kazakevich, Emmanuil Genrikhovich, 398–399, 402, 403, 404, 405, 413, 417, 421–422, 451, 457, 461, 475
Kennedy, John Fitzgerald, 469
Kerensky, Alexander Fyodorovich, 26, 34, 281, 560
Kern, A. P., 5*n*, 6
Kerzhentsev, Platon Mikhailovich, 75
Khalatov, Artemy Bagratovich, 270, 287, 288, 297
Khardzhiev, Nikolai Ivanovich, 275, 317
Kharms, Daniil Ivanovich, 487, 564
Khatsrevin, Zakhar Lvovich, 501
Khlebnikov, Velimir, 25*n*, 30
Khodasevich, Anna Ivanovna, 137, 163
Khodasevich, Vladislav Felitsianovich, 81, 98
Khomyakov, Alexei Stepanovich, 305
Khrapchenko, Mikhail Borisovich, 400, 511
Khrushchev, Nikita Sergeevich, 410, 417, 451, 469, 470, 471, 477, 479, 482, 484*n*, 485, 496, 531
Kierkegaard, Søren, 396
Kinney, Mr. and Mrs., 120, 121–122, 123, 133–134, 137–138, 148
Kipling, Rudyard, 16, 163–164, 564
Kirianovna, Nadezhda, 4
Kirov, Sergei Mironovich, 304, 305–306, 307, 309
Kirpotin, Valery Yakovlevich, 322, 335
Kiselyova, Yelena Andreevna, 523
Kleist, Heinrich von, 338
Klyachko-Lvov, Lev Moiseevich, 117–118, 126, 130, 149, 166, 171, 174, 184, 186, 187, 383, 563
Klyuchevsky, Vasily Osipovich, 207
Klyuev, Nikolai Alexeevich, 207
Knipovich, Yevgenia Fyodorovna, 96
Knipper, Olga Leonardovna, 387
Kobetsky, Mikhail Veniaminovich, 132
Kochetov, Vsevolod Anisimovich, 462, 463

Kogan, Iosif Afanasyevich, 344
Kogan, Pyotr Semyonovich, 89
Koltsov, Mikhail Yefremovich, 215–216,
    233, 235, 236, 255–256, 258–259, 270,
    290, 314, 316, 487
Koltsova, Yelizaveta Nikolaevna, 215, 261,
    296
Komarovskaya, Nadezhda Ivanovna, 135
Komsomol, 280, 321, 325, 355–356, 542
Komsomol'skaia Pravda, 323, 506
Kon, Lidia Felixovna, 463
Konashevich, Vladimir Mikhailovich, 130,
    132, 291, 307, 361, 422
Koni, Anatoly Fyodorovich, 25, 43–44, 81,
    120, 188, 490, 495
Konovalov, Sergei Alexandrovich, 458, 506
Kopelev, Lev Zinovyevich, 471, 487
Korneichukova, Maria, 161
Korneichukova, Yekaterina Osipovna, 151,
    161*n*, 164, 166
Kornilov, Boris Petrovich, 459, 474–475
Korolenko, Sofia Vladimirovna ("Sonya"),
    239
Korolenko, Vladimir Galaktionovich, 20,
    164, 214, 423, 485, 503
Kosarev, Alexander Vasilyevich, 321
Kosygin, Alexei Nikolaevich, 532
Kotlyarevsky, Nestor Alexandrovich, 81,
    168
Kozhevnikov, Vadim Mikhailovich, 450–
    451, 463, 499
Kozlov, Ivan, 243*n*
Krasin, Leonid Borisovich, 123
Krasnaia gazeta, 175, 177, 180, 183, 185,
    190, 197, 199, 206, 213, 263, 276
Krasnaia nov', 191, 232*n*, 336, 389
Krasnova, Sofya Petrovna, 423, 463, 494,
    534, 548
Kristi, Mikhail Petrovich, 81
Kron, Alexander Alexandrovich, 412
Kropotkin, Katerina Nikolaevna, 32
Kropotkin, Pyotr Alexeevich, 32–35, 559–
    561
Krotky, Emil, 562–563
Kruchonykh, Alexei Yeliseevich, 533
Krug Publishers, 123–124, 186
Krupskaya, Nadezhda Konstantinovna, xiii,
    215, 325, 405

Krylov, Ivan Andreevich, 76, 467
Kryuchkov, Pyotr Petrovich, 233, 274, 310,
    464
Kubuch (Commission for the Improve-
    ment of Scholars' Living Conditions),
    163, 169, 178, 181, 183, 188
Kudashin, Mitrofan Stepanovich, 50
Kudashin, Stepan Stepanovich, 50
Kugel, Iona Rafailovich, 177, 183, 185, 190
Kuibyshev, Valerian Vladimirovich, 314
Kukolnik, Nestor Vasilyevich, 241
Kún, Agnes, 432
Kún, Bela, 432
Kún, Nikolai Nikolaevich, 432
Kuprin, Alexander Ivanovich, 16, 44, 72,
    332–333, 383, 431, 495, 498, 523
Kuzmin, Mikhail Alexeevich, 81, 191, 562
Kuznetsov, Yevgeny Mikhailovich, 183–
    184, 206
Kvitko, Lev Moiseevich, 430

Lagerkvist-Volfson, Suzanna Eduardovna,
    210
Laplace, Pierre Simon, 62
Lashkova, V. I., 527*n*
Lazhechnikov, Ivan Ivanovich, 61
Leaf, Munro, 478
Lebedenko, Alexander Gervasovich, 236
Lebedev, Boris Fyodorovich, 32
Lebedev, Vladimir Semyonovich, 473, 508–
    509
Lebedev, Vladimir Vasilyevich, 236
Lebedev-Polyansky, Pavel Ivanovich, 192–
    193, 322
Le Corbusier, 284
Lenin, Vladimir Ilyich, 43, 287, 351*n*, 451,
    500, 501; and Chukovsky's work, 215,
    265; family background of, 526; and in-
    telligentsia, 58, 288, 314, 422; Red Ter-
    ror of, 55*n;* veneration of, 94, 154, 245,
    313*n;* writings of, 22*n*, 205, 490
Leningrad Institute of Precision Mechan-
    ics and Optics, 449–450
Leonov, Leonid Maximovich, 359, 380, 384–
    385, 390, 416, 420, 472; on censorship,
    371; on the economy, 375, 376; on other
    writers, 358, 386; personal traits of, 356,
    384; as writer, 385, 457, 459, 475, 508

Lepeshinsky, Panteleimon Nikolaevich, 322
Lermontov, Mikhail Yuryevich, 27, 60, 68–69, 82n, 108n, 127, 128, 155, 243, 253, 355, 371, 378, 445n
Lerner, Nikolai Osipovich, 60, 67, 107, 110, 156, 497
Leskov, Nikolai Semyonovich, 20, 152
Lesyuchevsky, Nikolai Vasilyevich, 459
Letopis' Doma literaterov, 85
Levidov, Mikhail Yulyevich, 459
Levinson, Andrei Yakovlevich, 74
Lewis, Sinclair, *Babbitt,* 120
Liberalism, 46, 274–275, 307, 426, 479, 499
Lidin, Vladimir Germanovich, 400, 419
Lifshits, Mikhail Alexandrovich, 304, 506
Lipkin, Semyon Izrailevich, 524
Literatura i zhizn', 456, 478
Literaturka. See *Literaturnaia gazeta*
Literaturnaia gazeta, 256, 257, 264–265, 274–275, 323, 340, 361, 362, 363–364, 380, 381, 387, 421, 485, 498, 505, 533, 534
Literaturnaia Moskva, 403, 404, 408, 412, 413, 416, 417–418
Literaturnaia mysl', 117, 132
Literaturnaia Rossiia, 478, 552
Literaturnoe nasledstvo, 440, 441
Litvinov, Maxim Maximovich, 527
Litvinov, Pavel Mikhailovich, 527–528, 536n, 537
Litvinova, Ivy, 528n, 537
Litvinova, Tatyana Maximovna, 448, 519, 527–528, 530, 531, 537n
Livshits, Benedikt Konstantinovich, 25, 111, 191, 435, 485, 487, 502
Lloyd George, David, 85, 94
Lomonosova, Raisa Nikolaevna, 175, 182, 250
London, Jack, 138, 155, 194, 515–516, 559
Lozinsky, Mikhail Leonidovich, 156
Lozovskaya, Klara Izrailevna, 380, 391, 434, 448, 451, 471, 530
Lucretius, 13
Lugovsky, Vladimir Alexandrovich, 261n, 491
Lunacharsky, Anatoly Vasilyevich, 36–38, 42, 52, 65–66, 75, 142, 154, 186, 199, 200–202, 503

Lunts, Lev Natanovich, 93
Lurie, Artur Sergeevich, 75, 98
Lyadova, Vera Natanovna, 259, 273, 282, 290–291, 296
Lyubimov, Alexander Mikhailovich, 15
Lyubimov, Yury Petrovich, 524, 531, 532

McKay, Claude, 124, 126, 127
Maeterlink, Maurice, 82–83
Maikov, Valeryan Nikolaevich, 31, 60
Maisky, Ivan Mikhailovich, 157
Makashin, Sergei Alexandrovich, 395, 459
Maklakova, Lidia Filippovna, 251–252
Malenkov, Georgy Maximilianovich, 378
Maltsev, Yelizar Yuryevich, 498, 544–545
Mandelshtam, Osip Emilyevich, 25, 75, 430, 435, 485, 487, 502; death of, xvi, 242, 453, 476; influence of, 191, 275; other writers on, 211, 275, 299, 312; writings of, 235, 298
Mao Tse-tung, 384
Marcinowski, Jaroslaw, 199, 201
Marinetti, Filippo Tommaso, 23
Marr, Nikolai Yakovlevich, 369
Marshak, Samuil Yakovlevich, 442, 489–490, 491–492; and censorship, 290; and children's literature, 236–237, 276, 280, 294–295, 318, 563; Chukovsky's talk about, 422, 423; and Chukovsky's work, 149, 349; death of, 494–495; and Gorky, 230, 291, 563; personal traits of, 237, 414, 491, 563–564; writings of, 147, 291, 363–364, 457, 469, 564
Martinists, 262
Martynov, Leonid Nikolaevich, 431
Marx, Adolf, 154–155
Marx, Karl, 13, 16, 171, 251, 378
Marxism, 194, 260, 303, 369n, 535
Maugham, Somerset, "Rain," 176, 178, 179, 180, 181, 184, 190
Mayakovsky, Vladimir Vladimirovich, 26, 38, 83, 90, 103, 142, 332, 533; and censorship, 89; Chukovsky's writings about, 51, 76, 104, 352, 375, 532; death of, xvi, 240–241, 454, 476, 485, 502, 525; and Lili Brik, 74, 75, 76, 77, 233, 241, 321, 440; *Ogonek* article about, 532, 534; personal traits of, 74, 191, 241, 242; remi-

Mayakovsky, Vladimir Vladimirovich (continued)
  niscences about, 243, 321, 360, 467, 476; visits to Leningrad, 74–77, 88–89; writings of, 124, 232, 233, 321, 382–383, 422, 440, 539, 551–552
Medvedev, P. G., 419
Medvedev, Zhores Alexandrovich, 474
Mekhlis, Lev Zakharovich, 314, 316
Melman, Ruvim Lazarevich, 186–187
Mencken, H. L., 120
Mensheviks, 157
Merezhkovsky, Dmitry Sergeevich, 38, 44, 52, 64–65, 230, 356, 453, 554, 561; and Gorky, 58–59, 77; and *Niva*, 28–29; writings of, 47, 56, 230, 561
Meshcheryakov, Nikolai Leonidovich, 123, 239–240, 322
Meyerhold, Vsevolod Emilyevich, 89, 166, 178–179, 206, 211, 325, 459
Mickiewicz, Adam, 160, 495
Mikhailov, Mikhail Larionovich, 305, 336, 430
Mikhailov, Nikolai Alexandrovich, 434, 442
Mikhailov, Nikolai Nikolaevich, 410
Mikhailovsky, Nikolai Konstantinovich, 34, 49, 50, 244
Mikhalkov, Sergei Vladimirovich, 351, 363–364, 388, 457, 515
Milyukov, Pavel Nikolaevich, 26*n*, 109*n*
Mirolyubov, Viktor Sergeevich, 26
Mirsky, Dmitry Petrovich, 313, 314, 320, 430, 435, 485, 487
Mitford, Nancy, 452
Modernism, 60
Modzalevsky, Boris Lvovich, 298–299
Molodaia gvardiia, 259, 270, 278, 282, 290–291, 302, 460
Molotov, Vyacheslav Mikhailovich, 259, 464
Monakhov, Nikolai Fyodorovich, 87, 140
Morton, Miriam, 489
Moskva, 413, 497, 500, 505, 506
Muizhel, Viktor Vasilyevich, 44, 107, 133
Muromtsev, Dmitry Nikolaevich, 236
Murzilka, 357*n*, 361
Musorgsky, Modest Petrovich, 20
Mussolini, Benito, 356

Nabokov, Konstantin, 550–551
Nabokov, Vladimir Dmitrievich, 29, 109, 452–453
Nabokov, Vladimir Vladimirovich, 22, 452, 503, 523
Nagrodskaya, Yelena Apollonovna, 562–563
Nakanune, 113, 114, 121*n*
Na literaturnom postu, 194, 261*n*
Nappelbaum, Moisei Solomonovich, 100
Nashi dostizheniia, 236, 289
Neizvestny, Ernst Iosifovich, 479, 480
Nekrasov, Nikolai Alexeevich, xiii, 33, 57, 191, 240, 562–563; Akhmatova's commentaries on, 125, 128; anniversary of, 97; on censorship, 533; Chukovsky's work on, xiii, xvi, 42, 51, 52, 63, 69, 73, 85, 97, 119, 125, 128, 151, 155, 169, 174, 178, 179, 180, 181, 183–184, 186, 188, 193–194, 195, 205, 207, 208–209, 242, 265, 274, 280, 281, 293, 298, 319, 322, 324, 335, 350, 352, 355, 358, 360–361, 362, 363, 367, 368, 370, 376, 379, 380, 385, 388, 409, 436, 441, 467, 480–481, 495, 519, 530, 535, 559; poetry by, 6*n*, 130*n*, 196, 208, 244, 303–304, 332, 362, 479, 480, 560
Nekrasov, Viktor Platonovich, xvi
Nekrasova, Yelizaveta Ivanovna, 145
Nemirovich-Danchenko, Vasily Ivanovich, 19, 43, 102, 283, 536
Neo-Romanticism, 59*n*
Neradovsky, Pyotr Ivanovich, 183
Nevedomsky (= Mikhail Petrovich Miklashevsky), 32
Nexø, Martin Andersen, 114–115
Nicholas I, Tsar, 69, 188, 520
Nicholas II, Tsar, 25, 29*n*, 75*n*
Nietzsche, Friedrich Wilhelm, 101
Nihilism, 46
Nikitin, Nikolai Nikolaevich, 60, 93
Nikulin, Lev Veniaminovich, 457
Niva, 25, 28–29
Novaia Rossiia, 107
Novaia russkaia kniga, 108
Novaia zhizh', 55
Novoe vremia, 90
Novyi mir, 258, 353, 361, 362, 363, 381, 383, 386, 390, 408, 411, 435, 453, 462,

469, 471, 477, 481, 484, 491, 508, 509, 517, 518, 520, 522, 534

Novyi zritel', 144*n*

Oblonskaya, Raisa Yefimovna, 512
Obolenskaya, Yekaterina Mikhailovna, 308
Obraztsov, Sergei Vladimirovich, 393, 416, 474, 478
October Revolution (1917). *See* Revolutions
Odesskie novosti, 7, 10*n*, 20, 21
Ogonek, 235, 362, 375, 380, 441, 532, 534
Oistrakh, David Fyodorovich, 284
Oksman, Yulian Grigoryevich, 363, 404, 407, 459*n*, 466*n*, 515–516
Oktiabr', 361, 400, 451, 499
Oldenburg, Sergei Fyodorovich, 53, 120, 156
Olesha, Yury Karlovich, 283–284, 412
Olminsky, Mikhail Stepanovich, 194
Opie, Iona and Peter, 468
Ordzhonikidze, Grigory Konstantinovich "Sergo," 258.
Orlova, Raisa Davidovna, 471, 502
Ostretsov, Ivan Andreevich, 153, 154, 169, 171, 172–173
Otechestvennye zapiski, 61
Otsup, Nikolai Ardievich, 55, 57, 66–67, 82
Ovsyannikova, Olga Nikolaevna, 255
Ozerov, Lev Adolfovich, 476

Panaeva, Avdotya Yakovlevna, 137, 199*n*, 210, 212, 213, 365, 562
Panfyorov, Fyodor Ivanovich, 314, 361
Panin, Grigory Ivanovich, 25
Panova, Vera Fyodorovna, 459
Pasternak, Boris Leonidovich, 250, 268–269, 270, 278, 299–300, 325; Chukovsky's visits to grave of, 486; Chukovsky's writings on, 507*n*, 508, 509, 515; death of, 444, 445, 455; denunciations and censorship of, 264, 359, 408, 434–438, 439, 441, 446, 502, 505, 518; *Doctor Zhivago*, 356–357, 359, 392, 399, 407–408, 431, 433, 434–436, 437*n*, 439–440*n*, 487, 489, 515; estate of, 454, 470–471, 476, 478, 486–487, 489; financial prob-

lems of, 166, 443; health problems of, 424–427, 444, 446, 470–471; and Nobel Prize, 434–436, 441; and other writers, 337*n*, 371, 389, 431–432; personal traits of, 262, 264, 357, 358, 364, 399, 431, 434, 437, 439, 442, 443, 446; poetry of, 257–58, 264, 315, 399, 408, 433–34, 439, 454, 487, 489, 507*n*, 508; reputation of, 191, 320, 454; translations by, 338, 358, 364, 373–374, 375, 408, 435, 470
Pasternak, Yevgenia Vladimirovna, 268–269, 285
Pasternak, Yevgeny Borisovich "Zhenya," 471, 497, 506, 508
Pasternak, Zinaida Nikolaevna, 264, 269, 286, 359, 406, 441, 445; and husband's estate, 446, 454, 470, 471, 472, 473, 478, 486–487; and husband's illness, 425–427; and husband's writings, 433, 435, 446, 454, 478, 506; and Nobel Prize, 434–435
Paustovsky, Konstantin Georgievich, 411, 418, 431, 457, 481–482, 483, 484, 513, 532
Pavlenko, Pyotr Andreevich, 398
Pavlov, Dmitry Vasilyevich, 447
People's Commissariat of Education, 67*n*, 68
Pertsov, Viktor Osipovich, 337, 393, 518
Peshkova, Nadezhda Alexeevna, 377, 431
Peshkova, Yekaterina Pavlovna, 377, 387, 430, 464, 472
Peter Pan (Barry), 118
Petrograd Municipal League, 50–51
Petrov, Sergei Mitrofanovich, 393
Petrovykh, Maria Sergeevna, 446, 506
Pilnyak, Boris Andreevich, 86, 114–115, 123–124, 232, 256–258, 269–270, 285–287, 316, 487
Pisarev, Dmitry Ivanovich, 31, 79, 408
Platonov, Andrei Platonovich, 256–257, 501
Podarsky, 8
Poe, Edgar Allan, 18
Pogodin, Nikolai Fyodorovich, 359, 412, 463
Polevoy, Nikolai Alexeevich, 430
Polezhaev, Alexander Ivanovich, 312, 430
Polikarpov, Dmitry Alexeevich, 400, 401, 435, 451, 477

Polonskaya, Klavdia Pavlovna, 59, 366

Polonsky, Vyacheslav Pavlovich, 231

Polonsky, Yakov Petrovich, 59, 209, 264

Ponedel'nik, 461

Ponomarenko Panteleimon Kondratyevich, 374, 375, 379, 383

Popov, Vasily Stepanovich, 374

Popov, Vsevolod Ivanovich, 235

Populism, 244, 322

Pospelov, Pyotr Nikolaevich, 383, 526

Postupalsky, Igor Stefanovich, 268

Pravda, 150, 271, 308, 310, 313, 316, 330n, 340, 351, 357, 358, 359, 369, 405, 409, 463, 481, 500

Prokofiev, Sergei, 209n

Proletcult, 67, 70, 81

Proshian, Prosh Perchevich, 37

Przybyszewski, Stanisław, 17

Punin, Nikolai Nikolaevich, 71, 74, 132, 148–149

Pushkin, Alexander Sergeevich, 28, 60, 79, 109, 128, 129, 209, 240, 253, 276, 305, 378, 539; anniversaries of, 81–82, 311, 324–325, 480; books about, 294, 316, 332, 338, 526; Chukovsky's article on, 366, 436, 480; comparisons of others with, 371; death of, 69n; *Eugene Onegin,* 10; letters of, 243, 298; poetry by, 4–6, 99, 150, 152, 155, 374, 523

Pushkin House, 194, 262, 263

Rachmaninoff, Sergei Vasilyevich, 508

Radio Center, Moscow, 282, 302

Radlov, Nikolai Ernestovich, 232

Radlova, Anna Dmitrievna, 97–98, 306, 335, 336, 394

Raikh, Zinaida Nikolaevna, 178n

Raikin, Konstantin Arkadievich, 529

RAPP (Russian Association of Proletarian Writers), xiii, 157n, 176, 181, 196, 271, 275–276, 410n, 441

Realistic art, 378n

Rech', 15

Redko, Alexander Mefodievich, 112

Red Terror, 55n

Reeve, Franklin D., 546

Reineke, Maria Nikolaevna, 277

Reisner, Larisa Mikhailovna, 179, 234

Rembrandt van Rijn, 153; *Danaë,* 127

Remizov, Alexei Mikhailovich, 13–14, 108, 356

Renan, Joseph-Ernest, 10

Repin, Ilya Yefimovich, 16, 25, 166, 204, 302; anecdotes of, 19–20, 368; Chukovsky's portrait by, 19–20, 265–266, 458, 555–558; Chukovsky's writings on, 85, 308, 311, 312–313, 319, 324, 335, 352, 353, 380, 494, 503, 550; *18 October,* 20; and Gorky, 26–28; paintings by, 22, 24, 29–30, 34, 36, 266, 479, 550; personal traits of, 15, 84, 159, 231; and Soviet Russia, 159–160

Repin, Yury Ilyich, 27

Republic, proclamation of, 29n

Resounding Shell, 100

Revolutions (1905, 1917), anniversaries of, 130, 250; battleship *Potemkin* mutiny, 11, 12n, 328, 333; Blok's poem of, 39n; Chukovsky's diary entries about, 11–13, 289, 301, 478; Chukovsky's imprisonment during, 397n; February (1917), 29, 307; Finland Station, 44; Gregorian calendar, 47n; Kronstadt events in, 84; October (1917), 47n, 52n, 89n; Repin's caricature of, 20; rites and rituals abolished by, 78; spirit of, 268, 313n, 481n; Volfila commitment to, 45n; Writers' Union on, 210, 301

Richardson, Samuel, 392

Rodchenko, Alexander Mikhailovich, 124

Rolland, Romain, 280, 318

Romanticism, 59n

Roskina, Natalia Alexandrovna, 484–485

Rossetti, Dante Gabriel, 14, 15

Rotov, Konstantin Pavlovich, 307

Rousseau, Jean-Jacques, 318

Rozanov, Vasily Vasilyevich, 12–13, 21–22, 49, 51, 266, 550

Rozenel, Natalia Alexandrovna, 200, 201

Rozenko, A., 282

Rozhdestvensky, Vsevolod, 152

Rubenstein, Ida, 303

Rudakov Konstantin Ivanovich, 293

Rudenko, Roman Andreevich, 439n

Rumanov, Arkady Veniaminovich, 32, 560–562

Russell, Bertrand, 521–522
Russia. *See* Soviet Union
Russian Museum, 183
Russian Telegraph Agency, 83, 91
Russkaia starina, 169
Russkii sovremennik, 138, 139, 142, 143, 148, 149, 150, 162; banned, 153–155, 157; writers' letters about, 151–152
Russkoe bogatstvo, 8, 558–559
Rykov, Alexei Ivanovich, 168, 179, 186, 232

Sadofyev, Ilya Ivanovich, 81
Sadovskaya, Xenia Mikhailovna, 87*n*
Sadovsky, Boris Alexandrovich, 70
Safonova, Yelena Vasilyevna, 324
Salinger, J. D., 447
Saltykov-Shchedrin, Mikhail Yevgrafovich, 195, 244, 315*n*, 495, 520
Samarin, Yury Fyodorovich, 370
Sapir, Mikhail Grigoryevich, 169, 173, 209
Schopenhauer, Arthur, 16
Scott, Walter, 61
Seifullina, Lidia Nikolaevna, 203, 259–260, 270, 301, 302
Selvinsky, Ilya Lvovich, 232*n*, 261*n*, 360, 376, 441
Semashko Nikolai Alexandrovich, 307–311
Serapion Brotherhood, 93–94, 115, 505
Sergeev-Tsensky, Sergei Nikolaevich, 413
Sergievsky, Ivan Vasilyevich, 365–366
Serov, Vladimir Alexandrovich, 409, 480
Severyanin, Igor, 65
Shaginyan, Marietta Sergeevna, 259–260, 263–264, 270, 301, 416, 526
Shakespeare, William, 9, 105, 122, 123, 144, 173, 306, 311, 319, 394, 435, 457, 491
Shamil (folk hero), 286
Shaskolskaya, Marianna Petrovna, 460, 530
Shaw, George Bernard, 85, 412
Shchepkina-Kupernik, Tatyana Lvovna, 304
Shcherbakov, Alexander Sergeevich, 476
Shcherbina, Vladimir Rodionovich, 511
Shchogolev, Pavel Yeliseevich, 81, 98, 117, 125
Shevchenko, Taras Grigoryevich, 21, 166–167, 208, 213, 286

Shileiko, Vladimir Kazimirovich, 66, 99, 134
Shklovsky, Isaak Vladimirovich (= Dineo), 52, 74–75, 93, 173, 211, 263, 551
Shklovsky, Viktor Borisovich, 59, 67, 82, 90, 155, 160, 212, 235, 250–251, 275, 279, 294, 319, 381, 460, 473, 478, 501
Shmakova, Manya, 334
Shmidt, Otto Yulyevich, 144
Sholokhov, Mikhail Alexandrovich, 302, 339, 340, 349, 383, 389, 431, 432, 483, 484, 516, 528
Shostakovich, Dmitry Dmitrievich, 467, 471, 513
Shteinberg, A. Z., 45*n*
Shut, 63
Shvarts, Yevgeny Lvovich, 163, 384, 429
Sibirskie ogni, 479
Simonov, Konstantin Mikhailovich, 356, 361, 362, 373, 380, 398, 404, 411
Sinclair, Upton, 110
Sinyavsky, Andrei Donatovich, 510, 513, 516,
Slater, Lydia Pasternak, 489
Slavin, Lev Isaevich, 501
Sleptsov, Vasily Alexeevich, 176, 244, 252, 271, 364, 365, 402, 423
Slezkin, Yury Lvovich, 43, 44
Slonimsky, Mikhail Leonidovich, xiv–xv, 64, 82, 93, 112, 152, 179, 206, 214, 242–243, 283, 293, 316, 332, 348
Smirnov, Alexander Alexandrovich, 156
Smirnov, Lev Nikolaevich, 493
Smirnov, Nikolai Ivanovich, 290–291, 293, 296, 390
Smirnov, Sergei Sergeevich, 513
Smirnov, Vasily Alexandrovich, 400, 411
Sobolev, Leonid Sergeevich, 362, 457, 478, 522
Socialism, 31–32, 34, 43, 129, 273
Socialist Realism, 450, 564
Sokolovsky, Marshal, 487–488
Soldatov, Alexander Alexeevich, 487, 511
Sologub, Fyodor Kuzmich, 29, 41, 60, 112, 130, 133, 134, 152, 153, 156, 166–167, 174, 371*n*, 495, 516, 526, 554, 558–559
Solovyov, Vladimir Sergeevich, 356*n*
Solts, Aron Alexandrovich, 301–302

Solzhenitsyn, Alexander Isaevich, 483, 484, 485, 490, 508n, 509–510, 522–523, 532, 538, 544; *The Cancer Ward*, 496, 513n, 517, 518, 519–520, 522, 526, 533n; and censorship, 518, 535, 536, 540–541; "Krechetova Station," 488, 492, 511; *One Day in the Life of Ivan Denisovich*, 462, 471, 477, 487, 511; opposition and attacks on, 481, 487–488, 509, 522, 523, 533, 534, 535; personal traits of, xvii, 486, 496, 510, 520, 522, 540; "Right Hand," 513

Somov, Konstantin Andreevich, 15

Soviet Union: arrests in, 48, 53, 58, 132, 162, 201, 236; artists' poverty in, 191, 195, 230, 256–257, 263; artists supported by, 252, 255–256, 258, 269–270; attacks and intimidation of intelligentsia in, xi, xv, xvi, 79–80, 82, 99, 181, 301, 309–310, 311–312, 403, 410n, 430, 441–442, 459, 463, 469, 474, 476, 479–480, 483–484, 487, 508, 509, 531n, 532, 533–535, 537–538, 557, 564–565; balloon flight in, 297; censorship in, xii–xv, 20, 24, 104–105, 112, 153–158, 160, 164, 176, 181, 200, 257, 263, 366, 410n, 520, 526, 533, 534, 536; Chukovsky in support of, 145, 244–245; copyright in, 122, 251; currency reform in, 375–376; dissident movement in, 510n, 527–528, 536n, 537n; food shortages in, 52, 54–55, 57, 59, 66, 71–72, 81, 82–83, 85–87, 104, 108, 114, 121–122, 130, 163, 265, 278, 280, 342, 376; Great Terror in, xvi, 301, 304, 313n, 436, 459, 473n, 481n, 487, 527, 557; housing shortages in, 123; industrialization in, 231, 234–235, 267, 270; kolkhoz in, xv, 240, 244–245, 246–247, 256, 374, 483, 507; literary establishment of, xii–xiv, xvii, 176, 237, 257, 261, 271, 275n, 369n, 374, 379, 394, 398–399, 410n, 416, 435–436, 438, 440–442, 450, 459n, 480, 483–484, 488, 501, 502, 504, 505, 511–512, 516, 552; New Economic Policy (NEP) of, 122, 150n, 192, 383; "new order" in, 374; Pantheon project, 324–325; paper shortages in, 44, 77, 177–178, 180, 181, 236, 270, 274; peasants in, 45, 46, 83, 86, 91; public facilities in, 91–92; revolution in (*see* Revolutions); sailing prohibited in, 201–202; self-criticism in, 262, 263; social approach to literature in, 155; social change in, 172, 192; space flights of, 455–456, 496, 545; travel in, 272–273, 280

Sovremennik, 33n, 462. See also *Russkii sovremennik*

Sovremennyi Zapad, 119, 150, 163

Speranskaya, Yelizaveta Petrovna, 395–396

Speransky, Georgy Nesterovich, 67, 395–396

Spesivtseva, Olga Alexandrovna, 77–78

Stalin, Iosif Vissarionovich: book by, 525; and censorship, 158, 258, 403; death of, xv, 373, 382, 396–397, 473; destruction of images of, 404–405, 463; and Gorky, 296, 297; and Great Terror, xvi, xvii, 304n, 404, 406, 436, 459, 473n, 481n, 487, 506, 508n, 557; and kolkhoz, xv, 244–245; speeches of, 268, 314n, 330, 386, 405; veneration of, xv, 325, 330, 405; and writers, xiv, xvi, 269–270, 321, 349, 351, 356, 369n, 398, 403, 410n, 459, 464, 475, 477, 480, 487–488; writings about, xv–xvi, 232, 258–259, 264, 320n, 404, 469

Stanislavsky, Konstantin Sergeevich, 231–232, 283, 387

Stasov, Vladimir Vasilyevich, 20

Stead, William Thomas, 410–411

Stendhal: *De l'amour*, 133; *The Red and the Black*, xii, 31

Stenich, Valentin Iosifovich, 242, 283, 430

Stetsky, Alexei Ivanovich, 308–310, 321

Stevenson, Robert Louis, 39, 72, 393, 397

Stolyarova, Natalya Ivanovna, 510

Stowe, Harriet Beecher, 515

Strindberg, August, 123

Studio of the Art Theater, 119

Stupniker, Alexander Maximovich, 362

Sudeikina, Olga Afansyevna, 97, 99, 106, 126, 148

Surkov, Alexei Alexandrovich, 348, 389, 398, 400, 404, 420, 423, 433, 454, 470, 523

Suvorov, Prince, 33

Sverdlova, Klavdia Timofeevna, 290
Swift, Jonathan, 122, 132
Symbolism, 59n, 61–62, 411, 442, 555
Synge, John Millington: Chukovsky's talk about, 122–124; *Playboy of the Western World*, xiii, 115–116, 119, 123–124
Syomin, Vitaly Nikolaevich, 528
Syrkina, Olga Yefimovna, 270
Sytin, Ivan Dmitrievich, 560–562

Tabidze, Titsian, 285–286, 299, 315, 434
Tager, Yelena Mikhailovna, 487, 502
Tagore, Rabindranath, 431–432
Tan, Vladimir Germanovich, 16, 107
Tarkovsky, Arseny Alexandrovich, 514
Tavrog, Marianna Yelizarovna, 537
Tendryakov, Vladimir, 418
Teplinsky, Mark Veniaminovich, 519
Thoreau, Henry David, 515
Tikhomirova, Nadezhda Vasilyevna, 427
Tikhonov, Alexander Nikolaevich, 53, 55, 144, 158, 232, 233, 316, 357, 362, 457, 475; arrest of, 162; and Blok, 80, 96; and Chukovsky's work, 39, 179, 180, 181, 184, 187, 214; and Gorky, 109, 287, 289; and Pasternak's estate, 471, 486; and *Russkii sovremennik*, 139, 153, 154; and Tolstoy's letter, 152; and World Literature project, 39, 73, 120, 122, 156, 162; and *Zavtra*, 51
Tikhonov, Nikolai, 93, 163–164
Times (London), 85
Tinyakov, Alexander Ivanovich, 191
Titian, 127
Titov, German Stepanovich, 455–456
Tolstaya, Lyudmila Ilyinichna, 431, 472
Tolstoy, Alexei Konstantinovich, 147
Tolstoy, Alexei Nikolaevich, 15, 232, 253, 262, 281, 320, 453; Chukovsky's writing about, 138, 143, 423, 424; and Gorky, 136, 300; and letters to authorities, 152, 349; personal traits of, 345–346; and *Russkii sovremennik*, 142, 143; writings of, 68, 121n, 134–135, 136–137, 140, 144, 212, 233–234, 323, 521, 529
Tolstoy, Lev Nikolaevich, 15, 60, 84, 137, 457; *Anna Karenina*, 72, 85, 130; attacks on, 4, 16; biographies of, 16n, 212, 423;

death of, 495; diary of, 395; and Gorky, x, 48–49, 61, 159; *The Kreutzer Sonata*, 7; personal traits of, 4, 164, 214, 239, 530; portraits of, 22, 30, 89, 160; *Resurrection*, 130; *War and Peace*, 130
Tomashevsky, Boris Viktorovich, 173, 303
Trenyova, Natalia Konstantinovna, 431
Trollope, Anthony, 413–414
Trotsky, Lev Davydovich, 142, 168, 215, 404; and censorship, 153, 154; Chukovsky described by, xii, 151, 281
Trotskyism, 157n, 281, 411
Tsarskoe Selo, 107, 144, 167
Tseitlin, Natan Sergeevich, 56, 275, 508–509
Tsitovich, Sergei Sergeevich, 489–490
Tsvetaeva, Anastasia, 371
Tsvetaeva, Marina Ivanovna, xvi, 250n, 371n, 412, 430, 453, 469, 476, 485, 487, 502
Tsypin, Grigory Yevgenievich, 323–324
Turgenev, Ivan Sergeyevich, 6, 22, 137, 194, 199, 423, 466, 495, 498
Tvardovsky, Alexander Trifonovich, 355, 402, 422, 471; and censorship, 383, 462, 518, 534; and Chukovsky's work, 414–415, 421, 423, 463; and *Novyi mir*, 383, 386, 462, 469, 481, 484, 517, 518, 522, 534; other writers described by, 389n, 414–415, 456–457, 496, 499; personal traits of, 456; and Solzhenitsyn, 462, 513, 517, 518, 519, 522; writings of, 383, 403, 410, 422n, 457
Twain, Mark, 42, 397–398, 409–410, 423
Tynyanov, Yury Nikolaevich, 152, 174, 194, 211, 303, 332, 372, 429; aging of, 338; Chukovsky's memoir of, 380, 515; on Chukovsky's work, 208, 212; family troubles of, 317–318, 322–323; on Fedin, 299; and Formalism, 160, 173; and Gorky, 300, 304, 318, 320; and Pasternak, 262, 300, 320; personal traits of, 208–209, 261–262, 320; and Stalin, xv, 244–245; writings of, 160, 163, 169, 187–188, 209, 279–280, 294, 299, 316, 318, 319–320, 338, 521
Tynyanova, Yelena Alexandrovna, 294, 317, 320, 322–323

Tyutchev, Fyodor Ivanovich, 60, 117, 139, 498

Union of Soviet Writers, 275n. *See also* Writers' Union
Union of the Artists of the Word, 43
Union of Workers in Education, 190
Universal Library, 189
Updike, John, 496
Urusova, Princess, 71–72, 156
Usievich (Kon), Yelena Felixovna, 275, 276
Uspensky, Gleb Ivanovich, 244
Uspensky, Nikolai Vasilyevich, 176, 244, 249, 274, 280
Utyosov, Leonid Osipovich, 335

Vaginov, Konstantin Konstantinovich, 191
VAPP (All-Russian Association of Proletarian Writers), 157n
Vasilevsky, Ilya Markovich, 461
Vasilyev, Pyotr Vasilyevich, 351n
Vatson, Maria Valentinovna, 82, 99
Vavilov, Nikolai Ivanovich, 474
Veksler, Alexandra Lazarevnas, 59
Veltman, Alexander Fomich, 61
Veltman, Sofya (= Yelena Ivanovna), 61
Vengerov, Semyon Afanasyevich, 11, 173–174
Vengrov, Natan, 26, 199, 214–215, 316
Verbitskaya, Anastasia Alexeevna, 433
Verlaine, Paul, 35n
Verne, Jules, 249
Vestnik znaniia, 23, 62
Vesy (Scales), ix
Vigdorova, Frida Abramovna, 411–412, 431, 449–450, 491
Vilmont, Nikolai Nikolaevich, 454
Vinogradov, Viktor Vladimirovich, 117, 355, 369, 372–373, 441, 475, 505
Virta, Nikolai Yevgenievich, 341–342, 385
Vishnyak, Mark Venyaminovich, 107
Vladimirtsev, Boris Yakovlevich, 120
Vlasov, Andrei Andreevich, 509n
Vlasov, Mikhail Fyodorovich, 426, 427
VLKSM. *See* Komsomol
Voitolovsky, Lev Naumovich, 195–196
Volin, B. (= Boris Mikhaiovich Fradkin), 267, 270, 307–310

Volkonsky, Prince, 71–72
Voloshin, Maximilian Alexandrovich, 129, 145
Voltaire, 318
Volynsky, A., 54, 57, 67, 110, 120, 153, 156, 158
Voronsky, Alexander Konstantinovich, 157n, 186, 187, 209, 251, 265
Voroshilov, Kliment Yefremovich, 417, 489, 491
Vostokov, Alexander Khristoforovich, 262
Voznesensky, Andrei Andreevich, 514
Vrubel, Mikhail Alexandrovich, 15
Vvedensky, Alexander Ivanovich, 487
Vyazemsky, Pyotr Andreevich, 5
Vygotsky, David Isaakovich, 263
Vygotsky, Lev Semyonovich, 507
Vyshinsky, Andrei Yanuaryevich, 473
Vysotskaya, Olga Nikolaevna, 459

Washington, Booker T., 41
Wasilewska, Wanda, 348, 414
Wells, H. G., 69, 72, 82, 84
Whitman, Walt, 35, 398, 495; Chukovsky's readings of, 30, 85, 373, 447; Chukovsky's writings on, 119, 270, 274, 373, 379, 380, 395, 502, 512, 531, 550, 561; *Leaves of Grass,* 30, 373, 512; Whitman Society, 103–104; World Literature project on, 110–111
Wilde, Oscar, 35, 42, 101, 119, 286, 415, 424, 436, 452, 453n, 467, 495, 551
Wilhelm II, Kaiser, 25
Wilson, Edmund, 521
Winnicott, D. W., 433
World Literature project: and arrests, 162; and Blok, xi, 18, 41, 45, 59, 60, 61–62, 68–69, 73–74, 77, 96; breakup of, 156–157, 158; and censorship, 79, 104, 122, 154; and Gorky, x, 39–42, 45–47, 55, 57–58, 61, 62, 63, 67, 68–69, 72–73, 77, 79–80; Gosizdat (*see* Gosizdat Editorial Division); Lenin Corner of, 154; readings in, 110, 120–121, 153
World War I, 25–26, 27–28, 191
World War II, 337, 349, 350
Wren, Christopher, 466
Writers' Congress, 278, 312, 394, 520, 522

Writers' House. *See* House of Writers
Writers' Organizational Committee, 301
Writers' Union, 152, 319, 374, 459; and
    Akhmatova, 131, 358, 514–515, 518; and
    Blok, 90; and censorship, 210, 275*n*, 349,
    383, 400; and Chukovsky, 82, 83–84, 85,
    186, 310, 348, 349, 373, 424, 500–501;
    criticism of, 339, 389; and Ivanov, 348,
    380, 398; leadership of, 361, 362, 380,
    383, 398, 400, 417, 424, 478, 501, 502,
    518, 540; and Pasternak, 359, 425, 435,
    446, 510; readings in, 110, 184, 189,
    348, 380, 416, 500–501; self-criticism in,
    262, 263; and Zoshchenko, 358, 375,
    377, 400, 501

Yarmolinsky, Avrahm, 137
Yasensky, Bruno (= Viktor Yakovlevich),
    430, 487, 502
Yashin, Alexander Yakovlevich, 416, 483
Yashvili, Paolo Dzhibrazlovich, 453
Yasinovskaya, Anna Viktorovna, 503, 526
Yefimov, Boris Yefimovich, 215–216
Yegolin, Alexander Mikhailovich, 426, 427,
    442, 532
Yermilov, Vladimir Vladimirovich, 310,
    362, 385, 386, 463, 481–482, 484
Yershov, Pyotr Pavlovich, 114*n*
Yesenin, Sergei Alexandrovich, xvi, 100*n*,
    174, 176, 178–179, 191, 241, 360, 430,
    476, 524, 525
Yevdokimov, Ivan Vasilyevich, 352
Yevgenyev-Maximov, Vladislav Yevgenyev-
    ich, 322
Yevreinov, Nikolai Nikolaevich, 516
Yevtushenko, Yevgeny Alexandrovich, xvii,
    474, 475, 485, 501, 504, 514, 539, 540–
    541, 545–546
Yezhov, Nikolai Ivanovich, xv–xvi, 321, 469
Yugov, Alexei Kuzmich, 460, 461, 463
Yuryev, Yury Mikhailovich, 314
Yushkevich, Semyon Solomonovich, 552–
    553, 554

Zabolotsky, Nikolai Alexeevich, 412, 435,
    459, 487, 538
Zagoskin, Mikhail Nilolaevich, 61
Zaitseva, Lyudmila Stepanovna, 345

Zakhoder, Boris Vladimirovich, 510
Zalygin, Sergei Pavlovich, 499, 526
Zamirailo, Viktor Dmitrievich, 132
Zamyatin, Yevgeny Ivanovich, 43, 80, 85,
    92*n*, 98, 126, 138, 152, 203, 204; per-
    sonal traits of, 105, 110; and *Russkii so-
    vremennik*, 139, 150; and World Litera-
    ture project, 60, 69, 120, 156; writings
    of, 76, 84, 104, 120–121, 129, 163; and
    Zavtra, 51
Zapiski mechtatelei, 104
Zaslavsky, David Iosifovich, 313–314, 322,
    396
Zavtra, 51
Zbarskaya, Yevgenia Borisovna, 381, 382,
    388, 483
Zbarsky, Boris Ilyich, 381, 382
Zbarsky, Lyova (= Felix), 339, 363, 381,
    382
Zelikson, Isaak Naumovich, 68
Zelinsky, Kornely Lutsianovich, 260–261,
    264, 393, 445–446, 518
Zhdanov, Andrei Alexandrovich, 236, 357*n*,
    360, 386*n*, 492, 508*n*
Zhemchuzhnikov, Alexei Mikhailovich,
    525*n*
Zhenya (servant), 65, 68, 72
Zhirmunsky, Viktor Maximovich, 59, 156,
    303–304
Zhitkov, Boris Stepanovich, 132, 262, 328,
    375, 379, 380, 384, 473, 523
Zhizn' iskusstva, 84
Zhukovsky, Vasily Andreevich, 54, 253
Zhurnalist, 124
Zilbershtein, Ilya Samoilovich, 213, 395,
    425, 440, 441
Zinovyev, Grigory Yevseevich, 58, 114–
    115, 143, 156, 158, 162, 168, 215, 305,
    311, 451
Zinovyevites, 144
Znamia, 376, 379
Zola, Emile, 318
Zorgenfrei, Vilgelm Alexandrovich, 96
Zoshchenko, Mikhail Mikhailovich, xvi,
    92*n*, 349, 380, 431; Chukovsky's writings
    about, 493, 495, 496, 497, 498, 500–501,
    505, 506; *Dear Citizens*, 200, 201; others'
    writings about, 204, 275; personal prob-

Zoshchenko, Mikhail Mikhailovich (continued)
lems of, 179, 201, 242; personal traits of, 198–199, 200, 201–202, 203, 206, 211, 213–214, 293, 334, 429–430; political attacks on, 357n, 358, 359, 360, 375, 400–401, 435, 476, 487, 492, 498, 501, 502; restoration of, 377; sailing trip with, 201–202; *Sentimental Tales*, 203, 211; *What the Nightingale Sang*, 202–203, 204; as writer, 179, 200, 201, 243, 413, 430; *Youth Restored*, 203n, 293, 299, 300

Zverev, Ilya (= Izold Yudovich Zamdberg), 485

Zvezda, 157, 242